THE DICTIONARY OF NAUTICAL LITERACY

"I did not wish to take a cabin passage,
but rather to go before the mast and on deck of the world,
for there I could best see the moonlight amid the mountains.
I do not wish to go below now."

Henry David Thoreau, *Walden* (1854)

Robert McKenna

The
DICTIONARY
of NAUTICAL
LITERACY

INTERNATIONAL MARINE

INTERNATIONAL MARINE / McGRAW-HILL

Camden, Maine • New York • Chicago • San Francisco • Lisbon • London • Madrid
Mexico City • Milan • New Delhi • San Juan • Seoul • Singapore • Sydney • Toronto

1 2 3 4 5 6 7 8 9 0 DOC DOC 0 9 8 7 6 5 4 3

Copyright © 2001 Robert McKenna

Paperback Edition ISBN 0-07-141950-0

Hardcover Edition Library of Congress Cataloging-in-Publication Data
McKenna, Robert.
  The dictionary of nautical literacy / Robert McKenna.
       p.   cm.
  ISBN 0-07-136211-8
  1. Naval art and science—Dictionaries. 2. Navigation—Dictionaries.
  3. Naval biography—Dictionaries. I. Title.
  V23 .M33 2001
  623.8'03—dc21   2001001471

Questions regarding the content of this book should be addressed to
International Marine
P.O. Box 220
Camden, ME 04843
www.internationalmarine.com

Questions regarding the ordering of this book should be addressed to
The McGraw-Hill Companies
Customer Service Department
P.O. Box 547
Blacklick, OH 43004
Retail customers: 1-800-262-4729
Bookstores: 1-800-722-4726

To my wife Tamara and daughters Julia and Daria.
You are my reason for being.

In Memoriam

Joseph P. Gribbins
1939–2001

A master interpreter of the great sea's voice

Preface

The history of man and the sea has kept abreast of the history of civilization. In recent years, however, we as individuals have become less dependent upon the sea, and its presence and importance have ebbed from our daily lives.

Still, the sea is eternal, and we cannot hope to measure ourselves or define who we are without a knowledge and awareness of its influence. Further, it would be unthinkable to look to the future without a lens of maritime history, and for those who have heard the sea's call, it would be useless to follow the traditions if we are unable to appreciate how they were brought about and why their contributions are important.

The Dictionary of Nautical Literacy is the first lexicon to chart our maritime culture. By identifying and defining a baseline of ideas, individuals, and events across the full spectrum of our relationship with the sea, it attempts to fix our position and facilitate our journey. All entries have historical value, hold literary or artistic merit, or are important to comprehending and placing in context the issues of our time.

The terms identified are those that invariably arise in the course of life or business or are encountered in maritime-related texts. Some serve as a foundation on which additional knowledge is based, and others are included to broaden readers' horizons.

The body of knowledge contained herein is based on reading and reviewing thousands of nautical books and periodicals, thousands of hours spent at sea on all types of vessels, hundreds of hours spent in maritime museums and at related historic sites, numerous conversations with experts in various marine fields, and a lifetime of absorbing the sea's role in our popular culture.

Like every compilation, *The Dictionary of Nautical Literacy* presents problems of inclusion and omission. While it presumes a basic acquaintance with the sea, it transcends the vernacular and technical terms that have up to now characterized most nautical dictionaries. *The Dictionary* contains the equivalent of the first magnitude stars of our maritime galaxy. Countless other potential entries certainly deserve mention and perhaps will find their way into some future volume. Issues concerning the treatment of some terms are bound to arise. A book twice this size could not do justice to the entries, and in many cases the entry is itself the subject of a book or larger body of work.

The Dictionary of Nautical Literacy was inspired by E. D. Hirsch Jr.'s best-seller *The Dictionary of Cultural Literacy* (1989). Whereas Hirsch set out to establish a baseline of information "every American needs to know" to be "culturally literate," this book identifies and defines the important and useful aspects of the "culture of the sea." *The Dictionary* was conceived as a concise reference text to identify a core of nautical knowledge. As the research process moved ahead, however, it became increasingly clear that the book has added value as a device. It has been written and designed specifically to engage the curiosity of the reader, and it is cross-referenced to maximize information in as many areas of interest as possible. Thus it contains 3,500 "points of entry" into a interesting, engaging, and meaningful world. It begs to be read, scanned, perused, and used as a recall vehicle and a catalyst for learning, as well as consulted as a reference.

I sincerely hope that the knowledge, lessons, and traditions contained in *The Dictionary of Nautical Literacy* will be read and remembered, will enter into the stream of life, and perhaps will move people to reflection, thought, and action.

Robert R. McKenna
Noank, Connecticut

Acknowledgments

Many people answered my call for assistance with *The Dictionary of Nautical Literacy*, but none more so than Gordon R. Ghareeb, who helped overcome many of the initial obstacles of the book's format and whose wit and wisdom eased the entire writing process, and William H. Barnum, who was always on call to field a question, research a topic, or review entries.

I am deeply indebted to those who helped shape the idea for *The Dictionary*, namely J. Russell Jinishian, Stephen Jones, James A. Mitchell III, and Kurt Volkan.

I am also thankful and humbled to have had the input of Captain Bob Bates, Fred Calabretta, Andrew German, and Joseph Gribbins, who has been a good friend and mentor.

The following people generously provided various kinds of information: Alex Agnew, Captain Richard Bailey, Phil Budlong, J. Revell Carr, John T. Gibbons, Dana Hewson, Martin Hillsgrove, William Hogan, Tom Manning, Paul O'Pecko, William Peterson, Andrew Price, John Rutchik, Quentin Snediker, Mary Anne Stets, Paul Stillwell, Don Treworgy, Bruce Vancil, Raymond Visel, Shawn Waldron, Greg Walsh, David Way, and Robert Weiss.

Special thanks are due to my family for their support: Tamara, Julia, and Daria McKenna; Pete and Pam McKenna; Bill and Robin McKenna; Kevin and Marga Huban; and William and Mary McKenna—my parents, who introduced me to a semidiurnal world and gave me the freedom to explore. Thanks go also to Arthur Suwalow, Nina Lapin, Cliff and Marina Morgenegg, Walter and Eleanor Grin, Victor and Dana Grin, and Kevin and Natasha Raymond.

Also important were the help and support shown to me and my family by James and Pam Adase, Chris and Barbara Arelt, Russ and Judy Barber, Tim and Peg Butler, Bart and Lori Calobrisi, Jim and Linda Chambers, Frank and Lorna Conahan, Owen and Sue Ehrlich, Skip Eisenlau, Charles and Mary Fernandes, John and Julie Haines, David and Linda Halstead, Stephen and Debbie Hayes, Lee Jinishian, Jon and Greta Jones, Davis Kong, Bill and Adrianne Loweth, Jim and Jeanine Lynch, Mark and Debbie Malloy, Jennifer Mongeon, Greg and Marina Quintana, Andrés and Cheryl Salinas, Steve and Pam Skillman, Marc Smith, Fred and Raney Studier, and the entire Tulevech family.

Many thanks also to my colleagues at Mystic Seaport—Donna Bellantone, Claire Calabretta, Katherine Cowles, Chris Cox, Jennifer Harmon, Maureen Hennessy, Bill and Lou Ellen Scheer, Corlyn Secchiaroli, Sarah Shrewsbury, Mike Smiles, and Ruffian Tittman—and to all the folks at Ram Island Yacht Club.

A final thanks to Ed Knappman of New England Publishing Associates, who got the idea for the book right away, and special thanks to Jonathan Eaton and the entire staff at International Marine.

Reader's Note

No dictionary can lay claim to completeness. The author and editors have made every effort to ensure as wide a coverage as possible within the range imposed by the scope and space limitations of this work.

In constructing *The Dictionary of Nautical Literacy*, the author and editors have sought to preserve a degree of authority while making the book approachable and easy to use—the information contained herein can be of no use if it is not read. The reader will immediately notice that it does not follow strict dictionary style and that cross-references, provided to help readers make connections and linkages, are contained within the text of a definition—such cross-references are in boldface type. *The Dictionary of Nautical Literacy* does, however, run alphabetically through many seemingly disparate terms. This is the real power of such a book.

Ships are alphabetized by name rather than by prefix (prefixes are defined below). Naval engagements are found under the location, such as **Trafalgar, Battle of.**

Faced with the task of defining many terms and concepts, the author realizes the limitations of this work and welcomes at all times suggestions from readers as to possible improvements and enlargement of *The Dictionary of Nautical Literacy*. These suggestions may be sent to Editorial Director, International Marine, P.O. Box 220, Camden ME 04843, www.internationalmarine.com, or via www.NauticalLiteracy.com.

Fleet Designations

CSS	Confederate States Ship
HMAS	Her/His Majesty's Australian Ship
HMCS	Her/His Majesty's Canadian Ship
HMS	Her/His Majesty's Ship
HMNZS	Her/His Majesty's New Zealand Ship
MS	Motor Ship
MV	Motor Vessel
NS	Nuclear Ship
RMS	Royal Mail Steamship
SS	Steamship
USCGC	United States Coast Guard Cutter
USNS	United States Naval Ship
USRC	United States Revenue Cutter
USS	United States Ship

U.S. Navy and Coast Guard Ship Types

AGSS	Auxiliary Oceanography Vessel
AGTR	Auxiliary Technical Research Ship
AH	Auxiliary Hospital Ship
BB	Battleship
C	Cruiser
CA	Heavy Cruiser
CC	Command Cruiser
CG	Guided Missile Cruiser

CGN	Nuclear Powered Guided Missile Cruiser
CL	Light Cruiser
CV	Aircraft Carrier
CVA	Attack Aircraft Carrier
CVAN	Nuclear Powered Attack Aircraft Carrier
CVN	Nuclear Powered Aircraft Carrier
DD	Destroyer
DDG	Guided Missile Destroyer
DE	Destroyer Escort
DLG	Destroyer
FF	Frigate
FFG	Guided Missile Frigate
LST	Tank Landing Ship
LV	Lightship
PR	Patrol Vessel
PT	Patrol Boat
SS	Submarine
SSBN	Nuclear Powered Ballistic Missile Submarine
SSN	Nuclear Powered Submarine
WLV	Lightship
WPG	Gunboat

A number following the specific ship type is the ship's hull number. It is assigned to a vessel, usually one of a class of vessels, by the U.S. Navy.

THE DICTIONARY OF NAUTICAL LITERACY

A

A-1, old **Lloyd's of London** classification indicating that a ship has met the highest standards of construction. The term is now used colloquially to describe anything that is the very best.

Aaron Manby, the first **steamship** to be built of iron and one of the first iron vessels ever. The 120-foot **paddle wheeler** was launched in Staffordshire, England, in 1821 and made her first voyage in 1822 across the English Channel and up the Seine to Paris. The use of iron plates instead of wood was a watershed event in shipbuilding, although some people opposed this method of construction because iron does not float.

AB, see **able-bodied seaman**.

Abandon Ship!, 1957 seagoing "survival of the fittest" saga that portrays the sinking of a luxury **liner** during World War II. The motion picture, based on a true story, starred Tyrone Power, Stephen Boyd, and Lloyd Nolan.

Abbott and Costello Meet Captain Kidd, 1952 spoof of Hollywood's swashbuckler movies, which shows Bud and Lou finding a treasure map. In addition to Bud Abbott and Lou Costello, the film featured Charles Laughton, who reprised his role from the 1945 film ***Captain Kidd***.

ABCD Ships, three **cruisers** and a dispatch boat—*Atlanta, Boston, Chicago,* and *Dolphin*—launched in March 1883 as the U.S. **Navy**'s first steel ships. Their commissioning ushered in the modern U.S. Navy, giving a notable boost to the nascent U.S. steel industry and what became the military-industrial complex.

Abeking and Rasmussen, boatbuilding company located near Bremen, Germany, best known in the United States for having built ninety-nine **Concordia yawls** between 1949 and 1966. Founded in 1907 by engineer George Abeking and yacht designer Henry Rasmussen, the company's building program included the design and building of naval vessels and special utility craft during World War I.

able-bodied seaman (AB), an experienced member of the deck crew aboard a merchant ship. The rank is higher than **ordinary seaman** and below that of a petty officer, such as a **boatswain**, or a licensed officer, such as a **mate**. Today they are referred to as "able seamen."

Able Manner, the largest search and rescue operation ever undertaken by the U.S. **Coast Guard**. It was in response to a massive increase in the number of Haitians fleeing their country in October 1991.

Able-Peter, the old international signal flag designation for "A-P," which meant "I am aground." Following the Korean War, the code was revised to adapt to dialects and accents better understood by military organizations within NATO and the United Nations. Today's designation would be "Alpha-Papa."

Above Us the Waves, British movie about the midget submarine hunt for the Nazi battleship *Tirpitz* and her ultimate destruction. Although a good sea story, the film is also a reminder that the winners of wars write the history books. The 1956 film starred Theodore Bikel and Lyndon Brook.

ABS, see **American Bureau of Shipping**.

The Abyss, 1989 underwater adventure film starring Ed Harris as the leader of a team of oil-drilling divers who are pressed into service by the U.S. **Navy** to locate an inoperative nuclear submarine. Directed by James Cameron, who later directed *Titanic*, the film was lauded by critics for its good underwater footage and musical score, and it captured an Academy Award for special effects.

Acapulco, originally the **P&O** *Mongolia* of 1923, the 15,182-gross-ton-passenger steamer was acquired by the Mexican government–owned Natumex Line in 1961 and refitted to run a fortnightly service between Los Angeles and Acapulco. The maiden positioning cruises were canceled because the **liner** failed to pass U.S. **Coast Guard** inspections. After surmounting that embarrassing obstacle, the vessel had a near-complete mechanical breakdown on her third voyage south from California. She served for six months at the Seattle World's Fair in 1962 as a hotel ship. Mexico's one and only ocean liner, she was **laid up** in 1963 and finally scrapped in 1964.

MS *Achille Lauro*, motor **liner** delivered in 1947 as the Dutch *Willem Ruys* and sold to the Lauro Line of Naples in 1964. Renamed *Achille Lauro* in 1972, she became a well-known cruise ship. After leaving Alexandria, Egypt, in 1985, the ship was boarded and hijacked by four Arab terrorists. While holding the ship, her crew, and her passengers hostage, the terrorists brutally murdered one American passenger, Leon Klinghoffer, and threw his body overboard. After three days, the terrorists surrendered and the liner was returned to her owners. The ship burned and sank in the Indian Ocean in December 1994 with the loss of two passengers' lives.

acoustic torpedo, torpedo fitted with a sensor that detects the sound of a ship's propellers. The sensor steers the torpedo toward the ship and detonates it when close to the ship's hull. The torpedo was introduced by the German navy in 1943 and was used with limited success during World War II. To counter this weapon, ships tow a device or an array behind them that emits more noise than the ship's machinery.

Action in the North Atlantic, excellent 1943 film—whose value as a recruiting instrument cannot be denied—showcasing the U.S. **merchant marine** in World War II. The film portrays the harrowing story of the fictitious **Liberty ship** *Sea Witch* as she is separated from her North Atlantic **convoy** and has to sail on to **Murmansk** alone. Based on an original story by **Guy Gilpatric**, it starred Humphrey Bogart, Raymond Massey, and Alan Hale Sr. and was nominated for Academy Awards for best writing and best original story.

Actium, Battle of, naval engagement in the Roman Civil War in which Octavian's fleet of four hundred ships defeated the combined five-hundred-vessel fleet of Mark Antony and Cleopatra in September of 31 B.C. off the coast of Greece. During the fighting, Cleopatra ordered her Egyptian **galleys** to flee, and Antony broke off with a few ships and followed her. The remainder of the fleet surrendered, and Octavian became the undisputed ruler of the Roman Empire as the emperor Augustus.

Acushnet, whaleship that left Fairhaven, Massachusetts, in 1841 with **Herman Melville** serving on board as an **ordinary seaman**. The ship voyaged around **Cape Horn** and into the South Pacific, where Melville jumped ship in the **Marquesas Islands** eighteen months later. The experience provided raw material for his novels *Typee* (1846), *Omoo* (1847), and *Moby-Dick* (1851).

Adams, Charles Francis (1866–1954), renowned American yachtsman and the first amateur to defend the **America's Cup**, as **skipper** of *Resolute* in 1920 against Sir **Thomas Lipton**'s *Shamrock IV*. In 1934 he skippered the **J-boat** *Yankee* in her losing contest with *Rainbow* in the America's Cup trial races. A descendant of John Quincy Adams, he served as secretary of the navy from 1929 to 1933 and was a tireless campaigner for increasing the size and scope of the U.S. military.

admeasurement, the confirmed or official dimensions, size, or capacity of a ship.

Admiral, streamlined **Mississippi River** excursion steamer built in 1906 as the *Albatross* (not to be confused with the *Albatros*). The 396-foot craft was completely rebuilt in 1940 to become the all-steel *Admiral*, which was capable of carrying four thousand passengers at a time on day trips. In 1979 the U.S. **Coast Guard** shut the operation down when the vessel's hull proved too weak in places to pass

Achille Lauro. (Courtesy Gordon R. Ghareeb)

safety inspection. The art-deco riverboat was refurbished in 1994 as the President Casino's *Admiral Riverboat* and was permanently docked on the Saint Louis waterfront not far from the Gateway Arch.

Admiral Cruises, U.S.-based cruise operation formed in 1987 by the consolidation of Eastern Cruise Lines, Western Cruise Lines, and Sundance Cruises. It came under the control of **Royal Caribbean Cruise Line** in 1990.

Admiral Graf Spee, widely known as the **Graf Spee**, German **pocket battleship** built in 1936 to conform to the terms of the **Treaty of Versailles** and named for Admiral **Maximilian von Spee** (1861–1914). After terrorizing the Atlantic Ocean in the early days of World War II, the sixteen-thousand-ton ship was **scuttled** to avoid capture by her British adversaries off Montevideo, Uruguay, during the Battle of the **River Plate** on December 17, 1939. Her captain, **Hans Langsdorff**, committed suicide the following day.

Admiral Kuznetsov, the only full-flight-deck aircraft carrier ever to be completed by the Soviets. Built at Nikolayev South Shipyard on the Black Sea in the Ukraine, the conventionally powered sixty-seven-thousand-ton Riga-class ship was laid down in 1982 and finally outfitted for full service in 1985. After making a tour of duty in the Mediterranean, the 885-

foot vessel was tied up in port for repair and modifications. The economic upheaval resulting from the 1991 breakup of the Soviet Union delayed this repair work for several years.

Admiral Popov, circular Russian battleship built in 1875. She was constructed to be a platform for her two twelve-inch guns regardless of the sea state. Along with her sister ship *Novgorod*, she performed reasonably well but proved difficult to keep on course at low speeds.

Admiral's Cup, unofficial world championship of offshore yacht racing, established in 1957 by Great Britain's **Royal Ocean Racing Club**. It is sailed every odd-numbered year at Cowes, **Isle of Wight**, England, and the races include the **Fastnet Race**.

Admiralty, the administrative department governing Britain's **Royal Navy**. It was founded by King Henry VIII (1491–1547) and was amalgamated into the Ministry of Defence in 1964. The offices are still located at **Whitehall** in London.

admiralty law (also known as "**maritime law**"), rules and principles—derived from custom, judicial decisions, legislative enactments, and international treaties—that govern the legal relationships arising from the transportation of passengers and cargoes on the high seas and other navigable waters.

Adney, Edwin Tappan (1868–1950), American artist and writer credited with saving the art of birchbark canoe construction. He built more than a hundred one-fifth-scale models of different types of canoes, which are now housed at the **Mariners' Museum** in Newport News, Virginia. With **Howard Irving Chappelle**, he wrote *The Bark Canoes and Skin Boats of North America* (1964).

Adrift: Seventy-Six Days Lost at Sea, best-selling 1986 account by solo sailor **Steven Callahan** of his two-and-a-half-month survival experience

in 1980 aboard a five-foot rubber life raft in the Atlantic after his twenty-foot sailboat sank in a violent storm.

Adventure Galley, thirty-four-gun vessel—a **galley-frigate** type with both sail and oar power—in which Captain **William Kidd** and a crew of seventy sailed from Plymouth, England, in April 1696 on an expedition to capture pirates. Kidd and an augmented crew turned to pirates themselves in the Indian Ocean and abandoned their ship, *Adventure Galley*, on the coast of Madagascar in favor of a captured ship, *Quedah Merchant*.

Adventures in Paradise, American television show that ran from 1959 to 1962, starring Gardner McKay as Adam Troy, a Korean War veteran who, as captain of the **schooner** *Tiki III*, drifted from adventure to adventure while carrying passengers and cargo around the Pacific.

The Adventures of Roderick Random, picaresque 1748 novel by **Tobias George Smollett**, which provides a graphic account of British naval life of the time by recounting the seagoing adventures of the fictional Scottish rogue **Roderick Random**.

Aebi, Tania (b. 1969), American teenager who, at age eighteen, became the youngest woman to sail solo around the world. Her twenty-seven-thousand-mile, two-and-a-half-year westward voyage in a Contessa 26 was recounted in her book *Maiden Voyage* (1989).

Aegean Captain, 210,257-gross-ton **supertanker** that ran into the tanker *Atlantic Empress* in 1979 while transporting a cargo of crude oil from Venezuela to Singapore. The combined loss of oil from both tankers into the Caribbean was estimated at 48,550 barrels. Both vessels caught fire, and the *Atlantic Empress* was lost. The *Aegean Captain* was salvaged without casualties and towed to Curaçao for repairs.

Aegir, Norse god of the sea.

Aegospotami, Battle of, naval engagement in 405 B.C. off the Dardanelles in which a Spartan fleet of 180 vessels captured 160 Athenian ships, killing their crews. The battle ended the Peloponnesian War—and Athenian naval supremacy.

Aeolia, a floating island described in **Homer**'s *Odyssey*.

An Affair to Remember, hit 20th Century Fox film about a millionaire bachelor and a single heiress who meet and fall in love aboard ship while en route from the Mediterranean to New York. It was filmed aboard the SS *Constitution*, with Deborah Kerr and Cary Grant, during a 1957 westbound crossing.

The African Queen, 1935 novel by **Cecil Scott "C. S." Forester** that takes place in German Central Africa during World War I. Rose Sayer, the sister of a slain English missionary, is rescued by Charlie Allnut, the captain of a **tramp** steamer. They both escape aboard the leaky launch *African Queen* and later sink the German gunboat *Königen Luise* on Lake Tanganyika. The 1951 film adapted from the novel was directed by John Huston and starred Katharine Hepburn and Humphrey Bogart, who won his second Academy Award for his role as the boozing, smoking, cussing captain.

afterguard, a group of crew members, frequently including the owner, who determine the course of action aboard a racing yacht. The term comes from the tradition that the **skipper** and officers aboard ship are stationed around the helm, at the after end of the vessel.

Against All Flags, classic 1952 motion picture, a no-holds-barred epic about an undercover espionage foray into a den of early-eighteenth-century Madagascar pirates. The quintessential swashbuckler was portrayed by Errol Flynn, and the film also starred Maureen O'Hara and Anthony Quinn.

HMS Agamemnon, **Royal Navy** ship launched in 1781 and commanded by **Horatio Nelson** from 1793 to 1796. She saw action in the 1801 victory at the Battle of **Copenhagen** and survived the Battle of **Trafalgar** in 1805. Named for the leader of the Greeks against Troy, who is immortalized both in **Homer**'s *Iliad* and in Aeschylus's tragedy *Agamemnon*, she ran aground in the **River Plate** and was abandoned in 1809.

Agassiz, Alexander (1835–1910), Swiss-born marine zoologist, oceanographer, and mining engineer who used his wealth to make important contributions to marine science. He co-published *Seaside Studies in Natural History* (1865) and also wrote *Marine Animals of Massachusetts Bay* (1871) and *Revision of the Echini* (1872–74). The son of Louis Agassiz, a world authority on living and fossil fish, Alexander was curator of the Harvard Museum from 1874 to 1885 and maintained a private laboratory at his summer residence in Newport, Rhode Island. He underwrote a number of scientific voyages in the Pacific that focused on coral reef studies.

Captain Ahab, fictional one-legged captain of the whaling ship *Pequod* in the novel *Moby-Dick; or, The Whale* (1851), by **Herman Melville**. Ahab is obsessed with avenging himself upon the great white whale Moby Dick, who had bitten off his leg.

aids to navigation (ATON), general term for buoys, beacons, lighthouses, daymarks, and other markers installed to assist navigators and warn of dangers or obstructions.

Aivazovky, Ivan Konstantinovich (1817–1900), Armenian painter embraced by Russian royalty and the Naval Ministry. He was commissioned to paint numerous canvases devoted to Russian ports, battles at sea, and the heroic past of the Russian fleet. Aivazovsky went on to become one of the most celebrated marine artists in Europe. He exhibited in the United States as well and traveled there in 1892.

Akagi, 855-foot Japanese aircraft carrier (whose name means "Red Castle") constructed in 1927 from the hull of an uncompleted battle **cruiser** to comply with the terms of the **Washington Naval Treaty**. She led the task force that attacked **Pearl Harbor** on December 7, 1941. The 36,500-ton ship was set on fire at the Battle of **Midway** from USS *Enterprise*–based aircraft assaults and was **scuttled** to prevent capture by American forces. *Akagi* and her sister ship *Hiryu* were the only carriers ever fitted with port-side islands.

CSS Alabama, most famous of the **Confederate raiders**, which preyed on Union merchant ships and whalers during the Civil War. Built secretly in England in 1862 along with sister ships CSS *Florida* and CSS *Shenandoah*, and commanded by **Raphael Semmes**, *Alabama* sank, burned, or captured sixty-four ships in the next two years. On June 19, 1864, the Union warship USS *Kearsarge* sank *Alabama* outside of the harbor of Cherbourg, France. Following the war, Britain had to pay the United States more than $15 million for damages inflicted on northern shipping by *Alabama* and other Confederate raiders. These reimbursements became known as the *Alabama* Claims.

USS Alabama (BB-60), thirty-five-thousand-ton U.S. **Navy** battleship of the *South Dakota* class built in 1942. After serving in action in the Atlantic Ocean in World War II, she was sent to the Pacific theater of operations. The 680-foot-long warrior earned nine battle stars and led the U.S. fleet into Tokyo Bay in 1945 to receive the surrender of the Imperial Japanese forces. Decommissioned in 1947, the battle-

ship was eventually towed to Mobile Bay in Alabama, where she continues to serve as the centerpiece of Battleship Memorial Park.

Alaska Marine Highway, state-owned and -operated line of ships that carry passengers, vehicles, and freight between Alaskan ports and to the ports of Seattle, Washington, and British Columbia.

Alaska Steamship Company, cargo and passenger operation formed in 1895 to maintain service between ports along the Pacific Coast and Alaskan ports. The 1899 Yukon gold rush insured the company's success. With scheduled service as far as Deering, Saint Michael, and Kotzebue, the American-owned company played a major role in bringing settlers to the frozen frontier. Passenger operations ceased in 1954, and the company sold all of its assets in 1970.

USS Albacore (AGSS-569), experimental U.S. **Navy** submarine completed in 1953. Carrying no weapons, the 205-foot vessel was used to test such new equipment as **sonar** and hydrophones as well as to provide data regarding submerged speed, maneuverability, and depth. The 1,692-ton *Albacore* was decommissioned in 1972 and thirteen years later was opened for tours as a display ship at the Portsmouth Maritime Museum Park in New Hampshire.

Albatros, North Sea pilot **schooner** built in Holland in 1921, a sister ship to the Tabor Academy's *Tabor Boy* and **Irving Johnson**'s *Yankee*. She was purchased by American author Ernest Gann in 1954 and was the subject of his book *Song of the Sirens*. Sold again in 1958, she became an American sail training vessel under Panamanian registry. Hit by a **white squall** in May 1961 while en route from Mexico to the Bahamas, the eighty-three-foot schooner sank in the Caribbean Sea with the loss of six lives. This tragic loss was the subject of the 1995 film *White Squall*.

Japanese carrier *Akagi*. (Courtesy The Mariners' Museum, Newport News, Virginia)

albatross, a large web-footed, soaring seabird inhabiting the Pacific and **Southern Ocean**s, with a wingspan sometimes exceeding twelve feet. Sailing lore has it that each bird bears the soul of a sailor lost at sea.

albatross around one's neck, "The **Rime of the Ancient Mariner**" by **Samuel Taylor Coleridge** tells the tale of a seaman who kills an **albatross**, bringing bad luck to his shipmates. He is forced to wear the bird around his neck as punishment. The phrase has come to mean a burden or something that causes deep anxiety.

Albion, Robert G. (1896–1983), American academic long considered the dean of American naval historians. He was a Harvard professor of Oceanic History and Affairs and served as U.S. historian of naval administration from 1943 to 1950, supervising a project that produced some two hundred volumes. He was the author or contributor to many additional volumes on maritime history.

Alcoa Steamship Company, subsidiary in charge of ocean transportation for the Aluminum Company of America, which was formed in 1940 by the consolidation of the already allied Aluminum Line, American Caribbean Line, and Ocean Dominion Steamship Company. The fleet's main function was to carry raw bauxite from world mines to aluminum plants in the United States. Following World War II, three new combi-**liners** were converted from attack transports for the company. The *Alcoa Cavalier, Alcoa Clipper,* and *Alcoa Corsair* were all on line between South America and New York by 1947. The line ceased to carry passengers after 1960, continuing solely as a cargo operation.

Alden, John (1885–1962), American yacht designer who was one of the first to gain fame through ocean racing. He incorporated a working knowledge of fishing **schooners** in yacht design, and in the 1920s his schooner-rigged ocean racers were thought to be among the few safe and reliable yachts for distance passages. His series of *Malabar*s were the most famous ocean-racing yachts of the 1920s.

Alert, the ship that along with the brig *Pilgrim* carried **Richard Henry Dana Jr.** on his adventure at sea from 1834 to 1836. Dana boarded the larger *Alert* in San Diego for a return trip back to Boston. Dana's voyage is immortalized in his book *Two Years Before the Mast* (1840). The *Alert* had been built for the **China trade** and was a whaleship when she was sunk by the CSS *Alabama* in 1862.

Aleutians, a volcanic island chain in the North Pacific stretching twelve hundred miles southwest from Alaska. The Japanese occupied two of the islands, Attu and Kiska, in 1942–43. Attu was retaken in May 1943 in the only ground fighting on North American soil in World War II.

Alexanderson, Leroy (b. 1910), final commodore of the **United States Lines** and last **master** of the **liner** SS *United States*. He also held the rank of rear admiral in the U.S. **Navy** Reserve.

Alexandr Pushkin, Soviet passenger **liner**, completed at the height of the Cold War in 1965, that inaugurated transatlantic service between Leningrad and Montréal the following year. The ill-designed and poorly decorated 19,861-gross-ton vessel was the second of five identical ships constructed by the Soviet Union to show the hammer and sickle in ports around the world. She was removed from liner operation in 1975, relegated solely to cruising, and then sold in 1991 to become the cruise ship *Marco Polo*.

Alliance, **Continental Navy frigate** that accompanied **John Paul Jones** and *Bonhomme Richard* in their attack on British shipping during the American Revolution. Captain **John Barry** took command of *Alliance* in

1780, and in 1781 she captured two British sloops. Following the war, she made several Atlantic crossings, including transporting the Marquis de Lafayette back to France. In 1783 she fought the last naval battle of the American Revolution. With the **Treaty of Paris**, *Alliance* was the only vessel still in commission in the Continental Navy. She was sold in 1785, and it would be ten years before the United States had another naval vessel.

Aloha Tower, distinctive structure overlooking the cruise ship and ocean **liner** docking facility in Honolulu Harbor that includes piers 9, 10, and 11. When built in 1925, this nine-story pink clock tower was the tallest structure in the territory of Hawaii.

Alter, Hobart "Hobie" (b. 1933), American surfer and outrigger canoe enthusiast who pioneered the development of fiberglass surfboards and a lightweight **catamaran**. In 1968 he designed and introduced the **Hobie Cat**, a popular sailing catamaran.

Altmark, German tanker that was used as a supply ship and floating prison for captured seamen during World War II. In February 1940 British Prime Minister **Winston Churchill** ordered the vessel boarded despite its location in neutral Norwegian waters. Discovered in *Altmark*'s holds while it was anchored in a fjord near Bergen were 299 British merchant seamen captured by the *Admiral Graf Spee*.

Alvin, the U.S. **Navy**'s first manned Deep Submergence Research Vessel (DSRV), commissioned in 1964. In 1966 *Alvin* located the hydrogen bomb that was lost in the Mediterranean when two U.S. planes collided over Spain. In 1986, with underwater explorer **Robert Duane Ballard** aboard, *Alvin* descended to the wreck of RMS *Titanic*. The name for the sub was a contraction of "Allyn Vine," the name of a **Woods Hole Oceanographic Institution** oceanographer and a reference to the popular cartoon chipmunk.

ambergris, a waxlike concretion that may be extracted from the intestine of a dead whale but may also be found floating on the sea or cast up on shore. Extremely valuable, it is used as a fixative for high-quality perfumes.

amberjack, large, fast-swimming game fish found in warm and tropical oceans that is prized for its fierce fighting ability when hooked.

Ambrose (LV-87), replacement **lightship** built in 1907 to send her beacon across the entrance to lower New York Bay between Coney Island and Sandy Hook. She served as a floating lighthouse until she was retired in 1963. *Ambrose* was later presented to New York's **South Street Seaport Museum** for refitting into an exhibit ship.

America, ninety-foot **schooner** built for **John Cox Stevens** and a syndicate of **New York Yacht Club** members both to accompany U.S. exhibits at the first World's Fair in London, England, in 1851 and to race the yachts of Britain's **Royal Yacht Squadron**. *America* defeated fifteen British vessels in a race around the **Isle of Wight** on August 22, 1851, to win the **Hundred Guinea Cup**, later renamed the **America's Cup** in her honor. Sold to a British yachtsman, *America* later returned to the United States, where she served as a Confederate **blockade runner** in the Civil War and a training vessel at the U.S. **Naval Academy**, before again racing for the America's Cup in 1870. **Scuttled** and saved once more, she raced again in the 1920s. She was donated to the Naval Academy, and lasted until the 1940s, when a shed collapsed on her.

America, former **Hamburg-America Line** passenger **liner** *Amerika*, which was built in 1905 and seized in 1917 by the United States for naval transport service. After World War I, she was overhauled and operated by the **United States Lines** and her name given the Yankee spelling. She was again converted for war service in 1941 as USS *Edmund B. Alexander*. **Laid up** in 1949, she was finally scrapped in 1958.

SS *America*, 26,454,-gross-ton U.S. passenger **liner** completed in 1940 to replace the recently retired SS ***Leviathan*** as the flagship of the **United States Lines**. Christened in 1939 by Eleanor Roosevelt, she entered World War II service in 1941 as the troopship USS *West Point*. She took up station on the North Atlantic run in 1946 and was sold in 1964 to **Chandris Line**, after which she became the ***Australis***, serving on emigrant duty to Australia. Sold again to operate short budget cruises from New York in 1978, she quickly reverted to Chandris ownership after a disastrous initial cruise to Nova Scotia as *America*. She was renamed the *Italis* by Chandris but was **laid up** the following year in Piraeus. In 1994, while being towed to Thailand as the *American Star*, she grounded off the Canary Islands and subsequently became a total loss.

***America*^{3}**, American yacht that defeated the Italian yacht *Il Moro di Venezia* in 1992 to retain the **America's Cup** for the United States. Cup newcomer Bill Koch, head of the *America*^{3} syndicate, defeated **Dennis Conner** for the privilege of defending the Cup.

American Bureau of Shipping (ABS), U.S.-based private **classification society** for merchant ships and other marine systems. Founded in 1862, the primary purpose of ABS is to determine the structural and mechanical fitness of ships and other marine structures and to establish design, construction, and operating standards for the same.

American Canoe Association, society founded in 1880 to promote and organize the activities of canoeists in the United States and Canada.

The American Coast Pilot, volume containing navigational information, first published in 1796 by James Furlong at Newburyport,

Massachusetts. Edward March Blount acquired the rights to the volume, but in 1866 the newly formed U.S. Hydrographic Office took over from the Blount family. Through the 1990s, the **National Ocean Service** published nine annual *Coast Pilot*s to supplement nautical charts of U.S. waters.

American Export Lines (AEL), American **steamship** company established in 1919 to carry cargo from New York to the Mediterranean. In 1931 the company entered the passenger business with the addition of the Excalibur-class **Four Aces** combi-**liners**. AEL later designed and operated the incomparable SS *Independence* and SS *Constitution* in the postwar world. In 1962 the Isbrandtsen Company of New York bought a controlling interest in the firm, and its name became the American Export Isbrandtsen Lines. The company stopped carrying passengers in 1968 and filed for bankruptcy in 1977.

American Hawaii Cruises, operating agency of the American Global Line that began inter-Hawaiian service with SS *Independence* in 1980. Two years later her sister ship, SS *Constitution*, also began sailings through the islands. From 1985 to 1987, this agency also operated the former *Argentina*—as SS *Liberté*—on cruises through French Polynesia.

American Legion, organization of former American soldiers and sailors who served in World War I, which later expanded to include veterans of all U.S. wars and conflicts. It was founded in Paris in 1919 at a meeting of representatives of all divisions of the American Expeditionary Force in France. Posts were later set up in each state and in some foreign cities.

American Line, U.S. transatlantic **steamship** line established in 1871, which became a subsidiary of the **Red Star Line** in 1884. In 1893 the line transferred the British-built **liners** *City of New York* and *City of Paris* to U.S. registry. The U.S. Congress permitted this

transfer on the condition that the line build two comparable ships in the United States, which it did—the *St. Louis* and the *St. Paul*.

American Maritime Officers (AMO), national union representing licensed officers in all sectors of the U.S.-flag merchant fleet. It was chartered in 1949 as the Brotherhood of Marine Engineers, an affiliate of the **Seafarers International Union**.

American Merchant Marine Library Association (AMMLA), organization founded in 1921 to provide portable libraries to U.S. merchant vessels. In addition to supplying mariners with entertainment, having books on board was intended to prevent seamen from reading the socialist propaganda distributed in many foreign ports. AMMLA became part of the **United Seamen's Service** in 1973.

The American Neptune, quarterly scholarly journal of maritime history and the arts published since 1950 by the **Peabody Essex Museum** in Salem, Massachusetts.

The American Practical Navigator, U.S. government publication that describes the modern principles of marine navigation and includes tables, data, and instructions required by navigators to perform computations associated with dead reckoning, piloting, and celestial navigation. Published on a five-year schedule by the **National Imagery and Mapping Agency** (formerly the **Defense Mapping Agency**), it contains sections addressing the practice of navigation, navigational safety, oceanography, weather, and electronic navigation. The publication is popularly known as *Bowditch*, because it was originally published by **Nathaniel Bowditch** in 1802.

American President Lines (APL), transpacific shipping company started by Captain Robert Dollar in 1900 as the **Dollar Line**. The company also acquired a controlling interest in the American Mail Line in 1923 and then assumed the more recognized moniker in 1938, when the whole operation was taken over by the U.S. **Maritime Commission** and reorganized to prevent bankruptcy. Well known for such passenger **liners** as *President Cleveland* and *President Wilson* as well as its fleet of freighters and container vessels, in 1995 the line was acquired by the Singapore-based Neptune Orient Lines.

American Queen, the largest Mississippi **paddle wheeler** ever constructed. Built in 1995 at a cost in excess of $65 million for the **Delta Queen Steamboat Company** in New Orleans, it embodies all the luxury and romance associated with these river vessels in American folk legend.

American Sail Training Association (ASTA), a nonprofit organization founded in 1972 for the promotion and support of sail training and sea education in the United States. Based in Newport, Rhode Island, it is the American arm of the International Sail Training Association (ISTA).

American Society of Marine Artists (ASMA), organization founded by the **National Maritime Historical Society** in 1976 to promote marine art and maritime history in the United States and to encourage cooperation among artists, historians, and other scholars and enthusiasts of marine art and maritime history. Britain's Royal Society of Marine Artists (RSMA) inspired the founding of ASMA.

American Victory, standard **Victory ship** freighter constructed in 1945. The 10,750-gross-ton vessel was used to ferry supplies between California and the Pacific front in World War II. She saw postwar service under charter to private operators and was one of the vessels of the **Military Sealift Command** during the Vietnam conflict. She was **laid up** in reserve in 1969 for thirty years, until rescued from oblivion by the American Victory Mariners Memorial, where she serves as a museum ship in Tampa, Florida.

American Waterways Operators (AWO), national trade association for the barge and towing industry and the shipyards employed in the repair and construction of these craft.

America's Cup, the world's most famous sailing competition and the longest-running international sporting event. In 1851, the **schooner** *America* won the ornate silver **Hundred Guinea Cup** by beating fifteen British yachts in a race around the **Isle of Wight** off the southern coast of England. The cup became known as the **America's Cup** and is currently challenged every 3 to 5 years or as agreed upon. The first team to win four races wins the match and the Cup. Races are now held on a triangular course, twenty-four nautical miles long, off the defending nation's coast. The **New York Yacht Club** dominated the event for 132 years.

America's Cup, the trophy, twenty-seven-inch, sixteen-pound, Victorian-era sterling silver ewer fashioned by London jeweler Robert Garrard as a yachting trophy for Britain's **Royal Yacht Squadron**. Originally called the **Hundred Guinea Cup**, it was presented to the winner of an invitational race around the **Isle of Wight** on August 22, 1851. Renamed after the **schooner** *America*, the winner of that race, it was presented in 1857 to the **New York Yacht Club** as a perpetual trophy open to challenge by any foreign yacht club. The names of the winning boats adorn the cup, and the club that sponsored the winner holds the trophy.

Amerika, proposed transatlantic superliner to be constructed for **North German Lloyd** as a replacement for the **scuttled** SS *Columbus* and to recapture the **Blue Riband** as a display of Nazi technology. The ship was to be 1,070 feet long and over eighty thousand gross tons. Her intended speed of thirty-eight **knots** was to be delivered by five steam turbine–driven propellers receiving three hundred thousand horsepower. The keel-laying ceremony was planned for 1939 in the presence of Adolf Hitler but was postponed indefinitely for more important military vessel construction. If built, *Amerika* would have wound up the ultimate white elephant because her thirsty machinery would have needed a hundred tons of bunker fuel an hour to maintain a record-breaking speed.

Amistad, coastal **schooner** on which fifty-three Africans sold into slavery initiated a shipboard revolt in 1839 in the waters off Cuba. *Amistad* wound up in U.S. waters, and the Africans were taken into custody in New London, Connecticut. American abolitionists mounted a legal defense on their behalves, and the case went all the way to the Supreme Court, where former president John Quincy Adams joined the abolitionists' legal team. In March 1841 the court upheld their freedom, and ten months later the thirty-five *Amistad* Africans who had survived the ordeal returned to their homeland. The story was the subject of a 1997 film directed by Steven Spielberg. A replica of the ship was launched in 2000 by **Mystic Seaport** in Connecticut and is sailed today to promote African-American history.

Amoco Cadiz, 233,690-deadweight-ton tanker built in Spain in 1971 for Amoco Oil Corporation to carry crude oil from the Arabian Gulf to Europe. On March 16, 1978, while en route to Rotterdam, the ship lost power in the English Channel and drifted onto rocks off the coast of Brittany, becoming a total constructive loss. The ship broke in two and disgorged some 223,000 tons of crude oil onto the French coastline. In 1988 Amoco was ordered to pay $83 million in fines.

Amphitrite, the goddess of the sea in Greek mythology. The daughter of the titan Ocean, she became the wife of **Poseidon** and the mother of **Triton**.

Amundsen, Roald (1872–1928), Norwegian polar explorer and leader of the first expedition to reach the South Pole, in December 1911. He arrived one month before the ill-fated expedition led by British naval officer and explorer Captain **Robert Falcon Scott**. From 1903 to 1906, he successfully cajoled the converted fishing smack *Gjøa* on the first trip through the **Northwest Passage**, also reaching the magnetic North Pole. He died when his plane was lost over the **Barents Sea** during a search for explorer Umberto Nobile and his airship *Italia*.

AMVER, acronym for Automated Mutual-Assistance Vessel Rescue, an international search and rescue system operated by the U.S. **Coast Guard**. Through international cooperation, ships and other vessels on the high seas report their positions and routes of travel so that, in an emergency, they may be called upon to render aid to a vessel in distress. When initiated in 1958 as Atlantic Merchant Vessel Emergency Rescue, the operation's scope was limited to the Atlantic Ocean north of the equator and west of the prime meridian.

anadromous, species of fish that reproduce in and inhabit fresh water but usually journey out to the ocean before returning to spawn. Anadromous species include salmon, steelhead trout, and striped bass.

Anchor Line, Scottish shipping firm established in 1856 that maintained cargo and passenger services on the Atlantic and to the Indian subcontinent. The company retained its own tartan character and image from 1912 until 1935, while it was operated by the **Cunard Line**. Anchor Line attained financial independence by reorganizing and was closely allied with the **Donaldson Line**. Anchor ceased transatlantic sailings in 1940, although the India passenger operation continued until 1965. Among the more famous vessels of its Atlantic fleet were the *California*, *Cameronia*, and *Transylvania*.

"Anchors Aweigh", unofficial U.S. **Navy** service march written in 1906 for the U.S. **Naval**

Academy class of 1907. The music was composed by Lt. Charles A. Zimmerman, bandmaster at the Naval Academy, and the lyrics were written by midshipman Alfred H. Miles. The march was first performed at the Army–Navy football game in Philadelphia in 1906.

SS *Ancon*, American passenger **liner** built in 1939 for the New York to **Panama Canal** service of the Panama Railroad. From 1942 to 1946, *Ancon* was taken over as a U.S. Army transport. The streamlined 10,021-gross-ton vessel was **laid up** in 1961 and sold the following year for use as the training ship *State of Maine*. She was broken up in 1973.

SS *Andrea Doria*, **Italian Line flagship** built in 1953 to reestablish Italy in the premier Genoa to New York trade, named for the Italian admiral (1466–1560) recognized as the father and liberator of Genoa. The single-funneled, 29,083-gross-ton beauty was rammed July 25, 1956, by MV *Stockholm* a hundred miles short of New York in heavy fog, killing forty-seven people in the collision. The **liner** settled onto her **starboard** side before sinking the following day, after 1,654 people had been saved by rescue vessels. *Stockholm* limped to New York for repairs. Very bad press followed, and the two shipping companies involved settled their lawsuits out of court. The wreck of *Andrea Doria* has become a popular dive site and continues to claim lives.

Andrea Gail, **Gloucester**, Massachusetts, swordfish boat whose story is portrayed in Sebastian Junger's best-selling book *The Perfect Storm* (1996), which was later made into a movie (2000). With a six-man crew, the *Andrea Gail* was lost at sea during an unexpectedly massive storm that developed off New England in 1991.

Angel Island, immigration staging facility located on the largest island in San Francisco Bay. Between 1910 and 1940, it was the major portal of entry to the United States for Asian immigrants, processing more than 175,000

Chinese newcomers alone. The U.S. Army used the island as a base from 1863 to 1946, and in World War II enemy prisoners of war were confined there. The compound has been restored and today is a museum, while the island is a state park.

Angel's Gate, name of the San Pedro breakwater entrance to Los Angeles Harbor.

Anglo-Dutch War, series of three seventeenth-century wars fought by England and the Netherlands over sea trade and fishing rights. The first war was from 1652 to 1654; the second, from 1664 to 1667; and the third, from 1672 to 1674. The second war resulted in the English possession of New Amsterdam, which was later renamed New York in honor of James II, the Duke of York, admiral and head of the British navy. The third war ended with signing of the Treaty of Westminster.

Anne of the Indies, a film of spying and piracy on the eighteenth-century **Spanish Main** in which the hero rescues the not-so-hapless damsel in distress. The 1951 B movie starred Louis Jourdan, Debra Paget, and Jean Peters.

Ann McKim, 143-foot, three-masted, square-rigged ship considered by some to have been the first **clipper ship**. She was designed and built in Baltimore in 1832 for railroad and shipping tycoon Isaac McKim. After twenty years of successful sailing, the ship was broken up at Valparaíso, Chile, in 1852.

Anson, Admiral George (1697–1762), British admiral who led a fleet of seven vessels on a circumnavigation (1740–44), which only one ship, HMS *Centurion*, completed. While attacking Spanish shipping in 1743, Anson took a treasure-laden **galleon**, a prize that enriched him for life. The expedition was partly chronicled by the ship's chaplain, Richard Walter, in *A Voyage Round the World* (1748). Anson served as Britain's **First Lord of the Admiralty** from 1751 to 1756 and from

Model of the *Ann McKim*. (Courtesy Addison Gallery, Phillips Academy, Andover, Massachusetts; model by Walter A. Simonds)

1757 to 1762 and is credited with building a more professional navy.

Antarctic Circle, imaginary line that forms the northern boundary of Antarctica. Points on the Antarctic Circle lie at 66°30′ South **latitude** and mark the edge of an area where the sun stays above the horizon one or more days each year.

Antilles, **French Line** steamer, sister ship to the *Flandre*, built in 1953 for the company's Caribbean service. The 19,828-gross-ton **liner** went aground on an uncharted reef off of the island of Mustique in the Saint Vincent and Grenadines group in 1971, resulting in the destruction of the ship by fire. All 635 people on board were rescued by the *Queen Elizabeth 2*.

antipodean day, the day gained when crossing the **international date line** (180th meridian) going east.

Antipodes, old British term for Australia and New Zealand because of their location in relation to England at opposite ends of the earth.

Anything Goes, classic Cole Porter song-and-dance extravaganza set aboard the make-believe transatlantic **liner** *American*, featuring the songs "I Get a Kick Out of You," "You're the Top," and the title song "Anything Goes." It opened on Broadway in 1934, starring Ethel Merman, William Gaxton, and Vivian Vance, and was made into a motion picture two years later, with Ethel Merman and Bing Crosby in the lead roles. The movie was refilmed in 1956 and featured Bing Crosby, Donald O'Connor, Mitzi Gaynor, and Phil Harris.

Anzio, Italian coastal town south of Rome that was the site of a major landing in the World War II Allied invasion of Italy. In January 1944 troops set up the beachhead, which was secured only after heavy fighting.

apparent wind, the speed and true direction from which the wind appears to blow in reference to a ship's motion.

April in Paris, film set in the mid-Atlantic aboard a **liner** bound for France, featuring shipboard songs, merriment, and mistaken identities. Doris Day kicking up her heels in the galley along with the ship's vast culinary crew while belting out "We're gonna rock the boat tonight" is the 1952 film's most improbable—and most entertaining—sequence. It also starred Ray Bolger and Paul Harvey.

aqualung, underwater diving device, now better known by its acronym **scuba** (self-contained underwater breathing apparatus) that permits free dives to considerable depths. Coinvented in 1943 by two Frenchmen—**Jacques-Yves Cousteau**, a naval officer, and Emile Gagnan, an engineer—it became available commercially in 1946.

Aquaman, DC Comics comic book superhero character created in 1941 who uses his abilities to fight crime. The son of an Atlantean and a human, Aquaman is king of the city of Poseidonis and the figurative king of the sea. He can breathe underwater, swim at high speeds, and control sea creatures through mental telepathy.

Aquarama, **Great Lakes** passenger and car ferry originally constructed in 1945 as the **C4 freighter** *Marine Star*. The vessel was rebuilt for lake operation in 1953, during which all structures more than fifty-five feet above the waterline were removed and stowed on deck to allow passage under bridges on the **Mississippi River** and the **Illinois Waterway**. Conversion was completed in the Great Lakes, and the 12,773-gross-ton *Aquarama* began regular service between Detroit and Cleveland in 1955. She was removed from active operation in 1977.

aquavit, alcohol spirit clear to pale yellow in color, distilled from fermented potatoes or grain mash, and flavored with caraway and other spices or citrus. Considered the vodka of Scandinavia, the name derives from *aqua vitae*, Latin for "water of life." Certain brands of aquavit require that it be stored in oak containers and make a long sea voyage—supposedly to improve the normal aging process. The same is said for armagnac, cognac, and whiskey.

SS Aquitania, famous 45,647-gross-ton **Cunard Line** passenger ship that served in both world wars. Built in 1914 to round out the transatlantic express service with RMS *Lusitania* and RMS *Mauretania*, her design was profoundly influenced by the size and salient features of the **White Star Line**'s RMS *Olympic,* introduced in 1911. *Aquitania* made varied cruises between the wars, including three-day "booze cruises" from New York, which catered to thirsty Americans tormented by Prohibition. Known as the "Ship Beautiful" for her elegant public rooms and perfect, four-**funnel** exterior lines, she operated on the emigrant service to Halifax, Nova Scotia, from 1948 to the end of 1949. She was sold for scrap after more than thirty-five years of continuous service for her owners.

The Cunard Line transatlantic veteran *Aquitania*. (Courtesy Gordon R. Ghareeb; photo by Everett E. Viez)

Arabia, cargo **steamboat** that sank in the **Missouri River** just north of Kansas City in 1856. Excavated in 1988, *Arabia* was a time capsule of remarkably preserved pre–Civil War frontier supplies, including bottled fruit, vegetables, clothing, dishes, tools, and weapons. The objects are showcased in the Arabia Steamboat Museum in Kansas City, Missouri.

SS Arabic, British passenger steamer that was torpedoed by a German **U-boat** on August 19, 1915, during World War I, resulting in the loss of two American lives. Occurring more than three months after the sinking of RMS *Lusitania* (with the loss of 128 American lives), the incident prompted Germany to issue the *Arabic* Pledge, which stated that unarmed passenger ships would not be sunk without warning. Apart from one incident, Germany stood by the pledge until unrestricted submarine warfare was reopened in February 1917.

Aral Sea, large saltwater lake in Kazakhstan and Uzbekistan. It is one of the world's largest inland bodies of water, covering about 15,500 square miles. Since the early 1960s, however, diversion of river water for irrigation has caused the lake to shrink to about sixty percent of its former size.

Arcadia. (Courtesy Gordon R. Ghareeb)

Arcadia, 29,734-gross-ton steamer built for the Australian service of the **P&O** in 1954. Starting in 1972, she did extensive cruising from California, especially pioneering cruises through Alaska's **Inland Passage** for large passenger ships. She was scrapped in 1979.

Archangel, one of the largest Far North cities in the world. Located in Russia, it lies about a hundred miles below the **Arctic Circle**. During World War I, Allied troops captured the port city to secure Western interests in the face of the Bolshevik Revolution. During World War II, Archangel was an important northern port for receiving supplies from the Allies.

Archer, Colin (1832–1921), Norwegian-born Scottish shipbuilder and designer of **pilot** boats and rescue **cutters**. He was famous for building seaworthy vessels, one of the most well known being the polar ship *Fram*, which carried the explorers **Fridtjof Nansen** and later **Roald Amundsen** on their voyages to the Arctic and Antarctic.

archipelago, group of islands that are closely related and form a distinct geographic entity.

SS *Arctic*, Collins Line transatlantic **side-wheel** steamer built in 1850. The 2,860-gross-ton **liner** featured such innovations as steam heat, bathtubs, and a barber shop. Her luxury far surpassed that to be found on the rival ships of the **Cunard Line** at the time. In 1854 she collided with the French liner *Vesta* in fog off Cape Race, Newfoundland, and sank with the loss of 322 lives. Among those lost were the wife and two children of the line's founder and owner, **Edward Knight Collins**.

Arctic Circle, imaginary line that runs through the northern parts of Canada, Alaska, Russia, and Scandinavia. All points on the Arctic Circle lie at 66°30′ North **latitude** and mark the edge of an area where the sun stays above the horizon one or more days each year.

Argentina, American passenger **liner** constructed in 1958 for the South American service of the **Moore-McCormack Line**. She was notable for having engine uptakes aft, while the dummy funnel contained a forward-facing observation platform and an enclosed solarium, which was intended—although never advertised—for nude sunbathing. In 1972 the 14,984-gross-ton vessel became **Holland America Line**'s SS *Veendam* before changing owners with great frequency thereafter.

Argo, in Greek mythology, the ship that carried **Jason** and his crew of **Argonauts** in quest of the Golden Fleece. A replica was built in 1984 by **Tim Severin** to retrace the route.

Argo Merchant, 18,743-gross-ton Greek tanker built in 1953 that grounded on a shoal twenty-five miles southeast of Nantucket on December 15, 1976, while en route from Venezuela to Boston with a cargo of 183,000 barrels of fuel oil. The ship broke up in rough weather, dumping her entire cargo into the ocean off the Massachusetts coast. Northeast winds kept most of the oil at sea, and it remained the worst spill in U.S. waters until bested by that of the *Exxon Valdez* thirteen years later.

Argonauts, in Greek mythology, a group of fifty sailors and adventurers who sailed with **Jason** on the *Argo* in quest of the Golden Fleece. The fleece was kept in a kingdom on the **Black Sea**.

USS *Arizona* (BB-39), U.S. **Navy Pennsylvania-class** battleship completed in 1916 that patrolled the East Coast during World War I. While lying at anchor in **Battleship Row** in **Pearl Harbor** on the morning of December 7, 1941, the vessel exploded after being hit by a 1,760-pound armor-piercing bomb during the Japanese strike on the U.S. naval base. The ship sank in less than nine minutes, with the loss of 1,177 sailors. She was never decommissioned or salvaged; nor were the dead entombed in her hull recovered. Instead, she remains on the harbor bottom at Ford Island as a national memorial to the attack. Her location required that every naval ship sailing from Pearl Harbor to fight the war in the Pacific pass her partially submerged remains as a reminder of the Japanese raid. In 1962 a permanent shrine was built above the wreckage, and the Arizona Memorial continues to be one of the most revered of all American historical sites.

USS *Arkansas* (BB-33), 27,243-ton U.S. **Navy** Wyoming-class battleship completed for duty in 1912. The 562-foot vessel was stationed in Scotland for most of World War I. She moved to the **Atlantic** for World War II, and in 1944 she shelled Omaha Beach from two miles offshore to support the Invasion of **Normandy**. Reassigned to the Pacific in 1945, she took part in the assault on **Iwo Jima**. The battleship was used as a target ship in **Operation Crossroads** at the **Bikini Atoll** in 1946 and was sunk during the second atomic bomb test there.

HMS *Ark Royal*, British aircraft carrier completed in 1939 and designed to be superior to the U.S. **Navy**'s *Yorktown*. Aircraft launched from her decks played an important role in the sinking of the *Bismarck*. In November 1941 *Ark Royal* was hit by a single torpedo from U-81 off Gibraltar and developed a bad **starboard** list. An attempt to tow the vessel into harbor failed, and she sank.

Arktika, Soviet nuclear-powered icebreaker that in 1975 became the first surface vessel to reach the North Pole.

USS *Arleigh Burke* (DDG-51), prototype U.S. **Navy** guided missile destroyer completed in 1991. The ship is noticeably wider in beam than her predecessors, and Admiral **Arleigh Burke**—a famous leader during World War II—said the ship was named for him because he too was broad in the beam. The 504-foot, steam-driven vessel gave her name to a class of forty ships built to the same design, which are capable of speeds far above their posted best of thirty-two **knots**. Their firepower make them the most powerful U.S. surface ships built since the **Iowa**-class battleships of World War II.

U.S. Army Corps of Engineers (USACE), unique division of the U.S. Army founded in 1775 to oversee civil works projects in support of the public and private sectors. Since 1924 the Corps has managed national water resource projects, including the construction of flood control works, and is responsible for managing and restoring U.S. wetlands and for charting most of America's inland waters. In addition to monitoring the nation's deep draft harbors, it has built an intracoastal and inland network of commercial navigation channels. It oversaw the canalization of the **Mississippi River** system with levees and locks, and it lined the river in many places. During times of war, the USACE handles the assault boats, rafts, and bridging during river-crossing operations.

Aronow, Donald (1927–1987), American speedboat designer, builder, and racer who transformed high-performance powerboating by founding four speedboat manufacturing companies: Formula, **Donzi**, Cigarette (see also **William Hand**), and Magnum. He made his

W. H. Aspinwall.

money in real estate development in New Jersey in the 1950s and moved to Miami Beach, Florida. Over the years, Aronow's powerboats have won more than eleven world and twenty-five U.S. championships and have held twenty-five world speed records. Aronow was shot to death in 1987 on Thunderboat Row, the very Miami street he made famous. The case involving his murder has not been closed.

Around Alone, single-handed, around-the-world sailing race held every four years since its inception in 1982. The course spans twenty-seven thousand miles of the world's roughest and most remote oceans. It was formerly known as the **BOC Challenge**—carrying the name of its founding sponsor, the British gas company BOC.

Around Cape Horn, 1980 award-winning video, narrated by Captain **Irving M. Johnson**, on the last days of commercial sail. It contains real film footage of Johnson rounding **Cape Horn** on board the **bark** *Peking* in 1929.

Around the World Submerged, 1962 book by Captain **Edward L. Beach** about the submarine USS *Triton*'s thirty-six-thousand-mile underwater circumnavigation in 1960.

ARPA, acronym for automatic **radar** plotting aid, a processing device that manipulates radar returns through a computer to display ship vectors and provide collision avoidance information.

Asama Maru, popular NYK (**Nippon Yusen Kaisha**) transpacific motor **liner** completed in 1929 for service between Yokohama, San Francisco, and Los Angeles. The 16,975-gross-ton vessel was taken over by the Imperial Japanese Navy in 1941 to be operated as a troop transport in the Pacific conflict and was sunk by the U.S. submarine *Atule* in 1944. She was sister ship to the *Tatsuta Maru*.

Ascension Island, volcanic island in the South Atlantic Ocean, seven hundred miles north-west of **Saint Helena**, said to be so named because it was discovered on Ascension Day. **William Dampier** shipwrecked there in 1699, and Captain **James Cook** called there in 1775. Great Britain established a naval base on the uninhabited island when **Napoleon I** was exiled to Saint Helena in 1815. In 1922 the island was made a dependency of Saint Helena.

ASDIC, a device used for detecting submarines. The name derives from the Anti-Submarine Detection Investigation Committee, a British-French collaboration after World War I. The American name for the device was **sonar**.

ash breeze, sailor slang for rowing, or the progress made with oars in a calm.

Ashley, Clifford W. (1881–1947), American painter, illustrator, and author of marine subjects. He wrote *The Yankee Whaler* (1926), a history of New England whaling, among other books, and is best known for his *Ashley Book of Knots* (1944), a guide to knot tying. Sales of the book surged when it was given fresh notice in Annie Proulx's *The Shipping News* (1993).

"As idle as a painted ship, Upon a painted ocean", lines from "The **Rime of the Ancient Mariner**," by **Samuel Taylor Coleridge**.

Aspinwall, William Henry (1807–1875), American merchant who created a shipping empire that contributed greatly to the development of the western United States. He entered the shipping business in the 1830s, ran early **clippers**, and established the **Pacific Mail Steam Ship Company** and the Panama Railroad. The city of Colón in Panama, founded in 1850 by Americans working on the trans-Panama railroad, was named Aspinwall until 1890.

Assault on a Queen, successful 1959 adventure novel by Jack Finney about a high-seas holdup aboard RMS *Queen Mary* carried out by a band of treasure hunters using a salvaged World War I German **U-boat**. The novel was adapted by Rod Serling for the 1965 Paramount film version, which starred Frank Sinatra, Virna Lisi, and Tony Franciosa, with a musical score by Duke Ellington. It was filmed aboard *Queen Mary* off the Bahamas while the **liner** was on a five-day cruise to Nassau.

Astor, John Jacob (1763–1848), richest American of his day, who first made his money in fur trading. In connection with his fur trade, Astor established the first line of fur trading stations and founded Astoria, Oregon. He engaged in import and export and owned his own shipping lines. The bulk of the family fortune derived from his real estate holdings in Manhattan.

Astor IV, John Jacob (d. 1912), great-great-grandson of **John Jacob Astor** and heir to the Astor fortune who went down with RMS *Titanic* on April 15, 1912. An avid yachtsman, Astor was the wealthiest passenger—with a fortune estimated at $100 million. After a long second honeymoon in Egypt and Paris, he was returning home with his second wife, Madeleine, who was five months pregnant. She survived the sinking.

astrolabe, ancient navigational instrument used to measure the altitude of celestial bodies in order to determine latitude. Developed by the Greeks and refined by the Arabs, astrolabes were used well into the eighteenth century. One advantage of an astrolabe was that it needed no horizon; however, ship motion made its readings inaccurate in any kind of sea.

Atalanta, 70-foot Canadian challenger to the **America's Cup** in 1881 who was soundly defeated by the American defender *Mischief* in two races off Sandy Hook, New Jersey. The competition was the first America's Cup raced between single-masted boats.

SS *Athenia*, Anchor-Donaldson **liner** built in 1923 to serve the company's Glasgow to Canada route. The 13,465-gross-ton ship was

torpedoed by U-30 two hundred miles west of the Hebrides Islands on September 3, 1939, shortly after Britain had declared war on Germany, making *Athenia* the first merchant ship to be sunk in World War II. Of the 1,418 passengers and crew onboard, 112 perished.

Atlantic, see **Atlantic Ocean**.

Atlantic, one of the most renowned sail racing yachts of the early twentieth century. She was designed by **William Gardner** and built in 1903 for Wilson Marshall. The three-masted, 185-foot, steel-hulled *Atlantic* won the **Kaiser's Cup** in 1905, setting a transatlantic speed record, while **skippered** by **Charles Barr**. The much-favored *Atlantic*'s defeat in the 1928 **Transatlantic Race** by *Elena* and *Niña* symbolized the change in sail racing from large yachts with professional crews to smaller yachts run by amateurs. Engaged in coastal patrol duty in World War II, *Atlantic* was broken up in the late 1970s.

SS *Atlantic*, 429-foot **White Star Line** steamer built in 1871 and employed in transatlantic passenger service. She departed Liverpool on March 20, 1873, en route to New York, but encountered rough seas. Low on coal, the ship altered course to the nearest port and ran aground April 1 on the rocky coast near Halifax, Nova Scotia. An estimated 250 people were saved, but at least 560 lost their lives.

SS *Atlantic*, U.S. passenger **liner** built in 1958 using the hull and machinery of the *Badger Mariner* for the American Banner Lines. Acquired by **American Export Lines** in 1960 when the decision was made not to build their proposed *Constellation*, she was sold to Orient Overseas Lines in 1971, renamed the *Universe*, and used for an at-sea college after the destruction of the *Seawise University* (ex–*Queen Elizabeth*) in Hong Kong.

Atlantic, Battle of the, continuous battle fought in the **Atlantic Ocean** during World

The front of an astrolabe.

The back of an astrolabe.

War II by the sea forces of the Allies against Germany to control the supply routes to the United Kingdom. The battle opened September 3, 1939, when the **liner** *Athenia*, sailing from Glasgow to New York, was torpedoed by a **U-boat**. On May 24, 1943, Admiral **Karl Dönitz** issued orders for his submarine **wolf packs** to return to home bases because, quite literally, the Americans were producing ships faster than the Germans could sink them. German submarine aggression was also countered by the efficiency the Allies had developed in **convoy** operation and protection. The Allies destroyed nearly eight hundred U-boats during the campaign, and at least twenty-two hundred convoys of seventy-five thousand merchant ships crossed the ocean protected by U.S. naval forces.

Atlantic Charter, declaration that outlined the post–World War II aims of the United States and Great Britain. It was signed by President **Franklin D. Roosevelt** and Prime Minister **Winston Churchill** in August 1941 during a conference aboard the ships USS *Augusta* and HMS *Prince of Wales*, which were anchored at Placentia Bay, off the coast of the Canadian province of Newfoundland.

Atlantic Conveyor, 14,946-gross-ton container ship built for the **Cunard Line**'s subsidiary Atlantic Container Line to maintain transatlantic cargo service. She was requisitioned by the British government in 1982 for duty in the Falklands War. While transporting Harrier Jump Jet aircraft, the *Conveyor* was hit by a French-built, Argentine-launched Exocet missile. Fire erupted and eventually engulfed the ship, which sank with the loss of twelve crew members.

Atlantic Empress, 128,398-gross-ton Greek **supertanker** built in 1974. She collided with the tanker *Aegean Captain* in 1979 while en route from Texas to the Persian Gulf. Both ships caught fire, and some 48,550 combined barrels of crude oil were released into the Caribbean Sea not far from the island of Little Tobago. The fire killed twenty-six crew members on the *Atlantic Empress* before she sank.

Atlantic Ferry, 1941 British motion picture about a race of two **steamships** across the **Atlantic** to prove the superiority of the owners, who just happen to be brothers. Set in 1840, the film—starring Michael Redgrave and Griffith Jones—is a broad exaggeration of the origins of the **Cunard Line**.

Atlantic High, 1982 novel by **William F. Buckley** describing his passage across the **Atlantic** aboard the **ketch** *Sealestial*.

Atlantic Neptune, series of 250 charts and views of the **Atlantic** coast of North America produced by British army engineer J. F. W. Des Barres around 1776.

Atlantic Ocean, named by the Greeks as the sea beyond the Atlas mountains, near the **Strait of Gibraltar**, and long thought to be home to the lost continent of **Atlantis**. Atlantis is now believed by most scholars to have been in the Mediterranean.

Atlantic Provinces, the four Canadian provinces of New Brunswick, Newfoundland, Nova Scotia, and Prince Edward Island. Three of the provinces—New Brunswick, Nova Scotia, and Prince Edward Island—are sometimes called the **Maritime Provinces**.

Atlantis, a legendary kingdom believed to have once occupied a large island in the **Atlantic Ocean**. The first mention of Atlantis appeared during the 300s B.C. in two works by the Greek philosopher Plato. According to Plato, a brilliant civilization once existed on Atlantis, but its people became corrupt and greedy and so the gods punished them. During one day and night, great explosions shook Atlantis, and the continent sank into the sea. Atlantis is now believed by most scholars to have been in the Mediterranean. Recent research suggests that the legend may have been inspired by the volcanic eruption of the Greek island of Thera in the 1620s B.C.

Atlantis, short-lived incarnation of the passenger **liner** *President Roosevelt* when purchased and extensively rebuilt by the **Chandris Line** in 1971. After a riotous cruise was aborted in New York with much unflattering press, the 24,458-gross-ton liner never gained the popularity Chandris hoped for. She was sold in 1972 to the Eastern Steamship Company and was renamed the *Emerald Seas*.

Atocha, see *Nuestra Señora de Atocha*.

Atomic Submarine, interesting futuristic motion picture tale of USS *Tiger Shark*, a state-of-the-art U.S. atomic submarine that encounters a submerged flying saucer in the frigid depths of the Arctic Ocean. The 1959 science fiction classic starred Arthur Franz and Dick Foran.

Aubrey, Jack, fictional **Royal Navy** officer in **Patrick O'Brian**'s **Aubrey-Maturin** series.

Aubrey-Maturin, refers to the two protagonists of the series of twenty books by **Patrick O'Brian** set in His Majesty's **Royal Navy** during the Napoleonic era. The series traces the mingled careers of Captain **Jack Aubrey** and ship's surgeon turned intelligence agent **Stephen Maturin**. The series begins with *Master and Commander* (1970) and ends with *Blue at the Mizzen* (1999).

Auld Mug, nickname for the **America's Cup** coined by Sir **Thomas Lipton**.

aurora, natural display of light in the sky that can be seen with the unaided eye only at night. An auroral display in the Northern Hemisphere is called the aurora borealis, or the northern lights. A similar phenomenon in the Southern Hemisphere is called the aurora australis, or the southern lights.

Aurora, Russian **cruiser** that fired the opening shots of the Bolshevik Revolution early on the morning of October 25, 1917. Anchored in the Neva River, the ship's crew fired a broadside of blanks, which signaled the storming of the Winter Palace at Saint Petersburg. Built in 1903, *Aurora* was a veteran of the 1904–5 Russo-Japanese War and is today a floating museum in Saint Petersburg.

Australia, Australian challenger for the **America's Cup** in 1977 and again in 1980. She was defeated by the American defenders *Courageous*, **skippered** by **Ted Turner**, and *Freedom*, skippered by **Dennis Conner**.

Australia II, Australian **twelve-meter sloop** that was the first non-American contender to win the **America's Cup**. Designed by **Ben Lexcen**, she had a winged keel, which improved her lateral resistance and maneuverability. Built and raced by a syndicate headed by **Alan Bond** and **skippered** by John Bertrand, "Winged Victory," as she would be called, defeated **Dennis Conner** and *Liberty* in 1983 in five races in the waters off Newport, Rhode Island.

SS Australis, the former **United States Lines** SS *America* while operating from 1965 to 1977 under the ownership of the **Chandris Line**. Renamed *American Star*, she ran aground while being towed to Thailand in 1994 and became a total loss.

SS Austria, **Hamburg-America Line** passenger and emigrant ship launched in 1857 and employed in North Atlantic service. During an 1858 crossing, the ship's surgeon ordered that the steerage compartments be fumigated. A fire broke out and engulfed the entire ship. Of the 538 passengers on board, mostly Germans and Hungarians, 471 either drowned or burned to death.

Automated Mutual-Assistance Vessel Rescue, see **AMVER**.

auxiliary, a sailboat carrying auxiliary power. Also, a noncombatant vessel that supports fighting ships with provisions, fuel, ammunition, and personnel.

avast, a seafaring interjection that means to stop.

Away All Boats, best-selling 1955 novel by Kenneth Dodson extolling the wartime services of the American sailor. It featured the fictitious story of USS *Belinda*—a World War II U.S. **Navy** attack transport—and the gradual enlightenment of her crew as they head for battle. Based on the novel and starring Jeff Chandler, Keith Andes, and Richard Boone, the 1956 feature film re-created an amphibious landing and employed two hundred U.S. naval ships and ten thousand marines off Vieques Island, Puerto Rico.

aweigh, the description of a ship's anchor as soon as it leaves the bottom. Also called "short stay."

Azores, volcanic **archipelago** composed of nine major islands in the North Atlantic about nine hundred miles west of Portugal. Settled by the Portuguese beginning in the fifteenth century, the islands are a part of Portugal today. On trade routes between Europe and the Caribbean, the islands took on special significance as staging posts and **coaling stations**.

B

backing and filling, stopping and going in a sailing ship, usually to hold position against a head tide, without moving ahead.

backstaff, a precision instrument designed especially for navigation. It was invented by English explorer **John Davis** around 1595. Also known as the **Davis quadrant**, it improved upon the **cross staff** in a number of ways, including the ability to measure the altitude of the sun while not having to look into it. The backstaff made possible a huge leap in navigational accuracy, and it remained in used for nearly two hundred years.

Baffin, William (1584–1622), English navigator who explored Greenland and led several expeditions in search of a **Northwest Passage** to Asia. His name was given to Baffin Bay, which he explored in 1616, and to Baffin Island. He was the first navigator to determine **longitude** at sea by observing the moon.

baggywrinkle, strands of old line wrapped around a stay or shroud and used as chafing gear on a sailing ship or sailboat to prevent damage to the sails.

Bahama Star, American passenger **liner** completed in 1931 as the *Borinquen*. She was acquired by the Eastern Steamship Company in 1959 and operated on three- and four-day cruises to Nassau from Miami while named in honor of her destination. She played a heroic role in saving survivors from the SS *Yarmouth Castle* tragedy of 1965. After being

Bahama Star at Prince George Wharf, Nassau, Bahamas. (From the collection of Everett E. Viez. Bahamas Ministry of Tourism)

sold in 1969, the liner was renamed *LaJenelle* and, while **laid up** at anchor off the California coast in 1970, was driven ashore in a gale and capsized at the entrance to Port Hueneme.

Lake Baikal, the world's deepest lake, located in Siberia, which contains more water than all five of the **Great Lakes** combined.

Bainbridge, William (1774–1833), U.S. naval officer in the **Barbary Wars** and the **War of 1812**. He commanded the **frigate** USS *Philadelphia* in the Barbary Wars and surrendered when it ran aground near Tripoli. He was held prisoner for more than a year. In 1812, he commanded a squadron of three ships composed of USS *Constitution*, USS *Essex*, and USS *Hornet* and destroyed the British frigate HMS *Java* in single-ship combat with *Constitution*.

Balboa, Vasco Nunez de (1475–1517), Spanish navigator and conquistador who explored South America and, in 1513, was the first European to see the Pacific Ocean from the Americas. He called the body of water the South Sea (it was renamed the Pacific by **Ferdinand Magellan** in 1520). Balboa found gold and pearls on the coast and hoped to be made governor of the region. Instead he and four colleagues were accused of treason and beheaded.

Balclutha, 256-foot, **full-rigged ship** built in Scotland in 1886. After carrying general cargoes and lumber for twenty-five years, she was used as a floating barracks and storage ship by the Alaska salmon fishery until 1930. For the next twenty years, she sailed the West Coast of the United States as a waterfront attraction. She was purchased in 1950 by the San Francisco Maritime Museum and restored to her former glory. She opened as a museum ship in 1955 and today is moored at the San Francisco Maritime National Historic Park.

baldheaded, term used to describe a **gaff rig** with no topmasts.

Balikpapan, Battle of, sortie on January 24, 1942, in which USS *John D. Ford*, USS *Parrott*, USS *Paul Jones*, and USS *Pope* sank four Japanese transports and a patrol boat in a surprise attack. The four-stacked **destroyers** found themselves in the first surface engagement involving U.S. warships since the **Spanish-American War**.

"The Ballad of the Yarmouth Castle", lyrical description of the fire aboard SS *Yarmouth Castle*, composed and recorded by Canadian folksinger Gordon Lightfoot in 1969, which realistically captures the grim details of the disaster that overtook the **liner** in 1965 off the Florida coast.

Ballard, Robert Duane (b. 1942), American oceanographer who has advanced underwater exploration. He discovered the remains of HMS *Titanic* on the floor of the North Atlantic in 1985 and subsequently made photographic surveys of the wreck site. He also discovered the grave of the German battleship *Bismarck* off the French coast in 1988. He has been involved in photographing and exploring the undersea wrecks of RMS *Lusitania* and USS *Yorktown* and has helped design deep-sea research vehicles. In the early 1980s, he developed *Argo-Jason*, a remote-controlled submersible with video cameras and a detachable robot to collect samples.

Baltic and International Maritime Council (BIMCO), shipowners group founded in 1905 and based in Copenhagen, Denmark. Its primary mission is to unite shipowners and to defend the interests of international shipping at large.

Baltic Exchange, the world's oldest international shipping exchange, established in the mid-1700s in London, England. It is the leading marketplace for the matching of ships and cargoes.

Baltimore clipper, type of topsail **schooner** developed in the Chesapeake Bay during the

A rendering of *Balclutha* in San Francisco harbor by David Thimgan. (Courtesy J. Russell Jinishian Gallery, Fairfield, Connecticut)

late eighteenth and early nineteenth centuries that combined speed and maneuverability. These vessels were normally seventy feet to more than ninety feet on deck and were instantly recognizable by their fine lines and raked masts. They were employed by privateers and **blockade runners**, and their design influenced many fast racing yachts.

Bancroft, George (1800–1891), American educator and diplomat and one of the most outstanding historians of the nineteenth century, a reputation based largely on his ten-volume *History of the United States* (1834–1874). He briefly served as secretary of the navy under President James K. Polk, and in the aftermath of the *Somers* **Mutiny,** he started the U.S. Naval School at Fort Severn in Maryland in 1845. The name was changed to the U.S. **Naval Academy** and the school was moved to Annapolis in 1850. The academy's dormitory, the school's largest building, is named Bancroft Hall.

band of brothers, Admiral **Horatio Nelson**'s term for the captains of British ships under his command. He was no doubt alluding to the monologue with which William Shakespeare's Henry V rouses his seemingly doomed British troops before the Battle of Agincourt: "We few, we happy few, we band of brothers" (*Henry V,* IV.iii).

Banks, Sir Joseph (1743–1820), renowned British naturalist and explorer who traveled extensively collecting natural history specimens. He volunteered to accompany Captain **James Cook** on his first expedition to the Pacific (1768–71), and he kept a detailed journal of the voyage. Cook named the harbor at New South Wales **Botany Bay** in honor of Banks's many discoveries there. Banks served as president of the **Royal Society** from 1778 to 1820.

Banning, Phineas (1830–1885), stagecoach driver who is often referred to as the "Father of Los Angeles Harbor." When the first San Francisco to San Pedro coastal shipping line was established in 1853, Banning began the twenty-mile freight service between the latter port and Los Angeles (one of his drivers was Wyatt Earp). He established New San Pedro, which later became the port of Wilmington, to shorten the distance to the inland city. As a California senator, he was instrumental in constructing the first breakwater at the Port of Los Angeles, which began the enlargement and modernization of the facility.

USS *Barb*, submarine that sank the most enemy tonnage of any U.S. sub in World War II. During one mission in 1945, *Barb* penetrated a harbor on the coast of China and fired upon some thirty Japanese ships at anchor. She retired at high speed on the surface through uncharted and heavily mined waters. For this patrol, *Barb*'s captain, Commander Eugene B. Fluckey, was awarded the **Medal of Honor**, and USS *Barb* was awarded the Presidential Unit Citation.

Barbarossa (1466–1546), nickname for a **Barbary pirate** named Khair-ed-Din, who, along with his brother, Aruj, controlled a powerful fleet that ravaged the western Mediterranean in the sixteenth century. He became an admiral of the Turkish navy and devoted his life to attacking Christian ships and enslaving thousands of Christians. He twice defeated the Genoese admiral Doria (after whom the Italian **liner *Andrea Doria*** was named five hundred years later). The Turkish naval supremacy that he helped to build was not destroyed until the Holy League fleet defeated the Turks at the Battle of **Lepanto** in 1571. The two brothers were often referred to as the Barbarossa Brothers, so named because of their red beards.

Barbary Coast, Mediterranean coastal region of the **Barbary States** and home to the **Barbary pirates**. This name also was given to the San Francisco waterfront, a rough and tumble place following the gold rush of 1849.

Barbary pirates, sea rovers of the **Barbary States** who plundered seaborne commerce in the Mediterranean from the sixteenth through the nineteenth centuries. They demanded tribute money, seized ships, and held crews for ransom or sold them into slavery. From 1795 to 1801, the United States paid large sums of money to the Barbary States for protection against these pirates, but continued attacks on U.S. vessels led to the **Barbary Wars**.

Barbary States, European term for the Muslim Ottoman city-states of North Africa—**Tripoli**, Tunisia, Algeria, and Morocco—extending from the western border of modern-day Egypt to the **Atlantic Ocean**. The terms "Barbary" and "Berber," the name of the people who make up a large part of the North African population, come from the Latin word *barbari*. Barbari, or "barbarians," was the name given in Roman times to peoples who lived at the fringes of the Roman Empire.

Barbary Wars, war fought from 1801 to 1805 and again in 1815 to combat the hostile acts of the **Barbary pirates**. The United States sent naval squadrons into the Mediterranean in 1801–5 and blockaded the coast, bombarded shore fortresses, and engaged in bitterly contested gunboat actions. In 1815 the navy sent two squadrons under Commodores **Stephen Decatur** and **William Bainbridge** to the

Mediterranean. Diplomacy backed by a show of force secured an agreement to end hostilities, which were also referred to as the War with **Tripoli** or the Tripolitan Wars.

Bard, James (1815–1897), American ship portraitist who painted—often in collaboration with his twin brother, John (1815–1856)—the **steamboats**, racing yachts, **schooners**, and tugboats that plied New York Harbor and the **Hudson River**. His work offers a colorful record of the many ships that traveled the waterways in and around New York City.

bareboat charter, agreement (also called a demise charter) under which a boat is chartered without a crew but usually fully equipped. The charterer assumes all responsibility for costs of manning, operation, repair, and insurance.

Barents, Willem (d. 1597), Dutch navigator who made three unsuccessful expeditions in search of the **Northeast Passage**. In 1597 he discovered Spitsbergen (Svalbard) in the Arctic Ocean north of Norway and explored what is now the **Barents Sea**, but after rounding **Novaya Zemlya** his vessel became trapped in the ice. His crew thus became the first Europeans to winter in the Arctic. Barents died on the return voyage.

Barents Sea, a major portion of the Arctic Ocean lying northeast of the Scandinavian peninsula. In World War II, Allied ships ran the **Murmansk Run**, and on December 30, 1942, the British scored an important naval victory there. The failure of a superior German force to destroy a **convoy** led to a series of disagreements between Adolf Hitler and Admiral **Erich Raeder**, with Raeder resigning as commander in chief of the German fleet soon thereafter.

bare poles, a ship with no sail set due to bad weather; said to be "under bare poles."

bark (also known as a "barque"), vessel with three or more masts, square-rigged on all but the mizzenmast, which is **fore-and aft-rigged**.

James Bard's painting of the steamboat *Harlem*, circa 1877. (The Mariners' Museum, Newport News, Virginia)

barkentine, vessel of at least three masts, differing from the **bark** in the **fore-and-aft rigging** of its mainmast. The foremast is square-rigged, but the mainmast and mizzenmast both carry fore and aft lower and gaff topsails. The addition of one or two fore-and-aft-rigged masts made the vessel a four- or five-masted barkentine.

Barney, Joshua (1759–1818), American naval officer who engaged in many daring missions during the American Revolution. He was originally chosen to command one of the first six **frigates** called for in the **Navy Act of 1794**, but he declined. He served instead in the French navy from 1796 to 1802 and turned to privateering in the **War of 1812**.

Barr, Charles (1864–1911), colorful Scottish yacht captain and one of the best-known professional racing **skippers** of all time. He successfully raced many vessels, including Morton F. Plant's *Ingomar* in 1904 and Alexander Smith Cochran's *Westward* in 1910. Three times he defended the **America's Cup**: in 1899 and 1901 aboard *Columbia*, and in 1903 aboard *Reliance*. The *Reliance* defense was the last for a professional skipper in the history of the competition. Barr won the 1905 **Kaiser's Cup** as captain of the **schooner** *Atlantic*, setting a transatlantic speed record.

barratry, fraud or gross negligence on the part of the **master** or crew of a ship, for some unlawful or fraudulent purpose, to harm the owners or insurers.

Barron, James (1769–1851), U.S. naval officer who played a prominent role in the events leading up to the **War of 1812.** While commanding USS *Chesapeake* in 1807, he was challenged by the captain of the British warship HMS *Leopard,* who demanded he surrender several American sailors accused of deserting from the **Royal Navy.** Barron refused, and *Leopard'*s guns fired on *Chesapeake'*s crew. After three men were killed and eighteen were wounded, Barron surrendered the suspects. He was later court-martialed and placed on shore duty. Barron killed **Stephen Decatur** in 1820 in a duel.

Barry, John (1745–1803), Irish-born U.S. naval officer who, along with **John Paul Jones,** was one of the most celebrated naval figures of the American Revolution. He was the senior officer and commodore of the first regular U.S. **Navy** when it was established under the **Navy Act of 1794.**

Barth, John (b. 1930), American author who focuses many of his novels in Chesapeake Bay. Among his most notable works are *The Floating Opera* (1956) and *The Last Voyage of Somebody the Sailor* (1991). His book *Sabbatical* (1982) is about a couple taking a last sailing cruise around Chesapeake Bay before their child is born.

Bartlett, Robert Abram (1875–1946), Canadian-American Arctic explorer famous for his skill in piloting ships through ice. He commanded the **steamship** *Roosevelt* for polar explorer **Robert Edwin Peary** from 1905 to 1909. Bartlett led an expedition in 1913 during which the ship *Karluk* was crushed by ice near Wrangel Island in the Arctic Ocean. He walked across the ice to Siberia and returned with a rescue party. Bartlett explored Alaska for air

base sites in 1925 and later made twenty Arctic voyages aboard his **schooner** *Effie M. Morrissey* (later called *Ernestina*).

Bartley, James, English sailor aboard the whaleship *Star of the East* who, according to legend, was swallowed in 1891 by a sperm whale and lived to tell about it. The whale was later captured by Bartley's shipmates, and two days later he was removed from the whale's stomach.

Bass, George (1771–1803), British naval surgeon best known for his exploration of the eastern coast of Australia. In 1795 and 1796, he and **Matthew Flinders** explored the coastline south of Sydney, Australia, in the tiny boat *Tom Thumb.* In 1803 Bass disappeared while on a trading voyage from Sydney to Peru.

Bass, George F. (b. 1932), American underwater archaeologist and a pioneer of modern scientific methods. In 1973 he founded the **Institute of Nautical Archaeology,** which is affiliated with Texas A&M University. His books include *Ships and Shipwrecks of the Americas* (1988).

Batavia, seaport city on the island of Java (present-day Jakarta) that was founded in 1619 by the **Dutch East India Company.** Batavia served as the headquarters of the company in East India.

bateau, French word for "boat." In the northeastern United States, a flat-bottomed flare-sided workboat.

Bates, Sir Percy (1879–1946), chairman of the **Cunard Line** from 1930 to 1946. He never lost his vision for the twin superships his company had proposed as giant weekly ferryboats to maintain its Atlantic service. He was instrumental in meeting government demands that resulted in Parliament's loaning Cunard the money to build RMS *Queen Mary* and RMS *Queen Elizabeth.* His tenacity was indefatigable, and the two **liners** played a major role in World War II by carrying half of all the

American and Canadian forces that landed in Britain during the conflict. He collapsed and died the day *Queen Elizabeth* made her peacetime **maiden voyage** to New York.

Bath Iron Works (BIW), shipyard located on the Kennebec River in Bath, Maine. Founded in the 1840s, the company built an excellent reputation for quality and initiated a long relationship with the U.S. **Navy**. In addition to yachts, fishing trawlers, and commercial vessels, the yard has provided battleships, **frigates**, **cruisers**, and **destroyers**. Today it is the largest private employer in Maine and, as part of **General Dynamics,** continues to be a lead designer and builder of surface combatants for the navy.

bathyscaphe, diving craft used for deep-sea observation. It can dive more than six miles to explore the deepest parts of the ocean. It was designed by Swiss scientist Auguste Piccard (1884–1962) and was first tested in 1948. In 1960 the bathyscaphe *Trieste* made a historic dive into the **Marianas Trench**.

"Battle of New Orleans", song about the famous battle of the **War of 1812**, sung by Johnny Horton, that hit number one on the pop charts in 1959. Written by Jimmy Driftwood, it opens, "In 1814 we took a little trip, Along with Colonel Jackson down the mighty Mississip, We took a little bacon and we took a little beans, And we caught the bloody British in the town of New Orleans."

Battleship Row, area of the **Pearl Harbor**, Hawai'i, naval base that was a primary target of the Japanese surprise attack of December 7, 1941. Seven U.S. **Navy** battleships—USS *Arizona*, USS *California*, USS *Maryland*, USS *Nevada*, USS *Oklahoma*, USS *Tennessee*, and USS *West Virginia*—were lost or severely damaged during the early morning bombing. Only two battleships of the Pacific fleet escaped the attack—the USS *Pennsylvania* was in drydock and the USS *Colorado* was being overhauled on the West Coast of the United States.

Bay of Fundy, an extension of the North Atlantic Ocean that divides New Brunswick from western Nova Scotia. The bay is about sixty miles wide at its mouth and reaches inland about a hundred miles. The upper part of the bay is famous for its tides, which are the highest in the world and rise and fall over a range that is sometimes greater than fifty feet.

Bay of Pigs, anglicization of Bahía de Cochinos, an area on the south coast of Cuba that was the site of a failed attempt by U.S. Central Intelligence Agency–trained Cuban exiles to invade Cuba in 1961. The fourteen hundred invaders had left after the revolution in 1959 and had returned to overthrow Fidel Castro. Most of them were killed or taken prisoner. The incident became a foreign policy debacle for President **John F. Kennedy**, who had approved the plan just three months into his presidency.

BB, U.S. **Navy** designation for a battleship. The USS *Texas*, considered the first U.S. battleship, was commissioned August 15, 1895.

Beach, Edward L. (b. 1918), U.S. naval officer and best-selling author who commanded submarines from World War II until the nuclear age. He was captain of USS *Triton* when it circumnavigated submerged in 1960. His works of fiction include the best-seller *Run Silent, Run Deep* (1955), *Dust on the Sea* (1972), and *Cold Is the Sea* (1978). His nonfiction titles include *Wreck of the Memphis* (1962) and his autobiography, *Salt and Steel* (1999).

HMS *Beagle*, 90-foot **bark** dispatched by the British government on a round-the-world mission of exploration and scientific discovery between 1831 and 1836. In addition to carrying twenty-two **chronometers** to fix the **longitudes** of foreign lands, the vessel also carried the twenty-three-year-old **Charles Darwin** as its medical officer and naturalist.

Beaglehole, John Cawte (1901–1971), New Zealand historian and a leading authority on the life and voyages of English explorer **James Cook**. He edited Cook's journals for the **Hakluyt Society** and wrote *The Exploration of the Pacific* (1966) and *The Life of Captain James Cook* (1974).

Bear, 198-foot **barkentine** launched in 1873 in Scotland. She spent her first ten years as a sealer off Newfoundland, and in 1884, having been purchased by the U.S. **Navy**, she led the task force that rescued **Aldolphus Greely** and his expedition. In 1885 *Bear* began a distinguished forty-one-year career as a U.S. **Revenue Cutter Service** cutter stationed in Alaska. **Laid up** in 1926, *Bear* became a museum ship in Oakland a year later and starred as the sealer *Macedonia* in the 1930 film version of **Jack London**'s *The Sea Wolf*. She was acquired in 1932 for Admiral **Richard Evelyn Byrd**'s second Antarctic expedition, and from 1941 to 1944 she served in the **Atlantic**. *Bear* was again laid up in 1948 in Halifax, and she sank off Long Island in 1963 while being towed to Philadelphia.

beat to quarters, old **Royal Navy** order for battle stations or **general quarters**. It was announced by drummers with rhythm: "heart of oak, heart of oak." The modern equivalent is "action stations."

Beatty, David (1871–1936), British admiral who commanded part of the force that stopped the German fleet in the Battle of **Jutland** in 1916. He succeeded Admiral **John Rushworth Jellicoe** to become the commander of the British fleet and, in 1918, accepted the surrender of the German navy. He was **First Sea Lord** from 1919 to 1927.

Beaufort Scale, a numerical scale for wind strength devised in 1808 by Admiral Francis Beaufort (1774–1857), the **hydrographer** of Britain's **Royal Navy** from 1829 to 1855. Beaufort made an extensive study of the effects of varying winds on the surface of the open sea and assigned them to twelve categories or "forces"—from 0 (calm conditions) to 12 (hurricane). The numbers originally corresponded with the amount of sail that a **man-o'-war** of the period could carry in different wind speeds.

USS *Becuna* (SS-319), 311-foot Balao-class submarine completed in 1944 that received four battle stars and a Presidential Unit Citation for her exploits in World War II, which included sinking five Japanese merchant ships. She also saw duty in the Korean and Vietnam Wars. Decommissioned in 1969, the 1,526-ton submarine, which once carried nuclear warhead–tipped torpedoes, is permanently moored as a museum ship alongside USS *Olympia* at the Independence Seaport Museum on the Philadelphia waterfront.

Beebe, William (1877–1962), American naturalist and writer who gained fame for his explorations into the depths of the sea. He designed a spherical steel vessel called a bathysphere and in 1934 was lowered into the sea to a record-setting depth of 3,028 feet. His many books include *Half Mile Down* (1934), in which he tells of his undersea adventures in his bathysphere, and *Beneath Tropic Seas* (1928) and *Book of Bays* (1942).

Beesley, Lawrence, thirty-four-year-old British science teacher who survived the sinking of RMS *Titanic*. His eyewitness account, *The Loss of SS Titanic* (1912), was published two months after the disaster and is one of the most descriptive accounts of that fateful night in April 1912.

Beetle Cat, a **one-design** centerboard gaff-rigged **catboat** designed by John Beetle and introduced in 1921 by the Beetle Boat Company of New Bedford. With a length of twelve feet, four inches, and a beam of five feet, this type of classic catboat is a frequent sight on the bays of **Cape Cod** and on Buzzards

Bay, Narragansett Bay, and Long Island Sound. Since 1946 Beetle Cats have been built by the Concordia Company of Padanaram, Massachusetts.

before the mast, term used to describe the hierarchy of seamen or those not in a position of authority, as compared with officers. It derives from the position of the crew, whose living quarters aboard ship were in the **forecastle**—forward of the mast. **Richard Henry Dana Jr.** wrote of his experiences sailing as a seaman in his book *Two Years Before the Mast* (1840).

Beken of Cowes, pioneering family of British marine photographers based in Cowes on the **Isle of Wight**. Since the late nineteenth century, members of this family have been the leading marine photographers in Great Britain. Beken & Son photographs document luxurious sail and steam yachts as well as transatlantic ocean **liners**.

belay, to secure a line to a pin or cleat, or to cancel a command.

USS *Belknap* (DLG-26), first of a series of nine identical steam turbine–powered, 547-foot guided missile **cruisers**. Completed in 1964, the 7,930-ton vessel was designed as an antisubmarine and antiaircraft escort for aircraft carriers. In 1975 *Belknap* incurred serious damage when the carrier *John F. Kennedy* came down off a swell and the overhanging support for the flight deck destroyed the superstructure of the frigate. *Belknap* was rebuilt between 1976 and 1978.

Bellamy, John Haley (1836–1914), American woodcarver who worked at both the Boston and the Portsmouth navy yards, carving **figureheads**, ornamental works for sterns, panels for gangways, and sundry decorations for other parts of naval and mercantile craft. Bellamy's eagle carvings were so popular that numerous imitators copied his work even in his own lifetime.

Bellamy, Samuel (d. 1717), English pirate known as "Black Bellamy" who attacked ships off the coast of New England. In April 1717 Bellamy's flagship *Whydah* sank off **Cape Cod**, Massachusetts, and he drowned. In 1984 divers began recovering artifacts from *Whydah*.

bell-bottoms, sailor's uniform pants that are flared at the bottom so that they can be rolled up when swabbing the deck or performing other wet chores.

HMS *Bellerophon*, British warship that accepted **Napoleon I**'s surrender in 1815. After abdicating his throne on June 22, Napoleon tried to escape to the United States but failed. He surrendered to Frederick Lewis Maitland, the captain of *Bellerophon*, and in August was sent into exile on the British island of **Saint Helena** in the South Atlantic Ocean.

Bellingshausen, Fabian von (1778–1852), Russian naval officer who is often credited with discovering Antarctica. He sailed around the South Polar region between 1819 and 1821 and discovered Peter I and Alexander I Islands. Elsewhere in the Pacific, he called at several unexplored islands in the Fiji Islands group.

Belloc, Hilaire (1870–1953), French-born British writer best known for his light verses for children. He is also considered one of the most literate of all writers of the sea and small boats. His works include *The Hills and the Sea* (1906), *The Cruise of the Nona* (1925), and *On Sailing the Sea* (1951).

bells, shipboard system of announcing the time and change of watch. The watch is changed every four hours (0400, 0800, 1200, 1600, 2000, and 2400/0000); these times are assigned as eight bells. Bells are sounded and added for each half-hour period until they reach eight.

Benchley, Peter (b. 1940), American author best known for his sea-themed novels *Jaws* (1974),

The Deep (1976), *The Island* (1979), *Beast* (1991), and *White Shark* (1994).

bend, to attach or fasten to a halyard, as with a sail or flag. To unbend is to remove the same.

the bends, so called because divers double over in pain; see **decompression sickness**.

Beneath the Twelve-Mile Reef, classic 1953 dive film that has two rival groups of divers competing for sponge beds off the Florida coast. Noted for its underwater photography, it starred Robert Wagner, Gilbert Roland, and Peter Graves, and it received an Academy Award nomination for cinematography.

"Benito Cereno", 1855 short story by **Herman Melville**, included in his *The Piazza Tales*, about Amasa Delano, the captain of a seal-hunting ship who encounters a slave ship with a human cargo that has revolted. Delano saves the slaver captain, Benito Cereno, and his remaining crew, and the leaders of the revolt are slaughtered. Melville based his plot on a few pages in the real **Amasa Delano**'s *Narrative of Voyages and Travels in the Northern and Southern Hemispheres* (1817).

Bennett, James Gordon, Jr. (1841–1918), American journalist and son of *New York Herald* founder James Gordon Bennett (1795–1872). He became the paper's owner in 1872 and continued his father's traditions of sensationalism and aggressive news gathering. A prominent yachtsman, he participated in the **schooner** racing of the era, and his *Henrietta* won a high-stakes **Transatlantic Race** in December 1866. He sponsored Henry M. Stanley's search in Africa for the missing British explorer David Livingstone in 1869. He also helped to finance the *Pandora*'s search for a **Northwest Passage** in 1875 and the ill-fated 1879–81 **Jeannette Expedition**. He was commodore of the **New York Yacht Club** in 1884 and 1885.

USS Bennington (CV-20), **Essex**-class aircraft carrier commissioned in 1944 and assigned to duty in the South Pacific for the duration of World War II. Planes from the 872-foot carrier participated in the destruction of the Japanese superbattleship **Yamato** in 1945. *Bennington* was crippled in 1954 by an exploding steam catapult, which left 103 dead and 201 injured. She was decommissioned in 1970 and scrapped in 1993.

Bentley, Helen Delich (b. 1923), American congresswoman and tireless advocate of the U.S. **merchant marine**. She started her career as a maritime reporter and editor for the *Baltimore Sun* and from 1969 to 1975 was the first female chair of the **Federal Maritime Commission**. She was elected to the House of Representatives in 1985, where she served for a decade on the **Merchant Marine and Fisheries Committee**. She was also the only woman to sail on the tanker *Manhattan* on that ship's historic voyage through the **Northwest Passage** in 1969.

Bequia, small island of the Saint Vincent and Grenadines group, which is a popular sail cruising destination located about two hundred miles north of Venezuela. The islanders have a long tradition of open-boat whaling that they still practice.

RMS Berengaria, flagship of the **Cunard Line** from 1921 to 1936. Completed in 1913 as the *Imperator* for Germany's **Hamburg-America Line** transatlantic run, the 52,226-gross-ton **liner** was confiscated after World War I, sold to the Cunard Line, and renamed for King Richard the Lion Hearted's queen. Known for stability problems, the liner nonetheless maintained the company's premier weekly New York service alongside SS *Aquitania* and RMS *Mauretania*, and later with RMS *Queen Mary*. She burned at her **Hudson River** pier in 1938 with no casualties and was returned to Southampton without passengers, where she was sold for scrap.

bergy bit, official term used to classify a piece of an iceberg less than three feet high and less than sixteen feet long.

Bering, Vitus Jonassen (1680–1741), Danish navigator in the Russian navy who in 1725 was appointed by **Peter I** to lead an expedition to see whether Asia and Alaska were connected. Bering traveled overland to Kamchatka, built ships, and in 1728 voyaged north. He sailed between the two continents in waters today known as the Bering Sea and the Bering Strait without sighting land. He sighted Alaska on a second expedition in 1741, but on his return voyage heavy fog forced him to land on present-day Bering Island, where he died of **scurvy**.

Bermuda Race, one of the major ocean races for sailing yachts, which is run biennially from Newport, Rhode Island, to Bermuda. Cosponsored by the **Cruising Club of America** (CCA) and the Royal Bermuda Yacht Club, it alternates with Britain's **Fastnet Race**. First sailed in 1906, the Bermuda Race was suspended in 1910 and then revived in 1923. In 1926 the CCA began to manage the race. From 1923 to 1936, the race started from New London, Connecticut. Winners are determined by a handicapping formula.

Bermuda rig, a sailboat rig that employs a triangular mainsail. It is also referred to as a "**Marconi rig**" and a "Bermudian rig."

Bert Dow, Deep Water Man, 1963 children's book by Robert McCloskey about a fisherman who catches a whale tail. He puts a Band-Aid on the hole in the whale's tail and later becomes a doctor to all of the other whales.

Bertram, Richard H. (b. 1916), American yachtsman who competed in both sail and power-boat racing. He founded Bertram Yachts, a Miami-based manufacturer of production pleasure boats, in 1960. Bertram Yachts began the first large production runs of boats with **C. Raymond Hunt**'s revolutionary deep-V hull design.

Bertrand, 161-foot **Missouri River steamboat** that sank in April 1865 north of Omaha, Nebraska, on her first passage upstream. In

RMS *Berengaria*. (Courtesy Gordon R. Ghareeb)

1968 her remains were excavated in a field far from the current path of the river. The vessel's remains—and nearly two million individual items—were covered by 26 feet of sediment.

Bessemer, 350-foot British steamer that was constructed in 1875 with a cabin suspended inside the ship that was supposedly capable of maintaining a level position despite the vessel's motion. It was pioneered by Sir Henry Bessemer (1813–1898), a British engineer best known for devising the process that converted pig iron into steel. Put to the test in 1875, the experiment failed miserably when the "Bessemer **saloon**" refused to remain still and the ship's helm would not respond. The volunteer passengers experienced their worst seasickness ever. In the end, the ship was refitted with traditional accommodations; however, the ship was withdrawn from service in 1880.

Betelgeuse (also known as Beetle Juice or Alpha Orionis), one of the fifty-two navigational stars and brightest star in the constellation of Orion.

Bethlehem Shipbuilding, shipbuilding facility of Bethlehem Steel Corporation located at Sparrow's Point, Maryland. During World War II, the yard was one of Bethlehem's fifteen shipyards, which built over 1,121 vessels—more than any other shipbuilder in the war.

"Bethship" delivered the first **Liberty ship**, *Patrick Henry*, as well as one of the last remaining ones, SS *John W. Brown*. The yard was sold in 1997 to a private investment group.

between the devil and the deep blue sea, phrase that is the nautical equivalent of "between a rock and a hard place." The devil is the deck nearest the rail on a wooden ship, which was difficult to caulk. If not caulked properly, the result could be disastrous.

Beyond the Poseidon Adventure, 1979 motion picture sequel to the 1972 box-office hit *The Poseidon Adventure*. Revolving around a plot to loot the capsized **liner** before she sank, the sequel is memorable only for the special effects of an upside-down, 81,000-ton ocean liner. It starred Michael Caine, Sally Field, and Shirley Jones and was based on the 1978 novel of the same name by Paul Gallico.

Bianca C, motor **liner** built as the French *La Marseilles* in 1949 and acquired by the **Costa Line** and renamed in 1959. While on a Caribbean cruise in 1961, the 18,427-gross-ton vessel caught fire after an explosion in the engine room and sank at the entrance of Saint George Harbor, Bermuda, with the loss of three lives out of the 673 people on board.

Bich, Marcel (1914–1994), French businessman who built the Bic empire of consumer products, including ballpoint pens, lighters, and shavers. Baron Bich competed four times to challenge for the **America's Cup** but came up short each time. He raced his **twelve-meter** yachts *France I, II,* and *III* off Newport, Rhode Island, in 1970, 1974, 1977, and 1980.

Biddle, Nicholas (1750–1778), American naval officer who was one of the original officers in the **Continental Navy**. As a young man, he served in the British navy, and during the American Revolution he raided British shipping off the American coast. He was killed in action off the coast of Barbados.

Bienville, Sieur de (1680–1768), a French-Canadian explorer who played a leading role in the European settlement of the Louisiana territory. In 1699, he and his brother Iberville explored the region around the mouth of the **Mississippi River**. He founded Mobile, Alabama, in 1702 and New Orleans in 1718.

The Big Broadcast of 1938, fanciful song-and-dance feature film of 1938 that revolves around the fictitious ultra-streamlined passenger ship *Gigantic* and her transatlantic race with the *Colossal*, an uncanny SS *Normandie* look-alike. No actual **liner** footage was used in the movie, but the sets give a good idea of the ambiance found on the Atlantic between the wars. It starred Bob Hope (singing "Thanks for the Memories"), Martha Raye, and W. C. Fields.

Big Missouri, the **steamboat** in **Mark Twain**'s *Adventures of Tom Sawyer*.

Big Muddy, endearing riverman's term for the **Missouri River**, which is said to be too thick to drink but too thin to plow. The Big Muddy River, a 135-mile waterway and tributary to the **Mississippi River**, is located in southwest Illinois.

Bikini Atoll, isolated atoll in the northwest **Marshall Islands** group in the Pacific Ocean. Bikini's approximately fifty-four-mile-long reef encircles a lagoon. Large breaks in the reef allow ships to enter and exit the lagoon, which was the site of **Operation Crossroads** in 1946 and is the present site of a **ghost fleet**.

Bikini Beach, classic 1964 beach movie, starring Annette Funicello and Frankie Avalon, in which a group of surfing teenagers joins forces with a British recording star to keep their beach from being turned into a retirement community. It was just one of American-International Pictures' Beach Party series, which usually costarred Annette and Frankie. The series started with *Beach Party* (1963) and included *Muscle Beach Party* (1964), *Pajama Party* (1964), *Beach Blanket Bingo* (1965), *How to Stuff a Wild Bikini* (1965), and *The Ghost in the Invisible Bikini* (1966).

billethead, carved scroll used in place of a **figurehead** on a ship.

bill of lading, the basic document of ocean transportation that is a contract between the carrier and the shipper listing the destination as well as all terms and conditions. It is also serves as a receipt issued to the shipper by the carrier to acknowledge that the carrier has received the goods. The U.S. Government stipulated the bill's characteristics, obligations, and liabilities in the **Carriage of Goods by Sea Act** of 1936.

Billy Budd, Foretopman, novel by **Herman Melville** written in 1891 and left unfinished at his death. First published in 1924, it tells of Billy Budd, a young sailor pressed into the service of the **Royal Navy** who accidentally kills John Claggert, the satanic master-at-arms aboard the ship *Indomitable.* Tried for murder and sentenced to be hanged, Billy goes willingly to his death. It is thought that much of the story derives from the *Somers* **Mutiny**. A 1962 film of the novel was produced by, codirected by, and starred Peter Ustinov. Terence Stamp was nominated for a best supporting actor Academy Award for his portrayal of Billy.

Bimini, two islands that belong to the Bahamas group but that lie far out in the **Atlantic**. Superstitious belief placed on them a marvelous fountain that had the power of restoring youth. This fountain was an object of eager quest for **Ponce de León**, who in his search for Bimini found Florida and claimed it for Spain.

Bingham, George Caleb (1811–1879), American painter known as "the Missouri Artist." Raised on the banks of the **Missouri River** near Saint Louis, he knew the history and lore of the busy waterway and chronicled in his highly realistic genre paintings the inexorable changes brought by progress and commerce. His paintings also often reflected his interest in politics.

binnacle list, daily sick list on board ship, so called because it was once kept at the compass housing, or binnacle, with the officer or mate of the watch.

Birch, Thomas (1779–1851), English-born American marine artist who settled in Philadelphia and became curator of the Pennsylvania Academy of Fine Arts in 1811. In addition to numerous marine scenes, he recorded naval engagements during the **War of 1812**.

HMS *Birkenhead*, iron **frigate** converted to a troopship in 1848 and employed by the British **Admiralty** to transport regiments to South Africa. One reinforcement left Queenstown, Ireland, in late February 1852 with 680 soldiers, sailors, and passengers, including families. The ship struck a reef off the **Cape of Good Hope** and began to take on water. The military commanders ordered the soldiers to assemble on deck and hold their ranks until all the women and children could be loaded into the lifeboats. All the women and children aboard were among the 193 survivors.

Birkenhead Drill, more commonly known by the phrase "women and children first." Its origin comes from the discipline and courage displayed on board HMS *Birkenhead* in February 1852.

USS *Birmingham*, U.S. **Navy** light **cruiser** that was the site of the first shipboard launch of an airplane. Professional test pilot Eugene Ely took off on November 14, 1910, in his Curtiss Model D biplane. Ely's feat was followed two months later by the first shipboard landing of an airplane on USS *Pennsylvania*.

Bismarck, the final **liner** of **Hamburg-America Line**'s "Big Three," which never saw service for the company that built her. The 56,551-gross-ton steamer was launched in 1914 and remained unfinished throughout World War I. She was completed and handed over to Great Britain as part of the **Treaty of Versailles**. The ship became SS *Majestic* in 1922 and was sold to the **White Star Line** as a replacement for the lost RMS *Britannic*, which had been sunk in 1916. *Bismarck* was sister ship to the *Vaterland* and the *Imperator*.

Bismarck, German battleship that was sunk in one of the most important naval actions of World War II. Her launching in 1940 was attended by Adolf Hitler, and the exploits of this 41,000-ton sister ship to the *Tirpitz* became well known after she sank the British battlecruiser HMS *Hood* in action off of Iceland in 1941, during her first sortie at sea. Two and a half days later, the German **dreadnought** was spotted and sunk by the British Atlantic fleet about six hundred miles off the French coast. American researchers found the ship in 1989, and an inspection revealed that the Germans may have **scuttled** the *Bismarck* to keep the British from seizing it. She was named for Otto von Bismarck (1815–1898), the Prussian statesman who united the German states into one empire.

Bismarck Sea, Battle of the, World War II engagement March 1–4, 1943, in which eight Japanese transports and four Japanese destroyers were sunk by American bombers between Rabaul and New Guinea.

bitter end, the free or loose end of a line, so named because the bitter end of a mooring line was taken to the bitt to secure it.

Bixby, Horace E. (1826–1912), **Mississippi River steamboat** pilot who in the 1850s took the young **Samuel Longhorne Clemens** on as cub **pilot** on the steamboat *Paul Jones*. Clemens, as

Mark Twain, later recounted the experience in *Life on the Mississippi* (1883).

Black Ball Line, American shipping line that began service in 1817 and pioneered **packet** service to the North Atlantic, scheduling monthly sailing service between New York and Liverpool whether full or not. Black Ball Line's innovation contributed to the growth of the Port of New York over rivals Philadelphia and Boston. The line ran under sail until folding in 1878.

Black Bart, nickname of the Welsh pirate **Bartholomew Roberts**.

Blackbeard (d. 1718), legendary British pirate who was born **Edward Teach**. He received his nickname from his habit of braiding his long, black beard and tying the braids with ribbon. Blackbeard terrorized the Carolina and Virginia coasts during 1717 and 1718 in his ship *Queen Anne's Revenge*. HMS *Pearl* and HMS *Lyme* were sent out to take him alive or dead, and Blackbeard was caught on November 21, 1718, off the North Carolina coast. He fought desperately with sword and pistol until he fell with twenty-five wounds in his body. His head was taken back to Virginia and displayed on a pole.

Blackbeard the Pirate, 1952 motion picture about the eighteenth-century buccaneer. The film starred Robert Newton, Linda Darnell, and Irene Ryan.

Black Book of the Admiralty, a collection of medieval and early modern **maritime laws**, including the **Laws of Oleron**, published in four volumes for the British **Admiralty**, by Sir Travers Twiss between 1871 and 1876.

Blackburn, Howard (1859–1932), **Gloucester**, Massachusetts, fisherman who rowed for five days straight to reach land after his dory became separated from the fishing **schooner** *Grace L. Fears* off the coast of Newfoundland in 1883. Blackburn lost all his fingers to frost-bite because his hands froze to the oars. He became a popular figure in Gloucester and later opened Blackburn's, one of the best-known saloons on the North Atlantic seaboard.

black gang, slang for the personnel in the engine department of a ship.

Black Magic, New Zealand yacht that swept the U.S. defender *Young America* five races to none in 1995 to win the **America's Cup**. Syndicate leader **Peter Blake** was knighted for his efforts and in 2000 became the first non-American in 149 years to defend the trophy successfully.

The Black Pirate, 1926 motion picture tale of eighteenth-century romance, revenge, and pirates on the **Spanish Main**, starring Douglas Fairbanks, Billie Dove, and Anders Randolf.

Black Sam, nickname of pirate **Samuel Bellamy**, captain of the *Whydah*.

Black Sea, tideless inland sea between Europe and Asia that is fed by the Don, Dniester, Dnieper, and Danube Rivers. The Bosporus Strait, the Sea of Marmara, and the Dardanelles Strait connect it to the Mediterranean Sea. Its name is believed to be derived from either its heavy fogs or its stormy character. In Greek myth, it was the sea **Jason** and the **Argonauts** sailed across in their search for the Golden Fleece.

Black Star Line, U.S. shipping line launched in 1919 by Jamaican-born black leader **Marcus Garvey** to provide passenger-cargo transportation to Africa and to connect black business throughout the world. The line proved to be a better propaganda instrument for Garvey than a business, and it suspended operations in 1922. Garvey was convicted of fraud because he had continued to offer stock to pay for mounting debt. Before he entered the federal penitentiary, he launched the Black Cross Navigation and Trading Company, which collapsed in 1925.

Black Swan, 1942 Academy Award–winning, swashbuckling motion picture starring Tyrone Power, Maureen O'Hara, George Sanders, and Anthony Quinn. The **Rafael Sabatini** story involves Sir **Henry Morgan** and his first mate, James Waring, who are dispatched to dispense of the redheaded villain Captain Billy Leach. O'Hara plays the young aristocrat Margaret Denby, who is abducted and, in the course of the film, changes her mind about Waring.

USCGC *Blackthorn*, 180-foot U.S. **Coast Guard** buoy tender that, in clear conditions on the evening of January 28, 1980, collided bow-on with the U.S. tanker SS *Capricorn* in Tampa Bay, Florida. The tanker's anchor became imbedded in the hull of the *Blackthorn*, eventually causing it to capsize. The incident, which came a little more than a year after the sinking of the Coast Guard **cutter** *Cuyahoga*, killed twenty-three Coast Guard personnel.

Black Tom explosion, World War I waterfront munitions facility located on Black Tom Island in Morgan, New Jersey, that exploded July 31, 1916, destroying a hundred barges, eighty-five loaded freight cars, thirteen brick warehouses, and six piers. Although the blast shattered windows from Manhattan and Brooklyn to Hoboken and Jersey City, and fallout from the explosion pelted the Statue of Liberty and **Ellis Island**, only seven people were killed. The cause of the blast was never pinpointed, but suspicion of German sabotage helped gain support for the U.S. declaration of war the following year.

Blackwall frigate, a type of merchant ship built in Blackwall, England, in the early nineteenth century.

Blake, Peter (b. 1948)), New Zealand sail racer who has won the **America's Cup**, the **Whitbread Race**, and the Trophée Jules Vern for the

Commander
Bligh of the
Bounty. (Courtesy
International Marine/
McGraw-Hill;
illustration by
Nathan
Goldstein)

fastest nonstop circumnavigation of the globe. Blake won the America's Cup in 1995 with **Black Magic** and successfully defended it with Team New Zealand in 2000. He wrote *Blake's Odyssey* (1982) about his 1981–82 Whitbread Round the World Race victory.

Blake, Robert (1599–1657), British admiral who commanded the British fleet in the first **Anglo-Dutch War** and wrote *Fighting Instructions*, a book of naval tactics. He is considered one of the greatest admirals ever.

Blane, Sir Gilbert (1749–1834), English physician who helped eradicate **scurvy** from the **Royal Navy** by encouraging the consumption of lemon juice. Credited with improving the navy's overall health and sanitary conditions, he wrote *Observations on the Diseases of Seamen* (1785).

Bligh, William (1754–1817), British naval officer who achieved fame as a result of the mutiny on HMS *Bounty* in 1789. His nearly four-thousand-mile, open-boat voyage to Timor after being set loose from the *Bounty* is considered one of history's greatest feats of seamanship. Bligh resumed his career in the British **Royal Navy** in 1791 and in 1806 became governor of New South Wales, Australia. He was promoted to rear admiral in 1811 and to vice admiral in 1814. He served as sailing **master** of HMS *Resolution* on Captain **James Cook**'s third voyage around the world (1776–79) and later wrote *The Mutiny on Board HMS Bounty* (1792).

Bligh Reef, a hazard to navigation located in Alaska's Prince William Sound that was the site of the *Exxon Valdez* grounding on March 24, 1989. The tanker disgorged some eleven million gallons of crude oil, leading to the **Oil Pollution Act of 1990**, which required that the U.S. **Coast Guard** install an automated light on the reef. Bligh Reef was named by Captain **James Cook** in honor of **William Bligh**, **master** of HMS *Resolution* on Cook's last voyage (1776–79).

Block, Adriaen (d. 1624), Dutch trader and explorer who, in 1613, led the first settlement of Europeans to live on Manhattan Island after their ship, *Tiger*, was destroyed by fire. They built a new ship, **Onrust**, and left the island in the spring of 1614, sailing up the Connecticut River and claiming Connecticut for the Dutch as part of their colony of New Netherland. Block named Long Island and Block Island, and some historians believe he also named **Hell Gate** and Rhode Island by calling an island in Narragansett Bay Roodt Eylandt (Red Island) because of the red clay on the shore.

blockade runners, fleet of fast coasting vessels that outran Union Navy ships blockading the coast to supply the Confederacy with badly needed food and supplies during the Civil War. Many were British vessels sailing out of Bermuda, the Bahamas, and Havana, Cuba. Blockade running was a very profitable business, in which the odds of being caught were better than one in four.

Blohm & Voss, shipbuilding and mechanical engineering company founded in 1877 in Hamburg, Germany, by Hermann Blohm and Ernst Voss. Over the years, the yard turned out the **liners *Vaterland*, *Bismarck*, SS *Europa*,** and ***Wilhelm Güstloff*;** the sail training ships *Gorch Foch I* and *II*; and the battleship ***Bismarck***, in addition to many other naval vessels, fast ferries, cargo ships, and mega-yachts.

Blood Alley, American action movie about a merchant ship that takes on board a cargo of fleeing Chinese expatriates and smuggles them on to Hong Kong. The 1955 sea story starred John Wayne, Lauren Bacall, and Anita Ekberg.

blood money, fee given by a ship's **master** to a **crimp** for procuring seamen.

"Blow the Man Down", song about the unfair beating of sailors that has its origin in the **Black Ball Line**. In the mid-nineteenth century, Black Ballers had a reputation for being the fastest ships between Britain and America, and captains of those ships relied on the whip for discipline. "Blow the man down" meant that the sailor was to be beaten.

USS *Bluejack* (SS-581), the final diesel submarine built for the U.S. **Navy**. Completed in 1959, the 219-foot-long vessel went on to establish a new submerged-distance travel record for a diesel sub. When retired in 1990, she was the last diesel sub serving in the navy. Five years later, the 2,158-ton vessel became a museum ship, the centerpiece of the Oregon Museum of Science and Industry in Portland.

bluejacket, an enlisted navy sailor as distinguished from a marine.

Bluejacket's Manual, a primer for newly enlisted sailors and the basic reference book for all U.S. naval personnel. It was first prepared in 1902 by Lieutenant Ridley McLean and has been continually updated.

Blue Jay, popular **one-design**-class centerboard racing sloop designed by **Sparkman & Stephens** in 1949. The overall length is thirteen feet, six inches; the beam is five feet, two inches, with a draft of five inches. Carrying mainsail and jib, with the ability to set a spinnaker, these small vessels are often used to train young people.

bluenose, name given to a Canadian inhabitant of the **Maritime Provinces**, especially Nova Scotia. The term is also used for a sailing vessel of Nova Scotia or a seaman on such a vessel.

Bluenose, Canadian fishing **schooner** designed by William J. Roue of Halifax, Nova Scotia, and launched at **Lunenburg**, Nova Scotia, in 1921. The schooner was used as a fishing vessel as well as for racing and won five consecutive International Fisherman's races, held in 1921, 1922, 1923, 1931, and 1938 between Canada and the United States. Beginning in 1942, she was used to carry cargo in the Caribbean Sea, and in 1946 she ran aground on a coral reef

near Haiti and sank. An image of the famous schooner appears on the Canadian dime.

Bluenose II, replica built in 1963 of the original **schooner *Bluenose***. Based in **Lunenburg**, Nova Scotia, she continues to ply the seas as a sail training vessel.

Blue Peter, a common nautical name for the signal flag P, or Papa, of the **International Code of Signals**, which is blue with a white center square. It is flown when a vessel expects to sail within twenty-four hours.

Blue Riband, nominal title awarded to the fastest passenger **liner** on the North Atlantic. It was first bestowed in 1838 on the British ship *Sirius*. In 1935 a tangible icon of its reality came into being with the **Hales Trophy**, which was created in Britain at the behest of a member of Parliament. Among the holders of the coveted azure pennant were the *Kaiser Wilhelm der Grosse*, RMS *Lusitania*, RMS *Mauretania*, *Bremen*, SS *Rex*, SS *Normandie*, RMS *Queen Mary*, and SS *United States*.

blue water, term that refers to deep or offshore waters, usually more than one hundred fathoms. Blue-water ships are suited to deep or open seas, as opposed to **brown-water** vessels, which operate in shallow waters and rivers.

bluewater sailing, open ocean sailing, as opposed to sailing in a lake or sound.

Blunt, Edmund March (1770–1862), American publisher of nautical books and charts based in Newburyport, Massachusetts. His sons Edmund (1799–1866) and George William (1802–1878) established a similar business in New York and published *Bowditch*, *Blunt's Coast Pilot*, and nautical charts of the world.

Blyth, Chay (b. 1940), Scottish sailor and circumnavigator and the first to sail around the world nonstop east to west (November 1970–August 1971). His boat, *British Steel*, was sponsored by the British steel industry and various other organizations. He wrote *The Impossible Voyage* (1972), recounting his experiences.

BMIN, see **Bureau of Marine Inspection and Navigation**.

BOAC-Cunard, division of British Overseas Airways Corporation formed in 1962 with the **Cunard Line** investing nearly $16 million plus two new Boeing 707 jetliners from the defunct **Cunard Eagle Airways**. The objective was to obtain a foothold in the lucrative transatlantic airline business once it finally had become clear that the era of the ocean **liner** as transportation was ending. Its slogan was, "One way air, one way sea." Cunard sold its thirty percent interest in the concern in 1966 to raise the capital necessary to finish building the *Queen Elizabeth 2* and to cover the operating losses of the liners RMS *Queen Mary* and RMS *Queen Elizabeth*.

The Boat, hilarious 1921 silent short film starring Buster Keaton, who destroys his entire house trying to extricate from his basement the boat he has just built. Naturally, once the boat is launched, it sinks.

Boat Day, pre–World War I term applied to the arrival of a passenger **liner** at Honolulu. Such arrivals were festive occasions, when native islanders would paddle out in ceremonial canoes to meet the incoming steamers with flower leis for the passengers and entertaining greetings of welcome.

The Boatniks, 1970 Disney comedy about an accident-prone U.S. **Coast Guard** ensign who finds himself in charge of busy Newport Harbor and on the trail of a gang of bumbling thieves in their attempt to recover stolen jewels at the bottom of the bay. The film starred Robert Morse, Stefanie Powers, and Phil Silvers.

boat people, the many refugees who left Vietnam in small boats, risking drowning and pirate attacks in the South China Sea, in the years after the Vietnam War. The term is also used to describe Cubans fleeing the Castro government.

boatswain, the highest unlicensed rating in the deck department of a ship. This person directs deckside operations and work parties and, in turn, comes under the orders of the **master**, chief mate, or **mate**. This is also a deck rating in the U.S. **Navy** and U.S. **Coast Guard**.

boatswain's pipe, peculiarly shaped shrill whistle used by a boatswain for signaling and to call orders. Most shipboard functions and salutes have their own distinctive calls.

The Boat Who Wouldn't Float, humorous 1969 account of **Farley Mowat**'s experiences with his Newfoundland **schooner** *Happy Adventure*.

BOC Challenge, former name of **Around Alone**, a solo, around-the-world sailing race. First held in 1982, it was sponsored by BOC (British Oxygen Company).

USS Boise (CL-47), 12,700-ton **Brooklyn**-class **cruiser** commissioned in 1938. The 608-foot ship was en route to Manila when she passed the eastbound Japanese task force that was headed for the attack on **Pearl Harbor** in December 1941. Her fifteen six-inch guns later came into play during the Battle of **Cape Esperance**, where she sustained severe damage from Japanese attacks. Decommissioned in 1951 and sold to Argentina, she became the *Nueve de Julio* the following year.

Bolitho, Richard, fictional **Royal Navy** officer in the **Napoleonic Wars** who is the main character in twenty-four novels by **Alexander Kent**—the pseudonym of **Douglas Reeman**.

Bond, Alan (b. 1938), Australian businessman and yachtsman who made four **America's Cup** challenges before winning. In 1983 Bond's *Australia II* defeated **Dennis Conner**'s *Liberty* to win for the Royal Perth Yacht Club. Bond's defense bid in 1987 lost to *Kookabura III*, which lost to Conner's *Stars & Stripes*.

bone in her teeth, colloquial phrase for the surge of foam raised at the forepart of a ship's stem, or cutwater, when she is moving rapidly.

Bonhomme Richard, American raider originally built in 1765 as the French **frigate** *Duc de Duras*. Given by the king of France to **John Paul Jones** in 1779 and renamed *Bonhomme Richard*—which means "Poor Richard"—in honor of Benjamin Franklin and his famous *Almanac*. She was sunk as a result of damage sustained during the Battle of **Flamborough Head** in September 1779, after Jones had captured her adversary, the British frigate HMS *Serapis*, in which he sailed away as victor in this famous sea fight.

Bonnet, Stede (d. 1718), Barbados plantation owner, known as the "Gentleman's Pirate," who purchased the **sloop** *Revenge* in 1717 and turned to piracy. In 1718 he received a pardon from the colonial governor of North Carolina and became a **privateer** while Great Britain was at war with Spain. Finally tired of working for the colonial governor, he again became a pirate and plundered ships along the Carolina, Virginia, and Delaware coasts. Bonnet's attacks eventually so angered the citizens of Charleston, South Carolina, that they sent out ships to capture him. He surrendered and was hanged in Charleston in 1718.

Bonny, Anne (c. 1720), Irish female pirate who was pirate **John Rackham**'s lover and comrade in arms. Both she and **Mary Read** fought alongside "Calico Jack" throughout the Caribbean. When Rackham's **sloop** *William* was captured in 1720, all aboard were tried and sentenced to death by hanging in Jamaica. Anne and Mary were reprieved when it was discovered that they were both pregnant at the time. Anne's fate is unknown, but it is commonly believed that her father purchased her freedom.

Bon Voyage!, typical 1962 Disney Studios light feature film with Fred MacMurray and Jane

Wyman in the lead roles. It was largely photographed aboard the SS *United States* both at sea and alongside Pier 86 on **Luxury Liner Row** in New York City.

boot topping, stripe of paint (usually black or white) at the waterline of a vessel that separates the hull paint from the antifouling underwater paint.

Bosporus, strait located in northwestern Turkey that connects the **Black Sea** and the Sea of Marmara, and part of the **Dardanelles** that flows from the Black Sea to the Mediterranean Sea. The city of Istanbul lies along the nineteen-mile strait.

Boston Light, first lighthouse in America, erected in 1716 on Little Brewster Island in Boston Harbor. In 1719 a cannon was installed to answer ships in the fog. The light was damaged by fire on several occasions, severely in 1751, and was blown up by the British during the American Revolution. It was replaced in 1783 and was ceded to the U.S. government in 1790.

Boston Tea Party, incident of December 16, 1773, in which a group of colonists, protesting the taxation of tea, disguised themselves as Mohawk Indians, boarded the British cargo ships *Dartmouth*, *Eleanor*, and *Beaver*, and emptied 342 crates of tea into Boston Harbor. The patriots, led by Samuel Adams, called themselves the "Sons of Liberty."

Boston Whaler, fiberglass production motorboat first built in 1958 by Richard T. Fisher in Braintree, Massachusetts. Its unique foam core construction made the boat durable and unsinkable. Since the first thirteen-foot model, more than seventy thousand Boston Whalers have been built in an array of sizes and styles. Today the company is headquartered in Edgewater, Florida.

Botany Bay, body of water in New South Wales, on the east coast of Australia about five miles

Nathaniel
Bowditch.
(Courtesy
International
Marine/
McGraw-Hill)

south of Sydney. In 1770, the British explorer **James Cook** became the first European to reach the bay, and his shipboard naturalist **Joseph Banks** named it for the many unusual plants growing on its shores. In 1788 eleven ships arrived there with 548 male and 188 female prisoners to set up the first British penal colony in Australia.

Bougainville, Louis Antoine de (1729–1811), French scientist and navigator who commanded the first French naval force to circumnavigate the globe (1766–69). He made many astronomical and botanical studies (bringing back samples of plant life, including the genus named for him—*Bougainvillea*) and published an account of the journey, which was widely read. His voyage opened the modern age of scientific exploration in the Pacific. He served with the colonial forces in the American Revolution but suffered a defeat in 1782 in the Caribbean and returned to France. He later served under **Napoleon I**.

bounding main, colloquial term for the sea.

HMS *Bounty*, British naval **frigate** launched in 1787 that was the scene of the noted 1789 **Mutiny on the** *Bounty*. Under the command of **William Bligh** and with a crew of forty-six men, it sailed from England for Tahiti in 1789 to carry a cargo of **breadfruit** trees to the **West Indies**. On the return voyage, the crew, led by second mate **Fletcher Christian**, mutinied and set Captain Bligh and eighteen others adrift in the *Bounty* launch. They sailed 3,618 miles to Timor and managed to get back to England. Some of the mutineers were later captured by HMS *Pandora*, while others settled on **Pitcairn Island**.

Bowditch, popular name for the navigation text *The American Practical Navigator* (formerly *The New American Practical Navigator*, which was first published in 1802 by **Nathaniel Bowditch**).

Bowditch, Nathaniel (1773–1838), American mathematician and astronomer from Salem, Massachusetts, best known for his extensive revision of J. H. Moore's *The Practical Navigator* (1799), the leading book on navigation at the time, which he named *The New American Practical Navigator* (1802). Between 1795 and 1803, he voyaged to various places around the world, first as a clerk and eventually as a supercargo and part owner, and studied and taught navigation on each voyage. He spent his career as an insurance executive.

USS *Bowfin* (SS-287), 311-foot Balao-class submarine built in 1943 that was responsible for sending 67,882 tons of Japanese shipping to the bottom of the Pacific. Heavily decorated for her service in World War II, the 1,525-ton sub was decommissioned in 1971. The national historic landmark is now part of the USS *Arizona* Memorial in **Pearl Harbor** along with the battleships USS *Arizona* and USS *Missouri*.

bowsprit, a spar projecting from the bow or stem of a sailboat or ship to which the forestays are attached. While supporting the mast or foremast, it allows additional sails to be set.

Boxer Rebellion, Chinese revolt against foreigners and Chinese Christians in 1898–99 by a secret society referred to by Westerners as Boxers. In 1900, after violence went unchecked, twenty thousand troops from Great Britain, Germany, Russia, France, and the United States were sent to protect foreign property. The Allied forces crushed the rebellion, and a peace protocol was signed in September 1901. The incident reinforced the need for the U.S. **Navy** to retain control of the Philippines and to maintain a strong presence in the Far East.

box the compass, the act of naming the thirty-two points of the compass in proper sequence, starting with north and proceeding through east, south, and west back to north, including quarter points. This knowledge was formerly required in the training of seagoing sailors.

Boy-Ed, Karl (1872–1943), German naval officer who served as an attaché in Washington, D.C., at the outbreak of World War I. He directed a network of spies and saboteurs who were so active that President Woodrow Wilson demanded his recall in 1917.

The Boy, Me, and the Cat, interesting narrative by Henry Plummer about a 1912–13 cruise aboard his **catboat** from Massachusetts to Florida and back—with his son and a cat.

Bradbury, Ray (Douglas) (b. 1920), American author best known for his science fiction novels, including *Fahrenheit 451*. With John Huston, he wrote the screenplay for the 1956 version of ***Moby-Dick***, which featured Gregory Peck as Captain **Ahab**.

Bradford, William (1830–1892), American artist from Fairhaven, Massachusetts, who is best known for his radiant paintings of the Arctic region and polar subjects.

Braer, Liberian-flagged tanker that went aground in the Shetland Islands off the coast of Scotland on January 5, 1993. The ship broke up a week later and dumped twenty-five million gallons of crude oil into the sea, twice as much as that released by the ***Exxon Valdez***.

The Brassbounder, classic 1921 novel by Scottish author David W. Bone (1874–1959) about sailing aboard a nineteenth-century merchant vessel. The term "brassbounder" was used in the British merchant service to describe an officer apprentice.

Brassey, Anna (1839–1887), English travel writer who made several long voyages with her husband, Thomas Brassey, a railroad magnate and millionaire member of the British Parliament. In the 1870s the couple made a circumnavigation on the yacht ***Sunbeam*** with their children, eleven other passengers, and a crew

of thirty-two, including a nurse, a ladies' maid, and a stewardess. Brassey chronicled the trip in *The **Voyage in the Sunbeam*** (1879). When she died, she was buried at sea.

brass monkey, a metal frame laid on the deck of a ship to help contain the bottom layer of a stack of cannon balls. The phrase "cold enough to freeze the balls off a brass monkey" meant that in extremely cold temperatures the brass frame shrank more than the iron cannon balls, and the stack would collapse.

Bravo Zulu, phonetic pronunciation of "BZ" from the **International Code of Signals**, which signifies "good job" or "well done."

Braynard, Frank O. (b. 1917), prolific and beloved American author and historian of passenger ships and shipping. He is well known for his exhaustive six-volume series on the liner SS ***Leviathan***, which is titled *Leviathan: The World's Greatest Ship* (1972–83).

HMS *Breadalbane*, 500-ton sailing ship that sank in the Canadian Arctic in 1853 while searching for the lost explorer Sir **John Franklin**. The ship was discovered, largely intact, in 1975 and has been the subject of ongoing diving expeditions.

breadfruit, a tropical fruit native to the Pacific Islands. It gets its name from its edible starchy pulp, which some people think tastes and feels like bread. Among the missions of HMS ***Bounty*** was to obtain breadfruit plants from Tahiti and transport them to the British **West Indies** for replanting and cultivation. After the *Bounty* mutiny, Captain **Bligh** became known as "Breadfuit Bligh" throughout the **Royal Navy**.

break-bulk, cargoes of nonuniform sizes, often on pallets, that require labor-intensive loading and unloading. Before containerization, most cargo—also called general cargo—was characterized this way. The term was coined to differentiate this type of cargo from **bulk** shipments.

A branch and fruit of the breadfruit tree. (Courtesy International Marine/McGraw-Hill; illustration by Nathan Goldstein)

breeches buoy, a ring buoy fitted with canvas breeches that is used for bringing shipwrecked persons ashore.

Breezing Up, popular 1876 **Winslow Homer** oil painting, subtitled "A Fair Wind," that depicts three young men and one veteran hand aboard the **catboat** *Gloucester*. It hangs in the National Gallery of Art in Washington, D.C.

Bremen, 938-foot **North German Lloyd liner** that, on her **maiden voyage**, took the speed record for the **Atlantic** away from RMS *Mauretania*. Near-sister to the *Europa*, she represented Germany's resurgence as a major player in the transatlantic passenger competition. *Bremen* fled New York Harbor in August 1939 on a harrowing fourteen-day, blacked-out voyage to Germany via **Murmansk**. It was intended that she would land troops during Hitler's proposed invasion of Britain, and preliminary work was done on board to ready her for this role. However, she was destroyed by fire in Bremerhaven in 1941 and was scrapped soon thereafter.

The Brendan Voyage, 1978 narrative by the author-adventurer **Tim Severin** recounting his 1976–77 voyage in the thirty-six-foot leather boat *Brendan* across the North Atlantic, re-creating the voyage of **Saint Brendan,** who according to Irish tradition sailed to North America before the Vikings and nine hundred years before **Christopher Columbus**.

Brierly, Oswald Walter (1817–1894), skilled British artist who served as marine painter to Queen Victoria. He had a close relationship with the **Royal Navy** and traveled extensively throughout the world on naval vessels.

brig, vessel with two masts, both of which are square-rigged. On the mainmast is a standing gaff to which is rigged a **fore-and-aft** sail. There are two other classes of brigs: **brigantine** and **hermaphrodite brig**.

brig, ship's area for confining prisoners, or a naval jail. During the **Napoleonic Wars,**

Horatio Nelson placed French prisoners in the type of ship known by the same name.

brigantine, sailing vessel with two masts. The foremast is square-rigged, and the mainmast carries a **fore-and-aft** mainsail and square-rigged topsails.

brightwork, woodwork on a boat that is varnished or otherwise finished to show its natural grain. Aboard ship it can refer to polished metal, particularly brass.

Brilliant, sixty-two-foot, two-masted **schooner** designed by **Olin James Stephens II** of **Sparkman & Stephens** and constructed in 1931 by **Henry B. Nevins** at **City Island**, New York. She served as a coastal patrol vessel in World War II and was sailed after the war by **Briggs Cunningham**. One of the finest-built yachts ever afloat, she is today one of the best preserved historic wooden boats. She continues as a sail training vessel and is among the watercraft collection of **Mystic Seaport** in Mystic, Connecticut.

Brinkley, William (b. 1917), American novelist and author of ***Don't Go Near the Water*** (1956), the best-seller *The Ninety and Nine* (1966), and the fictional thriller *The Last Ship* (1988), about the guided missile **destroyer** USS *Nathan James* that becomes the last ship afloat after a nuclear holocaust.

Brinnin, John Malcolm (1916–1998), American poet, editor, and social historian who wrote three histories of North Atlantic **steamship** travel, including *The Sway of the Grand Saloon* (1963).

Briscoe, Arthur (1873–1943), British yachtsman and marine artist best known for his etchings of scenes aboard merchant sailing vessels. He served in the **Royal Navy** in World Wars I and II and wrote *A Handbook of Sailing* under the pen name Clovehitch.

Bristol, industrial city and seaport in southwestern England. As a yachting center, it was the reference for the expression "Shipshape and Bristol Fashion," used to describe something maintained in a seamanlike style. The phrase also applied to Bristol, Rhode Island, home to the Herreshoff Manufacturing Company, which served as one of America's leading yachting centers.

Britannia, one of the most raced, successful, and revered sailing yachts of all time. The racing **cutter** was designed by **George L. Watson** and launched in 1893 for the Prince of Wales, later King Edward VII. A sister ship of the Earl of **Dunraven**'s *Valkyrie*, *Britannia* was sold in 1897 but was later returned to royal ownership. Upon Edward's death in 1913, *Britannia* continued racing, with his son King George V often at the helm. After the death of George V in 1936, and in deference to his wishes, the forty-three-year-old yacht was towed into the English Channel and **scuttled**.

HM Yacht *Britannia*, 412-foot British Royal yacht completed in 1954 and decommissioned in 1997 by direction of Queen Elizabeth II because of the cost of upkeep. She carried a crew of 270, and the wheel of King George V's racing yacht *Britannia* was used in the wheelhouse, fitted to a modern steering system.

SS *Britannia*, wooden **paddle wheel** steamer built in 1840 as the first ship for the **Cunard Line** (then the British and North American Royal Mail Steam Packet Company). She embarked on her **maiden voyage** from Liverpool to Boston on July 4, 1840—a date chosen specifically because it was American Independence Day. The 1,156-gross-ton vessel had a crew of 89 and carried 115 passengers for the thirteen-day crossing to Halifax, thence to the American port where she arrived amid much celebration on July 19. SS *Britannia* was sold in 1849 after making twenty round trips of the **Atlantic** and was scrapped in Kiel in 1880.

MS *Britannic*, motor **liner** built in 1930 for the **White Star Line**. The 26,943-gross-ton sister ship to MS *Georgic* came under the control of the **Cunard White Star Line** with the amalgamation in 1934. She was the last White Star Line ship remaining in operation when she was scrapped in 1960.

RMS *Britannic*, third giant ship of the **White Star Line**, which was originally conceived to operate a balanced Southampton to New York service with her two sisters, RMS *Olympic* and RMS *Titanic*. Her name was intended as *Gigantic*, consonant with the names of the previous twin **liners** but was changed to the more conservative sounding moniker after *Titanic* rendezvoused with destiny. The 48,158-gross-ton liner was finished as *Britannic* in 1915 as a British hospital ship. She was sunk by a mine in the Aegean Sea in 1916, with 21 lives lost of the 1,134 on board.

British East India Company, powerful trade organization founded in 1600 that eventually controlled all of India and dominated trade with China. The company practically ruled these places until the mid-nineteenth century, when the regions formally became part of the British Empire and the company ceased to exist. The British East India Company was also responsible for the illegal opium trade that led to the **Opium War** with China.

Brooking, Charles (1723–1759), British marine artist who grew up in the dockyards of London and started painting at an early age. He spent a considerable time at sea and knew his subject well. Unscrupulous art dealers caused his career to struggle, and he died at the early age of thirty-six. Today his work is considered some of the best and most important of the period.

USS *Brooklyn* (CL-40), namesake lead unit of a class of eleven U.S. **Navy** light **cruisers**. The 12,700-ton vessel was commissioned in 1938 and attached to duty in the North Atlantic. She rescued 1,100 men from the burning naval transport USS *Wakefield* —formerly SS *Manhattan* of the **United States Lines**—in

1942. She shelled targets to support beach-head landings in North Africa, **Anzio**, and Normandy. She was decommissioned in 1945 and transferred to Chile in 1951 as the *O'Higgins*. Decommissioned again in 1992, she sank while being towed to India for scrapping.

Brown, Margaret "Molly" (1867–1932), spirited Denver millionairess who rallied fellow RMS *Titanic* survivors aboard lifeboat number six to work together in order to save all their lives until rescue arrived. She was decorated by the British government for her decidedly "Rocky Mountain" brand of heroism and is remembered today as "the Unsinkable Molly Brown." She was the subject of the Broadway musical and film, *The* **Unsinkable Molly Brown**.

Brown on Resolution, 1929 novel by **Cecil Scott "C. S." Forester** that describes the exploits of a British petty officer stranded on Resolution Island when it was being attacked from the sea by Germans in World War I. Published as *Single-Handed* in the United States, the story was filmed in Britain as *Sailor of the King*.

brown water, shallow water or shallow draft, especially a ship (or a force whose ships are) not suited to deep or **blue water** operations.

Brunel, Isambard Kingdom (1806–1859), English engineer who was one of the greatest and most innovative engineers of the nineteenth century. After designing railway bridges and tunnels, he turned his attention to **steamships**. He designed SS *Great Western*, *Great Britain*, and *Great Eastern*, three vessels that set records for speed, power, size, and construction.

Brunswick Corporation, Lake Forest, Illinois–based marketer and manufacturer of many leading boating brands, including **Mercury** and Mariner outboard engines; Mercury MerCruiser sterndrives and inboard engines; Sea Ray, Bayliner, and Maxum pleasure boats; Baja high-performance boats; and **Boston Whaler** and Trophy offshore fishing boats.

buccaneer, one of many pirates and **privateers** who had bases in the **Spanish Main**. The word derives from the French *boucan*, a grill for cooking meat, because the pirates needed to obtain and cook meat from uninhabited islands to avoid arrest.

The Buccaneer, the Hollywood version of the story of pirate **Jean Lafitte** and his band in the **War of 1812**, as envisioned and directed by Cecile B. DeMille. The 1938 action-packed adventure spectacle starred Fredrick March, Spring Byington, Walter Brennan, and Anthony Quinn.

Buccaneer's Girl, wildly entertaining 1950 American motion picture about a spunky tavern girl in colonial New Orleans who manages to get involved with a good-natured band of pirates. It starred Yvonne De Carlo, Phillip Friend, Elsa Lancaster, and Jay C. Flippen.

Buchanan, Franklin (1800–1874), U.S. naval officer who in 1845 was chosen by **George Bancroft** to be the first superintendent of the U.S. Naval School, which later became the U.S. **Naval Academy**. He later served in the Mexican War and sailed with the **Perry Expedition** to Japan in 1853. In 1860 he resigned from the U.S. **Navy** to become the **Confederate States Navy**'s first admiral. He commanded CSS *Virginia* at the beginning of the Battle of **Hampton Roads** and captained CSS *Tennessee* at the Battle of **Mobile Bay**.

Buchheim, Lothar-Günther (b. 1918), German author of *Das Boot* (1973), the classic novel of World War II **U-boat** warfare, which was later made into an award-winning documentary and motion picture of the same name. Buchheim was an official naval correspondent and served on one patrol aboard U-96. Buchheim also produced *U-Boat War*, an epic essay about Germany's U-boats at war.

Buckley, William F., Jr. (b. 1925), American editor, author, and sailor, and one of the best-known spokesmen for political conservatism. He founded the magazine *National Review* in 1955. He has told of his own at-sea adventures in *Airborne* (1970), ***Atlantic High*** (1982), *Racing through Paradise: A Pacific Passage* (1987), and other books.

Buffett, James "Jimmy" (b. 1946), American singer and songwriter whose music often includes Caribbean rhythms and evokes images of the sea, sailing, and laid-back living.

bugeye, distinctive double-end workboat with two masts of equal height, developed in Chesapeake Bay in the later nineteenth century. Commonly fifty feet or longer, this type of boat was an outgrowth of the **Chesapeake log canoe**. It featured a large centerboard, two raking masts with **leg-o'-mutton** sails, and a jib; later many had a counterstern. The name is believed to be derived either from the hawseholes or from the running lights, which resemble a bug's eyes.

"The Building of the Ship", 1849 poem by **Henry Wadsworth Longfellow** published in his compilation *The Seaside and the Fireside*. It begins, "Build me straight, O worthy Master! Stanch and strong, a goodly vessel, That shall laugh at all disaster, And with wave and whirlwind wrestle!"

bulbous bow, rounded appendage at the lower forward end of a ship designed to reduce wave-making resistance as the ship moves through the water. This feature was pioneered by **David Watson Taylor** and was first employed on the battleship USS *Delaware* in 1907.

bulk, cargo—such as coal, ore, oil, and grain—that is shipped unpackaged in the holds of specially designed ships. Bulk service is generally not offered on a regularly scheduled basis, but rather as needed. Many companies that ship these cargoes operate their own fleets or charter **tramp** vessels.

bulker, vessel designed to carry **bulk** cargo.

Bullen, Frank Thomas (1857–1915), English author who recounted his experience as first **mate** aboard a New Bedford whaleship in *The Cruise of the Cachalot* (1897). He wrote thirty-five other books about the sea and ships, including *Idylls of the Sea* (1906) and *Our Heritage the Sea* (1906).

HMS *Bulwark*, British **Royal Navy** battleship launched in 1902 that was ripped apart by a massive internal magazine explosion while loading ammunition at anchor at the Naval Dockyard at Sheerness, England, on November 26, 1914. Only twelve men out of a complement of nearly eight hundred survived. Subsequent investigation found that the explosion was caused by improper storage of cordite.

bunker, fuel consumed by the engines of a ship. Also, the place on a vessel where fuel is stored. "Bunkering" refers to the act of refueling.

USS *Bunker Hill* (CV-17), U.S. **Navy Essex**-class aircraft carrier commissioned in 1943. She saw extensive action against the Japanese in the South Pacific in World War II, including strikes on Rabaul, the Gilbert Islands, Tarawa, and the **Marshall Islands**. The ship was damaged by two **kamikazes** in 1945, killing 429 men and wounding an additional 264. Decorated with eleven battle stars for her wartime service, *Bunker Hill* was **laid up** in 1966 and scrapped in 1973.

Buntline, Ned, pseudonym of E. Z. C. Judson (1823–1886), American adventurer and writer who penned hundreds of dime novels. His stories often included swashbuckling heroes and seafaring exploits. He began his career as a cabin boy in the U.S. **Navy** in 1844.

Bureau of Marine Inspection and Navigation (BMIN), U.S. government bureau that emerged from the consolidation of the **Steamboat Inspection Service** and the **Bureau of Navigation** in 1932. BMIN was established within the Department of Commerce in 1936 to address many of the flaws in the existing system of certifying vessels and personnel—flaws that manifested themselves in the 1934 burning of the **liner** *Morro Castle*. In 1942 BMIN was placed under the jurisdiction of the U.S. **Coast Guard**, and its responsibilities were permanently transferred to the service in 1946.

Bureau of Navigation, federal bureau established under the control of the Treasury Department on July 5, 1884, to supervise U.S. merchant mariners. It was combined with the **Steamboat Inspection Service** in 1932 within the Department of Commerce and named the Bureau of Navigation and Steamboat Inspection. In 1936 it was renamed the **Bureau of Marine Inspection and Navigation**.

Bureau Veritas, one of the world's oldest classification societies, headquartered in Paris, France.

Burgess, Edward (1848–1891), American yacht designer who produced the successful **America's Cup** defenders *Puritan* (1885), *Mayflower* (1886), and *Volunteer* (1887). Burgess was a Harvard professor of entomology who turned his passion for mathematics and yachting into a business in which he designed 207 vessels in his short lifetime. His son **W. Starling Burgess** continued his fine work.

Burgess, W. Starling (d. 1947), American yacht designer, son of **Edward Burgess**, and a pioneer of American aviation. He built the Wright brothers' planes under license and later designed seaplanes for the U.S. **Navy**. During World War I, Burgess turned out eight planes a day from his factory in Marblehead, Massachusetts. The factory burned in 1918 and was never rebuilt. In the 1930s he designed the **America's Cup J-boats** *Enterprise* (1930) and *Rainbow* (1934) and collaborated with **Olin James Stephens II** on *Ranger* (1937). He also designed many sailing yachts, including the staysail **schooner** *Niña*. Burgess and R. Buckminster Fuller designed the experimental three-wheeled car Dymaxion.

Burke, Arleigh Albert (1901–1996), U.S. naval officer in World War II who won recognition for his excellent handling of **destroyers** in the South Pacific. Popularly referred to as "31-Knot Burke," he served an unprecedented three terms as **Chief of Naval Operations**, from 1955 to 1961. The lead ship in the modern class of U.S. **Navy** destroyers is named for him.

Burns, George (1795–1890), British shipowner who, in 1840, along with **Samuel Cunard**, founded the **Cunard Line**. He served for many years as head of the company and was succeeded by both his son, John, and his grandson, George.

Bushnell, David (c. 1742–1824), Yale College student who designed the *Turtle*, a one-man submarine powered by a hand-cranked propeller. In 1777 the *Turtle* failed in an attempt to sink the British warship HMS *Eagle* in New York Harbor.

Butler, Rhett, fictional character in Margaret Mitchell's Civil War epic *Gone with the Wind* (1936). Captain Butler is a **blockade runner** captain who consorts with the North but eventually joins with the South. Clark Gable played Butler in the 1939 Academy Award–winning film.

Buttersworth, James Edward (1817–1894), English marine artist who emigrated to the United States in the late 1840s. The son of English marine painter Thomas Buttersworth (1797–1842), he painted in New York City during the mid-nineteenth century—an era in which American shipping was undergoing continuous and momentous change. His oil paintings include naval battle scenes and the evolution of the **America's Cup**. His work, featured in many major American art museums as well as in private collections, records fifty years of dramatic developments in the maritime history of America. Many of his paintings were made into popular lithographs by Nathaniel Currier and later by **Currier and Ives**.

James E. Buttersworth's *The Yacht* Magic *Defending America's Cup*, circa 1870. (The Terra Museum of American Art, Chicago, and South Street Seaport Museum, New York)

Byng, John (1704–1757), British admiral who in 1756 was held responsible for losing the island of Minorca to the French during the **Seven Years' War**. Byng was brought to trial, court-martialed, and sentenced to death. In 1757 he was shot on the quarterdeck of HMS *Monarch*. His execution is behind Voltaire's famous line in *Candide*: "In this country we find it pays to kill an admiral from time to time to encourage the others."

Bynkershoek, Cornelius van (1673–1743), Dutch writer on international law, best known for his classic *De Domino Maris* (1702) on **maritime law**. Bynkershoek suggested that a maritime state's jurisdiction—or **territorial sea**—should extend as far as a cannon could fire. At the time, a cannon shot carried approximately three miles. *De Domino Maris* was a compromise between the concepts of *mare liberum* by **Hugo Grotius** and *mare clausum* by John Selden.

Byrd, Richard Evelyn (1888–1957), U.S. **Navy** admiral, aviator, and explorer who piloted planes over the North Pole in 1926 and the South Pole in 1929. He led a total of five naval expeditions to Antarctica, opening the continent to scientific exploration.

C

C&C, Canadian production boat manufacturer founded in 1961 by George Cuthbertson and George Cassian. C&C excelled at race boats but also designed and produced family cruisers.

C1 freighter, small, standardized cargo vessel constructed in accordance with the **Merchant Marine Act of 1936**. Built in four models weighing seventy-two hundred tons and measuring 418 feet in length, these general cargo ships could operate as **tramps** or on trade routes. The ships were either steam or diesel powered and were capable of making sixteen **knots**. Between 1940 and 1945, 173 C1s were constructed, sixteen of which were lost during the war. The need for such small vessels for "island hopping" in the South Pacific led to a request by General **Douglas MacArthur** for the development of the **C1-M**.

C1-M freighter, shallow draft cargo ship, 239 of which were delivered for service in the South Pacific during World War II. With a length of 320 feet, the ships had low fuel consumption and high endurance, and they were capable of lifting heavy war cargo. To enable navigation

of the South Pacific's many shallow harbors and bays, diesel engines and machinery were positioned aft. Like the **C1**, these ships proved quite popular when sold under the **Merchant Ship Sales Act of 1946**.

C2 freighter, standard intermediate dry cargo vessel constructed under the **Merchant Marine Act of 1936**. Mostly steam turbine powered, the vessels were capable of 15.5 **knots**. Considered the U.S. **Maritime Commission**'s finest design, the C2s were 459 feet in length and measured nine thousand tons. Approximately 315 of the ships, often named for famous American **clipper ships**, were built between 1939 and 1947.

C3 freighter, the largest and fastest class of cargo vessels, 258 of which were constructed under the **Merchant Marine Act of 1936**. Powered by either diesel engines or steam turbine, measuring 492 feet in length and twelve thousand tons, their top speed was in excess of 16.5 **knots**.

C4 freighter, a class of seventy-five vessels designated by the U.S. **Maritime Commission**

and built between 1943 and 1945. Of the total produced, thirty-three were completed as troop transports, while the remaining forty-two were finished as cargo ships.

C5 freighter, eight specially designed ore-carrying ships built under the aegis of the U.S. **Maritime Commission** between 1945 and 1948.

cabin class, term coined in the mid-1930s to represent what had previously been **first class** in order to allow **steamship** companies to charge lower fares for the top grade of passenger accommodation. Before World War II, the best grade to be found on SS *Normandie*, RMS *Queen Mary*, and other transatlantic **liners** was cabin class. Following the war, the term "first class" was reapplied to the best accommodation on board, and the term "cabin class" was used to describe what had been tourist class before the conflict.

cabin cruiser, a small to medium-sized engine-driven yacht specially designed for inland or coastal use rather than use on the open seas. It places comfort and accommodation above seaworthiness and performance.

cable, unit of measurement equal to one tenth of a **nautical mile**, or 608 feet. The length of a ship's hemp anchor cable was formerly 101 fathoms, or 606 feet.

Cabot, John (ca. 1450–1498), Italian navigator born Giovanni Caboto, who settled in Bristol, England. Sailing under the English flag, he left Bristol in 1497 in the ship *Matthew* in search of a **Northwest Passage** to Asia. He landed in Nova Scotia and later explored **Cape Breton** and Newfoundland, claiming the land for England. Cabot returned to England, believing he had reached Asia, and was given a reward and pension. Cabot set sail again in 1498 with five ships and was lost at sea.

Cabot, Sebastian (1484–1557), Venetian-born navigator, explorer, and mapmaker who was the second son of **John Cabot**. He led unsuccessful searches for both a **Northwest Passage** and a **Northeast Passage**.

USS *Cabot* (CV-28), seventh **Independence**-class aircraft carrier, completed in 1943 and assigned to patrols in the South Pacific. She was hit by a **kamikaze** in 1944, resulting in the deaths of sixty-two crew members. She participated in strikes against Luzon, Formosa, **Iwo Jima**, and the Japanese home islands. Decommissioned in 1955, the eleven-thousand-ton ship was transferred to Spain in 1967. She returned to U.S. ownership in 1989 but was scrapped in 2000 because the necessary funds could not be raised to preserve her.

cabotage, French term meaning "by the capes" that is used to describe the coasting trade and shipments made between ports of a nation, which are commonly referred to as coastwise or intercoastal navigation or trade. Many nations, including the United States, have cabotage laws (for example, the **Jones Act**) that require national flag ships to provide the domestic interport service. Waivers in the United States may be obtained through an act of the U.S. Congress.

Cabral, Pedro Alvares (c. 1467–1520), Portuguese navigator who, planning to sail around the African continent to India, sighted Brazil in 1500 and claimed it for Portugal. His voyage helped Portugal develop its large overseas empire in the 1500s.

Cabrillo, Juan Rodriguez (d. 1543), Portuguese-born Spanish conquistador who was the first European explorer to sail along the California coast. In 1542 his ship dropped anchor in San Diego Bay and claimed for Spain the west coast of what became the United States. He continued to sail northward along the coast, reaching San Francisco Bay. Soon afterward, the expedition turned south. The explorers anchored at San Miguel Island, about fifty miles west of Santa Barbara, where Cabrillo died.

Cabrillo National Monument, statue erected in 1913 near San Diego, California, to honor the Portuguese-born explorer and navigator **Juan Rodriguez Cabrillo,** who in the service of Spain was the first to explore California.

The Caine Mutiny, 1951 novel by **Herman Wouk** about a group of officers on board the **destroyer**-minesweeper USS *Caine* in the Pacific in World War II who revolt against a captain they consider mentally unfit. Much of the book focuses on the court-martial and its aftermath. Wouk's first novel, it won the Pulitzer Prize in 1952. The 1954 film featured Humphrey Bogart as **Captain Queeg** as well as Fred MacMurray, Lee Marvin, and E. G. Marshall.

USS *Cairo*, Union **ironclad** that was one of the seven Pook Turtles designed by **Samuel H. Pook** and built by **James B. Eads** of Saint Louis during the Civil War. On December 12, 1862, *Cairo* struck two mines and sank in less than twelve minutes, with no loss of life, in the Yazoo River, approximately ten miles north of Vicksburg, Mississippi. The Civil War vessel was salvaged in 1964 and is presently on display at Vicksburg National Military Park.

caisson disease (also known as "**decompression sickness**" or "the bends"), condition first diagnosed during the construction (1869–83) of caissons—dry construction compartments sunk into a riverbed—for New York's Brooklyn Bridge.

Calico Jack, nickname of the English pirate **John Rackham,** who was known to wear colorful clothes made of calico, a coarse cotton.

SS *California*, two-hundred-foot **side-wheel** steamer operated by the **Pacific Mail Steam Ship Company** that sailed with mail and a few passengers on a trip from New York to San Francisco in October 1848. When she reached Panama in January 1849, she was greeted by hundreds of Americans who sought

passage after they heard that gold had been discovered in California. In February 1849 she became the first **steamship** to enter San Francisco Bay.

USS *California* (BB-44), thirty-two-thousand-ton Tennessee-class battleship that was the flagship of the Pacific Fleet from her commissioning in 1921 to the beginning of World War II. Moored in **Battleship Row** in **Pearl Harbor** the morning of December 7, 1941, the ship was sunk in the attack and lost ninety-eight crew members, with another sixty-one wounded. Refloated and rebuilt, the 624-foot vessel was made ready for duty in 1944 and saw action in the invasion of the Mariana Islands, the Battle of **Leyte Gulf**, and the assault on **Okinawa**. She was decommissioned in 1947 and scrapped in 1959.

California Maritime Academy, Vallejo campus of the California State University system that has provided professional maritime training since 1929. The academic program is designed to qualify students for bachelor of science degrees in marine transportation, marine engineering technology, business administration, mechanical engineering, and facility engineering. The school also offers professional courses that provide certification in maritime skills, environmental protection, and health and safety.

SS *Californian*, small British passenger freighter of the Leyland Line that played a major role in the RMS *Titanic* disaster of 1912. It is claimed by many that the **master** of *Californian* disregarded the wireless pleas for assistance sent out by the foundering *Titanic* while some of the ship's crew watched distress rockets from the great **liner** only fifteen miles distant. Although all parties testified at subsequent hearings, the findings were inconclusive. *Californian* continued in service until she was torpedoed and sunk off Cape Matapan, Greece, in 1915.

Callahan, Steven (b. 1952), American sailor, vessel designer, and writer who spent seventy-six days adrift in a raft in the North Atlantic after his **sloop** *Napoleon Solo* sank during a 1982 crossing. His account of the ordeal appears in his book *Adrift: Seventy-Six Days Lost at Sea* (1986).

Callison, Brian (b. 1936), popular Scottish author of nearly twenty action-packed maritime thrillers, many of which revolve around the notorious Captain Trapp. Callison served twenty-seven years in the **Royal Navy** Auxiliary Service, and his novels are highly acclaimed for their attention to detail. His novels include *A Flock of Ships*, *Sextant*, *Trapp's Crocodile*, and *A Web of Salvage*.

call sign, a code comprising four alphabet flags that is traditionally assigned to every registered ship as her visual flag hoist and radio call sign. All four-letter call signs have now been assigned, and in recent years authorities have assigned letter and number designations.

Calvert, James F., U.S. **Navy** officer who was the commanding officer of the submarine USS *Skate* when it surfaced at the North Pole on February 1959. Calvert achieved the rank of Vice Admiral and served as Superintendent of the U.S. **Naval Academy** from 1968 to 1972.

calving, process by which a piece of ice breaks off from an iceberg, a glacier, or an ice shelf to form a calf, or small piece of ice.

Calypso, converted British minesweeper, built in the United States in 1942, that in 1950 began serving as the research platform for French explorer **Jacques-Yves Cousteau**. Appropriately, Calypso was the name of the sea nymph who detained **Odysseus** for seven years on the island of Ogygia; thus the name suggests a beautiful seductress. *Calypso* served Cousteau for more than fifty years, until she was replaced by *Calypso II*.

Camarioca boatlift, the first large-scale exodus of Cuban immigrants to the United States. In September 1965 Fidel Castro announced that Cubans with relatives in the United States could leave the country provided that an American vessel picked them up at the port of Camarioca, near Havana. Nearly five thousand people made the trip.

Cambria, 108-foot British **schooner** that in 1870 was the first yacht to challenge for the **America's Cup**. Owned by British yachtsman James Ashbury, she faced a fleet of twenty-three American boats in a course off New York and finished tenth. The schooner *Magic* won the race. Ashbury challenged, and lost, the following year in the schooner *Livonia*.

Campania, **Cunard Line** passenger steamer that, on her 1893 **maiden voyage**, took the honor of the fastest transatlantic passage away from the **Inman Line liner** *City of Paris*. Sold for scrap in 1914, the 12,950-gross-ton *Campania* was repurchased by the British government and converted into an aircraft carrier. She sank in 1918 after colliding with HMS *Revenge* in the **Firth of Forth**.

Camper & Nicholson, renowned British yacht builder founded in 1855 by William Camper and Ben Nicholson. In the 1880s **Charles E. Nicholson** brought the firm worldwide acclaim with his innovative designs. Among the most famous yachts the company launched were four **America's Cup** challengers, including the **J-boats** *Shamrock V*, HMS *Endeavour*, and *Endeavour II*. Today the firm, which has facilities in Southampton and Gosport, remains on the cutting edge of yacht design and construction.

Camperdown, Battle of, decisive British naval victory over the Dutch fleet on October 11, 1797, during the **French Revolution**. The Dutch fleet was intending to help the French land in Ireland. The battle, fought off the coast of Holland, effectively marked the end of significant Dutch naval power.

Canadian Pacific Hotels, magnificent chain of palatial hotels built across Canada at the very beginning of the twentieth century to provide havens of civilization for passengers making the transcontinental railroad journey, often as a segment of the **Canadian Pacific Steamships** option of travel from Great Britain to the Orient. The Empress in Victoria, Banff Springs in the Rockies, and the Château Frontenac in Québec are among the chain's best-known hostelries.

Canadian Pacific Railway, company that opened trans-Canadian railway service in 1886 and also operated an assortment of coastal vessels on the Pacific Coast as far north as Alaska as an extension of the railroad. The most notable among these vessels were the *Princess Louise* and the *Princess Patricia*. At one time the Canadian Pacific was the largest travel operation in the world, capable of furnishing the finest transportation and lodging under one house flag between Great Britain and the Orient. The company also branched into the airline business following World War II, until that concern was swallowed up into Air Canada.

Canadian Pacific Steamships, diversification of the **Canadian Pacific Railway** to provide continuous transportation from Great Britain, across Canada, and on to the Orient, thus avoiding the extremely harsh climatic changes one had to endure traveling via the **P&O** line from Europe to the Far East. Passenger service from Vancouver to Yokohama began in 1887, and the transatlantic division was started in 1903. The company's version of the **Atlantic** voyage was appealing because more than a thousand miles of it was on the sheltered inland waterway of the Saint Lawrence River. The line operated the famous *Empress of Britain* in the 1930s in addition to other very

fine **liners**. It ended transpacific services at the start of World War II, and its Atlantic operations ceased in 1972.

Canaletto (1697–1768), Italian painter best known for his elegant views of his home city of Venice. He was known as Giovanni Antonio Canal until he adopted the name Canaletto, meaning "little canal," in about 1720. In search of patrons, Canaletto made extended visits to England, where his style had a profound effect on British marine painting.

Canary Islands, group of volcanic islands located about sixty-five miles off the coast of Northwest Africa. Controlled by Spain, the principal islands in the group are Tenerife, Palma, Gomera, Hierro, Grand Canary, Fuerteventura, and Lanzarote. **Horatio Nelson** attacked Santa Cruz de Tenerife Harbor in 1797 in search of a Spanish treasure ship. He was defeated by the defenders of the town, losing his arm in the process.

Canberra, ocean **liner** built in 1960 as the last passenger ship for the Australian service of the **P&O** line. She was revolutionary when built, with twin **funnels** set abreast and very far aft, while lifeboats were slung on davits below the superstructure. She saw action as a troopship during the 1982 Falklands Campaign. Known in shipping circles as "the Great White Whale," she was scrapped in Pakistan in 1997.

Cannery Row, 1945 novel by **John Steinbeck** about down-and-outers who live in the sardine cannery district of Monterey, California. The story follows the adventures of Mack and the boys, a group of unemployed men who inhabit a converted fish-meal shack and try to please Doc, the owner of a biological supply house.

Canton, Western name for Guangzhou, the largest city in southern China, which served as the center of China's foreign trade from the 1780s until the 1840s. Foreign traders were limited to areas containing warehouses, called "hongs," a term later applied to the groups of Chinese merchants who had the privilege of trading with Europeans and Americans.

Cap Arcona, passenger **liner** completed in 1927 at **Blohm & Voss** for Germany's Hamburg–South America Line. The splendid 27,560-ton steamer was taken over for Axis service in 1940. While transporting more than five thousand concentration camp inmates and more than a thousand crew and military personnel from the collapsing Eastern front to western Germany, the three-**funneled** vessel was attacked by British airplanes and caught fire on May 3, 1945. Panic ensued on board as the liner capsized in the shallow waters of Neustadt Bay, near Kiel on the Baltic Sea, taking the lives of well over five thousand people only days before the war came to an end.

Cape Agulhas, the southernmost point of Africa, lying about a hundred miles east and about thirty miles farther south of the **Cape of Good Hope**.

Cape Breton Island, large island off the Atlantic coast of Canada that forms part of the province of Nova Scotia and covers 3,981 square miles. A saltwater lake called Bras d'Or Lake—a favorite of cruising yachtsmen— occupies about a sixth of the island.

Cape Cod, sixty-five-mile-long, hook-shaped peninsula on the coast of Massachusetts. British sea captain **Bartholomew Gosnold** christened it Cape Cod around 1602 because of the codfish caught off its shores.

Cape Cod Canal, 17.5-mile sea-level waterway that cuts through the strip of land that joins **Cape Cod** to the rest of Massachusetts. The canal connects Buzzard's Bay with Cape Cod Bay and eliminates the hazardous passage around the cape and decreases the sea route between Boston and New York City by seventy miles. Work on the canal began in 1909

Canberra. (Courtesy Gordon R. Ghareeb)

when August Belmont, a banker, sponsored the project. It opened in 1914 as a toll waterway; the U.S. government purchased the canal in 1928 for $11.4 million and today operates it toll-free.

Cape Disappointment, promontory located on the north side of the mouth of the Columbia River in southwest Washington, which is the site of some of the heaviest surf in the continental United States. It was named in 1798 by English explorer John Meares, who rounded the cape but could not enter the river due to its treacherous breaking bar. Known as the Graveyard of the Pacific, it is the site of the U.S. **Coast Guard**'s National Motor Lifeboat School and the Cape Disappointment Lighthouse.

Cape Engaño, Battle of, World War II naval engagement fought on October 25, 1944, in the Battle of **Leyte Gulf** that resulted in the loss of seven Imperial Japanese Navy **capital ships** at the hands of the U.S. **Navy**.

Cape Esperance, Battle of, World War II U.S. naval victory over a Japanese squadron on October 11–12, 1942, off the Solomon Islands. The USS *Boise* was severely damaged and the USS *Duncan* was sunk while intercepting a

Japanese "**Tokyo Express**" troop convoy en route to **Guadalcanal**. The Japanese lost one **cruiser** and three **destroyers**, while two other cruisers were badly damaged.

Cape Horn, known simply as The Horn, the most southerly part of South America, which lies at the southern tip of Horn Island in Chile. It was first sighted by Sir **Francis Drake** in 1578, but Willem Schouten (1527–1625), a Dutch navigator, named it in 1616 for his native town of Hoorn. It is known for the severity of its storms and the difficulty in rounding it, especially from east to west. **Square-rigger** sailors called it Cape Stiff because of its stiff winds.

Cape Horner, a **square-rigger** employed on a trade route that required **doubling a cape**, in this case **Cape Horn**. The term also applies to a seaman who has been on this passage.

Cape Leeuwin, peninsula at the tip of southwest Australia. Along with **Cape Horn** and the **Cape of Good Hope**, it is the third milestone cape.

Cape of Good Hope, peninsula at the southern tip of the African continent, which was first rounded, in 1487, by **Bartholomew Dias**, who named it Cabo Tormatoso (Stormy Cape). King John II of Portugal renamed it Cabo del Buonza Esperanza (Cape of Good Hope) lest future seamen be deterred from rounding it to find a sea route to India. The Portuguese explorer **Vasco da Gama** sailed around the Cape of Good Hope and, in May 1498, reached India.

Capes, Battle of the, decisive French naval victory over a British fleet off the mouth of Chesapeake Bay during the American Revolution. The September 5, 1781, action prevented the British from entering the Chesapeake with food and supplies for their troops at Yorktown, Virginia. Lord Cornwallis was eventually forced to surrender on October 19, 1781, at the Battle of **Yorktown,** ending the war.

Cape Saint George, Battle of, World War II naval action in the Pacific off New Ireland on November 25, 1943, between five Japanese and five U.S. **destroyers**. The U.S. force, led by **Arleigh Albert Burke**, sank three Japanese ships while itself sustaining no damage.

Cape Saint Vincent, Battle of, important naval engagement of the **French Revolution** in which a British force of fifteen vessels, under the command of Sir **John Jervis** aided by **Horatio Nelson**, defeated a Spanish fleet of twenty-seven ships off the coast of Portugal. The February 14, 1797, British victory scuttled French plans for an invasion of Great Britain and resulted in the capture of four Spanish ships and three thousand prisoners.

Capital Construction Fund (CCF), tax benefit for operators of certain U.S.-built U.S.-flag ships by which taxes may be deferred on income deposited in a fund to be used for the replacement of vessels.

capital ship, term that has historically described a navy's most important vessels. Under sail, such a ship was called a **ship of the line**. Through the years, the term has come to apply to **cruisers**, battleships, battle aircraft carriers, and even submarines.

captain, title accorded the **master** of a merchant ship or a commanding officer of a military vessel regardless of rank.

Captain Blood, 1922 novel by **Rafael Sabatini** that tells the story of an English doctor who escapes after being sold into Caribbean slavery for aiding enemies of King James. Captain Blood becomes a renegade—but good-hearted—**buccaneer** and chivalrously rescues the damsel in distress. The 1935 film was the silver screen debut of Errol Flynn and also starred Olivia de Havilland and Basil Rathbone.

Captain Horatio Hornblower, classic 1951 motion picture drawn from the novel by **Cecil Scott "C. S." Forester**. The British naval hero thwarts the 1807 French and Spanish Navies in a remarkably action-packed seagoing epic. It starred Gregory Peck, Virginia Mayo, and Christopher Lee.

Captain January, 1936 Shirley Temple movie about an orphan who is saved from a shipwreck by a crusty lighthouse keeper. He raises the castaway and fights to keep her. In addition to Temple, the film starred Guy Kibbee and Buddy Ebsen.

Captain Kidd, 1945 film about the famous pirate and his scheme to capture a treasure ship bound from India to England. Charles Laughton played Captain Kidd and reprised the role in the 1952 comedy ***Abbott & Costello Meet Captain Kidd***. The movie also starred Randolph Scott and Barbara Britton.

Captain of the Port (COTP), U.S. **Coast Guard** officer who is stationed at certain ports or places on navigable waters, with authority conferred by the U.S. Congress, to oversee port safety and security. COTPs supervise the enforcement of anchorage regulations, oversee the loading and discharging of hazardous materials, and control the movements of vessels in harbors and other congested water areas. The explosion of the ***Mont Blanc*** in Halifax in 1917 prompted congressional leaders to increase the powers and responsibilities of COTPs.

Captains Courageous, nautical adventure novel by **Joseph Rudyard Kipling**, which was first published in 1897. The story tells of Harvey Cheyne, a rich man's spoiled son who falls from a transatlantic **liner** and is rescued by the fishing **schooner** *We're Here* out of **Gloucester**, Massachusetts. Instead of being returned to shore, he is forced reevaluate the meaning of life while working his way to port. The 1937 film, directed by Victor Fleming and known for its fine footage while under way, starred Spencer Tracy, Lionel Barrymore, and Mickey Rooney.

Tracy won the Academy Award for best actor for his portrayal of Captain Disko Troop.

captain's mast, a hearing in which the commanding officer of a ship imposes punishment on violators of discipline or regulations. Under the **Uniform Code of Military Justice**, such punishment is deemed nonjudicial punishment.

The Captain's Table, delightful English comedy about a former cargo ship captain who finds commanding a luxury ocean **liner** a very different experience. The 1960 film starred John Gregson, Peggy Cummins, and Donald Sniden.

Cap Trafalgar, exceptional 18,805-gross-ton **liner** built in 1914 for Germany's Hamburg–South America Line. Requisitioned for war service the same year, she was outfitted as an armed merchant **cruiser** and, on September 14, 1914, engaged the **Cunard Line**'s SS ***Carmania*** in close-range naval action off the coast of Brazil. The *Cap Trafalgar* sank as a result of intense gunfire from the British-armed **auxiliary**, with the loss of sixteen lives. This was the only time two refitted passenger ships ever engaged each other in battle.

caravel, type of ship most commonly used by Spanish and Portuguese explorers of the fifteenth and sixteenth centuries. The ship had no standard size or arrangement of sails but generally had three masts and measured between eighty and one hundred feet.

cardinal buoyage system, system of buoys and other **aids to navigation** in which the shape, color, and number are assigned in accordance with location relative to the nearest obstruction. Common in waters having numerous small islands and hazards to navigation, the system is compatible with the **Maritime Buoyage System.**

cardinal points, the four principal points of the compass: north, east, south, and west.

Intercardinal points are the points in between the four main points.

careen, to beach a ship and list her to expose her bottom so that marine growth can be scraped off. The word comes from the old French word *carine*, which refers to the bottom of a ship.

cargo preference, cargo reserved by a nation's laws for transport only aboard ships registered in that nation. Usually such cargo is being transported because of a direct or indirect activity of the government. Agricultural aid is one example, which is often referred to as a "set-aside."

Carlssen, Henrik Kurt, tenacious **master** of the *Flying Enterprise* when she was crippled with cracks in her hull by a North Atlantic gale in 1951. Captain Carlssen courageously remained on board his command for two weeks while the stricken vessel was towed to Falmouth, England. He was forced to abandon his ship thirty miles short of her destination when the craft's port rail dipped under the waves and she subsequently went down off the English coast.

SS *Carmania*, first turbine steamer built for the **Cunard Line** and completed in 1905. Her sister ship *Caronia* was fitted with reciprocating engines to see which machinery setup was more efficient. The turbine installation won hands down, and this type of propulsion was designed into the currently under construction RMS *Lusitania* and RMS *Mauretania*. Taken over by the **Admiralty** in 1914 and outfitted as an armed merchant **cruiser**, the 19,524-gross-ton *Carmania* engaged the similarly refitted German **liner** *Cap Trafalgar* in a two-hour, close-range gun battle on September 14, 1914. *Carmania* sank the other liner but lost nine men. She was refitted for passenger service in 1918 and was eventually scrapped in 1932.

Carnegie, 155-foot nonmagnetic **brigantine** built in 1909 by steel magnate Andrew Carnegie to study the earth's magnetic fields. To accomplish this research, she was built entirely iron-free—engines, anchors, and other fittings were made of either bronze or wood. Between 1909 and 1921, she completed six voyages for the Carnegie Foundation, during which she performed magnetic surveys across all the oceans. After being **laid up** for a time, she was destroyed by fire following a gasoline explosion while lying in Apia Harbor, Samoa, in December 1929.

Carnival Airlines, experimental air carrier intended to transport passengers from various gateway cities throughout the United States to the cruise ships of the **Carnival Cruise Lines** from Miami. It ceased operation without incident in the mid-1990s.

Carnival Cruise Lines, Miami-based cruise ship operation started by Ted Arison in 1972 with the *Mardi Gras*, originally the *Empress of Canada*. Low fares coupled with the phenomenal popularity of the television series *Love Boat* spurred unprecedented growth. It was responsible for the first passenger ship weighing more than one hundred thousand gross tons, the *Carnival Destiny*, and today operates sixteen major cruise vessels, with more on order, as well as wholly owns the **Holland America Line**, **Costa Line**, and **Cunard Line**.

Carnival Destiny, first passenger ship to exceed one hundred thousand gross tons. She was built for **Carnival Cruise Lines** and made her **maiden voyage** in 1996 to New York before taking up station on weeklong Caribbean cruises out of Miami. The 101,000-gross-ton ship has accommodations for 2,642 passengers and is staffed by an 1,100-member crew.

Carnivale, the second passenger **liner** for **Carnival Cruise Lines**. Formerly the Canadian Pacific *Empress of Britain* of 1956, the ship was sold to the Greek Line in 1964 to replace the destroyed MS *Lakonia*. She was purchased by Carnival in 1975 to partner the

Mardi Gras year-round in the company's booming weekly cruise service out of Miami.

SS *Caronia*, Cunard Line liner built in 1947 expressly for the high-end cruise market. She was nicknamed the Green Goddess for the five shades of green (except the **funnel** and **boot topping**) that she was painted to emphasize that she was vastly different from the transatlantic units of the line. The 34,183-ton steamer was sold in 1968 for further trading as the *Caribia* under the short-lived Universal Cruise Line. She was destroyed in a typhoon at the entrance to Apía Harbor in Guam while under tow to the scrapyard in 1974.

Carousel, classic Rodgers & Hammerstein musical based on the play *Liliom* by Ferenc Molnar about an ill-fated carnival barker who falls in love. Filmed on location in Boothbay Harbor, Maine, it includes wonderful waterfront scenery and sailing footage. The 1956 film starred Gordon MacRae as Billy Bigelow and Shirley Jones as the object of his affections.

SS *Carpathia*, second-string **Cunard Line liner** most remembered for rescuing the 703 survivors of the RMS *Titanic*. In 1918 the 13,564-gross-ton ship was sunk by a German **U-boat** 120 miles west of Ireland while en route from Liverpool to New York, with the loss of five people.

carrack, large seagoing vessel that was a hybrid of the square rig of northern Europe with the **lateen** rig of the Mediterranean. Popular in the fourteenth through sixteenth centuries, it was superseded by the **galleon**, a finer-lined vessel lying lower in the water.

Carriage of Goods by Sea Act (COGSA), complex and much-amended law first enacted in 1936 covering the transportation of merchandise by sea to or from ports of the United States and in foreign trades.

carrier, a person or entity who, in a contract of carriage, undertakes to perform or to procure the performance of carriage by sea.

Caronia. (Courtesy Gordon R. Ghareeb; photo by Stewart Bale, LTD)

Carrier Action off Korea, 1951 U.S. **Navy** film that covers three years of action off Korea.

carronade, short-barreled cannon of heavy caliber widely employed by Britain's **Royal Navy** around the time of the **Napoleonic Wars**. Its ball produced great destruction of wooden hulls at short range. The name comes from the foundry Carron Iron Works in Scotland, where the cannons were first made around 1779.

Carry On Cruising, jovial British 1962 motion picture set aboard the cruise ship *Happy Wanderer*—actually the *Orsova*—that follows the predicaments of her captain, whose crew has been replaced by totally inexperienced men—the Carry On bunch. The comedy starred Sidney James, Kenneth Williams, Liz Fraser, and Kenneth Connor.

Carry on, Mr. Bowditch, award-winning 1955 novel by Jean Lee Latham for young readers that blends mathematics and adventure while relating the real-life story of navigation pioneer **Nathaniel Bowditch**.

Carson, Rachel Louise (1907–1964), American marine biologist and science writer. She wrote several books that reflected her lifelong interest in seas and seashores, including **The Sea around Us** (1951), which won the 1951 National Book Award for nonfiction; *The Edge of the Sea* (1955); and *Under the Sea Wind*. She is best known for *Silent Spring* (1962), which called public attention to the destructive use of pesticides.

Carthage, city-state and maritime power on the North Coast of Africa that often came into grim and unrelenting conflict with Rome in the third and second centuries B.C. These conflicts, which resulted in the **Punic Wars**, ended in Roman victory.

Cartier, Jacques (1491–1557), French explorer and navigator who, in search of a **Northwest Passage**, discovered the Saint Lawrence River and estuaries in a series of voyages in 1534 and 1541. He discovered Prince Edward Island and sailed up the Saint Lawrence to the site of modern-day Montréal. Cartier's explorations established the basis for France's claims to territory in what is now Canada.

cartouche, section of a map or chart, often decorated, that carries the name, distances, scale, and other information.

carvel-built, wooden hull made with plank edges meeting flush. This technique produces a smooth surface, in contrast to the overlapping planks of **lapstrake** in **clinker-built** construction.

Caspian Sea, largest inland body of water in the world, which also has no outlets. Famous for producing Beluga caviar, this salt lake is bordered by Iran, Russia, Azerbaijan, Kazakhstan, and Turkmenistan.

Cassandre, A. M. (1901–1968), French art-deco artist and designer renowned for his posters advertising ocean **liners**. Born Adolphe Jean-Marie Mouron in the Ukraine, he adopted the pseudonym Cassandre when he began making posters. Famous works include *Statendam*,

Ocean liner poster by A. M. Cassandre, ca. 1931.

Cote d'Azur, and *L'Atlantique*. Cassandre's poster of the *Normandie* is regarded as a **flagship** of deco graphic design.

The Casting Away of Mrs. Lecks and Mrs. Aleshine, classic 1886 comic novel by American author Frank Stockton (1834–1902) about two middle-aged women who are shipwrecked and set up house on a deserted island.

Castle Garden, round fortress built in lower Manhattan to defend New York City shortly before the **War of 1812**. Initially named Castle Clinton after New York City mayor **De Witt Clinton**, it was renamed in 1824 when it became a show hall and exposition center. From 1855 to 1890, it was the principal East Coast immigrant landing and processing depot (**Ellis Island** opened in 1892). From 1896 until

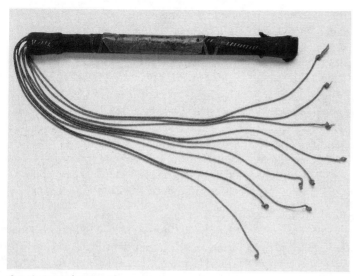

Cat-o'-nine tails. (National Maritime Museum, Greenwich, England)

Island and the Port of Los Angeles. She was retired in 1975 after making 9,807 round-trips and is currently rotting on the bottom of the harbor in Ensenada, Mexico.

catamaran, twin-hulled vessel, usually powered by sail, used for racing or cruising.

catboat, sailboat with a single sail on a mast set well up in the bow of the boat, normally gaff-rigged. Shallow in draft and beamy, it usually carries a centerboard. Measuring up to forty feet in length and traditionally used as a workboat on the East Coast, this type of boat has been adapted for racing and recreation.

catch a crab, rowing phrase used to describe catching the tip of an oar in the water, which results in the oar hitting the rower in the chest, slowing and disrupting the progress of the boat.

C. A. Thayer, California-built **schooner** used in the Pacific Coast lumber trade out of Seattle. Completed in 1895, the 453-gross-ton craft also saw service in Alaskan waters before being retired in 1950 as the last commercial sailing vessel in operation. She was opened as a museum ship in 1963 in what is today the San Francisco Maritime National Historic Park and was granted status as a national historic landmark in 1984.

cat-o'-nine tails, short piece of rope that was unlayed and braided into nine tails to be used for flogging.

Cavalcade, melodramatic but effective 1931 Noel Coward play about the impermanence of

the 1940s, it housed the New York Aquarium, and in 1946 it was declared a national historic monument. Today it is a national park service visitor's center.

Castor and Pollux, twin heroes in Greek mythology who are often called the Dioscuri, which means "sons of Zeus." The two brothers were protectors of sailors at sea and received sacrifices for favorable winds. Castor and Pollux are also stars in the constellation Gemini, forming the eyes of the twins after whom they are named. The brightest star in the constellation, Pollux is one of the fifty-two navigation stars.

Catala, small coastal **liner** built in 1925 for the Union Steam Company of Vancouver, Canada. She was moored in Seattle during the 1962 World's Fair for use as a hotel ship along with the *Acapulco* and the *Dominion Monarch*. Taken to Ocean Shores, Washington, in 1963 to serve as a base of operations for sports fishermen, she capsized during one-hundred-mile-per-hour winds during a storm on New Year's Day 1965 and was subsequently scrapped.

Catalina, famous "Great White Steamer" built in 1924 for day service between Santa Catalina life and the mystery of its direction. On the moonlit deck of an ocean **liner** a starry-eyed honeymoon couple profess their undying love for each other and their anticipation of what wonders the future may hold in store for them. After a romantic embrace by the vessel's railing, the couple moves off to reveal the ship's life ring with "**Titanic**" emblazoned on it in full view for the audience. Made into an English feature film in 1933, it was last produced on American television in 1973, with Julie Andrews and Keith Mitchell.

USS *Cavalla* (SS-244), 1,820-ton Gato-class submarine built in 1944 that sank 34,180 tons of Japanese shipping—including the carrier *Shokaku*—during World War II. After a retirement of five years, the 307-foot craft was recommissioned as a hunter-killer submarine. Removed from active operation in 1971, she was sent to Seawolf Park in Galveston as a memorial to the crews lost aboard the fifty-two U.S. subs sunk in World War II.

SS *Central America*, American **side-wheel** steamer that left Havana, Cuba, for New York on September 8, 1857, carrying nearly six hundred passengers, many of whom were successful miners returning from California, and an estimated $1 billion in gold. She was commanded by **William Herndon**, brother-in-law of **Matthew Fontaine Maury**. On September 11 the ship developed a leak that extinguished her boilers, and the following day all women and children were transferred to another vessel. Later that evening, *Central America* foundered and sank in a gale off South Carolina. In all, 423 passengers and crew were lost. The wreck was discovered in the 1980s, and the cargo of gold was salvaged in the 1990s. The wreck and the recovery were the subject of *Ship of Gold in the Deep Blue Sea* (1998) by Gary Kinder.

Chadburn, **Great Lakes** term for the **engine order telegraph**. It is named after the manufacturer, Chadburn and Company of England.

HMS *Challenger*, two-hundred-foot British screw steam vessel that was the first ship designed and constructed for ocean research. Sponsored by Britain's **Royal Society** and aided by the **Royal Navy**, *Challenger* made a landmark round-the-world scientific voyage (68,890 miles) from 1872 to 1876 collecting data about the oceans and ocean life—the first oceanographic survey of its kind. Scottish naturalist Sir **John Murray**, who made the voyage, finished editing the expedition's fifty volumes of scientific reports nineteen years later.

Chambers, George (1803–1840), British marine artist whose promising career was cut short by tuberculosis. He went to sea at a very young age and earned his living by painting, lettering, and decorating ships. He is said to have arrived in 1831 when King William IV purchased his painting of the opening of the new London Bridge. Chambers's paintings displayed nautical expertise, and he is best known for his naval commissions.

Champlain, Samuel de (1567–1635), French explorer of North America and founder of the colony of New France (Canada). Starting in 1603, he explored the Atlantic coast from **Cape Breton** to **Cape Cod**. He established a colony at the mouth of the Saint Croix River and, exploring the Saint Lawrence River, founded Québec City. He discovered Lake Champlain in 1609 and traveled up the Ottawa River to Lake Huron in 1615.

Chandris Line, Greek shipping concern established in 1915 that entered passenger operation in 1959 with the acquisition of the *Patris*. The line was noted for buying and rebuilding outdated **liners**. Some of their more notable vessels include the *Australis* (former **America**), *Ellinis* (former **Lurline**), and *Regina Magna* (former **Pasteur**). The company became Chandris Fantasy Cruises in 1988 and then Celebrity Cruises in 1989.

WRECK OF THE STEAMSHIP CENTRAL AMERICA.

APPALLING DISASTER.

On Saturday, September 12th, 1857, Capt. Herndon, bound to New York, from California, with the Pacific Mails, Passengers and Crew, to the number of 592 persons, and treasure to the amount of over $2,000,000, foundered in a hurricane, off Cape Hatteras.

Whole number on board, 592.   Number saved, 166.   Number on board whose names are known, 134.   Names unknown, 292.

Wreck of the steamship *Central America*. (Courtesy National Maritime Museum, Greenwich, England; engraving by J. Childs)

channel fever, state of euphoria felt by English seamen upon entering the English Channel after a long voyage. The term is used today to describe the condition of a crew when a vessel is on the homestretch.

chantey, shipboard song sung while performing a specific task, such as hoisting a sail or walking a capstan. A chanteyman would usually lead the singing, and the crew or work party would join in. On some ships, the officers would join in song as well.

Chapelle, Howard Irving (1900–1975), American yacht designer, naval architect, maritime historian, and writer. He served in the U.S. Army during World War II as head of the army's shipbuilding program. As the longtime curator and historian of the Museum of Transportation at the Smithsonian Institution, he authored *The Baltimore Clipper* (1930), *American Small Sailing Craft* (1936), *Yacht Designing and Planning and Boatbuilding* (1936), *The Search for Speed under Sail* (1941), *Boatbuilding* (1941), *The History of the American Sailing Navy* (1949), and *The American Fishing Schooners* (1973).

Chapman's, common name for *Chapman Piloting: Seamanship and Small Boat Handling*, the navigation tome developed in 1917 by small-boat enthusiast Paul F. Chapman, editor of *Motor Boating* magazine. *Chapman's* remains a text for boating schools and has long stood as the standard reference for powerboaters and sailors alike.

Charcot, Jean-Baptiste (1867–1936), French polar explorer who in 1908–10 surveyed many miles of Antarctic coastline aboard his ship *Pourquoi Pois?* (French for "why not?"). The vessel, known for carrying the finest stock of wines ever taken to the polar regions, made many important discoveries. Charcot died when *Pourquois Pas?* was wrecked off the coast of Iceland.

Charles de Gaulle, French nuclear-powered aircraft carrier completed in 1999. The 40,550-ton ship took over ten years to build, and the $200 million overrides on her contract price resulted in a final cost for the 858-foot vessel of more than $3.3 billion. When the ship was finished, it was determined that the carrier's angled flight deck was too short to handle the Hawkeye aircraft she was designed for and that the shielding from her nuclear furnace was inadequate by present standards. She was returned to the shipyard for costly and lengthy reconstruction.

Charles W. Morgan, last surviving American wooden sailing whale-ship. Launched in 1841, she completed thirty-seven voyages during an eighty-year career and is today preserved and on display at **Mystic Seaport** in Mystic, Connecticut. The vessel is named after Charles Waln Morgan (1796–1861), the New Bedford shipowner and businessman who had her built.

Charlie Noble, slang term for a ship's galley smokestack. It was named after a British ship **captain** who insisted his ship's copper galley stack be kept polished at all times.

Charlotte Dundas, the world's first tugboat of record. The fifty-five-foot, steam-powered sternwheel paddleboat, designed by Scottish

HISTORIC PRESERVATION

Postage stamp depicting the *Charles W. Morgan*.

engineer William Symington, was built in 1801 and in 1802 towed barges through Scotland's Forth and Clyde canal. Her motto was "Fair Wind Ahead," and she was broken up in 1861.

Charon, the mythological ferryman who pilots the souls of the departed across the river **Styx**.

charter party, written contract between the owner of a vessel and the party desiring to charter the vessel. It sets forth the terms of the arrangement, including duration, rates, and ports.

Chart No. 1, U.S. government publication that contained a description of the symbols, abbreviations, and terms that appear on nautical charts produced by the **National Imagery and Mapping Agency**, the **National Ocean Service**, and the International Hydrographic Organization. The government discontinued printing *Chart No. 1* in the late 1990s.

Chase, Owen (1796–1869), twenty-three-year-old first mate aboard the American whaleship *Essex* when it was stove in by a sperm whale in the Pacific Ocean in 1820. He wrote *Narrative of the Most Extraordinary and Distressing Shipwreck of the Whaleship Essex of Nantucket* (1821) about the terrible sufferings of those who survived the ordeal by resorting to cannibalism. The story was read and studied by **Herman Melville** and is known to be the basis for the climax of his novel *Moby-Dick; or, The Whale* (1851). After the ordeal, Chase went on to become the **master** of a whaleship and made several other voyages.

Chatterton, E. Keble (1878–1944), **Royal Navy** officer and one of Great Britain's best-known yachtsmen and maritime writers. He wrote nearly forty books, including *Sailing Ships* (1909), *Steamships and Their Story* (1910), *King's Cutters and Smugglers* (1912), *Ships and Ways of Other Days* (1913), *Seaman All* (1924), and *On the High Seas* (1929).

Chelsea clock, clock manufactured by the Chelsea Clock Company of Chelsea, Massachusetts. Established in 1897, Chelsea has produced many ship's clocks for the U.S. government that have seen service aboard U.S. **Navy**, U.S. **Coast Guard**, and U.S. **merchant marine** vessels.

Chelsea Piers, docks on New York City's West Side Chelsea district. Piers 54 through 62 were the staging facilities for the departures and arrivals of the **Western Ocean**'s most famous passenger ships from 1907—when the docks were built—until the **liner** companies moved north to the midtown **Luxury Liner Row** in 1935.

cheng, term (pronounced "chang") for the chief engineer. On merchant vessels, "cheng" is written as an abbreviation along with C/E, but on ship he or she is known as "Chief" or "the Chief." The date of the first engineering license issued to a woman in the U.S. **merchant marine** was November 18, 1919.

Cheops ship, 143-foot vessel discovered in an airtight vault during the excavation of the Great Pyramid at Giza, Egypt, in 1954. More than 1,200 separate pieces of wood were recovered, and the vessel was reconstructed and placed on exhibit in 1982. It is believed that the vessel was a ceremonial barge used for Cheops, an Egyptian pharaoh, around 2700 B.C., to make his trip to the afterworld.

Chesapeake, best-selling 1978 historical novel by **James Albert Michener** about the history

and people of the Chesapeake Bay region and Maryland's Eastern Shore.

USS *Chesapeake*, one of six original **frigates** authorized under the **Navy Act of 1794** to form the U.S. **Navy**. In 1807 she was involved in the ***Chesapeake* Affair**. In the **War of 1812**, she was badly damaged and was captured by the British frigate HMS *Shannon* in a fierce but short battle off the coast of Boston on June 1, 1813. On the U.S. side, sixty sailors died and eighty-five were seriously wounded. Captain **James Lawrence**'s dying words—**"Don't give up the ship"**—became an American battle cry.

Chesapeake, Battle of the, see Battle of the Capes.

***Chesapeake* Affair**, naval incident of June 22, 1807, off **Hampton Roads**, Virginia, in which HMS *Leopard* fired on USS *Chesapeake*, boarded her, and seized four seaman said to be deserters from the **Royal Navy**. The incident created an outcry in the United States for war against Great Britain and was a contributing factor to the **War of 1812**. At the time of the incident, *Chesapeake* was under the command of **James Barron**, the same man who killed **Stephen Decatur** in a duel in 1820.

Chesapeake & Delaware Canal (C&D Canal), waterway built in 1829 connecting Chesapeake Bay and the Delaware River. It shortened the trip for ships bound for Baltimore from northern ports by nearly three hundred miles. The U.S. government assumed control of the canal in 1919, and the canal remains a primary passage for pleasure boats traveling the **Intracoastal Waterway**.

Chesapeake & Ohio Canal, waterway planned to connect the Potomac and Ohio Rivers. Construction began in 1828, above the falls of the Potomac River at Washington, D.C. Although never completed, the canal was used until 1924 as far as Cumberland, Maryland, where

Sir Francis
Chichester.
(Courtesy Chichester
Archive; photo by
Eileen Ramsey)

building ended. In total the C&O Canal was 184 miles long and sixty feet wide, and it averaged six feet deep. Today, the canal is a national historical park.

Chesapeake Bay Maritime Museum, nonprofit institution founded in 1965 in Saint Michaels, Maryland, to further an interest, understanding, and appreciation of the culture and maritime heritage of Chesapeake Bay and its tributaries. The seventeen-acre waterfront site features historic vessels, structures, and interpretive exhibits.

Chesapeake log canoe, double-ended sailing craft ranging up to thirty-five feet, developed in Chesapeake Bay in the early nineteenth century and commonly made from two or more large logs hollowed out and fastened together. Originally employed in fishing and oystering, the vessel's large sails made it capable of high speeds. The boat was later raced with big crews, often hiking out of springboards to prevent capsizing.

Cheyne, Harvey, a rich man's spoiled son who in **Joseph Rudyard Kipling**'s novel *Captains Courageous* (1897) falls off an ocean **liner** and is rescued by the fishing **schooner** *We're Here* out of **Gloucester**, Massachusetts.

Chicago Mackinac Race, the world's longest freshwater sailing race, which is run each July on Lake Michigan from Chicago to Mackinac Island, a north Michigan island summer resort in the Straits of Mackinac. Sponsored by the Chicago Yacht Club, the 331-mile yacht race was first sailed in 1898.

Chicago River, waterway in Chicago whose natural course was reversed in 1900 to flow westward through the **Chicago Sanitary and Ship Canal**. Before completion of the canal in 1900, Chicago sewage was dumped into Lake Michigan, causing pollution of water used in the city water system. The river, now an outlet instead of an inlet of Lake Michigan, was the first river in the world to flow away from its mouth.

Chicago Sanitary and Ship Canal, waterway completed in 1900 to connect the Chicago River with the Des Plaines River, enabling ships to travel between Lake Michigan and the **Mississippi River** via the Chicago, Des Plaines, and Illinois Rivers—a system called the **Illinois Waterway**. Sometimes called the Chicago Drainage Canal, the waterway carries Chicago's treated sewage into the Des Plaines River, near Lockport, Illinois.

Chichester, Sir Francis Charles (1901–1972), English adventurer and author who, in 1960, won the first solo sailing race across the **Atlantic**. In 1967, at age sixty-four, he circumnavigated the globe aboard his fifty-five-foot yacht *Gipsy Moth IV*, making only one port of call—Sydney, Australia—and setting a solo speed record of 274 days. He was knighted in May 1967 by Queen Elizabeth II with the sword of Sir **Francis Drake**, the first Englishman to circumnavigate. Chichester's books include *Atlantic Adventure* (1962); his autobiography, *The Lonely Sea and the Sky* (1964); and *Gipsy Moth Circles the World* (1967).

chief mate, also known as the first **mate**, the officer in the deck department of a merchant ship next in rank to the **master**. The chief mate assumes the position of the master in his or her absence.

Chief of Naval Operations (CNO), the highest-ranking officer in the U.S. **Navy**. His equivalent in the U.S. **Marine Corps** and U.S. **Coast Guard** is the commandant.

Childers, Robert Erskine (1870–1922), Irish author, politician, and accomplished yachtsman who wrote the enormously popular nautical thriller *The Riddle of the Sands* (1903). His knowledge of the German coast, of which he wrote about in his only novel, proved invaluable to Great Britain's **Royal Navy** during World War I. After the war, he devoted himself to Irish independence and was later shot by a Free State firing squad. Childers is credited with launching the spy novel genre.

China Seas, 1935 motion picture blockbuster about an English passenger ship bound from Hong Kong to Singapore. En route the vessel and her captain become embroiled by pirates, typhoons, and love triangles. With excellent shipboard sets and dockside footage, the film starred Clark Gable, Jean Harlow, Rosalind Russell, and Wallace Beery.

China trade, European and American trade with China that spanned the sixteenth through the nineteenth centuries. The U.S.–China trade opened in 1784 when the ***Empress of China*** left New York for **Canton** and returned with tea, porcelain, and silks.

chine, line at which the bottom of a flat- or V-bottomed hull meets the side. In such a hull, this line coincides with the turn of the bilge. A hard-chine is the simple joining of the two surfaces—side and bottom; a round-chine uses a shaped timber to provide a rounded edge; and a multi-chine uses several joints to form a roughly rounded corner between the sides and the bottom.

Chinese School, attribution given to paintings fashioned by a series of anonymous Oriental painters in the early to mid-nineteenth century whose works depicted American and European ships, their captains, and Far East harbor scenes.

chip log, a device for determining the approximate speed of a vessel. It comprises three parts: the chip, which is a thin wooden quadrant; a line on a reel, knotted at intervals of forty-seven feet, three inches; and a twenty-eight-second glass. When the chip was thrown overboard, the glass was inverted and the line let to run. The number of knots leaving the reel in the twenty-eight seconds was approximately equal to the vessel's speed in **knots**. Fairly accurate speeds of up to about ten knots

A 1940 Chris-Craft seventeen-foot runabout. (Courtesy The Mariners' Museum, Newport News, Virginia)

could be measured. The chip log was replaced by the **patent log** and the speedometer.

chock-a-block, situation in which two blocks of a tackle are pulled firmly together and can go no farther—a condition also called two-blocked.

Chris-Craft, production boat company founded in Michigan in the 1880s by Christopher Columbus Smith as Chris Smith & Sons Boat Company. Early in the twentieth century, Chris and his sons were building gasoline launches and by 1916 were building the fastest boats in the world. In the 1920s, the Smiths dominated the market for mahogany speedboats and in the 1930s, after surviving the Great Depression, began to dominate the market for cruisers as well. In the boating boom following World War II, Chris-Craft became the largest and most successful recreational boatbuilder in the world, with a brand name as familiar as Ford or Boeing. By 1959 the company had nine plants in the United States, producing eight-thousand-plus boats that range from fifteen to sixty-six feet. When sold to a Detroit-based conglomerate in 1960, it was the largest boatbuilding enterprise ever. Chris-Craft survives today as a corporation with principal holdings in broadcasting and, under license, as the boatbuilding properties of the **OMC** (Outboard Marine Corporation).

Christian, Fletcher (1764–1793), rebellious lieutenant in the **Mutiny on the *Bounty*** incident. Angered by the tyranny of Captain **William Bligh**, Christian led a mutiny and succeeded in taking control of HMS ***Bounty*** in 1789. After setting Captain Bligh adrift in a small boat, Christian and his group of mutineers landed at **Pitcairn Island**. He most likely died in an uprising on the island, although rumors persist that Christian made his way back to England.

Christian Radich, a 205-foot Norwegian sail training **tall ship** built in 1937. The vessel was named for a successful businessman who, having died childless, provided in his will the funds to build a school ship for Norway. During World War II, she was seized and used as an accommodations ship for German **U-boat** crews. After the war, she was found capsized at Flensburg, Germany, and stripped of all of her fittings. She was rebuilt and resumed sail training in 1947, and she continues to sail today.

chronometer, timepiece used aboard ship essential for celestial navigation, especially for determining **longitude** at sea. The first accurate instruments were produced in the mid-eighteenth century by clockmaker **John Harrison**, who won a competition to develop a timepiece that was unaffected by temperature, ship's motion, or changes in gravitational force.

Churchill, Winston (1871–1947), American author of popular historical novels and an 1894 graduate of the U.S. **Naval Academy**. His novels *Richard Carvel* (1899) and *The Crossing* (1904), about a navy hero who serves under **John Paul Jones** in the American Revolution, sold one million copies. His fame was such that Sir **Winston Churchill** reclaimed the "Spencer" in his name to avoid confusion with the American author.

Churchill, Sir Winston [Leonard Spencer] (1874–1965), charismatic British prime minister, statesman, and author. He served as **First Lord of the Admiralty** from 1911 to 1915 and pressed for a naval buildup to counter the growing threat from Germany. He returned to that position at the outbreak of World War II in 1939 and upon Neville Chamberlain's forced resignation in 1940 was elected prime minister and minister of defense. He and his party were surprisingly turned out of office after World War II, and he turned to writing *The Second World War* (1948–53), for which he won the Nobel Prize in Literature. He again served as prime minister from 1951 to 1955, and in 1963 an act of the U.S. Congress declared him an honorary U.S. citizen.

church pennant, blue-and-white pennant flown during divine services at sea. It is the only pennant allowed to be flown above the national ensign.

cigarette boat, general name for a V-hull, planing, "go fast" boat. It is also the brand name of a manufacturer of such vessels. The name Cigarette was used for a series of long, narrow commuter yachts built between 1905 and 1928. The most famous of these was designed by **William Hand** and built for L. Gordon Hammersley in 1919. Capable of making forty-five **knots**, she raced and beat the New York Central train up the **Hudson River** to Albany.

Cinderella Liberty, 1973 novel by Darryl Ponsican about a U.S. **Navy** snafu involving the loss of a seaman's records, which meant that officially he did not exist. It was made into a 1973 motion picture, starring James Caan and Martha Mason, that was nominated for three Academy Awards.

Cinderella liberty, shore leave that terminates at midnight.

Cinque, Joseph (b. 1815), African slave born Sengbe Pieh and given a new name by Spanish

City of Honolulu (1904). (Courtesy Gordon R. Ghareeb)

slave traders. He led the 1839 revolt on the **schooner *Amistad***. Cinque ordered the navigator to take the fifty-three enslaved men on board back to Africa, but after sixty-three days at sea the ship was intercepted by the revenue **cutter** *Washington* off the shore of Long Island. The court case that followed reached the U.S. Supreme Court, and former president John Quincy Adams was so moved by the plights of Joseph Cinque and the others that he volunteered to represent them. The court ordered their release, and Cinque and thirty-four other survivors returned to Sierra Leone.

City Island, island in the far western corner of Long Island Sound that is part of the Bronx in New York City. Due to its protected waters and its location fifteen miles east-northeast of midtown Manhattan, the island—which measures one and a half miles by half a mile—served as the city's major yachting and boat-building center from the late nineteenth century to the mid-twentieth century.

City of Benares, 486-foot Ellerman passenger ship built in 1936 for the Liverpool to Bombay service. While serving as a transport during World War II, the **liner** was torpedoed in the mid-Atlantic on a voyage from Liverpool to Canada in September 1940. Out of 406 people onboard, 248 died, including 77 children. The tragedy brought an end to the British plan of evacuating children from the war zone by sea.

City of Detroit III, magnificent **Great Lakes** steamer believed by many to be the finest **side-wheel** passenger vessel ever built. The **liner** was completed in 1912 for the Detroit & Cleveland Navigation Company service between Detroit, Cleveland, and Buffalo and was **laid up** in 1950. When the ship was scrapped in 1956, the smoking room was removed intact, and the seven and a half tons of carved oak have been reassembled as the Gothic Room exhibit at the Dossin Great Lakes Museum in Detroit.

City of Glasgow, **Inman Line** passenger steamer launched in 1850. It left Liverpool in March 1854 en route to Philadelphia with a full complement of 480 persons. The ship was reported missing in April, and by May it was assumed that the ship had struck an iceberg in the North Atlantic.

City of Honolulu, the second steamer of the **Los Angeles Steamship Company** to be installed on the Los Angeles to Hawai'i run. Originally built as the German *Friederich der Grosse* in 1896, it was seized by the United States during World War I and subsequently chartered for the Honolulu service. While homeward bound from the islands on her **maiden voyage** in October 1922, the ship caught fire four hundred miles off the California coast. All aboard were rescued without incident, and the derelict hulk was sunk by gunfire from the U.S. **Coast Guard cutter** *Shawnee*.

City of Honolulu, former *Kiautschou*, which was built in 1904 for the **Hamburg-America Line**'s Atlantic service. She served as a U.S. **Navy** transport during World War I and was sold to

City of Los Angeles, flagship of the Los Angeles Steamship Company fleet. (Courtesy Gordon R. Ghareeb)

the **Los Angeles Steamship Company** in 1926 to replace the first *City of Honolulu*. She was rebuilt to match the style and luxury then offered on the route by the **Matson Line**'s SS *Malolo*. The second *City of Honolulu* burned dockside at the **Aloha Tower** in 1930 and was eventually scrapped in Osaka, Japan, in 1933.

City of Los Angeles, American passenger **liner** that more than any other vessel embodied the vision of a stately white cruise ship bound for tropical lands. Completed in 1900 as the *Grosser Kurfurst* for **North-German Lloyd**, she was chartered to the **Los Angeles Steamship Company** in 1922 after service as an American transport during World War I. The liner opened the Los Angeles to Honolulu service and was the first to give the established steamers of the **Matson Line** any serious competition to the Hawaiian Islands. She was sold for scrap in Osaka, Japan, in 1937.

City of New York, **Inman Line liner** built in Scotland in 1888, which along with her sister *City of Paris* received special dispensation from the U.S. Congress in 1892 to be transferred to U.S. registry. She served as the U.S. naval transport USS *Harvard* in the **Spanish-American War** and the USS *Plattsburg* in World War I. She was scrapped in Italy in 1923.

City of Paris, magnificent passenger **liner** built in 1888 for the **Inman Line**. Along with her sister the *City of New York*, she ushered in the era of the true transatlantic **steamship**. She captured the **Blue Riband** on her second crossing and later traded it on and off with other vessels, including her sister. In 1892 the *City of Paris* and the *City of New York* received approval from the U.S. Congress to be registered in the United States as the *Paris* and the *New York* and transferred to the **American Line**. A condition of this move was that the line had to build stateside two comparable ships; as a result, the *St. Louis* and the *St. Paul* were launched in 1895.

Clancy, Thomas (b. 1947), American author of thriller novels, often with a naval theme, including *The **Hunt for Red October*** (1984), *Red Storm Rising* (1986), and *Debt of Honor* (1994). He also wrote the nonfiction *Submarine: A Guided Tour Inside a Nuclear Warship* (1995).

Clark, William (1770–1838), U.S. explorer who, with **Meriwether Lewis**, led the government-sponsored **Lewis and Clark expedition** to investigate a water route to the Pacific coast in 1804–6.

classification society, group involved in establishing and administering standards or rules for the design, construction, and operational maintenance of marine vessels and structures. It surveys ships and places them in grades or classes of quality and condition according to the society's rules for each particular vessel type. Classification of a vessel is directly tied to insurance and employment. Examples of such societies include **American Bureau of Shipping**, **Bureau Veritas**, **Lloyd's Register**, and **Det Norske Veritas**.

Clearwater, a replica **Hudson River sloop** built in 1969 to promote environmental awareness on the Hudson. The movement to construct the vessel was started by folk singer Pete Seeger.

Clemens, Samuel Langhorne (1835–1910), one of America's most popular humorists, correspondents, and travel writers who wrote under the pseudonym **Mark Twain.**

Cleopatra's Barge, eighty-three-foot **hermaphrodite brig** considered the first deep-water yacht built in the United States. Launched in 1816 as a pleasure vessel for Captain **George Crowninshield Jr.**, she had high style for a time. Upon Crowninshield's death aboard the yacht in 1817, she was stripped and sold at auction and then sailed as a cargo and packet vessel. She later became the royal yacht of Hawaii's King Kamehameha II and was shipwrecked off Hawaii in 1824. Her remains were discovered in 1995 and are today an underwater archaeological site.

Clermont, wooden-hulled paddle steamer that, in 1807, was the first **steamship** to engage in commercially successful operations. Designed by **Robert Fulton**, it sailed in regular passenger service on the Hudson River between New York City and Albany. Registered as the *North River Steam Boat*, the 150-foot, wood-burning ship was generally called the *Clermont* after the home of Fulton's business partner, **Robert R. Livingston.** The ship was dismantled in 1815.

Clevely, John (1712–1777), English marine artist known for his dockyard scenes, ship launches, harbor views, and naval battles. His twin sons, John (1747–1786) and Robert (1747–1809), were also marine painters.

clinker-built, the construction of a wooden boat's hull with the lower edge of each plank overlapping, and fastened to, the upper edge of the plank below it. This construction, also called **lapstrake**, contrasts with the smooth surface of a **carvel-built** vessel.

Clipper cards. (Courtesy The Mariners' Museum, Newport News, Virginia)

clinometer, shipboard instrument for determining degree of inclination of a list, roll, or heel.

Clinton, De Witt (1769–1828), American statesman who as early as 1809 advocated the building of the **Erie Canal**. Clinton served as a canal commissioner during the early years of its construction and was governor of New York when the waterway was completed in 1825. The Erie Canal is sometimes referred to as "Clinton's Ditch."

clipper card, card used to advertise vessel qualifications and sailing dates, particularly during the competitive period of the 1850s, when **clipper ships** sped people and products from the East Coast around **Cape Horn** to San Francisco during the California gold rush.

clipper ship, fast, slender sailing vessel—so named for the way it "clipped" off the miles—developed in the United States in the mid-1800s. The era of the clipper ship was short because it was eclipsed in the late 1800s by

The clipper ship *Eagle*, rendered by James E. Buttersworth, 1857. (South Street Seaport Museum)

steamships and **square-riggers**, which were designed to carry large cargoes at slower speeds.

close-hauled, adjective for a sailing vessel with sails trimmed as close to the wind as possible in order to make the maximum speed to windward. Sailing close-hauled with the wind on one bow, and then on the other, is called "beating to windward."

Clydebank, famous shipbuilding area of western Scotland lying downstream from Glasgow on the River Clyde. Among the yards in the area were the firms of Alexander Stephen & Sons, Fairfield Shipbuilding & Engineering Company, John Brown Shipbuilders and Engineers, and J. & G. Thompson.

coaling station, a coal depot established for refueling coal-fired ships. In the late 1800s, **steamships** had limited range and had to regularly load coal. As a result, places previously considered unimportant—such as the Falkland Islands and **Midway Islands**—were suddenly essential as coaling stations to service steamship lines and navies. In this way, steam power led directly to the colonization of many strategically located islands and ports.

Coastal Warning Display Program, network of yacht clubs, marinas, and U.S. **Coast Guard** stations that hoisted flags, pennants, and colored lights to warn mariners of storms at sea. The display stations were notified by the National Weather Service, and signals indicated a **small craft advisory**, **gale warning**, storm warning, or hurricane warning. The system was formally retired in 1989, in favor of telephone recordings and radio, after being in use for more than a hundred years. Individual stations continue to display the signals.

U.S. Coast and Geodetic Survey (C&GS), see U.S. **Coast Survey** and **National Ocean Service** (NOS).

U.S. Coast Guard (USCG), U.S. armed force and the nation's oldest continuous maritime service. The USCG comprises five federal services, agencies, and bureaus that are no longer in existence. The **Revenue Marine**, established on August 4, 1790, under the Department of Treasury, later became the U.S. **Revenue Cutter Service**. In 1915, the latter merged with the U.S. **Life-Saving Service** to form the U.S. Coast Guard. The U.S. **Lighthouse Service** joined the Coast Guard in 1939, and in 1946 the **Bureau of Marine Inspection and Navigation** (formerly two separate bureaus) was added to the mix. The Coast Guard was transferred from the Treasury Department to the Department of Transportation in 1967. It becomes part of the U.S. **Navy** in times of war.

U.S. Coast Guard Academy (USCGA), service school of the U.S. **Coast Guard** located in New London, Connecticut. Candidates for commission in the Coast Guard attend a four-year undergraduate bachelor of science program and upon graduation are commissioned as ensigns in the Coast Guard. The first academy was started in 1876 aboard the revenue **cutter** *Dobbin* as a combination training ship, classroom, and berthing quarters. Cadets had their winter quarters at New Bedford, Massachusetts, and later at Arundel Cove, Maryland. A more formal school was established in 1910 at Fort Trumbull, in New London, and in 1932 the school moved to its present site.

U.S. Coast Guard Auxiliary, civilian volunteer arm of the U.S. **Coast Guard** whose members donate their time, boats, and expertise to help improve boating safety. The Auxiliary was established in 1939 as the Coast Guard Reserve and in 1941 was made a separate organization.

Coast Guard Hymn, song whose lyrics read, "Eternal Father, Lord of hosts, Watch o'er all those who guard our coasts. Protect them from the raging seas, And give them light and life and peace. Grant them from thy great throne above, The shield and shelter of thy love."

Coast Guard Reserve, organization administered by the U.S. **Coast Guard** to provide trained and qualified personnel available for active duty in time of war or national emergency and at such other times as the national security requires. Established in 1939 and composed primarily of boatowners, its mission was to promote boating safety and to assist the Coast Guard. In 1941, this organization's name was changed to **Coast Guard Auxiliary**, and the Coast Guard Reserve was established as a military service.

Coast Pilot, publication of the **National Ocean Service** that provides mariners with in-depth information necessary for voyage planning and safe and efficient navigation. (Its predecessor, *The American Coast Pilot*, dates back to 1796.) Through the 1990s, nine regional volumes provided data on channels, hazards, winds and currents, restricted areas, port facilities, pilotage services, and more. By 2000, as a cost-cutting measure, the government was seeking a commercial publishing partner to print the pilots.

U.S. Coast Survey, agency of the U.S. government established in 1807 by President **Thomas**

Clydebank, Scotland, was the site of many launchings: here, the launch of RMS *Queen Mary*.

Jefferson to survey the nation's coast. With the increasing focus on westward expansion, its mission soon included surveys of the interior of the United States. In 1878 the agency was reorganized and given the new name of Coast and Geodetic Survey (C&GS), which it maintained until the creation of the **National Oceanic and Atmospheric Administration** (NOAA) in 1970. Under NOAA, the Coast Survey and the National Geodetic Survey became separate functions. Today the Coast Survey administers NOAA's nautical chart data collection and information program to promote safe navigation.

USS *Cochino*, U.S. **Navy** submarine that sustained several internal explosions while on patrol off Norway in September 1949. All hands were forced to the sail of the sub and were rescued by her sister ship USS *Tusk*. In all, thirteen crew members were lost—six to exposure when their life raft overturned in the Arctic water. *Cochino* was the first U.S. sub to sink after World War II.

Cochrane, Thomas (1775–1860), daring and skillful British naval officer known as "the Sea Wolf," whose exploits were the inspiration for many fictional seagoing characters in novels by **Frederick Marryat, Cecil Scott "C. S." Forester**, and **Patrick O'Brian**.

cockbill, positioning of the yardarms of a **square-rigger** as a sign of deference or mourning. Main yards were sloped down to **starboard**, fore yards sloped down to port, and lower booms were dropped.

Cockburn, George (1772–1853), British admiral who commanded the **Royal Navy** squadron in Chesapeake Bay in the **War of 1812**. In retaliation for the burning of the Canadian capital (present-day Toronto) by the United States, his forces burned the White House on August 24, 1814, forcing President James Madison and his wife, Dolley, to flee. Cockburn also commanded the squadron that carried **Napoleon I** to captivity on **Saint Helena** in 1815, and he remained there as governor until 1816.

Code of Liner Conduct, convention drafted under the auspices of the United Nations Conference on Trade and Development that provides that all shipping traffic between two foreign countries is to be regulated regarding the quantities of shipments on certain percentages—forty percent country of origin, forty percent country of destination, and twenty percent other. The United States is not a signatory of this agreement.

coffee grinder, a large deck winch on a pedestal used on modern racing yachts. Its vertical handles make it resemble an old-fashioned coffee mill, and the operator is called a "grinder."

cofferdam, watertight temporary structure sunk in a river or seabed, or often a box or chamber attached to a ship below the waterline, that has been pumped dry to enable workers to build, examine, or make repairs. Aboard ship, a cofferdam is an empty tank used to separate cargoes or engine spaces.

Coffin, Long Tom, daring protagonist in **James Fenimore Cooper**'s *The Pilot* (1823), the first American novel about the sea. The character's exploits are based on the naval adventures of **John Paul Jones**.

coffin ship, a vessel whose seaworthiness is questionable. This term is often applied to the British "coffin **brigs**" that were used to carry the mail between Great Britain and the United States. These ships were built for speed, not safety.

Colcord, Lincoln (1883–1947), American author and maritime historian. His novel *The Drifting Diamond* (1912) was well received, and his books of sea stories include *The Game of Life and Death* (1914) and *An Instrument of the Gods* (1922). He also compiled the *Record of Vessels Built on the Penobscot River and Bay* (1932) and was instrumental in the establishment of the Penobscot Marine Museum in Searsport, Maine.

cold-molding, technique in wooden boatbuilding that involves bonding together layers of thin planks or veneers to make a strong, lightweight, watertight hull.

USS *Cole* (DDG-67), U.S. **Navy destroyer** that was the target of a suicide bombing on October 12, 2000, while refueling in the port city of Aden in Yemen. A small boat carrying terrorists exploded alongside, crippling the *Cole* and killing seventeen U.S. sailors and injuring thirty-nine others.

Cole, Thomas (1801–1848), British-born American artist who was a founder of the **Hudson River School**. He first gained fame in 1825 for his scenes of the **Hudson River** Valley in New York. Among his most famous paintings are the four symbolic works known collectively as *The Voyage of Life* (1840).

Coleridge, Samuel Taylor (1772–1834), English poet well known for his work "The **Rime of the Ancient Mariner**" (1798). Coleridge, who had never been to sea, is said to have gotten the idea for the poem from a neighbor who mentioned dreaming of a skeleton ship. Coleridge created the plot during a four-day hike in the English countryside with William Wordsworth. Others say Coleridge was inspired by the tale of the *Flying Dutchman*.

Coles, Kaines Adlard (1901–1985), British yachtsman and ocean racer who was a prolific writer of books on sailing, including *Heavy Weather Sailing* (1967), the standard text on seamanship under gale conditions. He won the **Transatlantic Race** in 1950 and founded Adlard Coles Nautical Publishing in Britain, which still publishes books about the sea.

collier, a vessel in the coal trade.

Collins, Edward Knight (1802–1878), visionary American shipowner and founder of the **Collins Line** in 1847. His enthusiasm for the project outran common sense, for the steamers of his operation were far too luxurious and ornate to turn profits at competitive fares. He tragically lost his wife, son, and daughter in the wreck of his company's *Arctic* in 1854. Born in New England and transplanted to New York's South Street district, he was always involved with shipping until the collapse of the firm that bore his name in 1858, at which time he retired completely from the shipping business.

Collins Line, American transatlantic **steamship** company founded in 1847 by Edward Knight Collins and largely financed through U.S. government **mail subsidies**. When the scheduled service came on line in 1850 with the SS *Atlantic*, *Pacific*, *Arctic*, and *Baltic* quartet, the vessels were in every way superior to the ships in operation by the **Cunard Line**. The line was criticized for providing luxury out of step with the competition, and the ships never posted a profit. The loss in 1854 of the *Arctic* along with 322 lives, including the family of the line's founder and owner, as well as the disappearance of the *Pacific* in 1856 with all 186 souls onboard, proved too much to recover from and the line collapsed financially in 1858.

"A collision at sea can ruin your entire day", quote most likely originating in the days when warships were propelled by oars, and the principal mode of attack was ramming the enemy vessel; speaker unknown.

Colossus of Rhodes, 120-foot statue honoring the Greek sun god, Helios, erected in 280 B.C., which towered over the harbor at Rhodes on the island of the same name in the Mediterranean. One of the seven wonders of the ancient world, it was said to have been cast from the metal of captured Macedonian weapons. Fifty years after its completion, the statue was destroyed by an earthquake.

COLREGS, a contraction of "Collision Regulations" that refers to the International Convention for the Prevention of Collisions at Sea, 1972, a multilateral treaty developed under the **International Maritime Organization** to formalize the international rules by which the world's ships navigate. Adopted internationally at London in October 1972, they are often referred to as the **International Rules**, and mariners must comply with COLREGS when outside established demarcation lines.

Columbia, the first ship to sail around the world under the U.S. flag. *Columbia* sailed from

Boston in 1787, bound for the North Pacific by way of **Cape Horn**. Once there she came under the command of Captain **Robert Gray**. After visiting China, she returned by way of the **Cape of Good Hope** in 1790. Gray set out again on the same route and sailed into the mouth of the Columbia River in 1792, naming the waterway after his ship. Gray's entrance into the river became a basis for U.S. claims to the Oregon Territory.

Columbia, centerboard **schooner** that along with the schooner *Sappho* defeated the British schooner *Livonia*, four races to one, to defend the **America's Cup** in 1871. After winning the first two races, *Columbia* lost a jib and her steering gear in the third race. As was the custom at the time, *Sappho* was allowed to sail in the next two races of the seven-race series, winning them both.

Columbia, American passenger steamer constructed in 1880 that was the first vessel to be fitted with electric lights. Under the direction of Thomas A. Edison, four generators, powered by two steam engines, were installed to light 115 lamps. The successful application of electricity prompted other shipowners to install electric lights on their ships. *Columbia* was rammed by a lumber **schooner** in July 1907 and sank, with the loss of eighty-eight lives.

Columbia, 131-foot racing yacht and successful **America's Cup** defender in 1899 and 1901, having defeated Sir **Thomas Lipton**'s *Shamrock* and *Shamrock II*. Commissioned in 1899 by a **New York Yacht Club** syndicate that included **John Pierpont "J. P." Morgan** and **Charles Oliver Iselin**, *Columbia* was designed and built by **Nathanael Herreshoff**. Skippered by **Charles Barr**, she was named after the successful 1871 defender. She was bronze below the waterline, with steel plating above and nickel steel topsides.

"Columbia, the Gem of the Ocean", American patriotic song written in 1843 by David T. Shaw and T. A. Beckett. It begins "O Columbia, the gem of the ocean, The home of the brave and the free, The shrine of each patriot's devotion, A world offers homage to thee."

SS *Columbus*, 32,354-ton transatlantic **liner** completed in 1923 for the **North German Lloyd** line. She was modernized in 1929 to bring her more in line with the larger *Bremen* and *Europa*. Her passengers were set ashore in Havana during an August 1939 Caribbean cruise from New York when the political climate in Europe was about to explode. *Columbus* was intercepted by the British **destroyer** HMS *Hyperion* off the Virginia coast in December 1939 and was **scuttled** by her crew to avoid capture.

Columbus, Christopher (1451–1506), Genoese-born mariner who, in the service of Spain, was the first European known to have seen Central and South America and the Caribbean Islands. In October 1492, in search of a western route to Asia and the Indies, he landed in the Bahamas and called the people who lived there Indians. In 1496 he made the first recorded landing on the South American mainland, in what is now Venezuela. He made four voyages in all, and on his final journey he faced famine and mutiny. He returned to Spain never really understanding the importance and extent of his discoveries.

Combat Information Center (CIC), a division of the Operations Department on board a naval vessel that is in charge of and responsible for coordinating the activities of the various departments and divisions during battle, including the gathering, evaluating, and delivering of information on all aircraft or surface craft within range.

Comet, popular **one-design** centerboard sailing **sloop** designed by C. Lowndes Johnson in 1932. With a length of sixteen feet, a beam of five feet, and a draft of two inches, she carries a crew of two.

USS *Comfort* (AH-20), U.S. **Navy** hospital ship and sister to USS *Mercy*. Originally the tanker *Rose City* completed in 1976, she was converted into a hospital ship in 1987. The steam turbine vessel has twelve operating rooms, four X-ray facilities. and an intensive care unit equipped to handle eighty patients. The ship was designed to turn over three hundred patients a day, with surgery anticipated to be performed on 60 percent of them.

commissioning pennant, long, narrow pennant flown from the main truck of a naval vessel when under the command of a commissioned officer. In the U.S. **Navy**, this pennant is red, white, and blue with seven stars.

Commodore Cruise Line, Norwegian shipping company that pioneered weekly cruises out of Miami in 1967 with the converted car ferry *Boheme*. Soon its fleet of three vessels became known as the Happy Ships, and the line began to offer themed voyages. In recent years, the line has offered Caribbean cruise service from alternative ports like New Orleans.

common carrier, a vessel engaged in transporting goods for hire and offering space to any shipper.

Communications Satellite Corporation (COMSAT), a leading provider of communications satellite services in the United States and overseas. COMSAT provides services to the shipping and offshore oil-drilling industries through **INMARSAT**, an international maritime satellite system. In 1962, the U.S. Congress authorized the establishment of COMSAT as a shareholder corporation.

Compagnie Générale Transatlantique, formal name of the **French Line**.

compass card, the card in a compass marking 360° to indicate the ship's heading.

compass rose, the points of a compass printed on nautical charts in a circle that usually includes annual **variation**.

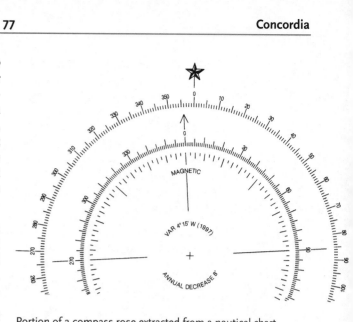

Portion of a compass rose extracted from a nautical chart.

Compass Rose, name of the **corvette** in **Nicholas Monsarrat**'s World War II novel *The Cruel Sea* (1953).

The Compleat Angler, a landmark discourse on the joys of fishing written by **Izaak Walton** and first published in 1653. In addition to sporting and fishing dialogue—between Piscator, a fisherman, and Venator, a hunter—it includes songs, poems, folklore, recipes, anecdotes, quotes from the Bible and classical literature, descriptions of country life and the English countryside, and lore about fishing.

The Compleat Cruiser, classic book by American yacht designer **L. Francis Herreshoff** about the pleasures of boating. Subtitled *The Art, Practice and Enjoyment of Boating*, the book uses the inspiration of **Izaak Walton**'s *The Compleat Angler* and takes the reader aboard all sorts of boats. It first appeared in serial form in the magazine the *Rudder* and was published in book form in 1956.

Concordia, a series of thirty-nine-foot and forty-one-foot **yawl** and **sloop** cruising-racing yachts designed by **C. Raymond Hunt**. The boats were introduced in 1938, but the majority were not built until after World War II. The ninety-nine yawl hulls were made in Germany by **Abeking and Rasmussen** and finished at the Llewellyn Howland Yard of South Dartmouth, Massachusetts. A total of 103 vessels were constructed, making them the most popular class of **one-design** seagoing wooden sailboats in the history of the sport. Concordia was the Roman goddess who personified harmony and amity.

Confederate raiders, group of 20 ships of the **Confederate States Navy** that preyed on Union merchant ships and whalers during the Civil War. CSS *Alabama*, *Florida*, *Shenandoah*, and seventeen other **cruisers** destroyed 257 Union ships. The Confederate raiders also forced more than 700 other Union ships to travel under foreign flags to avoid attack. The raiders had little effect on the outcome of the Civil War, but their actions disrupted trade and nearly destroyed the U.S. **merchant marine**.

Confederate States Navy (CSN), service operated from 1861 to 1865 by the Confederacy for the protection of harbors and coastlines from blockade and to establish local superiority over the Union Navy during the Civil War. Stephen R. Mallory, a U.S. senator and chairman of the Congressional Naval Affairs Committee, was appointed secretary. The service's strategy was to harass Union commerce and challenge the Union Navy for control of the southern coast. Ships of the service carried the prefix **CSS,** for Confederate States Ship, paralleling the Union Navy's *USS*, for United States Ship.

conference, affiliation of shipowners operating over the same routes who agree to charge uniform rates and other terms for the carriage of cargo. A conference is "closed" if one can enter only by the consent of the existing conference members. It is "open" if any carrier can enter by meeting certain standards.

USS *Congress*, one of the original six **frigates** of the U.S. **Navy** called for in the **Navy Act of 1794**. The thirty-six-gun frigate was launched in August 1799 and saw action in the **Quasi-War**, the **Barbary Wars**, and the **War of 1812**. By 1834 she was declared unfit for service and was broken up at the Norfolk Navy Yard in Virginia.

conn, to direct the course and speed of a ship. The person giving orders to the helmsman is said to have the conn and to be conning the ship.

Conner, Dennis (b. 1942), American sailor and four-time **America's Cup** winner. He was aboard *Courageous* (1974) when it won, and he **skippered** victories in *Freedom* (1980), *Stars & Stripes* (1987), and *Stars & Stripes II* (1988). He also holds the dubious distinction of having lost the cup twice: in 1983, when Australia's *Australia II* beat *Liberty*, and in 1995, when New Zealand's *Black Magic* swept his crew aboard the borrowed *Young America*.

Conrad, Joseph (1857–1924), Polish-born mariner and author who wrote many of the best-known novels and short stories about the sea. Born Josef Teodor Konrad Nalecz Korzeniowski, he ran away from Poland at age sixteen to become a sailor, and at age thirty-eight he began to write (in English) seafaring novels of great moral complexity. He later settled in England and used his seafaring experience to provide him with much material for his novels and stories. His body of work includes many of the most powerful novels in the literature of the sea, including *Heart of Darkness* (1899), *Lord Jim* (1900), *The Nigger of Narcissus* (1897), and *Typhoon* (1903). His autobiography, *The Mirror of the Sea* (1906), includes a reflection on his twenty years of sea experience.

Conrad the Sailor, humorous theatrical cartoon short about Daffy Duck and a feline mascot aboard a U.S. **Navy** battleship. The 1942 animated Warner Brothers production featured the unmistakable voice of Mel Blanc.

USS *Constellation*, thirty-eight-gun U.S. **frigate** built in 1797, the second of the six frigates (the others being USS ***United States***, USS ***Constitution***, USS ***President***, USS ***Congress***, and USS ***Chesapeake***) authorized by the **Navy Act of 1794**. **Thomas Truxtun**, who had supervised the construction of *Constellation*, also commanded her, and his naval victories made him a national hero. She captured the French frigate *L'Insurgente* on February 9, 1799, during the **Quasi-War** with France and went on to serve in the **Barbary Wars** and the **War of 1812**.

USS *Constellation*, twenty-four-gun **sloop of war** built during the mid-1850s in Baltimore. Her first assignment was interdicting the slave trade off the coast of Africa. After service in the Civil War, she saw various duties, including carrying famine relief stores to Ireland and serving both as a U.S. **Naval Academy** training vessel and as a relief **flagship** during World War II. In the 1990s, *Constellation* underwent a $9 million restoration and is today a museum ship in Baltimore. It was thought for some time that many of the timbers from the original USS *Constellation* of 1797 were used in the construction of her namesake—it was even thought that the second vessel was a rebuild of the first. However, recent evidence has proven otherwise.

SS *Constitution*, U.S. passenger ship, sister ship to SS ***Independence***, built in 1951 at the Bethlehem Steel shipyard in Quincy, Massachusetts, for **American Export Lines**. In 1956 she carried American actress Grace Kelly on a voyage to Monte Carlo, where she wed Prince Rainer. Lucille Ball was aboard for filming of an *I Love Lucy* episode, as were Deborah Kerr and Cary Grant for the filming of *An Affair*

As a vehicle for Grace Kelly, *I Love Lucy*, and *An Affair to Remember*, SS *Constitution* has forever earned a place in Hollywood history. (Bruce Vancil)

to Remember. The ship was rebuilt in 1959 to increase her passenger capacity, at the expense of her perfect external symmetry. Withdrawn from service in 1968, she wound up in Hong Kong as part of the Orient Overseas conglomerate before being refitted and sold to **American Hawaiian Cruises** in 1981 for interisland voyaging. **Laid up** in 1996, the 20,269-gross-ton **liner** sank in the Pacific while under tow to a scrapyard in Taiwan.

USS *Constitution*, most famous ship in the U.S. **Navy** and the oldest warship afloat in the world. Authorized by the **Navy Act of 1794**, she was launched October 21, 1797. The 204-foot **frigate** engaged the enemy in the **Barbary Wars** and the **War of 1812**, and it was during her victory over HMS *Guerrière* in August 1812 that she earned the nickname **Old Ironsides**. Falling into disrepair, she has been the subject of several rebuilds and restorations over the years. She inspired the poem **"Old Ironsides"** by **Oliver Wendell Holmes**, and between 1927 and 1931, American children raised money to help repair and restore the vessel so she could be preserved as a memorial. Today *Constitution* is docked at

A painting of USS *Constitution* by Tim Thompson. (Courtesy J. Russell Jinishian Gallery, Fairfield, Connecticut)

the Charlestown Navy Yard in Boston. She went to sea under sail in 1998, following her latest rebuild.

construction differential subsidy (CDS), a direct-cash government subsidy program to offset the high cost of constructing ships in U.S. shipyards. Established by the **Merchant Marine Act of 1936**, it was intended to decrease the cost and improve the competitiveness of the U.S. ocean shipping industry. Ships built with CDS had to be available for national defense or military purposes in times of war or national emergency and thus had to meet

certain design criteria. In 1981 the U.S. government ceased letting new contracts under the CDS program.

containerization, cargo system that originated in the early twentieth century but not employed until the 1950s by trucker **Malcolm McLean**. Consisting of sealed boxes, or containers, stacked on a ship and loaded directly—from or to a flatbed truck—the system replaced **break-bulk**. It launched **intermodalism**, changed ship and port design requirements, reduced pilferage, lowered cargo handling costs, speeded up loading and discharge, and lowered insurance rates. It resulted in the quicker delivery of goods and had a profound effect on shipboard and shoreside labor.

SS *Conte di Savoia*, spectacular 48,502-gross-ton **Italian Line** running mate to SS *Rex*. Constructed in 1932, she was the pet project of Benito Mussolini, and her intended name was *Dux*, after her benefactor. Stylish and sleek, the ship is best remembered for her experimental 600-ton gyroscopic stabilizers, which—while effective—proved unsafe in many sea conditions, resulting in their use being quietly discontinued altogether. **Laid up** near Venice from the outset of World War II, the **liner** was attacked by Allied aircraft and set on fire. She was scrapped in 1950.

SS *Conte Grande*, Lloyd Sabaudo **liner** completed in 1928 for the North Atlantic run. She came under the auspices of the **Italian Line** in 1932 and was seized by the Brazilian government in 1941 and sold to the U.S. **Navy** the following year to become the troop transport USS *Monticello*. She maintained the South Atlantic service of the Italian Line after the war, with occasional crossings to New York in the summer months. The steamer was brought back to the North Atlantic service permanently in 1956 to replace the lost SS *Andrea Doria*. She was scrapped in 1961.

contiguous zone, area of water contiguous to the **territorial sea** in which a coastal state has limited powers. Usually for the purpose of enforcing customs, fiscal, sanitary, and immigration laws or regulations, the maximum limit that a nation may claim is twenty-four miles.

Continental Navy, service established by the Continental Congress in October 1775 "for the protection and defense of the United Colonies" during the American Revolution. Initially it outfitted a series of converted merchantmen under the command of **Esek Hopkins**. Congress later ordered thirteen new **frigates**: seven never got to sea because they

had to be destroyed to prevent their capture, and the six others were captured or destroyed in their initial engagements. Many of the early officers had seagoing experience as **privateers** in the **Seven Years' War**, and most of the sailors were motivated by **prize money**. In all, more than fifty ships served without great success. The service was disbanded in 1785, leaving the United States without a navy for the next ten years.

convoy, grouping of ships that sail together under naval escort. At the outset of World War I, convoys were used primarily for troop ships, but the system was adopted for merchant shipping in the face of unrestricted submarine warfare in 1917 and was used continuously in World War II.

Cook, James (1728–1779), British navigator and one of the world's greatest seagoing explorers of all time. He exhibited outstanding intellectual powers as a scientific observer and cartographer from 1769 to 1779, when he led three voyages, aboard the ships HMS *Endeavour* and HMS *Resolution*, to the Pacific Ocean and sailed around the world twice. Cook became the first European to visit Australia's east coast. He reached the Sandwich (Hawai'ian) Islands on his third expedition but was killed there in a scuffle with the native inhabitants. His voyages led to the establishment of colonies throughout the Pacific region by several European nations.

Cooke, Edward William (1811–1880), English marine painter who specialized in river and coastal scenes. He traveled extensively throughout Europe and North Africa during his career and was considered the doyen of marine painters during the later years of his life. His collection of prints *Shipping and Craft* (1929) is considered an important contribution to marine art.

Cooper, James Fenimore (1789–1851), first major American novelist and the author credited with developing the genre of the American sea novel. Following early pioneer novels, including the renowned Leather-Stocking Tales, Cooper's novel *The Pilot* (1823) inaugurated a series of popular seafaring tales that included *The Red Rover* (1828), *The Water-Witch* (1830), *Homeward Bound* (1838), *The Two Admirals* (1842), *Wind and Wing* (1842), *Ned Myers* (1843), *Afloat and Ashore* (1844), *Miles Wallingford* (1844), and *The Sea Lions* (1849). Having served in the U.S. **Navy** from 1808 to 1811, Cooper also wrote a well-researched *History of the Navy of the United States* (1839).

Copenhagen, Battle of, naval engagement on April 2, 1801, between British and Danish fleets. Sir Hyde Parker was in command of the British fleet, with **Horatio Nelson** as his second-in-command. In response to the power of the shore fortresses, Parker signaled Nelson to discontinue and withdraw. Nelson failed to see the signal because he put his telescope up to his blind (right) eye. Britain won the day, and fourteen Danish ships were captured or destroyed.

Copley, John Singleton (1738–1815), well-known American portrait painter who later settled in England. He is best known in marine art circles for his powerful painting *Watson and the Shark* (1778), which is considered the first marine painting by an American artist. He based the painting on the real-life trauma of a fourteen-year-old English boy named Brook Watson who lost a leg to a shark while swimming in Havana Harbor in 1749. Today the painting hangs in the National Gallery of Art in Washington, D.C.

Coral Sea, part of the Southern Pacific Ocean between the northeast coast of Australia, the Solomon Islands, and the **Vanuatu** island group. The reefs along the western shores of the Coral Sea have the finest specimens of coral.

Coral Sea, Battle of the, World War II naval engagement fought entirely between aircraft from U.S. and Japanese warships in the **Coral Sea** on May 7 and 8, 1942. Although the carrier USS *Lexington* and two other ships were lost in the action, U.S. forces, led by the carrier USS *Yorktown*, inflicted the first major damage to the Japanese fleet and prevented the Japanese from landing on southeast New Guinea—thus saving Australia from the threat of Japanese invasion.

corinthian, in yachting parlance, an amateur. The term corresponds to a late-nineteenth-century movement in sail racing to move away from owners and professional crews and more toward individual seamanship and sport.

Corné, Michele Felice (1762–1832), French marine painter who was forced from his country by the **French Revolution**. He was brought to Salem, Massachusetts, by American merchant Elias Haskett Derby, where he specialized in ship portraits—decorating the interior of the Salem East India Marine Society in 1805—and naval actions of the **War of 1812**.

Coronet, 133-foot **schooner** built in 1885 as the private yacht of New York millionaire Rufus Bush. After two ocean crossings and one circumnavigation, Bush sold the vessel in 1889. Following a succession of **New York Yacht Club** owners and numerous voyages, *Coronet* was acquired in 1905 by the Kingdom, a non-denominational Christian organization, which employed her in missionary work. In 1995 the Kingdom donated *Coronet* to the International Yacht Restoration School in Newport, Rhode Island, which began an extensive restoration of what they dubbed "America's most historic yacht."

Corps of Discovery, name given by President **Thomas Jefferson** to the group of thirty-one explorers, led by Captains **Meriwether Lewis** and **William Clark**, that he sent on a mission to

Schooners *Dauntless* and *Coronet* by artist Donald Demers. (Courtesy J. Russell Jinishian Gallery, Fairfield, Connecticut)

explore the uncharted West after the Louisiana Purchase. The mission is also known as the **Lewis and Clark Expedition**.

Corregidor, island located at the entrance to Manila Bay in the Philippines. During World War II, it was taken by Japanese forces in May 1942 and was retaken by U.S. forces in February 1945.

corsair, French word meaning "sea raider." The name has been applied to pirate ships and men of the **Barbary States** and has often been used to describe **privateers**.

Corsair, a series of four steam yachts by the same name owned by **John Pierpont "J. P." Morgan** and his family. The vessels ranged from 185 to 343 feet and were fixtures of the American yachting scene from 1882 to 1939. The first *Corsair* was already named when J. P. Morgan purchased her from a member of the **New York Yacht Club** in 1882. Morgan used the 185-foot vessel, built in 1880 by William Cramp and Sons of Philadelphia, as a ferry between his office in Manhattan and his home up the **Hudson River**.

Corsair II, the second steam yacht of the same name to be owned by **John Pierpont "J. P." Morgan**. Ordered in 1891 and designed by naval architect J. Frederick Tams, the new 241-foot *Corsair* was sleek and black and in the **clipper** style. When the **Spanish-American War** broke out with Spain in 1898, *Corsair II* was requisitioned by the U.S. government for $225,000 to serve in the war. Painted gray and renamed USS *Gloucester*, she performed with distinction at the Battle of **Santiago**. She stayed on naval duty through World War I and was sunk in 1919 when she hit a reef while charting a region of the Gulf of Mexico. She was later salvaged and sold.

Corsair III, the third steam yacht of **John Pierpont "J. P." Morgan**, the 304-feet *Corsair* was described by many as the most perfectly proportioned steam yacht ever built in the **clipper** style. Delivered in 1899 in time for Morgan to serve as commodore of the **New York Yacht Club** (NYYC), she carried fifty-five officers and crew. With the outbreak of World War I, *Corsair III* was acquired by the U.S. **Navy** in 1917, her **bowsprit** was removed, and she was painted gray. She returned home from service in 1919 and underwent another refit, just in time to once again become **flagship** of the NYYC as Jack Morgan (J. P.'s son) served as commodore in 1920. Renamed *Oceanographer, Corsair III* eventually went back into government service for the U.S. Coast and Geodetic Survey (later the **National Oceanic and Atmospheric Administration**, or NOAA). Armed for combat in World War II, she engaged in survey work in the Pacific. She was decommissioned in September 1944 and broken up.

Corsair IV, the fourth and final *Corsair* yacht built for the Morgan family. *Corsair IV* was designed by Henry J. Gielow and was delivered in 1930 by **Bath Iron Works** for J. P. Morgan Jr. The 343-foot, oil-fired, steam-turbine, electric-driven motor yacht has been described as "the most nearly perfect power yacht ever built." *Corsair IV* served the Morgan family for ten years until she was turned over to the **Royal Navy** during World War II. After the war, she was converted to a cruise **liner** to travel Southern California to Acapulco, and on her **maiden voyage** in 1949 she was stranded on the rocky shore of Acapulco and ended up being scrapped.

corsair fleet, private vessels, including seagoing yachts and fishing **schooners**, that were loaned to the U.S. government to patrol the fifty-fathom curve of **Atlantic** coast in World War II. Also known as the "picket patrol" or the **Hooligan Navy**, the owners and crews of these vessels were made members of the U.S. **Coast Guard Reserve**. Their duty was to supplement forces employed in antisubmarine, rescue, and patrol duties. Walt Disney studios designed the fleet's emblem.

corvette, originally a small sailing warship designed for scouting and patrol duties. The term was revived during World War II to describe a class of small antisubmarine escort vessels.

Costa Line, trade name of the well-recognized shipping firm of Giacomo Costa fu Andrea, Genoa, which was also widely known as Linea "C." Founded in 1924, it attained notoriety after World War II by rebuilding worn-out ships into splendid passenger and emigrant **liners**. It branched out into cruising in the 1960s and became a leader in the industry but lost four ships—*Bianca C, Fulvia, Angelina Lauro*, and *Daphne*—to fire, while a fifth—*Columbus C*—sank at its pier. The company was swallowed up by **Carnival Cruise Lines** in 1996.

Countess of Dufferin, 107-foot **schooner** that in 1876 mounted the third challenge for the **America's Cup**. The Canadian yacht was defeated two races to none by the defender, *Madeleine*, on a course off Sandy Hook, New Jersey.

Count Luckner, the Sea Devil, popular book by Lowell Thomas, first published in 1927, that concerns the exploits of Count **Felix Von Luckner**.

The Count of Monte Cristo, novel by Alexander Dumas (1802–1870) in which a young sailor, Edmond Dantes, is unjustly accused of aiding the exiled **Napoleon**. He is incarcerated for fourteen years in a gloomy island prison in Marseilles Harbor. After a daring escape by simulating death and being cast into the sea in a sack, he takes possession of a treasure on the Isle of Monte Cristo and ultimately brings vengeance to bear on each of his persecutors.

Courageous, two-time successful **America's Cup** defender. Designed by **Sparkman & Stephens**, she measured sixty-six feet in length. *Courageous*, **skippered** by Robert Bavier, defended the Cup in 1974, defeating the Australian challenger *Southern Cross*. In 1977, with **Ted Turner** at the helm, *Courageous* soundly defeated another Australian challenger, *Australia*.

Cousteau, Jacques-Yves (1910–1997), French oceanographer and filmmaker best known as the co-inventor, with Emile Gagnan, of the **aqualung**. He popularized the study of marine environments through numerous books, films, and television programs. He gained international recognition with the publication of *Silent World* (1953), and he produced and starred in the U.S. television series *The Undersea World of Jacques Cousteau* (1968–76). He made many research expeditions aboard his converted British minesweeper *Calypso* and in 1973 formed the nonprofit marine conservation group the Cousteau Society.

Cowes Week, the world's largest sailing **regatta**, held annually at the **Isle of Wight** off England's South Coast during the first week in August. Run since 1822, the event now has more than two hundred races, with nearly a thousand entries, which start and finish in front of the **Royal Yacht Squadron**'s castle. The week is also a stage for an array of social functions, from society balls to cocktail parties.

coxswain, steersman and individual in charge of a boat, be it oar or power driven.

Cozzens, Frederick Schiller (1856–1928), American marine artist and yachtsman who specialized in yachting scenes in watercolor.

CQD, emergency signal that was the forerunner of **SOS**. Introduced around 1904, CQ was the signal for "all stations," and D meant "distress." It was popularly thought to stand for "Come Quickly, Danger."

Cracker Jack, snack food first introduced at the 1893 Chicago World's Fair. The combination of caramel-coated popcorn and peanuts is believed to have been inspired by a number of sea dishes, including "crackerjack," a combination of preserved meat and broken biscuits, and "dandyfunk," a mixture of broken biscuits and molasses. In 1916 product advertisements began to feature a young sailor boy, Jack, with his dog, Bingo.

Cramp, Charles H. (1828–1913), well-known American shipbuilder who was the son of William Cramp, founder of the William Cramp & Sons Ship and Engine Building Company in Philadelphia, and a pioneer of American shipbuilding. Under Charles Cramp's leadership, the yard became the nation's premier builder of iron and steel vessels, especially for the U.S. Navy. The Cramp yard closed in 1927.

Crane, Clinton (d. 1959), American engineer and yacht designer. He designed **six-meters**, **twelve-meters**, **J-boats**, and various **one-design** vessels, including speedboats. He designed the first two twelve-meters that were built in the United States—*Seven Seas* and *Gleam*—as well as the J-boat *Weetamoe*.

Crane, Stephen (1871–1900), American author best known for his Civil War novel *The Red Badge of Courage* (1895). His classic short story "The **Open Boat**" (1897) is based on his own experience of being shipwrecked.

Crash Dive, flag-waving 1943 motion picture released to glamorize the horrors of submarine warfare. The story followed the crew aboard the fictitious USS *Corsair* and their World War II North Atlantic assignments. It starred Tyrone Power, Anne Baxter, and Harry Morgan.

Crimean War, conflict fought from 1853 to 1856 between Russian forces and the allied armies of Britain, France, the Ottoman Empire, and Sardinia. The war's name derives from the

A depiction of a crossing the line ceremony from the 1850s. (Courtesy National Maritime Museum, Greenwich, England; engraving by J. C. Anderson.)

Crimean Peninsula, in the **Black Sea** region, an area of present-day Ukraine where much of the fighting took place. The Crimean War was the first war to be covered by newspaper reporters and photographers at the front.

crimp, shoreside agent or boarding house master who, in the later days of sailing ships, supplied sailors to captains in need of crewmen. Crimps maintained almost complete control over crews as soon as they appeared on the waterfront.

"Crossing Brooklyn Ferry", long poem by **Walt Whitman** that is a detailed record of his thoughts and observations while aboard a ferry between Brooklyn and Manhattan. First published in 1856, it provides a panoramic period description of the activity in New York Harbor.

Crossings, 1986 American television miniseries derived from Danielle Steele's best-selling novel of the same name. It involved romance, sex, and relationships aboard a great **liner** at sea and included wonderful interior footage of the retired RMS *Queen Mary*. It starred Lee Horsley, Christopher Plummer, and Jane Seymour.

crossing the bar, phrase that refers to the death of a mariner. Most rivers and bays develop a sandbar across their entrances, and "crossing the bar" meant leaving the safety of the harbor for the unknown.

"Crossing the Bar", classic, short 1889 poem by Alfred, **Lord Tennyson** that describes a ferry trip to the **Isle of Wight** and concerns Tennyson's death and his hopes to "meet his Maker face to face."

crossing the line, at sea, the act of crossing a significant mark, such as the equator, **international date line**, or Arctic Circle. It is accompanied by a seagoing ceremony, overseen by "King **Neptune**," that includes an initiation rite. "**Pollywogs**" become "shellbacks" upon crossing the equator; "Golden Dragons" when crossing the international date line; and "Blue-noses" when entering the Arctic circle.

cross staff, early navigational instrument used to determine **latitude**, consisting of a calibrated wooden staff approximately three feet in length, with a sliding vane. One would sight the celestial body along the top of the vane and the horizon along the bottom. Often referred to as a fore-staff or Jacob's staff, it was introduced at sea around 1515 and was widely used during the sixteenth century.

Crowhurst, Donald (1932–1969), English adventurer and sailor who tried to pull off one of the greatest hoaxes in sailing history. He set out from England in 1968 in his trimaran **ketch** *Teignmouth Electron* as a competitor in the first single-handed, nonstop, around-the-world sailboat race. Although he radioed his position to reflect he was sailing around the world, it turned out he never left the **Atlantic Ocean**. His vessel was found eight months after the start, structurally intact, but with no one on board.

Crowley Maritime Corporation, the largest operator of tugs and barges in the United States, founded in 1892 in San Francisco by Thomas Crowley. Crowley earned much goodwill from bankers and other businessmen during the earthquake of 1906 when he stored money, bonds, and records in a barge in the middle of San Francisco Bay until vaults and offices could be rebuilt. Through the years, the business expanded to Alaska and Puerto Rico, and in the 1970s Crowley Maritime entered the ocean shipping business.

Crowninshield, George, Jr. (1766–1817), member of the prominent and wealthy Crowninshield mercantile family of Salem, Massachusetts. In 1801 he built *Jefferson*, a **sloop** that he used for pleasure sailing along the New England coast. When war with Great Britain erupted in 1812, he obtained a **letter of marque** and operated the vessel as a licensed **privateer**. At the end of war in 1815, Crowninshield built a large private yacht, which he named *Cleopatra's Barge*. He died aboard the yacht following a yearlong cruise to the Mediterranean.

The Cruel Sea, classic 1951 novel by **Nicholas Monsarrat** about British **convoys** and German **U-boats** fighting the Battle of the **Atlantic**. Monsarrat picks two men, Ericson and Lockhart, and follows their service together from 1939 to 1945, first on the **frigate** *Compass Rose* and then the frigate *Saltash*. A powerful and dramatic, technically authentic 1953 documentary-style movie of the same name—arguably the finest naval movie ever made—was filmed based on the book. The motion picture starred Jack Hawkins, Denholm Elliot, and John Warner.

Cruise of the Alerte, classic 1896 narrative by E. F. Knight about a voyage to the island of Trinidad in search of plunder from the Peruvian revolution.

The Cruise of the Cachalot, wonderful 1897 narrative by British marine author **Frank Thomas Bullen** about his voyage aboard the New Bedford whaleship *Cachalot*.

The Cruise of the Snark, 1908 account by **Jack London** of a cruise from San Francisco to Hawaii, the **Marquesas**, and Tahiti, and ending on **Guadalcanal**. London, his wife, and their friend Roscoe designed and built *Snark*, a fifty-five-foot **ketch**, with the intention of sailing around the world. The extensive planned itinerary was cut short when London's ill

Donald Crowhurst, before he embarked on his strange last voyage. (Courtesy Peter Dunne/*Sunday Times*)

health forced him to forsake the voyage and return to California.

cruiser, a warship designed to operate with strike and amphibious forces against all threats. Today's cruisers employ special anti-air weaponry and sensors to protect aircraft carriers.

Cruising Club of America, nonprofit organization founded in the United States in 1922 by **William Washburn Nutting** and other yachtsmen to promote offshore and ocean racing and the development of cruising boats. Based on Great Britain's **Royal Cruising Club**, it has managed the biennial **Bermuda Race** since 1926 and it offers the Blue Water Medal for "the year's most meritorious example of seamanship" among all amateur sailors. The club's motto is "Nowhere is too far."

Crusoe, Robinson, fictional English seaman who is shipwrecked on an island for twenty-eight years in **Daniel Defoe**'s novel *Robinson Crusoe*. Crusoe's character was based on the real-life **Alexander Selkirk**.

CSS, prefix meaning Confederate States Ship, used for warships of the **Confederate States Navy** during the Civil War.

Cuauhtemoc, 270-foot **tall ship** built in 1982 to serve as a goodwill ambassador and training vessel for the Mexican navy. The **bark** is named for the last Aztec emperor.

Cuban Missile Crisis, the most serious of all Cold War confrontations between the United States and the Soviet Union. In October 1962 the Soviets were found to be secretly deploying medium- and intermediate-range ballistic missiles to Cuba to target the United States. The U.S. **Navy**'s monthlong naval blockade of Cuba was a major contributing factor to Soviet leader Nikita Krushchev's cancellation of his plans; the United States in turn pledged not to invade Cuba. The crisis was the subject of the 2001 movie, *Thirteen Days*.

cuddy, small covered area over the forward part of an otherwise open boat.

Cuffe, Paul (1759–1817), American seaman and merchant who encouraged the colonizing of blacks in Sierra Leone, Africa, after sailing there in 1810. Part black and part Indian, Cuffe was born on Cuttyhunk Island, Massachusetts. He financed the voyage of thirty-eight free blacks in 1815. He also sought to strengthen the legal position of blacks in the United States, and his efforts led to a law in 1783 that gave blacks in Massachusetts the right to vote.

cumshaw, naval slang for the procurement of materials outside the supply chain, usually by swapping or barter. It invariably involves food, usually coffee, in exchange for needed items.

Cunard, Samuel (1787–1865), Nova Scotia–born shipowner who was a founder of the British and North American Royal Mail Steam Packet Company—more commonly known as the **Cunard Line**—in 1840 to operate a regularly scheduled fortnightly transatlantic service. SS *Britannia* made the company's first voyage in 1840. Cunard was made a baronet for services the Cunard Line rendered to Great Britain during the **Crimean War**.

Cunard Eagle Airways, English airline formed in 1960 when the **Cunard Line** bought into the already established Eagle Airways. The new concern's application to fly to New York from London was denied because Cunard already operated the largest passenger fleet on the **Atlantic**. Left with only the Miami and Caribbean air routes from Britain, the **steamship** company sold the airline back to Eagle and—taking their two brand-new Boeing 707 jetliners, which were now redundant—allied themselves with a 30 percent interest in the North Atlantic routes of BOAC to form **BOAC-Cunard** in 1962.

Cunard Line, British **steamship** company founded in 1840 by **Samuel Cunard** and **George Burns** to maintain a regularly scheduled North Atlantic passenger and mail service. Unquestionably the most famous shipping house of all time, its ship names traditionally ended in "ia" and recalled such ancient Roman provinces as *Lusitania* (Portugal), *Mauretania* (North West Africa), and *Aquitania* (southern France)—exceptions to the rule being *Berengaria* (the queen of Richard the Lion-Hearted) as well as *Queen Mary* and *Queen Elizabeth*. Cunard merged with the **White Star Line** in 1934 to form the **Cunard White Star Line**. It returned to the singular company name in 1950 and maintained **steamship row** head offices at 25 Broadway in New York City. It was sold in 1971 to Trafalgar Investments and eventually wound up as a wholly owned division of **Carnival Cruise Lines** in 1998, with headquarters in Miami.

Cunard White Star Line, shipping conglomerate formed by the 1934 merger of the **Cunard Line** and **White Star Line** at the behest of the British government in return for loans to build the RMS *Queen Mary* and RMS *Queen Elizabeth*. The *Mary* (originally to be named *Victoria*) broke with the Cunard "ia" and White Star "ic" suffix nomenclature to signify the beginning of a new corporate era. The *Elizabeth* followed suit, although the original intention was to name her the *King George V*, but the death of the monarch in 1936 gave the new company the opportunity for an advertising coup with twin Queen **liner** monikers. "White Star" was dropped from the company name in 1950.

Cunningham, Briggs (b. 1907), American yachtsman who was a successful **six-meter** sailor in the 1930s. For a time he owned the **schooner** *Brilliant* before donating the vessel to **Mystic**

Cunard Line poster illustrating RMS *Queen Elizabeth* (top) and RMS *Queen Mary*.

Seaport. He was winning **skipper** of *Columbia* in the 1958 **America's Cup**. The cunningham, which allows a sailor to adjust the tension on the luff of a sail, is named for him. Cunningham is also a champion race car driver and was the first American to compete at the Le Mans.

HMS *Curacao*, **Royal Navy** vessel that was assigned to escort RMS *Queen Mary* as she ferried ten thousand U.S. troops to Britain in World War II. On October 2, 1942, the **liner** *Queen Mary* sliced through the **cruiser**, killing 340 *Curacao* crew members.

Currier and Ives, Nathaniel Currier (1813–1888) and James Merritt Ives (1824–1895), two early American printmakers who fashioned many nautical scenes. Currier opened his own firm in New York City in 1834 and in 1852 hired Ives as his bookkeeper and soon made him a partner. Many of the duo's hand-tinted prints were done in assembly-line fashion by women who each applied a particular color.

Cushing, William Barker (1842–1874), U.S. naval officer who commanded several Union warships with distinction in the Civil War. In October 1864 he led an expedition that sank the Confederate ram *Albemarle* in the Roanoke River at Plymouth, North Carolina, and in January 1865 he led an assault on **Fort Fisher**, North Carolina.

Cussler, Clive (b. 1931), best-selling American author of seventeen adventure novels, most with nautical elements, that revolve around the main character **Dirk Pitt**. Cussler began writing the adventures in 1973, and today nearly one hundred million copies are in print. His novels include *Iceberg* (1975), *Raise the Titanic!* (1976), *Treasure* (1988), and *Shock Wave* (1995). In 1978 Cussler founded the **National Underwater and Marine Agency**, a nonprofit foundation established to locate, identify, and preserve shipwrecks of historical significance.

U.S. Customs Service, an agency of the Department of the Treasury that enforces the laws passed to protect import and export revenues and assesses and collects taxes on imported merchandise. Established in 1789 and located in the nation's major seaports, the Customs Service supervised the U.S. **Revenue Cutter Service**. Customs revenue funded the entire U.S. government for nearly 125 years, and today customs provides the nation with its second-biggest revenue source.

Cutler, Carl (1878–1966), American lawyer and author, a leading American maritime historian of his time. In 1929 he was one of the three founders, along with Edward Bradley and Dr.

Charles Stillman, of the Marine Historical Association, now **Mystic Seaport**, in Mystic, Connecticut. He was the author of *Greyhounds of the Sea: The Story of the American Clipper Ship* (1930) and *Queens of the Western Ocean* (1961), a history of American **packet** ships.

cut of his jib, phrase from the days of sailing ships when sailors could identify a certain vessel by the shape and size of its sails.

cutter, single-masted sailboat with a mainsail and at least two headsails, a forestaysail, and a jib. These fast, seaworthy coastal craft were traditionally used as **pilot** vessels and revenue **cruisers** in the eighteenth and nineteenth centuries.

cutter, U.S. **Coast Guard** vessel sixty-five feet or longer, with adequate accommodations for crew to live on board. The name is a holdover from the fast sailing **cutters** used by the **Revenue Cutter Service**.

Cutty Sark, one of the fastest and most celebrated **clipper ships** and the only survivor of the breed. Launched in 1869 (her name was taken from Robert Burns's poem "Tam O'-Shanter"), she was initially engaged in Britain's tea trade with China. After the opening of the **Suez Canal**, she abandoned the tea trade, leaving it to the larger cargo steamers, and began regular voyages in the Australian wool trade. At 212 feet in length, *Cutty Sark* carried a large sail area in proportion to her size and could achieve a top speed of seventeen **knots**. In 1895 she became the Portuguese *Ferreira* and was used for transatlantic voyages. She returned to British ownership in 1922, and in 1957 she was preserved and placed on display in a dry dock built especially for her at Greenwich, England, near the **National Maritime Museum**.

USCGC *Cuyahoga*, 125-foot U.S. **Coast Guard cutter** that, in clear conditions on the night of October 20, 1978, collided with the Argentian bulk carrier M/V *Santa Cruz II* in Chesapeake

Watercolor of *Cutty Sark*, circa nineteenth century. (Courtesy National Maritime Museum, Greenwich, England; painting by Gregory Robinson.)

Bay. The **bulker** struck the *Cuyahoga* amidships, and the cutter sank in two minutes, taking the lives of eleven of the twenty-nine Coast Guard personnel on board.

CV, U.S. **Navy** designation for an attack aircraft carrier, a warship designed to support and operate aircraft, engage in attacks on targets afloat and ashore, and engage in sustained operations in support of other forces.

CVN, U.S. **Navy** designation for a nuclear-powered aircraft carrier, or **CV**.

Cyane, U.S. **Navy frigate** that in 1820 carried freed slaves to Africa in order to help establish the colony that later became Liberia.

USS *Cyclops*, 14,500-ton U.S. **Navy** collier built in 1910. She left Guyana bound for Norfolk in 1918 with 309 people on board and vanished without a trace. Despite an exhaustive search carried out by the American and French Navies, nothing in the way of wreckage or debris was ever found and there has never been a plausible explanation for her disappearance.

Cynthia Olson, the first U.S. **merchant marine** ship sunk by the Japanese in World War II. One hour before the Japanese bombed **Pearl Harbor**, the ship, carrying lumber to Hawai'i, was attacked by the Japanese submarine I-26. The **liner** SS *Lurline*, en route to California, picked up the *Cynthia Olson*'s distress call indicating a submarine attack but could not contact Pearl Harbor. The *Cynthia Olson* went down with no survivors.

D

Dahlgren gun, an improved form of cannon first developed in 1850 by John Adolphus Dahlgren (1809–1870), a U.S. naval officer and ordnance expert. Thick in proportion to pressures in the barrel, the bottle-shaped guns were employed on launches and most Union naval vessels during the Civil War.

SS Dakota, American passenger vessel built in 1905 in Groton, Connecticut. For twenty-five years the largest ship built in the United States, she ran aground in 1907 near Yokohama, Japan, and was later destroyed by a storm and finally scrapped where she lay. She was sister to SS *Minnesota*.

Dalrymple, Alexander (1737–1808), English chartmaker and first **hydrographer** to the **Royal Navy**. He previously worked as the first hydrographer for the **East India Company**. He was charged with producing charts based on the voyages of Captain **James Cook** and is credited for his high standards and accuracy.

Dame Pattie, Australian **twelve-meter** yacht that challenged for the **America's Cup** in 1967. She was defeated in four straight races off Newport, Rhode Island, by the U.S. defender, *Intrepid*.

Damn the Defiant, accurate 1962 film about mutiny and strife aboard a British warship in the **Napoleonic Wars**. It starred Alec Guiness, Maurice Denham, and Dirk Bogarde and was based on the 1958 novel *Mutiny* by Frank Tilsley about a mutiny on a British **frigate** in 1796.

"Damn the torpedoes! Full speed ahead!", famous battle cry of Admiral **David Glasgow Farragut** during the Battle of **Mobile Bay** on August 5, 1864. Mobile Bay was strongly defended by two forts and a double row of **torpedoes** (mines) and Confederate warships. When the **monitor** USS *Tecumseh* struck a mine and sank, other ships in the column stopped. Fearing that his squadron was drifting into confusion, Farragut uttered his command and ordered his **flagship** USS *Hartford* through the mines, which failed to explode.

Dampier, William (1652–1715), English navigator, mariner, and Pacific explorer. During a circumnavigation, Dampier explored Australia and the South Pacific and wrote one of the first English accounts of the region, *A New Voyage Around the World* (1697). From 1703 to 1707, he led an expedition that again circumnavigated the globe and was especially notable because **Alexander Selkirk**, the model for **Robinson Crusoe**, was left by Dampier on one of the Juan Fernández Islands off Chile on this expedition.

Dana, Richard Henry, Jr. (1815–1882), American author and lawyer who wrote the personal narrative *Two Years Before the Mast* (1840) based on his experiences as a common sailor. Dana had discontinued his law studies at Harvard because of eye problems and sailed in 1834 on the **brig** *Pilgrim* for a voyage from Boston around **Cape Horn** to California. He returned to Boston aboard the **ship** *Alert*. Dana also wrote *The Seaman's Friend* (1841), a manual of maritime law based on his voyages as well as his legal practice.

Daniels, Josephus (1862–1948), secretary of the navy in the Woodrow Wilson administration (1913–21). He was criticized for not preparing the U.S. **Navy** for World War I, but he is perhaps best known as the man responsible for abolishing all alcohol on board U.S. Navy vessels. **Franklin D. Roosevelt** served as his assistant secretary, and later, when president, FDR appointed Daniels ambassador to Mexico.

Danmark, 253-foot Danish **tall ship** built in 1933. To avoid having the ship fall into German hands during World War II, Denmark offered her services to the United States in 1939, and she spent the war as a school ship at the U.S. **Coast Guard Academy** in New London, Connecticut. Returning to Denmark following the war, some of her crew assisted the **Coast Guard** in sailing the new **bark** *Eagle*, formerly the German *Horst Wessel*, from Bremerhaven to the United States. President **John F. Kennedy** displayed a model of *Danmark* in the Oval Office. The Danish

Maritime Authority operates the ship as a training vessel.

Dante's Inferno, 1935 motion picture drama set on an offshore gambling ship. The movie starred Spencer Tracy, Claire Trevor, and Rita Hayworth.

Dara, British-India Line passenger ship that exploded and sank in the Persian Gulf on April 8, 1962, with the loss of 236 lives. An investigation later exposed that the explosion was caused by a time bomb.

Dardanelles, strategically important narrow strait that connects the Mediterranean Sea to the **Black Sea** (via the Aegean Sea, Sea of Marmara, and **Bosporus**). Overlooking this strait is the narrow **Gallipoli** Peninsula, site of one of the biggest stalemate battles of World War I.

Darwin, Charles (1809–1882), English naturalist and scientist who originated the theory of evolution by natural selection. During a five year voyage (1831–36) aboard the surveying ship HMS *Beagle* he spent much of his time making observations of the flora and fauna in South America, particulary the **Galápagos Islands**, and Australia. He wrote *The Voyage of the Beagle* (1839), later revised in 1860. He published *The Origin of Species by Means of Natural Selection* (1859), and his ideas reached wider recognition with the publication of *The Descent of Man* (1871).

Das Boot, 1981 German-made film with English subtitles that paints a realistic portrait of life in a **U-boat** during World War II. Originally it was a six-hour movie specially made for German television and based on the book of the same name (1975) by **Lothar-Günther Buchheim**. Costing over $40 million to produce, the movie was at the time the most expensive German movie ever filmed. As accurate a re-creation of cramped diesel submarine life as one will ever see, the production was a tribute to the 40,000 German World War II submariners—30,000 of whom were lost in action. The picture was later dubbed in English and rereleased in the United States as *The Boat*.

Dauntless, 124-foot **schooner** yacht built in 1866 at Mystic, Connecticut. Originally named *L'Hirondelle*, she was sold to flamboyant newspaper editor **James Gordon Bennett Jr.** and renamed *Dauntless* in 1867. In 1869 she made a record-setting transatlantic crossing and in 1870 participated in the first defense of the **America's Cup**. Later *Dauntless* served as the family yacht for firearm executive Caldwell Colt. Converted to a houseboat in 1903, she later sank and was broken up in 1915.

David Balfour, dramatic 1893 sequel to the **Robert Louis Stevenson** classic *Kidnapped*. Set in Stevenson's native Scottish Highlands, this story centers on Balfour's efforts to exonerate the national hero James Stewart.

David Taylor Research Center, one of the world's largest and most comprehensive ship research facilities. The facility was established by the U.S. **Navy** in 1967 when the David Taylor Model Basin at Carderock, Maryland—the nation's first ship model basin, opened in 1898—was merged with the Marine Engineering Laboratory in Annapolis. In the late 1990s, the facilities were consolidated and renamed the **Naval Sea Systems Command** Hydrodynamics Directorate.

Davis, Charles Henry (1807–1877), U.S. **Navy** officer and scientist who served as chief of the Navy's **Bureau of Navigation** from 1862 to 1865 and superintendent of the U.S. **Naval Observatory** from 1865 to 1867 and 1874 1877. He introduced the *American Ephemeris* and *Nautical Almanac*.

Davis, Howell (d. 1719), Welsh slave trader who turned to piracy when captured off the African coast by pirate Edward England. He became a well-known raider in the **Atlantic** and Caribbean, eventually succumbing to a

Portuguese ambush at the governor's palace at Principe Island off the West African coast.

Davis, John (1550–1605), English mariner, explorer, and inventor who made three unsuccessful voyages to Canada in search of a **Northwest Passage** (1585–87). The strait between Greenland and North America that connects Baffin Bay to the **Atlantic** is named after him. He fought against the **Spanish Armada** and in 1592 discovered the Falkland Islands. He published two treatises on navigation, *The Seaman's Secrets* (1594) and *The World's Hydrographical Description* (1595), and designed such navigation instruments as the **Davis quadrant**. He was killed by pirates during a voyage to the **East Indies**.

Davis quadrant, simple instrument that enabled seamen to find **latitude**. Invented by **John Davis** in 1594, it provided a simple method of finding the angle of the sun above the horizon without having to sight directly on it. It is also referred to as a **backstaff**.

Davy Jones, personification of the spirit who rules over the souls of the sea.

Davy Jones's locker, phrase used to describe the bottom of the ocean—the final resting place of lost articles, sunken ships, and sailors who have drowned or been buried at sea.

Dawson, Montague (1895–1973), British marine painter who is best known for his magnificent, big **square-rig** sailing ship pictures. He served in the **Royal Navy** during World War I and by the 1930s was considered one of the greatest living marine artists. During World War II, he was employed by the **Admiralty** and various magazines to paint sea battles and naval activities. His patrons included Presidents Dwight D. Eisenhower and Lyndon B. Johnson as well as the British Royal family.

Day, Thomas Fleming (1861–1919), American yacht designer, nautical journalist, and founder-editor of the *Rudder*. He is considered by many to be the father of American yachting and day sailing. He designed and built the twenty-five-foot **yawl** *Sea Bird*, the first practical, home-built type of sailing yacht capable of ocean voyages, and sailed her from Providence, Rhode Island, to **Gibraltar** and Italy in 1911. He wrote *Across the Atlantic in Sea Bird* (1926) and *The Voyage of the Detroit* (1929).

dazzle-painting, patterned camouflage technique invented by British marine artist **Norman Wilkinson** and first applied to ships during World War I. The bold abstract patterns were intended to break up the constructional lines so that when viewed through an enemy periscope the range, course, and speed were difficult to estimate. When combined with a zigzag course, the ship was thought to stand a far greater chance of survival. Dazzle-painting employed many marine painters of the time, but it was never conclusively proven to be effective.

DD, U.S. **Navy** designation for a **destroyer**, a high-speed warship designed to operate offensively with strike forces, with hunter-killer groups, and in support of amphibious assault operations.

D-Day, military code name for a special date, the most famous of which was June 6, 1944, the day on which Allied forces landed on five beaches—code named Utah, Omaha, Gold, Juno, and Sword—on the northern coast of France to commence **Operation Overlord**, the invasion of German-occupied France. A total of 127,000 Allied troops landed on the day, and 2,500 were killed, with 8,500 wounded. The entire operation is also called the **Normandy Invasion**.

DDG, U.S. **Navy** designation for a guided missile **destroyer**. These destroyers are equipped with standard guided missiles, naval guns,

long-range **sonar**, and antisubmarine warfare weapons.

DE, acronym for a **destroyer** escort, a warship developed by the U.S. **Navy** during World War II that was smaller and less heavily armed than a destroyer and was used extensively for **convoy** duty and antisubmarine warfare.

dead horse, a debt incurred by a seaman by advance of a month's wages, usually to pay for boarding bills and saloon tabs while ashore. It was occasion for a celebration among the crew aboard ship when their advanced money was worked off. During the celebration, an effigy of a horse was hoisted over the ship's rail and sent overboard.

Dead Man's Chest, island located in the Caribbean, now called Dead Chest Island, that was immortalized by **Robert Louis Stevenson** in *Treasure Island*. Stevenson wrote, "Fifteen men on the Dead Man's Chest, Yo-ho-ho, and a bottle of rum! Drink and the devil had done for the rest."

dead reckoning, the process of determining the position of a vessel by tracking course and speed for a given time. From the phrase "deduced reckoning," the plot is called a "DR."

Dead Sea, landlocked salt lake, with no outlet, located between Israel and Jordan, with the Jordan River as its source. The high salt content, which makes it difficult to sustain any life forms, is a result of rapid evaporation of the water. The Dead Sea is the lowest exposed point on the earth's surface.

deadweight tonnage, abbreviated "dwt," the number of tons of cargo, stores, and bunker that a vessel can transport. It is the difference between the number of tons of water a vessel displaces when light and when submerged to the deep load line.

Debussy, Claude (1862–1918), French composer whose musical works *La Mer* and *Sirènes* were inspired by the sea.

Decatur, Stephen, Jr. (1779–1820), U.S. naval officer who rose to fame during the **Barbary Wars**. In 1804 he and his men stole into **Tripoli** Harbor and destroyed the captured **frigate** USS *Philadelphia*. **Horatio Nelson** declared Decatur's deed "the most bold and daring act of the age." In the **War of 1812**, Decatur commanded three vessels, including USS *United States*. When tensions with the **Barbary pirates** arose again in 1815, he used his squadron to force a treaty that ended American payments to the **Barbary States**. He was killed by **James Barron** in a duel at Bladensburg, Maryland. Cities in Illinois, Alabama, and Georgia are named for him.

Decca, hyperbolic radionavigation system similar to **loran** that was first developed by the British around World War II. It is accurate for short to medium ranges.

Declaration of Paris, 1856 agreement that brought an end to the practice of privateering. Signatory nations included Britain, France, Austria, Prussia, Russia, Sardinia, and Turkey. The United States refused to accept the declaration, claiming that **privateers** were necessary if a nation did not have a strong navy. The United States became a signatory during the Civil War.

decompression sickness, painful, sometimes fatal illness caused by the formation of nitrogen bubbles in the bloodstream and body tissue as a result of the sudden lowering of atmospheric pressure (as when a diver ascends too quickly to the water's surface). It is characterized by tightness in the chest and pain in the limbs, joints, and abdomen. Also called "the bends," it was originally diagnosed as "**caisson disease**" because it first appeared among workers digging bridge footings.

The Deep, 1977 action-adventure film based on the best-selling novel by **Peter Benchley** about an innocent couple on vacation who discover the sunken wreck of a World War II freighter and unearth a treasure of gold and morphine. Afterward they battle drug dealers and treasure hunters. The film—which starred Robert Shaw, Jacqueline Bisset, Nick Nolte, Louis Gossett Jr., and Eli Wallach—was famous for Bisset's wet T-shirt scene.

deep six, euphemism for throwing something overboard that has come to mean to discard any object. It comes from the custom of burials at sea in which the ceremony took place in waters more than six **fathoms** deep.

Defender, 123-foot gaff-rigged **sloop** that successfully defended the 1895 **America's Cup** against the British challenge of *Valkyrie III*. **Nathanael Herreshoff** designed *Defender* using manganese bronze hull plating and aluminum topsides to save weight. *Defender* was a victim of electrolysis in later years as she nearly melted away. She was the first defender to be fitted with a fin keel.

Defense Mapping Agency (DMA), U.S. government agency created in 1972 to consolidate all military mapping activities. It published nautical charts and navigation directories until it became part of the **National Imagery and Mapping Agency** in 1996.

Defoe, Daniel (1660–1731), English author and journalist who was well versed on the subject of maritime affairs. He is best known for his popular adventure narrative *Robinson Crusoe*, based on the real-life adventures of castaway **Alexander Selkirk**. Defoe also completed *A General History of the Pyrates* (under the pen name Captain **Charles Johnson**), a volume that serves as a major source of information about piracy in the early eighteenth century.

degaussing, a magnetic mine countermeasure used on warships in which electrical cables are installed around the circumference of a ship's hull. A measured electrical current is passed through these cables to cancel out the ship's magnetic field, thus making the ship invisible to the sensors of magnetic mines.

de Hartog, Jan (b. 1914), Dutch mariner and author of popular seafaring novels. He sailed as a mate on Dutch oceangoing tugboats and in World War II served as a war correspondent for the Dutch **merchant marine**. His novels include *Captain Jan* (1940), *The Distant Shore* (1952), *The Captain* (1966), and *The Commodore* (1986). Nonfiction titles include *The Lost Sea* (1951) and *A Sailor's Life* (1955).

Delancey, Richard, fictional **Royal Navy** officer in the **Napoleonic Wars** series by **C. Northcote Parkinson**. The five novels are *Devil to Pay* (1973), *The Fireship* (1975), *Touch and Go* (1977), *Dead Reckoning* (1978), and *So Near, So Far* (1981).

Delano, Amasa (1763–1823), American sea captain who served as a **privateer** in the American Revolution at age fifteen. He later explored the sealing grounds of the South Atlantic and was the first to hear of *Topaz*'s discovery of the HMS *Bounty* mutineers on **Pitcairn Island**. Delano's experiences at sea are recorded in his *Narrative of Voyages and Travels in the Northern and Southern Hemispheres, Comprising Three Voyages Round the World* (1817), which **Herman Melville** used in writing **"Benito Cereno"** (1855). President **Franklin Delano Roosevelt** was a descendant.

Delilah, 1941 novel by Marcus Goodrich of life aboard an aging U.S. **Navy destroyer** policing the Philippines in the early twentieth century. Goodrich, who enlisted and served in the navy in World War I, spent fifteen years working on the fictionalized account. The book was published just prior to World War II and stayed unknown for many years. It ranks among the best sea stories ever written and is one of the finest accounts of life in the steam navy.

De Long, George Washington (1844–1881), U.S. naval officer and Arctic explorer who in the 1870s convinced newspaper publisher **James Gordon Bennett Jr.** to fund an expedition to reach the North Pole. De Long and the

Jeanette Expedition sailed from San Francisco to Alaska in July 1879, then headed north through the Bering Strait. On September 5, 1879, his ship, the *Jeanette*, became caught in the ice and drifted for twenty-one months before it was crushed on June 13, 1881. De Long died in the Siberian Arctic of starvation while trying to reach safety in a lifeboat. His diary *Voyage of the Jeanette* was published in 1883.

USS *Delphy* (DD-296), Clemson-class **destroyer** that led a flotilla of seven sister vessels down the California coast in 1923. The formation was traveling at twenty **knots** in thick fog when the **flagship** *Delphy* ran onto a rock outcropping seventy-five miles north of Santa Barbara. One by one, the destroyers followed the lead vessel aground onto the rocks, resulting in one of the greatest peacetime naval disasters in history. All seven ships were total constructive losses, and twenty-two men were killed. The six other wrecked flush-deckers were USS *Chauncey*, USS *Fuller*, USS *Nicholas*, USS *Woodbury*, USS *Young*, and USS *S. P. Lee*.

Delta King, stern-wheel paddle steamer prefabricated in Scotland and assembled in San Francisco in 1926 to provide night passenger service from Sacramento to San Francisco in tandem with her sister ship, the ***Delta Queen***. After falling into horrible disrepair after government service on San Francisco Bay during World War II, she was rescued and restored. The *Delta King* became a dockside hotel and restaurant ship at her Old Sacramento dock in 1990.

Delta Queen, 1,837-gross-ton flat-bottomed **paddle wheeler** prefabricated in Scotland and assembled in San Francisco in 1926 for operation between Sacramento and San Francisco with her sister ship, the ***Delta King***. She served on San Francisco Bay during World War II and was purchased by Greene Line Steamers in 1948 for continued passenger operation on the

Daniel Defoe.
(Courtesy National Maritime Museum, Greenwich, England)

Delta Queen. (Delta Queen Steamboat Company)

Mississippi, Ohio, and Cumberland Rivers. Beautifully restored, the largely wooden craft today operates under special dispensation from Congress now that she has attained national historic landmark status. She is currently owned and operated by the **Delta Queen Steamboat Company**.

Delta Queen Steamboat Company, U.S.-flagged cruise line that operates steam-powered **paddle wheelers** on many of the rivers of heartland America. Origins of the company date back to 1890 and the Greene Line. The company, a subsidiary of American Classic Voyages, operates the *Delta Queen*, *Mississippi Queen*, and *American Queen*.

demise charter, agreement that allows the charter to take over the vessel without captain or crew. It is also known as a **bareboat charter**.

demurrage, fee levied by a shipping company upon a port or supplier for not loading or unloading a vessel by a specified date agreed upon by contract.

depth charge, explosive antisubmarine weapon dropped from a ship or aircraft.

Derbyshire, 965-foot British **bulk** carrier with forty-two people on board that disappeared in September 1980 without a trace during a typhoon in the Pacific Ocean, south of Japan. That the ship was only four years old, well maintained, and manned by an experienced crew adds to the mystery.

Der Fliegende Höllander, see at *Fliegende Höllander*.

DESCO, acronym for the American Diving Equipment and Salvage Company, which in 1937 introduced a mixed gas system in combination with a fully sealed suite and set a depth record of 420 feet.

Desolation Islands, popular name for the Kerguelen Island group in the South Indian Ocean. The remote islands were a favorite stopping point for sealers.

de Soto, Hernando (ca. 1460–1542), Spanish explorer named governor of Cuba and Florida in 1539 who began a three-year expedition throughout much of the southeastern United States in search of gold, which he never found. He was the first European to see the **Mississippi River**. He caught a fever and died in 1542.

Desperate Voyage, best-selling 1949 autobiographical account of former merchant seaman John Caldwell's eighty-five-hundred-mile voyage across the Pacific in a twenty-nine-foot **cutter** from Panama to return to his wife in Australia following World War II.

Destination Tokyo, engrossing 1943 action film made as much for entertainment as for recruitment. It relays the story of USS *Copperfin*, a fictitious American submarine engaged in some risky espionage on Tokyo Bay to gain information needed by Jimmy Doolittle and his raiders before they can take off from USS *Wasp*. The movie features excellent acting by Cary Grant, John Garfield, and Alan Hale Sr.

destroyer, high-speed warship designed to operate offensively with strike forces and in support of amphibious assault operations, and defensively in **convoys** against submarine and surface threats. It was introduced in the late nineteenth century and employed as an anti-submarine vessel during both World Wars.

Destroyer, 1943 film, starring Edward G. Robinson and Glenn Ford, about close-quartered life and sibling rivalry on board a World War II U.S. **Navy destroyer**.

Destroyers for Bases Agreement, September 1940 pact between the United States and Great Britain that provided the United States with ninety-nine-year leases of British naval and air bases in Newfoundland and the Caribbean in exchange for fifty U.S. **Navy destroyers**. The agreement allowed the United States to defend the bases and help Britain fight World War II without becoming embroiled in the hostilities. It was followed up in 1941 with the **Lend-Lease** program.

Det Norske Veritas (DNV), Norwegian classification society established in 1864 and based in Oslo. DNV classifies nearly 15 percent of the world's commercial fleet.

deviation, the angle a boat's compass makes with magnetic north. It is caused by the magnetism in the boat's hull and equipment and can be corrected by compass adjustment through compensating magnets or by applying a correction from the ship's deviation table.

Devil's Island, small island six miles off the coast of French Guyana in South America. From 1895 to 1938, it was the site of a French penal colony, and it was made famous in the 1973 film *Papillon*, starring Steve McQueen and Dustin Hoffman.

the devil to pay, caulker's phrase for the difficult task of paying (caulking) one of the ship's seams that is known as the devil—the seam nearest the outboard edge of the deck. The phrase has come to mean trouble to be faced as a result of one's actions.

The trading dhow that Alan Villiers traveled on along the East African coast during the 1920s. (Courtesy National Maritime Museum/Villiers Collection, Greenwich, England; photo by Alan Villiers)

Dewey, George (1837–1917), commodore who commanded the U.S. **Navy** Asia squadron that entered the Philippines on May 1, 1898, and defeated the Spanish fleet without losing a ship or a man. Dewey is famous for his remark **"You may fire when you are ready, Captain Gridley!"** The remark started the Battle of **Manila Bay**. The battle—and the U.S. victory in the **Spanish-American War**—led to the eventual U.S. acquisition of the Philippines, who later gained their independence.

dhow, **lateen**-rigged coastal trading vessel native to the Red Sea, Arabian Gulf, and Indian Ocean.

Diamond Shoals, treacherous stretch of water off Cape Hatteras, North Carolina, formed by the northbound **Gulf Stream** colliding with cold currents coming down from the Arctic, which has earned itself the name **Graveyard of**

the Atlantic. A **lightship** was set on station in 1824, which repeatedly snapped her moorings. Through the years many passing ships rammed the lightship, and in 1918 a German **U-boat** torpedoed Diamond Shoals Lightship No. 71. Diamond Shoals Light Tower was erected in 1967 thirteen miles off the coast.

Dias, Bartholomeu (c. 1450–1500), Portuguese navigator and explorer who in 1478 led an expedition of three ships around the southern tip of Africa, establishing the possibility of a sea route to Asia. **Vasco da Gama**, another Portuguese explorer, led the first successful voyage to India in 1497. In 1500, Dias commanded four ships in the thirteen-vessel expedition led by **Pedro Alvares Cabral** that mistakenly reached what is now Brazil. Dias died during the voyage from Brazil when a storm sank his ship.

Dick Deadeye, hunchbacked sailor and pirate in Gilbert and Sullivan's *HMS Pinafore*. He is the foil of hero Ralph Rackstraw.

The Dictionary of American Fighting Ships, the foremost reference regarding U.S. naval vessels. Known as DANFS, it is published by the U.S. **Navy** in nine volumes (1959–91) and gives a history for virtually every U.S. naval vessel.

Diego Garcia, British atoll in the middle of the Indian Ocean. In 1982 the U.S. **Navy** finished building a $200 million complex that can accommodate the navy's largest ships and the biggest military cargo jets. The base played an important role in the Gulf War.

dinghy, small boat used for rowing or sailing. Its name is from the Hindi *dingi*, which means "small boat."

Dirigo, 312-foot four-masted steel **bark** built in 1894 by Arthur Sewall & Co., Bath, Maine. She was the first American-built steel-hulled sailing vessel, and her name was taken from the Maine state motto, "I lead." She was sunk with

gunfire from a German **U-boat** in 1917 in World War I.

HMS *Discovery*, ship that accompanied HMS ***Resolution*** on Captain **James Cook**'s third and final voyage of discovery (1776–79).

HMS *Discovery*, ship built in 1789 and commanded by Captain **George Vancouver** during his 1792–94 expedition to explore the Pacific coast of North America. *Discovery* sailed a hundred miles up the Columbia River, as far as the present site of Portland, Oregon. Vancouver's book, *A Voyage of Discovery to the North Pacific Ocean and Round the World in the Years 1790–1795*, was published in 1798.

HMS *Discovery*, British research ship built in Scotland in 1901 and commanded by **Robert Scott** during his 1901–4 Antarctic expedition. The **bark** is today a museum ship in Dundee, Scotland.

Dismal Swamp Canal, canal that is regarded as the oldest man-made waterway in the United States. Dug by slave labor in the 1790s, it runs through the heart of the Great Dismal Swamp, thereby connecting rivers flowing into the Chesapeake Bay in Virginia with North Carolina's Albemarle Sound.

displacement, statement of a ship's weight expressed in the actual weight of the water a vessel displaces when floating at a given draft. Salt water weighs sixty-four pounds per cubic foot. See **deadweight tonnage**.

Disraeli, Benjamin (1804–1881), British statesman and prime minister who was a skilled diplomat and empire builder. He arranged the purchase of Egypt's shares of the **Suez Canal**, thereby opening the gateway to India and eventually adding Empress of India to Queen Victoria's many titles.

ditty bag, small bag used by sailors to hold small tools, necessities, and other items. Sailors often used a ditty box to store such valuables as letters and photographs.

Enola, Dismal Swamp Canal, circa 1910, photograph by H. C. Mann. (Courtesy The Mariners' Museum, Newport News, Virginia)

Diver Dan, 1960s American children's television show that starred Frank Freda as the deep-sea explorer Diver Dan and Suzanne Turner as the beautiful and elusive mermaid Miss Minerva. The rest of the cast consisted of marionette fish puppets, and the show was filmed through a large fish tank, giving it an unusual look.

Diving to Adventure, 1951 best-selling book by Hans Hass about diving with whales, sharks, manta rays, and other sea creatures. The book enhanced diving's image as an adventure pastime.

documented vessel, according to U.S. **Coast Guard** regulations, a vessel of at least five net tons and wholly owned by a U.S. citizen. Vessels of at least five net tons that are used commercially must be documented. Instead of a state registration number, these vessels are assigned a six- or seven-digit federal documentation number.

Dodd, Robert (1748–1815), English marine artist who was one of the principal recorders of naval actions in both the American Revolution and the **French Revolution**.

Dodsworth, 1936 classic motion picture in which an affluent off-to-Europe American couple find themselves embroiled in heart games aboard a speeding ocean **liner**. A very young David Niven is outstanding as the shipboard gigolo. Directed by William Wyler and produced by Samuel Goldwyn, the film also starred Walter Huston, Ruth Chatterton, Mary Astor, John Payne, and Spring Byington.

dog, to close tightly a hatch, porthole, watertight door, or **scuttle**.

Dogger Bank, extensive sandbank in the middle of the North Sea where a German naval force of thirty ships encountered a detachment of the British **Grand Fleet** of forty-two ships on January 24, 1915. The ensuing battle lasted three hours, with the Germans losing one armored **cruiser**.

dogwatch, two-hour watch aboard ship that is usually inserted in the 1600–2000 schedule, one half between 4 and 6 P.M. and the other half between 6 and 8 P.M. Watches are "dogged" to enable those on watch to eat the evening meal and to rotate duty periods.

dog zebra, military term for a "darkened ship." All hull fittings, usually porthole covers, designated "DZ" must be closed.

doldrums, an equatorial trough of low atmospheric pressure that extends five degrees north and south of the equator. It is characterized by light winds and unsettled weather.

Dollar Line, American **steamship** company founded in 1900 by Captain Robert Dollar as the Dollar Steamship Company. Dollar Line served for many years as the main U.S. line in the transpacific trade until Japanese and other foreign lines became more competitive. In 1938 the company's stock was purchased by the U.S. **Maritime Commission**, and a new company, **American President Lines**, was formed.

dolphin striker, a short spar projecting downward under the **bowsprit** of a sailing vessel to spread the stays that counteract the upward pull of the rigging. Its name comes from the fact that it would hit a dolphin if one were to leap out of the water below the bowsprit.

Dominion Monarch, splendid 27,155-gross-ton motor **liner** completed in 1939 for the Shaw Savill Line's run from England to New Zealand. Taken up for duty in World War II and returned to passenger operation in 1948, she was retired from service in 1962 and, after

serving for six months as a hotel ship at the Seattle World's Fair, was sold later in the year for scrap.

Donald Duck, quick-tempered Walt Disney cartoon character and one of America's best-loved sailors. Although always dressed in a sailor's blouse and hat, he has never worn pants. The animated duck first appeared in print and on film in 1934.

Donaldson Line, Scottish shipping company started in 1858 to maintain North Atlantic operation to Canada. In 1916 the passenger service was financially allied with the **Cunard**-owned **Anchor Line** to form the Anchor-Donaldson Line. With a corporate reorganization in 1935, Donaldson again became an independent concern and was then known as the Donaldson Atlantic Line. Its SS *Athenia* was the first merchant ship to be sunk in World War II. The company ceased passenger services altogether in 1967.

Doña Paz, Philippine passenger ferry that collided with the Philippine coastal tanker *Vector* in the Sibuyan Sea on December 20, 1987. Both vessels sank, taking with them nearly 4,400 passengers and crew members—the largest-ever peacetime loss of life at sea.

Dönitz, Karl (1891–1980), German admiral who commanded the German navy's **U-boat** force from 1939 to 1943. He devised the "wolf pack" strategy that proved so destructive to Allied shipping. He succeeded Admiral **Erich Raeder** as commander-in-chief of the navy in January 1943 and was later nominated by Adolf Hitler to be his successor. As leader of the Third Reich, Dönitz negotiated its surrender. He was tried at Nuremberg in 1946 and sentenced to ten years' imprisonment.

"Don't give up the ship", dying plea of Captain **James Lawrence** after being mortally wounded in an engagement between his ship, the U.S. **frigate** *Chesapeake*, and HMS *Shannon*, on

June 1, 1813, in the **War of 1812**. The phrase was later used as the battle flag motto for Commodore **Oliver Hazard Perry** at the Battle of **Lake Erie**.

Don't Give Up the Ship, 1959 feature comedy film about a madcap officer aboard a U.S. **destroyer** who manages to misplace the ship during decommissioning. Jerry Lewis pulled out all the gags he is famous for and then some. It also starred Dina Merrill, Claude Atkins, and Gale Gordon.

Don't Go Near the Water, hilarious 1956 novel by **William Brinkley** about a group of publicity men who get drafted into the U.S. **Navy** and wind up in the Pacific in World War II. The 1957 film version starred Glenn Ford, Gia Scala, and Eva Gabor.

Donzi, speedboat manufacturer established in Miami, Florida, in 1965 by **Donald Aronow**. The company's name came from a critique that Aronow's previous boat had been built with a less-than-macho interior and was called a "Donsy."

Doolittle, James Harold (1896–1958), U.S. Army Air Force lieutenant colonel who led the **Doolittle Raid on Tokyo** and other Japanese targets on April 18, 1942. Doolittle was awarded the **Medal of Honor**. He later served tours in North Africa, Europe, and again in the Pacific.

Doolittle Raid on Tokyo, an attack by B-25 bombers on the Japanese capital from the carrier USS *Hornet*, which was led by Lieutenant Colonel **James Harold Doolittle** on April 18, 1942. Sixteen B-25 bombers successfully struck targets in Kobe, Nagoya, Tokyo, and Yokohama before flying on to airfields in China. It was a major psychological victory for U.S. forces, proving that the "Land of the Rising Sun" was not immune to attack.

Dorade, fifty-two-foot **yawl** designed by **Olin James Stephens II** for his father and built in 1929 at **City Island**, New York. In 1931 the racer-cruiser, sailed by Olin and his brother, **Roderick Stephens Jr.**, went on to win the **Transatlantic Race** as well as the **Fastnet Race**. She returned to New York, where her crew was received with a ticker-tape parade. *Dorade* went on to win an additional Fastnet Race, a **Bermuda Race**, and many others. She has been sold a handful of times and continues to sail the West Coast of the United States.

Dorade ventilator, type of ventilator that employs a box fixed to the deck that allows fresh air to enter but effectively traps and releases water. It was first used aboard the yacht *Dorade*.

USS *Dorchester*, U.S. troopship that was torpedoed in **convoy** in the North Atlantic off the coast of Greenland on February 3, 1943. Of the 904 men aboard, 605 were lost, including the **Four Chaplains**, who gave away their life jackets and remained aboard the sinking ship to comfort the injured.

Doré, Gustave (1833–1883), French artist and illustrator who was skilled at carrying the imagination into unknown depths of suffering. In addition to Dante's *Inferno* and Milton's *Paradise Lost*, his powerful illustrations accompanied **Samuel Taylor Coleridge**'s "The **Rime of the Ancient Mariner**."

Dorothy Alexander, coastal **liner** built in 1907 for the Pacific Coast Steamship Company. After wartime operation by the **Matson Line**, she was sold to the Admiral Line in 1922 and renamed after the wife of the company's owner. She pioneered the West Coast version of the weekend "booze cruise," which transported liquor-starved Prohibition-era passengers from Los Angeles to Ensenada, Mexico, for serious drinking south of the border. She was eventually scrapped in 1952 after further varied services.

doubling a cape, the act of sailing around or passing beyond a cape or promontory.

doubloon, Spanish and Spanish-American gold coin, weighing slightly less than an ounce, that was widely used in America until the 1800s. The name comes from the Latin *duplus*, which means "double."

Dove, 1972 adventure narrative by **Robin Lee Graham** about his five-year circumnavigation of the globe. Graham returned home to California in 1970, married and with a daughter, and became the youngest person to solo sail around the world. Named for his twenty-four-foot sloop, the story was first serialized in *National Geographic*. The 1974 film of the same name starred Joseph Bottoms.

Strait of Dover, body of water separating Great Britain and France and connecting the English Channel with the North Sea. It was the site of the defeat of the **Spanish Armada** and is today the world's busiest shipping sea lane.

"Dover Beach", classic Victorian poem by English poet Matthew Arnold (1822–1888), which was written during his honeymoon to the European continent and published in 1867. It begins, "The sea is calm tonight. / The tide is full, the moon lies fair."

Down East, sailors' term for Maine because the prevailing southwesterly winds blew sailing ships leaving Boston downwind to the east.

Down Easter, merchant **square-rigger** that combined a large carrying capacity with a sharp hull design. This type of ship was built in Maine for the California grain trade following the Civil War.

Downes, John (1784–1854), U.S. **Navy** officer who distinguished himself in the **Barbary Wars**. He served with **David Porter** on board USS *Essex* during the **War of 1812** and commanded the *Essex Junior* in 1814 when the two ships raided British shipping in the Pacific Ocean.

Down Periscope, 1995 motion picture comedy dealing with the 1990s return to sea of the fictitious World War II vintage submarine USS *Stingray* and the crew of misfits selected to take her out on maneuvers. The 20th Century Fox film starred Kelsey Grammer, Lauren Holly, and Bruce Dern. USS *Pampanito* was used to portray *Stingray*. The film included outstanding shots of the U.S. reserve lay-up fleet in Benicia, California, as well as of USS *Pampanito* underway.

Down to the Sea in Ships, 1922 silent adventure film about a female stowaway aboard a nineteenth-century Massachusetts whaleship. The drama was Clara Bow's movie debut and also starred the **Charles W. Morgan**.

Down to the Sea in Ships, classic 1949 motion picture about an old captain and the journey he makes with his grandson aboard his whaleship. Atmospherically filmed, it starred Lionel Barrymore, Richard Widmark, and Dean Stockwell.

Drake, Sir Francis (1540–1596), English mariner, adventurer, and **privateer** who achieved fame by raiding Spanish shipping and colonies in Europe and the Caribbean. After viewing the Pacific Ocean from the Panamanian Isthmus, he sold Queen Elizabeth I on a plan to sail around the world and disrupt Spanish control on the west coast of South America. Aboard the **Golden Hind**, he was the second captain, and the first Englishman, to sail around the world (1577–80), resulting in his being knighted by the queen. He was second in command of the fleet that defeated the **Spanish Armada** in 1588, gaining worldwide fame by defying the world's most powerful empire. He died at sea while raiding Spanish Caribbean settlements. Legend says he will return to defend England in any future emergency, a legend widely repeated during World War II, when England stood alone against Nazi-dominated Europe.

dreadnought, general term for the class of battleship built by all navies following the launch of HMS *Dreadnought* in Britain in 1906. Previous battleships had carried a combination of light, medium, and heavy guns. The 526-foot prototype HMS *Dreadnought* carried ten twelve-inch guns in five turrets, which made control of long-range firing easier. With an eleven-inch belt of armor for protection and with steam turbines capable of twenty-one **knots**, it remained the basis of battleship design. HMS *Dreadnought* was scrapped in 1923, having given her name to a class of ship, the heavy battleship of the twentieth century.

Dreyfuss, Henry (1904–1972), popular American industrial designer who was given a free hand in 1938 with the New York Central Railroad's *20th Century Limited*. The understated streamlined elegance of the train's design showed inside and out, and the train was noted for its cool tones, its modern styling, and even its own signature crockery designed by Dreyfuss. He was hired by **American Export Lines** to provide similar design coordination for their outstanding passenger **liners** *Independence* and *Constitution* of 1951.

driftnet, type of **gillnet**, suspended by floats and weighted by a foot rope, that is employed on or near the surface. These nets have caused considerable controversy because of their effectiveness in capturing all species. Modern synthetic fibers allow these nets to be thin, nearly invisible, and tens of miles long—they are called "curtains of death." The United Nations has called for a worldwide ban on the use of driftnets longer than two and a half kilometers.

USS *Drum* (SS-228), Gato-class submarine completed in 1941. The 312-foot vessel was responsible for the destruction of 80,580 tons of Japanese shipping during World War II, for which she was decorated with twelve battle stars. The submarine was decommissioned in 1969 and taken to Battleship Memorial Park on Mobile Bay, Alabama, to become a museum ship alongside USS *Alabama*.

"The Drunken Sailor", traditional heaving **chantey** that poses the question "What shall we do with a drunken sailor?" Some of the answers include "put him in a longboat 'til he's sober"; "pull out the bung and wet him over"; and "tie him to the taffrail when she's yard-arm under."

DUKW, nicknamed "Duck," an American six-wheeled amphibious truck developed by **Sparkman & Stephens** and used during World War II. DUKWs carried men and supplies from transport ships to shore and were first used in the **Sicily Invasion** in July 1943. They later played a vital part in almost every amphibious operation performed by Allied troops.

Dulcibella, **cutter** sailed by Davies and Carruthers around the North Sea in **Robert Erskine Childers**'s nautical thriller *The Riddle of the Sands* (1906).

Dunkirk, French seaport village that in World War II was the site of the largest naval evacuation in history. In May 1940 Germany had won control of Belgium, forcing thousands of English, French, and Belgian troops to retreat to Dunkirk. From May 26 to June 4, 1940, some eight hundred vessels of all sorts—**cruisers**, **destroyers**, gunboats, minesweepers, fishing boats, motorboats, and yachts—ferried some 337,100 Allied troops from the beaches of Dunkirk to England. The evacuation ranks as one of the most dramatic military movements in history and is often called the "Miracle of Dunkirk."

dunnage, loose wood or other material used in a ship's hold for the protection of cargo.

Dunraven, Earl of (1841–1926), wealthy English lord and yacht racing enthusiast who twice challenged for the **America's Cup**. In 1892 Lord Dunraven ordered a new yacht to replace his *Valkyrie* and then issued a challenge through the **Royal Yacht Squadron** for the

Cup. In 1893 Dunraven's *Valkyrie II* was defeated by the American defender, *Vigilant*. *Valkyrie II*, with Lord Dunraven at the helm, sank a year later when rammed in a yachting contest in Scotland. The 1895 America's Cup contest, which saw Dunraven's *Valkyrie III* defeated by *Defender*, was marked by the **Dunraven Affair.**

Dunraven Affair, controversial **America's Cup** incident that created ill feeling between American and British yachtsmen. During the second race of the 1895 contest, the Earl of **Dunraven**'s *Valkyrie III* bumped the American boat *Defender* and was disqualified. Dunraven blamed the incident on a fleet of spectator craft and wanted the races moved to less crowded waters. His request went unheeded, and he withdrew in the third race, giving the cup to *Defender*.

Dutch East India Company (Verenigde Osst Indische Compagnie, or VOC), Amsterdam-based company founded in 1602 that specialized in the lucrative deep-water trade to Asia. In 1609 the company started shipping tea to Europe from China and in 1619 established a colony in **Batavia**, marking the beginnings of the Dutch Empire in the **East Indies**. It was the first modern "public company" established for the purpose of expanding trade in Asia. The VOC—then the largest private company in the world—closed due to bankruptcy in 1799 when France invaded Holland.

Dutchman's log, buoyant object thrown overboard at the bow to determine the speed of a vessel. Knowing the vessel's length and time required for the object to travel that length will yield an approximate speed.

Dutch West India Company, company of Dutch merchants chartered by the government of the Netherlands in 1621 and given trading and colonizing privileges in the Americas, the **West Indies**, and West Africa. At its height, the company controlled some eight hundred ships. It founded the colony of New Netherland, which included parts of what are now the U.S. states of New York, New Jersey, Delaware, and Connecticut.

dwt, see **deadweight tonnage.**

ε

Eads, James B. (1820–1887), American engineer who pioneered **steamboat salvage** efforts on the **Mississippi River** and designed and built **ironclad** warships used in the Civil War. He was also responsible for the design and construction of the steel-arch Eads Bridge, a railroad bridge at Saint Louis that was completed in 1874 and was viewed as a marvel of its time.

USCGC *Eagle*, U.S. **Coast Guard cutter** acquired from Germany after World War II as part of war reparations. The 295-foot sailing ship has been the U.S. **Coast Guard Academy**'s training ship since 1946, teaching cadets basic seamanship. Built by **Blohm & Voss** in Hamburg, Germany, in 1936, the three-masted **bark** was christened *Horst Wessel* for an early leader of the Nazi Party. *Eagle*'s sister ships include the Ukraine's ***Tovarisch***, Portugal's ***Sagres II***, and Romania's *Mircea*. Germany's *Gorch Foch II* was built in 1958 on the same lines as *Eagle*.

Eagle Boat, two-hundred-foot, steel-hulled patrol vessel of simple design built by the Ford Motor Company during World War I. Henry Ford was awarded a contract to construct 112 boats, but only 9 were launched and 2 commissioned prior to the Armistice on November 11, 1918. After the war the contract was reduced to 60 boats. The Eagle's flat plate design, while facilitating construction, resulted in a hull form that was unkind in rough seas. The name is attributed to a *Washington Post* editorial that called for the construction of "an eagle to scour the seas" and destroy every German submarine.

Eakins, Thomas (1844–1916), Philadelphia-based American artist who painted portraits and many scenes of outdoor life and such sporting events as swimming and rowing. Among his famous outdoor paintings is *Max Schmitt in a Single Scull* (1871), which hangs in New York's Metropolitan Museum of Art.

East China Sea, Battle of, last stand of the Imperial Japanese Navy in World War II. The April 7, 1945, encounter with the U.S. **Navy** resulted in the loss of the battleship *Yamato*, which carried 2,498 crew members to the bottom with her. Five other Japanese **capital ships** were sunk by the U.S. task force.

Easter Island, remote forty-seven-square-mile island in the South Pacific Ocean, twenty-three hundred miles west of Chile, which is famous as the site of enormous statues of unknown origin. Scientists believe that Easter Island was settled about A.D. 400, but they are not sure who the first inhabitants were. Dutch explorer Jacob Roggeveen was the first European to see Easter Island, and he gave the island its name because he discovered it on Easter Sunday 1722. Since 1888, Easter Island has been governed by Chile.

Eastern Solomons, Battle of the, inconclusive World War II naval engagement in which a Japanese troop **convoy** was turned back and prevented from landing major reinforcements at **Guadalcanal**. The August 23–24, 1942, sortie cost the Japanese an aircraft carrier, a troop transport, and many aircrews.

East India Company, large and powerful English trading organization incorporated by Elizabeth I in 1600 to trade with India, the **East Indies**, and the Far East. It had a monopoly on trade in the region and was eventually given the right to acquire territory, make treaties, and wage war.

East Indiamen, name applied to large British passenger-cargo ships that traded with the **East Indies**, which included the India subcontinent, and the islands off Southeast Asia, including Borneo, Celebes, Java, and Sumatra.

East Indies, the islands of the Malay Archipelago and parts of southeastern Asia. Today it includes the Republic of Indonesia, formerly the Netherlands Indies. The term "Indies" was first used in the 1400s to describe the group (because of their proximity to India). When **Christopher Columbus** thought he was finding a short route to the rich Indies when he landed in America, he also called the islands the Indies. Later, these islands were named the **West Indies**, and the Pacific islands were called the East Indies, in order to distinguish the two groups.

Eastland, **Great Lakes** excursion steamer built in 1903 for the Eastland Navigation Company. While preparing to cast off from her Chicago pier on July 24, 1915, with 2,500 passengers aboard for a Western Electric company picnic to Michigan City, Indiana, the *Eastland* heeled over onto her port side and capsized into the twenty-one-foot-deep **Chicago River**, taking the lives of 841 people. She was later raised and refitted as a Great Lakes naval training vessel and was finally scrapped in 1947.

ebb tide, a falling tide.

E-boat, World War II term for the German motor torpedo boat, or *schnellboat*. The 106-foot vessels carried two torpedo tubes and antiaircraft guns and were capable of making nearly forty **knots**.

ECDIS, Electronic Chart Display Information System, a nautical chart displayed on a screen that is the legal equivalent of a paper chart.

economy class, American term coined in the post–World War II era describing shipboard accommodations that would have been called **third class** before the war. This class designation was prominently featured aboard the *President Cleveland* and *President Wilson* when their emigrant quarters were updated in the 1950s after Chinese immigration was curtailed.

Eddystone Light, 135-foot-high lighthouse completed in 1882 that sits on dangerous rocks in the English Channel. Probably the world's most famous lighthouse, it is the fourth light on the site. The first lighthouse was destroyed in a storm in 1703, and a replacement was completed in 1708 but was destroyed by fire in 1755. The third was dismantled in 1877 because the rock it stood on was crumbling. The Eddystone Light is the subject of a popular folk song, "The Keeper of the Eddystone Light," which begins, "Me father was the keeper of Eddystone Light, And slept with a mermaid one fine night, From this union there came three; A porpoise and a porgy and the other was me!"

HMS *Edinburgh*, British **cruiser** that was torpedoed by a German **U-boat** in the **Barents Sea** in 1942, after receiving heavy damage while fighting German surface vessels. In 1981, British divers retrieved about 4.5 metric tons of gold bars from the *Edinburgh*, the greatest amount of salvage that was ever recovered from a sunken ship.

Edmund Fitzgerald, 13,623-gross-ton American straight deck bulk carrier built in 1958. While en route from Superior, Wisconsin, to Detroit, Michigan, on November 10, 1975, with a load of iron ore, the Columbia Transportation steamer disappeared sometime after 7:10 P.M., with all twenty-nine hands, during the height of a howling storm on Lake Superior. Earlier in the evening, she had reported some damage from the sixteen-foot seas driven by winds over fifty **knots**. Memorialized in Gordon Lightfoot's ballad "The **Wreck of the Edmund Fitzgerald**," the tragedy has now attained prominence in American folk history.

EEZ, see **exclusive economic zone**.

Egypt, **P&O** passenger **liner**, built in 1897, that sank quickly when rammed by the French icebreaker *Seine* in fog off the coast of France in 1922. Along with eighty-six passengers and crew, eight tons of gold ingots and coins and forty-three tons of silver, valued at more than £1,000,000, went down with the ship. Most of the treasure was salvaged—at a depth of four hundred feet—by 1934.

Eight Bells, oil painting by **Winslow Homer**, showing two mariners clad in oilskins determining **latitude** by the noon sun. One of the men is thought to be Homer's father. Painted in 1886, the original oil hangs in the Addison Gallery of American Art on the campus of Phillips Academy at Andover, Massachusetts.

Elba, Italian island in the Tyrrhenian Sea off the northwest coast of Italy. In April 1814, after

Eight Bells, circa 1886, by Winslow Homer. (Courtesy Addison Gallery, Phillips Academy, Andover, Massachusetts)

abdicating the imperial throne, **Napoleon I** was exiled from France and made ruler of the island. On Elba, Napoleon planned his return to France, and in February 1815, he sailed from the island with eleven hundred followers who had shared his exile. They marched to Paris, gathering supporters along the way, and Napoleon again crowned himself emperor.

Elcano, Juan Sebastián de (c. 1476–1526), Spanish navigator who was the first to circumnavigate the globe in one voyage. He commanded *Concepción*, one of the five vessels in **Ferdinand Magellan**'s voyage of discovery, and assumed control of the expedition in 1521 after Magellan's death. Elcano returned to Spain in 1522 aboard *Victoria*, the only ship of the five to complete the entire voyage.

Elco, the Electric Launch and Navigation Company, later the Electric Launch Company (Elco), which began building electric launches in the 1890s and in the next sixty years designed and built more than six thousand powerboats. Elco built nearly five hundred sub-chasing boats during World War I for the British and four hundred **PT boats** for the United States and the Allies during World War II. Based in Bayonne, New Jersey, it became a division of **Electric Boat**, and later **General Dynamics**, and eventually wound down its operations.

Electric Boat (EB), world's largest builder of submarines, which is located in Groton, Connecticut. The company was founded in 1899 to bring to completion the fifty-four-foot submersible developed by **John Philip Holland**. A year later, the submarine USS *Holland* was accepted by the U.S. **Navy**. EB built eighty-five submarines during World War I and seventy-four during World War II. The EB subsidiary **Elco**, located at Bayonne, New Jersey, also constructed submarine chasers and **PT boats**. In 1951 Electric Boat built USS *Nautilus* as well as nearly every other significant submarine since. In 1952 it became a subsidiary of **General Dynamics**.

Electronic Chart Display Information System, see **ECDIS**.

Elephant Island, twenty-four-mile-long, mountainous, ice-covered island in the South Shetlands in the South Atlantic Ocean. It was here that the **Shackleton Expedition** landed after their ship *Endurance* became trapped in the ice of the Weddell Sea and sank.

Elissa, three-masted, iron-hulled **bark** built in 1877 for British owners. She was discovered in the 1960s by archaeologist Peter Throckmorton serving as a motor ship in the Mediterranean. Throckmorton succeeded in securing the vessel, and following a fifteen-year campaign by the **National Maritime Historical Society**, she was purchased in 1975 by the Galveston Historical Foundation. One of the last **square-riggers** in existence, *Elissa* was restored to sailing condition and found a permanent home at the Texas Seaport Museum in Galveston. She was named a national historic landmark in 1991.

Ellis Island, federal immigration depot in New York Harbor that opened in 1892 and closed sixty-two years later, processing a total of twelve million immigrants. Now part of the Statue of Liberty National Monument, the island was opened to tourists in 1976; in 1990 an immigration museum was opened.

Ellsberg, Edward (1891–1983), U.S. **Navy** admiral, renowned diving and salvage expert, and author. He served in World War I and later pioneered the salvage of U.S. submarines, including **S-51**. He returned to active duty in World War II and played a key role in supporting Allied forces in the Middle East and for the invasion of **Normandy** in 1944. His books include *On the Bottom* (1929), *Hell on Ice* (1938), *Captain Paul* (1941), *Under the Red Sea Sun* (1946), and *Cruise of the Jeanette* (1949).

Ellsworth, Lincoln (1880–1951), American civil engineer and polar explorer who was the first person to fly over the North and South Poles. He explored regions of the Arctic Ocean and Antarctic, claiming territory for the United States. He financed the Norwegian explorer **Roald Amundsen**, who in 1911 became the first person to reach the South Pole. Ellsworth's books include *Search* (1932) and *Beyond Horizons* (1938), and Antarctica's Ellsworth Land and Ellsworth Mountains are named after him.

Embargo Act, law passed by Congress in 1807 that prohibited all ships from entering or leaving American ports. The act was passed to put pressure mainly on Great Britain and France during the **Napoleonic Wars**. The act kept belligerents from capturing neutral American traders and the British from impressing American sailors, but it reduced the large profits to be gained by foreign trade. In 1809, Congress passed the **Non-Intercourse Act**, which canceled the embargo for all nations except Great Britain and France.

SMS *Emden*, German light **cruiser**, launched in 1908, that achieved worldwide notoriety for its attacks on British and Allied shipping and seaports in World War I. *Emden* was driven ashore in the Indian Ocean by the Australian cruiser HMAS *Sydney* in November 1914 and destroyed.

Emergency Fleet Corporation (EFC), subsidiary of the U.S. **Shipping Board** that was created in 1917 and empowered to undertake a huge shipbuilding program for merchant ships. The EFC built three new yards, which employed modern methods of standard-assembly construction. The most famous of the yards, and the largest shipyard in U.S. history, was the American International Shipbuilding Corporation Plant at **Hog Island**, Pennsylvania. Although only 113 ships were delivered prior to the Armistice on November 11, 1918, a total of 2,382 ships were delivered up to 1921. In 1927 EFC was renamed the Merchant Fleet Corporation and later was abolished by the **Merchant Marine Act of 1936**.

emergency position-indicating radio beacon, see **EPIRB**.

Empress Augusta Bay, Battle of, World War II naval engagement between U.S. and Japanese forces off Bougainville in the Solomon Islands of the Pacific Ocean on November 2, 1943. The Japanese lost one **cruiser** and one **destroyer**, while the rest of the squadron was reduced to shambles. The USS *Foote* was the only U.S. vessel to sustain any damage out of a force of twelve ships.

Empress of Britain, finest **liner** ever built for the **Canadian Pacific Line**. Completed in 1931, the 42,348-gross-ton beauty was intended to cross the **Atlantic** in season and to spend the winter months cruising around the world, a concept copied by the **Cunard Line** in 1949

for their ***Caronia*** and again in 1968 for the ***Queen Elizabeth 2***. Taken over by the **Admiralty** for troopship duty in World War II, *Empress of Britain* was attacked by a German bomber seventy miles northwest of Ireland, resulting in the loss of forty-nine lives. The burning liner was torpedoed by a **U-boat** two days later, and she sank on October 28, 1940.

Empress of Canada, final transatlantic **liner** constructed for the **Canadian Pacific Line** in 1961. The 27,284-gross-ton vessel was sold in 1972 to Arison Shipping, who renamed her ***Mardi Gras*** to launch **Carnival Cruise Lines**.

Empress of China, 104-foot **ship** built in 1783 that was the first U.S.-flag ship to sail to China. She left New York in February 1784 with a cargo of ginseng, silver, wine, and brandy, and she reached **Canton** in August 1784. The *Empress of China* is credited with opening the American **China trade**.

Empress of Ireland, **Canadian Pacific Line** transatlantic passenger steamer engaged in the Liverpool to Québec service. The 570-foot **liner** was carrying 1,477 passengers and crew when it was rammed in the Saint Lawrence River in Canada on May 30, 1914, by the Norwegian **collier** *Storstad*. The *Empress of Ireland* sank in minutes, with the loss of 1,078 lives. The *Storstad* was slightly damaged and was found by a court of inquiry to be entirely to blame for one of the worst maritime disasters ever.

HMS *Endeavour*, **bark** used by Captain **James Cook** on his first voyage of exploration in the **South Seas** (1768–71). The one-hundred-foot **ship** with a crew of thirty-four charted and explored the east coasts of Australia and New Zealand.

HMS *Endeavour*, Charles E. Nicholson–designed **J-boat** owned by British aviation pioneer Sir **Thomas Octave Murdoch "T.O.M." Sopwith** that challenged for the **America's**

Cup in 1934. She was defeated by **Harold Stirling "Mike" Vanderbilt**'s *Rainbow*, four races to two. *Endeavour* was judged to be the better boat, but clever tactics on the part of *Rainbow*'s crew and bungling on the part of Sopwith made the difference.

Endeavour II, Sir **Thomas Octave Murdoch "T.O.M." Sopwith**'s second challenger for the **America's Cup**, designed by **Charles E. Nicholson**. In 1937 the 136-foot **sloop** proved no match for **Harold Stirling "Mike" Vanderbilt**'s *Ranger*, losing in four straight races. *Endeavour II* was restored by Elizabeth Meyer in the 1980s and sails out of Newport, Rhode Island, today.

Endless Summer, classic 1966 surf documentary in which director Bruce Brown follows two young surfers around the world in search of the perfect wave.

Endurance, author Alfred Lansing's 1959 account of Sir **Ernest Shackleton**'s 1914 expedition to cross Antarctica that failed when their ship, *Endurance*, was wrecked in the ice. The narrative tells how they survived after a thousand-mile voyage in an open boat and an overland trek through glaciers and mountains.

HMS *Endurance*, 144-foot, three-masted, coal-burning **ship** that in 1914 left Great Britain carrying the **Shackleton Expedition**. The three-hundred-ton wooden **barkentine** became icebound and eventually sank in the Weddell Sea, twelve hundred miles from the fringes of civilization, stranding explorer Ernest Shackleton and his men. Schackleton saved his crew by an epic voyage through mountainous seas to South Georgia in one of the ship's boats. He named the Norwegian-built ship after his family motto: "By Endurance We Conquer."

The Enemy Below, suspenseful 1957 World War II drama detailing the duel between the fictitious American **destroyer** USS *Haynes* and a German **U-boat** in the South Atlantic. Directed by Dick Powell, the movie starred Robert Mitchum, David Hedison, and Theodore Bikel.

engine order telegraph (EOT), communications device, also called an "annunciator," that for many years connected the bridge of a ship to the engine room. Engine orders, or bells, were "rung up" and sent to the engine room watch standers, where they were carried out and confirmed. In recent years, the bridge watch has had direct control of a ship's propulsion equipment.

England, Edward (c. 1724), prolific British pirate known for his successful high-seas raids in the Caribbean, Atlantic, and Indian Oceans. After a bad run of luck—including being deserted by his crew—he died penniless.

Enigma, cipher machine developed by the German navy in World War II to encrypt the text of radio messages. In one of the great Allied triumphs of the war, British and American cryptoanalysts solved the Enigma system and broke the code. In this success, they were greatly helped by Polish patriots who smuggled over an early version of the machine.

enrollment, enlistment of a vessel in the coastwise trade. A commercial vessel is enrolled in the coastwise or domestic trade or is registered in the foreign trade.

Ensign O'Toole, American television comedy series that ran from 1962 to 1963 and was contemporarily set aboard a fictitious **Fletcher**-class **destroyer** named USS *Appleby*. The series, which gave a good—albeit highly romanticized—idea of life aboard a navy destroyer, starred Dean Jones, Jay C. Flippen, Jack Albertson, and Beau Bridges.

Ensign Pulver, 1964 sequel to *Mister Roberts* that details the further exploits of USS *Reluctant* and her crew during the closing days of World War II in the Pacific. It portrays American sailors trying their best to overcome hormone overload and boredom, both forced

Painting of USS *Enterprise* (CVAN-65), by Jim Griffiths. (Courtesy J. Russell Jinishian Gallery, Fairfield, Connecticut)

upon them by the war. The film starred Robert Walker Jr., Burl Ives, and Walter Matthau.

Enterprise, American **steamboat** that in 1815 made a round-trip between Pittsburgh and New Orleans, the first upstream travel on the **Mississippi River** system as far as Louisville, Kentucky. The *New Orleans* had made trips upstream to Natchez, Mississippi, as early as 1812.

Enterprise, **America's Cup** defender in 1930 that cost owner **Harold Stirling "Mike" Vanderbilt** $1 million. The **J-boat** was the dream yacht of designer **W. Starling Burgess**, a leading aeronautical engineer, and was one of the most innovative yachts that had ever been built. Her features included a weight-saving duralumin mast and special web frames, and her winches were below decks. Her "Park Avenue" boom, which was so large and flat that crew members could walk its length, allowed a curve to be put into the foot of the mainsail, thus achieving a more aerodynamic

shape. *Enterprise* defeated Sir **Thomas Lipton**'s *Shamrock V*, four races to none.

USS *Enterprise* (CV-6), **Yorktown**-class aircraft carrier completed in 1938. She was en route to Honolulu from **Wake Island** when the Japanese carried out their attack on **Pearl Harbor**. The ship saw intensive action at the Battle of the **Philippine Sea**, the **Okinawa Invasion**, and **Iwo Jima**. With twenty battle stars, she was the most decorated warship of World War II. Decommissioned in 1947, she was sold for scrap in 1958.

USS *Enterprise* (CVAN-65), the first nuclear-powered aircraft carrier, which was completed in 1961. The 93,384-ton vessel's eight Westinghouse reactors provide steam to drive the 280,000-horsepower quadruple screw craft along at well over thirty **knots**. In 1969 an explosion on the flight deck from a Zuni rocket left twenty-seven crew members dead and eighty-two injured while also destroying fifteen airplanes. When she was constructed, the expected life span of the 1,123-foot "Big E" was estimated to be forty years. She is scheduled to be decommissioned in 2013 (which will have been fifty-two years in continuous service) and replaced by the CVN-78, an as-yet-unnamed eighth aircraft carrier of the nuclear **Theodore Roosevelt** class.

EPIRB, emergency position-indicating radio beacon, a portable radio beacon carried by vessels and aircraft that when activated, by hand or automatically, transmits radio signals to be used by search and rescue authorities.

Epirotiki Lines, once-prolific Greek operator of smaller cruise ships that began passenger operation in 1955 with inter–Greek Island sailings of the *Semiramis*. The company's ships were traditionally named after classic Hellenic mythological figures. Their *Neptune* sank after collision in 1988, the *Pegasus* was lost to fire in 1991, and the *Oceanos* sank with irreparable results later that year. The *Pallas Athena* (once the *Princess Carla*) caught fire in 1994 and was completely destroyed, shortly after the ailing company came under the financial umbrella of **Carnival Cruise Lines**.

Erebus, lead **ship** in the ill-fated **Franklin Expedition** of 1845 in search of a **Northwest Passage**. For three years the two sister ships *Erebus* and *Terror* were trapped in the Arctic ice at King William Island in Victoria Strait. The crew eventually abandoned the ships they believed were hopelessly ice-locked and attempted to travel south by foot. All 135 men perished. Previously the ships *Erebus* and *Terror* were used by **James Clark Ross** on his 1839–43 voyage to Antarctica.

Ericsson, John (1803–1889), Swedish-born American engineer whose accomplishments included introducing screw propellers for use in place of paddle wheels on **ships**. In 1833, he began experimenting with screw propellers, and in 1837 he built the first propeller-driven commercial ship. Ericsson came to the United States in 1839 and became a citizen in 1848. He designed a number of vessels, including USS **Princeton**, the first propeller-driven warship. He won fame for his design and construction of USS **Monitor** in 1862, one of the earliest **ironclad** warships, and which also had the first revolving gun turret.

Eriksson, Leif (ca. 999), Norse explorer, son of **Erik the Red**, who visited Norway, was converted, and then introduced Christianity to Greenland. Many scholars believe that Eriksson landed on some part of North America, an area he called **Vinland**. A settlement on Newfoundland's north shore has been identified as his.

Erie Canal, the first great U.S. canal, an engineering marvel that cut a 325-mile artificial river across New York State from Albany to Buffalo. Construction began in 1817, and the canal opened in 1825, making it possible to travel from the **Hudson River** to the **Great Lakes**, a linkage that spurred westward trade and migration as well as the development of midwestern cities. Shortly after the canal's opening, cities like Syracuse sprung up along its route. It is often referred to as "Clinton's Ditch," in honor of New York governor **De Witt Clinton**, who originated the scheme.

Erik the Red (c. 950–1010), Norse explorer who discovered Greenland. He brought colonists from Iceland to establish permanent settlements—having given Greenland its attractive name to encourage settlers. His son was **Leif Eriksson**.

escutcheon, board fixed to a vessel's stern that is ornamented with her name and **hailing port**.

Esmeralda, 371-foot Chilean sail training vessel that is the longest **tall ship** in the world. The four-masted **barkentine**, built in Spain in 1952 from a design by **Camper & Nicholson**, is the near sister ship to Spain's tall ship **Juan Sebastián de Elcano**. Controversy follows *Esmeralda* because reports circulated that the ship was used as a prison ship for political prisoners during the rule (1973–88) of General Augusto Pinochet.

Essex, Nantucket whaleship that was stove in and sunk by a sperm whale in 1820 in the Pacific Ocean. Her twenty crewmen took to three small open boats and drifted for three months. Having run out of food, they finally resorted to cannibalism, and when the final eight survivors were rescued, they were said to be still sucking on the bones of their shipmates. The incident, written in **Owen Chase**'s *Narrative of the Most Extraordinary and Distressing Shipwreck of the Whaleship Essex of Nantucket* (1821), influenced **Herman Melville** when writing his novel *Moby-Dick; or, The Whale* (1851).

USS Essex, one of the most admired vessels in the U.S. **Navy**. She fought with distinction in the **Barbary Wars**, and in the **War of 1812** under the command of **David Porter** and with a young **David Glasgow Farragut** on board, she rounded **Cape Horn** to be the first U.S. Navy vessel to enter the Pacific Ocean. There she captured twelve British whaling ships in the South Pacific. *Essex* was defeated by the British **frigate** HMS *Phoebe* and the **sloop** HMS *Cherub* in March 1814 at Valparaiso, Chile. The American prisoners were permitted to escape to the United States in *Essex Junior*, a smaller vessel that they had earlier taken as a prize.

USS Essex (CV-9), first of a class of twenty-four aircraft carriers built for World War II. *Essex* was commissioned on the last day of 1942 and saw action throughout the Pacific theater of war, including the Battle of **Leyte Gulf** and the **Okinawa Invasion**. The 872-foot ship survived a devastating typhoon in 1944 and went searching for survivors from less fortunate warships afterward. She also saw action in the Korean conflict. *Essex* was **laid up** in 1969 and sold for scrap in 1973.

Estonia, Estonian **roll on–roll off** car ferry that capsized and sank in heavy weather in the Baltic Sea on September 27, 1994, while en route from Talinn, Estonia, to Stockholm, Sweden. Over nine hundred people went down with the ship.

"Eternal Father, strong to save", see the **Navy Hymn**.

SS Europa, ocean **liner** completed in 1930 for **North German Lloyd**'s North Atlantic service. Sister vessel to the **Bremen**, she won the **Blue Riband** on her **maiden voyage** and held the speed title until 1933, when she lost it to SS **Rex**. *Europa* was used as a German naval accommodations ship in the early part of World War II, and work was begun to adapt her to a massive troop carrier to deploy men for the proposed invasion of Britain. She was seized by U.S. forces in 1945 and served as an Allied troopship until being handed over to France and renamed SS *Liberté* the following year as partial compensation for the destruction of SS *Normandie*.

EUSC, U.S. government acronym used to describe a ship owned by a U.S. citizen or corporation and registered as foreign. It emphasizes that, while not U.S. flagged, the vessel is under "Effective U.S. Control" and can be called to serve U.S. interests in times of emergency.

Euterpe, British **East Indiaman** built in 1863 on the **Isle of Man** for the Great Britain to India trade. The **ship** was transferred to U.S. registry in 1901 and renamed *Star of India*. Today she is the oldest surviving iron-hulled sailing ship in the world and is on display at the San Diego Maritime Museum.

Evans, Robley D. "Bob", U.S. naval officer who commanded the battleship USS *Iowa* at the Battle of **Santiago Bay**. As a rear admiral, he commanded the **Great White Fleet** on its round-the-world cruise from 1907 to 1909.

Evergreen Marine Corporation, Taiwan-based shipping company that is the world's second-largest container carrier (behind **Mærsk**). Established in 1968 by Dr. Yung-fa Chang, Evergreen grew from a **tramp** operator to a **containerized** marine carrier with a young fleet of nearly 120 specially built ships. It is part of the Evergreen Group, Taiwan's leading company, which has diversified holdings around the world.

Evers, Carl (1907–2000), German-born American watercolor artist and illustrator renowned for his precise, lifelike marine paintings. He completed many commissions for the **Cunard Line**, **Grace Line**, **Farrell Lines**, **United Fruit Lines**, and others, as well as many magazine and book covers.

Every, Henry (c. 1665–1697), Bahamian **privateer** and slave trader who was arguably the most successful pirate of all time. He led a six-ship pirate armada in the Red Sea against ships carrying treasure from India in 1694 and captured more than £600,000 of gold, silver, and jewels. He returned to the Bahamas the following year but had a bounty placed on his head by the **British East India Company** for his torture and rape of Indian citizens taken prisoner during the Red Sea raids. He sailed to Ireland in 1695 and thereafter maintained such a low profile that he disappeared from record. He survived to live off his plunder and proved to be an inspiration to other would-be pirates.

Evinrude, engine company founded in 1909 in Milwaukee by **Ole Evinrude** and Bess Evinrude that pioneered the first commercially successful outboard motor. The company was purchased, along with Elto and Lockwood, in 1929 by the engine manufacturing firm Briggs & Stratton to form **OMC** (Outboard Motors Corporation), with Ole Evinrude as president. In 1936, under the leadership of Ralph Evinrude, OMC acquired the **Johnson** outboard

company. OMC then set out to sell engines under both the Evinrude and Johnson nameplates. During World War II, Evinrude manufactured thousands of engines to propel **Higgins boats** and other troop assault ships.

Evinrude, Ole (1877–1934), mechanical genius who, along with his wife, Bess, cofounded the Milwaukee-based **Evinrude** outboard motor company. Supposedly inspired by melted ice cream while picnicking with Bess, who was then his girlfriend, he introduced a two-cycle, one-cylinder, water-cooled, detachable boat engine in 1909; his business soon took off, attracting investors and thousands of orders. Ole sold his interest in the company when Bess fell into ill health in 1913. The couple then founded the Elto outboard motor company in 1920, which was successful but was bought out in 1929. Ole was appointed head of the newly formed **OMC** (Outboard Motors Corporation) and retrieved the Evinrude name. He died in 1934.

exclusive economic zone (EEZ), offshore zone in which exclusive fishing and management rights are held by the coastal nation, however many of the freedoms of the high seas are preserved. In the United States, the EEZ is defined as extending two hundred nautical miles from the baseline from which the **territorial sea** is measured.

Execution Dock, dock at Wapping on the banks of the Thames River in London where criminal sailors and pirates were executed by hanging or by being confined in a cage below the high-tide mark.

Exodus, best-selling 1957 novel by American author Leon Uris (b. 1924) about the founding of Israel in the days following World War II. The novel featured the saga of the *Exodus 1947*. The 1960 movie was directed by Otto Preminger and starred Paul Newman as an Israeli resistance fighter and Eva Marie Saint

The Privateers, by Carl Evers. (Courtesy J. Russell Jinishian Gallery, Fairfield, Connecticut)

as an American nurse. The musical score won an Academy Award.

Exodus 1947, 320-foot passenger steamer built in 1928 as the *President Warfield.* Renamed *Exodus 1947* after World War II, the former **Old Bay Line** ferry was used to transport more than 4,500 Jewish refugees from France to Palestine. British warships stopped *Exodus 1947* and sent the refugees to Hamburg.

Explorers Club, professional society founded in 1905 that promotes the scientific exploration of land, sea, air, and space. Since its inception, the club has served as a meeting point and unifying force for explorers and scientists worldwide. In addition to its headquarters building at 46 East 70th Street in New York City, the club has some thirty regional chapters in the United States and abroad.

ex scientia, tridens, motto of the U.S. **Naval Academy,** adopted in 1898. It is Latin for "sea

power comes from knowledge." See also ***scientae cedit mare.***

Exxon Valdez, very large crude-carrying (**VLCC**) vessel built in 1986. In 1989 the 987-foot supertanker, carrying 1,264,155 barrels of North Slope Alaskan crude oil, grounded on **Bligh Reef** in Prince William Sound, ripping open ten of the fifteen cargo compartments in the ship. In less than eight hours, some 215,000 barrels of crude had been lost into the waters of the sound. The spill, driven by heavy winds, contaminated over 3,190 miles of shoreline and drifted as far as 470 miles from the site of the wreck. The blunder was compounded by the fact that the government and the oil company argued for two weeks over who was going to clean up the mess while the oil seeped farther south, making it the worst spill ever in American waters. She was later renamed *Sea River Mediterranean.*

470, popular international **one-design** sailboat, which is fifteen feet, five inches in length and carries a crew of two. Designed by Andre Cornu and introduced in 1963, it first competed in the Olympics in 1976.

"the face that launched a thousand ships", phrase used by author Christopher Marlowe in his sixteenth-century play *The Tragicall History of D. Faustus* to describe the beauty of **Helen of Troy**.

factory ship, large fishing vessel that has onboard facilities for processing a catch before bringing it to port. These ships usually operate in conjunction with catcher boats.

Fairplay, weekly newsmagazine founded in Great Britain in 1883 by Thomas Hope Robinson, still reporting today on the international shipping industry.

fairway, a navigable channel in a body of water, or a shipping lane established in offshore waters.

Falconer, William (1732–1769), Scottish poet and sailor best known for *A Universal Dictionary of the Marine* (1769), a lexicon of sea terms. He drowned when HMS *Aurora* went down off South Africa with all hands.

Falkland Islands, Battle of the, decisive World War I British naval victory over German forces in the Falkland Islands in the South Atlantic. During the December 8, 1914, engagement, a British force of ten warships destroyed a German squadron of five ships, including the heavy **cruisers** *Gneisenau* and *Scharnhorst*. In all, the Germans lost 2,100 men, including Admiral **Maximilian von Spee**.

Fallingwater, famous house designed by Frank Lloyd Wright (1869–1959) that is located in Bear Run, Pennsylvania. The house is built cantilevered over a waterfall.

Fall River Line, renowned shipping company that provided luxurious overnight passenger service between Boston and New York from 1847 to 1937. Its run went from New York to Fall River, Massachusetts, with a rail connection to Boston. Among the "floating palaces" operated by the company were the steamers *Priscilla*, *Puritan*, *Providence*, and *Plymouth*.

A rendering of the Fall River Line's New York terminal by Steven Cryan. (Cryan Studio, Old Saybrook, Connecticut)

Falls of Clyde, the last iron-hulled, full-rigged, four-masted sailing **ship** in existence. Built in Scotland in 1878, the vessel came under the ownership of the **Matson Line** in 1898 and took up station on the California to Hawai'i passenger and freight service. She later traveled the world as a tanker and a fuel barge. Restored and rerigged to her former glory in the 1960s and 1970s, she is today the centerpiece of the Hawai'i Maritime Center in Honolulu Harbor. Permanently moored at Pier 7, the *Falls of Clyde* rests in the very shadow of the **Aloha Tower**.

Fanning, Edmund (1769–1835), American mariner and merchant who in 1797 sailed from New York around **Cape Horn** for a trading expedition to China and discovered the Line Islands in the central Pacific Ocean. He returned via the **Cape of Good Hope** and two

years later made another circumnavigation of the globe.

Far Tortuga, powerful 1975 novel by **Peter Matthiessen** about a doomed turtle-fishing voyage in the Caribbean aboard the decrepit **schooner** *Lillias Eden*.

Farragut, David Glasgow (1801–1870), U.S. **Navy** admiral who started his naval career at the age of ten as a midshipman aboard the **frigate** USS *Essex*, commanded by his guardian, Captain **David Porter**. In 1854 he established Mare Island Shipyard near San Francisco. Siding with the Union in the Civil War, he was the most outstanding naval commander of the conflict. Aboard his **flagship** USS *Hartford*, he commanded the fleet that captured New Orleans in 1862, and he was the hero of the decisive Battle of **Mobile Bay** on

August 5, 1864, with his famous cry "**Damn the torpedoes! Full speed ahead!**" He was the first officer in the U.S. Navy to receive the ranks of vice admiral and admiral.

Farrell Line, American shipping company formed in 1925 by John and James Farrell as the American South African Line to serve South Africa from eastern U.S. ports. In 1947 the name was changed to the Farrell Line, and service to West Africa was added. In 1978 the New York–based Farrell purchased the ships of **American Export Lines** and expanded its service to the Mediterranean from U.S. North Atlantic ports. Farrell was acquired by **P&O** Nedlloyd in 2000.

Fastnet Race, sailing race first sailed in 1925 and named after the rock off the southwest coast of Ireland called Fastnet Rock. Held biennially by the **Royal Ocean Racing Club**, the race alternates with the **Bermuda Race**. One of the most challenging races in the sport, the competition through the Irish Sea begins at the **Isle of Wight**, rounds Fastnet Rock, and finishes at Plymouth, Devon, for a total of 605 miles. The 1979 Fastnet Race made world headlines when five yachts sank and fifteen sailors died as hurricane-force winds hit the fleet.

fathom, unit of nautical measure equal to six feet. The word derives from the Old English Faethm, which means "embracing arms." A fathom was defined by the British Parliament as "the length of a man's arms around the object of his affections."

"Fear God and dread nought", motto of British admiral **John Arbuthnot "Jackie" Fisher**. Fisher was responsible for building HMS *Dreadnought*, the first modern battleship.

Federal Barge Lines, federally subsidized shipping company established in 1924 to operate on the **Mississippi River** and other rivers. Also known as the **Inland Waterways Corporation**, it—along with the Army Corps of Engineers'

lock and dam system and deepened channels—revitalized shipping on the Mississippi River. The company ceased operations in 1954.

Federal Boating Act of 1910, set of statutes that placed on the federal government the responsibility to regulate recreational boating in the United States. It was the beginning of what would become the U.S. **Coast Guard**'s regulatory responsibilities over pleasure boating in the United States. The Federal Numbering Act of 1918 instituted a numbering system for all undocumented vessels.

Federal Boating Act of 1958, legislation that set forth legal requirements governing most aspects of pleasure boating in U.S. navigable waters. It shifted the responsibility of numbering undocumented vessels from the federal government to the states and amended earlier acts regarding accident procedures and penalties.

Federal Boating Safety Act of 1971, legislation aimed at recreational boating that entrusted states and territories with ensuring minimum registration requirements set by the federal government. Among these requirements are navigation rules, vessel numbering, safety equipment, lights and day shapes, pollution rules, and distress assistance.

Federal Maritime Board (FMB), U.S. government agency created in 1950, along with the U.S. **Maritime Administration**, to replace the U.S. **Maritime Commission**. Set up under the Department of Commerce, it was created to decide all issues affecting government assistance and regulation of ocean transportation. It was succeeded in 1961 by the **Federal Maritime Commission**.

Federal Maritime Commission (FMC), independent agency of the U.S. government responsible for administering ocean shipping affairs, including tariffs, licensing, approving conference or other **carrier** agreements, and enforcing conditions of **Shipping Acts**. The five-member panel was established in 1961 to replace the **Federal Maritime Board**.

felucca, fast Mediterranean sailing vessel used primarily for fishing and coastal trading. It is long and narrow with large **lateen** sails.

"Ferry Boat Serenade", song performed by the Andrews Sisters that hit number 1 on the charts in 1940. It begins, "I have never been aboard a steamer, I am just content to be a dreamer, Even if I could afford a steamer, I will take the ferry boat every time."

Ferry to Hong Kong, classic 1959 sea thriller about the captain of the *Fat Annie*, played by Orson Wells, and a heavy drinking passenger without a passport, played by Curt Jurgens. The two put aside their differences to combat a group of pirates who threaten the lives of the passengers.

FEU, or Forty-foot Equivalent Units, a container shipping size standard of forty feet. Two twenty-foot containers, or **TEU**s, equal one FEU.

FF, U.S. **Navy** designation for a **frigate**, a warship designed to operate independently—or with strike, antisubmarine warfare, or amphibious forces—against submarine, air, and surface threats.

FFG, U.S. **Navy** designation for a **frigate** equipped with guided missiles.

fiddlehead, ornamental timbers at a ship's bow curved in the shape of the head of a violin.

Fiddler's Green, in folklore, a large ship lying on the bottom of the ocean at the equator that is the last home of souls of drowned sailors. It is a happy place filled with music, ale, and tobacco.

Fife, William, Jr. (1821–1902), Scottish boat designer and builder who in 1835 joined the family boatbuilding business in the town of Fairlie on the west coast of Scotland. As his father, William Fife, designed and built workboats, William Jr. turned to yacht design and construction. His designs, fine workmanship, and reliability reinforced the fine reputation of the "Fifes of Fairlie."

Fife, William, III (1857–1944), first-class Scottish yacht designer and builder who expanded his family's firm, the Fifes of Fairlie, and brought it into the modern age with new machinery and construction techniques. He designed **Thomas Lipton**'s *Shamrock I* and *Shamrock III* as well as many other successful racers and cruisers. The Fifes of Fairlie did not survive past World War II, and in 1985 their construction site was demolished to make way for a housing development.

"Fifteen men on the Dead Man's Chest, Yo-ho-ho, and a bottle of rum!", lines from the pirates' song in *Treasure Island* by **Robert Louis Stevenson**. The song continues, "Drink and the devil had done for the rest."

The Fighting Seabees, patriotic 1944 action film that depicts the forming of the U.S. **Navy Seabees** in the Pacific in World War II. The film made John Wayne a box-office hero, and the musical score was nominated for an Academy Award. The movie also starred Susan Hayward as a reporter and William Frawley.

The Fighting Sullivans, emotionally gripping 1944 film about the loss of the **Sullivans**—five brothers. The movie, which starred Thomas Mitchell and Anne Baxter, served as a tribute to all Americans who gave their lives in World War II. A **destroyer** named for the brothers, USS ***The Sullivans***, is preserved today in Buffalo, New York.

The Fighting Téméraire, 1839 painting by **Joseph Mallord William Turner** that depicts the sailing **ship** *Téméraire*—once the pride of the British fleet and the key to **Horatio Nelson**'s victory at **Trafalgar**—being towed to the breakers by a steam tug. It is one of Turner's most

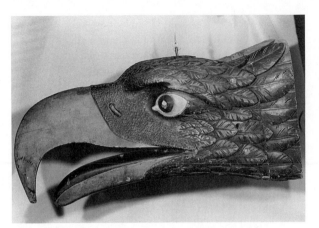

Figurehead from the four-masted bark *Great Republic*. (Courtesy Mystic Seaport Museum)

famous paintings. *Téméraire*'s final journey of 1838 was an expression of the changes sweeping across Europe at the time, particularly the age of steam.

figurehead, ornamental carved wooden statue or bust fitted forward on a vessel. Historically, ancient **galleys** carried rostrums, or beaks, on the bow to ram enemy vessels. These were often surmounted by figureheads representing national or religious emblems. This tradition has been brought forward through the ages.

The Final Countdown, science fiction motion picture dealing with the time-warp disappearance of a contemporary nuclear-powered U.S. **Navy** aircraft carrier. In this 1980 film, USS *Nimitz* finds herself and her nuclear arsenal transported to the waters off Honolulu on December 6, 1941. The fascinating story was filmed largely aboard the carrier, on which the action centered, and looks closely at the inner workings of the ship. It starred Kirk Douglas, Martin Sheen, and Katherine Ross.

a fine kettle of fish, literally, fish cooked in a kettle. It has come to mean a muddle, or an awkward or embarrassing situation.

Finisterre, thirty-eight-foot centerboard **yawl** designed by **Sparkman & Stephens** and built in 1954 for American yachtsman **Carleton Mitchell**. Among a list of ocean races, *Finisterre* won an unprecedented three **Bermuda Races**—in 1956, 1958, and 1960—and she continues to sail today.

Fink, Mike (1770–1823), legendary American frontiersman, hunter, trapper, and keelboatman on the **keelboats** of the Ohio and **Mississippi Rivers**. Stories of **flatboat** life are associated with his name in a manner similar to the connection of Paul Bunyan stories with lumbering.

Finn, **one-design** sailboat introduced in 1949 that measures fourteen feet, nine inches in length. The one-person boat has been competed in the Olympics since 1952.

finnan haddie, lightly salted and smoked haddock popular in Britain as a breakfast dish. It is named after Findon, Scotland, a fishing village near Aberdeen.

fireship, wooden **ship** of any kind that was loaded with combustible or explosive material and launched in flames toward an enemy fleet, preferably at anchor.

first class, generally the finest grade of service, food, and accommodations available aboard passenger vessels. During the mid-1930s, the top class carried on the **Atlantic** run was restyled as **cabin class** to allow companies to charge cheaper fares for the best accommodations rather than sail without passengers due to the financial restraints caused by the Great Depression. The term "first class" reemerged at sea following World War II.

First Class, theatrical film short produced in 1968 and shot entirely aboard the Italian ocean liner *Raffaello* between voyages in New York. The cast of seventeen characters was portrayed by French lyric mime artist Marcel Marceau. The film is not unlike a private guided tour of the ship, because Marceau is the only person ever seen on the otherwise deserted liner.

first lieutenant, individual in charge of general seamanship and deck evolutions and usually the ship's deck department. He or she oversees the care and maintenance of the exterior of the ship as well as its rigging, ground tackle, moving lines, towing gear, and so forth.

First Lord of the Admiralty, Great Britain's navy minister. The U.S. equivalent would be the secretary of the navy.

first rate, traditionally the largest ships in the **Royal Navy** fleet—usually with a hundred guns or more. The smallest vessels in the fleet were sixth-rate ships. See **rates**.

First Sea Lord, the professional head of Britain's **Royal Navy**. The U.S. equivalent would be the **chief of naval operations**.

Firth of Forth, important river in Scotland (*firth* means "river") that empties into the North Sea. Along it are many shipyards, an important naval base, and Leith, the port of Edinburgh.

Fischer, Anton Otto (1882–1962), German-born marine artist and illustrator who became a U.S. citizen in 1916. He illustrated the **Glencannon series** for the *Saturday Evening Post* and in 1942 was appointed official painter for the U.S. **Coast Guard**. He was also an experienced sailor who made many deep-sea passages and wrote and illustrated *Fo'c'sle Days* (1947).

Fisher, John Arbuthnot "Jackie" (1841–1920), British admiral who in the early twentieth century recognized the potential German threat and put in place many reforms. In 1904 he was appointed **First Sea Lord** and soon began construction of the HMS *Dreadnought* battleship and pressed hard for more naval construction programs. He also encouraged the development of submarines and the switch from coal-powered ship to oil-fired vessels. Fisher resigned as First Sea Lord in 1910 but returned in 1914 at the outbreak of World War I. He resigned again in 1915, due to differences in war strategy.

Fisher, Mel (1922–1998), American underwater explorer and treasure hunter. In 1972 he and his group of divers found the remains of the slave ship *Henrietta Marie* and also uncovered scattered traces of the Spanish treasure ship *Nuestra Señora de Atocha*. In 1985 they found the main body of the 1622 wreck along with nearly $400 million in gold, silver, emeralds, and historic artifacts. Many of the items are on display at the Mel Fisher Maritime Museum in Key West, Florida.

Fisherman's Prayer, "God grant I may live to fish, Until my dying day. And when it comes to my last cast, I then most humbly pray, When in the Lord's safe landing net, I'm peacefully asleep, That in His Mercy I be judged, As big enough to keep." Author unknown.

fisherman's staysail, a four-sided sail set between fore and main topmasts on a **gaff-rigged schooner**.

Fishery Conservation Management Act, law passed by the U.S. Congress in 1976 that established a two-hundred-mile conservation zone, thus quadrupling the offshore fishing area controlled by the United States. Also known as the **Magnussen Fishery Conservation Management Act** or the Magnussen Act, after Washington State senator Warren Magnussen.

Fitch, John (1743–1798), American inventor who designed the first workable **steamboat** in the United States. Fitch demonstrated his boat on the Delaware River near Philadelphia on August 22, 1787. A steam engine powered six paddles on each side of the forty-five-foot boat, which reached a speed of about three **knots**. In 1788 Fitch launched a sixty-foot boat propelled by paddles at the stern, and in 1790 a more powerful boat that reached a speed of about eight knots. It operated in regular passenger service between Philadelphia and Trenton, New Jersey. For all of his breakthroughs, however, Fitch never succeeded in attracting enough public support to make his boats profitable, and he committed suicide in 1798.

Fitzroy, Robert (1805–1865), British naval commander and explorer who captained HMS *Beagle* from 1828 to 1836 on expeditions to South America. He recruited **Charles Darwin** as the ship's naturalist for the 1831–36 voyage.

flag of convenience, national register offering registration to merchant ships not owned in the **flag state**. Vessel operators turn to flags of convenience because of low fees, low or non-existent taxation of profits, and skimpy manning or maintenance requirements. Sometimes associated with substandard ships, they are also referred to as "open registers." Flags of convenience were used to get around Prohibition laws in the United States and really took off after World War II. Panama and Liberia have traditionally been the principal open-registry countries, with the Marshall Islands now edging them out of the lead.

flag officer, naval rank that warrants flying a flag. A rear admiral's flag has two stars, a vice admiral's has three stars, an admiral's has four stars, and a fleet admiral's has five. The rank of commodore, usually reserved for wartime, has a flag with one star. In recent years, one star has been used to distinguish rear admiral (lower half). In the **merchant marine**, one star decorates the most senior captain.

flagship, navy ship that carries an admiral, or in merchant shipping, the ship of the most senior captain. "Flagship" in the general parlance has come to mean the finest, largest, or most important one of a series (as in a chain's flagship store).

flag state, nation in which a ship is registered and that holds legal jurisdiction over the operation of the vessel.

Flamborough Head, Battle of, famous naval engagement of the American Revolution off the east coast of England in which **John Paul Jones**, aboard *Bonhomme Richard*, attacked a British **convoy** escorted by HMS *Serapis*. Jones captured *Serapis*, but his own ship was so badly damaged that it sank. During the September 23, 1779, battle, Jones was asked to surrender, to which he replied, "I have not yet begun to fight." Following the battle, Jones sailed the captured *Serapis* to Holland.

flank speed, the fastest speed of which a ship's engines are capable. Only the captain can order this speed.

USS *Flasher* (SS-249), U.S. **Navy** submarine that sank 100,231 gross tons of Japanese shipping during World War II—more than any other U.S. submarine. *Flasher* was launched from **Electric Boat** in Groton, Connecticut, in 1943 and was placed in the reserve fleet in 1946.

flatboat, large, raftlike barge with a flat bottom and square ends that is used to haul freight and passengers, mostly downstream, on **Western rivers** (**keelboats** were used to transport goods up- and downstream prior to the introduction of **steamboats**). These boats, which carried goods during the westward movement in the United States, were moved by the current and by long oars that were also used for steering. A vast flatboat freight business grew on the **Mississippi River** and its tributaries from the late eighteenth through mid-nineteenth centuries.

flat top, naval slang for an aircraft carrier.

Flat Top, 1952 film about training U.S. **Navy** carrier pilots in World War II. **Sterling Hayden** played the strict **skipper**, and actual combat footage greatly enhanced and added realism to the picture.

flense, process of stripping a whale carcass of its blubber.

Fletcher, Frank J. (1885–1973), U.S. **Navy** admiral in World War II who commanded forces in the Battle of **Coral Sea.** During the Battle of

Midway, his **flagship** USS *Yorktown* was damaged, and Admiral **Raymond Ames Spruance** took command. After disagreements with his superiors, led by Admiral **Chester W. Nimitz**, he was transferred to command the Northern Pacific fleet.

USS *Fletcher* (DD-445), 376-foot namesake lead unit of a class of 119 **destroyers** launched during World War II. The 2,940-ton vessel was commissioned in 1942. Of the ships in the class, 21 were sunk during the war, 32 were transferred to foreign navies, and the remaining 66 units were scrapped by 1975.

Der Fliegende Höllander, 1843 opera by German composer Richard Wagner (1813–1883) that was inspired by the legend of the **Flying Dutchman**. Wagner used the overture to paint a graphic seascape as well as to outline the central characters.

Flinders, Matthew (1774–1814), British navigator who led an 1801–3 expedition to Australia to explore and survey the coastline. He was the first to observe that the increasing use of iron on ships created errors in compass bearings. He continued to work on his theory of magnetism and compass errors while a French prisoner of war for more than six years. Around 1812 he reported his findings to the **Royal Society** and suggested that a compass could be corrected by adding a bar of iron, which today is known as a **Flinders bar**.

Flinders bar, bar of soft iron used to help counteract **deviation** in a marine compass caused by magnetism. The bar is placed on the side of the compass opposite to the magnetic source.

Flipper, 1963 film about a fisherman's son who nurses and befriends an injured bottlenosed dolphin. It starred Chuck Connors and Luke Halpin and was followed by sequels and a popular television series that ran from 1964 to 1968. It is credited with changing popular attitudes toward marine mammals.

flood tide, a rising tide.

Flood Tide, action and adventure novel written in 1997 by **Clive Cussler** that features his famous lead character, **Dirk Pitt**, on a chase to apprehend SS *United States*, which is being used to smuggle illegal Chinese immigrants into America.

Florida, coastal **liner** built in 1931 for Henry Flagler's Peninsular and Occidental (P&O) Steamship Company. The 4,923-gross-ton craft maintained a regular service between Miami and Havana—except for U.S. Army transport service during World War II—until 1967, when she was sold for use as a floating hotel at the Montréal World's Fair. She was scrapped in 1968.

CSS *Florida*, **Confederate raider** built at Liverpool during the Civil War under a cloak of secrecy, with her true identity hidden by a false Italian name, the *Oreto*. Completed in 1862, she left Liverpool, fully armed and fully crewed, in January 1863. During her first cruise, she captured twenty-five Union merchant vessels, including the **clipper** *Jacob Bell* with a **China trade** cargo worth $1.5 million. *Florida* was captured by the Union sloop USS *Wachusett* off Brazil on November 1864 and was taken to Newport News, Virginia, where she sank in a collision. She was the second most successful Confederate raider, behind CSS *Alabama*, taking thirty-seven prizes worth a total of $4 million.

flotsam, floating articles, particularly those that have been tossed overboard to lighten a vessel in distress. Under the rules of **salvage**, flotsam must be returned only if the owner makes a proper claim.

Flying Cloud, one of the fastest **clipper ships** ever built. Launched in 1851 from **Donald McKay**'s East Boston yard, she departed New York on June 6 and sailed around **Cape Horn** to San Francisco in eighty-nine days and twenty-one hours—a record at the time. She

A rendering of the clipper ship *Flying Cloud* by J. Spurling, 1928. (© Smithsonian Institution)

bettered that record three years later. In the ensuing years, she performed well for her owners in a number of trades but ran aground in 1874 and, her back broken, was burned for her metal fastenings.

Flying Dutchman, apparition of a Dutch ship, said to be encountered off the **Cape of Good Hope**, that is regarded as a portent of evil. Legend relates that the ship's **Captain Vanderdecken** gambled his salvation by rounding the Cape of Good Hope in a storm and by doing so has condemned his ship and crew to that course for eternity, without reaching a haven. One superstition has it that any mariner who sees the ghost ship will die within the day.

Flying Enterprise, **C1 freighter** built in 1944 as the *Cape Lumukakai* and sold in 1947 to the Isbrandtsen Company of New York. She was disabled by a fierce North Atlantic storm in 1951, which left her with a thirty-degree list. Rescue vessels safely removed the ship's company, while salvage efforts began to tow her to England, some five hundred miles distant. Captain **Henrik Kurt Carlssen** refused to leave his command until thirteen days later, when the ship was rolling eighty-five degrees. The ship was only thirty miles from land when she finally capsized onto her port side and sank.

FMC, see **Federal Maritime Commission.**

Foch, Gorch, pseudonym of Hans Kinau (1880–1916), a popular German writer of sea stories. Kinau perished aboard the **cruiser** *Weisbaden* when it was sunk during the Battle of **Jutland** in May 1916. The German **bark** *Gorch Foch*, launched in the 1930s (now the training vessel *Tovarisch* from Ukraine), and Germany's **tall ship** *Gorch Foch II* were named in his honor.

Follow the Fleet, 1936 Fred Astaire and Ginger Rogers dance extravaganza set against the backdrop of the U.S. **Navy** in San Francisco. The musical score by Irving Berlin included "Let's Face the Music and Dance," "Get Thee Behind Me, Satan," and "I'm Putting All My Eggs in One Basket." The all-American classic motion picture also starred Lucille Ball, Betty Grable, Harriet Hilliard, and Randolph Scott.

Forbes, Edward (1815–1854), eminent British marine biologist who is often called the "founder of oceanography." He was the first to investigate the distribution of marine organisms at various depths in the sea.

Forbes, Robert Bennet (1804–1889), American merchant who specialized in the **China trade**. He was a strong supporter of marine safety, and his efforts led to the first iron-hulled tugboats. In 1847 Forbes captained the *Jamestown*, one of two **ships** sent by the U.S. government to carry supplies to Ireland for relief during the effects of the potato famine. He wrote *Voyage of the Jamestown on her Errand of Mercy* (1847), which included an illustration of the ship by **Fitz Hugh Lane**.

fore-and-aft rig, arrangement of sails on a sailing vessel in which the sails run parallel to the keel, in contrast to a **square-rigger**, on which sails are set perpendicular to the keel, crosswise to the ship.

forebitter, ballad sung by sailors while off watch. It was also called a "**forecastle** song" or "main hatch song." A **chantey**, on the other hand, was traditionally a work song.

forecastle, forward section of a vessel. Originally a fighting station on a warship, and thus was named the "fore castle," it was later used for the crew's quarters. It is pronounced "fo'c'sle," which is also a variant spelling.

Fore River Shipyard, legendary shipbuilding facility established in 1885 in Quincy, Massachusetts. During World War II, Fore River, which was operated by Bethlehem Steel Corporation, turned out more ships than any other shipyard in the country. The yard was later purchased by **General Dynamics** and was closed in 1985. It reopened in 1996 and is the site of American Overseas Marine Corporation and the home of the U.S. Naval Shipbuilding Museum and USS *Salem*.

Forester, Cecil Scott "C. S." (1899–1966), acclaimed English author who won fame for his fictional creation of **Horatio Hornblower**, a British naval hero of the 1800s. His adventure novel *The African Queen* (1935) was made into a popular motion picture in 1951. He also wrote *The Captain from Connecticut* (1941), *The Ship* (1943), *The Good Shepherd* (1955), and *Sink the Bismarck!* (1959). He lived in the United States from 1945 until his death.

Forrestal, James Vincent (1892–1949), U.S. politician who served as the first secretary of defense from 1947 to 1949 and committed suicide shortly after his resignation. He served as undersecretary of the navy from 1940 and as secretary of the navy from 1944. The aircraft carrier USS *Forrestal* was named in his honor.

USS *Forrestal* (CVA-59), the first "supercarrier" built after World War II. Delivered in 1955, she was the first carrier designed to carry jet aircraft. While the ship was on station in the Gulf of Tonkin in July 1967, a Zuni rocket was accidentally launched from an idle F-4 Phantom on the aft end of the flight deck. The missile slammed into parked planes at the fore end of the carrier's deck and punctured a fuel tank, culminating in a horrible fire and further detonation of armament. The resulting inferno claimed the lives of 134 men and left another 62 wounded. It also destroyed sixty-one airplanes. The seventy-six-thousand-ton, 1,046-foot ship was **laid up** in 1993. Three sisters in her class were USS *Saratoga*, USS *Ranger*, and USS *Independence*.

Fort Fisher, Confederate earthenwork fortification built to guard the port of Wilmington, North Carolina, and control the Cape Fear River. It was the site of one of the last large battles of the Civil War, and the fort was captured by Union forces on January 15, 1865. Fort Fisher is today a historic site.

Fort Schuyler, fort built in the 1850s in Throgs Neck, New York, to defend the Long Island Sound approaches to New York Harbor. The fort, named for American Revolutionary general John Philip Schuyler (1733–1804), is now on the grounds of the Maritime College of the State University of New York and houses the Maritime Industry Museum.

Fort Stikine, British munitions freighter that caught fire while docked in Bombay, India, on April 14, 1944. The ship exploded, showering the city with blazing cotton. Nearly thirty vessels in the port were sunk, and all of the waterfront buildings were damaged. In all, 1,400 people were killed or injured, and it took some 7,000 Allied soldiers a week to extinguish the blaze. It was the biggest accidental explosion of World War II.

Fort Sumter, U.S. fort on an island in the harbor of Charleston, South Carolina. On April 12, 1861, Confederate forces fired on the fort—the first shot fired in the Civil War. Although no one was killed, the Union troops withdrew from the fort on April 14.

fouled anchor, symbol used as a design and insignia for the U.S. **Navy** and **merchant marine**, which depicts an anchor entwined in rope or chain. Its origins date back to the British **Admiralty** in the 1500s. Despite representing the worst possible scenario associated with anchoring, it has become the symbol and insignia of deck officers the world over.

Four Aces, two generations of four combination cargo-passenger **liners** of **American Export Lines**. The first generation of Four Aces (1931–41) comprised *Excalibur*, *Exorchordia*, *Exeter*, and *Excambion*. The postwar class (1948–64) shared the same names.

Four Chaplains, four U.S. Army chaplains who gave away their life jackets when the Army

transport USS **Dorchester** was torpedoed and sunk in the North Atlantic off the coast of Greenland on February 3, 1943. Of the 904 men aboard, 605 were lost, including chaplains George Lansing Fox (Protestant), Alexander David Goode (Jewish), John P. Washington (Roman Catholic), and Clark V. Poling (Protestant). A U.S. postage stamp commemorating "Interfaith in Action" was issued in 1948 in their honor.

Fox, Uffa (1898–1972), English sailboat racer, designer, and author. He designed many small sailing dinghies and is considered the father of modern planing sailboats. His books include *Sailing, Seamanship and Yacht Construction* (1934), *Sail and Power* (1936), *Racing Cruising and Design* (1937), *Sailing Boats* (1959), and *Seamanlike Sense in Powercraft* (1968).

FPO, U.S. **Navy** acronym for Fleet Post Office, a system of using numbers for different ports to disguise mailing addresses. Established in World War II, it remains in use today.

Fram, 128-foot auxiliary topsail **schooner** built by **Colin Archer** in 1892 for explorer **Fridtjof Nansen**. The vessel was designed to withstand the Arctic ice—her hull was shaped so that when the ice closed in it would push the vessel upward. Nansen used the vessel from 1893 to 1896 to prove the theory of Arctic drift and to trace the polar currents. Explorer **Roald Amundsen** took *Fram* out of retirement in 1910 for his successful 1911 voyage to the South Pole. She is presently on exhibit at the Fram Museum in Oslo, Norway, not far from the **Kon-Tiki** Museum.

Franca C, well-known **Costa Line** passenger ship originally built in 1914 as the *Medina*. She was extensively rebuilt by Costa in 1952 and was operated quite successfully on the emigrant route to South America from Genoa. Rebuilt for luxury cruising, she paved the way for year-round Caribbean cruises out of Miami in 1959 and pioneered the short-cruise

A brand-new *France* enters Le Havre from her sea trials as the retired *Liberté* awaits her sale to the ship-breakers, circa 1962. (Courtesy Gordon R. Ghareeb)

market from Ft. Lauderdale to Nassau in 1965. Sold in 1977 and renamed *Doulos*, she is still trading as an interdenominational Christian book fair vessel.

SS *France*, spectacular four-**funneled**, 23,666-gross-ton **liner** built for the **French Line** in 1912, which had the grave misfortune to make her **maiden voyage** only a week after the demise of RMS *Titanic*. The whirl of news surrounding the lost steamer nearly caused a total eradication of publicity for the French Line vessel. She served in World War I as an armed merchant **cruiser**, hospital ship, and troop transport and returned to the French Line North Atlantic operation in 1919. Scrapped in 1935, she was noted for the elegance her public rooms expertly executed in various French "period" styles.

SS *France*, last **liner** built for the **French Line** and the longest liner ever built, at 1,035 feet (6 feet longer than RMS **Queen Elizabeth**). The 66,348-gross-ton vessel was noted for her winged twin **funnels**. She was removed from service after an onboard strike by her crew in 1974. She became the **Norway** of **Norwegian Cruise Lines** in 1979 and was still in cruise service as of 2001.

Francis in the Navy, outstanding cast in an improbable 1955 motion picture comedy about a talking four-footed mule who winds up aboard ship in the U.S. **Navy**. The film starred Donald O'Connor, Martha Hyer, Clint Eastwood, David Janssen, Martin Milner, and Jim Backus.

Franconia, famous **Cunard Line liner** built in 1923 for the transatlantic trade but that gained enormous popularity as a cruise ship. The 20,158-gross-ton steamer was taken over for Allied troopship service during World War II and was used by Sir **Winston Churchill** in

1945 as his headquarters for the Yalta Conference. She was returned to Cunard Line service in 1949 and scrapped in 1956.

USS *Frank E. Evans* (DD-754), U.S. **Navy destroyer** that was run down and cut in two by the Australian aircraft carrier HMAS *Melbourne* on June 3, 1969, in an international exercise in the South China Sea. The bow section sank quickly, taking 74 sailors with it. The stern section, carrying 199 crew members, remained afloat and was lashed to *Melbourne* before she returned to port.

Frank Leslie's Sporting Journal, American periodical founded by journalist Frank Leslie (1821–1880). It was one of the first to carry news and articles about recreational boating and fishing.

Franklin, Sir John (1786–1847), distinguished British naval officer and Arctic explorer. A veteran of the Battle of **Copenhagen**, in 1801, and the Battle of **Trafalgar**, in 1805, he also took part in the exploratory voyage of his cousin **Matthew Flinders** to Australia (1801–3). From 1818 to 1827, he went on a number of expeditions, during which he and his team endured terrible hardships and starvation. In 1845 he led an ill-fated expedition, known as the **Franklin Expedition**, in search of a **Northwest Passage**. He and all 128 of his men died.

USS *Franklin* (CV-13), **Essex**-class carrier completed in 1944. The 872-foot ship saw action almost immediately upon reaching the Pacific in World War II. On March 19, 1945, she was the target of two Japanese armor-piercing bombs. The resulting carnage and damage would have been untenable had it not been for the guts and stubbornness of the 710 men who survived the attack and kept the carrier afloat. The ship was wracked by fire and explosions that resulted in the death of 724 men, with a further 265 wounded. *Franklin*'s crew was presented with more medals and commendations

than any other unit in naval history. She was decommissioned in 1947 and **laid up** until sold for scrap in 1968. Nicknamed the "Ship that Wouldn't Die," she was the subject of a 1985 documentary film narrated by Gene Kelly.

Franklin Expedition, lost polar expedition of 1845 led by veteran British Arctic explorer Sir **John Franklin**. Two ships, *Erebus* and *Terror*, and 128 men sailed from Greenland in May 1845 in search of a **Northwest Passage**. They were never seen again after they spoke to two whaling ships on July 26. Over the next eleven years, thirty-five relief expeditions were sent out from Britain and America to find the men. Later it was discovered that the ships had been deserted after being icebound for nearly two years. After 24 officers had died of unknown causes, the 105 survivors embarked on an unsuccessful nine-hundred-mile trek inland in an attempt to find safety.

freebooter, person who pillages and plunders, especially a pirate or **buccaneer**.

Freedom, American defender of the **America's Cup** in 1980. The match marked **Dennis Conner**'s first Cup victory as a **skipper** as his sailboat defeated **Alan Bond**'s *Australia* four races to one in the waters off Newport, Rhode Island.

freedom of the seas, internationally agreed upon doctrine stating that the open seas, beyond territorial limits, are free and open to shipping of all nations.

freight forwarder, person or business that arranges shipments for customers but does not actually carry the cargo or conduct business for the ship.

French and Indian War, American phase of the **Seven Years' War**, fought between Britain and France from 1754 to 1763.

The French Atlantic Affair, 1979 television miniseries adapted from the best-selling novel by Ernest Lehman. The basic plot is the midocean hijacking of an ocean **liner** that is being ransomed for $70 million. **Carnival Cruise Lines'** *Festivale* was used as the seagoing damsel in distress. The miniseries featured an all-star cast, including James Coco, Chad Everett, Jose Ferrer, Carolyn Jones, Louis Jordan, John Rubinstein, Stella Stevens, and Shelly Winters.

French Line, English name of Compagnie Generale Transatlantique (CGT), the famous French shipping firm founded in 1855 by Emile and Isaac Pereire. The company's most famous ships, including the *Île de France*, *Paris*, and *Normandie*, ran between Le Havre and New York. The service concluded with the abrupt withdrawal of the *France* in 1974.

The French Line, 3-D movie extravaganza produced by Howard Hughes. The 1954 musical comedy showcased a buxom Jane Russell prancing seductively around the **French Line** ocean **liner** *Liberté* in stiletto heels and torpedo bra. The film was quite controversial due to the overt suggestiveness of its dance sequences and the brevity of its costumes. It also featured Gilbert Roland and Arthur Hunnicut.

French Revolution, revolution fought from 1789 to 1799 that had far-reaching effects for the rest of Europe concerning the spread of democratic ideals. It started on July 14, 1789, when a crowd of Parisians rushed the Bastille. Later, King Louis XVI and his wife, Marie Antoinette, were executed, and thousands of others met the same fate in a period known as the Reign of Terror. The revolution ended when **Napoleon I** seized the government.

Fresnel, Augustin (1788–1827), French physicist who revolutionized the design of lighthouse lenses and shipboard lighting at the beginning of the nineteenth century. He invented a system of annular lenses, refractors, and reflecting prisms, all of glass, that surrounded a single lamp. The first **Fresnel lens** to be installed in the United States was at Navesink Lighthouse in New Jersey in 1841.

A Fresnel lens on display at the Maritime Museum, Monterey, California. (Maritime Museum, Monterey, California)

Fresnel lens (pronounced "fray-nuhl"), glass lens used widely from running lights to lighthouses that is named for Frenchman **Augustin Fresnel**. Lighthouse lenses are classified by "order," the first order being the largest (approximately six feet inside diameter) and the sixth order the smallest (approximately one foot inside diameter).

Friendship sloop, popular **sloop**-rigged keel sailboat that is a classic example of a workboat that influenced yacht designers. The name refers to the town of Friendship, Maine, at the head of the Muscongus Bay just west of Penobscot Bay. The design features a clipper bow and broad low stern, a low freeboard, and a **gaff-rigged** mainsail with a staysail and a jib. Before power engines, the vessels comprised Maine's lobster fleet.

frigate, fast and seaworthy warship, too small to be a **ship of the line**. Used primarily for scouting, it engaged in independent action. As a modern warship, it is smaller than a **destroyer** and is used for antisubmarine, escort, and patrol duties.

Frobisher, Sir Martin (1535–1594), English navigator and mariner who made three unsuccessful voyages to discover a **Northwest Passage**. In 1576 he discovered Frobisher Bay in Canada but lost two of his three ships. He captured a Spanish treasure ship in 1588 and was knighted for his services.

frocking, naval practice of personnel assuming the uniform of the next higher rank, because of service needs, prior to actual promotion.

The Frogmen, 1951 film about the exploits of the U.S. **Navy**'s underwater demolition teams. It starred Richard Widmark and Dana Andrews.

frostbite racing, cold-weather sailboat racing, commonly in **dinghies** of around twelve feet.

Fuca, Juan de (ca. 1570–1610), Greek sailor—whose real name was Apostolos Valerianos—employed by the Spanish to sail northward from Mexico to search for a **Northwest Passage** from the Pacific to the **Atlantic**. In 1592 he entered the body of water now named after him—the **Strait of Juan de Fuca**.

full-and-by, said of a sailing **ship** with all sails set and full that is sailing **close-hauled** or as close to the wind as possible while keeping good headway.

full dress, to dress a ship with flags for a national holiday or other special event. To full dress a ship, the flags of the **International Code of Signals** are arranged in a specified order starting from the waterline forward, then over the masts and down over the stern to the waterline.

"Full Fathom Five", poem sung by the sea nymph Ariel in act 1, scene 2 of William Shakespeare's *The Tempest*. She sings, "Full **fathom** five thy father lies; / Of his bones are coral made; / Those are pearls that were his eyes: / Nothing of him that doth fade / But doth suffer a **sea-change** / Into something rich and strange: / Sea nymphs hourly ring his knell."

Full Fathom Five, 1947 abstract painting by Jackson Pollock (1912–1956) featuring his drip technique. The oil on canvas, whose shading and sea-green hue produces an idea of water and depth, includes nails, tacks, buttons, coins, matches, and cigarettes.

full-rigged ship, a fully square-rigged **ship** with three or more masts. It is also called a square-rigged ship, a **square-rigger**, or a ship.

Fulton, Robert (1765–1815), American inventor who pioneered the first economically viable **steamship**. In 1807 his *North River Steam Boat*, later renamed the *Claremont*, made a test run on New York City's East River. Soon, "Fulton's Folly" began regular runs on the **Hudson River** between New York and Albany. In 1800 Fulton built the *Nautilus*, a twenty-one-foot copper-covered submarine, and tried to sell it to France and Britain. Neither nation showed much interest, even though it sank several ships in demonstrations.

Fulton Fish Market, the largest fresh fish market in the United States. It is tucked in the shadows of the Brooklyn Bridge just two blocks from Wall Street in New York City. When it opened in 1822, boats brought the fish into the market alongside the East River. Over time the fishing boats were replaced with refrigerated trucks.

funnel, a **steamship**'s smokestack. Many of the early transatlantic ocean **liners** would carry false, or "dummy," funnels for aesthetic reasons and because passengers believed that more smokestacks indicated greater power and a speedier crossing. One of RMS *Titanic*'s four funnels was a "dummy."

Furuseth, Andrew (1854–1938), national labor leader who, as head of the **Sailors' Union of the Pacific** and the International Seamen's Union, championed the cause of American seamen. Among his major accomplishments was pressuring for the passage of the **La Follette Seamen's Act** of 1915.

Futility: Or the Wreck of the Titan, 1898 novel by **Morgan Robertson** that came close to predicting the RMS *Titanic* disaster of 1912. The far-fetched tale told of an unsinkable passenger **liner**, the *Titan*, that sank on its **maiden voyage** after hitting an iceberg.

G

gaff rig, any sailboat rig in which the principal sail is set on a gaff, which is a spar that extends the head of a quadrilateral **fore-and-aft** sail.

Galápagos, group of thirteen volcanic islands in the Pacific Ocean approximately six hundred miles west of Ecuador. The Spanish word for turtles, *galápagos*, gave the islands their name, and they are renowned for their fauna and flora. **Charles Darwin** made extensive observations there in 1835.

Galápagos, 1985 novel by Kurt Vonnegut (b. 1922) that is set one million years in the future. The cruise **liner** *Bahia de Darwin* embarked on a nature cruise in 1986 just as World War III began. After the ship was wrecked, the passengers became stranded on the Galápagos Islands and ended up as the only survivors of the war. Future humans that evolve from this pool are called "fisherfolk" and have certain traits of sea creatures.

Galatea, 103-foot **cutter** that was the British challenger for the **America's Cup** in 1886. She was defeated by the American defender, *May-flower*, in two races off Sandy Hook, New Jersey. Until 1956 it was required that yachts competing in the Cup competition had to sail to the competition on their own bottoms. *Galatea*'s owner, William Henn, sailed his vessel across the **Atlantic** along with his wife, several dogs, and a monkey.

USS *Galena*, the U.S. **Navy**'s first oceangoing **ironclad**, built in 1862 in West Mystic, Connecticut. Along with USS *Monitor* and USS *New Ironsides*, it was one of the first three ironclad designs accepted by the Navy. During the Civil War, *Galena* was badly damaged by Confederate batteries as it led a flotilla up the James River in Virginia in an attempt to capture Richmond. Her iron plating was removed and she served the rest of the war as a wooden gunboat, playing a role in the 1864 Battle of **Mobile Bay**. *Galena* was decommissioned in 1892.

The Gale Storm Show, mid-1950s situation comedy that brought the weekly zaniness of life aboard a passenger **liner** onto the television screen. Set aboard the make-believe *Ocean*

A rendering of *Galatea* racing *Mayflower* by artist Richard Loud. (Courtesy J. Russell Jinishian Gallery, Fairfield, Connecticut)

Queen (for which footage of the *President Cleveland* and *President Wilson* of **American President Lines** was used), stories centered around the shenanigans of Susanna Pomeroy, Elvira Nugent, and Cedric the Steward, who all delighted in tormenting stalwart Captain Huxley.

gale warning, alert issued to mariners by the National Weather Service to indicate that winds within the range of thirty-four to forty-seven **knots** are forecast for a certain area.

galleon, large merchant ship and warship originating in the early 1500s. It became the principal trading ship for the Spanish, Portuguese, and English (although the English rarely used the name for their own ships).

galley, low seagoing vessel propelled by oars and often equipped with a square of **lateen** sail, once common in the Mediterranean.

Gallipoli, port and peninsula in Turkey on the **Dardanelles**. From February 1915 to January 1916, Allied troops—chiefly forces from Aus-

tralia and New Zealand—landed on Gallipoli and tried to force their way through the Dardanelles and link up with Russia. The nine-month engagement was one of the most tragic naval and military operations of World War I, with thirty-six thousand Commonwealth troops killed.

gam, social visit or conversation between crews of **ships** at sea, especially whaling ships. Since ships stayed at sea for months, the occasion was used to catch up on news of home or of the seas.

Gama, Vasco da (c. 1460–1524), Portuguese nobleman and explorer who, in 1497–98, led the first European maritime expedition to India. He sailed around the **Cape of Good Hope** and across the Indian Ocean. He made a second voyage in 1502.

Gardiners Island, three-thousand-acre island off the east coast of Long Island, New York, that is the oldest family-owned estate in the United States. Dating to the reign of Charles I of England, it was settled by Lion Gardiner in 1639.

Gardner, William (1859–1934), distinguished American boat designer and principal of Gardner & Co. He designed the **schooner** *Atlantic* and the **sloop** *Vanitie*, which lost to *Resolute* in the **America's Cup** trials of 1914. His firm developed the design that became the internationally raced **Star** class. He wrote *The Development of the Sail Yacht, Steam Yacht, and Motor Yacht in American Waters* (1915).

Garvey, Marcus (1887–1940), Jamaican-born black leader who started a Back-to-Africa movement in the United States. He moved to America in 1916 and in 1919 launched the **Black Star Line** to provide **steamship** transportation to Africa and to connect black business throughout the world. The line suspended operations in 1922, and Garvey was convicted of fraud. Before entering the federal penitentiary, he launched another line, the Black Cross Navigation and Trading Company, which collapsed in 1925. President Calvin Coolidge commuted Garvey's sentence in 1927, and he was deported to Jamaica. Garvey moved to London in 1934, where he lived until his death.

Gar Wood, one of a succession of production mahogany runabout boats built in Algonac and Marysville, Michigan, by designer-builder **Garfield A. "Gar" Wood**. It is estimated that nearly ten thousand Gar Woods were constructed by the Gar Wood Boat Company between 1921 and 1947, excluding the World War II years, when production facilities were employed in the war effort.

Gatún Lake, 163-square-mile, artificial, freshwater lake that is part of the system to supply the **Panama Canal** locks with water. For many years, captains would use the lake for a freshwater washdown of their ships.

Gaugin, Paul (1848–1903), French painter who deserted his life in Paris to explore the **South Seas**. He kept a notebook of his thoughts and impressions during his ten years there, and his Marquesan and Tahitian works after 1891, for which he is best known, are considered some of his finest.

Gdansk, Polish seaport city on the Baltic, formerly known as Danzig. It was home to Solidarity, Poland's first independent trade union under Communism, which was founded by Lech Walesa, a shipyard worker at the Lenin Shipyard, in 1980. Walesa was awarded the Nobel Peace Prize in 1983, and the Solidarity union contributed to the downfall of the Communist system in the late 1980s.

USS *Gearing* (DD-710), lead unit giving her name to a class of ninety-eight U.S. **Navy destroyers**. Completed in 1945, the class was slightly bigger than the **Fletcher**-class destroyers. The 3,480-ton, 389-foot ship had a top speed of thirty-five **knots**. Construction on fifty-seven units of the series was halted in 1951.

geedunk, naval term for dessert, candy, junk food, or a place to buy same.

General Belgrano, Argentinian **cruiser** launched as USS *Phoenix* in 1939. The ship was sunk by the British submarine *Conqueror* on May 2, 1982, in the Falklands War. Approximately 370 of her 1,091 crew members were lost with the ship.

General Dynamics, U.S. defense contractor that is the world leader in shipbuilding and marine systems. Subsidiaries include **Bath Iron Works**, **Electric Boat**, **National Steel and Shipbuilding Company**, and American Overseas (formerly the Quincy Shipyard in South Boston). The company was officially established in 1952 when shareholders of the Electric Boat Corporation approved a change in the company's name.

general quarters (GQ), term used aboard **Navy** and **Coast Guard** vessels for the call for all hands to man stations for battle or other emergency aboard ship.

General Slocum, wooden **side-wheel** excursion boat that caught fire at **Hell Gate**, New York,

A rendering of the burning of the *General Slocum*, artist unknown. (Seamen's Chuch Institute's Water Street Gallery)

on May 5, 1904. The conflagration claimed the lives of 1,031 people, most of whom were women and children on a Sunday school outing. The tragedy resulted in the tightening of safety regulations for American excursion vessels. The hull was raised, refitted as a coal barge, and renamed the *Maryland.* She finally sank off the coast of New Jersey in 1912.

General W. P. Richardson, ninth vessel of a class of eleven U.S. transports designated as **P-2** troopships. She was laid down as the *General Blatchford* but was changed on the stocks when it was learned that this name had already been allotted to a ship under construction. She entered U.S. **Navy** service in 1944 and was transferred to private service in 1949 as the *La Guardia.* Subsequently rebuilt and renamed successively the *Leilani, President Roosevelt, Atlantis,* and *Emerald Seas,* so far she has had fourteen different names and is currently sailing on global cruises as the *Ocean Explorer I.*

Genesta, ninety-six-foot British **cutter** that challenged for the **America's Cup** in 1885. The copper-bottomed beauty was narrowly de-feated by the U.S. defender, ***Puritan***, in two races. The competition was marked by good sportsmanship in that the **skipper** of *Genesta* did not take advantage of a ***Puritan*** disqualification in an earlier race.

genoa jib, very large jib often used on racing and cruising boats. It takes its name from Genoa, Italy, where the sail was first used in a 1927 regatta by Sven Salén, the Swedish owner of the **six-meter sloop** *Lillian.* It is often referred to as a Genny or a jenny.

Gentlemen Prefer Blondes, smash 1949 Broadway musical set aboard an eastbound crossing of the **liner *Île de France*** during the Roaring Twenties. It launched Carol Channing into stardom with her rendition of "Diamonds Are a Girl's Best Friend," but the real gem of the show was sung by Yvonne Adair, "It's High Time," exalting the virtues of the great **French Line** liner, her varied public rooms, and the availability of liquor therein. The musical was adapted for the screen in 1953, but all references to the *Île de France* were removed, leaving Marilyn Monroe and Jane Russell to cavort around a fictitious liner that looked strikingly like RMS *Titanic*, about which a film was being made simultaneously on the lot.

geographic poles, the North Pole, located at 90°00′ North, and the South Pole, located at 90°00′ South.

George Prince, Louisiana state-run ferryboat that collided with the Norwegian tanker *Frosta* on October 20, 1976, twenty miles north of New Orleans, killing seventy-seven people. The U.S. **Coast Guard** found both vessels at fault.

Georges Bank, important fishing ground off the New England and Canadian coasts. The shallow sandbar, covering almost 1,000 square miles, is approximately 120 miles southeast of **Gloucester**, Massachusetts, and is known as the "Codfish Capital of the World." English colonists named the area for Saint George.

Georges Philippar, 17,539-gross-ton French motor **liner** built in 1931 for the Marseilles to Far East service. She caught fire in the Gulf of Aden while on the homeward leg of her 1932 **maiden voyage** from French Indo-China with 767 people onboard. The liner sank three days after the fire was first detected, taking fifty-four lives with her.

USS *George Washington* (SSBN-598), lead ship of a class of five nuclear-powered 6,888-ton ballistic missile submarines. Commissioned in 1959, the 381-foot vessel carried sixteen **Polaris** missiles tipped with thermonuclear warheads and was capable of steaming underwater at speeds well above her posted thirty **knots**. Her test firing of a Polaris missile in 1960 established the possibility of a nuclear-armed submarine force.

MS *Georgic*, outstanding motor **liner** built as the final **White Star Line** ship in 1932. She came under the control of the **Cunard White Star Line** in 1934. The 27,759-gross-ton vessel was seriously damaged by German aircraft in 1941 but was eventually rebuilt as a troop-

ship and reentered operation in 1944. She engaged in immigrant service to Australia from 1949, with seasonal North Atlantic voyages for Cunard in the summer months. *Georgic* was scrapped in 1956. Her sister ship was the MS *Britannic*.

Gerbault, Alain (1893–1941), French tennis champion, yachtsman, and solo circumnavigator. He was the first man to cross the Atlantic Ocean west to east alone and the third man ever—the first Frenchman—to sail around the world single-handed. He traveled westward via the **Panama Canal** aboard his thirty-nine-foot **cutter** *Firecrest* in 1923 and arrived back in **Le Havre** in 1929. His books include *Alone Across the Atlantic* (1925) and *Running After the Sun* (1929).

The Ghost and Mrs. Muir, 1945 novel by R. A. Dick about the ghost of an old sailing ship captain that hangs around his old house overlooking the sea, which is now inhabited by a young widow and her two children. Made into a film in 1947 with Rex Harrison as Captain Daniel Gregg and Gene Tierney as Mrs. Lucy Muir, it also featured George Sanders and Natalie Wood. A U.S. television series ran from 1968 to 1970, with Hope Lange as an updated Carolyn Muir and Edward Mulhare as the specter.

ghost fleet, general term used to describe inactive vessels. After the shipbuilding surges that occurred in the world wars had ended, ghost fleets began to form in little-used upstream waters.

The Ghost Ship, 1943 film about a mariner who signs aboard the *Altair* as third officer. After a couple strange deaths of crew members, he begins to think the captain is a psychopathic madman obsessed with authority. The thriller starred Richard Dix, Russell Wade, and Edith Barrett.

Gibbons v. Ogden, 1824 U.S. Supreme Court case that ruled that federal regulation of interstate commerce takes precedence over the state. The plaintiff, Thomas Gibbons, operated a **Hudson River** ferry that carried passengers across the river between New Jersey and New York. But New York claimed jurisdiction over the entire river up to the western shore, and it had granted a **steamboat** monopoly to **Robert Fulton** and **Robert R. Livingston**. The defendant, Aaron Ogden, held a license for a trans-Hudson ferry from Livingston's and Fulton's heirs. The ruling invalidated New York State's grant of a monopoly over steam navigation in state waters.

Gibbs, William Francis (1885–1967), genius American naval architect whose **liner** designs include the passenger liners SS *Malolo*, SS *America*, and SS *United States*. He founded the marine engineering firm Gibbs & Cox and was an authority on ship design. His obsession with fire prevention at sea resulted in the SS *United States* being virtually fireproof—the only publicized wood on board was that of the pianos in the lounges and the butcher blocks in the kitchens (the **lignum vitae** bearings of the propeller shafts and the balsa wood in the bilge keels were never mentioned). Every other item used in outfitting the ship was rendered in aluminum or nonflammable materials.

Gibraltar, 1,400-foot-high peninsula at the southern end of Spain, at the western end of the Mediterranean, noted for its rocky promontory. Approximately 2.25 square miles, it has traditionally been the ideal site for controlling the **Strait of Gibraltar**. It was captured by the British in 1704 in the War of Spanish Succession and made a British colony. Today it is a self-governing dependency of Great Britain.

Gidget, classic 1959 Hollywood film based on the novel of the same name by Frederick Kohner about a boy-crazy teenage girl who discovers romance and wisdom on the beaches of Malibu. It starred Sandra Dee and helped launch a national surfing fad and a fascination with California beach culture. It was followed by a number of sequels as well as a short-lived television show.

Gift from the Sea, book by Anne Morrow Lindbergh (1906–2001), wife of aviation pioneer Charles Lindbergh (1902–1974), that uses the seashore as a setting to reflect on life's stages. First published in 1955, the book remains relevant and inspirational and continues to be a tool for self-realization for readers.

The Gift Horse, 1952 film about an aging **destroyer** given to Great Britain in 1940 by the United States that ends up playing a key role in a subsequent World War II sea battle. The movie starred Trevor Howard and Richard Attenborough.

gig, commanding officer's personal boat.

Gilligan's Island, classic American television series that ran from 1964–1968 about the preposterous castaway plight of the seven survivors from a Hawai'ian day-tour boat that became shipwrecked in a sudden storm. The hornpipe theme song has become an American folk staple, and the dotted eighth-note rhythmatic **chantey** has made the terms "three-hour tour" and "the *Minnow* would be lost" recognized vernacular. The series starred Bob Denver, Alan Hale Jr., and Jim Backus.

gillnet, fishing nets consisting of a panel or panels of net held vertically in the water. Fish are caught by their gills in the net.

Gilpatric, Guy (1896–1950), American writer and author of the **Glencannon series**, about the dipsomaniac Scottish chief engineer Colin Glencannon aboard the British **tramp** steamer *Inchcliffe Castle*. The series ran in the *Saturday Evening Post* from the 1930s to the 1950s. As an expatriate living in France in the 1930s, Gilpatric pioneered the use of rubber goggles for skin diving and wrote *The Compleat Goggler* (1938), widely regarded as the first book to popularize recreational snorkeling. He also

Gipsy Moth IV sailing down the English Channel. (Courtesy Chichester Archive/Sunday Times)

wrote ***Action in the North Atlantic*** (1943), which was later made into a popular motion picture and for which he was nominated for an Academy Award for best original story.

Gimcrack, fifty-one-foot **schooner** designed and built by **John Cox Stevens** for his own use. It was in *Gimcrack*'s **saloon** on July 30, 1844, while at anchor off New York City's Battery, that the **New York Yacht Club** was founded.

Gipsy Moth IV, Sir **Francis Charles Chichester**'s fifty-five-foot yacht in which he circumnavigated the globe in 1966–67, making only one port of call. In 1960 Chichester set a transatlantic speed record in his boat *Gipsy Moth III*. As a young aviator, Chichester set several long-distance flying records and in 1931 attempted a flight around the world in his Moth biplane *Gipsy Moth*. He was badly injured when he crashed into high-tension wires in Japan, and he decided that any future attempts at circum-

navigation would be made by boat. *Gipsy Moth IV* is now on public view at Greenwich, England.

Gipsy Moth Circles the World, 1967 book by Sir **Francis Charles Chichester** that recounts his famous circumnavigation in **Gipsy Moth IV**, in which he set the solo speed record.

Girard, Stephen (1750–1831), French-American merchant, banker, and shipowner who was so wealthy that he helped finance the United States in the **War of 1812**. Girard contributed greatly to the improvement of his home city of Philadelphia and bequeathed several million dollars to found Girard College. He was the wealthiest individual in the United States at the time of his death.

give-way vessel, vessel that in a right-of-way situation that—under the ***Navigation Rules***—must keep out of the way of another vessel, the **stand-on vessel**. "Give-way vessel" replaced the term "burdened vessel."

Gjøa, seventy-foot reinforced fishing vessel, commanded by **Roald Amundsen**, that was the first ship to transit the **Northwest Passage**. *Gjøa* sailed from Oslo, Norway, on June 16, 1903, and reached Nome, Alaska, on August 31, 1906. She transited to San Francisco, passing through the Golden Gate on October 19, 1906, and received a warm welcome from the city, which was just recovering from the recent earthquake. *Gjøa* was placed on display in San Francisco until 1974, when she returned to Norway and was put on exhibit in Oslo.

Glencannon series, series of popular short stories by **Guy Gilpatric** featuring Colin Glencannon, the fictional Scottish chief engineer aboard the British **steamship** *Inchcliffe Castle*. The stories of the dipsomaniac Glencannon, who craves Duggan's Dew of Kirkintilloch, first appeared in the *Saturday Evening Post* in the 1930s and were subsequently compiled into book form.

Glomar Challenger, American drillship operated by the Deep Sea Drilling Project, now the **Ocean Drilling Program**, from 1968 to 1983. It extracted core samples from the ocean floor that confirmed the theory of continental drift.

Glomar Explorer, 618-foot vessel built in the early 1970s by the Central Intelligence Agency (CIA) to retrieve a Soviet nuclear submarine from the floor of the mid–Pacific Ocean—the Soviet sub K-129, carrying three nuclear missiles, which sank February 23, 1968, to a depth of thirteen thousand feet. The CIA asked billionaire Howard Hughes to serve as a cover, and it was explained that the *Hughes Glomar Explorer* was being constructed by Hughes with a big claw that would extend to the ocean floor and vacuum up magnesium nodules. In July 1974 the *Hughes Glomar Explorer* grabbed K-129, but the claw broke when it was halfway to the surface. Eventually a thirty-eight-foot section of the sub was retrieved—with no missiles or code books. The *Hughes* was converted for use as an oil-drilling ship and renamed the *Glomar Explorer.*

GLONASS, satellite navigation system started by the USSR and now operated by Russia, analogous to the U.S. global positioning system (**GPS**).

Gloria, 249-foot Colombian **tall ship** built in 1968 to train future naval officers. It is one of four **barks** built for Latin American nations in the 1960s and 1970s to serve as goodwill ambassadors and training ships (the others are the ***Guayas*** of Ecuador, the ***Simón Bolívar*** of Venezuela, and the ***Cuauhtemoc*** of Mexico). The ship was named for the wife of the Colombian defense minister.

Glorious First of June, naval engagement of June 1, 1794, in the **French Revolution** in which a British force of 25 **ships** attacked a French force of 26 ships, four hundred miles off the coast of Brittany. Both sides claimed a victory. For France, the battle allowed a grain convoy of 116 ships from the United States to safely reach French harbors. This was a great moral victory for the British because they captured six French ships and sank one, which proved they had some naval might following their defeat in the American Revolution.

Glory of the Seas, shipbuilder **Donald McKay**'s last great **clipper ship**. Launched in 1869, she was initially engaged in the grain trade between San Francisco or Australia to England, around **Cape Horn**. The 240-foot versatile vessel served her owners well for forty years in various capacities. In 1923, while serving as a floating cannery in Alaska, she was burned for her scrap metal.

Gloucester, an important fishing center settled in 1623 in northeastern Massachusetts about thirty miles from Boston. A statue, Fishermen's Memorial, overlooks the small, well-protected harbor and is a tribute to the many people from Gloucester who have lost their lives in fishing accidents.

Glückauf, the world's first modern-design oceangoing tanker. Built in 1886 in Newcastle, England, the skin of the ship formed the sides of the vessel's tanks. She went aground off Long Island in 1893.

GMDSS, Global Maritime Distress and Safety System, a worldwide network of satellite and radio communications systems set in place under the auspices of the **International Maritime Organization** so that a ship in distress anywhere in the world can be heard, even if her crew does not have time to radio for help, because the message will be transmitted automatically.

Goethals, George W. (1858–1928), U.S. Army colonel and chief engineer responsible for building the **Panama Canal**—ahead of schedule and under budget. The waterway opened to traffic August 15, 1914. Goethals was governor of the Panama Canal zone from 1914 to

1916 and was the first chairman, briefly, of the **Emergency Fleet Corporation** in 1917.

going down to dinner, term coined in the transatlantic heyday of the great **liners**. The dining room was always located lower down in the ship's hull, where the effects of rolling would be less noticeable. **First-class** accommodations were invariably located on decks higher than the **saloon**, so—once properly dressed—one had to make the grand descent to partake of meals.

Gokstad ship, Viking vessel found in a burial mound at Gokstad in southern Norway in 1880. Dating from about A.D. 850, the seventy-nine-foot ship was reassembled in Oslo's Viking Ship Museum along with the **Oseberg ship**.

Gold Cup, Tiffany-designed urn presented as the top prize in the premier American racing event for powerboats. It was first offered in 1904 under the rules of the newly established American Power Boat Association. Under the terms of the Cup's deed of gift, each race is conducted by the club whose representative won the previous year's race, and each winner may select the locale of the next year's contest. Winners have included **Garfield A. "Gar" Wood** in *Miss America* and band leader Guy Lombardo in *Tempo VI*. In recent years, the race has been run on the Detroit River. The 2000 winner was *Miss Budweiser*.

Golden Bear, the name of three training ships for the **California Maritime Academy**. The first *Golden Bear* was a U.S. attack transport laid down in 1944 and delivered to the school in 1946. The second was originally the *Del Orleans* of 1940. The 7,997-gross-ton **C3 liner** was commandeered by the U.S. **Navy** in 1941 for transport service as the *Crescent City*. **Laid up** in 1948, she was transferred to the academy in 1971. The third, and current, *Golden Bear* is the former oceanographic deep survey vessel USNS *Maury*, which was delivered to the school in 1995. Prior to the arrival of the first

Golden Bear, the school's training ships were the *California State/Golden State* (1931–46) and the *Jamestown* (1876–78).

Golden Hind, originally called the *Pelican*, the **flagship** of Sir **Francis Drake** during his legendary voyage around the world (1577–80), during which, among other exploits, he raided Spanish ships and ports on the western coast of South America. His expedition—the first English circumnavigation of the world—made a four hundred percent profit over expenses.

golden rivet, mythical last rivet that completes a ship. The story is often told to inexperienced seamen that one of the rivets in the lower parts of the ship's hull is made of gold and is sent in search of it.

Golden Thirteen, group of black sailors who attended the U.S. **Navy**'s Officer Candidate School in March 1944 and were commissioned as the service's first African-American officers on active duty. Until that time, the navy had one hundred thousand African-American enlisted men but no African-American officers.

Goliath Awaits, 1981 science fiction movie that tells the story of a self-contained microcivilization that develops inside the watertight sections of a luxury **liner** that was torpedoed and sunk in World War II. The only redeeming feature of the film is the extensive footage—shot aboard RMS **Queen Mary** in Long Beach—of the fictional wrecked *Goliath*, . The film starred Christopher Lee, Eddie Albert, and John Carradine.

gollywobbler, large, quadrilateral staysail hoisted between the masts of a **schooner** to increase sail area with a reaching wind.

The Good Shepard, gripping 1955 novel by **Cecil Scott "C. S." Forester** about the U.S. **destroyer escort** USS *Keeling*, which was engaged in North Atlantic convoys during World War II.

Gordon, Sir James Alexander (1782–1869), colorful **Royal Navy** officer who rose from a midshipman to become admiral of the fleet and who is believed to have been a model for **Cecil Scott "C. S." Forester**'s **Horatio Hornblower**.

Gorgas, William Crawford (1854–1920), U.S. Army colonel who oversaw sanitary work and reduced the deaths caused by malaria and yellow fever during construction of the **Panama Canal** (1906–14). Earlier in his career, Gorgas was stricken with yellow fever and recovered, making him immune to the disease. He served as U.S. surgeon general from 1914 to 1919 and wrote *Sanitation in Panama* (1915).

Gosnold, Bartholomew (1572–1607), English navigator who in 1602 explored the coast of New England in his ship *Concord*, becoming the first European known to have sighted **Cape Cod**, Martha's Vineyard, and Nantucket. He was a leader of the English colony established in 1607 in **Jamestown**, Virginia, but died of swamp fever later that first year.

Gould, Rupert (1890–1948), English naval officer whose career was cut short by a series of nervous breakdowns. Among his passions was antiquarian horology, and it was while writing his definitive book, *The Marine Chronometer, Its History and Development* (1923), that he discovered the great timekeepers built by **John Harrison**, in Britain's Royal Observatory storeroom. His efforts to restore the clocks to operating condition occupied much of the rest of his life.

GPS, acronym for global positioning system, a satellite-based radio navigation system developed and operated by the U.S. Department of Defense. It permits users to determine their three-dimensional position, velocity, and time twenty-four hours a day. The system consists of twenty-four satellites in six circular orbits 10,900 **nautical miles** above the earth that continuously broadcast position and time data to users throughout the world.

GQ, see **general quarters**.

Grace Line, shipping concern established in the 1870s by Irish-American emigrant William R. Grace to handle the South American import-export trade. In 1892 the firm became the New York & Pacific Steamship Company and acquired several other ship lines. To tie everything together, the Grace Line was formed in 1916. Its fleet of vessels with the prefix "Santa" served in both world wars and operated on routes between South America, the Caribbean, and New York and the West Coast. The Prudential Line obtained a controlling interest in the company in 1969, and the name was changed to Prudential-Grace Line, with the famous family name removed altogether four years later. What was left of the company was sold to Delta Line in 1978.

Graf Spee, see *Admiral Graf Spee*.

Graf Zeppelin, the only aircraft carrier to be constructed for the German navy during World War II. The 861-foot ship was completed in 1943 but—due to the reshuffling of the Kriegsmarine's command and policies—never saw action against the Allies. Her armament was removed and installed in various artillery locations in Norway. In 1945 the twenty-three-thousand-ton carrier was **scuttled** to prevent her capture by advancing Soviet troops. Refloated by the Soviets, the *Graf Zeppelin* was sunk as a weapons testing target in 1947.

Graham, Robin Lee (b. 1949), American sailor and circumnavigator. In 1965, at age sixteen, he departed San Pedro, California, in his twenty-four-foot Ranger **sloop**, *Dove*. Five years later, married and with a daughter, he returned to port, in a Luders 33, to become the youngest person to solo sail around the world. His voyage was chronicled in *National Geographic*, and he wrote the best-selling book *Dove* (1972), which was also made into a popular 1974 movie.

Grand Banks, shallow plateau—three hundred miles long and four hundred miles wide—in the North Atlantic ocean southeast of Newfoundland that makes for fertile fishing grounds. It is a prolific breeding ground for cod and many other fish species. Most of the area, which is known for its persistent dense fog, falls under Canadian jurisdiction.

Grandcamp, **French Line Liberty ship** that exploded while loading ammonium nitrate fertilizer in Texas City, part of the Port of Galveston, on April 16, 1947. The blast touched off fires in the surrounding chemical plants and oil refineries and caused two more freighters, the *High Flyer* and the *Wilson B. Keene*, to explode. The nightmare took at least 581 lives, left more than 3,500 wounded, and caused more than $67 million in damage. The *Grandcamp*'s 1.5-ton anchor was found two miles from the blast, and the explosions were heard 150 miles away.

Grand Fleet, term used to describe the home-based British fleet during the **French Revolution**, the **Napoleonic Wars**, and World War I—the Great War.

Grand Republic, **paddle wheeler** built in 1876 that was the largest period **steamboat** to ply the **Mississippi** and Ohio Rivers. It was said that *Grand Republic* had calendar dimensions: 365 feet long, fifty-two feet wide, a twelve-foot draft, seven decks high, and a cost of $365,000. There were several other *Grand Republics* in her era.

Grant, Gordon (1875–1962), American artist, illustrator, and writer who is best known for his maritime drawings and watercolor paintings. His early voyages on sailing vessels started a lasting fascination with the sea, and in 1906 prints of his painting of USS *Constitution* were sold by the thousands to help raise money for preservation of the historic vessel (the painting was hung in the Oval Office at the White House). Grant devoted the rest of his life to painting images of ships and the sea. The books he illustrated include *Eagle of the Sea: The Story of Old Ironsides* (1949), *Sail Ho!* (1931), *The Story of the Ship* (1919), *Greasy Luck* (1932), *Ships under Sail* (1939), *The Book of Old Ships* (1924), *Forty Famous Ships* (1936), and *The Sea Witch* (1944?).

Grasse, François Joseph Paul de (1722–1788), French admiral who commanded the French fleet sent to aid the Continental forces during the American Revolution. After defeating Admiral **Samuel Hood** in 1781 and capturing Tobago, he came north and was instrumental in blockading the York and James Rivers, thus contributing to the British surrender at Yorktown. After the revolution, he was soundly defeated at the Battle of the **Saints** in 1782 by Admiral **George Brydges Rodney**.

Graveyard of the Atlantic, treacherous stretch of coast off Cape Hatteras, North Carolina. Here the northbound **Gulf Stream** collides with cold currents coming down from the Arctic to form **Diamond Shoals**. More than six hundred ships have been wrecked along the coast since the sixteenth century.

graving dock, basin or structure—also called a dry dock—in which ships are repaired and hulls cleaned and painted. It has a gate that can be closed so the dock can be pumped dry.

Gray, Robert (1755–1806), American explorer who was the first person to sail around the world under the U.S. flag. Gray sailed from Boston in 1787 in the **sloop** *Lady Washington* on the first U.S. voyage to the Pacific Northwest. There he took command of the **ship** *Columbia* and visited China, returning by way of the **Cape of Good Hope** in 1790. Gray set out again on the same route and sailed into the mouth of the Columbia River in 1792. He named the river after his ship *Columbia*, and his entrance into the river became a basis for U.S. claims to the Oregon Territory. Gray's calculation of **longitude** at the mouth of the river gave Americans a first glimpse of the size of the North American continent.

Gray Lady Down, motion picture action drama about the rescue of the crew from the sunken USS *Neptune*, a fictitious nuclear-powered submarine that was sunk when rammed by a Norwegian freighter off the coast of New England. The 1978 fare starred Charlton Heston, David Carradine, Stacey Keach, and Ned Beatty. The film was based on the book *Event 1000* (1971) by David Lavallee.

SS *Great Britain*, the first oceangoing iron steamer and the first to be driven by a screw propeller. Launched in Bristol in 1843, she was the largest and most powerful ship of her day. Designed by engineer **Isambard Kingdom Brunel**, the 302-foot ship was at first too big and too heavy to leave her dock. During a long career, she served as a transatlantic **liner**, an emigrant ship to Australia, and a troop carrier in the Crimean War, and she was converted to a sailing ship and employed as a storage vessel in the Falkland Islands. *Great Britain* was returned to her builder's dock in Bristol in 1970. Restored there, she serves today as an educational resource and national monument.

great circle, a course plotted on the surface of a globe that is the shortest distance between two points. Lines of **longitude** are great circles. Lines of **latitude**, with the exception of the equator, are not. Great-circle sailing, usually employed on long voyages, requires a series of course changes along chords of the arc.

SS *Great Eastern*, seven-hundred-foot, five-funneled, iron passenger **steamship**, was the last creation of **Isambard Kingdom Brunel**. Built for the England-to-India service of the Great Ship Company to solve the problem of ships' having to load coal numerous times in one voyage, she took many attempts to launch in 1858. Sold at a great loss even before her **maiden voyage**, the giant **paddle wheeler** never served the route for which she

was developed and was deemed a commercial failure. She entered the Southampton to New York transatlantic service from 1860 to 1864. Dubbed a "white elephant," she served successfully in various transoceanic cable laying ventures from 1866 to 1874. **Laid up** in 1875–86, she was broken up in 1888.

Greater Buffalo, sister ship to the **Greater Detroit**. The original plans called for turbine-driven twin-screw vessels but an unwillingness to retrain the company's engine room crews resulted in **side-wheel** propulsion for both ships. Built in 1925, *Greater Buffalo* was requisitioned for service in World War II and was rebuilt into a aircraft carrier, USS *Sable*, for training navy pilots on the **Great Lakes**. She was scrapped after the war.

Greater Detroit, 7,820-gross-ton overnight **Great Lakes** passenger steamer built in 1924 for the Detroit & Cleveland Navigation Company. Designed by **Frank Kirby**, the *Greater Detroit* and her sister, the **Greater Buffalo**, each costing over $3.5 million, were the largest and most powerful **side-wheelers** ever constructed except for the **Great Eastern**. *Greater Detroit* was scrapped in 1956.

Great Harry, the first war vessel built for the **Royal Navy**. Built under King Henry VIII at the same time as the **Mary Rose**, she served from 1514 to 1553 and was the largest and most powerful ship of her time.

Great Lakes, according to the *Navigation Rules*, the waters of the five Great Lakes—Erie, Huron, Michigan, Ontario, and Superior—and their connecting and tributary waters, including parts of the Calumet and **Chicago Rivers** and the Saint Lawrence River as far east as the Saint Lambert Lock, near Montréal.

Great Lakes Maritime Academy (GLMA), one of six state maritime academies authorized by the federal government to train future officers for the U.S. **merchant marine**. Located in

A rendering of the clipper ship *Great Republic* by Antoine Roux.
(© Smithsonian Institution)

Traverse City, Michigan, it is the only freshwater school with the particular mission of training men and women for licensed officer positions aboard **Great Lakes** commercial bulk carriers.

The Great Lover, 1949 American movie comedy set aboard a transatlantic passenger **liner**. Complete with gambling, murder, royalty, and a super-sleuth troop of Boy Scouts, the film starred Bob Hope, Rhonda Fleming, George Reeves, and Jim Backus.

Great Marianas Turkey Shoot, phrase applied to the World War II air battle during the Battle of the **Philippine Sea** on June 20, 1944, when the U.S. fleet of 15 carriers and 956 aircraft shot down some 300 Japanese planes.

The Great Pacific War, 1925 novel by British naval correspondent Hector Bywater that foretold the events of World War II in the Pacific. Subtitled *A History of the American-Japanese Campaign of 1931–33*, the book included Japan striking a surprise blow on the United States, an island-hopping campaign toward the Japanese mainland, and a U.S. victory.

Great Republic, four-masted **bark** launched in 1853 by renowned American shipbuilder **Donald McKay**. At 335 feet, she was the largest ship built in the United States up to that time—and the largest **clipper ship** ever built. While loading at New York for her **maiden voyage** to Liverpool, the ship caught fire and burned to the waterline. *Great Republic* was raised and rebuilt with three decks (versus the original four) and with a reduced sail plan. Sailing again in 1855, she was renamed *Denmark* in 1869 and met her demise in a North Atlantic storm in 1872.

Great Salt Lake, shallow body of salt water located in northeast Utah. Its size and depth vary according to weather changes. It was discovered in 1824 by mountain man Jim Bridger (1804–1881), who initially thought its briny water was an arm of the Pacific Ocean.

Great Steamboat Race, hotly contested showdown between the steamboats **Natchez** and **Robt. E. Lee** that made headlines across the United States in 1870. The *Robt. E. Lee* earned boasting rights as the fastest boat on the **Mississippi River** by winning the twelve-hundred-mile race, from New Orleans to Saint Louis, in three days, eighteen hours, and fourteen minutes.

Great Tea Race, 1866 race between five British **clipper ships**—*Ariel*, *Fiery Cross*, **Taeping**, *Taitsin*, and *Serica*—that started after loading tea at Foochow, China. The first ship to England would be able to command a far higher price for her cargo. Three of the ships reached the English Channel in just under a hundred days, and the clipper *Taeping* docked an hour ahead of her nearest rival, *Ariel*.

"The Great Titanic", one of the most popular children's summer camp songs in the United States. Written around 1915, it was among the many songs about the 1912 RMS **Titanic** disaster. Often titled "Husbands and Wives" or "It Was Sad When That Great Ship Went Down," its opening lines are: "It was on one Monday morning just about one o'clock, When that great *Titanic* began to reel and Rock; People began to scream and cry, Saying, 'Lord, am I going to die?'" The chorus: "It was sad when that great ship went down, It was sad when

Artist Jim Griffith's *The Fourth to Leave*, depicting the start of the Great Tea Race. (Courtesy J. Russell Jinishian Gallery, Fairfield, Connecticut)

that great ship went down, Husbands and wives and little children lost their lives, It was sad when that great ship went down."

SS *Great Western*, 236-foot, wooden, **paddle wheel** passenger **steamship** designed by **Isambard Kingdom Brunel** and put into transatlantic service in 1837. She launched transatlantic steamship service on her **maiden voyage** when she sailed from Bristol with 111 passengers and arrived in New York less than sixteen days later. Scheduled transocean service was not established until 1840.

Great Whaling Fleet Disaster of 1871, fleet of thirty-one American whaling ships that became trapped in the Arctic ice off Alaska in late August 1871. All 1,219 men, women, and chil-

dren climbed into small boats and made it safely to seven rescue ships. In 1872, one of the ships was salvaged, but the remainder sank, were stripped of their wood by local natives, or were crushed by the ice.

Great White Fleet, fleet of U.S. **Navy** ships sent around the world by President **Theodore Roosevelt** from December 16, 1907, to February 22, 1909, as a grand pageant of sea power. The fleet, consisting of sixteen new battleships of the Atlantic fleet, which were painted white with gilded scrollwork on their bows, covered forty-three thousand miles and made twenty port calls on six continents. It marked the first circumnavigation by a fleet of steam-driven warships and was particularly aimed at Japan,

Great White Fleet souvenir. (Courtesy The Mariners' Museum, Newport News, Virginia)

who had recently defeated Russia's fleet in the **Russo-Japanese War**. The voyage galvanized support for a strong U.S. merchant fleet in that the navy ships had to be supported by foreign merchant vessels.

Great White Fleet, originally the colloquial name for the vessels of the **United Fruit Company** because of the color they were painted. In 1990 the parent company, Chiquita Brands, decided to dissolve United Fruit and call the shipping unit the Great White Fleet. The term has also been applied to the ships of the U.S. **Coast Guard**.

Greely, Adolphus Washington (1844–1935), U.S. army officer and Arctic explorer who led an 1881 expedition to Greenland to establish a meteorological station. He and his party of twenty-four officers and men mapped unknown portions of Greenland and achieved a

new northern record. Relief ships failed to reach the expedition in 1882 and 1884, and Greely and six others were finally rescued later in 1884 by a mission headed by **Winfield Scott Schley**. Near death when rescued, another man died on the voyage home. Greely's account of the tragic polar expedition is chronicled in his *Three Years of Arctic Service* (1886). He later wrote *Handbooks of Alaska* (1925) and *The Polar Regions in the Twentieth Century* (1928), and in 1935 he was awarded the **Medal of Honor**.

green flash, phenomenon sometimes seen at sunrise and sunset when the spectrum of light of the sun's upper edge changes and gives a sudden, brief appearance of the color green.

Greenhill, Basil (b. 1920), a leading English maritime historian and writer who served as the director of Britain's **National Maritime Museum** from 1967 to 1983.

Greenpeace, grassroots environmental advocacy group formed in 1971, taking its name from a rented boat it used to protest nuclear weapons testing in the Aleutian Islands. Greenpeace's initial efforts focused on the Save the Whales campaign and was expanded to encompass other sea animals, including the Stellar sea lion and dolphins. Over the years, the group extended its scope to all environmental issues, from nuclear disarmament to Antarctic protection. In 1985 the Greenpeace vessel *Rainbow Warrior* was sunk in Auckland, New Zealand, by the French Secret Service.

USS *Greeneville* (SSN-772), U.S. **Navy** submarine that collided with the Japanese fisheries research and training vessel *Ehime Maru* on February 9, 2001, in the waters south of Hawai'i. The 360-foot *Greeneville* surfaced beneath the 180-foot Japanese vessel, sinking it and killing nine students, teachers, and crewmen.

green water, solid water on the deck of a ship, so deep that it appears green.

Greenwich Hospital, home for old and disabled seamen chartered in 1694 and built in Greenwich, England. Architect Christopher Wren was responsible for the original design, and construction was completed in 1714. When the hospital closed, the vacated buildings were transferred to the **Royal Navy** College and later to the **National Maritime Museum**.

Greenwich Mean Time (GMT), name for mean solar time at the Royal Observatory in Greenwich, England, site of the **prime meridian**. GMT was established to aid worldwide oceanic navigation. In 1884 it was adopted universally, and the twenty-four times zones were created along with the **international date line**. In 1928 the International Astronomical Union changed the designation of the standard time of the prime meridian to universal time. It changed again in 1964 to **universal coordinated time**, or UTC. GMT or UTC may be listed as **zulu time**, or Z.

Greenwich meridian, line of 0° **longitude**, chosen in 1884 as the world's **prime meridian**. The line runs through Britain's Royal Observatory in Greenwich, which was founded in 1675, then the world's leading scientific center.

Gretel I, Australian **twelve-meter** that challenged for the **America's Cup** in 1962. She was defeated by the American defender, **Weatherly**, four races to one. The races off Newport, Rhode Island, drew large crowds, including President **John F. Kennedy** aboard the **destroyer** USS *Joseph P. Kennedy*.

Gretel II, Australian challenger for the **America's Cup** in 1970. After winning the first-ever international challenger series, the Aussie yacht was defeated by the American defender, *Intrepid*, four races to one off Newport, Rhode Island. The competition was marred by accusations of cheating on the part of the **New York Yacht Club**.

Grey, Zane (1872–1939), American storyteller and the best-selling author of Westerns of all time. His success as a writer allowed him to pursue his lifelong passion for angling, and Grey is credited with introducing sportfishing to millions. He roamed the world's game-fishing grounds in his own **schooner** and held several deep-sea fishing records for decades. In all, he wrote nearly ninety books, of which sixty are Westerns and nine concern fishing.

Grey Seas Under, gripping 1958 nonfiction adventure by **Farley Mowat** about the Canadian seagoing tug *Foundation Franklin* and her rescue of shipping throughout the North Atlantic from the 1930s through World War II.

Gridley, Charles Vernon (1844–1898), U.S. naval officer who was the **flagship** commander under Commodore **George Dewey** aboard USS *Olympia* at Manila in 1898. Dewey's command to him—"**You may fire when you are ready, Captain Gridley!**"—began the May 1 Battle of **Manila Bay** in the **Spanish-American War**. Gridley, already ill, died later that year while returning to the United States.

Griffiths, John Willis (1809–1882), American naval architect who in 1845 began a new era in shipbuilding by designing the extreme **clipper ship** *Rainbow*. A year later *Sea Witch* was launched, and Griffiths's ships proved to be the fastest of their time. He was a leading spokesperson for the scientific approach to shipbuilding and made many contributions to the field, including inventing a timber-bending machine, a bilge keel, and an improved rivet. He was the author of *The Ship-builder's Manual and Nautical Referee* (1853) and *The Progressive Ship Builder* (1874–75).

MS Gripsholm, well-known motor **liner** completed in 1925 for the **Swedish America Line** as a running mate to the *Kungsholm*. The 17,716-gross-ton passenger ship spent World War II sailing for the International Red Cross and transported more than twenty-five-thousand civilians between Europe and North America. She was returned to her owners after the war

MS *Gripsholm*. (Courtesy Gordon R. Ghareeb)

and placed back in transatlantic and cruise service in 1949. She became the **North German Lloyd** liner *Berlin* in 1954 and was scrapped in 1966.

grog, a ration of rum diluted with two parts water that replaced the rum ration aboard British ships in 1740. A staple in the **Royal Navy** for many years, it was named for Admiral **Edward Vernon**, who introduced its issue. Vernon was referred to as Old Grog for his habit of wearing overcoats made of a material called "grogram." From this, we have the word "groggy," for those who have had too much. The grog ration was finally abolished in the Royal Navy in 1970.

gross registered tonnage (grt), the measure of total internal volume of a ship, in units of one hundred cubic feet, excluding machinery spaces, bridge and navigation spaces, and other minor spaces essential to the operation of the ship. This measure is applied only to merchant vessels.

Grotius, Hugo (1583–1645), Dutch jurist and statesman whose legal writings laid the foundation for modern international law. He wrote *Mare Liberum* (translated as *The Free Sea*) in 1609 challenging the right of any nation to exclusively claim part of the open sea as its own.

groundfish, species or group of fish that spends most of its life on or near the seafloor.

growler, official term used to classify an iceberg whose size is from three to fifteen feet high and fifteen to forty-six feet long.

Guadalcanal, the largest island of the nation of Solomon Islands in the Pacific Ocean. It was the scene of heavy fighting in 1942 and 1943, when U.S. forces landed and forced the invading Japanese to evacuate the island.

Guadalcanal, Battle of, bitter World War II naval campaign that began on August 7, 1942, over control of an airstrip to be constructed on the island of **Guadalcanal**. The six-month engagement was drawn out because of the effective nighttime landings of supplies and troops—known as the **Tokyo Express**—made by the Japanese navy to reinforce their positions in the islands. The ultimate price for the island and its attendant airfield was 23,000 Japanese lives and 1,600 American lives, with 4,200 Americans wounded.

Guam, Invasion of, World War II confrontation that secured the largest island in the Marianas group. Begun on July 21, 1943, the amphibious assault on the island lasted twenty days and cost the Japanese forces more than 18,250 men. Some of the Japanese soldiers fled to the interior of the island, the last of whom surrendered in the 1960s. American casualties included 1,744 men killed and 5,970 wounded.

guano, concentrated bird droppings used as fertilizer that were mined from islands in the **Humboldt** Current off the west coast of South America, where seabirds gathered to feed off abundant fish stocks. Guano was a staple cargo for many late-nineteenth-century sailing ships because the value of guano was too slight to warrant using expensive transport by **steamship**.

Guantánamo Bay, U.S. naval station on the island of Cuba. The forty-five-square-mile base was leased to the United States in 1903 in a treaty that was renewed in 1934. Consent of both governments is needed to break the lease. Since 1960 the Cuban government has refused to accept the token annual rent of $5,000.

HMS *Guerrière*, British **frigate** originally taken from the French in 1806. She was captured by USS **Constitution** on August 19, 1812, in the first naval encounter of the **War of 1812**. During the engagement, *Constitution* earned the nickname **Old Ironsides**. In 1821 the U.S. **Navy** began using *Guerrière* as a training school.

Gulf of Tonkin incident, August 2, 1964, torpedo boat attack on the **destroyer** USS *Maddox* off the coast of North Vietnam. The destroyer, engaged in information gathering about the coastal defense forces, managed to evade the North Vietnamese boats and received some machine gun fire. The incident prompted the U.S. Congress to pass the Gulf of Tonkin Resolution, which basically gave President Lyndon B. Johnson a blank check to use all necessary measures to deal with the "aggression" in North Vietnam.

Gulf Stream, warm ocean currents—with an average speed of four **knots**—flowing clockwise from the Gulf of Mexico to Newfoundland, across the North Atlantic, and along the coast of Northwest Europe. It was first described by Spanish explorer **Ponce de León** and first charted in the mid-1700s by the American Benjamin Franklin while traveling to England.

Gulliver's Travels, classic 1726 novel by Irish author Jonathan Swift (1667–1745) that chronicles the adventures of Lemuel Gulliver, an eighteenth-century English surgeon and ship captain. In the four-part novel, Gulliver is shipwrecked on Lilliput, where the people are six inches tall. His second voyage takes him to Brobdingnag, a land inhabited by giants. Gulliver's third voyage takes him to several strange kingdoms, and in his last voyage, he discovers a land of wise and gentle horses called Houyhnhnms, who ruled a vicious population of humanoids called Yahoos.

gunboat diplomacy, general phrase used to define a nation's foreign policy objectives through force, military intervention, or coercion. Gunboat diplomacy had its origins in the **Opium War**, when the Chinese rebelled against British importation of opium into China, and the British response was to send a gunboat up the **Yangtze River**.

Gun Cargo, 1949 motion picture about the adventures of a cruel captain and a crew of misfits in the Caribbean in 1906. It starred Rex Lease, Smith Ballew, and William Farnum.

gunkhole, small indentation in a shore, cove, bay, or river where the water usually is too shallow for larger craft but navigable by small craft. To go gunkholing is to cruise uncrowded coastal waters in a small boat, visiting and often stopping in gunkholes.

gybe, see **jibe**.

gyrocompass, shipboard navigational system that incorporates a gyroscope controlled in such a way that its spin axis is made to seek and maintain alignment with the earth's north–south meridian. Thus, the gyrocompass points consistently true north. It was patented in 1908 by German engineer Herman Anschutz and American inventor **Elmer Sperry**. In 1911 Sperry installed the first gyrocompass on the Old Dominion Line's *Princess Anne* for a trial run from New York down the coast to **Hampton Roads**, Virginia. It worked!

H

HA-8, Japanese midget submarine captured during World War II. The forty-six-ton HA subs were designed to be launched from seaplane tenders, where the submersible's two-man crew would then navigate their craft and its twin torpedoes closer to the intended target. The *HA-8* is today on exhibit at the Historic Ship *Nautilus* & Submarine Force Museum in Groton, Connecticut.

Hacker Craft, boatbuilding company specializing in high-speed **runabouts**, established in 1915 in Mt. Clemens, Michigan, by John L. Hacker. His designs were innovative, and he manufactured both custom and production boats, called Hackers, until the 1950s.

Hadley's quadrant, a navigational instrument invented in 1731 by English amateur scientist John Hadley (1682–1744), which enabled much more accurate navigation measurements to be made from the deck of a ship. The easy-to-use instrument, also known as an "octant," employed two mirrors that allowed for measurements of up to ninety degrees despite the device being only forty-five

degrees, or one eighth of a circle. It evolved into the **sextant** around 1757.

Hague Line, popular name for the international boundary that divides U.S. and Canadian waters on **Georges Bank**.

hailing port, port where a vessel is registered or enrolled, or the place in the same district where the vessel was built, or where one or more of the owners resides. The hailing port along with the ship's name must be shown on a **documented vessel**'s stern.

The Hairy Ape, 1923 **Eugene O'Neill** play in which Yank Smith, a stoker aboard a transatlantic **liner**, is jilted by a millionaire's daughter and vows to get even with her. His plan to destroy a factory owned by her father fails and he wanders into a zoo, where he releases an ape that kills him. The 1944 screen adaptation starred William Bendix and Susan Hayward.

Hakluyt, Richard (pronounced "Hack-loot") (1552–1616), English geographer and maritime historian who published *Principal Navigations, Voyages, Traffics and Discoveries of the*

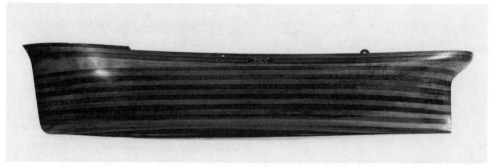

Half model of the ship *Frolic*, circa 1869. (Courtesy Mystic Seaport Museum)

English Nation (1589) (also published as *Hakluyt's Voyages*), consisting of eyewitness accounts and other records of more than two hundred voyages. These stories stirred up interest in navigation and colonization.

Hakluyt Society, organization founded in Britain in 1847 to continue the work of **Richard Hakluyt** and publish scholarly editions of primary sources on the voyages and travels undertaken by individuals from many parts of the globe.

Hakluyt's Voyages, common name for *Principal Navigations, Voyages, Traffics and Discoveries of the English Nation* (1589), one of the more famous compilations of collective voyage accounts that sometimes include important information from little-known voyages. Compiled by **Richard Hakluyt**, the ten volumes contain primary source reports and finely engraved maps and illustrations.

halcyon days, period of calm weather before and after the shortest day of the year, about December 21. The phrase is taken from the halcyon, an ancient Greek mythical bird who nested on the surface of the ocean and was able to quiet the winds while its eggs were hatching.

Hales Trophy, a four-foot-high silver trophy awarded to the commercial vessel that makes the fastest crossing of the **Atlantic Ocean**. Named after British parliamentarian Harold K. Hales, who offered the award, it shows the sea

god **Neptune** sitting on a marble base surrounded by mermaids. The mermaids are supporting a globe in their uplifted arms, around which is tied a blue silk ribbon representing the **Blue Riband**. First awarded in 1934, the trophy has been held by the **liners Rex**, *Normandie*, *Queen Mary*, and *United States*. The trophy has been captured in recent years by a series of high-speed ferries and yachts, but merchant mariners disregard these efforts and feel the superliner SS *United States* really retains the trophy.

Haley, Alex P. (1921–1992), renowned novelist and author of the worldwide best-seller *Roots*, which won a Pulitzer Prize in 1977, and *The Autobiography of Malcolm X*, among others. Haley enlisted in the U.S. **Coast Guard** in 1939 and served in various capacities as a writer and editor before becoming the service's first journalist. He retired in 1959, after serving in World War II and Korea as a chief journalist.

half model, carved wooden model of one side of the hull of a ship with little or no deck details. In early times, half models were used to design a ship and by the nineteenth century were used as an intermediate stage between the plan and the full-size vessel.

Half-Safe, 1955 book by Australian adventurer and author Ben Carlin (1912–1981) about his round-the-world trip in a World War II surplus amphibious jeep, which was named *Half-Safe* because Carlin believed it was "half-safe."

The book begins with his leaving Montréal with his wife, Elinore, in 1950 and ends with his reaching Europe and having the vehicle totally rebuilt in England from 1952 to 1954. Carlin's follow-up book, *The Other Half of Half-Safe* (1989), tells about the rest of the 9,600-**nautical-miles** and 39,000-mile journey. *Half-Safe* is now on permanent display in Perth, Australia.

half seas over, term used to describe the condition of a vessel that has stranded on a reef or rock with the seas washing over her deck. It also describes someone who is well on the way to being drunk.

Hall, Charles Francis (1821–1871), American explorer of the Arctic who in 1859 raised his own funds and went in search of the **Franklin Expedition**. Although finding no clues on that trip, he returned to the Arctic in 1864 and remained there for five years, coming upon some traces of the ill-fated expedition. In 1871 the U.S. Congress granted Hall funding for an expedition to the North Pole. In the 140-foot tug USS *Polaris*, he reached 82°11´ North, a record for the time, but died soon thereafter.

Hall, James Norman (1887–1951), American writer best known for his work with **Charles Bernhard Nordhoff** on *Mutiny on the Bounty*. In addition to his many collaborative efforts as part of the **Nordhoff and Hall** team, his other novels include *Dr. Dogbody's Leg* (1937), *Lost Island* (1944), and *The Far Lands* (1950).

Halliburton, Richard (1900–1939), American adventurer, writer, and lecturer. He traveled throughout the world and wrote many books about his trips, including *The Glorious Adventure* (1927), *New Worlds to Conquer* (1929), *The Flying Carpet* (1932), *Seven League Boots* (1935), and *Richard Halliburton's Complete Book of Marvels* (1937). In 1928 Halliburton swam the **Panama Canal**, paying a toll of thirty-six cents. In 1939, he and his crew attempted to sail a Chinese **junk**, the *Sea Dragon*,

from Hong Kong to San Francisco as a publicity stunt. The vessel was unseaworthy and went down in a storm, and everyone on board was lost. Halliburton's last message was, "Southerly gales, squalls, lee rail under water, wet bunks, hard tack, bully beef, wish you were here—instead of me!"

Halsey, William Frederick "Bull," Jr. (1882–1959), U.S. **Navy** admiral during World War II whose handling of carrier fleets played a significant role in defeating Japan. He launched the **Doolittle Raid on Tokyo** in 1942, and in 1944 led the U.S. fleet at the Battle of **Leyte Gulf**. He was promoted to fleet admiral in 1945.

Halve Moen, vessel commissioned in 1609 for the **Dutch East India Company** and captained by the Englishman **Henry Hudson**. Hudson set out to find a **Northeast Passage** to China north of Russia, but ice blocked the route one month into the voyage. The decision was made to alter course and search for a **Northwest Passage** instead. The *Halve Moen* probed the east coast of North America as far south as the Carolinas. Hudson then headed north and discovered the mouth of the **Hudson River**. The *Halve Moen* sailed upriver hoping to reach the Pacific and journeyed as far north as Albany. After it became apparent that this was a freshwater route, the *Halve Moen* returned to the mouth of the river and claimed the land (New Amsterdam) for Holland.

Hamburg, first major newly built passenger liner for German owners in the post–World War II era. She was completed in 1969 and advertised as "the Space Ship" by her German-Atlantic Line owners. Sold in 1973 for cruising under the Soviet flag, the 25,022-gross-ton steamer was briefly renamed *Britannic* for her starring role in the movie *Juggernaut*. She was refitted for cruising in 1974 as the *Maxim Gorki*.

Hamburg-America Line, German shipping line established in 1847 as the Hamburg-

Amerikanische Packetfahrt-Actien-Gesellschaft (HAPAG). North Atlantic service opened in 1848 and, under the directorship of Albert Ballin, Hamburg-America pioneered the "cruise." The line's *Deutschland* won the **Blue Riband** on her **maiden voyage** in 1900, but World Wars I and II resulted in the loss of the company's entire fleet. In 1970 Hamburg-America merged with **North German Lloyd** to form **HAPAG-Lloyd**.

Hamilton, Alexander (1755–1804), U.S. secretary of the treasury under President George Washington. In organizing the finances of the young republic, Hamilton realized that tariffs on imported goods were the primary means of generating revenue and that smugglers were inhibiting the collection of these funds. He proposed the construction of ten **cutters** to safeguard revenue by combating smuggling, and on August 4, 1790, Congress established the **Revenue Marine** and authorized the cutters' construction. Hamilton is regarded as the "Father of the U.S. **Coast Guard**," and August 4 is recognized as Coast Guard Day. Hamilton was killed in a duel with Aaron Burr.

Hamilton, Emma (c. 1765–1815), wife of Sir William Hamilton, the British ambassador to Naples, and the mistress of **Horatio Nelson**. Her influence over Nelson became so great that he disobeyed his orders to leave Naples and join a squadron in the Mediterranean. She gave birth to Nelson's daughter Horatia in 1801, and after his death at the Battle of **Trafalgar** in 1805, she tried and failed to procure a government pension. Lady Hamilton died in poverty.

Hampton Roads, natural channel and harbor formed at the place where the James, Nansemond, and Elizabeth Rivers meet in Virginia. These rivers flow through Hampton Roads into Chesapeake Bay. The name derives from the Earl of Southhampton, who granted the colonial charter.

Hampton Roads, Battle of, naval engagement fought March 8 and 9, 1862, off Norfolk,

Hamburg. (Courtesy Gordon R. Ghareeb)

Virginia. After CSS *Virginia* sank USS *Cumberland* and destroyed USS *Congress*, the Union **ironclad** USS *Monitor* arrived from New York. On the morning of March 9, the two vessels exchanged gunfire for four hours—the first battle ever to be fought between two ironclad ships. No winner emerged, but the match forever changed the nature of warfare at sea.

USS *Hancock* (CV-19), 888-foot **Essex**-class aircraft carrier completed in 1944, which launched air strikes in World War II. During action at Okinawa, one of her returning planes exploded, killing fifty crew members and injuring another seventy-five. The 27,100-ton ship was modernized in 1952 and was the first American carrier to be fitted with steam catapults for launching jet aircraft. Active off the coast of Vietnam during the war in Southeast Asia, she was decommissioned in 1976 and sold for scrap later in the year.

Hand, William (1875–1946), American yacht designer who was innovative in both power and sail. He is best known for pioneering the motorsailer, a marriage of the motorboat and auxiliary sailboat, and for designing a **cigarette boat**.

Hanseatic League, group of northwest German towns, or *hansas*, that created a trading confederation in the twelfth century and united for mutual protection against the pirates of the Baltic Sea. Powerful in shipping and fishing, the league established a near-monopoly in Baltic and North trade but declined in importance during the fifteenth century.

MS *Hans Hedtoft*, 2,875-gross-ton Danish motor **liner** built for operation between Denmark and Greenland by the Royal Greenland Trading Company. While on her return **maiden voyage** in January 1959, with ninety-five passengers and crew on board, she struck an iceberg forty miles south of Cape Farewell, the southernmost point of Greenland. Rescue ships arriving at the scene the following day found no trace of the wreck nor any survivors.

HAPAG, acronym for the **Hamburg-America Line**. It was established in 1847 as the Hamburg-Amerikanische Packetfahrt-Actien-Gesellschaft.

Hapag-Lloyd, German shipping line formed in 1970 by the merger of **Hamburg-America** and **North German Lloyd** lines. Since then the line has specialized in container shipping and cruises. Among its cruise ships are the *Europa*, *Bremen*, *Sea Cloud*, and *Sea Cloud II*.

harbor chart, chart with a scale larger than 1:50,000, used for harbors and smaller waterways.

harbormaster, person who administers the berthings and vessel movements that take place within a particular port. He or she has the experience of a certified **master** mariner and an excellent working knowledge of the characteristics of the port.

hardtack, hard biscuits baked without salt and dried in a hot oven, also called **sea biscuits**. They were a staple provision for ships on long sea voyages before refrigeration, because they resisted spoilage.

Hardy, Thomas Masterman (1769–1839), British naval officer, later admiral and **First Sea Lord**, who is one of the most famous captains in the **Royal Navy**. He fought in the American

Revolution and was present at all of **Horatio Nelson**'s great victories, commanding HMS *Victory* at the Battle of **Trafalgar** in 1805, where he was exhorted by the dying Nelson to "Kiss me, Hardy."

Harland and Wolff, shipbuilder founded in Belfast, Ireland, in 1853, which achieved fame by building many of the most famous ships for Great Britain's **White Star Line**, including RMS *Titanic*. During both world wars, the yard delivered hundreds of vessels, and the site was a prime target for German bombers during World War II. Today it is one of the best-equipped shipbuilding facilities in the world.

Harlow, Frederick P. (1856–1952), American sailor and author of the classic *The Making of a Sailor, or Sea Life Aboard a Yankee Square-Rigger* (1928), a colorful firsthand account of the excitement and danger aboard a **square-rigged** ship in the 1870s. He also wrote *Chanteying Aboard American Ships* (1962), published posthumously, one of the principal sources for nineteenth-century sea music.

Harmsworth Trophy, popular name for the British International Cup for Motorboats. It was introduced in 1903 by Irish-born newspaper publisher Sir Alfred Harmsworth to be awarded to boat racing teams, not individuals. The competition was dominated in the late 1920s and 1930s by **Garfield A. "Gar" Wood**.

Harriet Lane, 180-foot **side-wheel** steam **cutter** that fired the first shot from a ship in the Civil War. Launched in 1858 for the U.S. **Revenue Cutter Service**, she was named for President Buchanan's niece, the bachelor president's unofficial first lady. Entering naval service in 1861, *Harriet Lane* challenged the steamer *Nashville* with a shot across her bow off Charleston, South Carolina, on April 14, 1861. Captured by Southern naval forces in 1863, she became the **blockade runner** *Lavinia* and flew the Confederate flag until the end of the war. Sunk in Havana in 1865, she was raised and renamed *Elliott Richie*, and she kept on steaming until 1884.

Harriman, W. Averell (1891–1986), American diplomat and businessman who inherited a fortune from his father, the railroad tycoon Edward H. Harriman. Harriman launched **United American Lines** in the early 1920s and sold it off by the end of the decade. He served as chairman of the board of Union Pacific Railroad from 1932 to 1946. During World War II, Harriman coordinated **Lend-Lease** supplies to Britain and the Soviet Union and later served as U.S. ambassador to each of those countries. He served as secretary of commerce from 1946 to 1948 under President Harry S. Truman, and from 1948 to 1952, he administered the **Marshall Plan**. He served as governor of New York from 1955 to 1958 and later in many other diplomatic roles.

Harriman Alaska Expedition, 1899 scientific expedition to Alaska sponsored by American railroad executive Edward H. Harriman. A group of 126 members, including some of the most esteemed American scientists, writers, photographers, and artists of the day, made the eight-week voyage from Seattle aboard the **steamship** *George W. Elder*. The expedition's findings were published by the Smithsonian Institution in a thirteen-volume series titled *Harriman Alaska Expedition* (1901–14).

Harrison, John (1693–1776), self-taught English clockmaker who built numerous precise timepieces in an effort to determine **longitude** at sea and win the £20,000 prize set forth in the **Longitude Act** of 1714. After nearly sixty years, numerous **chronometers**, and many trials, Harrison was awarded the prize by an act of Parliament in 1773 and was finally recognized as having solved the longitude problem.

USS *Hartford*, 225-foot U.S. **Navy** screw **sloop** built in 1859 that served as the **flagship** of Admiral **David Glasgow Farragut** during the Civil War. She played an important role in the

capture of New Orleans in 1862, the capture of Vicksburg in 1863, and the Battle of **Mobile Bay** in 1864. After the war, *Hartford* continued to serve in the navy as a warship and later as a training vessel. After spending time in Washington, D.C., and Norfolk, Virginia, she was finally broken up in 1956.

Hart Nautical Collections, museum founded in 1921 as a component to the Department of Naval Architecture and Marine Engineering at the Massachusetts Institute of Technology. Officially the Francis Russell Hart Nautical Museum, its focus is the technical history of ship and small craft design, construction, and propulsion. The most visible component of the collection is the more than forty ship models on display.

Harvard, California coastal **liner** built in 1907 along with her sister ship *Yale*. Originally intended for East Coast operation, both ships were brought to the Pacific for charter work. After troopship service in World War I, the pair was purchased by the **Los Angeles Steamship Company** for $1,755,000 to provide regular, fast service between Los Angeles and San Francisco. *Harvard* ran onto rocks off Point Arguello, California, in 1931, without casualties. The 3,818-gross-ton liner became a constructive total loss and was eventually destroyed by the pounding surf.

Harvard vs. Yale Regatta, the first intercollegiate sporting event, first competed in 1852. It introduced intercollege athletics and the popularity of rowing as a sport. The event continues to be held each year on the Thames River in New London, Connecticut.

Hashimoto, Mochitsura (1909–2000), one of the few Japanese submarine commanders to survive World War II. As captain of I-58, he sank USS ***Indianapolis*** during the last days of the war. Hashimoto testified at the court-martial of Charles McVay, captain of the *Indianapolis*, that he would have spotted and torpedoed the ship even if it had been zigzagging. During his last years, Hashimoto supported the *Indianapolis* survivors' fight to clear McVay's name.

Hawaii Calls, fanciful 1938 movie about an island-bound stowaway who is discovered aboard ship and sings his way across the Pacific entertaining the passengers. The film starred Bobby Breen, Pua Lani, and Ward Bond.

Hawkins, John (1532–1595), English sea captain who played an important role in defending England against the **Spanish Armada** in 1588. He was knighted in the battle. In 1595 he and Sir **Francis Drake** were sent to raid Spanish settlements in the **West Indies**, where they both died.

hawsepipe, steel tunnel through which the anchor chain runs at the bow of a ship.

hawser, heavy fiber or wire rope used for towing or docking.

Hayden, Sterling (1916–1986), American actor, sailor, and author. During the Hollywood blacklisting of the 1950s, Hayden confessed prior membership in the Communist party and named colleagues as members. His autobiography, *Wanderer* (1963), tells the story of his 1959 voyage to Tahiti with his children aboard his 1938 **schooner** *Wanderer* after a California court threatened to take the children away. Hayden's novel, *Voyage: A Novel of 1896* (1976), was his first and only foray into fiction. He appeared in nearly seventy films, including *Dr. Strangelove* (1962) and *The Godfather* (1972).

Hayes, William A. "Bully" (1829–1877), legendary **South Seas** adventurer and pirate. Among his trademarks was hiring on as a captain of a vessel and then either selling it to others or selling the goods on board for personal profit. His name became known from San Francisco to Sydney and throughout the Pacific. Late in his career, Bully was immortalized in popular novels.

head, toilet on a vessel. The use of the word comes from the days when sailors relieved themselves at the water's edge from the bow or head of the ship.

headboat, vessel that is chartered or hired on a per-person basis, usually engaged in recreational fishing.

headsail, any triangular sail set forward of the foremast.

Healy, Michael (1839–1902), known as Hell-Roaring Mike, the son of a Georgia slave and her master. He served a distinguished career in the U.S. **Revenue Cutter Service** and is best known as captain of the **cutter** *Bear* from 1887 to 1895. In 1890 Healy initiated the successful program that transferred herds of reindeer from Siberia to Alaska in order to help feed the native population. He was the service's foremost Arctic navigator, and he maintained American laws in Alaska in the absence of established courts. Healy retired as the third-highest ranking officer from the Revenue Cutter Service.

Heart of Darkness, 1902 novella by **Joseph Conrad** in which Marlow tells of his voyage in command of a **steamboat** far up the Congo River to relieve the mad ivory trader Kurtz. The story was adapted to fit the Vietnam War in Francis Ford Coppola's 1979 film *Apocalypse Now*.

"Heart of Oak", authorized march tune for Britain's **Royal Navy**. The music was written by Dr. William Boyce (1711–1779), and the words were taken from actor David Garrick's (1716–1779) song "Harlequin Invasion," written and composed in 1759 to commemorate the naval victories of that year. The chorus goes, "Heart of oak are our ships, jolly too are our men; We always are ready, steady, boys, steady! We'll fight and we'll conquer again and again!"

Heavy Weather Sailing, classic 1967 how-to book by veteran English yachtsman and book publisher **Kaines Adlard Coles** about storms at sea and the handling of small craft. It has been revised and reprinted a number of times.

Hebrides, group of islands off the west coast of Scotland, divided into the Inner Hebrides and the Outer Hebrides.

hedgehog, bow-launched antisubmarine weapon used in World War II to combat the German **U-boat** threat. The small-depth charges exploded on impact.

Helen of Troy, in Greek mythology, the daughter of Zeus. She was considered the most beautiful woman in the world, and her abduction by Paris led to the Trojan War. Author Christopher Marlowe described her beauty as "the face that launched a thousand ships," because the entire Greek army sailed to Troy to get her back.

Heligoland Bight, Battle of, important World War I British naval victory over German forces in the Heligoland Bight, the stretch of water between Heligoland Island and the northwest coast of the German mainland. The August 28, 1914, success by battle **cruisers** of the **Grand Fleet**, under the command of Admiral **David Beatty**, was a severe blow to German naval morale.

Hellcats of the Navy, 1957 movie about the U.S. submarine service in the Pacific during World War II. The stars of the film—Ronald Reagan and Nancy Davis—had been married for five years before this production was made and well before its leading man went off to tackle politics. It is the only film in which the couple starred together.

Hell Gate, channel in New York City's East River that lies between Wards Island and the Queensborough portion of Long Island. Early Dutch settlers of New York may have named it Hell Gate because of its dangerous tidal whirlpool, swift current, and submerged rocks. The rocks were removed and the channel deepened during the last half of the 1800s. Nine hundred feet

wide and thirty-four feet deep, the channel is spanned by the Triborough Bridge and is often referred to as the "Back Door" to New York Harbor.

Hemingway, Ernest (1898–1961), American novelist and short story writer who has become a literary icon. His novel *The **Old Man and the Sea*** (1952) won the 1953 Pulitzer Prize for fiction. Other sea-related novels include *To Have and Have Not* (1937) and *Islands in the Stream* (1970). The latter, published posthumously, is about an American artist living in **Bimini** who is drafted into the service of American intelligence in World War II. Hemingway was often seen fishing the waters of the Caribbean in his 1934 Wheeler Playmate cruiser *Pilar*.

hen frigate, vessel on which the captain's wife went along for the voyage.

Henley Royal Regatta, international rowing regatta held each summer since 1839 (except during the two world wars) on the Thames River above London. A highlight of the social season, the regatta was extended to five days in 1986.

Henrietta Marie, seventeenth-century slave ship that was wrecked off the coast of Florida in 1700 with no survivors. The wreck was first discovered in 1972 off Key West by **Mel Fisher**. Fisher donated his claim to the wreck site and all its artifacts to his Maritime Heritage Society, which organizes exhibitions of what are considered the world's most important sources of artifacts from the early period of transatlantic slave trade.

Henry B. Hyde, celebrated **Down Easter** built in Bath, Maine, in 1884 and considered by many to have been the finest American **ship** of the post-**clipper** era. The 290-foot vessel made numerous passages between New York and San Francisco and was driven ashore off Cape Henry, Virginia, and wrecked in 1904 while being towed from New York to Baltimore.

Henry the Navigator (1394–1460), Portugese nobleman who has been described as "the Father of Modern Navigation." Prince Henry sponsored many expeditions to the north and west coasts of Africa and in 1450 established a naval observatory at Cape Sagres, Portugal, for teaching astronomy, cartography, and navigation. A grand monument to Henry stands in the harbor in Lisbon, Portugal, where he stands before the human wave set in motion by his pioneering the Age of Discovery.

Henson, Matthew Alexander (1867–1955), African-American sailor and explorer who accompanied **Robert Edwin Peary** on the last leg of his journey to the North Pole in 1909. He had traveled on expeditions with Peary for more than twenty years. He wrote the book *A Negro Explorer at the North Pole*.

Herald of Free Enterprise, **P&O** auto ferry that had just departed Dover, England, on March 6, 1987, for Zeebrugge, Belgium, when she capsized onto her port side and sank in less than two minutes, taking the lives of 193 of the 623 people on board. The cause of the disaster was determined to be the open bow loading doors, which allowed the sea to flood into the car deck. The loss of life would have been greater if the ship had not settled onto a sandbank in thirty feet of water.

Here Comes the Navy, 1934 romantic comedy motion picture about a land-based feud carried out at sea aboard USS *Arizona*. Excellent footage of the battleship is provided because the film was actually shot on board. The movie starred James Cagney, Pat O'Brien, and Gloria Stuart.

hermaphrodite brig, a two-masted sailing vessel with the foremast of a **brig** and the mainmast of a **schooner**. It is sometimes called a "half brig."

HMS *Hermione*, **frigate** that was the site of the bloodiest mutiny in **Royal Navy** history. In 1797, while off the coast of Venezuela,

Hermione's crew revolted against Captain Hugh Pigot and his extreme punishment, killing ten officers. The British **Admiralty** responded by hunting down all of the mutineers—the last in 1805—and executing them. The story is told in **Dudley Pope**'s *The Black Ship* (1963).

Herndon, William (1813–1857), subject of the U.S. **Navy**'s only monument to a peacetime hero, at the U.S. **Naval Academy**. As captain of SS *Central America*, Herndon went down with his ship after seeing to the rescue of many passengers. Herndon's timely heroism inspired a small Virginia town to name itself after this famous native Virginian. Herndon's chronicle of his exploration of the Amazon Valley, *Exploration of the Valley of the Amazon*, published by the U.S. Navy in 1853–54, inspired reader **Samuel Clemens** to head for Brazil, only to be stranded on a **Mississippi River** dock, where he found his destiny, first as a riverboat **pilot** and then as the writer **Mark Twain**. Herndon's brother-in-law, **Matthew Fontaine Maury**, achieved his own measure of nautical and literary fame.

Herreshoff, L. Francis (pronounced "Herreshoff") (1890–1972), American naval architect and sailor nicknamed Skipper and son of **Nathanael Greene Herreshoff**. As a yacht designer, he created racing and cruising yachts as well as small sailing craft. In the 1940s he began writing his famous articles for the *Rudder* magazine, which formed the basis for his books *The Common Sense of Yacht Design* (1974), *Capt. Nat Herreshoff* (1953), *The Compleat Cruiser* (1956), and *Introduction to Yachting* (1963), among others. His most enduring vessels include *Ticonderoga* and *Rozinante*.

Herreshoff, Nathanael Greene (1848–1938), prominent American naval architect and yacht designer who owned and operated the Herreshoff Manufacturing Company in Bristol,

Rhode Island, which was unequaled in its day. Known as the Wizard of Bristol, he designed five successful **America's Cup** defenders—*Vigilant* (1890), *Defender* (1895), *Columbia* (1899 and 1901), *Reliance* (1903), and *Resolute* (1920).

Heyerdahl, Thor (b. 1914), Norwegian anthropologist who undertook many sea voyages in an attempt to prove his various theories. In 1947 he and five others drifted forty-three hundred miles aboard the balsa raft *Kon-Tiki* to prove that Polynesians came from South America, not Southeast Asia. In 1970 he sailed from Africa to the **West Indies** in the papyrus boat *Ra II* to contend that sailors from Egypt or Phoenicia reached South America or Mexico and built pyramids there. *Kon-Tiki* and *Ra II*, as well as other artifacts from Heyerdahl's expeditions, are on display at the Kon-Tiki Museum in Oslo, Norway.

SS H. F. Alexander, steamer built in 1915 as the *Great Northern* for Pacific coastal operation by the Great Northern Pacific Steamship Company. After World War I service as a navy transport, she was sold in 1922 to the Admiral Line and renamed *H. F. Alexander*. The twenty-five-**knot** speedster was known as the Galloping Ghost of the Pacific Coast for her ability to beat railroad schedules between San Francisco and Seattle by more than three hours. Used as a U.S. Army transport during World War II and renamed the *George S. Simonds*, she was scrapped in 1948 at Philadelphia.

Higgins boat, thirty-six-foot, shallow-draft, World War II landing craft built by Higgins Industries of New Orleans. Constructed of wood and steel, this type of boat was also used for transporting troops, light tanks, artillery, and other mechanized equipment for amphibious operations. Founded by Andrew Jackson Higgins, Higgins Industries also manufactured **PT boats**. The combined output by Higgins Industries during the war was 20,094 boats.

SS *H. F. Alexander*. (Bruce Vancil)

high seas, the seas beyond a country's declared territorial waters and **exclusive economic zone**. They are usually international waters and open to the shipping of all nations. In recent years, territorial waters have been extended to twelve miles, and most countries claim a two-hundred-mile economic zone in which only certain laws can be enforced.

Hikawa Maru, Japanese **liner** built for the transpacific trade of the NYK Line (**Nippon Yusen Kaisha**) in 1930. The 11,622-gross-ton motor ship, the only Japanese passenger vessel to survive World War II, returned to her Kobe-to-Seattle route in 1950. She was retired in 1961 and was used at various times as a youth hostel, exhibit, and restaurant ship in Yokohama, Japan.

Hildebrand, Arthur Sturgis (1887–1924), American cruiser and nautical writer who was lost at sea in the Arctic. He designed the Blue Water Medal for the **Cruising Club of America**, which continues to be the ultimate recognition of an outstanding offshore voyage.

Hiryu, Japanese aircraft carrier built in 1939 that took part in the December 7, 1941, raid on **Pearl Harbor**. The 746-foot ship was set on fire by planes from USS *Enterprise* and USS *Yorktown* during the Battle of **Midway** in 1942 and was subsequently **scuttled** to prevent capture.

Hiryu and her sister *Akagi* were the only aircraft carriers ever built with portside islands, or superstructures. Each was meant to work with a **starboard**-island ship so as to improve the flight patterns around the carriers.

Hispaniola, fictional vessel used by Jim Hawkins in search of Captain Flint's treasure in **Robert Louis Stevenson**'s novel *Treasure Island* (1883).

Historic American Merchant Marine Survey (HAMMS), 1936–37 Works Progress Administration project for the watercraft collection of the Smithsonian Institution. The resulting seven volumes record the plans and specifications of 426 vessels. HAMMS was administered by the Department of the Interior and was a personal favorite of **Franklin D. Roosevelt** because of his keen interest in ship models.

History Is Made at Night, schmaltzy 1937 feature film drama climaxing aboard a European-bound passenger ship in some extraordinarily unbelievable circumstances. It contained excellent ocean **liner** sets in an otherwise melodramatic story. It starred Charles Boyer, Jean Arthur, and Leo Carrillo.

History of the American Whale Fishery, important reference book on whaling history compiled by Alexander Starbuck and first published in 1878. It recounts the techniques and ships of the great days of whaling and includes comprehensive tabular lists of American whaling voyages up to 1876.

History of the Navy of the United States of America, comprehensive 1839 work in two volumes of the history of the early U.S. **Navy**, beginning in 1605 and continuing through 1815, by **James Fenimore Cooper**.

The History of United States Naval Operations in World War II, thorough and meticulously detailed fifteen-volume "shooting history" account of the American fight at sea during World War II, written between 1947 and 1962 by Rear Admiral **Samuel Eliot Morison**, USNR. Wanting to chronicle the battle from the inside, Morison approached President **Franklin D. Roosevelt** early in 1942 about the proposed project. Roosevelt OK'ed the plan, and Morison was commissioned as a lieutenant commander in the U.S. **Naval Reserve** in order to author the epic, serving on eleven different ships in far-flung campaigns to record the history while it was being made. Accurate and dependable, the work has become the standard reference on the subject.

Hit the Deck, 1955 musical about three U.S. sailors on shore leave in San Francisco. While prowling for dames, they become involved in a brawl and are chased by the **Shore Patrol**. The film starred Jane Powell, Debbie Reynolds, and Ann Miller.

CSS H. L. Hunley, forty-foot **Confederate States Navy** submarine that became the first underwater vessel to sink a ship in wartime. The hand-cranked *Hunley*, built from locomotive boilers, carried an explosive attached to a long spar on its bow. On February 17, 1864, it rammed the Union blockade ship USS *Housatonic* in Charleston Harbor in South Carolina. The explosion sank the *Housatonic*, but the *Hunley* also went to the bottom with its victim. In 1995, a search team led by author and amateur marine archaeologist **Clive Cussler** found the wreckage of the *Hunley*, which was raised in 2000.

HMS, ship prefix meaning "His or Her Majesty's Ship," long used by Britain's **Royal Navy**. British Empire/Commonwealth navies used their own versions, such as HMCS for Canada, HMNZS for New Zealand, and HMAS for Australia.

HMS Pinafore, 1878 comic operetta by William Gilbert and Arthur Sullivan about the marriage of the daughter of the captain of HMS

Pinafore. The production contains the notable songs "I'm Called Little Buttercup" and "When I Was a Lad."

Hobie Cat, a series of **catamarans** introduced by **Hobart "Hobie" Alter** in the 1960s. Measuring fourteen, sixteen, and eighteen feet, the boats are capable of speeds upward of twenty-four **knots**.

USS *Hobson*, destroyer-minesweeper that was rammed by the aircraft carrier USS *Wasp* during night maneuvers in the North Atlantic on April 26, 1952. The force of the collision rolled USS *Hobson* over, breaking her in two, and she sank with 176 lives lost.

Hodges, William (1744–1797), British artist appointed by the **Admiralty** to accompany Captain **James Cook** on his second expedition. Hodges made on-the-spot drawings from which he worked up larger oil paintings for exhibition. Some of his designs were engraved for Cook's *A Voyage Towards the South Pole and Around the World 1772–1775* (1777).

hog, vessel whose bow and stern have drooped. It is the opposite of sag.

Hog Island, site of the largest shipyard in the United States, located on the Delaware River south of Philadelphia. The U.S. **Shipping Board** and the **Emergency Fleet Corporation** established the facility in 1917 with fifty shipways to mass-produce simply designed 401-foot freighters and 448-foot troop transports for World War I. The American International Shipbuilding Corporation Plant at Hog Island delivered 122 "Hog Islanders" before it was closed in 1921. The land was sold to the City of Philadelphia in 1930 and eventually became the site of the city's airport.

Hokusai, Katsushika (1760–1849), Japanese artist who is considered one of the masters of Ukiyo-e, or woodcut art. Among his most famous works are *In the Hollow of a Wave off the Coast at Kanagawa*, often referred to as *The Wave*, and his series *Thirty-six Views of Mt. Fuji*.

Hole in the Wall, maritime landmark located on the southwest coast of Great Abaco Island in the Bahamas. It is a favorite spot of whale watchers and dolphin researchers, and it was a hideout for Butch Cassidy and the Sundance Kid.

holiday routine, U.S. **Navy** and **Coast Guard** term for a day when no nonessential work or drills are conducted. It is a day off at sea.

Holland, John Philip (1841–1914), Irish-American inventor who was primarily responsible for the development of the submarine. His vessel, the *Holland*, built in 1898, proved that the submarine was practical and provided the model for later submarines. In 1900, the U.S. **Navy** bought the *Holland* and asked the inventor to build several more ships like it. Holland's firm, the **Electric Boat Company** (now the Electric Boat Division of **General Dynamics** Corporation), has continued to build most U.S. Navy submarines.

USS *Holland* (SS-1), first U.S. **Navy** submarine. In 1898, inventor John Holland built and launched a fifty-three-foot submarine powered by a gasoline engine and electric batteries. It could reach a speed of six **knots** submerged and carried four torpedoes and a crew of seven. The U.S. Navy purchased the vessel for $150,000 on October 12, 1900, and commissioned it USS *Holland*. The purchase date is considered the birth date of the navy's submarine force. *Holland* was scrapped in 1910.

Holland America Line, shipping line founded in 1873 as the Netherlands-America Steamship Company to run a transatlantic steamer service. The line was a principal carrier of emigrants from Europe to the United States until well after the turn of the twentieth century, carrying 850,000 people to new lives in the

New World. Some of its more famous **liners** included SS *Rotterdam*, SS *Nieuw Amsterdam*, and SS *Statendam*. In 1971 the line suspended its transatlantic service and turned to offering cruise vacations full-time. Purchased by **Carnival Cruise Lines** in 1983, the company has managed to maintain much of its renowned Dutch character.

Holmes, Oliver Wendell (1809–1894), American physician, writer, and poet. In 1830, while still a college student at Harvard, he won national acclaim with the publication of his poem **"Old Ironsides,"** which aroused public sentiment against the destruction of the **frigate** USS *Constitution*. "Oh, better that her shattered hulk should sink beneath the wave," he stated, than be plucked by the "harpies on the shore." Congress appropriated funds to restore the shattered vessel.

holystone, large brick of sandstone used by crew members to scour a wooden deck of a ship. Its name comes from the fact that sailors used the stone while on their hands and knees as if in a position of prayer.

"Home is the sailor, home from the sea", line from the 1887 poem "Requiem" by **Robert Louis Stevenson**. Stevenson died at age forty-four, and "Requiem" is inscribed on his gravestone as an epitaph: "Under the wide and starry sky, / Dig the grave and let me lie. / Glad did I live and gladly die, / And I laid me down with a will. // This be the verse you grave for me: / Here lies where he long'd to be; / Home is the sailor, home from the sea, / And the hunter home from the hill."

Home Lines, multinational passenger shipping house started in 1947 with secondhand **Swedish America Line** vessels refitted for the South Atlantic service. Growth followed success, and the firm was operating on the North Atlantic route by 1949. The company specialized in running older tonnage. The first **liner** specifically built for them—SS *Oceanic* of 1965—was also their best known. The company was sold in 1988.

home port, port where a vessel is kept or out of which it usually sails. U.S. regulations specify that a home port must be recorded on the vessel's document; however, it need not be the port (the **hailing port**) written on the stern of a vessel. In many cases, a vessel's hailing port is different from its home port.

Homer (late eighth century or early seventh century B.C.), author of the *Iliad* and the *Odyssey*, the two greatest epic poems of ancient Greece.

Homer, Winslow (1836–1910), American artist famous for his intense and stirring paintings of the human activity associated with the sea. Homer illustrated battlefield scenes for *Harper's Weekly* during the Civil War, and in the early 1880s he settled permanently at Prout's Neck on the coast of Maine. Most of his sea paintings were done at Prout's Neck, but he often traveled to the Adirondack Mountains and to Florida, Bermuda, and Nassau. He developed his watercolor technique on these trips. He skillfully applied transparent washes to his work to instill a dramatic quality and fine feeling for light.

Homeric, 34,351-gross-ton motor ship laid down as the first *Columbus* for **North German Lloyd**. The hull, launched but unfinished, lay idle during World War I and was awarded to Britain per conditions of the **Treaty of Versailles**. She entered **White Star Line** transatlantic service in 1922 as the *Homeric* and operated in tandem with the SS *Majestic* and RMS *Olympic* on their premier New York run. After 1932 she was relegated to the role of cruise ship, sailing from Southampton to European ports. **Laid up** in 1935, she was sold for scrap two years later.

homeward bound pennant, long narrow pennant flown by ships after being away from their

home port for more than a year. It formerly was equal to a foot for every man aboard and was later cut up for souvenirs.

Honolulu Race, see **Transpacific Race**.

Hood, Samuel (1724–1816), British admiral who fought many naval engagements during the American Revolution. He was second-in-command when Admiral Sir **George Brydges Rodney** led the British fleet to victory over a French force under **François de Grasse** at the Battle of the **Saints** off the island of Dominica in 1782.

HMS *Hood*, British battle **cruiser** completed in 1920 and equipped with eight 15-inch guns as her main arsenal. Her deck armor was known to be inadequate, but in 1941 she engaged the brand-new German battleship ***Bismarck*** in action off Iceland. *Hood* was hit by the fifth salvo from the German **dreadnought**, and the explosion of her own magazines resulted in the nearly instantaneous destruction of the British craft, which broke in two. She sank quickly, taking all but three of the 1,421 crewmen on board with her.

Hook, Captain, infamous villain in the classic 1904 tale ***Peter Pan*** by Sir James Barrie. So named for his hook-shaped prosthesis on his lower right arm, Hook is relentlessly pursued by the crocodile that wounded him. The two classic screen portrayals of the comically foppish English pirate captain of the *Jolly Roger* were achieved by Hans Conried in the 1953 Disney animated feature film and by Cyril Ritchard in the critically acclaimed 1955 television production.

Hook, motion picture update of the ***Peter Pan*** saga. Wonderful characterizations bring this story to life in an endearing way. The 1991 film was directed by Steven Spielberg and starred Dustin Hoffman as Captain Hook, Julia Roberts, Maggie Smith, and Robin Williams.

Hooligan Navy, nickname for the U.S. **Coast Guard** that was first applied during World War II as it was perceived that the military matters and manners were not as enforced as the other armed services. It particularly applied to the many civilian yachtsmen who manned the **corsair fleet**.

USNS *Hope*, C4 transport constructed in 1944 and completed as the hospital ship USS *Consolation*. She was chartered in 1960 by the non-profit Project HOPE (Health Opportunities for People Everywhere) and sent on medical mercy missions to Third World nations. Carrying a nursing staff of 112 and 30 volunteer doctors, as well as an able-bodied crew of 92, she set out on her first tour under the aegis of the **American President Lines**. **Grace Line** took over the running of the vessel in 1972. The *Hope* was **laid up** in 1973 and scrapped two years later.

Hopkins, Esek (1718–1802), American merchant mariner from Rhode Island who was first commodore of the **Continental Navy**, appointed in 1775. His rank was to correspond with that of George Washington. He carried out a successful raid against the British in the Bahamas, capturing valuable guns and supplies, but in 1776 the Continental Congress became disappointed in his performance, censured him, and later dismissed him.

Hopper, Grace Murray (1906–1992), U.S. **Navy** rear admiral who was a pioneer in developing computer technology. She helped to devise Univac I, the first commercial electronic computer, and wrote languages so computers could be used for naval applications. She retired from active duty in 1986 at the age of 79. Hopper coined the term "bug" to refer to unexplained computer failures.

Hormuz, Straits of, body of water that links the Arabian Gulf to the Gulf of Oman. Two-thirds of the world's seaborne oil passes through these straits.

Hornblower, Horatio, fictional British naval officer who is the hero of twelve books by novelist **Cecil Scott "C. S." Forester**. Set in the **Napoleonic Wars**, Hornblower's exciting adventures, his coolness and inventiveness under stress, and his weakness for women endear him to a large reading public. Hornblower rises from midshipman to admiral in a series of novels, which includes *Mr. Midshipman Hornblower* (1950), *Lieutenant Hornblower* (1952), *Flying Colours* (1938), *A Ship of the Line* (1938), and *Lord Hornblower* (1946).

USS *Hornet* (CV-8), 809-foot aircraft carrier commissioned by the U.S. **Navy** in 1941. In 1942 she made history by being the takeoff site for Lieutenant Colonel **James Harold Doolittle** and his squadron of sixteen B-25 bombers who set off to attack Tokyo. After being a major player in the Battle of **Midway**, she was set afire by Japanese bombs and torpedoes during the Battle of the **Santa Cruz Islands** in October 1943. To prevent her capture, the ship was sent to the bottom by a further nine torpedoes from American ships.

USS *Hornet* (CV-12), 894-foot **Essex**-class aircraft carrier completed in 1943. The 41,200-ton ship was the most decorated aircraft carrier of World War II. Planes from the *Hornet* shot down 1,410 Japanese aircraft, and the Japanese battleship *Yamato* was sunk by her aircraft. She retrieved *Apollo 11* and its astronauts, Neil Armstrong, Buzz Aldrin, and Mike Collins, after their splashdown from the first manned lunar landing. She was stricken from the **Navy** register in 1989 and donated to the Aircraft Carrier *Hornet* Museum, where she opened in 1998 as a museum ship at Alameda, on San Francisco Bay in California.

hornpipe, wind instrument popular with sailors that accompanied, and eventually gave its name to, the traditional sailor's dance—a lively vigorous dance performed by a single person.

horse latitudes, two areas of variable and fickle winds located on either side of the **doldrums**, at about thirty degrees in each hemisphere, in both the **Atlantic** and Pacific Oceans. Sometimes called the "calms of Cancer" and the "calms of Capricorn," the term supposedly originates from becalmed Spanish vessels having to throw some horses overboard to conserve water.

Houqua (1769–1843), most prominent and wealthiest Chinese merchant of the **China trade**. His Hong, or trade guild, ruled virtually all foreign trade—including tea, silk, and export porcelain—transacted through **Canton**. Houqua's personal wealth in 1834 was estimated at $26 million, and he lived in a magnificent home on a large estate.

USS *Housatonic*, U.S. warship that was blown up by the Confederate submarine *H. L. Hunley* in the Civil War—the first warship to be sunk by a submarine. CSS *H. L. Hunley*, operating on the surface with a spar torpedo, was sunk along with the Union ship.

house flag, the distinguishing flag of a shipping company, which was traditionally flown at sea from the mainmast to identify the firm to which a merchant ship belonged. The ship's smokestacks also carried distinguishing characteristics and were called "house **funnels**."

house of refuge, one of a series of stations first established in the 1850s by the U.S. government along the Atlantic coast in which emergency supplies and equipment were maintained for the rescue of ships in distress. They preceded the establishment of the U.S. **Life-Saving Service**.

Houston ship channel, sixty-mile-long waterway running from Galveston Bay on the Gulf of Mexico to Houston, Texas. Opened in 1914, it continues to provide vital shipping access to the petroleum ports of Houston.

Howe, Richard (1726–1799), British admiral who commanded the British fleet in the first years of the American Revolution. He resigned in 1778, partly because he favored a negotiated peace with the Americans. At the end of the war, Howe became **First Lord of the Admiralty**. When England and France went to war in 1793, he took command of the Channel Fleet. The next year, he won the victory known as the Glorious First of June in the Bay of Biscay. Howe became admiral of the fleet in 1796. His brother William Howe was commander of the British army in America during the early years of the American Revolution.

Howland Island, small island located in the central Pacific Ocean that served as a source of **guano**. It is today a U.S. possession.

How to Be a Sailor, theatrical short, animated by Walt Disney, about oceanic conquest from prehistoric man to the technological wonders of the modern warship—all demonstrated by the inimitable character of Goofy. The 1944 cartoon was narrated by John McLeish.

Hoyne, Thomas Maclay (1923–1989), American marine artist who was heavily influenced by his friend and fellow artist **Gordon Grant**. He served in the U.S. **Navy** during World War II and later became a successful painter specializing in ships and marine scenes, especially New England fishing **schooners**.

Huckins, American manufacturer of motor yachts and sportfishing boats. Founded in 1928 by Frank Pembroke Huckins, the company turned out vessels renowned for their fine design and style. The Huckins Yacht Corporation, located on the Saint Johns River in Jacksonville, Florida, continues to build custom yachts and fast cruising powerboats.

Huckleberry Finn, great American adventure novel of 1884 by **Mark Twain** about a young-

ster who runs away from his abusive father and sets off with a runaway slave on a raft voyage down the **Mississippi River**. Along the way, the two companions encounter many characters and adventures.

Hudson, Henry (d. 1611), English navigator and explorer who led several expeditions to find the **Northwest Passage**, a long-sought northern water route through the Americas to Asia. Failing to find a passage northeast above Russia, on his third voyage (1609) he sailed along the American coast from Virginia northward and took his ship, *Halve Moen*, 150 miles up what would later be called the **Hudson River**, giving up his search only when he encountered increasingly fresh river water. On his last expedition, setting sail in 1610, he passed through the strait that now bears his name and entered what is now Hudson Bay. Following a winter spent icebound, he was set adrift in 1611 by a mutinous crew and never heard from again.

Hudson River, waterway that winds for 315 miles through New York State, from its source in the Adirondack Mountains to its mouth in New York Harbor, and is navigable for 150 miles. One of the richest estuaries of the East Coast, it was discovered in 1524 by **Giovanni da Verrazano** and was fully explored in 1609 by **Henry Hudson**, who sailed his ship *Halve Moen* to the end of the navigable river in Albany. Long a vital avenue to the interior, the Hudson River became New York's link to the West when the **Erie Canal** opened in 1825.

Hudson River School, collective name of the first group of American artists to develop a characteristic style of landscape painting. The school flourished from 1825 until the late 1800s, and its early artists painted many scenes of the **Hudson River** Valley in New York with dramatic landscape and atmospheric effects. Later artists of the school painted landscapes of various areas of North and South America. Members included Thomas Cole, Albert Bierstadt, Frederick E. Church, Jasper F. Cropsey, and Thomas Moran.

Hudson River sloop, **sloop**-rigged sailing craft that carried the bulk of commerce on the **Hudson River** from the 1700s through the mid-1800s and contributed greatly to the growth of the Port of New York. Approximately seventy to eighty feet in length, its design originated from seventeenth-century Dutch vessels.

Huggins, William John (1781–1845), British marine painter who went to sea at a young age with the **East India Company**. He specialized in ship portraits, particularly of **East Indiamen**, general shipping scenes, and sea battles. His works are an important contribution for understanding the period in which he painted.

Hughes, Langston (1902–1967), African-American author whose fascination with the sea provided him with inspiration for a number of short stories and poems. As a young man, he shipped out aboard a series of freighters. He recounted his adventures in his autobiography, *The Big Sea* (1940).

Hull, Isaac (1773–1843), U.S. naval officer from Connecticut who commanded USS *Constitution* when it defeated the British **frigate** *Guerrière* in the **War of 1812**. The celebrated engagement earned *Constitution* the famous nickname **Old Ironsides.**

hull down, said of a ship that is over the horizon, her hull hidden due to the curvature of the earth but whose stacks, superstructure, or rigging is visible.

Humboldt, Baron Alexander von (1769–1859), German scientist, explorer, and philosopher best remembered for his scientific studies in and around South America. The cold ocean current that runs up the west coast of the continent today bears his name.

Humphreys, Joshua (1751–1838), Philadelphia shipbuilder who designed ships for the **Continental Navy** as well as three of the six new **frigates** called for in the **Navy Act of 1794**— USS *Constitution*, USS *Constellation*, and USS *United States*.

Hundred Guinea Cup, race so called because of the cost of the trophy when it was crafted by Robert Garrard, the queen's jeweler, around 1844. It was awarded by Britain's **Royal Yacht Squadron** to the **schooner** *America*, winner of the 1851 race around the **Isle of Wight**. Thereafter, the Hundred Guinea Cup was known as the **America's Cup.**

Hunt, C. Raymond (1908–1978), American sailor and boat designer best known for designing the **Concordia yawl**, the **Boston Whaler**, and the deep-V hull for motor boats.

The Hunt for Red October, 1984 best-selling suspense novel by **Thomas Clancy** and first published by the U.S. **Naval Institute** Press about the defection of a Soviet nuclear submarine. The compelling 1990 nail-biting movie starred Sean Connery as the Soviet captain Marko Ramius and Alec Baldwin as CIA analyst Jack Ryan.

Hurley, Edward N. (1864–1933), American businessman who served as chairman of the U.S. **Shipping Board** during World War I. He oversaw the buildup of the U.S. merchant fleet and, after his retirement from public office in 1919, continued to be a vigorous proponent of a strong **merchant marine**. His writings include *The New Merchant Marine* and his World War I memoirs, *Bridge to France* (1927). He developed the pneumatic rivet gun and other pneumatic tools that affected shipbuilding, and in 1930 he made a gift to Notre Dame University to build the Edward N. Hurley College of Foreign and Domestic Commerce.

HMS *Hussar*, British **frigate** in the American Revolution that sank in **Hell Gate** in New York City while moving the army's payroll. The ship went down November 24, 1779, carrying what has been estimated to be between $2 million and $4 million in gold. While many attempts have been made, nothing has ever been salvaged.

huzzah, shout used aboard ship, and elsewhere, to express joy, encouragement, or triumph.

hydrofoil, surface vessel with underwater blades or foils that enable the vessel to rise above the water, thus reducing hull drag and increasing speed. Hydrofoils are practical only in calm waters.

hydrography, branch of physical geography that deals with the surface waters of the earth, especially with regard to navigation. Hydrographers make surveys of navigable water, including oceans, rivers, and lakes. They publish charts and maps that show water depths and the position of coastlines, channels, reefs, shoals, and other hazards to navigation. Hydrographers also study and track tides, currents, and winds.

hydroplane, racing powerboat designed with planing surfaces that provide lift for the hull.

𝓘

IACC, acronym for International **America's Cup** Class boats, which are designed to specific measurement rules to qualify for competition in the America's Cup races. Adopted after the 1988 race, the IACC is a design formula for a lightweight sailboat measuring approximately seventy-five feet long, constructed primarily of carbon fiber, and having a mast more than ten stories tall. IACC succeeded the **twelve-meter** class, which originated in the early 1900s and was used in cup competition from 1958 to 1987.

IALA, acronym for International Association of Lighthouse Authorities, the original incarnation of the current International Association of Marine Aids to Navigation and Lighthouse Authorities. Based in France, the organization was founded in 1957 and serves authorities, manufacturers, and consultants related to aids to navigation.

Iceberg Alley, term for an area of the North Atlantic Ocean approximately 250 miles east-southeast of Newfoundland, Canada. Icebergs and sea ice flowing south here with the Labrador current pose great hazards for shipping—and were responsible for the RMS *Titanic* disaster of 1912.

Ice Station Zebra, 1963 novel by Scottish author **Alistair MacLean** about a U.S. nuclear submarine that races the Soviets to find film from a Russian satellite hidden under the polar ice cap. The 1968 film starred Rock Hudson, Ernest Borgnine, Patrick McGoohan, and James Brown.

ICW, see **Intracoastal Waterway**.

USS *Idaho* (BB-42), final unit of the **New Mexico**–class battleships to be built. Commissioned in 1919 and modernized in 1931, the vessel spent all of World War II fighting in the Pacific theater, including the **Iwo Jima** and the **Okinawa Invasions**. She steamed into Tokyo Bay with the occupation forces on August 27, 1945.

Ideal X, converted T-2 tanker that ushered in the era of **containerization**. American trucker **Malcolm McLean** sent the ship to sea on April 26, 1956, with fifty-eight 33-foot intermodal

Île de France. (Courtesy Gordon R. Ghareeb)

containers stowed on her deck to showcase his revolutionary idea.

idler, shipboard crew member (also known as a dayworker) who works during the day and does not stand night watches. The term has taken on a negative meaning and is used to describe someone who avoids work and duty.

"I have not yet begun to fight!", reply of **John Paul Jones** during the Battle of **Flamborough Head** on September 23, 1779, when asked by Captain Richard Pearson of HMS *Serapis* whether he had surrendered.

Île de France, venerable 43,153-gross-ton **French Line Atlantic** steamer built in 1927. Known for her revolutionary art-deco interiors, she came to be loved by thousands as the "Rue de la Paix of the Atlantic." She served the British during World War II as an invaluable troop transport. Refitted in 1949 to reflect a more modern example of French design, the **liner** presented a sleeker profile after her three **funnels** had been reduced to two. She earned the nickname Saint Bernard of the Atlantic for her various involvements in open-sea rescue, including saving 753 people from the sinking SS *Andrea Doria* in 1956. She was sent to Osaka, Japan, for scrapping in 1959, but the undertaking was deferred until after *The Last Voyage* was filmed on board.

Iliad, ancient poem by the Greek poet **Homer**, written in the 700s B.C. The *Iliad* describes events in the final year of the ten-year Trojan War, which was fought between the Achaeans in southern Greece and the city of Troy. According to the *Iliad*, the Trojan War was fought over **Helen of Troy**, the beautiful wife of King Menelaus of Sparta. Helen had been taken from Sparta to the city of Troy by Paris, a son of the Trojan king Priam.

USS Illinois (BB-65), fifth **Iowa**-class battleship, which was laid down early in 1945. Her construction was canceled after eight months, and the unfinished hull—which was a quarter complete—was broken up on the building slip.

Illinois & Michigan Canal, ninety-seven-mile man-made waterway that opened in 1848 connecting the **Great Lakes** to the Illinois and **Mississippi Rivers**. The canal was a big factor in turning Chicago into a major port, because goods from the Great Lakes could be shipped along its length to the Mississippi River. By the twentieth century, canal barges were primarily transporting waste material from Chicago, and in the 1930s, following the establishment of the **Illinois Waterway**, the I&M Canal ceased operation.

Illinois Waterway, 336-mile waterway linking Lake Michigan with the **Mississippi River**, thus connecting the **Great Lakes** with the Gulf of Mexico. The waterway, built primarily by the channelization of certain rivers, extends from the **Chicago Sanitary and Ship Canal** to the Des Plaines and the Illinois Rivers to the Mississippi. Principal cargoes, carried mostly by barge, include coal, petroleum, and grain products.

I Love Lucy, one of the most popular American television situation comedies of all time. Two episodes telecast in January 1956 were set aboard the eastbound **liner** SS *Constitution*. The shows were so effective that the U.S. **Maritime Administration** requested copies of the two programs to use as promotional films for the U.S. **merchant marine**.

IMO, see **International Maritime Organization**.

Imo, outbound Norwegian grain carrier that collided with the inbound French munitions

ship *Mont Blanc* in the Narrows of Halifax Harbor, Nova Scotia, on December 6, 1917, creating the largest man-made explosion ever detonated before the first atomic bomb.

Imperator, first of designer Albert Ballin's "Big Three" transatlantic **liners** built for the **Hamburg-America Line**, the other two similar ships being *Vaterland* and *Bismarck*. The 52,117-gross-ton steamer was completed in 1913 and could carry 4,594 passengers in the days before immigration restrictions. In order to outstrip the length of the under-construction SS *Aquitania* by eight feet, the German ship was given a huge bronze eagle **figurehead** mounted on her bow to stretch her overall dimension to 909 feet. She was ceded to Great Britain after World War I and renamed SS *Berengaria* as flagship of the **Cunard Line** (without the huge figurehead) to replace their torpedoed *Lusitania*.

impressment, the practice of forcing individuals to serve in the army or navy. The British taking of American sailors off U.S. ships and forcing them into the service of the **Royal Navy**, with the claim that they were British subjects, led largely to the **War of 1812**.

IMS, see **International Measurement System**.

Inchcape Rock, two-thousand-foot-long sandstone reef in the North Sea twelve miles off the coast of Scotland. Also called Bell Rock, it is exposed for a few feet at low tide but submerged at high tide. After hundreds of shipwrecks, a one-hundred-foot lighthouse was erected on the rock in 1811.

Inchon, Invasion of, September 15, 1950, amphibious assault on the Korean peninsula. Two days of shelling from U.S. **Navy** support ships and aircraft paved the way to success for the Korean War mission that led to the capture of Seoul ten days later.

The Incredible Mr. Limpet, 1964 movie combining live action and animation to portray a salty fairy tale of the sea in which a man gets his wish, is turned into a fish, and inadvertently becomes a hero as he saves the U.S. **Navy** during World War II. The movie starred Don Knotts, Jack Weston, and Andrew Duggan.

SS *Independence*, American Export Lines steamer completed in 1951 for the Mediterranean service alongside her sister SS ***Constitution***. Fugazy Travel tried to run a series of budget cruises on the ship, with meals at an extra charge, "op art" decor throughout, and a million-dollar psychedelic exterior paint job. Needless to say, the scheme failed dismally, and the ship was **laid up** in 1969. She was sold to the Orient Overseas group in 1974 and was renamed the *Oceanic Independence*. The ship was eventually transferred to an American-registered division of the company, **American Hawaii Cruises**, and today maintains inter–Hawai'ian Island operations.

USS *Independence* (CV-22), namesake lead vessel of a class of nine aircraft carriers converted from the incomplete hulls of heavy **cruisers**. Completed in 1943, the ship was severely damaged by a Japanese torpedo during one of her first forays into the South Pacific in World War II. Repaired, the carrier returned as a major participant in the assault on the Philippine Islands. She was decommissioned in 1946 and used for testing during the atomic bomb detonations in the **Bikini Atoll**. After surviving two nuclear blasts less than fifteen hundred feet from ground zero, the 622-foot carrier remained afloat and was towed to **Pearl Harbor**, then to San Francisco for additional examination. The extremely dangerous hulk was sunk in further weapon testing off the West Coast in 1951.

India House, club founded in 1914 at Hanover Square in New York City for those interested in maritime affairs and foreign trade. The name was chosen because the "Indies"—**West Indies** or **East Indies**—stood for overseas

trade. The club has a very fine collection of pictures, models, and other objects connected with sailing and seafaring life. The clubhouse was opened in 1999 as a fine restaurant for the general public, where only moguls had dined before.

USS *Indianapolis* (CA-35), 12,575-ton Portland-class heavy **cruiser** commissioned in 1933. The 610-foot ship had a main armament of nine 8-inch guns. In 1936 she carried President **Franklin D. Roosevelt** on his monthlong tour of South America. The vessel was on maneuvers not far from Honolulu at the time of the Japanese surprise attack on **Pearl Harbor** and therefore escaped damage in the harbor. She sustained a **kamikaze** attack in March 1945 and after repairs in California returned to the South Pacific. She transported the atomic bomb used to destroy Hiroshima to its staging position, reaching Tinian on July 26, 1945, where it was loaded aboard the B-29 bomber *Enola Gay*. Less than four days after delivery of her historic cargo, *Indianapolis* was torpedoed by Japanese submarine I-58 under the command of **Mochitsura Hashimoto** and sank in twelve minutes. *Indianapolis* was not noticed as missing until four days later, by which time only 316 of her 1,196 crewmen were rescued—many of the men lost were eaten by sharks. It was the U.S. **Navy**'s second-greatest loss of life from a single ship (after USS ***Arizona***). The captain of the ship, Charles B. McVay, was court-martialed for failing to order a zigzag course.

India Pale Ale, style of beer developed in England in the late eighteenth century to survive the temperatures and rolling seas during the long sea voyage to the British troops and civilians living in India. The increased alcohol and hops served to combat infections from bacteria during transit.

The Influence of Sea Power upon History, 1660–1783, 1890 book by U.S. **Navy** captain

Alfred Thayer Mahan that today has great historical significance. In it Mahan argued that naval power was the key to success in international politics and that the nation that controlled the seas held the decisive factor in modern warfare. The book coincided with the navy arms race leading up to World War I and was immediately translated into several languages. It greatly influenced **Theodore Roosevelt** and other proponents of a big navy and overseas expansion.

Ingalls Shipbuilding, shipbuilding facility in Pascagoula, Mississippi, that has been in continuous operation since 1938. Ingalls has built a variety of commercial ships and other structures over the years and today specializes in U.S. **Navy** surface ships and commercial marine structures. A division of Litton Industries, it is Mississippi's largest private employer.

USCGC *Ingham* (WPG-35), Secretary-class U.S. **Coast Guard cutter** built in 1936 that saw extensive Atlantic convoy escort duty during World War II. The 2,656-ton cutter also saw service around Korea and Vietnam during those conflicts. She was retired in 1988 and opened the following year at Patriots Point in South Carolina as a national memorial to the 912 Coast Guard personnel killed in World War II and Vietnam.

In Harm's Way, classic 1965 American film directed by Otto Preminger that centers on U.S. **Navy** personnel after the Japanese attack on **Pearl Harbor**. The stellar Hollywood blockbuster starred John Wayne, Kirk Douglas, Patricia Neal, Tom Tryon, Paula Prentiss, Jill Haworth, Dana Andrews, Stanley Holloway, Burgess Meredith, Carroll O'Connor, and Slim Pickens.

in irons, condition of a sailboat headed into the wind and unable to bear away on either **tack**. It particularly applies to **square-rigged** vessels,

but **fore-and-aft-rigged** vessels can also fall into this state.

Inland Passage, also called the Inside Passage, a 950-mile natural protected waterway from Puget Sound to Skagway, Alaska. One of the world's most scenic sea routes, it includes views of mountain, waterfalls, and glaciers.

Inland Rules, navigation rules to be followed by all vessels while navigating upon certain defined waters of the United States. These waters are inside the **COLREGS** demarcation lines and are defined in *Navigation Rules* as inland waters.

Inland Waterways Corporation, federal corporation established in 1924 under the supervision of the U.S. secretary of war to coordinate water transportation on America's navigable rivers. It operated as the Federal Barge Lines on the **Mississippi**, **Missouri**, and Warrior Rivers. The IWC was terminated in 1954.

Inman Line, British shipping line founded in the 1850s as the Liverpool, New York & Philadelphia Steamship Company. For a time it was the largest maritime operation on the North Atlantic, operating such vessels as the *City of Glasgow*, *City of Montreal*, and the *City of Rome*. It merged with the **Red Star Line** in 1886 and became known as the Inman and International Steamship Company. In 1888 the *City of New York* and the *City of Paris* came on line as the largest and fastest **liners** of the period. The two liners were transferred to American registry in 1892 to form the resurrected **American Line** in 1893. In 1902 Inman became part of **International Mercantile Marine**.

INMARSAT, acronym for international marine satellite system, a system of satellites that provides exclusive ship-to-ship, ship-to-shore, and shore-to-ship communications services.

Innes, Hammond (1913–1998), Scottish sailor and novelist known for his adventure stories that pit their characters against the environment. Among his twenty-nine best-selling novels are *The **Wreck of the Mary Deare*** (1956), *Atlantic Fury* (1962), *North Star* (1974), and *The Last Voyage: Captain Cook's Lost Diary* (1978). Several of Innes's works have been adapted into screen productions, and *Sea and Islands* (1967) is an autobiographical sketch of his life afloat.

The Innocents Abroad, humorous 1869 travel narrative by **Mark Twain** about his 1867 **steamship** voyage to Europe, Egypt, and the Holy Land. Also called *The New Pilgrim's Progress*, it sold seventy thousand copies its first year and remained the best selling of Twain's books throughout his lifetime.

Institute of Nautical Archaeology (INA), nonprofit scientific and educational organization incorporated in 1972 for the purpose of gathering knowledge of human past from the physical remains of maritime activities. It became affiliated with Texas A&M University in 1976, and a permanent institute has since been established there. Over the years, INA's excavations have included the **Uluburon shipwreck**, **Port Royal**, and **Sieur de La Salle**'s **flagship**, *La Belle*.

intermodalism, practice of moving containers directly from ships to trains, trucks, and barges. Pioneered in the 1960s, by the 1970s intermodalism was providing "door-to-door" service in the United States, Western Europe, and the Pacific Rim.

International America's Cup Class, see **IACC**.

International Association of Marine Aids to Navigation and Lighthouse Authorities, see **IALA**.

International Code of Signals, standardized code in which meanings are assigned to signals for visual, sound, and radio communications. It came into use January 1, 1902, and has since been revised extensively. Transmis-

sion commonly is by code flags and pennants, each representing a letter or numeral. The current system consists of twenty-six alphabet flags, ten numeral pennants, three repeater pennants, and one answering pennant. The U.S. government publication describing the code is *H.O. 102*.

international date line, line that runs roughly along the 180th meridian of **longitude**—without bisecting any islands or groups. In 1883 it became the point at which the calendar day changes by one day as the line is crossed—crossing it in an easterly direction, it is the same calendar day two days in succession (called an **antipodean day**); crossing westward eliminates one day completely. The line is twelve hours each way from the **prime meridian**, 0° longitude, running through Greenwich, England.

International Ice Patrol, international agreement financially supported by seventeen nations and managed by the U.S. **Coast Guard** since 1914 to monitor icebergs and field ice in the North Atlantic and warn mariners of any danger. Ice observation in the general region of the **Grand Banks** of Newfoundland begins in February and concludes in August. The sinking of RMS *Titanic* in 1912 spurred the creation of the patrol, and not a single ship has been lost to ice in the patrolled area since that disaster.

International Load Line Convention, international agreement drafted in London in 1930, and adopted in the United States in 1931, that requires **load lines** or **Plimsoll marks** to be easily visible on the sides of ships.

International Longshoremen's and Warehousemen's Union (ILWU), labor union organized in 1937 to represent waterfront workers on the West Coast.

International Longshoremen's Association (ILA), labor union organized in 1892 to represent longshoremen in the **Great Lakes** and on the East Coast and the Gulf Coast.

International Maritime Organization (IMO), specialized agency established through the United Nations to promote cooperation among world governments in matters involving international shipping, navigation safety, ship design and equipment, crew standards, and pollution control. Headquartered in London, the IMO began in 1959 as the Inter-Governmental Maritime Consultative Organization (IMCO) and took its present name in 1982.

International Measurement System (IMS), handicap rating system used for sailboat racing.

International Mercantile Marine (IMM), federation of several shipping companies assembled by American financier **John Pierpont "J. P." Morgan** in 1902 to operate mostly under foreign flags. At the time, Atlantic shipping companies were in a rate war that was hurting all parties involved. Morgan's plan was to buy all rival lines and place them under one controlling trust. IMM controlled a million tons of shipping through managing ownership of the **White Star Line**, **Red Star Line**, Leyland Line, Atlantic Transport Line, and portions of the **Holland America Line**. IMM faced strong competition from the **Cunard Line**, **Hamburg-America Line**, and **North German Lloyd**, and the loss of RMS *Titanic* and the effects of World War I weakened the holding company. IMM acquired **United States Lines** in 1931 and by 1936 operated only U.S.-flag vessels. It rolled all operations into United States Lines in May 1943.

International Offshore Rule (IOR), yacht-racing rule introduced in 1968 to replace both the American and the British rules and to equate yachts of different sizes and speeds.

International Rules, rules and regulations governing the conduct of vessels operating in waters outside **COLREGS** demarcation lines. Also referred to as COLREGS.

International Sailing Federation (ISAF), governing body of all international sailboat racing that administers racing rules such as the **International Offshore Rule**. Before the 1990s, the organization was called the International Yacht Racing Union (IYRU).

international waterways, straits, inland and interocean canals, and rivers that separate the territories of two or more nations. Provided no treaty is enforced, merchant ships and warships have the right of free and unrestricted navigation through these waterways.

International Yacht Racing Union (IYRU), see **International Sailing Federation**.

Interstate Commerce Commission (ICC), independent U.S. government agency established in 1887 and charged with regulating carriers engaged in transportation between states. It jurisdiction included water carriers engaged in coastwise and intercoastal trade. The ICC was terminated in 1995, and its remaining functions were transferred to the new National Surface Transportation Board.

In the Heart of the Sea, best-selling 2000 National Book Award–winning account of the whaleship *Essex* by Nathaniel Philbrick. The 1820 *Essex* incident, which involved whaling, a shipwreck, and survival by cannibalism, inspired **Herman Melville's** *Moby-Dick* (1851).

"In the Navy", pounding-beat disco song recorded by the Village People in 1979. The hit made it to the number three position on the popular song charts. In 1980 the U.S. **Navy** was in the process of using the group to perform the ditty on board a **capital ship** for recruiting, but the project was abruptly canceled.

In the Navy, comedy motion picture that had Bud Abbott and Lou Costello bound for duty

The retired aircraft carrier USS *Intrepid* is the setting for a successful aerospace museum in midtown Manhattan. (Courtesy Gordon R. Ghareeb; photo by Frank Desisto)

on the high seas. They befriend a singing star who is trying to escape the limelight for a quiet enlisted life. It includes lots of good footage of the pre–World War II U.S. fleet. The 1941 film also starred Dick Powell and the Andrews Sisters.

Intracoastal Waterway (ICW), a largely sheltered, three-thousand-mile water route consisting of a series of rivers, estuaries, inland bays, sounds, and inlets, linked by canals, along the **Atlantic** and Gulf Coasts of the United States from Boston to Key West, Florida, and from Apalachee Bay, Florida, to Brownsville, Texas. Vessels are exposed to the open ocean for only about fifty miles along the Rhode Island coast, for a thirty-seven-mile stretch along the New Jersey coast, and along the Gulf Coast of Florida. The waterway was authorized by Congress in 1919 and is maintained in most sections by the U.S. **Army Corps of Engineers**.

USS *Intrepid*, sixty-foot **ketch** built for **Napoleon** as *L'Intrépide* in 1798. She was later sold to **Tripoli** and renamed *Mastico*. Captured by **Stephen Decatur Jr.** during the **Barbary Wars** and renamed USS *Intrepid*, in September 1804 the ship, under the command of Lieutenant Richard Somers, was used as a fireship to attempt to destroy the Barbary fleet at anchor. It exploded prematurely, killing the entire crew. Along with Decatur's exploits a few months earlier in burning the captured USS *Philadelphia*, the act set valorous examples for the young naval service.

USS *Intrepid* (CV-11), **Essex**-class aircraft carrier delivered to the U.S. **Navy** in 1943. The

27,100-ton ship saw extensive duty in the Pacific during World War II. The carrier retrieved astronaut Scott Carpenter in 1962 after his *Aurora 7* Mercury space capsule splashed down into the **Atlantic**. The 872-foot vessel also picked up astronauts Virgil Grissom and John Young after their successful splashdown following the first manned *Gemini 3* orbital flight in 1965. After service off Vietnam, the carrier was retired and now serves as home to the Intrepid Sea-Air-Space Museum at Pier 86 on the **Hudson River** in New York City.

Intrepid, two-time victorious American defender of the **America's Cup**. Considered by many to be the greatest **twelve-meter** ever built, the **Olin Stephens**–designed yacht took on the Australian challenger *Dame Pattie* in 1967 and won, four races to none. *Intrepid* returned in 1970 to win a controversial series over another Australian challenger *Gretel II*, four races to one.

In Which We Serve, gripping World War II film about the sinking of the fictional British destroyer HMS *Torrin* during the Battle of Crete, told by three survivors who recount their lives aboard the sunken vessel. Noel Coward scripted, scored, codirected, and co-starred in the 1942 film and won an Oscar for outstanding production achievement. Nominated for best picture and best original screenplay Academy Awards, the film also starred John Mills, Celia Johnson, and Richard Attenborough.

IOD, international **one-design**, a term for internationally recognized classes of one-design vessels.

IOR, see **International Offshore Rule**.

USS *Iowa* (BB-61), first and namesake vessel of a class of 887-foot superbattleships laid down for the U.S. **Navy**. Each of the six 45,000-ton Iowa-class battlewagons carried a price tag of over $100 million. The lead ship was commissioned in 1943, and one of her first assignments was to carry President **Franklin D. Roosevelt** to the Tehran Conference. She saw extensive action during 1944 in the South Pacific, with her battery of nine 16-inch guns providing firepower during many amphibious assaults. She saw further action in the Korean War. Decommissioned in 1958, she was reactivated as part of President Ronald Reagan's plan to revitalize the military. In 1989 an explosion in one of her 16-inch gun turrets killed forty-seven crew members. She is currently **laid up** in Newport, Rhode Island. Her sisters include *New Jersey*, *Missouri*, *Wisconsin*, *Illinois*, and *Kentucky* (the latter two were never completed).

Ironbottom Sound, name given to the body of water off **Guadalcanal** in the Solomon Islands because of the many ships sunk there during World War II in the Battle of **Savo Island** and the subsequent Battle of **Guadalcanal**, from August 1942 to February 1943.

ironclad, a vessel protected by iron plating. From the 1860s onward, cladding a ship in armor made it nearly unsinkable with the guns then in existence. Ironclads spurred the evolution of **steamship** and weapons design.

iron coffin, nickname applied to German **U-boats** during World War II.

iron genny, yachting term for the auxiliary motor of a sailboat ("genny" for "**genoa jib**").

iron mike, the automatic steering system aboard a vessel that utilizes input from the ship's **gyrocompass** or other electronic navigation aids. When introduced by **Elmer Ambrose Sperry** in 1921, it was known as "**metal mike**."

ISAF, see **International Sailing Federation**.

Iselin, Charles Oliver (1854–1932), American shipowner and yachtsman who as a member of the **New York Yacht Club** was an active partner in the syndicates that built and raced *Vigilant* (1893), *Defender* (1895), *Columbia* (1899), and *Reliance* (1903) for the **America's Cup.**

Isherwood, Benjamin Franklin (1822–1915), U.S. **Navy** officer who is considered by many to be the service's greatest engineer. Isherwood pioneered steam power and ship design and was responsible for the buildup of the steam navy from before the Civil War to his retirement in 1884. His two-volume work *Experimental Researches in Steam Engineering* (1863, 1865) became a standard text upon which future steam experimentation was based. The engineering building at the U.S. **Naval Academy** is named Isherwood Hall in his honor.

Ishmael, fictional sailor on board the whaleship *Pequod* who narrates the novel ***Moby-Dick; or, The Whale*** (1851) by **Herman Melville**. The story opens "Call me Ishmael," but his real name is never revealed.

Island of the Blue Dolphins, award-winning 1960 children's novel by American author Scott O'Dell about a young Indian girl and her brother, who are shipwrecked on a Pacific island. A wicked sea captain lands on the island, bringing with him death and destruction. A film of the same name was made in 1964 and starred George Kennedy, Celia Kaye, Larry Domasin, and Ann Daniel.

Isle of Man, self-governing dependency of the United Kingdom located in the Irish Sea between Great Britain and Ireland. Residents are called Manxmen.

Isle of Wight, 147-square-mile, diamond-shaped island off the south coast of England. The Solent separates the island from the mainland county of Hampshire and the ports of Portsmouth and Southampton. Cowes, its leading port, is a world yachting center. The course for the **Hundred Guinea Cup**—later

called the **America's Cup**—race was around the Isle of Wight.

Ismay, Bruce (1861–1937), president of the **White Star Line** and survivor of RMS *Titanic*'s **maiden voyage**. Ismay inherited control of the White Star Line after his father, Thomas Ismay (1837–1899), the company's founder, died in 1899. Ismay proved an able leader, and the company flourished. In 1904 White Star became part of the American-controlled **International Mercantile Marine**, with Ismay heading up the entire operation. He had planned to retire in 1913 and was traveling to New York on board *Titanic* to experience the new ship and to meet with IMM officials about his decision. His decision to save his own life when so many passengers died was widely criticized, and he lived his later life as a recluse.

MS *Italia*, originally the **Swedish America Line**'s *Kungsholm* of 1928, the passenger ship was renamed upon her sale to **Home Lines** at the conclusion of World War II. She was operated in the **Atlantic** service of her new owners and also became very popular as a cruise ship sailing out of New York. She was sold in 1964 to become the dockside Imperial Bahama Hotel at Freeport, Bahamas. The hotel never became a profitable venture, because gambling was not legally permitted on board. She was sold for scrap after one year of hotel operation.

Italian Line, North Atlantic shipping house formed in 1932 by the government-induced (at Mussolini's recommendation) merger of Italy's three major North Atlantic passenger companies. In much the same way that the **Cunard Line** and the **White Star Line** came together to eliminate in-house competition, the Navigazione Generale Italiana, Lloyd Sabaudo, and Cosulich Line banded together to form the "Italia." It operated SS *Rex*, SS *Conte di Savoia*, and SS *Michelangelo*, to name a few of its famous **liners**, and ceased operation with the removal from service of the **Leonardo da Vinci** in 1976.

Ivy Bells, code name for U.S. activity of intercepting cable communications between the Soviet Union and its submarines. So named because, without penetrating the cable, information was gathered by a bell-shaped device placed on the ocean floor over the Soviet cables.

Iwo Jima, tiny Japanese-held island lying nine hundred miles south of Tokyo, which was the site of a U.S. World War II amphibious assault. The bloody monthlong battle began February 19, 1945, and resulted in the U.S. possession of an airfield with which to launch an all-out bomber offensive against the enemy's home islands. The last Japanese encampments on Iwo Jima were finally subdued on March 24, 1945, and the final tally showed that 21,788 Japanese and 6,891 Americans had been killed in the fighting. *Iwo Jima* is Japanese for Sulfur Island.

IYRU, see **International Sailing Federation** (ISAF).

J

jack-of-the-dust, in the U.S. **Navy** and **Coast Guard**, the individual in charge of food issue. In Britain's **Royal Navy**, "Jack Dusty" was the name for a sailor assigned responsibility for the bread room, where flour was stored.

Jack Tar, slang term for a sailor. It is derived from the word "tarpaulin," for canvas impregnated with pine tar for waterproofing that is used for hatch covers, among other things, aboard ship. "Jack" is a nickname for the name John and was used to describe any common fellow.

Jacobsen, Antonio (1850–1921), prolific Danish-American marine artist who specialized in ship portraits. He emigrated to the United States in 1873 and began his career in New York decorating safes. He chronicled the transition from sail to steam, and his body of work is an important period history of the ships that called on the Port of New York. He was a friend and contemporary of such other artists as **Frederick Pansing**, **James Edward Buttersworth**, and **Frederick Schiller Cozzens**. It is estimated that Jacobsen painted upward of 6,000 paintings in his lifetime—3,300 that are identified.

Jacob's ladder, portable rope ladder with wooden rungs that is slung over a ship's side to

Antonio Jacobsen, date unknown. (Courtesy The Mariners' Museum, Newport News, Virginia)

provide temporary embarkation. The term is based on the ladder on which the biblical Jacob, in his dream, saw angels ascending and descending (Genesis 28:12).

JAG, acronym for Judge Advocate General, an officer in charge of legal matters in the U.S. **Navy**. The offices, known as the JAG Corps, provide legal services, including prosecuting, defending, reviewing courts-martial, and offering legal assistance. The American television show *JAG*, about fictional U.S. naval officer Harmon Rabb Jr., who crashed his F-14 and later joined the JAG Corps, premiered in 1995.

jake, a fully equipped deep-sea diving outfit, including suit or dress, helmet, suit, shoes, weight belt, air hose, and knife.

Jamaica Inn, 1939 drama about an orphan girl who becomes involved with a band of pirates who lure unsuspecting sailing ships onto the rock-bound coast of Cornwall in England, and then plunder the stricken vessels. Based on the Daphne du Maurier novel of the same name, the film was directed by Alfred Hitchcock and starred Maureen O'Hara and Charles Laughton.

James, Joshua (1827–1901), perhaps the most celebrated lifesaver in world history, he is credited with saving more than six hundred lives during a long and distinguished career that spanned nearly sixty years with the **Massachusetts Humane Society** and the U.S. **Life-Saving Service**. He died while still serving at his Point Allerton, Massachusetts, Life-Saving station. His most famous rescue was in November 1888, when he and his crew saved twenty-nine people from five different vessels. During the *Portland* **Gale** of November 1898, he saved twenty people from six ships.

James, Naomi (b. 1948), New Zealand sailor, the first woman to sail single-handed around the world via **Cape Horn**. Her voyage in the fifty-three-foot **sloop** *Express Crusader* began in September 1977 and ended in June 1978.

She wrote *At One with the Sea* (1978) about the journey.

James Caird, twenty-three-foot lifeboat that Sir **Ernest Shackleton** and five others sailed eight hundred miles in sixteen days to South Georgia to find help to rescue their ill-fated Antarctic expedition.

Jamestown, the first permanent English colony in North America, founded on May 13, 1607, on the banks of the James River in Virginia. A total of 144 colonists sailed from England aboard the ships *Susan Constant*, *Godspeed*, and *Discovery*, and landed on a little peninsula about sixty miles upriver. They named both the river and their settlement in honor of King James I of England.

Jane's Fighting Ships, annual publication regarded as the standard reference book about warships of all nations. First published in Britain in 1897 as *All the World's Fighting Ships*, it was founded by journalist and novelist Frederick Thomas Jane (1865–1916). Today the *Jane's* series includes reference books on merchant ships and survey vessels.

Jason, hero in Greek mythology who traveled with the Argonauts to seek the Golden Fleece. He fell out of favor with the gods and was later killed when his old ship, the *Argo*, fell on him.

Jason Jr., remote operated vehicle (ROV) equipped with imaging systems and a manipulator arm, which is designed to operate to a maximum depth of nearly twenty thousand feet. It was tethered to *Alvin* and used by **Robert Duane Ballard** to explore the wreck of RMS *Titanic* in 1986.

HMS Java, British **frigate** destroyed by USS *Constitution* in a famous engagement off the coast of Brazil on December 29, 1812, during the **War of 1812**.

Java Sea, Battle of, World War II naval engagement between Japanese and Allied forces fought

February 27–28, 1942, in the Java Sea. The fifteen U.S., British, Australian, and Dutch ships were routed by the Japanese fleet—only four badly damaged U.S. **destroyers** managed to escape.

Jaws, best-selling 1974 novel by **Peter Benchley** (b. 1940) about a giant great white shark that terrorizes a fictional Long Island, New York, beach. The 1975 blockbuster film was directed by twenty-six-year-old Steven Spielberg and starred Roy Scheider, Richard Dreyfuss, and Robert Shaw. Three sequels were produced, all of which fell well short of the popularity of the original.

Jay Treaty, agreement negotiated by U.S. diplomat John Jay (1745–1829) in 1794 with Great Britain to settle problems stemming from the **Treaty of Paris** of 1783 and to regulate commerce and navigation. The treaty improved U.S. relations with Britain and incensed the French, thus contributing to the **Quasi-War**.

J-boat, class of large, magnificent racing yachts built in the United States and Great Britain in the 1930s to compete for the **America's Cup**. Expensive to build, maintain, and race, only ten were built for eight seasons of racing (1930–37; three races). They measured between 76 and 87 feet on the waterline, and their overall length exceeded 120 feet. Yachts built to the J-class of the American Universal Rule included *Endeavour*, *Endeavour II*, *Enterprise*, *Yankee*, *Rainbow*, *Ranger*, *Shamrock V*, *Velsheda*, *Weetamoe*, and *Whirlwind*, and the yachts in the United States and Great Britain that were altered to race with them were *Astra*, *Britannia*, *Candida*, *Resolute*, *Vanitie*, and *White Heather II*.

Jeanette, 145-foot ship used in the ill-fated 1879 **Jeanette Expedition**. The wooden ship was built in Wales in 1861 and was originally named HMS *Pandora*. She was purchased in 1876, strengthened for work in the ice, and renamed *Jeanette* by **James Gordon Bennett**

Jr., who funded the expedition. The loss of the *Jeanette* inaugurated the U.S. **Revenue Cutter Service**'s Bering Sea patrol when the **cutter** *Corwin* was dispatched in 1880 to search for the missing ship.

Jeanette Expedition, 1879 U.S. **Navy** Arctic expedition seeking a passage to the North Pole led by Lieutenant **George Washington De Long** and funded by *New York Herald* publisher **James Gordon Bennett Jr**. Their ship, the *Jeanette*, departed San Francisco on July 8, 1879, sailed through the Bering Strait, and made way for Wrangell Island. *Jeanette* became locked in the ice in September and drifted with the floes for twenty-one months, until June 1881, when it was crushed and sank. The crew made off in three boats, but only eleven men survived. De Long died in October 1881 but kept a diary prior to this death, which was published in 1883. The scientific failure of the voyage and heavy loss of life were an embarrassment for the U.S. Navy and prompted congressional hearings. The discovery in 1884 of crew members' possessions off the coast of Greenland confirmed the theory of a continuous Arctic current.

Jebel Ali, largest man-made harbor in the world. It occupies sixty-five square miles of desert in the United Arab Emirates.

Jefferson, Thomas (1743–1826), third president of the United States, author of the Declaration of Independence, and architect of the Univeristy of Virginia. He is viewed by some as the father of the U.S. **Navy** because he built up the service following the **Quasi-War** and it was first used as an offensive weapon during the **Barbary Wars**. Jefferson served as president from 1801 to 1809, overseeing the Louisiana Purchase, the **Lewis and Clark Expedition**, the *Chesapeake* **Affair**, and the **Embargo Act**, and establishing the U.S. **Coast Survey**.

Jefferson's gunboats, series of two hundred small coastal defense vessels called for by Presi-

Jeremiah O'Brien.

dent **Thomas Jefferson** in 1807 as a result of the **Barbary Wars**. Along with a buildup of shore and floating batteries and land-based artillery, they were designed to be a low-cost alternative to ships to protect the harbors and waterways of the United States.

Jellicoe, John Rushworth (1859–1935), British naval officer who achieved the rank of admiral prior to World War I. He commanded the British **Grand Fleet** at the Battle of **Jutland** in May 1916, the only time the main British and German fleets met in combat. While the British suffered greater losses, the German fleet never again contested British control of the North Sea. As **First Sea Lord**, Jellicoe then directed the campaign against German submarine warfare until December 1917, when he was dismissed by Prime Minister David Lloyd George for failing to fully implement the **convoy** system. He was promoted to admiral of the fleet in 1919.

Jenkins' Ear, War of, war fought between Spain and Great Britain from 1739 to 1742. Britain went to war with Spain over the mistreatment of English seamen whom the Spaniards accused

of smuggling. The war took its name from Robert Jenkins, captain of the English **ship** *Rebecca*, who claimed the Spanish had cut off his ear in 1731. He displayed the ear in the House of Commons and so aroused public opinion that the government declared war on October 23, 1739. Another cause of the war was the boundary dispute between Spanish Florida and Georgia, over which a number of bloody battles were fought between the settlers. The war merged into the War of Austrian Succession 1740–48 (also known as King George's War) and ended with the inconclusive Treaty of Aix–La Chapelle in 1748.

Jeremiah O'Brien, U.S. **Liberty ship** commissioned in 1943 that saw service in the **Atlantic**, Pacific, and Indian Oceans during World War II. She was **laid up** in 1947 at Suisun Bay, California, and in 1978 was designated a U.S. national monument to memorialize the **merchant marine** in World War II. Restored by volunteer labor, the vessel currently is moored in San Francisco Bay as a testimonial to the era of her construction and operation. In 1994 she steamed on a five-and-a-half-month voyage to Normandy, France, for the fiftieth anniversary celebration of the **D-Day** invasion.

Jervis, Sir John (1735–1823), British admiral who served in the American Revolution and in the **French Revolution** and **Napoleonic Wars**. He was Britain's **First Lord of the Admiralty** from 1801 to 1804. Jervis was a model of character for **Royal Navy** officers and had a profound influence on his subordinate **Horatio Nelson**.

SS *Jervis Bay*, 13,839-gross-ton ocean **liner** built for the emigrant service from Britain to Australia. Refitted as an armed merchant **cruiser** in 1939, she alone engaged the German **pocket battleship** *Admiral Scheer* in gunfire while escorting thirty-seven ships in **convoy** in November 1940; most of the convoy steamed off to safety. The hopelessly outclassed *Jervis Bay*

Steamboat *J. M. White*. (Delta Queen Steamboat Company)

was sent to the bottom, taking with her 190 of the 259 crew members.

jetsam, portion of a jettisoned cargo that sinks or is washed ashore. Under the rules of **salvage**, jetsam must be returned only if the owner makes a proper claim.

jibe, to turn a sailboat away from the wind to change from one **tack** to the other (also known as to "gybe"). In a large **square-rigger**, this is called "wearing ship."

J. M. White, elegant and opulently appointed **paddle wheeler** that was acclaimed by many to be the finest **steamboat** of her day and perhaps the grandest of all time. She was built in 1878 for the passenger and cotton trade of the lower **Mississippi River**.

john boat, a type of **scow**, flat bottomed, square-ended, and relatively narrow. Usually propelled by oars or poles, this type of boat found use on the **Western rivers** of the United States.

John Brown Shipyard, legendary shipyard on the River Clyde in **Clydebank**, Scotland, that produced some of the most famous vessels in history, including RMS *Queen Elizabeth*, RMS *Queen Mary*, HMS *Hood*, HMY *Britannia*, and *Queen Elizabeth 2*. Launching of the ships required digging out the riverbank on the opposite side of the Clyde to accommodate their lengths. Today the yard specializes in converting vessels and constructing offshore structures.

Johnson, marine outboard manufacturer founded in 1911 in South Bend, Indiana, by four brothers with the last name Johnson. In 1921 the company introduced a small air-cooled outboard engine that was lighter than those built by **Evinrude**, and by 1922 it had thousands of orders, soon becoming a major player in the burgeoning industry. The company fell on hard times during the Great Depression and was sold to **OMC**, which kept the Johnson nameplate.

John W. Brown.

Johnson, Captain Charles, reputed pen name of **Daniel Defoe**. His book *A General History of the Pyrates* (1724) is one of the most important period accounts of pirates and related activities.

Johnson, Irving M. (1905–1991), American seaman, author, and lecturer who first went to sea in the German four-masted **bark** *Peking* in a **Cape Horn** passage in the nitrate trade in 1929. Johnson and his wife, Electa, circumnavigated the globe aboard their boats, all named *Yankee*, seven times between 1933 and 1958, then dedicated seventeen years to sailing the inland waterways, canals, and seas of Europe and Egypt. The Johnsons documented each voyage extensively, often visiting remote islands and capturing images of traditions, customs, and lifeways that in many cases no longer exist. These experiences were extensively reported in *National Geographic* and in the Johnsons' books, which include *Westward Bound in the Schooner Yankee* (1936), *Sailing to See* (1939), *Yankee People and Places* (1955), *Yankee's Wander-World* (1949), and *The* Peking *Battles Cape Horn* (1977).

John W. Brown, U.S. **Liberty ship** launched in 1942 that had an active and distinguished war record in World War II. From 1946 to 1982, "Brownie" served as a floating high school in New York City and is presently preserved in Baltimore. She steams as a working monument to the U.S. **merchant marine**, making trips up and down the East Coast of the United States. She was named for John W. Brown (1867–1941), an early union organizer at **Bath Iron Works**.

Jolie Brise, seventy-two-foot French **pilot cutter** launched in 1913. She became an English yacht in 1920 and went on to win countless ocean races. She was purchased by Britain's Exeter Maritime Museum in 1977 and continues to be used for sail training, ranging afield.

Jolliet, Louis (1645–1700), French-Canadian explorer and **hydrographer** who in 1673, with **Jacques Marquette**, was the first European to travel down the **Mississippi River**, reaching as far as its junction with the Arkansas River. He later explored and mapped parts of Hudson Bay and the coast of present-day **Labrador**.

jolly boat, small rowing or sailing craft used as a general-purpose ship's boat.

Jolly Roger, pirate flag, commonly a skull and crossbones, that was designed to strike fear in victims and encourage a hasty surrender. Pirates also flew a red flag, which meant that no mercy would be shown in battle (**no quarter given**). Jolly Roger likely got its name from the French *jolie rouge*, or "red flag."

Jonah and the Whale, story in the Old Testament of the Bible (Jonah 1–4) in which Jonah, an Israelite, refuses God's mission for him to become a prophet and instead sets off on a sea voyage. In his anger, God raises a great storm. Realizing that it was Jonah's disobedience that caused the storm, his fellow sailors throw him overboard and Jonah is saved from drowning when he is swallowed by a great whale. He lives inside this fish for three days until he is "vomited out." Thankful that his life has been saved, Jonah takes up God's mission.

Jones, John Paul (1747–1792), Scottish-born sailor who was one of the original officers of the **Continental Navy** and whose ideas of naval service were adopted by the U.S. **Navy**. He began his career at sea in the British merchant fleet but fled to Virginia after killing another seaman in self-defense. During the American Revolution, he commanded the *Providence* and *Ranger* and became the scourge of British shipping. Aboard *Bonhomme Richard* he engaged and captured HMS *Serapis* in the Battle of **Flamborough Head**, uttering the statement **"I have not yet begun to fight!"** when asked to surrender. In 1788 he accepted a commission as a rear admiral in the Russian navy and saw action against the Turks. He resigned from that position two years later and lived the rest of his life in Paris, dying in poverty. His remains were carried to the United States a century later and now rest in the chapel of the U.S. **Naval Academy** in Annapolis, Maryland.

Engraving of *John Paul Jones* shooting a sailor. (Courtesy The Mariners' Museum, Newport News, Virginia)

Jones, John Treasure (1906–1993), thirty-third and final **master** of RMS *Queen Mary*, who brought the great **liner** into Long Beach, California, on December 9, 1967, and retired with his famous ship. He was a cantankerous, lovable old salt who is remembered for his satirical remarks during that final cruise. While slowly working their way across the sweltering equator, Jones announced on the ship's public address system: "Ladies and gentlemen, it is my duty to inform you that we are hopelessly lost. However, I am happy to report we are making wonderful time."

Jones, Tristan (1924–1995), legendary Welsh sailor and author who during his lifetime covered a distance of more than 450,000 miles—many single-handed—in small ocean craft. Born at sea off the island of Tristan de Cunha, in the South Atlantic, he served in the **Royal Navy** in World War II and was wounded. As a result of his injuries, one leg was amputated in 1982, but he continued to sail to inspire other amputees. He wrote sixteen books about his worldwide adventures, including *The Incredible Voyage* (1977), *Saga of a Wayward Sailor* (1979), and *Yarns* (1983).

Jones Act, name applied to section 27 of the **Merchant Marine Act of 1920** requiring that all U.S. domestic waterborne trade be carried by U.S.-flag, U.S.-built, and U.S.-manned vessels. The section was named for Senator Wesley L. Jones (1863–1932) of Washington, chairman of the Senate Committee on the Merchant Marine.

Jones-White Act, government legislation that empowered the U.S. Treasury to offer loans of up to seventy-five percent to American ship-owners for the building and conversion costs of U.S. passenger **liners** and to let mail subsidies to provide active income for the vessels. The act made possible the construction of the **California**-class liners of 1928, the *Morro Castle* and her sister in 1930, three **Matson Line** sisters in 1932, and the **United States Lines** passenger liners *Manhattan* and *Washington*. Also known as the **Merchant Marine Act of 1928**, it was largely repealed by the **Merchant Marine Act of 1936**. It was sponsored by Senators Wesley Jones of Washington and Wallace H. White of Maine.

Jordan River, two-hundred-mile river that is formed by headwaters in North Israel that flow south between Israel and the Golan Heights, through the Sea of Galilee, to the Dead Sea. The unnavigable river forms the boundary between Israel and the West Bank, and the country of Jordan. It is viewed by many as a sacred stream and is mentioned in the Bible as the scene of Jesus' baptism.

Joseph Conrad, sail training ship, originally named *Georg Stage*, built in 1882 for cadets in the Danish merchant service. She operated in this role until 1934 when, under the command of **Alan John Villiers**, the renamed ship circumnavigated the globe (1934–36). Since 1947 the ship has been featured as an exhibit at **Mystic Seaport** and continues to house sailing students after nearly 120 years afloat.

The Journal of Commerce, daily newspaper founded by Samuel F. B. Morse (1791–1872) in 1827 that has long been considered the bible of shipping and international trade. In 2000 it dropped its daily print version in favor of an online presence and a weekly magazine.

Juan Sebastián de Elcano, 370-foot Spanish **tall ship** built in 1927 as a training ship for midshipmen and ensigns of the Spanish navy. The 370-foot, four-masted topsail **schooner** is named for the captain of the *Victoria*, the only ship of **Ferdinand Magellan**'s exploratory fleet to complete the 1519–22 global expedition.

Juggernaut, 1974 action film in which the ocean **liner** *Britannic* is being held hostage for ransom. The film starred Richard Harris and Omar Sharif in a story based on a similar real-life scenario involving the *Queen Elizabeth 2* in 1972. Almost all of the movie was shot aboard the *Hamburg*, and the aerial footage of the liner slamming her way through a gale-force sea is spectacular. A novelization of the movie was also done in 1974.

USS *Juneau* (CL-52), U.S. **Navy cruiser** that was torpedoed and sank on November 13, 1942, during action off the island of **Guadalcanal**. More than six hundred crew members were lost, including the **Sullivans**, five brothers from Waterloo, Iowa, who served together in the navy to avenge the death of a friend killed at **Pearl Harbor** aboard USS *Arizona*.

Juniata, 4,330-gross-ton American passenger steamer designed by **Frank Kirby** for upper **Great Lakes** operation along with her sister ships *Octorara* and *Tionesta*. She was completed in 1905 for the **Anchor Line** service between Buffalo and Duluth and was retired in 1937 with the tightening of U.S. marine safety regulations. She was sold in 1940 to become the *Milwaukee Clipper*.

junk, Western term for a type of sailing vessel used in China and other countries of East Asia. With a flat bottom, a broad and flat bow, and a broad and high stern, a junk is used for fishing, for transporting goods and people on rivers and seas, and sometimes as houseboats.

Junyo Maru, Japanese cargo ship carrying 2,300 Dutch, British, American, and Australian prisoners of war and 4,200 Indonesian slave laborers that was torpedoed off the coast of Sumatra on September 18, 1944, by the British sub HMS *Tradewind*. More than 5,620 people perished.

Jutland, Battle of, naval engagement fought May 31, 1916, off Denmark between the British and German main fleets. It was perhaps history's last **line of battle** engagement, and losses on both sides were heavy. Admirals **Reinhold Scheer** and **John Rushworth Jellicoe** each claimed victory: Germany for having sunk more ships than they lost and Britain because the German navy retired to its bases and never again disputed the surface control of the seas during World War I.

$\mathcal{K}$

Kaga, Japanese aircraft carrier originally laid down as a battleship but completed as a carrier in 1928 that carried part of the strike force that attacked **Pearl Harbor** on December 7, 1941. At the Battle of **Midway** in May 1942, it was hit by four U.S. bombs from aircraft from the USS *Enterprise*. Uncontrollable fires caused violent explosions, and the 812-foot converted battleship sank.

Kaiser, Henry J. (1882–1967), popular American industrialist who established giant businesses in cement, aluminum, chemicals, steel, tourism, and health care. During World War II, he and his corporations made exceptional contributions to the war effort, producing ships, planes, and military vehicles in vast numbers. His shipbuilding firms won renown for their mass production of **Liberty ships**. The record time for construction of a Liberty was set at the Kaiser Shipyard in Richmond, California, in late 1942. The SS *Robert E. Peary* was completed in four days, fifteen hours, and began operating three days later.

Kaiser's Cup, also known as the Emperor's Cup, a yachting trophy designed and sponsored by **Wilhelm II**, emperor of Germany, and awarded to the winner of the 1905 **Transatlantic Race**. Eleven sailing yachts made up the open field in the contest from Sandy Hook, New Jersey, to the Lizard lighthouse at the entrance to the English Channel. The American **schooner** *Atlantic* won the race, setting a speed record. The kaiser's "solid gold" cup became a propaganda weapon in World War I when it was found to be fashioned of gilded pewter.

Kaiser Wilhelm der Grosse, 627-foot **North German Lloyd liner** launched in 1897 to capture the speed record of the North Atlantic from the **Hamburg-America** liner *Deutschland*—a distinction she achieved shortly after her entry into service. The first liner with four **funnels**, *Kaiser Wilhelm der Grosse* set the design trend for the **Atlantic** greyhounds that continued until World War I. Requisitioned as a German navy **auxiliary cruiser** in 1914, she was engaged by the British cruiser HMS

Highflyer off West Africa later in the year. The two ships slugged it out for ninety minutes, and the *Kaiser Wilhelm der Grosse* was abandoned after running out of ammunition. The liner was **scuttled** by her crew to avoid capture by the British.

Kaiulani, 250-foot **bark** built in Bath, Maine, in 1899 for service between San Francisco and Hawai'i. In World War II she carried lumber from Washington State to South Africa by way of **Cape Horn**, sailing on to Sydney, Australia, as the last American **square-rigger** in regular commercial service. In Sydney, *Kaiulani* was converted into a barge to support U.S. forces during the island-hopping campaign in the Pacific. In 1964 *Kaiulani* was donated to the United States by the Philippines, but efforts to raise funds for her restoration and return were unsuccessful and she was broken up in 1974.

Kalakala, ferry built in 1926 as the *Peralta* for service across San Francisco Bay. Brought to Puget Sound after sustaining some fire damage in 1933, she was redesigned by engineers from the Boeing Aircraft Company into a streamlined, stainless steel, 1,526-ton, art-deco vessel. Renamed *Kalakala*, she began service between Seattle and Bremerton in 1935. Retired from passenger service in 1967, she was relegated to fish processing in Alaskan waters. In 1997 she was towed to Seattle for restoration as a floating museum of Puget Sound history.

Kalmar Nyckel, Swedish ship that in 1638, along with *Fagel Grip*, established the first permanent European settlement in the Delaware Valley. The 116-foot, three-masted **pinnace** carried soldiers, sailors, and a party of twenty-four settlers from Sweden, Germany, Finland, and Holland. A replica of the ship was launched in 1997 and, home-ported in Wilmington, serves as Delaware's seagoing "Ambassador of Good Will."

kamal, navigational instrument used for centuries by Arab seamen to measure the altitude of a celestial body. It consisted of a small board with a hole drilled in the center and a knotted string that passed through the hole. The observer would hold the board so that the upper and lower edges coincided with the celestial body and the horizon. In this position, the string was held tight to the observer's eye and its length was used to measure the height of the observed body, thereby determining the ship's **latitude**.

Kamehameha I (ca. 1758–1819), founder of the Kingdom of Hawai'i. He rose to power through ability and strength and united the islands with help from Europeans who visited the islands and traded guns for goods.

kamikaze, Japanese suicide bomber flights of World War II, the idea of Admiral Ohnishi. Begun in October 1944, these missions, crash-diving into U.S. ships, were carried out in a final defense of the home islands to half the inevitable U.S. invasion. The pilots were extremely young men who were given funeral rites before their departures. The term *kamikaze* translates as "divine wind," alluding to the wind that scattered the fleet of Kublai Khan as it was crossing the Strait of Tsushima to invade Japan in 1281.

Kane, Elisha Kent (1820–1857), U.S. naval physician and Arctic explorer who in 1850 led an unsuccessful expedition to Greenland in search of the British explorer Sir **John Franklin**, missing since 1845. In 1853 Kane led another expedition in search of Franklin and to establish whether there was an open sea around the North Pole. He and his crew were forced to abandon their ship after it became icebound, and they made an eighty-three-day journey to Greenland. Kane and his party were rescued and returned to New York in 1855.

kapok, buoyant material used to stuff life jackets and life buoys, replacing the earlier use of cork, before the advent of Styrofoam. It is made up of the silky fibers that surround the seeds of the tropical ceiba tree.

Kashiwara Maru, the largest and fastest passenger **liner** ever built for Japanese operation. Construction of the 27,200-gross-ton NYK (**Nippon Yusen Kaisha**) vessel was taken over by the Japanese navy in 1940 and completed as an aircraft carrier named the *Junyo*. She was torpedoed by U.S. submarines off of Nagasaki in 1944 and, although she didn't sink, was so badly damaged that she served no further part in the war effort. She was scrapped in 1947.

USS *Kearny* (DD-432), U.S. **Navy destroyer** that was struck by a torpedo fired by a German **U-boat** on October 16, 1941, while escorting a British **convoy** from Newfoundland to Iceland. The eleven men killed were the first U.S. fatalities of World War II.

USS *Kearsarge*, Union navy **sloop of war** that engaged and sank the **Confederate raider** CSS *Alabama* outside the harbor of Cherbourg, France, on June 19, 1864. During the battle, Captain **John Ancrum Winslow** slung chains along the length of *Kearsarge*'s wooden hull to protect the engine room. During the battle, a Confederate shell lodged in the ship's rudder post but did not explode, and *Kearsarge* suffered only minor damage. An estimated fifteen thousand French citizens watched the battle from the shoreline cliffs. After a number of rebuilds, *Kearsarge* was stricken from the navy list in 1894.

USS *Kearsarge* (CV-33), **Essex**-class aircraft carrier completed in 1946 and modernized in 1950 to land jet aircraft. She saw action in the Korean War and in 1962 retrieved astronaut Wally Schirra and his Mercury *Sigma 7* spacecraft after they had orbited the earth six times. Later that year, she collided with the British **liner** *Oriana* in fog off Long Beach, California. She retrieved another astronaut, Gordon Cooper, in 1963 after splashdown following

twenty-two orbits above the earth in his *Faith 7* Mercury space capsule. The 888-foot ship was stationed in the Gulf of Tonkin to provide air support to ground forces during the Vietnam War. Decommissioned in 1970, she was sold for scrap in 1973.

kedge, to move a ship by laying out an anchor by boat and then heaving in on the line out to the anchor. Often a special anchor, called a "kedge anchor," is used.

The Kedge Anchor, popular American manual on seamanship by William N. Brady. Since it was introduced in 1876, it has been published in eighteen editions.

keelboats, double-ended vessels used from the late eighteenth through the mid-nineteenth centuries on the **Mississippi**, Ohio, and **Missouri Rivers** and their tributaries to transport goods and people. Important to the westward expansion of the United States, they ranged in length from thirty feet to over a hundred feet. They were the only sizable form of watercraft that could travel upstream—**flatboats** could only travel downstream—on the **Western rivers** prior to the introduction of **steamboats**. They were propelled by oars, setting poles, sails, and cordelle (a line running from the boat to crewmen walking along the shore), depending on conditions.

keelhaul, a means of punishing a sailor by tying him to a line, rigged yardarm to yardarm and passing under the ship. He was hoisted up to one yardarm and then dropped into the sea, hauled under the ship, and lifted to the opposite yardarm. The punishment was repeated after the sailor had time to catch his breath. In modern times, the term has come to mean a severe reprimand.

Kendall Whaling Museum, museum located just south of Boston in Sharon, Massachusetts, that was founded in 1956 around the Kendall family collection begun in 1899. Twelve galleries house an international collection of art, history, and ethnology celebrating the age-old human fascination with whales. The museum includes the world's finest collection of **scrimshaw**.

Kennedy, John F. (1917–1963), thirty-fifth president of the United States. He was a recreational sailor who enlisted in the U.S. **Navy** in September 1941 and became commander of a **PT boat** in the Pacific during World War II. In action off the Solomon Islands in August 1943 his boat, **PT-109**, was sunk, and Kennedy was credited with saving the life of at least one of his crew. For being wounded in combat, he was awarded the Purple Heart. During his presidency, he oversaw the abortive **Bay of Pigs** invasion of Cuba by Cuban exiles in April 1961, and he ordered a naval blockade of the island in October 1962 during the **Cuban Missile Crisis**.

Kent, Alexander, the pseudonym of **Douglas Reeman** for his popular **Richard Bolitho** series of **Napoleonic**-era naval fiction.

Kent, Rockwell (1882–1971), American artist and author who found material for his books and drawings on his travels to remote parts of the world. Kent's profound respect for the outdoors is evident in his stark and powerful landscapes. Among his major works of art are *Down to the Sea* and *Toilers of the Sea*, and he is well known for his illustrations in an early-twentieth-century printing of *Moby-Dick*. He traveled to the southern tip of South America, making the last part of his trip in a lifeboat, and chronicled the journey in *Voyaging: Southward from the Strait of Magellan* (1924). Other books of his include *N by E* (1936) and his autobiography, *It's Me, O Lord* (1955).

ketch, two-masted sailing vessel with the shorter mizzenmast abaft the mainmast but stepped forward of the rudder post.

Kiangya, Chinese passenger ship carrying refugees fleeing Communist troops that struck a mine and sank off Shanghai on December 3, 1948, with the loss of an estimated three thousand lives.

Kiche Maru, Japanese **steamship** that sank off the coast of Japan in a storm on September 28, 1912, with the loss of more than a thousand lives. News of the tragedy was overshadowed by the loss of RMS *Titanic* months before.

U.S. postage stamp issued in 2001 and depicting one of Rockwell Kent's illustrations from the 1930 Random House edition of *Moby-Dick*. (© Plattsburgh State Art Museum)

Kidd, William (c.1645–1701), Scottish-born English **privateer** who became a pirate in 1695 off the coast of Madagascar and became renowned as Captain Kidd. After a very profitable career of high-seas raiding, he arrived in the **West Indies** to find he had a bounty on his head. He purportedly buried part of his treasure on eastern Long Island before being captured and sent to London for trial, where he was publicly hanged. His corpse was tarred and hung in a cage as a warning to would-be pirates.

Kidnapped, 1886 story by **Robert Louis Stevenson** set in Scotland in the mid-1700s. After the death of his father, David Balfour is cheated out of his inheritance by his uncle, kidnapped, and shipped off to the Carolinas in the brig *Covenant*. Balfour escapes and eventually claims what is rightfully his. Balfour's adventures continue in Stevenson's sequel *David Balfour* (1893).

Kiel Canal, sixty-one-mile waterway through northern Germany that provides a shortcut for ships sailing between the North Sea and the Baltic Sea. It leads from Brunsbuttelkoog, at the mouth of the Elbe River, to Holtenau, near Kiel, and shortens the trip around Denmark by more than three hundred miles. Built by Germany in 1895, the canal was declared an international waterway by the **Treaty of Versailles**. It was formerly called the Kaiser Wilhelm Canal, and today its official German name is Nord-Ostsee Kanal (Northeast Sea Canal).

Kimball, Sumner I. (1824–1923), American **Revenue Marine** officer, the man responsible for organizing the U.S. **Life-Saving Service** in 1878. He served as its head for its entire existence, through its merger with the U.S. **Revenue Cutter Service** in 1915 to form the U.S. **Coast Guard**. In 1876 Kimball established a school of instruction aboard the revenue cutter *Dobbin* to train officers, the forerunner of the U.S. **Coast Guard Academy**. He wrote *Organization and Methods of the U.S. Life Saving Service* (1889) and *Joshua James, Life Saver* (1909).

Kimmel, Husband Edward (1882–1958), U.S. **Navy** admiral who in February 1941 was appointed commander in chief of the U.S. Pacific fleet. He was relieved of his command ten days after the Japanese surprise attack on **Pearl Harbor** and was made a scapegoat. He reverted to the rank of rear admiral and retired in 1942. The Roberts Commission later cleared him of all charges but never returned his rank. The debate over his part in the disaster continues to this day.

King, Ernest Joseph (1878–1956), U.S. admiral who commanded the U.S. fleet—the greatest naval fleet in history—during World War II. Early in 1942, he also became **chief of naval operations**, holding both assignments until after the war—the only officer in U.S. naval history to occupy both posts.

HMS *King George V*, one of five 40,990-ton Duke of York–class British battleships. The 745-foot vessel was completed in 1940 and as **flagship** of the Home Fleet played an instrumental role in tracking down and sinking the German battleship *Bismarck* in 1941. Active in the **Atlantic**, she carried Prime Minister

Winston Churchill home from the Teheran Conference—the first meeting of the main Allied leaders during World War II—after December 1, 1942. She was assigned to active duty in the Pacific war in 1944 and was present at the surrender of Japan in September 1945. She was decommissioned in 1949 and scrapped in 1958.

King Neptune, ruler of the seas, from the Roman god **Neptune**.

King of Spain Cup, name for the 1928 **Transatlantic Race** from New York to Santander, Spain, which was sponsored by Spain's King Alfonso, an ardent yachtsman. The race was won by William B. Bell's 135-foot **Herreshoff schooner** *Elena*, commanded by John Barr, nephew of **Charles Barr**.

Kings Point, site of the U.S. **Merchant Marine Academy**, located on the former estate of automobile magnate Walter P. Chrysler, on Long Island Sound in Kings Point, New York.

king spoke, the spoke on a ship's steering wheel that is up and vertical when the ship's rudder is amidships. It is usually longer than the other spokes and marked by a **Turk's head** or brass cap.

Kingston, William H. G. (1814–1880), prolific British author who turned out more than 150 adventure books, at least 80 relating to the sea and seafaring. His first big success was *Peter the Whaler* (1851), which related the adventures of a wild son of an Irish vicar.

Kipling, Joseph Rudyard (1865–1936), British poet and author best known in maritime circles for his classic novel ***Captains Courageous*** (1897), set aboard a fishing **schooner** on the **Grand Banks**. Other books include *A Fleet in Being* (1898), *Fringes of the Fleet* (1915), and *Sea Warfare* (1916). He also compiled many short stories and poems about the sea, including "The Day's Work" (1899) and "Traffics and Discoveries" (1904).

Kirby, Frank (1848–1929), renowned American designer of vessels for operation on the **Great Lakes**. Among his most famous commissions were the *City of Detroit III*, *Greater Buffalo*, *Greater Detroit*, *Seeandbee*, and the *Juniata* trio.

Kitchener, Horatio Herbert (1850–1916), army officer who served as Great Britain's war minister during World War I and was drowned when HMS *Hampshire* struck a mine on June 5, 1916. He was featured on a recruitment poster that showed him pointing his finger above the legend "Your Country Needs You." Uncle Sam's famous finger-pointing poster surely followed suit.

USS *Kitty Hawk* (CVA-63), lead aircraft carrier of the class, the other two being USS ***Constellation*** and USS ***America***. Completed in 1961, the 81,780-ton ship saw extensive action during the Vietnam War. In 1984 she collided with a submerged Soviet Victor-class submarine in the Sea of Japan. By 2000 she had earned the distinction of being the oldest aircraft carrier still in active service. The 1,069-foot ship is scheduled to be decommissioned in 2008 and replaced by the as-yet-unnamed nuclear-powered CVN-77, which will be the seventh carrier of the **Theodore Roosevelt** class.

knee, timber or metal support fashioned into an angle that is used when two structural members come together at or close to a right angle. In wooden ships, knees are fashioned from naturally grown timbers in which the grain of the wood follows the desired angle, thus keeping full strength against splitting. Trees chosen for shipbuilding may be artificially bent during growth to provide the desired angle. Pasture oak, which provides tight-angle knees because it has room for branches to spread out horizontally, was much prized for natural knees. The root of the hackmatack, or larch, tree is most commonly used today.

Knight's Modern Seamanship, standard text on seamanship, considered by many to be the sail-or's bible, that was first published by Austin Knight in 1901.

knot, unit of speed in navigation that is the rate of one **nautical mile** (6,080 feet, or 1,852 meters) per hour.

Knox, Dudley Wright (1877–1960), U.S. **Navy** officer and author credited with improving and expanding the navy's archival and historical operations. In 1921, after a twenty-five-year naval career, he was assigned as Officer in Charge, Office of Naval Records and Library, and as curator of the Navy Department. During World War II, he was given the additional responsibilities of Deputy Director of Naval History, retiring as a commodore in 1946 after another twenty-five-year career. His books include *The Eclipse of American Sea Power* (1922), *The Naval Genius of George Washington* (1932), and *A History of the United States Navy* (1936), one of the best single-volume histories ever written.

Knox-Johnston, Sir Robin (b. 1939), English mariner who was the first to complete a non-stop solo circumnavigation. He was awarded the Golden Globe prize, established by Britain's *Sunday Times*, for his efforts in racing 30,123 miles in 313 days, from June 1968 to April 1969. Knox-Johnston was the sole finisher in a field that included **Bernard Moitessier**, **Chay Blyth**, John Ridgway, and **Donald Crowhurst**. Knox-Johnston completed the voyage in his teak-hulled **ketch *Suhaili***, which he built himself while stationed in India. He later wrote *A World of My Own: The Single-Handed, Nonstop Circumnavigation of the World in Suhaili* (1970).

Koga, Mineichi (1885–1944), Japanese admiral who succeeded **Isoroku Yamamoto** as commander in chief of the Japanese fleet in 1943. He continued Japan's reckless expenditure of aviators and was himself killed in an aircraft accident. He was succeeded by Admiral Soemu Toyoda.

Kon-Tiki, balsa raft built and sailed by Norwegian anthropologist **Thor Heyerdahl** and five others to test the theory that the Pacific Islands were first explored by the Incas. The raft was built on the lines of an early Peruvian craft and named *Kon-Tiki* after an Indian god. They set sail from the South American port of Callao, Peru, on April 29, 1947, and after 101 days of sailing and drifting, made landfall forty-three hundred miles away on a coral reef of an atoll near Tahiti. *Kon-Tiki* is now housed in the Kon-Tiki Museum in Olso, Norway, along with the *Ra II*. Heyerdahl's book about the expedition, *The Kon-Tiki Expedition*, has been translated into at least sixty-six languages, and a documentary of the voyage won an Oscar in 1951.

Kookabura III, Australian **sloop** that failed to defend the **America's Cup** in 1987 against the U.S. challenger *Stars & Stripes*. **Dennis Conner** became the first man to win back the Cup, and the trophy's new home became the San Diego Yacht Club.

Kortum, Karl (1917–1996), American mariner and ship preservationist who helped found the San Francisco Maritime National Historic Park and New York's **South Street Seaport Museum**. Kortum sailed aboard the **bark** *Kaiulani*, the last American merchant **square-rigger** under sail, and served in the **merchant marine** during World War II. He was instrumental in preserving the big square-riggers *Balclutha*, *Falls of Clyde*, *Wavertree*, *Elissa*, and *Moshulu* as well as inspiring the saving of the early steamer *Great Britain* in England, the square-rigger *Glenlee* in Scotland, and the *Polly Woodside* and *James Craig* in Australia—plus a host of lesser vessels, including the **schooner** *C. A. Thayer* and the steam schooner *Wapama* in San Francisco.

Kraken, legendary sea monster long feared by sailors. Seamen from northern Europe and Scandinavia believed Kraken would float on the waves so that passing ships would think it was a small island. It would then grab the vessel with its tentacles and pull it under the water, devouring all men on board. The Kraken of legend was probably a giant squid. Alfred, **Lord Tennyson** penned a short poem entitled "Kraken" in 1830 about the hideous beast.

Kretschmer, Otto (1912–1988), German World War II **U-boat** ace who was responsible for sinking forty-seven Allied ships and damaging six others—the most of any U-boat commander. Kretschmer's U-99 was trapped by British destroyers in March 1941, and he and his crew were taken prisoner after they **scuttled** the sub. Kretschmer's motto was, "One torpedo . . . one ship."

Kronprinzessin Cecilie, 19,360-ton **North German Lloyd liner** built in 1906 for the Bremen to New York service. At the start of World War I, the liner was en route to Germany with a cargo that included forty million marks of gold. Rather than risk sinking or capture, she returned to the neutral United States and was interned at Boston. She was seized by the U.S. government in 1917 and was outfitted as the U.S. **Navy** transport USS *Mount Vernon*. Plans to place her in passenger service after the war fell through, and she was **laid up** in Chesapeake Bay from 1919 until 1940, when she was scrapped.

Kronprinz Wilhelm, 14,908-ton **North German Lloyd liner** launched in 1901 for the Bremen to New York service. She captured the **Blue Riband** in September 1902 from the *Deutschland* for the fastest westbound Atlantic crossing. In World War I, she was outfitted as an armed merchant **cruiser** and destroyed 60,552 tons of Allied shipping off the coast of South America. With no friendly ports to load coal, she entered neutral Newport News, Virginia, in April 1915 and was interned at Philadelphia. In 1917 *Kronprinz Wilhelm* became the U.S. **Navy** transport USS *Von Steuben*. After the war, she was transferred to the U.S. **Shipping Board** and was scrapped in 1923.

Kruzenshtern, Adam Johann von (1770–1846), Russian navigator and oceanographer who circumnavigated the globe (1803–6). His *Atlas de l'Ocean Pacifique* (1827) contributed greatly to the knowledge of the **hydrography** of the North Pacific coast of North America.

Kruzenshtern, 376-foot Russian **tall ship** built in 1926 in Germany as the sailing cargo ship *Padua.* The four-masted **bark** carried nitrates from Chile and wheat from Australia. Following World War II, *Padua* was surrendered to the Soviet Union for use as a training vessel. Renamed for the Russian sailor and oceanographer **Adam Johann von Kruzenshtern**, the ship's home port is Saint Petersburg.

Kudirka, Simonas, Lithuanian seaman who leaped from the Soviet factory ship *Litva* to the decks of the U.S. **Coast Guard cutter *Vigilant*** on November 23, 1970, seeking political asylum, while the two ships were moored together off Martha's Vineyard for a discussion of fish-eries issues. The captain of the *Vigilant* allowed Soviet sailors to board the cutter and remove Kudirka. The *New York Times* described the event as "one of the most disgraceful incidents ever to occur on a ship flying the American flag," and all ranking Coast Guard officials involved in the incident were either court-martialed or severely reprimanded. Kudirka was imprisoned in Siberia but eventually made his way to the United States via diplomatic channels.

Kursk, Russian nuclear submarine that sank in the icy waters of the **Barents Sea** on August 12, 2000, with her crew of 118. More than a week later, Norwegian divers opened the rear hatch of the sub but found no survivors. The cause of the accident is believed to have been an internal torpedo explosion.

Kwajalein, atoll in the **Marshall Islands** in the Pacific Ocean that was the site of fierce fighting between U.S. and Japanese troops during World War II. It was taken by American forces in February 1944, with no survivors from the Japanese garrison of eight thousand men.

L

Labrador, peninsula between the Atlantic Ocean and Hudson Bay that is the northeastern corner of the Canadian mainland. The western part belongs to Québec, and the eastern coast forms part of Newfoundland.

Labrador Current, cold ocean current that rises in the Arctic Ocean and flows along the shores of **Labrador** to a point near the island of Newfoundland, where it meets the **Gulf Stream**.

SS *Laconia*, 19,680-ton passenger **liner** completed for the **Cunard Line** in 1922. She was taken up for service as an armed merchant **cruiser** in 1939 and began troop transport operations the following year. In 1942 she was sunk in the South Atlantic with 2,372 souls on board, including 1,800 Italian prisoners of war. The **U-boat** that sank her took on what survivors it could and radioed for additional help from neighboring German vessels and U-boats to assist the rescue efforts. An American Liberator bomber flew over and—regardless of the fact that the submarine was towing lifeboats and was clearly marked with a red cross—

bombed the U-boat. *Laconia* survivors were put into the remaining lifeboats, and the U-boats escaped. French vessels eventually pulled 1,111 people from the sea. Admiral Dönitz issued the directive, known as the *Laconia* Order, that forbade U-boats from further rescue operation after sinking an enemy vessel.

A Lady Fights Back, ten-minute American film, narrated by John Nesbitt, detailing the salvage of USS *Lafayette* (former SS **Normandie**) from the frozen muck of the **Hudson River**. The 1944 short was reedited in the mid-1950s with an added voice-over by Walter Lance and was shown often on television's *Woody Woodpecker Show* into the early 1960s. The final added scenes of the ship being scrapped against Woody's comments made many postwar American kids ask the question, "Where did the metal in my bike come from?"

USS *Laffey* (DD-724), Allen M. Sumner–class **destroyer** completed in 1944. After **convoy** duty and support operations for the **Normandy Invasion**, the twenty-two-hundred-ton ship was dispatched to the South Pacific, where she was heavily damaged by **kamikaze** attacks. The efforts of her crew to keep her from sinking earned her the nickname "the ship that would not die." The 377-foot vessel received five battle stars for service in World War II and two more for her role in the Korean War. Decommissioned in 1977, the destroyer is one of the museum ships at Patriot's Point Maritime Museum in South Carolina.

Lafitte, Jean (1780–1826), American **privateer** who, commissioned by Latin American countries, primarily preyed on Spanish cargo from bases in the Caribbean, and as far north and west as New Orleans and Galveston, in the early nineteenth century. With some fifty pirate ships at his command, combined with his dislike for the British, he was instrumental in the American victory at the 1815 Battle of **New Orleans** and was granted pardons by President James Madison—as were all one thousand members of his band—for his participation in the battle during the **War of 1812**.

La Follette Seamen's Act, law passed by the U.S. Congress in 1915 protecting the rights of U.S. seamen by regulating working conditions and establishing safety requirements for oceangoing ships. The act was named for Senator Robert La Follette (1855–1925) of Wisconsin.

La Guardia, test ship of the U.S. **Maritime Commission** used to show the worth of the **P-2** design in commercial peacetime operation. She was converted in 1949 from the troopship *General W. P. Richardson* for operation by **American Export Lines** to Mediterranean ports from New York. Her wartime design was ill-equipped to anticipate the financial needs of the postwar world, and even with full passenger complements, the ship failed to turn a profit. She was returned to the government lay-up fleet in 1952 as the only true P-2 transport–type conversion to serve commercially and was sold

in 1955 to become the *Leilani* for West Coast service to Hawaii.

laid up, said of a vessel that has been taken out of active service.

Lake, Simon (1866–1945), American inventor and pioneer of submarine design and construction. He invented the periscope in 1902, which used mirrors and magnifying lenses to enable a submerged submarine to sight distant targets. Lake designed and built submarines for salvage operations, but he was largely unsuccessful in selling subs to the U.S. **Navy**.

USS *Lake Champlain* (CV-39), **Essex**-class aircraft carrier commissioned in 1945. In 1961 the twenty-seven-thousand-ton ship recovered Commander Alan B. Shepard and his *Freedom 7* Mercury space capsule after they splashed down in the Atlantic following the first manned space flight. She also recovered astronauts Gordon Cooper and Charles Conrad after their *Gemini 5* capsule splashed down in the **Atlantic** following an eight-day multiorbital flight in space. She was decommissioned in 1966 and sold for scrap in 1972.

Lake Champlain, Battle of, two naval actions, one during the American Revolution and the other in the War of 1812. The 1776 battle was a series of naval engagements—the first of the Revolution, apart from single-ship encounters—between squadrons of small British and American vessels in October 1776. The lake was of great strategic importance as it linked New England and Canada, and while the British seized control of the lake, it was too late in the year for them to make use of it. Among the skirmishes was the Battle of **Valcour Island**. The second battle, thirty-six years later, was a major American victory in the **War of 1812** that occurred on September 11, 1814. An outgunned U.S. squadron under the command of thirty-year-old **Thomas Macdonough** engaged a British squadron at close range off

Plattsburg, New York. Macdonough anchored his vessels in such a way that they could be turned without needing wind, and the force captured one British **frigate**, one **brig**, and two **sloops of war**. Described as the greatest naval battle of the war, it occurred almost exactly one year after **Perry**'s victory in the Battle of **Lake Erie**.

Lake Erie, Battle of, pivotal battle in the **War of 1812**. On September 10, 1813, Commodore **Oliver Hazard Perry** led nine small ships in victory over a British squadron of six vessels in Put-in-Bay, Ohio. Perry sent the message, **"We have met the enemy, and they are ours."** The victory led to the reopening of American supply lines on the upper **Great Lakes** and ensured America's hold on the Northwest. During the battle, Perry's **flagship**, *Lawrence*, was disabled. Perry transferred his command to the *Niagara* and hoisted his battle flag, which was inscribed with the motto: "Don't Give up the Ship."

Lake Itasca, source of the **Mississippi River**, located in Minnesota.

laker, type of ship that trades only in the **Great Lakes**. Long and narrow with a pilothouse either forward or aft (or both), it usually carries grain, salt, and ore cargoes. The term is also used for vessels built on the Great Lakes during World War II by the U.S. **Shipping Board**. Named for lakes, ninety-nine were built for ocean service.

Lake Sakajawea, the largest man-made lake in the United States. Located in the **Missouri River** Basin and managed by the U.S. **Army Corps of Engineers**, it is maintained for flood control, hydroelectric power, recreation, and irrigation.

Lake Washington Ship Canal, waterway completed by the U.S. **Army Corp of Engineers** in 1934 in Washington State to link Lake Washington to Puget Sound. The canal required digging cuts and includes a series of locks.

MS *Lakonia*, Greek Line motor ship that caught fire while on a Christmas cruise to the **Canary Islands** from Southampton, England, in 1963. Built as the Dutch *Johan van Oldenbarnevelt* in 1930, the **liner** had 1,036 people on board, of which 89 perished. The hulk sank while in tow to **Gibraltar**, and the Greek Line wasted no time in replacing her with the *Empress of Britain* of 1955, which they renamed *Queen Anna Maria*.

Lambdin, Dewey, American author of a naval adventure series set in the late eighteenth century that featured fictional **Royal Navy** officer **Alan Lewrie**. The nine-volume series began with *The King's Coat* (1989) and includes *The Gun Ketch* (1993) and *A King's Commander* (1997).

SS *Lancastria*, **Cunard Line** passenger steamer built in 1922 and well known for her prewar Caribbean cruises out of New York. In 1940, while serving as a transport in World War II, the **liner** was evacuating British personnel from Occupied France when she was attacked by German bombers and sank in less than thirty minutes. Officially the ship was loaded with 5,310 people and crew, and an estimated 2,500 were saved. The tragedy was not reported to the British people until more than a month later.

Land, Emory S. "Jerry" (1879–1971), U.S. **Navy** admiral who was chairman of the U.S. **Maritime Commission** from 1938 to 1946 (succeeding Joseph P. Kennedy) and served as head of the **War Shipping Administration** from 1942 to 1946. Land oversaw the buildup and operation of the U.S. merchant fleet—the world's largest—during World War II. In 1958 he published his memoirs, *Winning the War with Ships*.

land bridge, a shipping activity in which cargoes and passengers are offloaded from a ship

Fitz Hugh Lane's *Gloucester Inner Harbor.* (Courtesy The Mariners' Museum, Newport News, Virginia)

and carried over land, usually by rail, to their destination. Sometimes they are loaded on another ship. Well before the construction of the **Panama Canal**, **Cornelius Vanderbilt** amassed a great fortune by establishing a land bridge across Nicaragua to carry gold rush prospectors and supplies from New York City to San Francisco.

landlubber, derisive term for a person who is not familiar with the ways of the sea.

Land's End, cape in Cornwall that is the westernmost point of land in England, across the English Channel from Finistère in France. Land's End is a granite promontory with cliffs up to 250 feet high that have been carved into strange shapes by the waves.

Lane, Fitz Hugh (1804–1865), American painter who had a lifelong devotion to the sea and

ships and became one of the most popular and respected marine artists of his time. He is best known for his luminous harbor scenes of Boston and of his hometown of **Gloucester**, Massachusetts. Today he is considered a master, and his marines are among the most valued nineteenth-century American paintings.

Lane Victory, 1945-built **Victory ship** used as a supply vessel in World War II, the Korean conflict, and the Vietnam War. **Laid up** in 1970, the ship was presented to the U.S. Merchant Marine Veterans of World War II to be preserved as a memorial to the more than seven thousand U.S. **merchant marines** who died in World War II. Towed to Los Angeles, she has been completely restored by volunteer labor and made fully functional. She was to steam to Normandy in 1994 to join the *Jeremiah O'Brien* for the fiftieth anniversary of

D-Day, but engine problems aborted the trip at the **Panama Canal**. Once a month during the warmer seasons, she is taken out with passengers for a day sail to Catalina Island, which is highlighted by a mock air attack at sea and a memorial service.

USS *Langley* (CV-1), ship originally built as the U.S. **Navy collier** *Jupiter* in 1913 and rebuilt in 1922 as the first U.S. aircraft carrier. The 11,500-ton ship proved the value of the floating airfield and provided the experience necessary to build USS ***Lexington*** and USS *Saratoga*, which were much bigger ships that were laid down as battle **cruisers** but completed as carriers under the terms of the **Washington Naval Treaty** of 1922. The 542-foot *Langley* was refitted to become a seaplane **tender** in 1937 and was sunk off Java in 1942 by five direct hits from Japanese aircraft.

Langsdorff, Hans (1894–1939), German naval officer and captain of the Nazi **pocket battleship** *Admiral Graf Spee* during the early days of World War II. He was forced to **scuttle** the ship after the Battle of the **River Plate**, off Montevideo, Uruguay, and on the following night, December 18, 1939, he shot himself while wrapped in the flag of Imperial Germany.

lapstrake, form of boat construction in which long, narrow planks are lapped one over another and fastened at close intervals along the overlapping edges.

Lapworth, William C. (b. 1919), American yacht designer and builder who is considered a pioneer in the evolution of successful fiberglass-production sailboats.

Larsen, Wolf, fictional captain of the *Ghost* in **Jack London**'s *The Sea Wolf* (1904).

La Salle, Robert Cavelier, Sieur de (1643–1687), French explorer and fur trader who, in 1682 explored the **Mississippi River** to its mouth,

claiming it for the king of France. He named the adjacent lands Louisiana after King Louis XIV and returned to France to gain permission to colonize the region. The king supported the project and a **convoy** set out in 1684, but La Salle miscalculated the position of the Mississippi's mouth and landed in Texas. Establishing a colony on Matagorda Bay, La Salle spent years looking for the Mississippi and was killed by some of his men on one such expedition. La Salle's **flagship** from this expedition, *La Belle*, was discovered in Matagorda Bay in 1995 and excavated.

Laser, one-design racing sailboat designed by Bruce Kirby and first built in 1971. Nearly fourteen feet in length, it has a twenty-foot mast and nearly seventy-six square feet of sail.

LASH, acronym for "lighter aboard ship" that refers a specialized container ship with an overhead crane that loads and discharges small barges known as **lighters**. This concept was designed to eliminate the need for specialized port or dock facilities.

The Last Grain Race, 1956 book by Eric Newby (b. 1919) recounting the *Moshulu*'s last voyage in the Australian grain trade. In 1938 the eighteen-year-old Newby signed on for a trip from Great Britain to Australia and back around the **Cape of Good Hope** and **Cape Horn** in the last commercial sailing fleet. His narrative is a gripping account of the adventures that took place during the six-month journey.

The Last Voyage, 1960 Metro-Goldwyn-Mayer epic about the demise at sea of the fictitious **liner** *Claredon*. The movie was filmed entirely aboard the retired *Île de France* off Japan in 1959, while the ship was waiting to be scrapped. Realism attained new heights as the former **French Line** ship was blasted, burned, and partly **scuttled** by director Andrew Stone to lend credibility to an otherwise awful screenplay. The film featured Dorothy Malone, Robert Stack, and George Sanders, who were in reality nothing more than supporting players to the great old liner.

lateen, ancient sailing rig on which a triangular, loose-footed sail is set on a long yard and attached, at an angle, to a short mast. Devised by Arab sailors in the Indian Ocean, it became the dominant rig in the Mediterranean in medieval times. It was found unsuitable for the boisterous conditions of **Atlantic** sailing, and its use died out there except as a steering sail aft on the classic **square-rigged** ship that evolved around 1500.

lateral system, the system of **aids to navigation** that has historically been used in the United States in which the shape, color, and number are assigned in accordance with their location relative to navigable waters. Vessels proceed in the given direction, for example, **"red, right, returning."** The **cardinal system** has historically been used in other countries. Both systems are giving way to the internationally accepted **Maritime Buoyage System**, which combines both the lateral and the cardinal systems.

latitude, the position of a point on the earth's surface measured in terms of its distance from the equator toward one of the earth's North or South Poles. Measured in degrees, where one degree equals sixty **nautical miles**, the equator is 0° and the poles are 90°.

SS *L'Atlantique*, innovative three-**funneled French Line liner** thought by many to be the precursor of SS *Normandie*. Her broad expanse of lofty public rooms was unlike any seen at sea until the arrival of the latter steamer. Completed for service from Bordeaux to Buenos Aires in 1931, she caught fire while en route to the shipyard for her yearly overhaul in 1933. No passengers were aboard at the time, but nineteen crew members lost their lives fighting the fire. After legal battles as to her dis-

position, the 42,512-gross-ton ship was sold for scrap in 1936.

Lawley, name applied to the many fine-quality yachts and boats built at George Lawley & Son Corporation in Neponset, Massachusetts. The firm was established in 1866 in Scituate, Massachusetts, before moving to South Boston and then Neponset. The yard employed upwards of eight hundred men in boom times and more than four thousand during World War II. Lawley closed its doors in 1945, the same year that its rival **Herreshoff** Manufacturing Company in Bristol, Rhode Island, ceased operations. It is estimated that Lawley constructed more than 1,100 yachts—among them the **America's Cup** yachts *Mayflower* and *Puritan*—and 1,900 **tenders** under thirty feet, not including war contracts.

Law of the Sea, international agreement regulating the use and exploitation of the world's oceans. The United Nations–sponsored Law of the Sea Treaty (1982) calls for limited, and controlled, mining of the seabed; establishes in general the twelve-mile limit for territorial waters; gives all nations' ships the right of "innocent passage" through crucial straits; and sets up international antipollution regulations.

Lawrence, James (1781–1813), U.S. naval officer who commanded the **frigate** USS *Chesapeake* in the **War of 1812**. In a fierce engagement with HMS *Shannon* on June 1, 1813, outside Boston, *Chesapeake* was badly damaged and later captured, despite Lawrence's dying plea, **"Don't give up the ship."** American losses were sixty seamen killed and eighty-five wounded in the action.

Lawrence, Thomas E. (1888–1935), British explorer, soldier, and writer known as Lawrence of Arabia. Shortly before his death in a motorcycle accident, he published one of the finest translations ever of Homer's *Odyssey*.

Laws of Oleron, the first code of laws for the maritime service. They derived from the Romans and were instituted on the Island of Oleron in the Bay of Biscay. The laws dealt mainly with the rights and responsibilities of ships' captains, and King Richard of England introduced these laws into Great Britain around 1190, having met them during the Crusades, where the forces included a contingent from the Island of Oleron.

lay up, to remove a vessel from active service.

lead line, piece of lead attached to a long line, which is marked off in **fathoms**, and used to find the depth of water. After the lead is "heaved" and the lead hits the seabed, the leadsman sounds out the measurements. Often, the piece of lead is hollowed at the bottom so it can contain a lump of animal fat. This fat can pick up material from the seabed to indicate the type of bottom. If it comes up clean, the leadsman knows the seabed is rock.

league, unit of measure, no longer used, equal to three **nautical miles**.

Leahy, William Daniel (1875–1959), career U.S. naval officer, diplomat, and chief of staff to President **Franklin D. Roosevelt** and Harry S. Truman. After serving as **chief of naval operations** from 1937 to 1939, he retired with the rank of admiral. Leahy was ambassador to France from 1940 to 1942 and was recalled to active duty in the navy and became chief of staff to the president. He was promoted to fleet admiral in 1944 and continued to serve as presidential chief of staff until 1949.

Ledyard, John (1751–1789), American mariner who sailed with Captain **James Cook** on his third and final voyage to the Pacific. He later wrote *A Journal of Captain Cook's Last Voyage to the Pacific Ocean* (1783). Ledyard fought in the American Revolution and died while preparing an expedition to find the source of the Niger River in Africa.

Leeward Islands, group of fifteen islands and many islets in the **West Indies** that are sheltered from the **trade winds** by the **Windward Islands**. The Leeward group includes Antigua, Barbuda, Saint Christopher, Nevis, Anguilla, the British Virgin Islands, Montserrat, Saint Eustatius, Saba, Saint Martin, Guadeloupe, and the U.S. Virgin Islands.

leg-o'-mutton rig, simple sailboat rig that uses a triangular sail. Although still used, it was the forerunner of the **Marconi** or **Bermuda rig**. Its name appears to have been taken from its resemblance to a leg of lamb.

Le Havre, important French seaport and industrial center that lies along the English Channel at the mouth of the Seine River. After World War II, Le Havre was rebuilt according to a master plan and was equipped with excellent facilities that can accommodate very large vessels. Today it is France's second busiest seaport —after **Marseille**.

Leilani, passenger **liner** built in 1944 as the *General W. P. Richardson*. After service as the *La Guardia*, the **P-2 transport** was sold to Textron of Rhode Island in 1956 for service between California and Honolulu. Her initial voyage from New York to Long Beach in 1957 cast such a disgraceful pall over the operation that the liner never proved her worth and was **laid up** in 1958. She was eventually bought in 1960 by **American President Lines** for further service as the *President Roosevelt*.

Lend-Lease, arrangement enacted by the United States in March 1941 to provide military and other aid to Allied nations engaged in World War II without expecting any immediate payment. It was a make-good on President **Franklin D. Roosevelt**'s promise in 1940 for the United States to be "the great arsenal of democracy." When Lend-Lease was halted in August 1945, it was estimated that $42 billion in goods and services had been supplied—mostly to Great Britain and the Soviet Union.

Lenin, Soviet icebreaker commissioned in 1959 that was the world's first nuclear-powered surface ship. She was designed to escort merchant ships through the **Northeast Passage**, and her nuclear propulsion obviated the need for refueling. In 1967 a nuclear accident killed thirty of her crew members, and she was **laid up** for repairs. She reentered service again in 1972 and was decommissioned in 1989 to serve as a stationary power station.

Leonardo da Vinci, replacement vessel constructed for the **Italian Line** after the loss of the ***Andrea Doria*** in 1956. Completed in 1960, *Leonardo da Vinci* was the first **liner** built with the potential to have her boiler installation removed and replaced with an atomic reactor in the event that nuclear power ever proved to be economical. The 33,340-gross-ton ship made her final transatlantic journey in 1976 and, after an unsuccessful stint at budget cruising from Florida, was **laid up** in 1978. She was gutted by fire in 1980 and scrapped in 1982.

HMS *Leopard*, British **frigate** that confronted USS *Chesapeake* on June 22, 1807, off **Hampton Roads**, Virginia. *Leopard* fired on *Chesapeake*, boarded her, and seized four seaman said to be deserters from the **Royal Navy**. The incident became known as the ***Chesapeake Affair***.

Leopoldville, Belgian troopship that was torpedoed by a German **U-boat** on Christmas Eve 1944, killing at least 802 American GIs. The ship was carrying 2,235 members of the U.S. 66th Infantry Division for action in the Battle of the Bulge when it went down six miles off Cherbourg, France.

Lepanto, Battle of, naval engagement of October 7, 1571, in which an allied Christian force of two hundred **galleys** defeated a larger Muslim Turkish fleet near its base at Lepanto, on the west coast of Greece. An estimated 30,000 Turks died in battle, 10,000 were taken pris-

Leonardo da Vinci making her maiden voyage arrival toward midtown Manhattan. (Courtesy Gordon R. Ghareeb)

oner, and 12,000 slaves were freed by the Christians. The Holy League fleet lost 7,500 men. It was a defining battle of the Crusades and was the last large sea battle to be fought between galleys.

Lesseps, Ferdinand de (1805–1894), French diplomat and engineer who achieved international acclaim by directing the construction of the **Suez Canal** from 1859 to 1869. Lesseps's 1879 attempt to build a canal across Panama ran into many difficulties, and ended in financial scandal. Lesseps, once a hero, was sentenced to prison in 1893.

Let's Go Navy!, 1951 film in which the Bowery Boys go at it in the U.S. **Navy** to apprehend some undercover thieves aboard ship. The film starred Huntz Hall, Leo Gorcey, and Paul Harvey.

letter of marque, commission or permit issued by a government or monarch to the captain of a privately owned ship or **privateer**, allowing the ship to act against the government's enemy. Without a letter of marque, such conduct

S. S. LEVIATHAN.

SS *Leviathan*. (Bruce Vancil. © J. Salmon)

would legally be piracy. The practice was abolished by an international convention signed in Paris in 1856, but the Confederacy issued letters of marque at the beginning of the Civil War.

let the cat out of the bag, to remove the **cat-o'-nine tails** from its bag in order to administer punishment. Today it means to reveal a secret.

Levant, old name for the eastern shore of the Mediterranean Sea that extended from western Greece to western Egypt. The region was a popular trading partner with the rest of Europe as well as America.

levee, artificial embankment built to limit flooding at the side of a river or channel.

Leviathan, massive and strange sea monster mentioned in the Bible's Book of Job (41:1–34 and Isaiah 27:1).

SS *Leviathan*, formerly the German **liner *Vaterland*** of 1914, the 54,282-gross-ton liner was interned in the United States during World War I, taken over by the U.S. **Navy** in 1917, and renamed USS *Leviathan* for operation as a troop transport. She entered transatlantic service for **United States Lines** in 1923 as the largest ship in the world. Her economic ruin

was sealed by the Prohibition because liquor was always plentiful aboard alternative foreign liners plying the same route. Finally **laid up** in 1934, the giant was sold for scrap in 1938.

Levick, Edwin (1869–1929), American marine photographer who is best known for capturing on film New York Harbor activity as well as **America's Cup** racing and preparation, vessel launchings, the evolution of the cup races, and important people who have figured in the cup's history.

Levy, Uriah P. (1792–1862), U.S. naval officer who served sixteen months in an English prison during the **War of 1812**. He was later court-martialed and dismissed from the service for his refusal to inflict corporal punishment on a young seaman. Levy fought the decision and was reinstated. He rose to command the Mediterranean fleet and received the honorary rank of commodore. An ardent admirer of **Thomas Jefferson**, Levy purchased Monticello, the late president's Virginia estate, in 1836, and the house and grounds remained in the Levy family until the estate was sold to the Thomas Jefferson Memorial Foundation in 1923.

Lewis, David (b. 1917), well-traveled physician, scientist, and adventurer who won fame in long-distance races and as a writer: *The Ship That Would Not Travel Due West* (1961); *We, the Navigators: The Ancient Art of Landfinding in the Pacific* (1972); *Ice Bird: The First Single-Handed Voyage to Antarctica* (1975); and *Shapes on the Wind* (2000). Among his many sailing accomplishments are his third place in the first single-handed transatlantic race (1960), behind winner Sir **Francis Chichester**, and his first circumnavigation in a multihull (1964–67).

Lewis, Idawalley Z. "Ida" (1842–1911), lighthouse keeper of the Lime Rock, Rhode Island, lighthouse near Newport for thirty-nine years. Taking over for her father, who had been incapacitated by stroke, she is credited with saving eighteen lives. She made her first rescue at age fifteen and her last at age sixty-five. In recognition for her outstanding career as the keeper at Lime Rock, the light was renamed Ida Lewis Light.

Lewis, Meriwether (1774–1809), American explorer named by President **Thomas Jefferson** to lead the **Lewis and Clark expedition**. Lewis brought his Newfoundland breed dog, Seaman, along on the expedition. A U.S. Army captain, he had also served as secretary to Jefferson. It is believed that personal and professional problems led Lewis to commit suicide.

Lewis and Clark Expedition, journey made by **Meriwether Lewis** and **William Clark** from 1804 to 1806 to explore the newly acquired Louisiana Purchase (1803) and to determine the feasibility of a water route to the Pacific coast. The expedition, made mostly by boat, started from Saint Louis, Missouri, and moved up the **Missouri River** and down the Columbia River to the Pacific Ocean. The brainchild of President **Thomas Jefferson**, the expedition was also known as the **Corps of Discovery**.

Lewrie, Alan, fictional hero in the nine-volume naval adventure series by American author **Dewey Lambdin**.

Lexcen, Ben (1936–1988), Australian yachtsman and self-taught marine architect who designed *Australia II*, the first non-American yacht to win the **America's Cup**. Lexcen left his original name—Bob Miller—with his old manufacturing company when he sold the enterprise and had a friend's computer create a new six-letter surname for him. As Bob Miller he had designed *Southern Cross*, the 1974 America's Cup challenger.

USS *Lexington* (CV-2), ship laid down as the battle **cruiser** *Lexington* in 1921 and completed as an aircraft carrier in 1927. The thirty-three-thousand-ton sister to USS *Saratoga* was en route from Honolulu to **Midway**

Postage stamp commemorating the anniversary of the Lewis and Clark Expedition.

when the Japanese attacked **Pearl Harbor** in 1941. In May 1942 planes from the Japanese carriers *Shokaku* and *Zuikaku* struck *Lexington* with two direct torpedo strikes and three bomb hits. The initial fires were brought under control, but internal explosions from igniting aviation gasoline vapors caused the vessel to be abandoned. *Lexington* was sent to the bottom by two torpedoes from the **destroyer** USS *Phelps*, the first U.S. aircraft carrier loss of World War II.

USS *Lexington* (CV-16), **Essex**-class aircraft carrier completed in 1943. The 27,100-ton "Lady Lex" saw action in all Pacific campaigns after Tarawa. Radio progagandist Tokyo Rose called the carrier the Blue Ghost because of her distinctive paint scheme, and she is also remembered as the first U.S. **Navy** vessel to have female crew members stationed aboard. Retired from active service in 1991, the 872-foot carrier opened in 1992 as a museum ship in Corpus Christi, Texas.

Leyte Gulf, Battle of, the biggest naval battle in history, fought October 17–25, 1944, in the waters off the Philippines. The series of separate actions (Battle of the Sibuyan Sea, Battle of **Surigao Strait**, Battle of **Cape Engaño**, and Battle of Samar) involved 216 U.S. warships, 2 Australian vessels, and 64 Japanese ships. The losses inflicted upon the Japanese fleet—4 aircraft carriers, 500 aircraft, 3 battleships, 10 **cruisers**, 11 **destroyers**, and 1 submarine—

and the damage done to surviving ships greatly crippled the ability of the Imperial Japanese Navy to stage any subsequent offensives. U.S. losses were 3 light and escort carriers, 200 aircraft, and 3 destroyers. The battle was initiated by Japan to stop the impending U.S. invasion of the Philippine Islands.

Libau, German merchant ship used to run guns and ammunition to the Irish Republican Army for the anticipated Easter uprising in April 1916. The ship sailed to Tralee Bay, where it was intercepted by British patrol boats. The German captain **scuttled** the ship and surrendered himself.

Liberdade, thirty-five-foot vessel built and sailed by Captain **Joshua Slocum**, his wife and two sons, and a crew of ten after their vessel, the *Aquidneck*, ran aground and was wrecked in 1886 off the east coast of South America. Slocum, his family, and crew made it to the United States aboard the *Liberdade* in 1887, after battling swift currents, gale-force winds, surging seas, and sharks. Slocum recounted his adventures in *Voyage of the Liberdade* (1890).

Libertad, 356-foot Argentine **tall ship** built in 1960 that was a regular participant in **Operation Sail**. The **full-rigged** navy training ship set a speed record in 1966, crossing the North Atlantic from Cape Race, Newfoundland, to the English Channel in eight days, twelve hours.

SS *Liberté*, **French Line** resurrection of the former **North German Lloyd liner *Europa***. It was seized by U.S. forces in 1945 and used as the troopship USS *Europa* before being ceded to France in 1946. It was the original intent to name the 49,746-gross-ton liner the *La Lorraine* but—in view of the circumstances surrounding her French acquisition—*Liberté* seemed much more appropriate. Tall domes were fitted to her twin **funnels** in 1954 and she, more than any other postwar passenger

liner, ingrained the image of a great liner with tall smokestacks into the mind of the traveling public. She was scrapped in 1962.

Liberty, American yacht that lost the **America's Cup** in 1983 to the Australian challenger *Australia II*, four races to three, on a course off Newport, Rhode Island. *Liberty*'s loss ended the **New York Yacht Club**'s 132-year reign of the Cup and made **Dennis Conner** the first **skipper** ever to lose the Cup.

USS *Liberty* (AGTR-5), U.S. communications ship that was attacked by Israeli jets and torpedo boats on June 8, 1967, in international waters in the Mediterranean Sea, fifteen miles north of the Sinai Peninsula, an action in which 34 U.S. seamen were killed and 169 were wounded. The Israelis later claimed the attack was a case of mistaken identity and apologized. The U.S. government accepted the apology but has never really explained why. *Liberty* was built in 1945 as the **Victory ship** *Simmons Victory* and was converted in the early 1960s.

Liberty Island, twelve-acre island in New York Harbor that is the site of the Statue of Liberty. Originally called Bedloe's Island, it was renamed in 1956. The 151-foot statue, erected in 1886, stands atop a 154-foot pedestal and base. Together with nearby **Ellis Island**, it is part of the Statue of Liberty National Monument.

Liberty ship, cargo ship built by the U.S. **Maritime Commission** during World War II to replace the vessels being sunk. Libertys constituted the largest shipbuilding program in history. The blunt-ended ships were 442 feet long and had simple-to-manufacture triple-expansion steam engines, capable of making eleven **knots**. Approximately 2,750 of the standardized dry cargo vessels were built in eighteen shipyards from 1941 to 1945. To facilitate mass production, yards pioneered new concepts in shipbuilding, including prefabrication and welding. The ships' slow speed made them easy prey for **U-boats** and led to the development of the **Victory ship**. They acquired the designation *Liberty* from a speech by President **Franklin D. Roosevelt** at the launching of SS *Patrick Henry*, the first of the new ships. Nicknamed "ugly ducklings," they were named for prominent Americans.

Lifeboat, classic 1944 Alfred Hitchcock thriller set entirely in a lifeboat in the open **Atlantic** after the sinking of an Allied freighter and a German **U-boat**. Tensions mount among the eight diverse survivors when the Nazi commander is brought on board. Based on a story by **John Steinbeck**, the film starred Tallulah Bankhead, William Bendix, and Hume Cronyn.

Life on the Mississippi, 1883 memoir by **Mark Twain** about the **steamboat** era on the **Mississippi River** before the Civil War. In addition to giving a history of the waterway, it describes Twain's career as a **pilot** and his observations in the face of progress.

"A Life on the Ocean Wave", 1838 song written by American writer Epes Sargent (1813–1880). It was set to music by Henry Russell and became an instant hit. It was also adopted as the official march tune of Britain's Royal Marines. The first verse goes: "A life on the ocean wave! / A home on the rolling deep! Where the scatter'd waters rave / And the winds their revels keep!"

Life Savers, hard candy introduced in 1912, so named because they resembled miniature life rings. One of the first marketing slogans for the roll candies was "for that Stormy Breath."

Life Saving Medal, medal established by the U.S. Congress, in the Life-Saving Act of 1874, for rescues of extreme and heroic daring. The act also set aside a silver medal for rescues that were slightly less outstanding. The medals are awarded primarily to civilians who endanger their own lives while saving or attempting to save another person from drowning or from a shipwreck or other perils of the water. Since

1874 more than six hundred gold and two thousand silver Life Saving Medals have been awarded.

U.S. Life-Saving Service, agency established under the Treasury Department in June 1878 to help those "in peril upon the seas." Since 1848 the federal government had provided funds for shore-based lifesaving stations, including those of the **Massachusetts Humane Society**. **Sumner I. Kimball** petitioned Congress to organize the stations as a separate agency, and in 1878 he was appointed the general superintendent of the new service. The Life-Saving Service merged with the U.S. **Revenue Cutter Service** in 1915 to form the U.S. **Coast Guard**.

ligan (or lagan), cargo that someone has sunk with the intention of recovering it later. The person usually ties a buoy to ligan to mark its location. Under international rules of **salvage**, ligan found by other persons must be returned to the owner.

The Light at the Edge of the World, **Jules Verne** story about three men guarding an isolated lighthouse near **Cape Horn** who are attacked by a band of mid-nineteenth-century pirates. It was translated to film in 1971 and starred Kirk Douglas, Samantha Eggar, and Yul Brynner.

lighter, general name for a broad, flat-bottomed boat used to transport cargo between a vessel and the shore.

Lighthouse by the Sea, 1924 silent film in which Rin Tin Tin rescues a lighthouse keeper's daughter who is threatened by smugglers.

U.S. Lighthouse Service, arm of the U.S. government founded in 1789 under the Treasury Department as the Lighthouse Establishment to oversee lighthouse construction. It was known as the Lighthouse Board from 1852 to 1910 and the Bureau of Lighthouses or Lighthouse Service until 1939, when it became part of the U.S. **Coast Guard**.

Light Lists, seven-volume annual publication of the U.S. **Coast Guard** that contains information on lighthouses and other aids used for general navigation that are maintained by or under the authority of the Coast Guard and located in the waters surrounding the United States and its territories. Information on foreign **aids to navigation** is listed in the *List of Lights, Radio Aids and Fog Signals*.

Lightning, international **one-design** centerboard **sloop** designed by **Sparkman & Stephens** and introduced in 1938. It measures nineteen feet in length, and has a beam of six feet, six inches. The fast, stable boats carry a racing crew of three and can carry up to five adults.

Lightning, 279-foot **clipper ship** built by **Donald McKay** in 1854 at his yard in East Boston for Liverpool shipowner James Baines's **Black Ball Line**. She was a successful ship in the U.K.-to-Australia passenger and wool trade but had a short career because she burned and was **scuttled** in the harbor at Geelong, Australia, in 1869. Under optimum conditions, she could achieve speeds of eighteen **knots**, and she set a speed record of 436 **nautical miles** under sail in twenty-four hours—a feat that has never been broken.

Lightoller, Herbert (1874–1952), British mariner who was the second officer of RMS *Titanic* and the highest-ranking officer to survive her sinking. He was the principal witness following the sinking and stuck by the **White Star Line** throughout his testimony in both U.S. and British inquiries. During World War II, he used his yacht *Sundowner* to evacuate 131 British soldiers from **Dunkirk**.

lightship, ship specially designed and marked to serve as a floating lighthouse. Lightships were anchored where conventional lighthouses could not be built. The first lightship in the United States was stationed in 1820 off Craney Island in Chesapeake Bay. At the height of

their popularity, in 1909, they numbered fifty-six. They have all since been replaced by platforms, towers, and buoys. The last lightship station, Nantucket Shoals, was decommissioned in 1985.

The Lightship, 1986 film about the crew of a U.S. **Coast Guard lightship** anchored off the Carolina coast who rescue three men from a disabled boat, only to find they are escaped killers. Klaus Maria Brandauer played the captain of the besieged ship, who must protect his men, and Robert Duvall played the leading psychopath.

lignum vitae, from the Latin phrase meaning "wood of life," the smooth, very hard wood of the genus *Guaiacum*, which is native to tropical regions. The wood, so dense that it does not float, was commonly used aboard ship for block-sheaves, deadeyes, and bull's-eyes. It was also used for stern tube bearings because its natural oils served as a lubricant.

limey (also limejuicer), colloquial name for a British sailor or a British ship. The name derives from the **Royal Navy** practice of issuing lime juice to the crews of its ships to combat **scurvy**.

Lincoln, Abraham (1809–1865), sixteenth president of the United States. Lincoln piloted **flatboats** and cargoes over four thousand miles in the years leading up to his initial run for public office in 1832. In 1849 he received a patent for his Improved Method of Lifting Vessels Over Shoals, which made him the only chief executive ever to hold a patent. He was the inspiration for **Walt Whitman**'s poem **"O Captain! My Captain!"** (1865).

Lind, James (1716–1794), British navy surgeon who was the first to identify fresh fruit and vegetables as helpful in preventing **scurvy** among seamen. He suggested that the concentrated juice of lemons and oranges could be

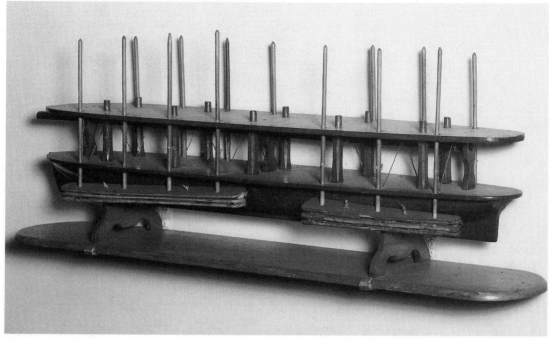

Abraham Lincoln's patent model for an improved method of lifting vessels over shoals. (© Smithsonian Institution)

used to both prevent and cure scurvy while at sea, and he published his findings in his *Treatise of the Scurvy* (1753).

line of battle, line formed by **ships** of a fleet when engaging an enemy force. In the days of sailing warships, the guns could only fire broadside. This formation led to the term **ship of the line** to describe the larger, less maneuverable vessels that were built to slug it out in this formation, which brought maximum firepower to bear upon the enemy.

liner, vessel operating between scheduled, advertised ports on a regular schedule with established rates.

Link, Edwin (1904–1981), American inventor who pioneered the first pilot trainers and flight simulators. After selling his company, Link Aviation, in 1954, he turned his attention to underwater archaeology and explo-

ration. He invented and improved underwater systems and equipment, including manned submersibles, to allow divers to go deeper, stay longer underwater, and explore more safely and efficiently.

Lipton, Sir Thomas (1850–1931), one of the most loved, admired, and respected yachtsmen ever. He challenged for the **America's Cup** five times from 1899 to 1930 with yachts named *Shamrock*. Born in Scotland of poor Irish parentage, Lipton acquired his wealth by developing a tea and grocery empire. He was knighted in 1898 for his contribution to charitable causes and is credited with returning sportsmanship to the America's Cup contest following the **Dunraven Affair**. Lipton's grand steam yacht *Erin* often escorted his five challengers. He died having never won what he termed the "auld mug" and having never married.

list, a vessel's angle of inclination to one side or the other that is caused by internal forces.

List of Lights, Radio Aids and Fog Signals, seven-volume annual publication of the **National Imagery and Mapping Agency**, which contains information on lights and other general **aids to navigation** that are maintained by or under the authority of foreign governments. The domestic version is called the **Light Lists**.

The Little Mermaid, classic 1846 fairy tale by Danish author Hans Christian Andersen (1805–1875) about a young mermaid who falls in love with a prince and then makes a deal with a witch to turn her into a human. It was reworked by Walt Disney for the 1989 animated film of the same name. The famous statue of Anderson's Little Mermaid, fashioned by Danish sculptor Edvard Eriksen, sits on a rock in the harbor of Copenhagen, Denmark.

The Little Red Lighthouse and the Great Gray Bridge, favorite 1942 children's picture book written by Hildegarde Swift and illustrated by Lynd Ward that celebrates Jeffrey's Hook Light on the **Hudson River**, which still stands next to the Manhattan tower of the George Washington Bridge.

Little Tim and the Brave Sea Captain, award-winning 1936 children's book written and illustrated by Edward Ardizzone (1900–1979) about a boy who stows away aboard a steamer and becomes a member of the crew. He befriends the captain and later survives a dramatic shipwreck.

Little Toot, 1939 children's book by Hardie Gramatky that features a mischievous little tugboat in New York Harbor that single-handedly rescues a stranded ocean **liner** during a howling Atlantic storm. The book had many sequels, including *Little Toot in the Grand Canal*

and *Little Toot through the Golden Gate*. The 1954 Walt Disney classic featured songs and narration by the Andrews Sisters.

Livingston, Robert R. (1746–1813), American statesman who helped write the Declaration of Independence in 1776. He was a member of the New York convention that ratified the Constitution in 1788, and in 1789 he administered the oath of office to the first U.S. president, George Washington. Livingston obtained a New York State monopoly for the operation of **steamboats** in New York waters in 1798 and assisted **Robert Fulton** in building the *Clermont*. After their initial success, the two men extended their operations to the **Mississippi River**.

Livonia, 127-foot **schooner** that was the second **America's Cup** challenger (*Cambria* in 1870 was the first). In 1871, off New York, she was defeated four races to one by the American tag team of *Columbia* and *Sappho*.

Lloyd's List, international newspaper, published by **Lloyd's of London**, that reports on shipping movements and casualties, maritime news, and other commercial information. In 1734 *Lloyd's List* began as a weekly journal of general commercial news and details of ships arriving at English and Irish ports, and in 1737 its frequency was increased to twice weekly.

Lloyd's of London, association of insurance underwriters incorporated by an act of Parliament that, among other things, specializes in marine insurance. The name is from the London coffeehouse operated by Edward R. Lloyd, where, in about 1688, underwriters began gathering to transact business, primarily in the shipping field. In 1734 Lloyd's began *Lloyd's List* as a weekly journal.

Lloyd's Register, British **classification society** founded in 1760. Although it has its origins with **Lloyd's of London**, it is a distinct organization. Since 1834 it has published annually its *Register of Ships*, which lists information on all seagoing, self-propelled merchant vessels of one hundred gross tons and over.

load line, line or marks on a vessel indicating the maximum depth to which that vessel is permitted to settle down into the water when loaded with cargo. Different lines correspond to the season and route of a specific voyage, with lighter loading mandated on, for example, a winter run in the North Atlantic. Usually referred to as **Plimsoll marks**—named for Samuel Plimsoll, who successfully fought for adoption of the marks by the British Parliament in 1876—they are required today under the **International Load Line Convention**.

Loblolly Boy, **Royal Navy** term for a surgeon's mate or ship's steward. Loblolly was a sailor's term for the gruel or soup fed to invalids aboard ship.

local apparent noon (LAN), the highest point in the sky to which the sun will climb on any day.

Local Notice to Mariners, weekly publication of U.S. **Coast Guard** districts that provides updated information concerning aids to navigation and other items of marine information of interest to mariners on the waters within that district. Information includes reports of channel conditions, obstructions, hazards to navigation, dangers, anchorages, restricted areas, regattas, information on bridges, and more.

Loch Ness monster, large animal that many believe lives in Loch Ness, a lake in Scotland. Hundreds of people have reported seeing the animal, which is nicknamed Nessie, and some observers believe the Loch Ness monster may be related to a dinosaur-like reptile or to a modern sea animal, such as the manatee or seal.

lodestar, a guiding star. The name derives from the Middle English *lode sterre*, which means a

"leading star." Sailors often use Polaris, also known as the North Star, as a guiding star.

lofting, laying out the lines of a ship at full scale on a large indoor floor. This activity is designed to eliminate errors involved in enlarging the lines from a sheet of paper.

Log from the Sea of Cortez, acclaimed 1951 novel by **John Steinbeck** that chronicles a 1940 research and collecting expedition he made with a biologist friend to the Sea of Cortez, now known as the Gulf of California.

L'Ollonais, Francois (d. 1668), colorful French pirate known for his ruthless exploits in the Caribbean Sea and his hatred of the Spanish. He was known to have licked the blood of his slain enemies off his sword and was said to have cut open a man's chest, pulled out his heart, and forced another captive to eat it. Shipwrecked in Nicaragua, he was eventually captured and eaten by cannibals.

London, Jack (1876–1916), popular American author, seaman, and wanderer. He went to sea **before the mast** at age seventeen and at age twenty-one joined the rush to Alaska in search of gold. He later served as a war correspondent in Japan in 1904 and in Mexico in 1915. During his lifetime, he became the most widely read American author. His books include *The Call of the Wild* (1903), *The Sea Wolf* (1904), *Tales of the Fish Patrol* (1905), *White Fang* (1906), *The Cruise of the Snark* (1908), and *The Mutiny of the Elsinore* (1914).

USS *Long Beach* (CGN-9), the first nuclear-powered surface warship and the first new U.S. **Navy cruiser** to be built after World War II. Completed in 1961, the 721-foot vessel saw service in the Mediterranean and in 1964 joined the nuclear-powered aircraft carrier USS *Enterprise* and **frigate** USS *Bainbridge* to form the first nuclear-powered task group. The three ships embarked on a circumnavigation without the need of replenishment, to showcase the flexibility of nuclear power. *Long Beach* was decommissioned in 1995 and **laid up** in Bremerton Washington Navy Yard.

Longfellow, Henry Wadsworth (1807–1882), the most popular American poet of the nineteenth century. Growing up in Maine, he developed a love of the ocean that greatly influenced his writing. His **"Wreck of the Hesperus"** (1841) helped to make Longfellow well known nationwide. His collection *The Seaside and the Fireside* (1850) conveyed one of his most characteristic themes—the sea—and contained "The **Building of the Ship**," which drew on Longfellow's familiarity with shipbuilding in Maine. In addition to his lyric poem "The Tide Rises, the Tide Falls," Longfellow also wrote many sonnets about the sea, including "The Tides," "The Broken Oar," and "Chimes."

longitude, the distance of a point on the earth from the **prime meridian**, measured to 180° east or west.

Longitude, best-selling 1995 book by Dava Sobel about eighteenth-century clockmaker **John Harrison** and his quest to build a truly functional marine **chronometer**.

Longitude Act, law passed by the British Parliament in 1714 that offered a £20,000 prize for the best method of determining **longitude** on a ship at sea. The act was prompted by the many maritime disasters that resulted from navigational error in not knowing longitude. The prize was won in 1773 by self-taught clockmaker **John Harrison.**

Long John Silver, fictional pirate in **Robert Louis Stevenson**'s novel *Treasure Island* (1883).

longline, fishing method that uses an extensive fishing line with many baited short lines attached. Also called a set line or trawl line. Vessels employed in this trade are called "longliners."

The Long Ships, 1964 action-packed seagoing motion picture, based on the novel by Frank G. Bengtsson, about an improbable encounter between a band of shipwrecked Vikings and a legion of Moorish soldiers in the Arabian desert, all in quest of a solid gold bell. The musical score by Dusan Radic contains one of Hollywood's most memorable main title themes ever composed for the screen. Richard Widmark , Sidney Poitier, and Lionel Jeffries starred in this epic.

longshoreman, worker employed along the waterfront to load and unload cargoes. Longshoremen are usually supervised by a **stevedore**.

long ton, standard of weight equivalent to 2,240 pounds that is used to determine a ship's **tonnage**. Its origin lies in the fact that wine was historically shipped in European sailing vessels in casks called "tuns." These casks weighed 2,240 pounds.

The Long Voyage Home, 1917 play by **Eugene O'Neill** about a crew of merchant seamen aboard the British freighter SS *Glencairn* in World War I. In 1940 it was adapted to the big screen with three other O'Neill plays (*Bound East for Cardiff, The Moon of the Caribbees*, and *In the Zone*) and set in 1939. The drama was directed by John Ford and starred John Wayne, Thomas Mitchell, Ward Bond, and Barry Fitzgerald. It was nominated for six Academy Awards, including those for best picture and best screenplay.

Looking for a Ship, 1990 narrative by author **John McPhee** in which he recounts his travels aboard a **Lykes Brothers Steamship Company** container ship during the 1980s. It doubles as a commentary on the state of the U.S. **merchant marine**.

Loomis, Alfred F. (1890–1967), American yachtsman and writer who is considered the dean of ocean-racing historians. He participated in seventeen **Bermuda Races**, eleven **Fastnet Races**, and innumerable other races and served in the U.S. **Navy** during both world wars. He was on the staff of *Yachting* magazine for thirty-four years, and his columns Under the Lee of the Longboat and Spun Yarn became international institutions.

LOOP, acronym for Lousiana Offshore Oil Port. Opened in the mid-1980s, the deepwater tanker offloading and temporary storage facility for crude oil transported on tankers, many too large for most U.S. ports, is located eighteen miles off the coast of Louisiana. Three single-point moorings with flexible hoses can handle ships up to seven hundred thousand **dead-weight tons**. The oil is then pumped ashore for storage in underground salt caverns.

loran, acronym for a long-range navigation system that was developed during World War II. This system established a hyperbolic pattern of radio transmissions used to determine lines of position to create a fix. Along with **radar**, it was among the closely guarded secrets of the war. It was state-of-the-art in the 1970s, providing complete coverage of the continental United States as well as most of Alaska. Loran's accuracy and coverage was surpassed by **GPS** in the 1990s.

Lord, Walter (b. 1917), American author and researcher best known for his book *A Night to Remember* (1956) about the sinking of RMS *Titanic*. Other works of his include *Day of Infamy* (1957), *Peary to the Pole* (1963), *Incredible Victory* (1967), *The Dawn's Early Light* (1972), *Lonely Vigil* (1977), and *The Miracle of Dunkirk* (1982).

Lord Jim, 1900 novel by **Joseph Conrad** about Jim, the first mate aboard the steamer *Patna*, an Arab pilgrim ship bound for Mecca. After the ship collides with an unseen object, Jim abandons ship, leaving the pilgrims to fend for themselves as the ship goes down. Dogged by his guilt, he spends years drifting around the East, eventually ending up in the forests of

Malaysia, where the indigenous people give him the title "Lord." The central theme of the book is the recovery of lost honor, and Jim dies having exorcised his demons. The 1965 film starred Peter O'Toole and James Mason.

Lorelei, high cliff that towers above the Rhine River in southwestern Germany. At that point, the river is swift and dangerous. Legend says the echo heard at the Lorelei is the voice of a beautiful but wicked **siren** called Lorelei, who is luring boatmen to destruction. The German writer Clemens Brentano may have invented the legend in his ballad "Die Lore Lay" (1801). The legend is also the subject of the German folk song "Die Lorelei."

L'Orient, French **flagship** that caught fire and exploded at the Battle of the **Nile** on August 1, 1798, killing Vice-Admiral François de Brueys and most of the crew.

USS *Los Angeles* (SSN-688), lead vessel of a class of sixty-one nuclear-powered attack submarines. The 362-foot craft displaces 6,927 tons and can travel at submerged speeds of over thirty-two **knots**. Commissioned in 1976 and manned by a crew of 127 members, it carries twelve Tomahawk and eight Harpoon missiles.

Los Angeles Steamship Company (LASSCO), company formed by the Los Angeles Chamber of Commerce, the *Los Angeles Times*, the Los Angeles Shipbuilding and Drydock Company, and local businessmen in 1921 to maintain the first direct regularly scheduled passenger and freight service from Los Angeles to Honolulu as well as a California coastal service. These services proved so popular, with their big white cruise ships *City of Los Angeles* and *City of Honolulu*, that the **Matson Line** was forced to follow suit and change the conservative operation of its **liners**. Loss of the *City of Honolulu* during the Great Depression caused the concern to be absorbed by the Matson Line in 1931.

Lost Colony, settlement established in 1585 under the authority of Sir **Walter Raleigh** on Roanoke Island off the Virginia coast (present-day North Carolina). The location was to be both mercantile, in that the latitude seemed to indicate a Mediterranean climate and was thought to yield similar commodities, and strategic, in that it would provide a foothold along Spain's treasure route. The colony of a hundred men, however, was found abandoned in 1586.

Louisbourg, important French fortress founded in 1713 on the east coast of **Cape Breton Island**, in Nova Scotia. Named for King Louis XIV, it developed into a strong trade and fishery center. British and French forces fought two battles over the fort during the mid-1700s. In 1758, during the **Seven Years' War**, the British demolished Louisbourg. In 1961, the Canadian government began the reconstruction of the town of Louisbourg, and today visitors can see the fortress, streets, and homes of Louisbourg as they were in the 1700s.

Love Affair, feature film romance comedy about a couple who meet and fall in love aboard an ocean **liner**. Starring Charles Boyer and Irene Dunn, the 1939 classic was nominated for six Academy Awards, including best picture and best actress. It was a precursor to *An Affair to Remember* some eighteen years later and was remade under the original title in 1994, with Warren Beatty, Annette Bening, and Katharine Hepburn.

The Love Boat, television show based on the novel *Love Boats*, which aired on the ABC Television Network from September 1977 until 1986. Most of the episodes were filmed on the *Pacific Princess* and the *Island Princess* during their regular voyages from the Virgin Islands to Alaska. *The Love Boat* was a major factor in making cruising popular for a whole new generation. The initial cast included Gavin MacLeod as Captain Merrill Stubing,

Bernie Kopell as the ship's doctor Adam Bricker, Fred Grandy as yeoman-purser Burl "Gopher" Smith, Ted Lange as bartender Isaac Washington, and Lauren Tewes as cruise director Julie McCoy. "The Love Boat Theme" was sung by Jack Jones.

Love Boats, autobiographical retelling of cruise ship cavortings by Jeraldine Saunders, who was the assistant cruise director aboard the *Princess Carla* at the time. First published in 1974, the book served as the basis for a screenplay and subsequent weekly television series called *The Love Boat* in 1977.

Love Boat: The Next Wave, 1998 television series attempting to resurrect the success of the original 1977 show *The Love Boat*. The action was set aboard the *Sun Princess*, with lots more space around the lido deck to parade loads of models in even skimpier swimsuits than were almost worn in the first production. The short-lived series starred Robert Urich, Phil Morris, and Stacey Travis.

Lowell's Boat Shop, boatbuilding business founded in 1793 by Simeon Lowell on the banks of the Merrimack River in Amesbury, Massachusetts. It is considered to be America's oldest operating boat shop and the birthplace of the American dory.

LST, U.S. **Navy** abbreviation for Landing Ship, Tank. The design of an oceangoing amphibious vessel was developed in World War II as a result of the British evacuation of **Dunkirk** in 1940. By 1942 the ships became workhorses and carried tanks and other vehicles in amphibious assaults throughout Europe, North Africa, and the Pacific. More than 1,500 LSTs were built for amphibious operations in World War II, and only 26 were lost to enemy action or weather.

Lt. Robin Crusoe, U.S.N., slapstick motion picture comedy about a stranded U.S. **Navy** pilot who sets up house—largely due to the fortuitous discovery of an abandoned submarine—on a desert island. The 1966 Walt Disney live-action film starred Dick Van Dyke, Nancy Kwan, and Akim Tamiroff.

lubber's line, reference mark on a compass or radar scope indicating the ship's heading.

Lubbock, Alfred Basil (1876–1944), British mariner and author, veteran of a **Cape Horn** passage in sail, who wrote many important books focusing on the glorious sailing ships, wanting to preserve their memories in writing. Lubbock's works include *The China Clippers* (1914), *The Colonial Clippers* (1921), *Log of the Cutty Sark* (1924), *The Western Ocean Packets* (1925), *The Last of the Windjammers* (two volumes, 1927 and 1929), *The Down Easters: The Story of the Cape Horners* (1929), and *The Arctic Whalers* (1937).

SS *Lucania*, 12,952-gross-ton ocean **liner** completed for the **Cunard Line** in 1893. Sister of the *Campania*, *Lucania* took the North Atlantic speed championship on her **maiden voyage** to New York. She caught fire in Liverpool in 1909 and was subsequently sold for demolition.

Luce, Stephen Bleecker (1827–1917), U.S. **Navy** admiral who was a strong advocate of education and improved training for seagoing officers. He was instrumental in establishing the U.S. **Naval War College** at Newport, Rhode Island, and was a strong advocate for the establishment of state nautical schools. His book *Seamanship* (1863) was for a long time the authoritative text on the subject.

Luckner, Count Felix von (1881–1966), German naval officer who in World War I disguised a sailing ship as a Norwegian lumber ship and sailed through the British blockade. He is said to have sunk about fourteen Allied ships. Luckner's ship, the *Seeadler*, eventually was wrecked, and he was captured by the British. Freed after the war, Luckner lived for several

SS *Lurline* turns seaward after having cast off from Honolulu's signature Aloha Tower passenger liner pier in 1952. (Courtesy Gordon R. Ghareeb)

years in the United States, where he lectured about his adventures.

lucky bag, compartment or locker aboard ship where various articles found adrift are stowed until claimed.

lugger, small coastal two- or three-masted sailing craft with a lugsail rig. A lugsail rig employs a four-sided sail set on a yard and is very much like a **gaff rig**.

Lunenberg, town in Nova Scotia, Canada, located southwest of Halifax, known for shipbuilding—especially of fine **schooners**—and for its fishing fleet.

Luny, Thomas (1759–1837), prolific English marine painter known for his portrayals of naval battles, shipping scenes, and ships. He served in the **Royal Navy** from the outbreak of the **French Revolution** and retired in about 1810, due to rheumatoid arthritis. It is estimated Luny painted close to three thousand pictures in his lifetime.

SS *Lurline*, quintessential Hawaiian **liner** built in 1932 for the **Matson Line**. Named for the wife of the company founder, she was constructed with two sisters, the *Monterey* and the *Mariposa*. *Lurline* was partnered when new with the older SS ***Malolo*** on the Honolulu service.

Luxury Liner Row. (Courtesy Gordon R. Ghareeb)

Operated as a U.S. **Navy** troopship during World War II, she returned to her designed operation in 1948 after a $19 million refit. Sold to the **Chandris Line** in 1963 and renamed *Ellinis*, she was scrapped in 1986.

RMS *Lusitania*, four-**funneled** British passenger **liner** built in 1907 for the **Cunard Line**. She broke the existing sea speed record on her **maiden voyage** but soon lost it to her sister ship, RMS *Mauretania*, in 1909. Retained on the North Atlantic service after the outbreak of World War I, *Lusitania* was torpedoed by German U-20 on May 7, 1915, off of the Old Head of Kinsale, Ireland, and sank in less than twenty minutes, with the loss of 1,198 lives—including 128 Americans. Controversy survives today as to whether or not the ship was carrying ammunition under the guise of a nonhostile passenger ship. Speculation continues that Sir **Winston Churchill** orchestrated the 31,550-gross-ton ship's destruction with American passengers on board in order to draw the still-neutral United States into the growing world conflict.

***Lutine* Bell**, bell from HMS *Lutine* (former French **frigate** *La Lutine*), which in 1799 was shipwrecked off Holland while carrying bullion and money. Salvage operations extended over many years, but much went unsalvaged. The ship's bell was recovered and today hangs in the rostrum of the underwriting room at **Lloyd's of London** and is rung to give warning of an important announcement.

Luxury Liner, 1948 musical comedy film set aboard a transatlantic greyhound. Featuring great scenes of the ***Conte di Savoia*** coming into dock, the film starred Jane Powell, Xavier Cugat, and George Brent.

Luxury Liner Row, midtown Manhattan Westside piers 82 through 94, where the major passenger **liners** called in New York. **Steamship** companies began moving to this area from the Chelsea Piers in 1935, when the advent of SS *Normandie* necessitated larger docking facilities.

Lykes Brothers Steamship Company, American shipping line founded in 1898 as part of the business concern of the seven Lykes Brothers, whose other interests included real estate, banking, energy, and citrus growing. Headquartered in New Orleans, Lykes Line connected the Gulf of Mexico ports with the Caribbean and, later, other world ports. The shipping company was a matter of great family pride, and each vessel was named after a Lykes wife or daughter. The company was sold out of bankruptcy in 1997 and continues to offer **liner** service.

Lyle Gun, line-throwing cannon developed in the 1870s by U.S. Army major David A. Lyle (1845–1937). It was initially used by the U.S. **Life-Saving Service** as a means of propelling a line to get a heavy **hawser** out to a wrecked ship. The term has since been used to describe any sort of line-throwing gun.

Lyman, general term for the high-quality boats built at the Lyman Boat Works of Sandusky, Ohio. Founded in 1875 by Bernard Lyman in Cleveland, the company began to specialize in rowboats and small motorboats around the turn of century. By the 1920s and 1930s, Lyman was delivering a line of wooden inboard cruisers and outboard boats. After turning to military production in World War II, Lyman was producing upwards of five thousand boats a year by the late 1950s. The company did not adapt quickly enough to the change in boat construction with the introduction of fiberglass and was forced to close its doors in 1972.

Lyman, John (1915–1977), pioneering U.S. maritime historian who specialized in detailed statistical studies of sailing ship construction and trades. He is the namesake of the North American Society for Oceanic History's award for outstanding maritime historical research.

MacArthur, Douglas (1880–1964), U.S. Army general of World War II and the Korean War. He is famous for returning as promised (the oft-quoted "I shall return") to liberate the Philippines in 1944. He presided over the Japanese surrender ceremony aboard USS *Missouri* on September 2, 1945, and then took over as commander of the Allied occupation forces in Japan. When the Korean War began on June 25, 1950, President Harry S. Truman appointed MacArthur head of the United Nations military force to defend South Korea. MacArthur was relieved of this command because of disagreements with Truman.

Macdonough, Thomas (1783–1825), U.S. naval officer and hero of the **War of 1812**. His command preparations and decisive victory at the Battle of **Lake Champlain** in September 1814 halted the British invasion of New York State and forced the British army to retreat into Canada. The action spurred British negotiators to give up territorial claims in America and settle the war with the **Treaty of Ghent**.

HMS *Macedonian*, fifth-rate British warship captured on October 25, 1812, by the **frigate** USS *United States*, under the command of **Stephen Decatur Jr.**, during a battle in the middle of the Atlantic Ocean. *Macedonian* was the only British warship captured and returned to a U.S. port during the **War of 1812**. She was later placed into service in the U.S. **Navy** as USS *Macedonian* and served with distinction until 1828.

MacGregor, John (1825–1892), Scottish adventurer who pioneered the sport of canoeing in Great Britain and America. He wrote about Native American paddling boats adapted for recreation and developed the double-paddle canoe *Rob Roy*. *The Voyage Alone in the Yawl Rob Roy* (1867) is his account of a single-handed voyage along the coast of France and across the English Channel.

Mackinac Race, see **Chicago Mackinac Race**.

MacLean, Alistair (1922–1987), prolific Scottish adventure author who served in Britain's **Royal Navy** in World War II. His first novel,

HMS Ulysses (1955), about a British light **cruiser** on the **Murmansk Run** in World War II, was well received. In addition to *The Guns of Navarone* and *Force Ten from Navarone*, his novels include *Ice Station Zebra* (1963), *When Eight Bells Toll* (1966), *Bear Island* (1971), *Seawitch* (1977), and *San Andreas* (1984). In 1972 MacLean produced the biography *Captain Cook.*

MacMillan, Donald Baxter (1874–1970), American polar explorer who traveled with **Robert Edwin Peary**'s Arctic expedition in 1908–9 and later led many of his own Arctic voyages on his **schooner** *Bowdoin*. In 1957, at age eighty-two, MacMillan made his thirty-first trip to the Arctic. He wrote several books about his experiences, including *Four Years in the White North* (1918), *Etah and Beyond* (1927), and *How Peary Reached the Pole* (1932). His one-hundred-foot schooner *Bowdoin*, built in 1921, is today used as a training vessel at the Maine Maritime Academy in Castine, Maine.

USS *Maddox* (DD-731), U.S. **Navy destroyer** that was involved in the **Gulf of Tonkin incident** that led to U.S. involvement in the Vietnam War. On August 2, 1964, *Maddox* was fired upon by three North Vietnamese gunboats while she was engaged in information gathering five miles off the coast.

Madeleine, 106-foot American **schooner** that defeated the Canadian challenger *Countess of Dufferin*, two races to none, in the 1876 **America's Cup** races. It was the third challenge, and the last time two schooners raced, for the Cup.

maelstrom, strong current off the northwest coast of Norway once believed capable of sucking in vessels at great distances. The word has come to mean any vortex of power, influence, or opinion that draws people into its orbit.

Mærsk Lines, Denmark-based shipping company founded in 1904 by Arnold Peter Møller

together with his father, Peter Mærsk Møller. Today it is the world's largest container ship line and part of the A. P. Møller Group of companies. In 1999 Mærsk acquired **Sea-Land** Service, Inc., America's largest shipping company, to create Mærsk-Sealand. The new company has more than 250 ships that log twenty thousand port calls annually in more than a hundred nations.

Mae West, an inflatable life vest used by aviators and aboard ship. Named for the shapely U.S. actress (1892–1980).

SS *Magdalena*, notable British Royal Mail Liner of 1949. While on the homeward portion of her **maiden voyage** from London to Buenos Aires, the 17,547-gross-ton steamer ran aground off of Rio de Janeiro without loss of life. Although refloated, the ship foundered and was scrapped later the same year. She was the fourth **liner** to be lost on her maiden voyage (after RMS *Titanic*, *Georges Philippar*, and MS *Hans Hedtoft*).

Magellan, Ferdinand (ca. 1480–1521), Portugese explorer and mariner who in the service of Spain commanded the first expedition to circumnavigate the globe (1519–22). In 1520 he passed around South America through the straits that now bear his name. There he sailed into a sea so calm he named it the Pacific (meaning peaceful). He crossed the Pacific to the Philippines, where he was slain in a local war. One of his lieutenants, **Juan Sebastián de Elcano**, brought one of Magellan's ships, the *Victoria*, home to Spain around the **Cape of Good Hope**, thus completing the first circumnavigation of the world and establishing a new route between Europe and Asia.

Magic, ninety-foot centerboard **schooner** that led a fleet of fourteen sailboats from the **New York Yacht Club**, including the *America*, in a single thirty-five-mile race off New York in 1870 to become the first successful defender of the **America's Cup**. The sole British challenger, *Cambria*, finished tenth.

magnetic mine, sea mine that is detonated by the magnetic field of a ship passing over or alongside. It was used effectively by the Germans at the beginning of World War II, nearly crippling British shipping. The British recovered one mine intact and, after dismantling and examining it, soon developed countermeasures.

magnetic poles, poles, both North and South, to which a compass needle points. Their exact locations change over time, but the magnetic North Pole is located south of the geographic North Pole in northern Canada, and the magnetic South Pole is located near the coast of Antarctica, hundreds of miles away from the geographic South Pole.

Magnuson Fishery Conservation and Management Act (MFCMA), landmark legislation signed into law in 1976 that ushered in a new era for U.S. marine fisheries management. The act established a two-hundred-mile fisheries limit around the shores of the United States (which in 1983 was named the **exclusive economic zone**) and set up eight regional Fisheries Management Councils. It has been amended numerous times, including in 1996 with the Sustainable Fisheries Act, which addressed overfishing, catch reduction, and habitat protection. Named after Senator Warren G. Magnuson (1905–1989) of Washington State, the MFCMA is sometimes referred to as the Magnuson Act.

Mahan, Alfred Thayer (1840–1914), U.S. naval officer, historian, and theorist. *The Influence of Sea Power upon History, 1669–1783* (1890) was his major work, which today has great historical significance. He was the best-known naval theorist of his day and served as the second president of the U.S. **Naval War College** in Newport, Rhode Island. Mahan's writings influenced **Theodore Roosevelt**, Henry Cabot Lodge, Kaiser **Wilhelm II**, and other proponents of a big navy and overseas expansion.

maiden voyage, first trip made by a vessel after she has been released to her owners by her builders.

mail subsidies, financial assistance in the form of mail contracts awarded by governments to shipowners. By the 1840s, overseas mail was taking on a volume and assuming an importance previously unknown, and ships were the only means of overseas communication. These contracts proved particularly vital during the transition from wood and sail to iron and steam. Great Britain was the first country to employ mail subsidies, followed by the United States and Germany.

USS *Maine*, U.S. **Navy** battleship completed in 1895. In January 1898 she was dispatched to the Spanish possession of Cuba to protect American interests from an ongoing revolution. While at anchor off Havana on February 15, 1898, *Maine* was destroyed by an explosion, which took the lives of 260 of the 350 men on board. The Spanish government was immediately held responsible, and Americans were so incensed that the United States declared war on Spain two months later. "**Remember the *Maine***" became a patriotic slogan during the **Spanish-American War**. The wreck was raised by army engineers at the request of Congress in 1912, taken out to sea, and sunk in a fitting ceremony. Recent evidence points to the likelihood that the explosion was caused by a shipboard accident.

SS *Majestic*, **flagship** of the **White Star Line** and the largest ship in the world from 1922 to 1934. Originally the German-built *Bismarck*, the 56,551-gross-ton ship was ceded to Britain following World War I and maintained White Star's first-string transatlantic service alongside RMS *Olympic* and *Homeric*. She was sold in 1936 to become the British cadet training ship HMS *Caledonia*. While plans to convert her into a transport were being finalized, she caught fire in 1939 and was sold for scrap the following year.

Malabar, name give to a series of thirteen **schooners, yawls,** and **ketches** that have earned their place in yacht racing and cruising history. Designed by **John Alden** starting in 1921, the yachts ranged in size from forty-two feet to fifty-four feet. The inspiration for the name was a spit of land off Monomoy Point on **Cape Cod** that disappeared during the eighteenth century.

Malacca, Straits of, five-hundred-mile-long passage between Sumatra and the Malay Peninsula that narrows, at a certain point, to thirty miles. Linking the Indian Ocean with the South China Sea, it contains one of the world's most important shipping lanes, making control of the passage supremely important. The amount of shipping has historically made it a hunting ground for piracy.

malacology, branch of zoology that relates to the structure and habits of mollusks.

SS *Malolo*, William Francis Gibbs–designed **liner** constructed for the **Matson Line** in 1927. She suffered a collision while on trials to prove the seaworthiness of the new 17,232-gross-ton vessel. She was originally introduced with a rust-colored hull, which shortly gave way to white as Matson took the lead in passenger shipping to Hawai'i, surpassing the **Los Angeles Steamship Company**. She was refitted as the *Matsonia* in 1937 to be a more substantial running mate to the new *Lurline*, with which she was partnered.

Malta, group of islands in the Mediterranean Sea between Sicily and Africa, the largest island of which is Malta, with the capital, chief city, and seaport of Valetta. Due to its strategic location and deep-water port, Malta has

Malolo. (Courtesy Gordon R. Ghareeb)

historically been subject to numerous foreign invasions, and it withstood heavy naval and aerial attacks during World War II.

"A man, a plan, a canal: Panama!", popular palindrome. Many believe that President **Theodore Roosevelt** had a hand in creating the country of Panama—formed around the canal zone—out of what was a northern province of Colombia. The **Panama Canal** greatly enhanced U.S. naval strength because ships could be dispatched fairly quickly from coast to coast.

Manhattan, U.S.-flag **supertanker** constructed in 1962 that was the first commercial vessel to voyage through the **Northwest Passage** across the top of Canada. In 1969, in an experimental voyage to try to open the northern route above Canada so that oil could flow from the fields of North Alaska to the East Coast of the United States, the tanker was strengthened and fitted with icebreaking capabilities. The ship left Philadelphia on August 24, 1969, with fifty-four crewmen and seventy-two scientists, scholars, and reporters. She reached Prudhoe Bay on the northern coast of Alaska on September 19, then sailed from Alaska on September 21 and reached New York on November 12. The trial venture proved uneconomical, but *Manhattan* remained in operation until 1987. In 1964 *Manhattan* sailed to the Soviet Union with the largest cargo of wheat ever loaded in a U.S. port.

Dorothy Marckwald.
(Courtesy Gordon R.
Ghareeb)

SS *Manhattan*, ocean **liner** built for **United States Lines** in 1932, sister ship to SS *Washington*. She carried the U.S. Olympic team, including gold medalist Jesse Owens, to the Berlin games in 1936 and later became the U.S. naval transport *Wakefield* in 1941. She caught fire while in **convoy** in 1942 but was rebuilt to U.S. **Navy** specifications by 1944. She was **laid up** in 1946 and finally scrapped in 1965.

Manila Bay, Battle of, decisive U.S. naval victory in the **Spanish-American War**. The seven-hour battle fought April 30, 1898, resulted in the Spanish fleet of ten ships, which was lying off Manila in the Philippines, being destroyed, silenced, or captured, with 381 casualties. The U.S. fleet—under the command of Commodore **George Dewey**, who started the battle by stating, "**You may fire when you are ready, Captain Gridley!**"—suffered no damage and had eight men wounded.

Manley, John (1734–1793), American sea captain, naval officer, and **privateer**. He was commodore of **Washington's Navy** in the American Revolution and was the second most senior officer when the **Continental Navy** was formed in 1776. He was captured three times during the American Revolution and was exchanged twice and escaped once.

man-o'-war, sailing vessel armed for war.

The Man without a Country, 1863 story written by Edward Hale (1822–1909) to inspire greater patriotism during the Civil War. It is about Lieutenant Philip Nolan, who, for having participated in the Burr Conspiracy, is convicted of treason and condemned to a lifetime at sea aboard U.S. **Navy** warships. A television movie based on the book was produced in 1973 with Cliff Robertson and Beau Bridges.

The Man with the Golden Gun, 1974 James Bond thriller based on the best-selling novel by Ian Fleming. It includes brief but magnificent vistas of the wreck of the *Seawise University* (former RMS *Queen Elizabeth*) in Hong Kong Bay while Agent 007 has a rendezvous inside the derelict hulk. The film starred Roger Moore, Christopher Lee, and Britt Ekland.

Manry, Robert (1918–1971), American sailor who in the summer of 1965 sailed his hand-built 13½-foot **sloop** *Tinkerbelle* from Falmouth, Massachusetts, to Falmouth, England. It was the smallest vessel to cross the **Atlantic** nonstop up until that time, and Manry chronicled the journey in his book *Tinkerbelle* (1966).

MarAd, see U.S. **Maritime Administration**.

Marckwald, Dorothy (1898–1986), American artist and decorator who designed the interior spaces of thirty-one U.S. passenger **liners**, including the *America* and the *United States*. She broke away from the traditional "period" interior style and brought American seagoing interior designs into the modern age with crisp, clear colors in simple but effective applications.

Marconi, Guglielmo (1874–1937), Italian inventor who gained international fame for his role in developing wireless telegraphy, or radio. At first Marconi overlooked the radio's value as a public broadcast medium, instead believing its principal application would be in the transmission of ship-to-ship or ship-to-shore messages, for which communication by wire was not feasible. In 1895 he sent the first telegraph signals through the air, and in 1901 he transmitted the first transatlantic wireless communication. He shared the 1909 Nobel Prize in physics.

Marconi rig, vessel with triangular **fore-and-aft** sails. The name comes from the resemblance of the mast and rigging to the transmitter antennas used by radio inventor **Guglielmo Marconi**. It is also referred to as jib-headed rig or a **Bermuda rig**.

Marder, Arthur Jacob (1910–1986), American historian whose main focus was British naval history. His greatest work was the five-volume *From the Dreadnought to Scapa Flow* (1961–70), a comprehensive naval history of the **Royal Navy** from 1904 to 1919. Other books of his include *The Anatomy of British Sea Power* (1940) and *From the Dardanelles to Oran* (1974) as well as three volumes on Admiral **John Fisher** titled *Fear God and Dread Nought* (1952–59).

Mardi Gras, the first ship to be operated under the banner of **Carnival Cruise Lines**. Originally completed in 1961 as the *Empress of Canada*, she was sold to Arison Shipping Company in 1972 for weeklong budget cruises out of Miami, with multinational crews under the command of Italian officers. The Carnival Cruise Line formula was so successful that a second ship, the *Carnivale*, was procured in 1975 to begin the seemingly limitless expansion of the corporation. *Mardi Gras* was removed from service in the early 1990s.

mare clausum, Latin for "closed sea," a sea under one nation's jurisdiction that is closed to vessels of all other nations.

Mare Clausum, 1631 work by John Seldon (1584–1654) that was a reply to *Mare Liberum* by **Hugo Grotius**. Seldon argued that the waters contiguous to a coastline of a country should be under the dominion of that country.

Mare Island Navy Yard, U.S. **Navy** shipyard located on an island in San Pablo Bay, opposite Vallejo, California. It was established in 1854 under the command of **David Glasgow Farragut** and was the first U.S. naval base on the Pacific coast. During World War I, the yard set many construction records, and during World War II it built nearly four hundred

ships and repaired some twelve hundred others. The yard was closed in 1993.

mare liberum, Latin for "free sea," a sea open to navigation by ships of all nations.

Mare Liberum, 1609 treatise by Dutch jurist **Hugo Grotius** challenging the right of any nation to claim part of the open sea exclusively as its own. The title translates as *The Free Sea*.

mare nostrum, Latin term for "our sea," the Romans' name for the Mediterranean.

Marianas Trench, oceanic trench that extends from southeast of Guam to northwest of the Mariana Islands in the Pacific Ocean. The part of the trench known as the Challenger Deep is the deepest place in the world. With a depth of 36,198 feet, it has a greater vertical dimension than the world's highest mountain—Mount Everest, at 29,028 feet. The **bathyscaphe *Trieste*** landed on its bottom in 1960.

Mariel boat lift, event in April 1980 during which the Cuban government permitted numerous Cubans to embark at Mariel, Cuba, for passage, via privately owned U.S. boats, to the United States. An exodus of enormous magnitude, the "freedom flotilla" embarked Cuban passengers with little regard for capacity or seaworthiness. The U.S. government had to direct numerous U.S. **Coast Guard** and U.S. **Navy** assets to patrol the waters off South Florida. It was one of the largest search-and-rescue operations conducted by the Coast Guard since World War II; by the end of that summer, approximately 125,000 Cubans had been ferried to Florida.

U.S. Marine Corps, branch of the armed services, formed in 1775, that is especially trained and organized for amphibious assault operations. Marines have fought in almost every major war involving the United States. The Marine Corps is closely aligned with the U.S. **Navy** (it falls under the oversight of the secretary of the navy), and marines are often referred to as "soldiers of the sea." The motto of the corps, adopted in 1880, is *semper fidelis*—"always faithful."

Marine Engineers Beneficial Association (MEBA), maritime labor union started in 1875 to secure better working conditions for engineers aboard U.S. steam vessels. MEBA merged with the **National Maritime Union** in 1988 and today represents a mix of engineers and deck officers aboard U.S. commercial ships.

marine exchange, organization established in a port to provide communications services and vessel information to the maritime industry in that port. Often a marine exchange runs in conjunction with a **vessel traffic service**.

Marine Protection, Research, and Sanctuaries Act of 1972, legislation approved by the U.S. Congress in 1972 to extend the kind of protection afforded by national park status to estuaries and coastal waters. It recognized that marine sanctuaries are "part of our collective riches as a nation" and charged the **National Oceanic and Atmospheric Administration** with managing the program. The first national marine sanctuary, designated in 1975, protects the remains of USS *Monitor*; today the system includes thirteen sites.

Mariner Class, series of thirty-five cargo ships designed by the U.S. **Maritime Administration** for military support for the Korean War. Construction contracts were placed with seven shipbuilders, who built five each. When the first ships were delivered in October 1952, they represented a quantum leap forward in American cargo ship technology and were considered a turning point in American ship design. The vessels were eventually sold for commercial use.

Mariner's Mirror, famous collection of sea charts of the sixteenth century compiled by Lucius Waghenaer and first published in Holland in 1583. Translated by Anthony Ashley and produced in England in 1588, the collection was widely used by British seamen for the next hundred years. The name of the collection is also used as the title of the quarterly journal of Britain's **Society of Nautical Research.**

Mariners' Museum, maritime museum founded in 1930 in Newport News, Virginia, by Archer M. and Anna H. Huntington. Archer Huntington was the son of Collis P. Huntington, founder of **Newport News Shipbuilding** and the Central Pacific Railroad. The museum has extensive holdings of maritime objects, books, and photographs.

Marine Rundschau, German periodical founded in 1890 that focuses on naval and maritime matters.

marine sanctuary, area established under provisions of the **Marine Protection, Research, and Sanctuaries Act of 1972**.

U.S. Marine Societies, charitable organizations established during the 1700s by ship captains in Boston, New York, Portland (Maine), and Philadelphia to advance maritime knowledge and to aid captains' widows and orphans.

Marine Society, British organization founded in 1756 to assist and prepare men and boys for service in the **Royal Navy**. As Britain's first secular charity, the society provided clothes and personal effects to poor boys and vagrants willing to go to sea.

Marine Sulphur Queen, 11,307-ton **T-2 tanker** built during World War II. In 1963 the 523-foot ship left Beaumont, Texas, bound for Norfolk, Virginia, with a crew of thirty-nine and cargo of 15,260 tons of molten sulfur brimstone. With her last reported position two hundred miles from Key West, the ship vanished. Despite a massive search by the U.S. **Navy** and **Coast Guard**, her wreckage was never located. Fifteen days after her disappearance, enough debris was recovered to determine that two crewmen survived the sinking but later died in the water from drowning or shark attack. The ship has never been found, and no reasonable explanation for her loss has ever been put forth.

U.S. Maritime Administration (MarAd), government agency that administers financial programs to develop, promote, and operate the U.S. **merchant marine**. It conducts research and development activities in the maritime field, maintains reserve fleets for national defense, operates the U.S. **Merchant Marine Academy**, and administers federal aid to state-operated maritime academies in California, Illinois, Maine, Massachusetts, New York, and Texas. MarAd was established in 1950 as one of the successors to the U.S. **Maritime Commission**, and in 1961 some of its regulatory functions were split off to a new agency, the **Federal Maritime Commission**. MarAd was transferred from the Department of Commerce to the Department of Transportation when the latter was established in 1967.

Maritime Buoyage System, uniform system of buoyage that has been implemented by most maritime nations. Promoted by the **International Association of Marine Aids to Navigation and Lighthouse Authorities**, it combines both the **cardinal buoyage system** and the **lateral system**. Maritime Buoyage System Region B is compatible with existing U.S. **Coast Guard** regulations and is used in North and South America and Japan; Region A is used elsewhere around the world.

U.S. Maritime Commission, independent government agency created under the **Merchant Marine Act of 1936** to further develop and maintain a **merchant marine** for the promotion of U.S. commerce and defense. First headed by Joseph P. Kennedy, this successor to the U.S. **Shipping Board** was authorized to regulate U.S. ocean commerce, supervise freight and terminal facilities, and administer funding to construct and operate commercial ships. In

1950 the functions of the Maritime Commission were transferred to the Department of Commerce, where they were assigned to the **Federal Maritime Board** and the newly formed U.S. **Maritime Administration**.

maritime law, body of law governing navigation and shipping that is based on customs and usages that developed between trading nations and were compiled beginning in the late Middle Ages. It is also known as "**admiralty law**."

Maritime Museum of the Atlantic, oldest and largest maritime museum in Canada. Established in 1948 in Halifax, Nova Scotia, it highlights Canada's and the region's marine history and contains art and objects relating to **steamships**, small craft, fisheries, the Royal Canadian Navy and merchant fleet, the Battle of the **Atlantic**, the Halifax explosion of 1917, and Nova Scotia's role in the aftermath of the RMS *Titanic* disaster.

Maritime Provinces (or Canadian maritimes), term applied to Nova Scotia, New Brunswick, and Prince Edward Island, in Canada. Before the formation of the Canadian confederation in 1867, they were politically distinct from Canada proper.

U.S. Maritime Service (USMS), service established in 1937 under the auspices of the U.S. **Maritime Commission** to train the men necessary to man the new ships called for in the **Merchant Marine Act of 1936**. The USMS, first established under the U.S. **Coast Guard** and later supervised by the U.S. **Navy**, was terminated as a separate service in 1954 and its responsibilities transferred to the U.S. **Maritime Administration**. The uniform often worn by U.S. **merchant marine** officers has its origin in the USMS.

Mark V, hard-hat diving helmet developed in 1838. Long considered the best design, it was standard issue for the U.S. **Navy** from 1916 to 1970.

marlinspike seamanship, the use of line in making knots, hitches, bends, and splices. The term comes from the seagoing use of the marlinspike, a pointed metal tool (or if wood, a "fid") used in separating strands of rope for splicing. Many sailors have developed marlinspike seamanship into an art form.

MARPOL, a contraction of "marine pollution," an international treaty that addresses accidental and operational oil pollution as well as pollution by chemicals, goods in packaged form, sewage, and garbage. Sponsored by the United Nations through the **International Maritime Organization**, it is formally named the International Convention for the Prevention of Pollution from Ships, 1973, as modified by the Protocol of 1978.

Marques, eighty-seven-foot-overall (72-foot-waterline) wooden sail training vessel that capsized, downflooded, and sank in a squall north of Bermuda in 1984, during a **tall-ships** race, with the loss of nineteen of the ship's company of twenty-eight. Built in Spain in 1917, the *Marques* was originally **schooner**-rigged but was a **bark** at the time of her loss. Rig and superstructure changes over the years had altered her stability to an unappreciated degree.

Marquesas Islands, fourteen small volcanic islands in the central Pacific Ocean that were discovered in 1595. **Herman Melville** described them in his novel *Typee* (1846).

Marquette, Jacques (1637–1675), French explorer and Roman Catholic missionary who in 1673 traveled with the French-Canadian explorer **Louis Jolliet** down the **Mississippi River**. They two men were probably the first whites to explore the upper Mississippi and parts of Illinois and Wisconsin. Marquette helped establish two Jesuit missions, at Sault Sainte Marie (1668) and Saint Ignace (1671).

Marr, Geoffrey (1908–1998), commodore of the **Cunard Line** fleet and final **master** of RMS *Queen Elizabeth*. He brought the great **liner** into Fort Lauderdale, Florida, on December 8, 1968, for refurbishment into a tourist center. When plans and money for the conversion were not forthcoming, Marr was brought out of retirement to take the ship, now renamed *Seawise University*, and her new Chinese crew on a very slow voyage to Hong Kong in 1971.

Marryat, Frederick (1792–1848), English naval officer and novelist known for his thrilling tales of sea adventure. After twenty-four years of **Royal Navy** service, including action in the **Napoleonic Wars**, Marryat settled down to a literary career. His experience provided rich background for his novels, which include *The Naval Officer* (1829), *The King's Own* (1830), *Peter Simple* (1834), and *Mr. Midshipman Easy* (1836). He also developed the **Marryat Code**.

Marryat Code, code of flag signals for merchant vessels developed by Captain **Frederick Marryat** that came into worldwide use following the **War of 1812**.

Marschall, Ken (b. 1950), American marine artist who was the foremost painter of RMS *Titanic* and is known for creating paintings that have artistic value beyond the photographic. His realistic work has appeared on the covers of *Time* and *Life* magazines. He served as the visual historian for James Cameron's epic film *Titanic* (1998).

Marseille, founded about 600 B.C., the oldest and second largest city in France (after Paris) and the country's main seaport. It is the largest port in the Mediterranean Sea as well as one of the world's busiest.

Marshall Islands, country comprising more than twelve hundred islands and islets located in the central Pacific Ocean. During World War II, the United States invaded the islands and defeated the Japanese in major battles at the **Kwajalein** and Eniwetak Atolls. Both the **Bikini Atoll** and the Eniwetak Atoll served as testing grounds for nuclear weapons from 1946 to 1962, and Kwajalein still serves as a missile testing range. The Marshall Islands became an independent republic in 1991 and today is a popular **registry** for shipping and is considered a **flag of convenience**.

Marshall Plan, U.S.-sponsored program to provide economic aid to European countries following World War II. The plan was proposed by and named for General George Marshall (1880–1959), secretary of state after the war. The plan provided some thirteen billion dollars in aid and kept the U.S. **merchant marine** busy transporting aid cargoes.

Martin Chuzzlewit, 1844 novel by Charles Dickens (1812–1870) in which the title character, after a long and unpleasant transatlantic crossing from Britain to the United States, states, "And, this . . . is the Land of Liberty, is it? Very well. I'm agreeable. Any land will do for me, after so much water!" Chuzzlewit's discomfort was directly based on Dickens's own experience during a 1842 transatlantic crossing aboard the **Cunard Line** steamer *Britannia*, when he became seriously seasick.

Martyr, Weston (1885–1966), English sailor and author who through his writings popularized coastal cruising. His books include *The Southseaman* (1926) and *The £200 Millionare* (1932).

maru, Japanese term meaning "sphere" or "circle." "Maru" is used in the names of most Japanese ships. In addition to implying completeness, it is a traditional term of endearment.

Mary Celeste, American **brigantine** found abandoned in the **Atlantic Ocean** in December 1872 while on a voyage from New York to Genoa, Italy. The ship was discovered between the Azores and Portugal in good order, with her cargo of seventeen hundred barrels of alcohol intact. There was plenty of food and water on board, but the lifeboat was gone. The mystery of the disappearance of Captain Benjamin Briggs, his wife and daughter, and eight crewmen has never been solved.

USS *Maryland* (BB-46), U.S. **Navy** warship commissioned in 1921 as the second of four Colorado-class battleships. The twenty-one-**knot** ship was stationed at **Pearl Harbor** the day of the Japanese surprise attack and, because she was moored inboard of the USS ***Oklahoma***, was spared when the outboard ship took all the direct hits. She participated in the assaults on Tarawa, Saipan, **Leyte Gulf**, the Surigao Straits, and **Okinawa**. The "Big Mary" was decommissioned in 1947 and sold as scrap in 1959.

Mary Powell, 295-foot American **side-wheel steamboat**, known as the "Queen of the Hudson," that carried people up and down the **Hudson River** from New York City to Kingston and Albany from 1861 into the 1920s.

Mary Rose, King Henry VIII's **flagship**, built in 1510 and updated in 1536, that capsized and sank while defending England from a French invasion in 1545. The **carrack** was raised from the waters off Portsmouth, England, in 1982 and placed on public display near HMS ***Victory***, where her shattered hulk serves as a magnificent time capsule of Tudor England.

Masefield, John (1878–1967), English poet and author best known as the "Poet of the Sea." He went to sea as a youth and spent several years in the United States. His first volume of poetry, ***Salt-Water Ballads*** (1902), contained the poem **"Sea Fever."** His other works include *A Mansail Haul* (1905), a collection of short nautical stories, and *A Tarpaulin Muster* (1907). He also wrote a number of novels but is best known for his poems. He was poet laureate of England from 1930 until his death in 1967.

mask painting, paint scheme adopted during the **Napoleonic Wars** in which ships' hulls were painted black with yellow, red, or white stripes along the gundecks, which were broken by black gunport covers. Merchant ships adopted similar schemes to resemble warships and thus ward off pirates.

USS *Mason*, U.S. **Navy** World War II **destroyer** escort (**DE**) commissioned in 1944 with a predominantly black crew that was a role model for the integration of U.S. Navy vessels. The ship's white captain, Bill Blackford, was the great-grandson of abolitionist Mary Berkeley Minor Blackford. The *Mason* was called Eleanor's Folly, a reference to First Lady Eleanor Roosevelt, a vocal advocate of desegregation of the armed forces.

USS *Massachusetts* (BB-59), 680-foot, South Dakota–class battleship completed in 1942. She was decorated with fourteen battle stars for her part in World War II. The thirty-five-thousand-ton vessel was acquired by her namesake state and has served since 1965 as a memorial and museum on the Fall River as well as being named a national historic landmark.

Massachusetts Humane Society, volunteer organization established in 1786 that operated the first small-boat rescue stations in the United States. The group operated eighteen stations with lifeboats and line-throwing equipment at dangerous locations on the Massachusetts coast. Its responsibilities were later assumed by the U.S. **Life-Saving Service**.

master, the highest officer aboard a merchant ship. He or she oversees all ship operations; keeps ships records; handles accounting and bookkeeping; takes command of vessel in inclement weather and in crowded or narrow waters; handles communications; and receives and implements instructions from home office. Also known as the "captain."

Masters, Mates & Pilots (MM&P), officially the International Organization of Master, Mates & Pilots, a union started in 1891 to represent licensed deck officers, state pilots, and other marine personnel on U.S.-flag commercial vessels. It is the International Marine Division of the **International Longshoremen's Association**.

mate, a **merchant marine** deck officer under the **master**.

Mathew, seventy-three-foot English **caravel** in which **John Cabot** explored the coast of Newfoundland and discovered **Cape Breton Island** in 1497. In 1996 a replica of *Mathew* was launched in Bristol, England, and sailed to North America for the five-hundred-year anniversary of Cabot's voyage.

Matson, William (1849–1917), American shipowner who pioneered the foremost shipping company to Hawai'i with the three-masted **schooner** *Emma Claudina* in 1882. His **Matson Line** outstretched competition from the Spreckles and **Oceanic** lines to maintain a service to Hawai'i that was second to none. The name "Matson" came to be virtually synonymous with "Hawai'i."

Matson Line, American shipping line founded by Captain **William Matson** in 1882 as a link between Hawai'i and California. Matson ran profitable cargo-passenger operations with small black-hulled ships, but when competition from the **Los Angeles Steamship Company** forced changes, Matson adapted a much more elegant and tropical appearance beginning with the *Malolo* in 1927 and culminating with the *Lurline* in 1932. The line operated a short-lived airline from 1946 to 1948 and maintained four Waikiki hotels in the 1950s: the Moana, the Royal Hawaiian, the Surfrider, and the Princess Kaualani. Today Matson Navigation Company provides container service to and from Hawai'i.

Matthiessen, Peter (b. 1927), American naturalist and author of both fiction and nonfiction. His *Far Tortuga* (1975) is considered a classic novel of the sea. Matthiessen's *Men's Lives* (1986) is a portrayal of the disappearing way of life of Long Island's commercial fishermen. Other works of his include *Blue Merid-*

RMS *Mauretania*'s arrival in New York from a Caribbean cruise, 1931. (Courtesy Gordon R. Ghareeb; photograph by Everett E. Viez)

ian Baikal: Sacred Sea of Siberia (1993) and *Lost Man's River* (1997).

Maturin, Stephen, fictional naval surgeon and intelligence officer in **Patrick O'Brian**'s seagoing series about the **Royal Navy** during the **Napoleonic Wars.**

RMS *Mauretania*, venerated four-**funneled Cunard Line** passenger vessel built in 1907. She held the speed championship across the **Atlantic** for twenty-two years until losing the **Blue Riband** to the sleek German steamer *Bremen* in 1929. The 31,938-gross-ton steamer had speeds in excess of twenty-six **knots** and is among the most famous ships ever built. She was painted with a white hull and sent cruising in the later years of her career. Her last departure from New York to Southampton, and ultimately the ship breakers, took place the same day in 1934 that her replacement—RMS *Queen Mary*—was launched.

RMS *Mauretania*, North Atlantic **Cunard Line** express steamer built in 1939 to augment the service of the MS *Britannic* and *Georgic* as well as serve as a backup relief ship for RMS *Queen Mary* or RMS *Queen Elizabeth* should the need arise. The splendid 35,738-gross-ton ship had the misfortune of being continually overshadowed by the two queens and, having been given the name of one of the most illustrious **liners** in history, never really came into her own among the oceangoing public and was only marginally successful on her intended route. She was used extensively for cruising and was finally sold for scrap in 1965 to cut losses and help raise capital to keep Cunard afloat while building the *Queen Elizabeth 2.*

Maury, Matthew Fontaine (1806–1873), U.S. naval officer and oceanographer. As superintendent of the U.S. **Navy**'s Depot of Charts and Instruments, Maury studied old log books

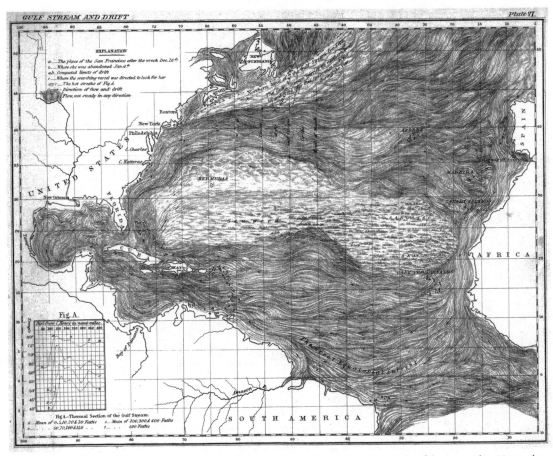

GULF STREAM AND DRIFT

Plate VI.

EXPLANATION

Fig A.

Thermal section of the Gulf Stream from Matthew Fontaine Maury's *The Physical Geography of the Sea, and Its Meteorology.*

and developed a series of **pilot charts** and a publication entitled ***Sailing Directions*** that helped mariners find the quickest and safest routes. He wrote *The Physical Geography of the Sea* (1855) and is credited with establishing the study of the sea as a distinct branch of science. During the American Civil War, Maury joined the Confederate forces, for which he was in charge of all coast, harbor, and river defenses. After the war he lived in England until President Andrew Johnson pardoned Confederate leaders in 1868. Maury returned home and became a professor of meteorology at the Virginia Military Institute.

Maxi Yacht, class of yacht designed expressly for ocean racing. Running from seventy-two to eighty feet in length, they are lightly built and carry minimal accommodations. They are usually sailed from series to series by delivery crews.

Mayagüez, U.S. container ship originally built in 1944 as the **C2 freighter** *Santa Eliana.* In May 1975 the **Sea-Land** vessel was seized by Cambodian forces (the Khmer Rouge), and her crew was charged with spying within Cambodia's territorial waters. President Gerald Ford's demands for the safe return of the ship and her thirty-nine crew members went unheeded. Three days after the seizure, a rescue mission was launched from USS *Coral Sea* and USS *Harold E. Holt*. The U.S. military rescue operation ended up with eighteen dead and fifty wounded service personnel. The crew of the *Mayagüez* was returned to the vessel unharmed, however, and she set sail the following day to resume her voyage to Hong Kong.

mayday, distress call for voice radio, for vessels and people in serious trouble at sea. The term was made official by an international telecommunications conference in 1948. It is the anglicized version of the French *m'aidez*, meaning "help me."

Mayflower, ninety-foot **galleon** built around 1610 in which 102 English separatists set sail on September 6, 1620, for America. Originally *Mayflower* was accompanied by another ship, the *Speedwell*, which was forced to turn back because of leaks. The Pilgrims arrived December 11 and founded the Plymouth Colony in Massachusetts. *Mayflower* returned to England in 1621 and resumed a career as a trading ship.

Mayflower, one-hundred-foot shallow-draft **cutter** designed by **Edward Burgess** that defeated *Galatea* in 1886 to defend the **America's Cup**. *Mayflower*'s syndicate was headed by General **Charles J. Paine**.

Mayflower II, 106-foot full-scale reproduction of the type of merchant vessel that brought the Pilgrims to America, given to the United States by Great Britain as a symbol of friendship. In spring 1957 *Mayflower II* traveled to America under the command of **Alan John Villiers** to commemorate the 350th anniversary of the Jamestown Colony. The trip took fifty-four days, which is eleven days fewer than the Pilgrims' trip in 1620. Today the ship is kept at Plimouth Plantation in Plymouth, Massachusetts, where she is regularly exercised under sail.

McDougall, Alexander (1845–1923), American **Great Lakes** ship captain who developed a series of **whaleback** vessels for carrying bulk grain and ore.

McFee, William (1881–1966), British mariner and author who became a U.S. citizen in 1924. He was an experienced shipboard engineer, and much of his writing is set during the age of steam. His novels include *Casuals of the Sea* (1916), *Swallowing the Anchor* (1925), *Harbourmaster* (1932), and *The Law of the Sea* (1950).

McGee, Travis, fictional private investigator in John D. MacDonald's series of twenty-four crime novels. McGee lives on his houseboat *Busted Flush* in Florida and calls himself a "**salvage** consultant."

McHale's Navy, hit American television comedy series that ran from 1962 to 1966 detailing the South Pacific exploits and shenanigans of the fictitious Squadron 19's **PT**-73 crew of the U.S. **Navy** during World War II. It captured the quintessence of the American sailor's ability to joke in the face of unopposable odds and to make the absolute best out of a lousy situation. The stories revolved around the **skipper** Quinton McHale and Ensign Chuck Parker in their underhanded dealings with "old lead bottom" Captain Binghamton. The series starred Ernest Borgnine, Tim Conway, and Joe Flynn.

McKay, Donald (1810–1880), Canadian-American shipbuilder and one of the greatest naval architects of his generation. He opened his Boston shipyard in 1844 and over the next thirty-plus years built some of the fastest and largest **clipper ships**, including *Stag Hound*, *Flying Cloud*, *Sovereign of the Seas*, *Great Republic*, *Lightning*, and *Glory of the Seas*.

McKenna, Richard (1913–1964), career U.S. **Navy** enlisted man and author of *The Sand Pebbles* (1962) and, posthumously, *The Left-Handed*

U.S. postage stamp issued in 1984 and depicting Herman Melville.

Monkey Wrench (1984), a collection of his stories and essays. McKenna died shortly after *The Sand Pebbles* was published, and he never got to see the now-classic 1966 film starring Steve McQueen, which was nominated for eight Academy Awards.

McLean, Malcolm (1913–2001), American shipping executive who is one of the most important figures in twentieth-century merchant shipping. In 1956, as the owner of an overland trucking company, he removed the piping and valves from a **T-2 tanker** and converted it to a metal box carrier, which he called a containership. He bought **Waterman Steamship Company** in 1955 to help with his experiment, and he launched **Sea-Land** in 1960 to pioneer container service along the East Coast and in the Gulf of Mexico. He sold Sea-Land in 1969 and purchased **United States Lines** in 1977, which subsequently went out of business.

McPhee, John (b. 1931), American author of *Survival of the Birch Bark Canoe* (1975) and *Looking for a Ship* (1990), among many other books.

Meander, ancient name of the Menderes River, which flows through Turkey into the Aegean Sea so slowly and by so many windings and turnings that its name has been used to describe persons who habitually wander slowly, circuitously, in a leisurely fashion.

measurement rule, system of measuring boats for racing so that different designs can compete on an equal basis. Boats are handicapped based on waterline length, sail areas, and so forth.

Medal of Honor, often called the Congressional Medal of Honor, it is the highest military

decoration that the United States grants to members of its armed forces. The award was initially approved by Congress in 1861 as the Navy Medal of Honor (the Army Medal of Honor followed in 1862). The first person to receive the Navy Medal of Honor was John Williams for his heroism on June 26, 1861, while serving as captain of the maintop of USS *Pawnee* in a Civil War attack.

Melville, Herman (1819–1891), American author best known for his novels of the sea. His novel *Moby-Dick; or, The Whale* (1851) is considered a masterpiece and one of the greatest American novels. Melville spent time at sea as a cabin boy, as a seaman aboard the whaleship *Acushnet*, and, briefly, in the U.S. **Navy** aboard the **frigate** USS *United States*. He based much of his writings on this sea experience. Although he achieved acclaim for his early novels *Typee* (1846) and *Omoo* (1847), he was virtually unknown at the time of his death. Other works of his include *Redburn* (1849), *Mardi* (1849), *White-Jacket* (1850), "**Benito Cereno**" (1855), and *Billy Budd* (1924).

The Memory of Eva Ryker, engrossing "who-done-it" thriller by Donald A. Stanwood set aboard RMS *Titanic* and told through flashbacks. What started out as a California State University of Long Beach writing assignment wound up eight years later as a 1978 best-seller for Stanwood.

USS *Memphis* (CA-10), U.S. **Navy cruiser** that was driven ashore and totally wrecked on August 29, 1916, at Santo Domingo in the Dominican Republic, by a **tidal wave** created by an underwater earthquake. Casualties included 41 sailors killed and 204 injured.

Men against the Sea, 1934 novel by **Charles Bernard Nordhoff** and **James Norman Hall** about the incredible 3,600-mile-voyage in an open twenty-three-foot launch by Captain **William Bligh** and eighteen crew members of HMS *Bounty*, who were set adrift after the

1789 mutiny. They reached the island of Timor and managed to get back to England.

Mendelssohn, Felix (1809–1847), German composer whose overture *The Hebrides* (1832), also called *Fingal's Cave*, was inspired by the sea.

Menoetes, pilot of the ship *Chimaera* in Vergil's *Aeneid*. For Menoetes's timidity in standing out from the shore, in order to avoid certain hidden rocks, and his consequent defeat by another craft, Gyas, the commander of the *Chimaera*, hurled him headlong into the sea. The word is used today to describe an overcautious person.

mercantile marine, see **merchant marine**.

mercantilism, an economic system followed by England, France, and other major trading nations from the 1500s to the late 1700s under which a nation's government strictly regulated international trade to enrich its treasury, especially by ensuring that exports exceeded imports.

Mercator, Gerhardus (1512–1594), born Gerhard Kremer, a Flemish geographer and mapmaker who was the first to use the names North America and South America. In 1569 he published a world map featuring a new type of projection of the round earth on a flat map. Called the "Mercator projection," it featured straight parallel lines of **latitude**; it is used today in ocean navigation.

merchant marine, fleet made up of a nation's commercial (nonmilitary) ships and the men and women who operate them. It includes both cargo and passenger ships but excludes tugs, fishing vessels, offshore oil rigs, and the like. The **Merchant Marine Act of 1936** established the U.S. merchant marine "as a naval or military auxiliary in time of war or national emergency."

U.S. Merchant Marine Academy, federal educational institution for training young men and

Recruiting poster for the post–World War II merchant marine.

women to be officers in the U.S. **merchant marine**. It was founded in 1943 at **Kings Point**, Long Island, New York, on the site of the estate of Walter P. Chrysler. Maintained by the U.S. **Maritime Administration**, it offers a four-year program emphasizing maritime and naval specialties and includes tours of service aboard merchant vessels. In addition to a degree, graduates receive the rank of third officer or third assistant engineer and a commission as an ensign in the U.S. **Naval Reserve**.

Merchant Marine Act of 1920, law prompted by efforts to dispose of a huge surplus of ships following World War I. The U.S. **Shipping Board** was given regulatory powers and responsibility for chartering and operating ships. The act reaffirmed coastwise laws by broadening the ban on domestic trade by foreign-owned or foreign-built vessels to include intercoastal and noncontiguous trades, a section referred to as the **Jones Act**. For the first time, the act enunciated that it is the policy of the United States to have a strong **merchant marine** for national defense purposes as well as for moving the nation's peacetime cargo.

Merchant Marine Act of 1928, also known as the **Jones-White Act**, legislation that stimulated an enormous growth in the U.S.-flag passenger fleet by providing liberal payments for mail carriage and shipbuilding loans. During the nine-year period the law was in effect, sixty-four large passenger ships were built and sixty-one existing ones were modernized.

Merchant Marine Act of 1936, legislation designed to modernize the U.S. merchant fleet. It established the U.S. **Maritime Commission** and set in motion a program of building fifty ships a year for ten years. It also authorized the Maritime Commission to develop a series of advanced ship designs. The act provided for direct **construction differential subsidy** and **operating differential subsidy** and authorized a training program for officer candidates and crews. Later it was amended to include a government-guaranteed loan and mortgage program to finance shipbuilding projects, which was referred to as **Title XI**.

Merchant Marine Act of 1970, legislation designed to increase the number of U.S.-flag ships by extending the **operating differential subsidy** to bulk carriers. The act, passed largely in response to the Vietnam War, set a goal of having 30 percent of U.S. foreign trade by weight carried on U.S.-flag ships, and it proposed the construction of three hundred new ships. The act did not achieve the desired results.

Merchant Marine and Fisheries Committee, standing committee of the U.S. House of Representatives that was established in 1887 to handle legislation affecting ocean transportation and maritime issues. The committee's power and prestige declined with that of the U.S. maritime industry, and the committee was dissolved in the 1990s and its responsibilities given to other transportation and environmental subcommittees.

Merchant Ship Sales Act of 1946, with a fleet of more than 4,100 merchant vessels after World War II, including 3,500 dry-cargo ships and 563 tankers, the U.S. government established a program for the disposition of the vessels. Under the act, the ships were to be sold, chartered, and **laid up** in reserve. U.S.-flag shipowners bought 850 ships, and 1,100 were sold to foreign shipowners. Approximately 1,500 ships were chartered to U.S. operators to carry **Marshall Plan** aid cargoes. At the close of the program in 1951, approximately 1,400 vessels were transferred to the **National Defense Reserve Fleet** to be ready for emergency needs.

Mercury, brand of outboard motor that was launched by Carl Kiekhaefer (d. 1983). In 1938 the young engineer bought the old Thor outboard manufacturing plant in Cedarburg, Wisconsin, and in 1940 began his own line of lightweight motors under the Mercury name. Kiekhaefer, who moved the company to Fond du Lac, Wisconsin, in 1950, constantly competed against **Evinrude** and **Johnson** and in 1962 was the first manufacturer to break the one-hundred-horsepower barrier. Mercury merged with the Brunswick Corporation in 1961, and Kiekhaefer left the company in 1970.

USNS *Mercy* (AH-19), hospital ship originally built in 1975 as the San Clemente–class **supertanker** *Worth*. When the $395 million financing collapsed for the planned 1981 government rebuilding of the **liner** SS *United States* into a hospital ship, the *Worth* and her sister *Rose City* were purchased instead. The 894-foot tanker was converted in 1986 to become the first hospital ship commissioned in the U.S. **Navy** in twenty years. The *Rose City* became the USNS *Comfort* (AH-20) a year later.

SS *Meredith Victory*, U.S. **merchant marine Victory ship** that performed the greatest rescue ever by a single ship by evacuating some 14,000 Korean civilians during the Korean War. In December 1950 the ship transported the refugees from the port of Hungnam, just ahead of the rapidly advancing Chinese army, down the coast of Korea to the island of Koji-Do, fifty miles southwest of Pusan.

USS *Merrimack*, U.S. **frigate** built in 1856 that was burned to the waterline in Norfolk by retreating Union forces in 1861. She was raised by the **Confederate Navy** and rebuilt as the 275-foot **ironclad** ram CSS *Virginia* the following year.

metal mike, gyropilot—more popularly known as "**iron mike**"—introduced by **Elmer Ambrose Sperry** in 1921 that led to the first automatic pilot in 1926. The term has come to describe the automatic steering system aboard a vessel that utilizes input from the ship's **gyrocompass** or other electronic navigation aids.

Meteor, series of five racing yachts owned and raced by Germany's Kaiser **Wilhelm II**. The first two were designed and built in British yards; *Meteor III* was designed by **Archibald Cary Smith** and was launched in New York in 1902; and *Meteor IV* and *Meteor V* were built in 1909 and 1914, respectively, and were launched in Germany.

Meteor, 233-foot German oceanographic ship that in 1925 used recently invented **sonar** to discover the Mid-Atlantic Range, the mountain range that lies under the **Atlantic Ocean**.

Miami–Nassau Race, 361-mile offshore powerboat race run annually since 1957 from Miami to the Bahamas.

SS *Michelangelo*, 45,911-gross-ton **Italian Line** passenger **liner** noted for her cagelike twin **funnels** set well aft. Built in 1965, both she and her sister, the *Raffaello*, were considered to be examples of government shortsightedness. Heavily subsidized, the transatlantic ships were built out of touch with the changing times, and both were **laid up** after only ten years of operation. In 1966 the *Michelangelo* slammed into an ugly storm that killed three people onboard and destroyed much of her forward-facing superstructure. She was sold to Iran as an accommodation ship in 1976 and was finally scrapped in 1991.

Michener, James Albert (1907–1997), American novelist best known for his fictional documentaries. His Pulitzer Prize–winning *Tales of the South Pacific* (1947) was based on his service as a naval historian in the South Pacific from 1944 to 1946. *Return to Paradise* (1951) was a sequel to *Tales*, and he later wrote *Chesapeake* (1978) and *Caribbean* (1989), among many other books.

middle passage, the ocean crossing from West Africa to the Caribbean and the Americas, usually involving slaves. As its name implies, this route initially formed the "middle leg" of a triangular trade between Europe, Africa, and the Americas. It is estimated that 10 to 12 million Africans were shipped to the Americas and perhaps 1.8 million died in the passage.

Middle Passage, 1990 novel by Charles Johnson (b. 1948) about freed slave Rutherford Calhoun, who escapes marriage and debt by stowing away on the illegal slave ship *Republic*. Once discovered, he is made part of the crew. After the slaves revolt, Rutherford is spared, and he is forced to reexamine his life. Johnson won the 1990 National Book Award for this work.

Midway, 1976 film epic dealing with the decisive naval battle of World War II in the Pacific. It contains excellent shipboard footage of aircraft carrier workings as well as—for the time—great special effects. The 1976 movie was scored by John Williams and starred Charlton Heston, Henry Fonda, Hal Holbrook, and Robert Mitchum.

Midway, Battle of, decisive naval engagement recognized as the turning point of World War II in the Pacific. Hopelessly outclassed by superior Japanese naval firepower, the American task force managed to sink four Imperial aircraft carriers—the *Akagi*, *Hiryu*, *Kaga*, and *Soryu*—as well as the heavy **cruiser** *Mikuma* during the four-day air engagement that started June 2, 1942. USS *Yorktown*, severely damaged in the confrontation, was sunk by a Japanese submarine following the battle.

Midway Islands, group of islands 1,134 miles west of Hawai'i claimed for the United States by Captain William Reynolds of the USS *Lackawanna* after discovery by the United States in 1859. Located midway between America and Asia, the islands served as a crucial **coaling station** for the U.S. **Navy** in the nineteenth century and later was the site of the turning point of the war in the Pacific—the Battle of **Midway**—during World War II.

Mikasa, Japanese battleship built in England in 1896 that was the **flagship** of Admiral Heihachiro Togo during the Battle of **Tsushima** in May 1905 during the **Russo-Japanese War**. She exploded and sank while undergoing repairs in 1906. Later refloated, she was preserved as a memorial. After World War II, she was stripped of all her fittings but today remains a memorial at Yokosuka.

MS *Mikhail Lermontov*, final unit of five lackluster motor **liners** built for the Soviet Union during the height of the Cold War. Completed in 1972, the vessel soon joined her younger sister, the *Alexandr Pushkin*, on the run to Montréal. Later that year, she made the first transatlantic call in New York by a Soviet liner. Economics caught up with the ship, and because the Soviet government became weary of funding a dying oceanic liner service simply for the sake of international public relations, the *Mikhail Lermontov* was permanently employed in cruise operations by 1975. She sank off New Zealand after running onto a rock outcropping in 1986, with the loss of one crew member.

Military Sealift Command (MSC), arm of the U.S. **Navy** that operates a fleet of approximately 110 ships around the world. These ships carry the **USNS** (United States Naval Ship) designation and are crewed by civilians.

Military Sea Transportation Service (MSTS), government entity formed in 1949 as part of the unification of the U.S. Armed Forces under the Department of Defense after World War II. The MSTS was established to consolidate all troop and cargo transport operations and supply functions of the army and navy. In 1970 the MSTS became the **Military Sealift Command**.

Miller, Doris (1919–1943), black U.S. **Navy** sailor, known as Dorie to his shipmates, who distinguished himself in action during the Japanese surprise attack on **Pearl Harbor** on December 7, 1941. Miller, assigned to the battleship USS *West Virginia*, manned a fifty-caliber machine gun during the air raid until he ran out of ammunition and was ordered to abandon ship. He received the **Navy Cross** for his extraordinary courage in battle. Miller was later assigned to the escort carrier USS *Liscome Bay*, which was sunk by Japanese aircraft on November 24, 1943. Miller was among the 646 sailors who perished.

Miller, Robert, see **Ben Lexcen**.

"Millions for defense, sir, but not one cent for tribute", supposed retort of U.S. diplomat Thomas Pinckney (1750–1828) when asked for a bribe of $250,000 from three French agents in 1797. The incident became known as the **XYZ Affair** and led to the 1798–1800

Quasi-War with France and the buildup of the U.S. **Navy**.

USS *Milwaukee* (C-21), 9,700-ton armored **cruiser** completed for the U.S. **Navy** in 1906. Dispatched in 1916 to assist in freeing the grounded American submarine H-3 from Samoa Beach near Eureka, California, the 426-foot cruiser helped evacuate the sub's crew of twenty-seven before attempting to pull the craft free from the sand. Not only did the 24,500 horsepower of the cruiser fail to extricate the sub, but the *Milwaukee* wound up becoming stranded herself. All actions to free the cruiser from the beach failed, and she broke in two during a storm in 1918. She was subsequently scrapped where she lay.

Milwaukee Clipper, resurrected guise of the *Juniata* of 1905. The ship originally designed by **Frank Kirby** was purchased in 1940 and rebuilt to the specifications of George Sharp to become a streamlined, fireproof passenger steamer between Muskegon, Michigan, and Milwaukee. The *Milwaukee Clipper* was **laid up** in 1970 and, after dockside stints at Chicago and Hammond, Indiana, was brought home to Muskegon in 1997 to be restored to her art-deco prime as a floating museum, restaurant, and hotel.

"Minesweepers" (1914), **Rudyard Kipling** poem that extolls the British fishermen whose **trawlers** swept the fairways for the safety of merchant ships during World War I.

SS *Minnesota*, 622-foot passenger-cargo **liner** built at Groton, Connecticut, in 1905 as a Seattle to Hong Kong extension of the Great Northern Railroad. She served in World War I as the U.S. **Navy** transport *Troy* and carried fourteen thousand servicemen back from Europe in three voyages when the war ended. Eventually scrapped in 1923, *Minnesota* and her sister ship the ***Dakota*** remained the largest passenger ships built in an American yard until 1927.

Minot's Ledge Light, lighthouse built in 1850 off Massachusetts as the first light built in a position directly exposed to the sweep of the open sea. It was washed into the seas in 1851, and two keepers drowned. Rebuilt as a stone tower in 1860, it was relit with one-four-three flash. Because this flash contains the same numerical count as the phrase "I love you," the lighthouse has become known as "Lover's Light."

The Mirror of the Sea, 1906 collection of short writings about the sea by **Joseph Conrad**. This work is often cited by sailors to people who want to understand their craft.

Mischief, sixty-seven-foot **cutter** designed by **Archibald Cary Smith** that represented the **New York Yacht Club** in its defense of the 1881 **America's Cup** series. She easily defeated the Canadian challenger *Atalanta*, two races to none.

Miss America, series of ten speedboats owned and raced by **Garfield A. "Gar" Wood** that ruled the racing circuit from 1920 to 1933. *Miss America I* set a long-standing **Gold Cup** speed record in 1920 of just over 70 miles per hour. In 1932 *Miss America X* reached speeds of over 124 miles per hour.

Mississippi Queen, flat-bottomed river passenger steamer built for the **Delta Queen Steamboat Company** in 1975 for operation on her namesake waterway. The 4,500-gross-ton sternwheel paddleboat cost over $27 million to construct.

Mississippi River, great waterway whose name meant "Big River" in the languages of the American Indians of the **Great Lakes** region. It is the second longest river in the United States (behind the **Missouri River**) and flows 2,340 miles from its source, **Lake Itasca**, in northwestern Minnesota to its mouth in the Gulf of Mexico. The Mississippi is the nation's chief inland waterway.

USS *Missouri* (BB-63), U.S. **Navy** warship completed in 1944 as the last of the 57,500-

ton **Iowa**-class battleships. The battlewagon mounts nine 16-inch guns among her formidable armament. After the ship saw action at **Iwo Jima** and **Okinawa**, the Japanese surrender to General **Douglas MacArthur** was signed on the ship's **starboard** quarterdeck while lying at anchor in **Tokyo Bay** on September 2, 1945. After serving in the Korean War, she was brought out of lay-up and participated in the attack on Baghdad during Operation Desert Storm in 1991. Decommissioned in 1992, the national historic landmark was towed to **Pearl Harbor** in 1998 and opened to the public the following year as a museum ship alongside the USS *Arizona* Memorial. *Missouri* is sister ship to USS *Iowa*, USS *New Jersey*, and USS *Wisconsin*.

Missouri River, the longest river in the United States, which flows 2,540 miles from its source, the Jefferson River at Red Rock Creek in southwestern Montana, to its mouth on the **Mississippi River**. Early explorers and American Indians called it the Big Muddy. During the early 1800s, the Missouri served as one of the main transportation routes of the fur trade in the West.

Mister Roberts, 1946 novel by Thomas Heggen about the crew of the USS *Reluctant*, an imaginary cargo ship in the backwaters of the Pacific during World War II. The successful novel was adapted to a popular Tony Award–winning stage play and, in 1955, a motion picture directed by Mervyn Leroy and John Ford. Henry Fonda starred in both the stage and the screen productions as cargo officer Lt. (jg) Roberts. Nominated for an Academy Award for best picture, it also starred William Powell and James Cagney. Jack Lemmon won the 1955 Academy Award for best supporting actor for his performance as Ensign Pulver.

Mitchell, Carleton (b. 1910), American sailor, author, and photographer who is best known

as the only **skipper** to win three consecutive **Bermuda Races**. He accomplished the feat in 1956, 1958, and 1960 in his thirty-eight-foot **yawl** *Finisterre*. Mitchell has written numerous books and magazine articles about his, and others', nautical adventures and introduced readers to such topics as cruising in the Caribbean. His books include *Islands to Windward* (1948), *Passage East* (1953), and *Summer of the Twelves* (1959).

Mitsui O.S.K. Lines (MOL), Japanese shipping firm formed in 1964 by the merger of Mitsui Steamship Company and O.S.K. Line. One of the biggest lines in the world, MOL today operates more than five hundred vessels worldwide, including container ships, tankers, car carriers, cruise ships, and domestic ferries.

Mobile Bay, Battle of, historic navy engagement of the Civil War fought August 5, 1864, which closed the last major Confederate Gulf Coast port to commerce. Aboard the **flagship** USS *Hartford*, Admiral **David Glasgow Farragut** ordered, **"Damn the torpedoes! Full speed ahead!"** when the lead ship of his flotilla, USS *Tecumseh*, struck a mine (then called a **torpedo**) and sank at the entrance to Mobile Bay. The Union fleet ran the minefield and the forts at the entrance and captured the small Confederate flotilla in the harbor.

Moby-Dick; or, The Whale, great American novel by **Herman Melville**, which was published in 1851. Narrated by a seaman who calls himself **Ishmael**, it relates the adventures of the whaling ship *Pequod*, led by the fanatical Captain **Ahab**, who after losing a leg in a first battle with the great white whale Moby Dick swears revenge. The captain's final three-day fight with the whale ends in the death of Ahab and the sinking of the *Pequod*. The screenplay for the 1956 Hollywood version was written by John Huston and Ray Bradbury, and the film starred Gregory Peck as Captain Ahab.

MODU, acronym for Mobil Offshore Drilling Unit, a movable platform used in offshore oil exploration and production.

Mohawk, U.S.-flagged passenger vessel that sank after colliding with the Norwegian motorship *Talisman* on January 24, 1935. The accident claimed the lives of 45 people and came five months after the *Morro Castle* burned at sea with 124 fatalities. The disasters led to the passage of more marine safety legislation in 1936–37 than had occurred during the previous twenty years.

Moitessier, Bernard (1925–1994), French circumnavigator and small boat sailor. In 1968 he set out in his steel-built Bermuda **ketch**, named *Joshua* for **Joshua Slocum**, in the first Golden Globe Race, a solo, nonstop circumnavigation rounding the **Cape of Good Hope**, **Cape Leeuwin**, and **Cape Horn**. Nearing the finish, Moitessier decided not to complete the race, instead sailing for another three months—circumnavigating the globe one and a half times (37,455 miles) without touching land and then landing in Tahiti. His account of the journey, *The Long Way* (1971), is considered a bible for the single-handed sailor.

Momsen, Charles Bowers "Swede" (1896–1957), U.S. **Navy** officer who led the rescue of thirty-three crewmen trapped in the bow of the submarine **USS *Squalus*** after it sank during tests off Portsmouth, New Hampshire, in May 1939. Momsen developed the diving bell used in the rescue, which served as a model for today's underwater rescue vehicles. Momsen was the subject of Peter Maas's *The Terrible Hours: The Man behind the Greatest Submarine Rescue in History* (1999). He also developed a submarine escape device that became known as the Momsen Lung.

Monamy, Peter (1681–1749), English marine artist who was influenced by **Willem van de Velde** the Younger. Monamy's paintings provide an accurate record of British naval history during the first half of the eighteenth century.

monitor, type of iron-plated warship (**ironclad**) designed by **John Ericsson** that carried heavy guns in revolutionary revolving turrets, having little draft and lying low in the water. The revolving turrets were protected by eight inches of armor and contained two eleven-inch guns. The sides of the vessels were protected by iron plating three to five inches thick with more than two feet of wood backing. The ships were moved by steam power with a screw propeller and were used extensively during the Civil War. Monitors had their limitation in that they were too heavy and unseaworthy for offshore travel.

USS *Monitor*, 179-foot **ironclad** built for the Union Navy by **John Ericsson** and launched in 1862. The first in a class of vessels called **monitors**, she sailed to **Hampton Roads**, Virginia, in March 1862 and engaged the Confederate ironclad CSS *Virginia* in battle. The four-hour fight resulted in a stalemate, but the lessons learned changed the terms of naval combat for all time. The steam-powered *Monitor* sank in a storm off Cape Hatteras on New Year's Eve 1862, with the loss of sixteen of her forty-seven crew members. After resting undetected for 111 years, the wreck was located in 1973 lying upside down in 235 feet of water. Numerous research expeditions to the wreck site have been carried out by the **National Oceanic and Atmospheric Administration**, working with the U.S. **Navy** and other partners.

monkey's fist, complex knot surrounding—and sometimes taking the place of—the weight on the end of a heaving line.

Monsarrat, Nicholas (1910–1979), English novelist whose best-known work, *The Cruel Sea* (1951), was based on his service with the **Royal Navy** in World War II. Other works of his include *H. M. Corvette* (1942), *The Nylon Pirates* (1960), *Monsarrat at Sea* (1975), and *The Master Mariner: Running Proud* (1979).

Mont Blanc, French munitions freighter that collided with the outbound Norwegian **tramp** steamer *Imo* in the Narrows of Halifax Harbor, Nova Scotia, on December 6, 1917. The ensuing explosion and fire destroyed many other vessels and devastated a square mile of structures as well as the entire waterfront area. The disaster took the lives of almost two thousand people afloat and ashore, injured nine thousand others, and left twenty-five thousand homeless. The tragedy is the central theme of the introduction to a series of animated training films on the **rules of the road** prepared by Walt Disney Studios for use during World War II.

Montagu, John, Fourth Earl of Sandwich (1718–1792), Britain's **First Lord of the Admiralty** from 1771 to 1782. He was criticized for his slow response to the American Revolution in 1775, but he did maintain a strong force in the English Channel to prevent a French invasion. He promoted Captain **James Cook**'s round-the-world research voyage in 1778 on which Cook discovered and named the Sandwich Islands (present-day Hawai'i). The modern-day sandwich is named for Lord Sandwich, who is said to have ordered meat between slices of bread while at the gambling tables.

USS *Montana* (BB-67), namesake lead vessel of a class of five 70,500-ton U.S. superbattleships intended to match the *Yamato* battleship type produced by Japan during World War II. The main armament of the 925-foot giants was to have been twelve 16-inch guns mounted in four triple turrets. The ships would have been too large to pass through the **Panama Canal**, but their speed would have been commensurate with that of the **Iowa** class. Acknowledging that naval air power was more important, the U.S. **Navy** canceled the work in 1943 in favor of constructing large aircraft carriers of the **Mid-**

way class. The four sisters of the *Montana* were intended to be the *Ohio, Maine, New Hampshire,* and *Louisiana.*

moonraker, small sail sometimes set in light winds above a **skysail.**

Moore-McCormack Line, U.S. shipping line founded in 1913 by Emmet J. McCormack and Albert V. Moore, which historically provided service from the United States to South America and Scandinavia. Eventually the shipping concern became a subsidiary of a larger company, Moore-McCormack Resources, which concentrated on energy, and in 1982 the shipping concern was acquired by **United States Lines.**

Moran, Edward (1829–1901), English-born artist who emigrated to America and specialized in marine and landscape painting. His younger brother Thomas (1837–1926) was an influential member of the **Hudson River School.**

Moran Towing, tugboat service founded in 1860 by Michael Moran in New York Harbor. The company's large white "M" on the stacks of its vessels has become a fixture in all the major ports on the East and Gulf Coasts of the United States. Today Moran operates more than ninety tugs and some twenty-six barges, and its business activities are divided among three areas of service: ship docking and general towage; marine transportation of petroleum and dry bulk products; and contract and specialty towing for barge owners and shipowners.

Morgan, John Pierpont "J. P." (1837–1913), American investment banker who at the turn of the twentieth century was one of the world's most powerful men. Between 1892 and 1902, he put together the financing to create General Electric, AT&T, International Harvester, and U.S. Steel. He was an avid yachtsman and a member and commodore of the **New York Yacht Club.** He owned a line of spectacular steam yachts named *Corsair* and sponsored the **America's Cup** yachts *Defender* and *Co-*

The wreck of the *Morro Castle* off of Asbury Park, New Jersey. (Bruce Vancil; Stickeler photo)

lumbia. He formed the shipping giant **International Mercantile Marine** in 1902.

Morgan, Sir Henry (1635–1688), Welsh-born British **buccaneer** famous for his extremely profitable ocean raids in the Caribbean Sea. He was appointed admiral of a powerful group of pirates that in 1670 sacked **Portobello**, Panama, Cuba, Maracaibo, and **Gibraltar**. After a treaty had been signed between England and Spain, Morgan was called to London to account for his actions. King Charles II dubbed him a knight in view of his enormous popularity and sent him back to Jamaica as the crown's lieutenant governor. He retired to become a wealthy plantation owner on the island.

Morison, Samuel Eliot (1887–1976), American historian, author, and naval officer. A longtime Harvard professor, he undertook many sea voyages and served on twelve U.S. **Navy** ships during World War II. His works include *The Maritime History of Massachusetts* (1921); *Admiral of the Ocean Sea* (1942), his Pulitzer Prize–winning biography of **Christopher Columbus**; the exhaustive *History of United States Naval Operations in World War II* (1947–62); *The Ropemakers of Plymouth* (1950); the two-volume *European Discovery of America* (1971 and 1974); and *John Paul Jones: A Sailor's Biography*.

Morro Castle, combination passenger-cargo vessel built in 1930 and operated on the New York to Havana route by the Ward Line. Early on the morning of September 8, 1934, the **liner**, en route to New York, caught fire off the New Jersey coast, killing 137 and injuring 224. The smoldering wreck, having run aground off Asbury Park, became a morbid tourist attraction. Ranking as the worst peacetime ocean disaster of a U.S.-flag vessel, the incident prompted the U.S. government to adopt stricter maritime safety regulations. Arson for insurance reasons has been suspected but never proven.

Moshulu, four-masted, steel-hulled sailing **bark** built in Scotland for German owners in 1904 as the *Kurt* for the nitrate trade. She came under American ownership during World War I, was renamed *Moshulu* after the war, and operated in the West Coast lumber trade until **laid up** in 1928. In 1935 she came under the Finnish flag and entered the Europe–Australia grain trade. She was the largest sailing ship still afloat in 1938 when Eric Newby sailed aboard her—a trip described in his *The **Last Grain Race*** (1956). *Moshulu* was completely restored and refitted in 1996 to serve as a floating restaurant at Pier 34 in Philadelphia.

Mosquito Coast, two-hundred-mile-long strip of land that lies along the northeast coast of Central America from the San Juan River in Nicaragua to the Aguan River in Honduras. The area received its name from the Mosquito Indians.

mosquito fleet, a group of vessels that take to the sea together "like a swarm of mosquitoes."

mothball fleet, ships that have been taken out of commission but are still maintained.

Mother Carey's chickens, sailor's term for storm petrels or similar seabirds. In folklore, Mother Carey is the woman in charge of ***Fiddler's Green***, the last home of the souls of drowned sailors. She sees to it that her guests are comfortable and, from time to time, lets them visit the upper world. When such visits occur, the souls take the form of seabirds known to sailors as storm petrels. For this reason, no real sailor will ever harm a storm petrel.

Motorboat Act of 1940, legislation that established legal requirements concerning safety for powerboats. It divided motorboats into four classes by length and prescribed the lights, sound signals, lifesaving equipment, fire extinguishers, and other equipment that must be carried. It also set forth rules that boaters must follow in case of accident or collision as well as specified penalties for various types of law infringement.

Mountbatten, Louis (1900–1979), British royal and military leader. Mountbatten was commander of the **destroyer** HMS *Kelly* when it was sunk by German bombers in the Battle of Crete in 1941. Mountbatten clung to the wreckage for four hours under enemy fire before being rescued. He was chief of combined British operations in 1942 and became commander in chief of Southeast Asia operations in 1943. He returned to naval service in June 1948, serving as **First Lord of the Admiralty** from 1955 to 1959. He was killed when a bomb, planted by the Irish Republican Army, exploded his fishing boat off the coast of Ireland.

Mowat, Farley (b. 1921), popular Canadian author who has written widely about the sea and wildlife issues. Among his more than twenty-six books are ***Grey Seas Under*** (1958), *The Serpent's Coil* (1961), *The Rock within the Sea* (1968), *The **Boat Who Wouldn't Float*** (1969), *A Whale for the Killing* (1972), and *Sea of Slaughter* (1984). Mowat also wrote the biography *Woman in the Mists: The Story of Diane Fossey and the Mountain Gorillas of Africa* (1987), which became the basis for the 1988 movie *Gorillas in the Mist*.

Mr. Midshipman Easy, 1836 novel by **Frederick Marryat** set in the time of the **Napoleonic Wars**. The main character is the spoiled son of a philosopher who enlists in the British navy and leads a dashing and adventurous life. Widely regarded as Marryat's best work, *Mr. Midship-*

A mothball fleet at Suisun Bay, California. (Captain James Nolan)

man Easy is based on the author's adventures sailing with Lord **Thomas Cochrane**.

Mr. Robinson Crusoe, 1932 **South Seas** adventure film in which a man makes a bet that he can live on a desert island for a year without the refinements of civilization. Shortly after he reaches the island, a woman arrives. The movie was written by and starred Douglas Fairbanks.

MS, letters designating a motor ship, which is usually diesel powered (in contrast to a **steamship**).

MSC, see **Military Sealift Command**.

MSTS, see **Military Sea Transportation Service**.

Mulberry harbors, two artificial harbors constructed by the Allied forces in Britain and floated across the English Channel to support the **Normandy Invasion** in 1944. The harbors'

primary function was to provide landing facilities for supplies and reinforcements after the **D-Day** landings.

Mulzac, Hugh (1886–1971), mariner who was the first African-American to command a U.S.-flag merchant ship. He sailed as a mate during World War I and commanded the racially integrated **Liberty ship** SS *Booker T. Washington* during World War II.

Munro, Douglas A. (1919–1942), U.S. **Coast Guard** signalman first class who was posthumously awarded the **Medal of Honor** for his actions in the rescue of a detachment of marines at the Matanikau River, **Guadalcanal**, on September 27, 1942. As coxswain of a thirty-six-foot **Higgins boat**, Munro took charge of the dozen craft that helped evacuate U.S. marines from the island. Munro was shot and died instantly while maneuvering his landing craft to serve as a shield against Japanese gunfire. He is the only U.S. Coast Guard member to have ever received the nation's highest military honor.

Muppet Treasure Island, **Robert Louis Stevenson**'s classic story *Treasure Island* retold on the silver screen with Kermit the Frog, Miss Piggy, and Fozzie Bear. The 1996 live-action movie starred Tim Curry, John Henson, and Frank Oz.

Murmansk, **Barents Sea** seaport on the northwest coast of the Kola Peninsula in northern Russia. Allied troops occupied the city for a time during World War I, and in World War II it served as the winter terminal for supplies from Britain and the United States. During the summer, supplies went to **Archangel**.

Murmansk Run, series of Allied supply **convoys** that sailed from Great Britain to the port of **Murmansk** in the Soviet Union during World War II. Casualties were often heavy because the natural hazards of transiting the Arctic waters were greatly increased by the activity of German **U-boats**, surface vessels, and aircraft operating from bases in northern Norway.

Murphy, Robert Cushman (1888–1973), American naturalist who worked on whaling ships and explored the world on fourteen expeditions, during which he cataloged tens of thousands of bird species. He was a global authority on oceanic birds and served as a curator at the American Museum of Natural History. His *Logbook for Grace* (1947), a logbook of his days on the whaling **brig** *Viola* in 1912, was written for his new wife.

Murray, Sir John (1841–1914), Scottish naturalist, oceanographer, and pioneer of deep-sea exploration who specialized in studying the ocean bottom. Aboard HMS *Challenger* he made a scientific study of oceans and ocean bottoms from 1872 to 1876 and later edited the expedition's fifty volumes of scientific reports.

He also wrote *The Depths of the Ocean* (1912) as well as *The Ocean* (1913), which is considered an important work in its field.

Musashi, second of three identical Japanese battleships laid down in direct defiance of the **Washington Naval Treaty**. Completed in 1942, the sixty-four-thousand-ton floating arsenal was sunk after being hit by twenty torpedoes and seventeen bombs from U.S. aircraft carrier–based planes in the Battle of **Leyte Gulf** in October 1944. *Musashi* was sister to the **Yamato** and the **Shinano**.

Musée de la Marine, France's national maritime museum and, along with the Russian Fleet Museum in Saint Petersburg, Russia, the world's oldest. Established in Paris in 1748, the museum's collections contain many objects related to seafaring through the ages, and particularly to the French navy. Among its prized possessions is a series of thirteen paintings of French ports by **Claude-Joseph Vernet** as well as a barge commissioned by **Napoleon I**.

Museum of the Sea, organization founded in 1968 to operate the oceanographic and historic museums to be constructed aboard RMS **Queen Mary** in Long Beach, California. As designed, the facility would have been the most phenomenal and spectacular display of its kind anywhere in the world. However, monetary overrides, scandals, and allegations of illegal activities resulted in the project's being stymied when it opened unfinished in 1971. The *Queen Mary* has continued to operate as a hotel with historical displays focusing on the **liner**'s own remarkable career.

The Mutineers, 1949 adventure movie about gunrunning and smuggling aboard a ship bound for Portugal. It starred George Reeves, Jon Hall, and Adele Jergens.

Mutiny, 1952 film about an American ship carrying $10 million in gold during the **War of 1812**. After a mutiny, the captain is set adrift.

The movie starred Mark Stevens, Gene Evans, and Angela Lansbury.

The Mutiny of the Elsinore, powerful 1914 novel by **Jack London** about a voyage around **Cape Horn** aboard one of the last of the great sailing cargo ships. At the time it was written, London was the highest-paid and best-known writer in the world.

Mutiny on the *Bounty*, famous mutiny that occurred in 1789 on board HMS *Bounty* near the island of Tofoa (now part of Tonga) in the South Pacific Ocean. Captain **William Bligh** and eighteen members of his crew were set adrift in a twenty-three-foot boat with little food or water. They suffered incredible hardships but sailed 3,600 miles across the Pacific to the Dutch colony of Timor, in what is now Indonesia. The mutineers on the *Bounty* sailed to Tahiti, where nine of them, led by **Fletcher Christian**, settled on **Pitcairn Island**. Two mutineers soon died in accidents. Christian and all but one of the rest were killed by natives they had abused.

Mutiny on the Bounty, 1931 novel by **Charles Bernard Nordhoff** and **James Norman Hall** based on the mutiny against Captain **William Bligh** on HMS *Bounty* in 1789. The story is narrated by Roger Byam and describes how **Fletcher Christian** and fifteen others revolted against Bligh and set him and eighteen crew members adrift in a small boat. Two sequels, *Men against the Sea* (1934) and *Pitcairn's Island* (1934), addressed the fate of the *Bounty* crew and the mutineers. The classic 1935 motion picture adaptation of the book starred Clark Gable, Charles Laughton, and Spring Byington. It was made into a controversial epic wide-screen Cinerama version in 1962, with Marlon Brando, Trevor Howard, and Richard Harris in the leading roles.

MV, motor vessel designation.

MY, motor yacht designation.

The Mysterious Island, 1872 adventure novel by **Jules Verne** about a group of castaways who build a community on an uncharted island and are later saved by a passing ship. The story includes the reappearance of Captain **Nemo**, who was introduced in Verne's ***Twenty Thousand Leagues under the Sea***. In the story, Nemo dies and is buried in his submarine.

The Mystery of the Mary Celeste, 1937 film based on the strange story of the *Mary Celeste*, an American ship found derelict and adrift on the **Atlantic Ocean** in December 1872. The movie starred Bela Lugosi and Shirley Grey.

Mystic Seaport, outdoor living history attraction and maritime museum in Mystic, Connecticut. Founded in 1929 on the site of nineteenth-century shipyards, it is the largest and most visited maritime museum in the United States. Ships in the museum's collection include the whaleship *Charles W. Morgan*, the ship *Joseph Conrad*, and the **Grand Banks** fishing **schooner** *L. A. Dunton* as well as many lesser vessels.

N

Nagato, 32,720-ton Japanese battleship completed in 1920. The 708-foot vessel was the first to mount sixteen-inch guns for her primary armament. She sustained serious damage in the Battle of the **Philippine Sea** and surrendered to U.S. forces at the end of World War II. The ship was taken to the **Bikini Atoll** in 1946 for the atomic bomb tests. She survived the first blast with only minor damage; however, test shot "Baker" sent her quickly to the bottom.

Nagumo, Chuichi (1886–1944), Japanese admiral who commanded the carrier strike force that attacked **Pearl Harbor**. His force was defeated at the Battle of **Midway** in 1942, and his aircraft strength was severely depleted in subsequent engagements. He was relieved of command in 1944 and placed in charge of the defense of Saipan. He committed suicide when the island was successfully taken by U.S. forces. He is often criticized for not mounting a third strike on Pearl Harbor on December 7, 1941, which could have destroyed U.S. fuel stores.

Nansen, Fridtjof (1861–1930), Norwegian explorer, scientist, and humanitarian who in 1893 set sail from Norway aboard **Fram** to trace the polar currents. By allowing the ship to become locked in the ice, Nansen's expedition drifted across the Arctic Ocean. While the team turned to scientific programs, Nansen left the vessel and traveled farther north than anyone before him. His writings include *Farthest North* (1897) and *In Northern Mists* (1911), a history of Arctic exploration. He received the Nobel Peace Prize in 1922 for his humanitarian and diplomatic efforts following World War I.

Nantucket (WLV-117), U.S. **Lighthouse Service lightship** on station off Nantucket. In January 1934, the **United States Lines'** SS *Washington* nearly rammed the lightship, scraping the sides and shearing off davits, a lifeboat, and antennas. Five months later, the lightship was sunk by RMS *Olympic*, with the loss of seven crew members.

Nantucket (WLV-612), the U.S. **Coast Guard**'s last active **lightship**. Decommissioned in 1985, she brought to a close the lightship era.

Nantucket Lightship basket, a style of simple, round basket first made in the early 1900s by the men stationed aboard the *No. 1 Nantucket New South Shoal Lightship* to sell to tourists once ashore.

Nantucket sleigh-ride, whaleman's term for the tow given a **whaleboat** by a whale after being harpooned.

Napoleon I (also Napoleon Bonaparte) (1769–1821), French soldier, general, and self-crowned emperor of France (1804–14 and 1815). He rose from obscurity to greatness through military power and intellect, and he created an empire that covered most of western and central Europe. He abdicated his throne in 1814 and was exiled to **Elba**. He returned to power in 1815 and shortly thereafter was defeated at Waterloo by the Duke of Wellington's English army—ending the **Napoleonic Wars**. Again he abdicated his throne, and the period from his return to Paris from Elba to his second abdication is known as the Hundred Days. After a failed attempt to escape to the United States, he surrendered to HMS *Bellerophen* and was exiled to **Saint Helena**, where he remained until he died.

Napoleonic Wars, series of military campaigns launched by **Napoleon I** during the **French Revolution** of 1789. In 1805 Admiral **Horatio Nelson** destroyed the fleets of France and Spain, France's ally, at the Battle of **Trafalgar**, giving Great Britain control of the seas and ending any chance of Napoleon's invading Britain. The wars ended with Napoleon's defeat at Waterloo in 1815.

SS *Naronic*, White Star Line steamer built in 1892 to carry cattle and passengers across the North Atlantic. The 6,594-gross-ton ship disappeared on her thirteenth voyage while due at New York on February 11, 1893. No legitimate trace of the vessel was ever found.

Natchez, 301-foot **side-wheel** steamer built in 1869 that was one of the fastest **steamboats** on the **Mississippi River**. In 1870 she faced the steamboat *Robt. E. Lee* in the **Great Steam-boat Race** from New Orleans to Saint Louis. The *Lee* won the race not because of its faster speed but because the *Natchez* had stopped at several ports on the way.

Nate and Hayes, 1983 swashbuckling adventure film that takes place in the South Pacific in the mid-1800s. The real-life pirate **William A. "Bully" Hayes** teams up with young Reverend Nate to face a cutthroat gang that has kidnapped Nate's wife. The film starred Tommy Lee Jones, Michael O'Keefe, Max Phipps, and Jenny Seagrove.

National Association of Underwater Instructors (NAUI), a dive training and certification organization founded in 1960 by Neal Hess and Al Tillman.

National Defense Reserve Fleet (NDRF), an inactive reserve source of basic merchant ships that can be activated within twenty to 120 days to meet both military and nonmilitary shipping requirements of the United States. Maintenance of this **mothball fleet**, established by the **Merchant Ship Sales Act of 1946**, is the responsibility of the U.S. **Maritime Administration**. Ships in the NDRF are regionally located at three sites—James River, Virginia; Beaumont, Texas; and Suisun Bay, California. Within the NDRF, the **Ready Reserve Force** (or RRF) vessels are maintained in a higher state of readiness.

National Imagery and Mapping Agency (NIMA), agency created in 1996 to centralize the U.S. government's mapping and imagery functions. It superseded the **Defense Mapping Agency**, and today NIMA's Marine Navigation Department publishes navigation charts and the *Notice to Mariners*, *List of Lights*, *Sailing Directions*, and *The American Practical Navigator*.

National Marine Fisheries Service (NMFS), unit of the **National Oceanic and Atmospheric Administration** that oversees the protection, study, management, and restoration of commercial and recreational fish stocks in the marine waters of the United States. It was initiated in 1871 as the U.S. Commission of Fish and Fisheries and was the first federal conservation agency. Later it was renamed the Bureau of Fisheries, and then the Bureau of Commercial Fisheries.

National Maritime Day, day of national recognition for the U.S. **merchant marine** and maritime industry. It was proclaimed by a congressional resolution in 1933 as May 22 of each year, the day in 1819 when SS *Savannah* became the first **steamship** to cross the Atlantic Ocean.

National Maritime Historical Society (NMHS), membership organization founded in 1963, under **Karl Kortum**'s leadership, with the primary purpose of saving the 1899 **bark *Kaiulani***. Failing in this mission, the society was reorganized in 1970 to raise the maritime awareness of Americans and involve them more in their maritime heritage. NMHS has played a leading role in saving several historic ships since the *Kaiulani* failure. It publishes the well-known magazine *Sea History*.

National Maritime Museum, museum established in 1934 at Greenwich, England, to illustrate the maritime history of Great Britain. The site is the former **Greenwich Hospital** and includes the Old Royal Observatory, home of the **prime meridian**. One of the world's premier maritime museums, its holdings include works and objects that exemplify Britain's **Royal Navy**, **merchant marine**, and fishing fleet.

National Maritime Union (NMU), maritime labor union founded in 1937 that was once the largest organization for seafarers in the United States. In 1988, with its influence greatly reduced, NMU merged with a chapter of the **Marine Engineers Beneficial Association**.

National Oceanic and Atmospheric Administration (NOAA), U.S. government agency established in 1970 within the Department of Commerce to unify many government departments and agencies with missions in the ocean and the atmosphere. Ancestor agencies include the U.S. **Coast Survey**, established in 1807; the Weather Bureau, established in 1870; and the Commission of Fish and Fisheries, established in 1871. Services within NOAA include the **National Marine Fisheries Service**; the **National Ocean Service**; the National Weather Service; the National Environmental Satellite, Data and Information Service; and the Office of Oceanic and Atmospheric Research.

National Ocean Service (NOS), service within the **National Oceanic and Atmospheric Administration** that manages the nation's coastal resources and charts the nation's oceans. The NOS grew out of the nation's oldest scientific agency, established as the U.S. **Coast Survey** in 1807 by President **Thomas Jefferson**.

National Steel and Shipbuilding Company (NASSCO), the largest West Coast ship construction facility in the United States. Founded in 1905 in San Diego, California, as California Iron Works, it began building ships in 1945. Today a part of **General Dynamics**, it designs, builds, and repairs cargo ships and tankers for commercial customers as well as auxiliary ships for the U.S. **Navy**.

National Underwater and Marine Agency (NUMA), organization founded in 1978 by best-selling author **Clive Cussler** for the historic preservation of underwater sites.

Naughty Marietta, popular 1935 motion picture musical romance about a French princess who switches identities with a mail-order bride and is captured by eighteenth-century pirates on the **Spanish Main**. It starred Jeanette MacDonald and Nelson Eddy—in their first matchup—and Elsa Lancaster and Frank Morgan.

NAUI, see **National Association of Underwater Instructors**.

Nautical Almanac, annual joint publication of the U.S. **Naval Observatory** and the Royal Greenwich Observatory. First issued in 1855, it provides basic information for celestial navigation.

Nautical Institute, international professional body of qualified mariners with thirty-eight branches worldwide and more than seven thousand members in over seventy countries. Based in England, the institute aims to coordinate nautical studies worldwide by promoting high standards of qualification, competence, and knowledge among those on or concerned with the sea.

nautical mile, standard unit of distance equal to one minute of arc on the earth's surface, or 1,852 meters (two thousand yards is used as the rough distance for navigation purposes). It was proposed by the International Hydrographic Bureau in 1929 and has been adopted by nearly all maritime nations, including by the United States on July 1, 1954.

Nautical Quarterly, handsome, hardcover, quarterly periodical for yachtsmen that expressed the aesthetics, technology, heritage, and pure pleasure of boats and the marine environment. Established in 1977, it ceased publication in 1990 with its fiftieth issue.

Nautical Research Guild (NRG), nonprofit society established in 1948 in the United States to link researchers, historians, collectors, and builders of ship models. The NRG publishes the quarterly *Nautical Research Journal*.

USS *Nautilus* (SSN-571), U.S. **Navy** submarine and the world's first nuclear-powered vessel. Built at the **Electric Boat** Division of **General Dynamics** in Groton, Connecticut, she was christened by Mrs. Dwight D. Eisenhower and launched in 1954. She was named specifically for the submarine in **Jules Verne**'s *Twenty Thousand Leagues under the Sea*. On its first voyage, the *Nautilus* broke all previous records for underwater speed and endurance. In 1958 she sailed beneath the Arctic ice and sent the famous message, "Nautilus 90 North" from the North Pole. Retired in 1980 after sailing more than three hundred thousand miles, the sub is the centerpiece of the Historic Ship *Nautilus* and Submarine Force Museum in Groton, Connecticut.

U.S. Naval Academy, U.S. **Navy** officer training school opened at Fort Severn in Annapolis, Maryland, in October 1845 by secretary of the navy George Bancroft. Initially called the U.S. Naval School, it combined existing school sites in New York, Boston, Philadelphia, and Norfolk. Its name was changed in 1850, and the first graduation exercises were held in June 1854. During the Civil War, the academy was temporarily moved to Newport, Rhode Island.

Naval Armament Limitation Treaty, see **Washington Naval Treaty**.

Naval Armed Guard, branch of the U.S. **Navy** in World War II that put gun crews aboard U.S. merchant ships to protect the ships, their cargo, and crew from enemy attacks and sabotage. By war's end, Naval Armed Guard training bases were located throughout the country, and more than 144,900 men served on over 6,236 American and Allied ships. Nearly 2,000 of these men died while performing their duty during World War II.

Naval Expansion Act of 1938, Congressional legislation that authorized a billion-dollar expansion of the U.S. **Navy** after both Japan and Germany had withdrawn from arms limitations treaties. It provided for the construction of **capital ships** and aircraft carriers for a two-ocean navy.

U.S. Naval Institute, private, nonprofit society for sea service professionals and individuals interested in naval and maritime affairs.

Established in 1873 at the U.S. **Naval Academy**, it publishes the magazine *Proceedings*—the main public forum for discussion and debate of subjects affecting the navy—as well as the bimonthly publication *Naval History* and many naval and maritime books.

U.S. Naval Observatory, scientific agency established in 1830 as the Naval Depot of Charts and Instruments. Its primary mission was to care for the U.S. **Navy**'s **chronometers**, charts, and other navigational equipment. It was named the Naval Observatory and Hydrographical Office in 1854 and received its present name in 1974. Today it monitors and disseminates time and astronomical data required for accurate navigation.

Naval Overseas Transportation Service (NOTS), governing body established in 1918 by the United States to maintain shipping to the American fighting forces in Europe during World War I. NOTS lost 8 vessels to enemy action out of the 450 ships they controlled during the conflict. Prior to World War II, the organization was superseded by the **Naval Transport Service**.

U.S. Naval Reserve, military force of men and women maintained by the U.S. **Navy** to meet the expanded needs of the regular navy. The tradition of a naval reserve dates back to 1887 when states organized naval militias. In 1915 Congress formally created a Federal Naval Reserve. Today's Naval Reserve numbers over 690,000.

Naval Reserve Officers' Training Corps (NROTC), organization established in 1925 to provide training and instruction in naval subjects at universities and colleges in order to train students for commissions in the U.S. **Navy** and **Naval Reserve**, U.S. **Marine Corps**, and Marine Corps Reserve.

Naval Sea Systems Command (NAVSEA), U.S. **Navy**'s central activity for designing, engineering, integrating, building, and procuring U.S. naval ships and shipboard weapons and combat systems. Ancestor agencies include the Bureau of Construction, Equipment and Repair; the Bureau of Ordnance and Hydrography, created in 1842; and the Bureau of Ships, established in 1940. NAVSEA also oversees the maintenance, repair, modernization, and conversion of in-service ships.

Naval Transport Service, U.S. **Navy** transportation agency that succeeded the **Naval Overseas Transportation Service**. It merged with the Army Transport Service in 1949 to become the **Military Sea Transportation Service**, and in 1970 the **Military Sealift Command**.

U.S. Naval War College, the highest professional educational institution in the U.S. **Navy**, which focuses on the theoretical and applied knowledge of naval warfare. Founded in 1884 by Rear Admiral **Stephen Bleecker Luce**, it is located in Newport, Rhode Island, and is the oldest school of its kind in the world.

Navarino, Battle of, naval engagement off the coast of Greece in the Ionian Sea in which the combined fleets of England, France, and Russia destroyed the joint Turkish-Egyptian fleet on October 20, 1827. The battle heralded Greek independence from the Ottoman (Turkish) Empire.

Navigation Acts, series of laws passed in the mid-1600s by the English Parliament to protect English trade and govern colonial commerce. An example of **mercantilism** among the laws was that all goods carried between British ports (including colonies) must be transported by British ships manned chiefly by British crews. Opposition to these acts was one of the main causes of the American Revolution.

navigational planets, the four planets commonly used for celestial observations: Venus, Mars, Jupiter, and Saturn.

Navigation Rules, statutory requirements to promote navigation safety established by international law and published by the U.S. **Coast Guard**. It includes **COLREGS** and **Inland Rules**. The official publication—which contains rules on steering and sailing, lights and shapes, and sound and light signals—is required to be carried on all vessels over forty feet in length.

The Navigator, 1924 silent feature film starring Buster Keaton, who, with his costar Kathryn McGuire, survives on an old abandoned ocean **liner** when the couple is set adrift. They fight off cannibals and are eventually saved when a submarine surfaces below them and lifts the ship into the air. Keaton purchased the liner SS *Buford* to make the film.

NAVSEA, see **Naval Sea Systems Command**.

Navtex, international automated system for instantly distributing maritime navigational warnings, weather forecasts and warnings, and search-and-rescue notices to vessels at sea. It is printed on a small roll of paper so that no one needs to be present to receive the message.

U.S. Navy, branch of the U.S. armed forces that acts to maintain command of the sea and serves as an instrument of peace. The Continental Congress established the **Continental Navy** in 1775, but it ceased operations after the American Revolution. A navy was called for in the U.S. Constitution of 1787, and during the late 1780s the **Barbary pirates** preyed on American merchant ships and killed or captured American sailors. Congress passed the **Navy Act of 1794**, and the launching of the **frigate** USS *United States* in 1797 marked the rebirth of the U.S. Navy.

Navy Act of 1794, act of the U.S. Congress approved on March 27, 1794, that created the U.S. **Navy** to address the problems of the **Barbary pirates**. The act provided for the building of six **frigates**, three with forty-four and three with thirty-six guns. The *United States*, *Constitution*, and *Constellation*, designed by

World War II recruiting poster for the U.S. Navy. (Courtesy The Mariners' Museum, Newport News, Virginia)

Philadelphia shipbuilder **Joshua Humphreys**, were launched in 1797. Events leading up to the **Quasi-War** led to the completion of the *President*, *Congress*, and *Chesapeake* in 1798.

Navy Blues, musical comedy aboard ship in **Pearl Harbor** in the placid days before the Japanese attack. The 1941 movie starred Ann Sheridan, Martha Raye, Jack Oakie, Jack Haley, Jackie Gleason, and Howard Da Silva.

Navy Board model, ship model built expressly for the Navy Board, a commission under the Lord High Admiral that supplied and administered the British Navy from the mid-sixteenth century until 1832. Usually at a scale of 1:48, models were used at the design stage to help

The Palm Court of the Nederland Plaza Hotel. (Courtesy Gordon R. Ghareeb; © RE White)

board members study the design and construction details of a proposed warship.

The Navy Comes Through, 1942 motion picture detailing the exploits of an American naval crew stationed aboard a **merchant marine** freighter and their struggle against the Nazis at sea. An effective vehicle for subliminal recruiting purposes, it starred Pat O'Brien, George Murphy, Jane Wyatt, and Desi Arnaz.

Navy Cross, naval decoration instituted in 1919 and awarded to a person who, serving in any capacity with the U.S. **Navy**, distinguishes himself or herself by outstanding heroism in action against the enemy.

"The Navy Hymn", text written in 1860 by American composer William Whiting (1825–1878). The first stanza reads: "Eternal Father, strong to save, / Whose arm doth bind the restless wave, / Who bidd'st the mighty ocean deep / Its own appointed limits keep, / O, hear us when we cry to Thee / For those in peril on the sea!"

Navy League, civilian organization founded in 1902 to support the men and women of the sea services. Nearly seventy thousand members work closely with the U.S. **Navy**, **Marine Corps**, **Coast Guard**, and U.S.-flag **merchant marine** through a network of more than 330 councils in the United States and around the world. The Navy League publishes *Sea Power* magazine.

Navy Log, dramatic American television series that ran from 1955 to 1958 representing with the pathos and humanity of the U.S. **Navy** sailor. The well-known theme song, the "Navy Log March," was composed by Fredrick Steiner.

Navy Pier, a Chicago Landmark that is a mix of year-round entertainment, shops, restaurants, attractions, and exhibition facilities. Built in 1909 as Municipal Pier, the 1½-mile stretch into Lake Michigan originally served as a freight terminal and public recreation facility. During the World Wars it served as a military training site, and then the temporary home for the University of Illinois Chicago campus into the early 1960s (it was officially renamed "Navy Pier" in 1927 as a tribute to U.S. **Navy** personnel who served during World War I). During the 1970s and 1980s the pier fell into disuse, but in 1989 the city turned over ownership to the Metropolitan Pier and Exposition Authority and contributed $150 million in funds to help redevelop it. Reopened in 1995, it is today the city's number-one tourist destination.

NAYRU, see **U.S. Sailing Association**.

"Nearer My God, to Thee", song that by many accounts was played by the orchestra of RMS *Titanic* as the great ship sank on April 14, 1912. Other accounts said the orchestra leader, Wallace Hartley, and his musicians remained steadfast at their posts and played "Autumn," an Episcopalian hymn.

Nederland Plaza Hotel, outstanding art-deco luxury hotel built in 1931 in Cincinnati, Ohio. The original hotel lobby, since renamed the Palm Court, was constructed to resemble in dimension and decoration the main lounge of a great transatlantic **liner**. The walls and clerestory of the room are paneled with more than half an acre of Brazilian rosewood.

Needles, group of tall rocks off the western end of the **Isle of Wight** that marks the beginning of the transatlantic run to New York.

Negro Seamen Act, law passed by the South Carolina legislature in 1822 requiring all free black sailors to be jailed while their vessels were in port. It was prompted by the fear that free blacks would spread ideas about freedom

Horatio Nelson. Painting attributed to Lemuel F. Abbott. (Courtesy The Mariners' Museum, Newport News, Virginia)

among Charleston's slaves. In later years, North Carolina, Georgia, Florida, Alabama, and Louisiana, as well as the Spanish colonies of Cuba and Puerto Rico, passed similar laws. The laws were modified in the 1850s because the acts particularly affected British ships loading cotton for textiles. The acts were abolished after the Civil War.

Nelson, Horatio (1758–1805), British vice-admiral who became the best-known naval leader in history. He began his naval career at age twelve and came of age during the **Napoleonic Wars**. He led the British fleet that crushed the French fleet at the Battle of the **Nile** in 1798 and was instrumental in destroying the Danish fleet at the Battle of **Copenhagen** in 1801. His arm was shattered and one eye blinded in other actions. On October 21, 1805, Nelson's fleet engaged a Franco-Spanish fleet in the Battle of **Trafalgar**, near Cadiz on Spain's Atlantic seaboard. Nelson was hit by a sniper's bullet and died aboard his **flagship** HMS *Victory* shortly after hearing the news of the enemy's defeat. His signal to the fleet at Trafalgar—"England expects that every man will do his duty"—has echoed through the years.

Nelson's blood, **Royal Navy** expression for rum that originates from the belief that after the Battle of **Trafalgar**, **Horatio Nelson**'s body was returned to England preserved in a barrel of rum. In fact, brandy and spirits of wine were used.

Nelson's prayer, prayer penned by Admiral **Horatio Nelson** in his diary on the morning of October 21, 1805, the day he died at the Battle of **Trafalgar**. It reads: "May the great God, whom I worship, grant to my country, and for the benefit of Europe in general, a great and glorious victory; and may no misconduct in any one tarnish it; and may humanity after victory be the predominant feature in the British fleet. For myself I commit my life to Him who made me, and may His blessing light upon my endeavours for serving my country faithfully. To Him I resign myself and the just cause which is entrusted to me to defend. Amen. Amen. Amen."

Captain Nemo, infamous arch-villain of **Jules Verne**'s 1870 underwater science fiction classic *Twenty Thousand Leagues under the Sea*. The semi-insane captain of the strangely powered submarine *Nautilus* is hell-bent on stopping warfare at sea no matter how many men

he has to kill in order to achieve his goal. Two years later, Verne fully redeemed the madman in the 1872 sequel, *Mysterious Island*. The character was consummately brought to life in 1954 by James Mason in the Walt Disney feature film *20,000 Leagues under the Sea*.

Neptune, in Roman mythology, the god of the sea. He married the sea nymph Amphitrite, and they had a son, **Triton**, who was half man and half fish. Many fountains, notably the Trevi Fountain in Rome, include a statue of Neptune. Neptune's Greek counterpart is **Poseidon**.

Neptunus Rex, Latin for **King Neptune**.

net registered tonnage (NRT), tonnage frequently shown on merchant ship registration papers. It represents the internal volume available for cargo and for passengers. Set at one hundred cubic feet per ton, it is used by port and canal authorities as a basis for tolls and charges.

USS *Nevada* (BB-36), 27,500-ton U.S. **Navy** battleship and sister vessel to USS *Oklahoma*. Commissioned in 1916 and modernized in 1929, her main armament consisted of ten 14-inch guns. While attempting to get under way when the attack on **Pearl Harbor** commenced, the 583-foot vessel was hit by one torpedo and four bombs, leaving 60 dead and 109 wounded. After the attack, she was beached to prevent her from sinking. She was repaired and stationed in the **Atlantic** until repositioned in the Pacific in 1945 for the invasions of **Iwo Jima** and **Okinawa**. She was sent to the **Bikini Atoll** atomic bomb tests in 1946, which she survived. Towed back to Pearl Harbor for further study, the vessel was sunk off Hawai'i in 1948 as a floating target.

Nevins, Henry B. (1878–1959), American boatbuilder who built yachts of world-class quality. He established the Henry B. Nevins Shipyard on **City Island**, New York, in 1906 and built many of the most famous yachts of the twentieth century, including *Brilliant*, *Stormy Weather*, *Columbia*, and *Bolero*. The Nevins yard ceased building boats in 1954.

Newbolt, Sir Henry John (1862–1938), British barrister, author, and poet who headed Great Britain's War Propaganda Bureau in World War I to help shape public opinion. His writings and poetry, which focused on the sea, were published in *Admiral's All* (1897), *The Island Race* (1898), *Sailing of the Longships* (1902), *Songs of the Sea* (1904), *Year of Trafalgar* (1905), *Songs of the Fleet* (1910), and *Book of the Blue Sea* (1914). He also published the last two volumes of the official five-volume *Naval History of the Great War* (1920–32) following the death of Sir Julian Corbett, who wrote the first three volumes.

USS *New Ironsides*, Union **ironclad** launched in 1862 and named in honor of **Old Ironsides**. The iron vessel was one of the most powerful ships afloat in the Civil War, but she did not handle well. She was **laid up** in 1865 and was destroyed by fire in 1866.

USS *New Jersey* (BB-62), U.S. **Navy** warship commissioned in 1943 as the second **Iowa**-class battleship. *New Jersey* was sent directly to the war in the Pacific and saw action throughout the area over the next two years. She participated in the assault on Korea in 1950 and saw two tours of duty shelling enemy targets in Vietnam with her nine 16-inch guns. She also saw action in the Middle East crisis of 1991. The veteran warrior was retired from the navy and towed to Camden, New Jersey, where she is being refitted as a museum ship in the Delaware River.

USS *New Mexico* (BB-40), first of a class of three thirty-two-thousand-ton battleships with a main armament of twelve 14-inch guns. *New Mexico*—nicknamed "The Queen" by her crew—was completed in 1918 and modernized in 1936. Sister ship to USS *Mis-sissippi* and USS *Idaho*, she spent World War II fighting in the Pacific and earned six battle stars for her service. In 1945 the 624-foot vessel was hit by two **kamikazes**, losing 54 men with another 119 wounded. She was decommissioned in 1946 and scrapped the following year.

***New Orleans*, side-wheel steamboat** built in Pittsburgh, Pennsylvania, in 1808, and owned by **Robert Fulton** and **Nicholas J. Roosevelt**. In 1811 *New Orleans* inaugurated steamboat service on the **Western rivers** by traveling down the Ohio River and the **Mississippi River** from Pittsburgh to New Orleans—becoming the first steamboat to call at the Port of New Orleans. The *New Orleans* was limited, lacking power to return upriver against the current. When more powerful engines came on the scene, her engine was removed to power a sawmill on land.

New Orleans, Battle of, bloody battle of the **War of 1812** that was fought from December 1814 to January 1815. The **Treaty of Ghent** had already ended hostilities, but word had not reached either party. The British fleet overpowered American warships in the **Mississippi River** and landed about six thousand troops in New Orleans. General Andrew Jackson defended the city, successfully driving the British back to their ships, with more than 2,200 British killed, wounded, or taken prisoner. The U.S. force lost 45 men.

Newport News Shipbuilding, shipyard founded in Newport News, Virginia, in 1886 by railroad magnate Collis P. Huntington to repair ships servicing his transportation hub. The company grew along with the U.S. **Navy** and soon specialized in battleships and aircraft carriers. During World War II, the yard employed some fifty thousand workers. In the postwar years, the yard survived on conversion and repair work and launched the **liner** SS *United States* in 1952. In 1960 it completed USS *Enterprise*, the first nuclear-powered aircraft carrier. The company was purchased by Tenneco Corporation in 1968 and was spun off in 1996.

New Providence, port city in the Bahamas, later renamed Nassau, that served as a base for pirates from the 1680s to the 1720s.

USS *New York* (BB-34), twenty-seven-thousand-ton battleship, sister ship to USS *Texas*. Completed in 1914 and extensively modernized in 1934, she participated mostly in the Atlantic theater during World War II, where she provided gunfire support for the 1944 **Normandy Invasion** with her ten 14-inch guns. She was transferred to the Pacific in time to see action at **Iwo Jima** and during the **Okinawa Invasion**. She was decommissioned in 1946 and taken to the **Bikini Atoll** for observation testing during the atomic detonations, which she survived. The still badly contaminated 573-foot hulk was then towed back to **Pearl Harbor** for study and was finally taken out to sea and sunk in 1948 as a floating target.

New York Yacht Club, America's oldest yacht club, founded on July 30, 1844, aboard **John Cox Stevens**'s **schooner *Gimcrack*** while anchored off New York City's Battery. In 1846 the first clubhouse was built on land donated by Commodore Stevens at the family estate in Hoboken, New Jersey. It served as the center of club activities for twenty-three years, following which the club moved to Staten Island and then Manhattan. In 1901 a permanent clubhouse was constructed at 37 West Forty-Fourth Street on land donated by then-commodore **John Pierpont "J. P." Morgan**. In 1988 the club opened an annex in Newport, Rhode Island. The club held the **America's Cup** for 132 years, successfully defending it twenty-five times.

New Zealand, 133-foot **sloop** that in September 1988 challenged for and lost the **America's Cup** to **Dennis Connor**'s sixty-foot **catamaran** *Stars & Stripes*. *New Zealand* owner Michael

Fay petitioned the courts to have the victory overturned, but after a series of legal wranglings, the New York Court of Appeals, in April 1990, declared *Stars & Stripes* the winner.

Next to No Time, entertaining 1958 English feature film shot onboard RMS *Queen Elizabeth* about a man who discovers himself on an Atlantic crossing. It starred Kenneth Moore and Betsy Drake.

Niagara, U.S. **brig** that was the relief **flagship** of Commodore **Oliver Hazard Perry** at the Battle of **Lake Erie** on September 10, 1813. After his flagship *Lawrence* was disabled, Perry transferred his command to the *Niagara* and hoisted his battle flag, which was inscribed with the motto **"Don't Give up the Ship"** (the dying words of **James Lawrence**, the ship's namesake, earlier that year). Following the battle, Perry sent his classic message of victory: **"We have met the enemy and they are ours."** A replica of *Niagara* was launched in 1988 and was commissioned in 1990 as the Flagship of Pennsylvania. An active sailing vessel built by Melbourne Smith, she is based in Erie, Pennsylvania, and regularly tours the **Great Lakes** and puts out to sea to visit U.S. East Coast ports.

Nicholson, Charles E. (1868–1954), English naval architect and builder whose bold and innovative designs include the **America's Cup** challengers *Shamrock IV*, *Shamrock V*, *Endeavour*, and *Endeavour II*. Son of Ben Nicholson, founder of the yacht-building yard **Camper & Nicholson**, Charles brought the firm into worldwide acclaim.

SS *Nieuw Amsterdam*, 36,982-gross-ton passenger vessel regarded by many to be the most perfectly proportioned ocean **liner** of all time. The **Holland America Line** liner was in many respects a scaled-down version of SS *Normandie*. Completed in 1938 for transatlantic service, the ship steamed five hundred thousand miles transporting four hundred thousand Allied personnel during World War II

The Dutch-registered *SS Nieuw Amsterdam*. (Courtesy Gordon R. Ghareeb)

before being returned to her owners in 1947. So beloved was the vessel that when her retirement was announced in the late 1960s, public sentiment in Holland led the owners to refit her for continued cruise service. She was finally scrapped in 1974.

The Nigger of Narcissus, 1897 novel generally regarded as **Joseph Conrad**'s first masterpiece. It is a challenging tale that chronicles the journey to self-understanding of the crew of the large merchant sailing vessel *Narcissus* during a **Cape Horn** voyage. Revolving around James Wait, a dying black sailor, it is perhaps the best portrait of a crew, and the best account of a passage, ever written.

A Night at the Opera, uproariously funny 1935 Marx Brothers movie set partly aboard a westbound transatlantic **liner**. The stateroom scene in which some thirty-two shipboard passengers and staff get stuffed into a two-berth cabin the size of a bathroom is one of the most hilarious comedy episodes ever put on film. In addition to Chico, Groucho, and Harpo, the classic motion picture also featured Kitty Carlisle, Margaret Dumont, and Allan Jones.

A Night to Remember, best-selling 1955 factual account by **Walter Lord** of the sinking of RMS *Titanic*. Regarded by many as the bible of the famous shipwreck, it was made into a technically excellent feature film in 1958 that starred Kenneth Moore. Some scenes were filmed in Southampton aboard the **liner** *Asturias*, before she was sent to the ship breakers later that year.

Nile, Battle of the, decisive **Royal Navy** victory over the French in the Mediterranean on August 1, 1798. The British fleet, commanded by **Horatio Nelson**, sailed into the harbor at Aboukir Bay, east of Alexandria, Egypt, and destroyed the French fleet, cutting off **Napoleon I**'s forces and leaving them to be defeated by the British army. The French **flagship** *L'Orient* exploded toward the end of the engagement, an incident immortalized in the

Chester W.
Nimitz. (U.S.
Naval Academy
Nimitz Library)

poem "Casabianca" by Felicia Hemans. Memorized by generations of British schoolchildren, the poem celebrates the heroism of the French captain's ten-year-old son, who refused to leave his station "on the burning deck, whence all but he had fled." He refused to leave his post unless so ordered by his father, but his father had already been killed. The boy died at his post.

Nimitz, Chester W. (1885–1966), American naval officer, World War II fleet admiral, and **chief of naval operations**. Following the Japanese attack on **Pearl Harbor**, President **Franklin D. Roosevelt** sent a message to Secretary of the Navy Frank Knox stating, "Tell Nimitz to get the hell to Pearl and stay there until the war is won." Nimitz assumed command of the Pacific fleet in December 1941 and four years later signed the Japanese surrender as the commander in chief of the largest naval force ever assembled. He served as chief of naval operations from 1945 to 1947.

USS *Nimitz* (CVAN-68), lead ship of three 1,089-foot, nuclear-powered aircraft carriers. Her sisters are USS *Dwight D. Eisenhower* and USS *Carl Vinson*. Completed in 1975, the 91,487-ton ship is capable of speeds well over thirty **knots**. In 1981 the crash landing of an aircraft on her deck resulted in the deployment of a Sea Sparrow missile that left fourteen crew members dead and thirty-nine wounded, and twelve planes destroyed or damaged.

Niña, seventy-foot **caravel** that, along with the *Santa Maria* and the *Pinta*, was one of the ships in **Christopher Columbus**'s first voyage of discovery that reached the New World in 1492. After the *Santa Maria* wrecked on a coral reef, the *Niña* became Columbus's **flagship**.

Niña, one of the favorite and most successful ocean-racing yachts ever. The fifty-nine-foot **staysail schooner** was designed by **W. Starling Burgess** and built (and named) for the 1928

transatlantic race to Spain. After winning that race on her **maiden voyage**, she went on to capture the 1928 **Fastnet Race**. *Niña* was purchased in 1935 by New York banker DeCoursey Fales and served as the **flagship** of the **New York Yacht Club**. She went on to win many races, including the 1962 **Bermuda Race**. Always beautifully maintained and seemingly immortal, *Niña* became a training vessel at the U.S. **Merchant Marine Academy** and later went into charter work, based in Antigua—a sad comedown for one of the immortals of the oceangoing world.

The Ninety and Nine, 1966 best-selling novel by **William Brinkley** about a landing ship and the amphibious invasion of Italy during World War II.

Nippon Yusen Kaisha (NYK Line), Japanese shipping house formed in 1885 to provide short-distance transport service between Japan, China, and the Philippines. Overseas passenger and cargo routes were extended to Seattle in 1896 and to San Francisco two years later. The firm eventually became a global operation, with service to North America, Europe, Asia, and Australia. The company resumed service after World War II with thirty-seven vessels and built the line up to be one of the world's largest.

Nitta Maru, Japanese passenger **liner** completed in 1940. Although she was intended for the service from Japan to Germany along with her sister the *Yawata Maru*, both ships were installed between Yokohama and San Francisco and Los Angeles due to the war in Europe. The 17,150-gross-ton *Nitta Maru* established the fastest crossing of the Pacific in 1941, just prior to her requisitioning by the Japanese navy for conversion into an escort aircraft carrier. She entered the Pacific War in 1942 as the *Chuyo* and was sunk by the submarine USS *Sailfish* the following year.

NOAA, see **National Oceanic and Atmospheric Administration**.

Noah's ark, according to the Bible (Genesis 6–9), a 450-foot ship built by Noah, the only righteous, God-fearing man of his time. Instructed by God, Noah took into the ark his family and enough birds and animals to repopulate the earth. After the rain poured for forty days and forty nights, the ark came to rest on Mount Ararat (in modern-day Turkey). Noah and the animals then left the ark to begin a new life.

Non-Intercourse Act, act signed by President **Thomas Jefferson** on March 1, 1809, that closed U.S. ports to France and England and outlawed their imports. The action was in retaliation for British and French interference with American commerce at sea. It was a modification of the **Embargo Act** passed by Congress in 1807, which prohibited all non-U.S.-flag ships from entering or leaving American ports.

Non-Vessel Operating Common Carrier (NVOCC), a cargo consolidator in ocean trades who buys space from a carrier and subsells it to smaller shippers. Although an NVOCC conducts itself as an ocean common carrier, it does not operate the vessel.

no quarter given, a saying from pirate times that meant that no mercy would be granted to a foe who surrendered. See also **Jolly Roger**.

Nordhoff, Charles Bernard (1887–1947), American adventurer and author who collaborated with **James Norman Hall** on a trilogy of books about the **Mutiny on the *Bounty***. In addition to publishing several books in collaboration with Hall as **Nordhoff and Hall**, he separately wrote *The Derelict* (1928). He was the son of Charles Nordhoff (1830–1901), author of *Man-of-War Life* (1895), *The Merchant Vessel* (1895), and *Whaling and Fishing* (1895).

Nordhoff and Hall, team of American authors —**Charles Bernard Nordhoff** and **James Norman Hall**—who collaborated on a number of important books, including three novels about the **Mutiny on the *Bounty*** of 1789. The trilogy includes *Mutiny on the Bounty* (1932), *Men against the Sea* (1934), and *Pitcairn's Island* (1934). The two met while serving as pilots in the Lafayette Escadrille, a French and American air squadron, during World War I. In 1920, Nordhoff and Hall sailed for Tahiti, where they lived for many years. The team also wrote *The Hurricane* (1936); *No More Gas* (1940), which was made into the film *The Tuttles of Tahiti*; and *Botany Bay* (1941), as well as a number of individual works.

Norfolk Island, fourteen-square-mile island lying in the South Pacific Ocean about a thousand miles northeast of Sydney, Australia. Many of the island's inhabitants are descendants of the mutineers of HMS *Bounty* who settled on **Pitcairn Island** in 1790. In 1856, 194 of their descendants moved to Norfolk Island, but the original settlement remains today.

Norgoma, the last overnight passenger vessel built for operation on Lake Huron and Lake Superior. Completed in 1950, the ship had cabin accommodation for a hundred passengers on her circuitous five-day schedule. Relegated to purely a car ferry in 1963, the craft was brought to Sault Sainte Marie, Ontario, in 1975 to be restored as a museum ship of Ontario's maritime heritage.

SS *Normandie*, 83,423-gross-ton vessel that is considered the most extravagant and lavishly decorated ocean **liner** of all time. She captured the **Blue Riband** from the *Rex* on her 1935 **maiden voyage**, with an average speed of 29.98 **knots** for the **Atlantic** crossing. She passed that honor back and forth with RMS *Queen Mary* until finally losing it to her British rival for good in 1938. *Normandie* was seized from

SS *Normandie*. (Courtesy Gordon R. Ghareeb)

the **French Line** and renamed *Lafayette* upon U.S. entry into World War II. The floating art-deco palace caught fire while being refitted as a troopship in New York City on February 9, 1942, and capsized the following day. Her salvage did not warrant rebuilding, and the hulk was scrapped in New Jersey in 1946.

Invasion of Normandy, Allied amphibious landings on the German-occupied beaches of northern France that began on **D-Day,** June 6, 1944. In the largest seaborne invasion in history, four thousand ships forged across the English Channel to unleash 176,000 combined Allied troops against the German army, thereby launching the Allied drive that liberated France in 1944 and led to the fall of Germany on May 8, 1945.

Noronic, 6,905-gross-ton steamer belonging to the Northern Navigation Company of Canada that was completed in 1914 for overnight passenger service on the **Great Lakes**. She maintained regular service between Sarnia, Detroit, Duluth, and Thunder Bay in addition to special extended cruises. The palatial **liner** caught fire while dockside in Toronto in 1949, taking 119 lives.

Norske Veritas, see at **Det Norske Veritas** (DNV).

North African Invasion, amphibious assault against French-held North African ports on both the **Atlantic** and Mediterranean coasts, carried out November 8–10, 1949, by the U.S. and British navies. During the assault, forty-nine thousand American and twenty-three thousand British troops were put ashore, launching a drive that cleared Africa of all Axis troops the following year.

North American Yacht Racing Union (NAYRU), see **U.S. Sailing Association.**

USS *North Carolina* (BB-55), 35,000-ton battleship—nicknamed The Showboat—completed

USS *North Carolina*. (USS North Carolina Museum, Wilmington, North Carolina)

for service in 1941. Earning fifteen battle stars for action in every Pacific campaign after **Guadalcanal**, the 728-foot-long vessel became the most decorated battleship of World War II. She was put into the **mothball fleet** following her decommissioning in 1947 and was rescued from the scrapyard by public subscription, which raised over $325,000 in 1960 to install her at Wilmington, North Carolina, as a museum ship and national historic landmark.

Northeast Passage, water route between the **Atlantic** and Pacific Oceans along the northern reaches of Europe and Russia. While not potentially as lucrative as finding a **Northwest** **Passage** would have been, this route attracted many voyages of exploration. It was first fully transited in 1878–79 by Nils Nordenskjöld (1832–1901) of Sweden, but it took the development of modern steamers to make the route commercially feasible. In the 1930s, a Northern Sea Route was established by the Soviet Union and has since been made navigable seasonally by Russian icebreakers. Used mostly by Russian shipping, it cuts the distance between Russian Atlantic and Pacific ports in half.

North German Lloyd (Norddeutscher Lloyd), German **steamship** company founded in 1857 to provide shipping service between Bremen and

New York. It operated the **liners** *Kaiser Wilhelm der Grosse*, *Bremen*, and *Europa*, among others. In 1939 the line was ordered by Adolf Hitler to carry out a very poorly booked South American cruise because the Führer wanted proof that the *Bremen* could actually pass through the **Panama Canal** if the military need arose. In 1970 the line merged with the **Hamburg-America Line** to form the **HAPAG-Lloyd**.

North River Steam Boat, also known as the *Clermont*, Robert Fulton's 150-foot **steamboat** that in 1807 carried forty passengers up the **Hudson River** from New York City to Albany, inaugurating commercial steamboat service in the United States.

North Star, first American steam yacht of great size, built for **Cornelius Vanderbilt** in 1853. Constructed of oak and rigged as a **brigantine**, the 270-foot **paddle wheeler** cost about $90,000. On her **maiden voyage**, she crossed the **Atlantic** in ten days, with the Vanderbilt family aboard to meet with the Russian imperial family. Upon her return, *North Star* was converted to a passenger ship.

Northwest Passage, water route between the **Atlantic** and Pacific Oceans along the northern reaches of Canada and Alaska. Discovery of a passage to Asia drove many voyages of exploration, including those of Sir **Martin Frobisher** and **Henry Hudson**, and the ill-fated **Franklin Expedition**. Existence of the Northwest Passage was confirmed in the 1850s, but it was not until 1903–6 that **Roald Amundsen**, aboard *Gjøa*, became the first to successfully transit the passage. In the 1960s, oil was discovered in North Alaska, and in 1969 the **supertanker** SS *Manhattan* became the first commercial ship to transverse the Northwest Passage.

Norway, successful cruise ship of **Norwegian Cruise Line** converted in 1980 from the famous ocean **liner** SS *France* of 1962. Her gross tonnage increased to 76,049 in 1990 with the addition of two new decks to the top of the existing superstructure, which increased her profitability at some cost to her classic appearance.

Norwegian America Line, shipping firm started in 1910 to establish a Norse transatlantic service to New York from Oslo. Vessel nomenclature follows names of well-known Norwegian fjords. The passenger division, including the *Sagafjord* and the *Vistafjord*, were sold in 1983 to Trafalgar Investments for assimilation into their **Cunard Line** fleet.

Norwegian Cruise Line (NCL), cruise company founded in 1966 by Knut Kloster and Ted Arison as the Norwegian Caribbean Line to create casual, one-class cruising in the Caribbean. Operations started with the *Sunward* on short-cruise service out of Miami, and Arison went on to found **Carnival Cruise Lines**. The NCL fleet continued to increase, and the *Norway* was added in 1980.

Nothing Sacred, 1937 motion picture about a small-town girl who gets caught up in a big-city publicity stunt. The film, starring Frederick March and Carol Lombard—some say in her finest performance—featured fine footage of **six-meters** sailing in New York. It was remade in 1954 as *Living It Up.*

Notice to Mariners (NTM), weekly publication of the U.S. government that provides timely marine safety information for the correction of all government-issued navigation charts and publications. NTMs should be used to update charts and related publications.

Novaya Zemlya, glacier-covered Russian **archipelago** in the Arctic Ocean that separates the **Barents Sea** from the Kara Sea. The name means "new land."

Novorossik, Soviet warship that mysteriously exploded in October 1955 in Sevastopol, killing some fifteen hundred sailors.

Now, Voyager, tearjerker 1942 motion picture classic about a repressed young Boston matron who blossoms and finds romance on a cruise to South America. It contains some excellent footage of the *Empress of Britain*, and the sets convey the realistic feel of a luxury cruise vessel. The movie starred Bette Davis and Paul Henreid.

Noyes, Alfred (1880–1958), popular English poet who filled his poems with colorful images of the sea and sea voyages. His epic poem "Drake" (1908) is about the famous English sea captain Sir **Francis Drake**. Other poems of his include "Tales of the Mermaid Tavern" (1913) and "Forty Singing Seamen." His best-known poem, "The Torch Bearers" (1922–30), is a trilogy in verse of man's scientific accomplishments. From 1914 to 1923, Noyes was a professor at Princeton University.

NROTC, see **Naval Reserve Officers' Training Corps.**

Nuestra Señora de Atocha, Spanish treasure **galleon** that sank in a hurricane off the Florida Keys in 1622 while returning to Spain from the New World. Of the 265 people on board, only 5 survived. Down with the ship went 900 silver bars, 161 gold bars or discs, and 255,000 silver coins. The wreckage was discovered by **Mel Fisher** in the early 1970s.

Nutting, William Washburn (1884–1924), American sailor, nautical journalist, and editor, and founder of the **Cruising Club of America**. His *Track of the Typhoon* (1922) is the story of his **ketch** *Typhoon* and her seven-thousand-mile **maiden voyage**. Nutting was lost at sea when *Typhoon* went down with all hands off Greenland in 1924.

NVOCC, see **Non-Vessel Operating Common Carrier.**

NYK Line, see **Nippon Yusen Kaisha.**

O

O'Brian, Patrick (1914–2000), English author and writer of the series of twenty **Aubrey-Maturin** novels, among other works. Born Patrick Russ, he adopted his new name sometime after World War II. He achieved international fame late in life with the widespread popularity of the Aubrey-Maturin series, which he continued to produce until his death. The *New York Times Book Review* called O'Brian's books "the greatest historical novels ever written."

O'Brien, Conor (1880–1952), Irish sailor and author. In his forty-two-foot **ketch**, *Saoirse*, he was the first yachtsman to circumnavigate the world (1922–25) by going south of **Cape Horn**, **Cape of Good Hope**, and **Cape Leeuwin**. He wrote *Across Three Oceans* (1927) about the voyage.

Observor Singlehanded Transatlantic Race (OSTAR), solo sailing race run from Plymouth, England, to Newport, Rhode Island. The race has been run every four years, in the Olympic year, since 1960, and until 1980 it was sponsored by Britain's *Observor* newspaper. The inaugural race was won in forty days by Sir **Francis Charles Chichester** in *Gipsy Moth III* against four other competitors.

"O Captain! My Captain!", popular three-stanza poem by **Walt Whitman** that is an elegy for President **Abraham Lincoln**. First published in 1865, the poem portrays Lincoln as the captain of the **ship of state**. The ship (the Union) successfully finishes its voyage (is victorious in the Civil War), but the captain dies.

Ocean Cruising Club, sailing organization formed in Britain in 1954, which ruled that members must accomplish an offshore passage in a boat no longer than seventy feet over a distance of not less than one thousand miles.

Ocean Drilling Program (ODP), international partnership in geological oceanography researching the history of the ocean basins and the nature of the crust beneath the ocean floor. Operated by Texas A&M University in College Station, Texas, ODP is sponsored by the U.S. National Science Foundation and more than twenty countries.

Patrick O'Brian, circa 1995. (W. W. Norton; photo by Cheryl Clegg)

Oceania, the islands of the Pacific and adjacent seas that comprise Polynesia, Micronesia, and Melanesia.

Oceanic, intended name of a sixty-thousand-gross-ton motor **liner** laid down for the **White Star Line** in 1928. If built, it would have entered service as the first one-thousand-foot ocean liner. The project was abandoned due to the Great Depression, and the ship's steel went into the line's smaller *Britannic* and *Georgic*, which were less than half her size. What had already been built of the *Oceanic*'s hull was broken up on the stocks.

Oceanic Steam Navigation Company Limited, the original name for the **White Star Line** when founded in 1867 by Thomas Ismay, father of **Bruce Ismay**.

Oceanos, in Greek mythology, a river that flowed around the world.

Oceanos, Greek cruise ship of the **Epirotiki Line**. Built in 1951 as the French *Jean Laborde*, the 7,554-gross-ton ship was acquired by Epirotiki in 1974. While on a cruise in 1991 from South Africa, with 571 people aboard, the vessel began taking on water in the engine room after a machinery explosion tore a hole in the ship's side. When the situation became serious, the captain was one of the first to leave the ship, to, as he put it, "direct the rescue operation from the shore." Fourteen South African Air Force helicopters lifted all passengers and crew to safety, and the *Oceanos* sank as the last straggler was being taken off.

ocean station, strategic employment of U.S. **Navy** and U.S. **Coast Guard** ships along major air and shipping routes in the mid-**Atlantic** and mid-Pacific Oceans to provide navigation, communications, meteorological, oceanographic, and search-and-rescue services. An ocean station was often referred to as a weather station. One ship was assigned to a two-hundred-square-mile block area that had a letter designation. By the mid-1970s, technology had eliminated the need for ocean stations, and the last ocean station patrol ended in 1977.

octant, see **Hadley's quadrant**.

Odessa, Ukrainean seaport lying on the **Black Sea**, near the Romanian border. An important industrial center as well as a strategic port and important transfer point for rail and ocean transportation, the city is also known for its health resorts.

ODS, see **operating differential subsidy**.

Odysseus, Greek hero in the Trojan War—prompted by the abduction of **Helen of Troy**—who helped bring about the fall of Troy by conceiving of and constructing the Trojan Horse. After the war he voyaged for ten years trying to return home and had many adventures along the way, including encountering the Lotus-Eaters, the **Sirens**, and **Scylla and Charybdis**. His journey is chronicled in **Homer**'s *Odyssey*.

Odyssey, Greek epic poem by **Homer** that is a sequel to the *Iliad*. **Odysseus** and his men experience many adventures on the wine-dark sea on their return from the Trojan War.

officer of the deck (OOD), aboard U.S. **Navy** and **Coast Guard** ships, a watch officer designated by the commanding officer to be in charge of the ship, including its safe navigation and general operation.

off soundings, navigating beyond the one-hundred-**fathom** curve. In early times, it referred to water deeper than could be sounded with a six-hundred-foot **lead line**.

USS *Ohio* (SSN-726), nuclear-powered ballistic missile submarine that gave her name to a class of eighteen sister ships. The 18,750-ton craft was commissioned in 1981 and carries forty-eight Trident missiles and forty-eight **torpedoes**. The 560-foot ship is driven by two steam turbines, which are capable of running the submerged vessel at speeds well above twenty **knots**.

Oil Pollution Act of 1990, environmental legislation approved by the U.S. Congress in 1990 to prevent oil spills in U.S. waters. A direct result of the *Exxon Valdez* shipwreck, the act extended the authority of the U.S. **Coast Guard** regarding its oversight of tankers and tanker personnel, and it mandated double-hulled tankers by 2015.

Okinawa Invasion, amphibious landing of U.S. forces on the Japanese home islands during World War II. During the invasion, which lasted from April 1 to June 21, 1945, more than 150,000 Okinawans, mostly civilians, were massacred by Japanese forces. The United States suffered 35,000 wounded and 1,200 dead. Japanese losses numbered nearly 60,000. The U.S. **Navy** lost five ships to **kamikazes**, while four more were damaged beyond repair.

USS *Oklahoma* (BB-37), second and final unit of the **Nevada**-class battleships. The 27,500-ton ship was completed in 1916 and modernized in 1936. Lying in **Battleship Row** on the morning of December 7, 1941, *Oklahoma* was hit by five Japanese torpedoes and capsized quickly in the waters of **Pearl Harbor**, with a loss of 415 men and 32 wounded. An additional 32 men managed to survive for days inside her upturned hull and were rescued by cutting out sections of the shell plating for their escape. In one of the most formidable **salvage** jobs of all time, the ship was righted and sent to Oakland. She sank while being towed to the California port in 1947.

Old Bay Line, nickname of the Baltimore Steam Packet Company, the venerable Chesapeake Bay **steamship** line that provided overnight **packet** service aboard fast and luxurious steamers between Baltimore and Norfolk from 1839 to 1962. Among Old Bay Line's many famous vessels was the *President Warfield*, later renamed *Exodus 1947*.

Old Ironsides, nickname given to USS *Constitution* during her engagement with HMS *Guerrière* on August 19, 1812. While six hundred miles east of Boston, *Constitution*, under **Isaac Hull**, defeated *Guerrière* in a short battle. During the battle, a cannonball bounced off the side of *Constitution*, prompting one sailor to exclaim that her sides were made of iron. In fact, her great strength came from live-oak frames set initially solid behind white-oak plankings.

"Old Ironsides", 1830 poem by then–college student **Oliver Wendell Holmes** that was written in protest against the proposed scrapping of the **frigate** USS *Constitution*. First printed in the *Boston Daily Advertiser*, it began: "Ay, tear her tattered ensign down! Long has it waved on high / And many an eye has danced to see, That banner in the sky." The poem generated public sentiment and was instrumental in saving the ship.

Old Ironsides, historically accurate 1926 silent film about the **frigate** USS *Constitution* during the **Barbary Wars** that includes some fictional exploits of **Stephen Decatur**. The adventure starred Esther Ralston, Wallace Beery, and Boris Karloff.

The Old Man and the Sea, short 1952 novel by **Ernest Hemingway** about a lonely and wise old Cuban fisherman, Santiago, who befriends a boy, Manolin. The old man catches a marlin, the largest fish ever caught in the Gulf of Mexico, and battles the elements and a mako shark in his attempt to secure the fish. He endures the heartbreaking loss of the fish but rises gallantly above his defeat. A Hollywood film with the same title was released in 1958, with Spencer Tracy in the title role.

Old Man of the Sea, monster encountered by **Sinbad the Sailor** in the *Arabian Nights*. It managed to fasten itself upon the sailor's shoulders so firmly that it could not be dislodged by the utmost efforts of its unfortunate

RMS *Olympic* entering New York Harbor. (Courtesy Gordon R. Ghareeb)

victim. After carrying it about for a long time, Sinbad at last succeeded in intoxicating it and effecting his escape. The phrase "Old Man of the Sea" is also used to describe **Proteus**.

Old Town Canoe Company, world's largest manufacturer of canoes and kayaks, which was founded in 1898 in Old Town, Maine. In 1974 the company was purchased by S. C. Johnson Wax, now Johnson Worldwide Associates.

USS *Oliver Hazard Perry* (FFG-7), namesake ship of a class of fifty-five gas turbine–powered guided missile **frigates**, named for Commodore and **War of 1812** hero **Oliver Hazard Perry**. The 3,638-ton ship was completed in 1977 and remained in active duty for twenty years until **laid up** in the Mayport, Florida, reserve fleet in 1997.

USS *Olympia* (C-6), 344-foot protected **cruiser**, launched in 1892, that served as **flagship** of the Asia Squadron and was the American flagship at the Battle of **Manila Bay**. She carried Commodore **George Dewey** into the battle that inspired his famous statement, **"You may fire when you are ready, Captain Gridley."** She saw further service during World War I and brought home the remains of the Unknown Soldier in 1921 for reinterment at Arlington National Cemetery. Retired from active duty in 1922, the ship is now a national historic landmark at Philadelphia's Independence Seaport Museum on the Delaware River. She is the oldest surviving steel-hulled U.S. naval vessel.

RMS *Olympic*, magnificent 45,324-gross-ton steamer of the **White Star Line** that was completed in 1911 as the first of a series of three particularly large and spacious **liners** for the Southampton to New York service. The other two, RMS *Titanic* of 1912 and RMS *Britannic* of 1915 never completed a voyage for the owners. *Olympic* earned the nickname Old Reliable as a result of her service in World War I as well as to remove her from the shadow of her unlucky sisters. The liner rammed the **Nantucket** lightship during a thick fog in 1934, with the loss of all seven men stationed there. *Olympic* was scrapped in 1935.

O'Malley, Grace (1530–1603), Irish seafarer and female pirate known as the Queen of the Irish Seas. Leading a band of some two hundred men and twenty ships, she was the scourge of English shipping. Twice widowed and imprisoned, she was pardoned by Queen Elizabeth I after a meeting between the two.

OMC, manufacturer of outboard boat engines formed in 1929 as Outboard Motors Corporation, when three major firms of the time—**Evinrude**, Elto, and Lockwood—were purchased by the engine manufacturer Briggs & Stratton. The motors continued to be sold under their former names, and in 1936 Outboard Motors Corporation acquired the **Johnson** Outboard Company and changed its name to the Outboard Marine and Manufacturing Company. Still referred to as "OMC," the company began to sell engines under just the Evinrude and Johnson names.

Omega, the first worldwide radio navigation system. Established in the 1960s, it operated on a low-frequency band and was in service for twenty-six years. Eight transmitter stations—in Norway, Liberia, Hawai'i, North Dakota, La Reunion, Argentina, Australia, and Japan—sent out radio signals, which would be turned into lines of position. A ship's position was estimated to be at or near the point where the lines crossed.

Omoo, 1847 novel by **Herman Melville** that is a sequel to *Typee* (1846). Subtitled *A Narrative of Adventures in the South Seas*, *Omoo* is based on Melville's own experiences and tells of the narrator's participation in mutiny on board the Australian whaleship *Julia* and his subsequent South Pacific wanderings with the former ship's doctor.

Onassis, Aristotle Socrates (1906–1975), Greek shipowner and financier who became one of the world's wealthiest individuals. In the 1930s, at age twenty-five, he began creating a large fleet of tankers and freighters. He was related by marriage to fellow Greek shipowners Stavros Livanos and Stavros Niachos, and together they formed the most powerful shipping clan in the world. He was famous for his romance with opera star Maria Callas and his marriage to Jacqueline Kennedy.

one-design, organized class of identical boats with the sole purpose of racing. In theory, all the yachts in a one-design class should have the same sailing performance, and the race results should depend on the skills of the crew.

O'Neill, Eugene (1888–1953), American playwright who drew from his experience on the waterfront and as a seaman aboard merchant ships. He chose the sea and sea life as the subject matter for several dramas, and his one-act plays *Bound East for Cardiff* (1916), *The Long Voyage Home* (1917), *Moon of the Caribbees* (1918), and *In the Zone* (1919) were adapted to film as *The Long Voyage Home* (1940). Other notable plays with seafaring aspects include *Beyond the Horizon* (1920), *Anna Christie* (1921), and *The Hairy Ape* (1922), and ships and shipping were an ever present undertone in his classic *Mourning Becomes Electra* (1931).

one-off, custom-designed vessel of which only one is made.

One of Our Submarines, 1952 narrative by Edward Young about his service aboard a British World War II submarine with other **Royal Naval** Volunteer Reservists. It is considered one of the best accounts of submarine warfare.

One Way Passage, 1932 Warner Brothers motion picture about an ill-fated romance set aboard a San Francisco–bound luxury **liner**. Largely filmed on board the *Calawaii* at sea, it starred William Powell and Kay Francis. It was remade in 1940 as *'Till We Meet Again.*

Onionhead, 1958 comedy film that was an attempt to cash in on the hillbilly high jinks of *No Time for Sergeants*, but here in the guise of a novice **Coast Guard** cook. The film starred Andy Griffith, Joey Bishop, Walter Matthau, and Claude Atkins.

The Only Way to Cross, 1972 book by John Maxtone Graham that blends details of the big twentieth-century transatlantic **liners**, from RMS *Mauretania* to the **Queen Elizabeth 2**, with anecdotes of transatlantic travel and style.

Onrust, forty-foot vessel built in 1614 on the island that is now Manhattan by explorer **Adriaen Block** and his crew of Dutch sailors to replace their original vessel, *Tiger*, after it was lost by fire. Aboard *Onrust* Block explored the southern New England coast as north in the Connecticut River as Hartford, east to Block Island (which bears his name), Rhode Island, and on to **Cape Cod**. At Cape Cod, he caught another ship home, while *Onrust* remained behind for use in coastal trading.

on soundings, waters whose depth can be measured with a six-hundred-foot **lead line**, usually within the one-hundred-**fathom** curve.

On the Town, hit 1949 film version of the successful Broadway musical about three sailors who search for romance in New York City while on a one-day leave during World War II. The movie starred Gene Kelly and Frank Sinatra and was choreographed by Jerome Robbins. The Academy Award–winning musical score by Leonard Bernstein, Betty Comden, and Adolph Green featured "New York, New York," "On the Town," and "That's All There Is, Folks."

On the Waterfront, 1954 motion picture about the lives of **longshoremen** and their struggle against corrupt union leaders. It includes great footage of New York Harbor and the **liner** *Nieuw Amsterdam*. The critically acclaimed film was directed by Elia Kazan and starred Marlon Brando, Rod Steiger, Karl Malden, and Lee J. Cobb. Brando won an Academy Award for best actor, and Eva Marie Saint took home the same for best supporting actress. In all, the film garnered eight Oscars, including the award for best picture.

"The Open Boat", short story by author **Stephen Crane**. In January 1897, Crane sailed as a newspaper correspondent on the steamer *Commodore* to cover the Cuban insurrection against Spain. The steamer sank shortly after leaving Jacksonville, Florida. With three others (the captain, the oiler, and the cook), Crane (Billie) reached Daytona Beach in a ten-foot **dinghy** on the following morning. Crane's story was carried in the *New York Press* and was published as "The Open Boat" in *Scribner's Magazine* in June 1898.

operating differential subsidy (ODS), a direct cash government subsidy given to U.S. ship operators to bridge the gap between U.S. costs and the lower operating costs of foreign-flag ships. Established by the **Merchant Marine Act of 1936**, it was intended to decrease the cost and improve the competitiveness of the U.S. ocean shipping industry. Made available only to ships owned and crewed by U.S. citizens, ODS replaced ocean mail contracts or **mail subsidies**. Administered by the U.S. **Maritime Administration**, it is being phased out.

Operation Crossroads, code name for two atomic bomb tests carried out in July 1946 at the lagoon in the **Bikini Atoll** and witnessed by more than forty-two thousand people—mostly U.S. **Navy** enlisted sailors. Anchored in the lagoon were ninety-seven vessels comprising surplus American as well as captured Japanese and German naval ships. The vessels were loaded with fuel and ammunition to see how they would fare in a nuclear attack. They also had live animals tethered to their decks to test the damage done to living tissue. The two detonations—Able, dropped from a B-29, and Baker, activated from beneath a ship anchored in the lagoon—sent twenty-four ships to the bottom. The seventy-three others that remained afloat were hopelessly irradiated and were **scuttled** or towed to such ports as **Pearl Harbor**, Seattle, and San Francisco for further examination. A total of sixty-seven blasts were set off at Bikini Atoll before the process was stopped in 1958.

Operation Overlord, code name for the **D-Day** landings in **Normandy** on June 6, 1944, and the subsequent invasion of German-occupied Europe.

Operation Pacific, classic submarine movie extolling the human factors of the U.S. **Navy**'s "silent service" in action against the Japanese in World War II. The 1951 classic starred John Wayne (as Commander "Duke" Gifford; the nickname remained his for the rest of his life), Patricia Neal, and Ward Bond.

Operation Petticoat, 1959 motion picture comedy about a fictitious U.S. **Navy** submarine in the Pacific during World War II that gets painted pink because the minimal quantities of **"red lead"** and "haze gray" paint had to be mixed in order to cover the exterior of USS *Sea Tiger* adequately. Directed by Blake Edwards, the classic starred Cary Grant, Tony Curtis, and Dina Merrill. It was made into a television series that ran from 1977 to 1979 and starred John Astin and Jim Varney; also in the cast was Jamie Lee Curtis.

Operation Sail (OpSail), organization founded in 1961 by President **John F. Kennedy** to promote the use of **tall ships** as a cultural exchange and to teach the importance of the ship, the ocean, and waterways in American history. OpSail events have included tall ship parades at the 1964 World's Fair, the 1976 Bicentennial Celebration, the 1986 Statue of Liberty Centennial, the 1992 Columbus Quincentennial, and the 2000 Millennium Celebration.

opium trade, illegal trade that developed in the early 1800s in which British ships would smuggle opium from India into China in demand for payment in silver (the Chinese government had outlawed opium in 1729). The illegal trade was fueled by the growing British appetite for tea, silk, and porcelain; the fact that the Chinese purchased few goods in return and would only sell their products for silver; British concern over the trade imbalance and that large amounts of silver were leaving the country; and widespread Chinese addiction to opium.

Opium War, war waged between Great Britain against China after Chinese officials tried to stop the illegal **opium trade** by seizing twenty thousand chests of opium from British merchants in Guangzhou in March 1839. Britain easily won the war, which ended with the Treaty of Nanjing in 1842. Among other things, the treaty gave the Chinese island of Hong Kong to Britain and opened five Chinese ports to British, as well as other foreign, residence and trade.

Optimist, the most popular class of youth sailing boat in the world. Developed in the 1960s by Clark Mills, it is an eight-foot, hard-chined, daggerboard **pram** with a small cat-rigged sail, which gives the boat high stability, making it very resistant to capsizing.

ordinary seaman (OS), deck crew member in the **merchant marine** who is subordinate to an **able-bodied seaman** (AB). The OS is sometimes called an "apprentice AB."

USS Oregon (BB-3), American battleship commissioned in 1896—the first U.S. battleship constructed on the West Coast—that made a journey of fifteen thousand miles from Puget Sound around South America to Florida in eighty days in 1898. Her purpose was to engage the Spanish fleet on July 3 in the Battle of **Santiago** at the beginning of the **Spanish-American War**. She was struck from the U.S. Navy list in 1942 and scrapped in 1956.

Orient Line, renowned British shipping house that began in 1877 to maintain a regulated mail operation to Australia. The last ship built for the line was the *Oriana* in 1960. The company merged with the **P&O** that same year to form the P&O-Orient Line.

USS *Oriskany* (CVA-34), 888-foot aircraft carrier, completed in 1950, that saw action in both the Korean and Vietnam Wars. While the ship was stationed in the **Gulf of Tonkin** in 1966, a magnesium parachute flare accidentally ignited below the hangar deck and the resulting fire soon engulfed five decks, claiming the lives of forty-three crew members and injuring sixteen others. She was **laid up** in 1976 and finally sold for scrap in 1995.

Oscar, the international signal flag for the letter "O," which is hoisted for "man overboard." It is also the name of the shipboard dummy used for man overboard drills.

Oscar II, Swedish passenger **liner** that was chartered by automobile magnate Henry Ford in 1915 in a failed attempt to end World War I by a negotiated peace. Termed the Peace Ship, she carried Ford and about 170 other people to Europe at Ford's expense. The group, which lacked approval by the U.S. government, failed to persuade the warring nations to settle their differences, and Ford was widely ridiculed for his efforts.

Oseberg ship, Viking vessel found in a burial mound in southern Norway in 1904. Dating from about A.D. 800, the ship was reassembled in Oslo's Viking Ship Museum along with the **Gokstad ship**.

MS *Oslofjord*, motor **liner** built for the New York service of the **Norwegian America Line** in 1949. She also became very popular among U.S. passengers for her extensive cruise programs. She was chartered in 1969 to the **Costa Line**, who renamed her the *Fulvia* for further cruising. An engine room explosion while off the **Canary Islands** in 1970 resulted in her becoming engulfed in flames. She sank thirty-six hours later without loss of life

OSTAR, see **Observor Singlehanded Transatlantic Race**.

Outboard Marine Corporation, see **OMC**.

Outerbridge Reach, 1991 novel by Robert Stone (b. 1937). It was inspired by the bizarre saga of **Donald Crowhurst**.

outflagging, the practice of transferring a vessel's registry out of country. Also called "flight from flag," its primary movement has been to **flags of convenience** for financial reasons. Other reasons have included Prohibition (particularly for passenger vessels), wars, and conflicts.

Out to Sea, 1997 comedy about two mature men who enlist as "dance hosts" aboard a Caribbean cruise ship. The film includes outstanding footage, both inside and out, of the **liner** *Westerdam*. The all-star cast includes Jack Lemmon, Walter Matthau, Gloria DeHaven, Elaine Strich, Dyan Cannon, Hal Linden, Donald O'Connor, Brent Spiner, Rue McClanahan, and Edward Mulhare.

Outward Bound, international educational organization that provides challenging wilderness experiences as courses of study. These experiences include seafaring and are intended to contribute to the self-discovery and personal growth of the participants. The first school was founded in 1941 as a survival program for British sailors during World War II. Outward Bound has about thirty schools in more than fifteen countries, including seven in the United States.

Outward Bound, eerie but popular mid-1920s Broadway play by Sutton Vane that is set aboard an ocean **liner** at sea. The dark drama eventually reveals the speeding ship to be a seaborne purgatory and the passengers to be the recently deceased, who are awaiting their ultimate fate.

Overland Expedition, 1897–98 mission to rescue the crews of eight whaleships trapped in heavy ice near Point Barrow, Alaska. On December 15, 1897, a rescue party led by U.S. **Revenue Cutter Service** lieutenant David Jarvis was put ashore some two thousand miles from the position of the trapped whalers. On March 29, 1898, the Overland Expedition, herding more than 130 reindeer, reached the trapped fleet, whose crews, near death, had already resorted to violent and animalistic behavior. Jarvis won the respect of the men and organized them until summer, when additional assistance arrived and the trapped ships could set sail.

"The Owl and the Pussycat", 1846 children's poem by Edward Lear (1812–1888) in which the two title characters "went to sea / In a beautiful pea-green boat. / They took some honey, and plenty of money, / Wrapped up in a five-pound note."

$\mathcal{P}$

P&I club, association of shipowners formed to provide mutual **protection and indemnity** insurance.

P&O, the Peninsular & Oriental Steam Navigation Company, founded in 1837 to provide regular mail service from England to the Iberian Peninsula. Service was later extended to India, Singapore, Hong Kong, and Sydney. P&O expanded into passenger and cargo service and soon became an Imperial institution and the premier British shipping company. P&O vessels served in both world wars, and over the years the company merged with other shipping concerns. Today P&O is many entities, including the container line P&O Nedlloyd and P&O **Princess Cruises**.

P-2 transport, type of U.S. **Maritime Commission** troopship built between 1943 and 1952. The ships were built in Kearny, New Jersey; Alameda, California; and Camden, New Jersey. Most were converted to civilian use.

SS *Pacific*, 2,860-gross-ton wooden-hulled steamer of the **Collins Line**. Completed in 1850, the **paddle wheeler** sailed from Liverpool for New York on January 23, 1856, and disappeared without a trace. It was long suspected that she sank after colliding with an iceberg, taking all 141 passengers and 45 crew members with her. In 1990, her remains were positively identified on the seabed off Anglesey, less than a day's run outside Liverpool, in the Irish Sea. The cause of her loss is still unknown.

Pacific Far East Line, company founded in 1946 to carry cargo between California and Asia. It established passenger operations by running the ***Leilani*** for two years under the auspices of the Textron Corporation. The line bought the *Monterey* and *Mariposa* in 1971—when **Matson Line** divested itself of its passenger operations—and operated them until 1978.

Pacific Liner, 1939 American film drama about a passenger **liner**—the *Arcturus*—leaving Shanghai bound for America with a full load of passengers and a festering plague of cholera onboard. It starred Chester Morris, Victor McLaglen, Wendie Barrie, and Barry Fitzgerald.

Pacific Mail Steam Ship Company (PMSS), U.S. **steamship** company founded in New York in 1848 by **William Henry Aspinwall** to take advantage of **mail subsidies**. The company reaped enormous profits from the gold rush of 1849 and subsequent westward expansion. Working in conjunction with the Trans-Panama Railroad from 1855 (which Aspinwall underwrote), the two companies were among the most lucrative U.S. corporations of the period. The completion of the transcontinental railroad in 1869 provided strong competition, and the PMSS redirected its activities toward transpacific shipping, providing passenger and freight service from San Francisco to Hong Kong, via Honolulu and Yokohama. The line was sold to the **Grace Line** in 1916, and was sold again in 1925, to the **Dollar Line**, which would become **American President Lines**.

Pacific Princess, cruise **liner** completed in 1971 as the *Sea Venture* for the **Norwegian Cruise Line**. She was sold to **P&O** in 1974 and assigned to their **Princess Cruises** division the following year as the *Pacific Princess*. She had the good fortune to be picked by ABC Television as the setting for its weekly television series *The **Love Boat***. The unprecedented success of the show insured the future of the ship and the cruise industry. The 20,636-gross-ton motor liner was arrested by Greek authorities in 1998 when fifty-six pounds of heroine was found hidden on board.

packet, fast sailing vessel or **steamship** that engaged in regularly scheduled mail, cargo, or passenger service. Transatlantic packet service was a maritime innovation introduced by the **Black Ball Line**, with the first sailing in January 1818.

paddlebox, protective casing or box enclosing each paddle wheel of a **paddle wheeler**. At times, paddleboxes were ornately decorated, and they always included the vessel name. Port and **starboard** paddleboxes were joined on top by a part of the ship that became known as the "bridge."

Paddle-to-the-Sea, magnificent panoramic children's book by Holling C. Holling first published in 1941 and still in print. It vividly details in text and illustrations the journey of a little carved Indian canoe from the Canadian North to the **Atlantic Ocean** while imparting the maritime history and majesty of the **Great Lakes** along the way. The story is viewed by many as an allegory to the passage through life.

paddle wheeler, **steamboat** driven by a paddle wheel. The most common arrangement was two paddle wheels mounted one on either side of the hull. American riverboats frequently had a single sternwheel.

PADI, Professional Association of Diving Instructors, a dive training and certification organization formed in 1966 by John Cronin and Ralph Ericson.

Paine, Charles J. (1833–1916), U.S. Army general who led three successful **America's Cup** defense efforts for the **New York Yacht Club**. In 1885 Paine managed what became known as the first modern America's Cup defense syndicate when *Puritan* defeated the British challenger *Genesta*. Paine's *Mayflower* defeated *Galatea* in 1886, and his *Volunteer* defeated *Thistle* in 1887.

painted ports, alternate black and white rectangles painted in a band along the hulls of merchant sailing ships to resemble gunports. The practice was also known as **mask painting**.

painter, rope line in the bow of a boat used for towing or making fast.

Palmer, Nathaniel Brown (1799–1877), American sea captain who, at age twenty-one, was the first to record sighting of the continent of Antarctica. In 1820 Palmer was searching for new sealing grounds in the South Atlantic aboard the forty-seven-foot scouting **sloop** *Hero*. Pushing farther south, Palmer came in sight of land not shown on his chart. For several days, he sailed along the coast of the peninsula that today is known as **Palmer Land**. Palmer Station on Antarctica was named for him, and he was commemorated by the U.S. Postal Service in 1988 on a block of stamps along with Antartic explorers Lieutenant **Charles Wilkes, Richard Evelyn Byrd**, and **Lincoln Ellsworth**.

Palmer Land, long arm of Antarctica extending into the **Southern Ocean** that was sighted and recorded in 1820 by Captain **Nathaniel Brown Palmer**. It is located due south of **Cape Horn**. Palmer was on the Pacific Ocean side when he sighted land. One of the islands along the peninsula was named Stonington by Admiral **Richard Evelyn Byrd** to honor Palmer's hometown of Stonington, Connecticut.

Pamir, 275-foot, steel-hulled, four-masted **bark** built in 1905 and employed in the grain and nitrate trades between Germany, Chile, and Australia. Along with the *Peking*, *Pamir* was one of the Flying "P" Line of sailing ships built for the House of Laeisz, a Hamburg mercantile family, and culminating with the *Padua* in 1926. In 1955 the ship was converted into a German sail training vessel and in September 1957 was en route from Argentina to Germany with thirty-five crewmen and fifty-one cadets when she ran into a hurricane and sank five hundred miles southwest of the **Azores**. The American freighter *Saxon* found only six survivors.

USS *Pampanito* (SS-383), Balao-class submarine completed in 1943. During her tour of duty in the South Pacific during World War II, the 311-foot vessel was responsible for sinking 27,332 tons of Japanese shipping. Decommissioned following the war, the 1,525-ton craft was presented to the San Francisco Mari-

time Museum Association in 1996 and is a museum ship at San Francisco's Pier 45.

U.S. postage stamp issued on the twenty-fifth anniversary of the opening of the Panama Canal.

pan, prefix for a priority marine radio communication that reports a priority situation requiring assistance. Repeated three times, it is less urgent than **mayday** but more urgent than a **securité** safety message.

Panama Canal, man-made waterway linking the **Atlantic** and Pacific Oceans. It extends across the Isthmus of Panama from Limon Bay on the Atlantic to the Bay of Panama on the Pacific, a distance of about fifty-one miles. Ships are raised and lowered eighty-five feet by a system of locks. The busiest canal in the world, it reduces the sea route between New York City and San Francisco by more than nine thousand miles. Construction on the waterway was started in 1881 by the French under **Ferdinand de Lesseps** but was abandoned. The United States resumed the construction in 1904, during **Theodore Roosevelt**'s presidency, and completed it in 1914. The opening of the canal had a profound effect on global trade patterns and world naval strategy. It played a vital role during World War II by enabling U.S. forces to move quickly and easily between the Atlantic and Pacific theaters. The waterway was remanded to Panama on December 31, 1999.

Panamax, short for "Panama Canal maximum," the maximum size of vessel, due to its length, beam, and draft, that can transit the **Panama Canal**. The dimensions of a Panamax vessel are 970 feet long, 105 feet wide, and 39 feet deep.

USS *Panay* (PR-5), U.S. **Navy** gunboat built in China in 1928 to protect U.S. interests during the Chinese civil war. The vessel was sunk in the **Yangtze River** near Nanking, China, by Japanese aircraft on December 12, 1937. Two Americans were killed, and the incident sparked a crisis in U.S.-Japanese relations. Japan claimed the attack was accidental and offered an apology, which the United States accepted.

HMS *Pandora*, Royal Navy frigate dispatched by the **Admiralty** in 1790 to apprehend the mutineers of HMS *Bounty*. Fourteen mutineers were captured at Tahiti and kept in chains in "Pandora's Box," a roundhouse on deck. Continuing her search for **Fletcher Christian** and *Bounty*, *Pandora* ran aground on a reef in August 1791. Thirty-one crew members and four mutineers drowned.

Pansing, Frederick (1844–1910), German-born marine artist who went to sea at age sixteen and later emigrated to America. A contemporary of artists **Antonio Jacobsen**, **James Buttersworth**, and **Frederick Cozzens**, he is best known for his fine paintings of passenger **liners**.

Paris, magnificent three-**funneled** passenger steamer of the **French Line** completed in 1921 after eight years of construction that was held up because of World War I. Following a fire on board in 1929, her splendid art-nouveau interiors were rebuilt in art-deco style to bring her in line with her larger running mate, the *Île de France*. *Paris* burned and capsized at her **Le Havre** pier in 1939, and the outbreak of World War II made **salvage** impossible.

Parkinson, C. Northcote (1909–1993), British scholar and author of well-known novels revolving around **Richard Delancey**, a fictional **Royal Navy** officer in the **Napoleonic Wars**. Parkinson's tongue-in-cheek story *Life and Times of Horatio Hornblower* (1970) is a history of **C. S. Forester**'s fictitious **Hornblower** and his family. He also wrote the nonfiction *Short History of the Royal Navy, 1776–1816*, and he is best known for his proverb, published in *Parkinson's Law* (1957), "Work expands so as to fill the time available for its completion."

passenger vessel, according to U.S. **Coast Guard** regulations, any vessel carrying passengers for hire.

Passenger Vessel Services Act (PVSA), U.S. legislation passed in 1886 that reserves the transportation of passengers directly between U.S. ports for vessels built in the United States, registered and crewed by U.S. citizens, and owned and operated by companies whose majority of stockholders consists of U.S. citizens. Similar statutes for the transportation of cargo were approved in the **Merchant Marine Act of 1920** and its amendments, popularly known as the **Jones Act**.

Pasteur, French ocean **liner** completed for the Cie. Sudatlantique in 1939. She was the first ship to have nude sunbathing facilities incorporated into her design. The revolutionary 29,253-gross-ton **liner** made her secret **maiden voyage** scurrying the French gold reserves to Halifax in June 1940 during the German invasion of France. She served as an Allied troopship during the war and continued in French government service before being sold amid great public displeasure to **North German Lloyd** in 1957 for conversion into their *Bremen* for the North Atlantic trade. She was sold to the **Chandris Line** in 1971 for cruising as *Regina Magna* and was later employed as a Saudi Arabian workers' hostel. She sank while being towed to the scrapyard in 1980.

patent log, mechanical device used for measuring the distance a vessel has sailed. It is also called a **taffrail log**.

Patna, rusty steamer that sank while carrying Moslem pilgrims to Mecca in **Joseph Conrad**'s *Lord Jim* (1900).

Patria, former French passenger **liner** that was chartered by the British in 1940 to carry 1,770

Jewish immigrants, who had been detained in Palestine, to the island of Mauritius. On November 25, a Jewish resistance group opposed to the British policy in Palestine hoped to bring attention to the plight of the refugees by **scuttling** the ship. Instead, when their explosives went off, instead of sinking slowly, the ship capsized in Haifa harbor, killing 202 passengers.

Patriot, cruise ship originally called the *Nieuw Amsterdam*, built in 1983 for the **Holland America Line**. The 33,930-gross-ton vessel was sold in 1999 and, by special dispensation from Congress, was reflagged in the United States as the *Patriot* for inter–Hawai'ian Island cruise service beginning in 2000 under the auspices of a new United States Lines—a subsidiary of American Classic Voyages—bearing no connection to the famed transatlantic **steamship** company.

Patterson, Charles Robert (1878–1958), British-born American marine artist and historian. Going to sea at an early age gave him the first-hand experience and knowledge later evident in his paintings.

Pax Britannica, an extended period of peace brought about by British supremacy at sea following the country's naval and military victories of the **Napoleonic Wars**. The period began in 1815 and lasted until the outbreak of World War I in 1914.

PBY Catalina, "flying boat" patrol aircraft first developed in 1935 and manufactured by Consolidated Aircraft during World War II. Its relatively fast speed and long range made it an ideal patrol craft during the war and a search-and-rescue asset after the war.

Peabody Essex Museum, the oldest continually operating museum in the United States and the first American maritime museum. Founded in 1799 in Salem, Massachusetts, it was based on the marine collection of the East India Marine Society, an organization of mariners who sailed

the oceans to China, Japan, India, Africa, the Pacific Islands, and the northwest coast of America, and carried back works of art and objects. In 1867 a gift from George Peabody established the Peabody Museum of Salem, and the museum added ethnographic and natural history materials. In 1992 the Peabody Museum merged with the nearby Essex Institute.

pea coat, heavy, short woolen jacket worn by sailors, which is also called a "pea jacket."

Pea Island, site of the U.S. **Life-Saving Service**, and later U.S. **Coast Guard**, station on North Carolina's Outer Banks that was the first to be manned entirely by African-Americans. Pea Island Station served with distinction from the 1880s until 1947, when the station was closed.

peapod, small rowing or sailing boat whose name comes from its shape, which is pointed at both ends and round-bottomed.

Pearl Harbor, Hawaiian base of operations for the U.S. **Navy**'s Pacific fleet. It was first established as a **coaling station** in 1887. On the morning of Sunday, December 7, 1941, the moored fleet was attacked by 191 aircraft of the Imperial Japanese Navy, launched from the carriers *Akagi*, *Hiryu*, *Kaga*, *Shokaku*, *Soryu*, and *Zuikaku*. In all, twenty-one U.S. ships were sunk or damaged (including four battleships), 2,403 Americans lost their lives, and 1,178 were wounded. The Japanese lost 28 planes and three midget submarines. President **Franklin D. Roosevelt** called December 7, 1941, a "date that will live in infamy."

Pears, Charles (1873–1958), British marine artist and illustrator whose best work depicted war at sea. He served as a war artist during World Wars I and II and helped design many of the propaganda posters of the time.

Peary, Robert Edwin (1856–1920), U.S. **Navy** rear admiral and Arctic explorer who is credited as being the first man to reach the North

Pole. In 1898, Peary set out in his ship *Windward* to reach the pole but fell short by about 390 miles. In 1905, Peary tried again, setting sail on the *Roosevelt*, a ship designed to navigate among ice floes, but fell short by 200 miles. He chronicled this journey in *Nearest the Pole* (1907). In 1908, Peary and his chief assistant, **Matthew Alexander Henson**, made a third attempt. Peary, without Henson, claimed that he reached the pole on April 6, 1909. Peary wrote an account of this trip in *The North Pole* (1910). Disputes as to whether Peary indeed reached the North Pole were put to rest in 1989, when the National Geographic Society credited him with the discovery.

Pease, Howard (1894–1974), popular and prolific American author of fifteen seafaring adventure novels for young readers. Many of the books chronicle the adventures of Tod Moran, who starts out as a mess boy on the steamer *Araby* in *The Tattoed Man* (1926).

Peking, four-masted German **windjammer** built by **Blohm & Voss** in 1911 for the Flying P Line's South American nitrate trade out of Hamburg. In 1926 *Peking* began carrying **merchant marine** cadets. **Irving M. Johnson** sailed aboard the **bark** as a young sailor in 1929 around **Cape Horn** to Chile and recorded the experience with still and movie cameras and a journal, which became the book *Round the Horn in a Square-Rigger* (1932). *Peking* was used as a stationary school ship in England beginning in 1932, and in 1975 she was permanently docked at Pier 16 at Manhattan's **South Street Seaport Museum**. A reissue of the *Peking* section of *Round the Horn*, with additional material, was published by the **National Maritime Historical Society** in 1977 as *The* Peking *Battles Cape Horn*.

pelagic, term used to describe fish—such as herring, tuna, and sharks—that spend most of their lives swimming, usually in schools, in the water column between the bottom and the surface, feeding on smaller fish or crustaceans. Also, of, relating to, or living in the open seas.

Peleliu, Invasion of, September 15, 1944, amphibious landings on a tiny five-square-mile island of the Palau chain, six hundred miles east of the Philippines. The island was finally won on November 25 at the cost of 1,460 American marines.

USS *Pennsylvania* (BB-38), 31,400-ton battleship commissioned in 1916. The 608-foot sister to USS *Arizona*—both armed with twelve 14-inch guns—was stationed in the Pacific after 1922. *Pennsylvania* was in drydock and escaped serious damage when the Japanese attacked **Pearl Harbor** in 1941. During World War II, she was assigned to action throughout the Pacific theater of war, including Attu, **Saipan**, **Guam**, the Palau Islands, **Leyte Gulf**, **Wake**, and the **Okinawa Invasion**. She sustained severe hull damage at Okinawa and, although temporary repairs were made, she was relegated to the atomic bomb test fleet at the **Bikini Atoll**. Decommissioned in 1946, *Pennsylvania* survived the initial blasts and was kept afloat to study the effects of radiation. She was towed to Kwajalein Lagoon, in the **Marshall Islands**, where she was finally sunk in 1948.

Penn Yan, name for the classic canoes and small lake boats built by the Penn Yan Boat Company, established in 1921 in Penn Yan, New York.

Penobscot Bay Expedition, one of the single worst military defeats of the American Revolution. On July 25, 1779, the **Continental Navy** and Army mounted an amphibious force of thirty-nine ships and three hundred marines to seize the British fortification at Castine, Maine. The British sent in ships, lightly digging in, and the American forces panicked, fleeing up the Penobscot River, and were trapped. American delays made the British victory possible. The British burned thirty-seven American ships and killed or took as prisoners five hundred colonists.

Pequod, fictional whaling ship in **Herman Melville**'s *Moby-Dick* (1851). Hailing from Nantucket, her tiller was made from the jawbone of a whale.

The Perfect Storm, best-selling 1996 book by Sebastian Junger recounting the tragic end of the six-man crew aboard the **Gloucester** (Massachusetts) swordfish boat *Andrea Gail*. The boat was lost at sea when it got caught in an unexpected nor'easter storm that developed off New England in October 1991. The book was made into a successful film in 2000 that starred George Clooney.

USS Permit (SSN-594), the second 319-foot **Thresher**-class nuclear-powered submarine, which was commissioned in 1962. After the loss of *Thresher* in 1963, the remaining thirteen subs of the series were referred to as the **Permit** class.

Perry, Matthew Calbraith (1794–1858), U.S. **Navy** commodore, younger brother of **Oliver Hazard Perry**, who played a leading role in the naval affairs of the Mexican War (1846–48). Known as Old Bruin, he is credited with opening up Japan to Western trade and diplomacy. Japan had virtually isolated itself from Western countries since the early 1600s and had resisted, sometimes by force, American and European attempts to establish business and diplomatic ties. In 1853 Perry led a squadron of ships into **Tokyo Bay** to "negotiate" a treaty between Japan and the United States, which was signed in 1854. Perry compiled the official record of the expedition, published as *Narrative of the Expedition of an American Squadron to the China Seas and Japan* (1856). Upon his death in New York City in 1858, he was accorded a state funeral.

Perry, Oliver Hazard (1785–1819), U.S. **Navy** commodore and national hero for his role as a lieutenant in the **War of 1812**, during which his younger brother **Matthew Calbraith Perry** also served as a midshipman. In 1813 he was given command of U.S. naval forces in Lake Erie and subsequently scored one of the most decisive victories of the war. Perry's success in the Battle of **Lake Erie**, in which he sent the message, **"We have met the enemy, and they are ours,"** gave the United States control of the lake and enabled General William Henry Harrison to regain territory lost to Canada.

U.S. postage stamp commemorating the opening of Japan to Western trade by Matthew C. Perry.

Perry Expedition, U.S. expedition led by **Matthew Calbraith Perry** to open up diplomatic relations with Japan. On July 8, 1853, four U.S. warships—USS *Susquehanna*, USS *Mississippi*, USS *Saratoga*, and USS *Plymouth*—sailed into a hostile Japan to begin diplomatic relations and to ensure the safety of shipwrecked Americans. Perry presented Japanese officials with a letter from U.S. President Millard Fillmore to the emperor proposing peace and friendship. On March 31, 1854, Japan entered into a treaty of peace and friendship with the United States. A treaty regarding trade with Japan followed in 1857.

SS Persia, the first iron vessel built for the **Cunard Line**. In 1856 she crossed the Atlantic to New York in nine days, one hour, and forty-five minutes, a record that would stand until 1862. She consumed approximately 143 tons of coal a day.

Peter I (1672–1725), Russian ruler who first served as czar of Russia and later became Russia's first emperor. Also called "Peter the Great," he transformed Russia from an isolated and backward country into a great European power and is regarded as the "Father of the Russian Navy."

Peter Pan, 1904 classic story by James M. Barrie (1860–1937) about a boy who refuses to grow up and lives on an island with a band of Indians and a den of vicious pirates headed by the infamous Captain **Hook**. The story was translated into a popular full-length animated motion picture by Walt Disney in 1953 and was fashioned into a Broadway musical the following year, with Mary Martin in the title role and Cyril Ritchard as Hook. The hit show was further adapted in 1955 for an unprecedented live television broadcast.

petty officer, a noncommissioned officer in the U.S. **Navy** or **Coast Guard**. Petty officer ranks begin with third-class petty officer and rises to master chief petty officer. The word comes from the French *petit*, meaning small.

Phantom Ship, 1937 motion picture account of the *Mary Celeste*, a ship found off Portugal in 1872 with her sails set but without anyone on board. Also known as *The Mystery of the Marie Celeste*, it includes lots of salty sailing ship footage as a background for outstanding acting by Bela Lugosi.

Pharos lighthouse, 440-foot lighthouse built in 270 B.C. on the small island of Pharos, outside the port of Alexandria, Egypt. One of the seven wonders of the ancient world, the white marble lighthouse served as a beacon for Mediterranean shipping for nearly nine hundred years. Connection of the name with the function became so strong that the word *Pharos* became the root of the word *lighthouse* in the French, Italian, Spanish, and Romanian languages. Its remains were discovered in 1994.

Philadelphia, American Revolution gunboat built in 1776 that is today the oldest preserved American warship. The fifty-three-foot, flat-bottomed vessel was sunk during the Battle of **Valcour Island** in 1776. It was raised from Lake Champlain in 1935 and—remarkably preserved by the cold freshwater—was used for many years as a floating attraction on the lake.

It was brought to the Smithsonian Institution in the 1960s, where it remains on display. A replica built in 1989 by the Lake Champlain Maritime Museum is actively sailed today.

USS *Philadelphia*, U.S. **Navy frigate** built in 1800 and commissioned for action in the **Quasi-War**. Having distinguished herself in that conflict, *Philadelphia* was sent to the Mediterranean for service in the **Barbary Wars**. In October 1803, with Captain **William Bainbridge** in command, *Philadelphia* ran aground on a reef and was forced to surrender to the **Barbary pirates**. As the captured ship was being refitted, Lieutenant **Stephen Decatur** led a mission into the harbor at **Tripoli** on February 16, 1804, slipped aboard, and set fire to the ship. Vice-Admiral **Horatio Nelson** declared his deed "the most bold and daring act of the age."

Philadelphia Experiment, alleged 1943 incident in which the **destroyer** USS *Eldridge* was made invisible and teleported from Philadelphia to Norfolk, Virginia. Supposedly, the crew of the civilian merchant ship SS *Andrew Furuseth* observed the arrival via teleportation of the *Eldridge* into the Norfolk basin. No one has ever confirmed the event, which is often referred to as Project Rainbow. A 1984 film, *The Philadelphia Experiment*, is based on the premise and has several participants of a navy experiment hurled forty-one years into the future.

Philippine Sea, Battle of the, desperate June 19–20, 1944, confrontation between 112 U.S. warships and 55 Imperial Japanese Navy vessels. It was a decisive U.S. victory and the last great aircraft carrier battle ever fought. Of the 430 Japanese carrier-based planes in the battle, only 35 survived. The Japanese aircraft carriers **Shokaku**, **Taiho**, and *Hiyo* were sunk in the Marianas Island encounter, which was so overwhelming that it became widely known as the **Great Marianas Turkey Shoot**.

Phoenix, the first **steamship** to transit in the open sea, taking thirteen days to travel the 150 miles from New York to Philadelphia in June 1808. Designed by **John Stevens** and built in Hoboken, New Jersey, the 101-foot vessel was captained by his son, Robert L. Stevens. **Robert Fulton** and **Robert R. Livingston** had a monopoly on **steamboats** in New York waters, so Stevens—forced to find other profitable routes in which to operate—transited around to the Delaware River, where he set up passenger and freight service between Philadelphia and Trenton.

USS *Phoenix* (CL-46), one of nine **Brooklyn**-class light **cruisers** built just prior to World War II. Commissioned in 1939, *Phoenix* saw action in World War II and was sold to Argentina in 1951—along with sister ship USS *Boise*—and renamed the *General Belgrano*. The 13,479-ton vessel was sunk by a British **torpedo** in 1982 during the Falklands War.

picket ship, ship employed at a distance from a target being defended to provide protection and an early warning, and to extend radar coverage.

Pidgeon, Harry (1869–1954), American sailor who completed the first solo circumnavigation of the world via the **Panama Canal** (1921–25). Seven years later, in his same home-built, thirty-four-foot **yawl**, *Islander*, he set out to be the first man to twice sail around the world single-handed and finished that trip in 1937. On his third attempt, he was shipwrecked in the New Hebrides. He wrote *Around the World Single-Handed* (1932) about his first voyage.

pieces of eight, legendary pirate coins that were silver dollars made by Native American craftsmen in Mexico, Peru, Colombia, and elsewhere in Central and South America who had been enslaved by the Spanish. The coins were produced for approximately three hundred years. Eight was the coin's denomination in reales. They became the standard trade coin, especially for European trade with China, and they were legal tender in the United States until about 1857. Gold coins came in the same denominations but were called "escudos," and the eight-escudo piece was known as a "**doubloon.**"

pierhead painter, marine artist who specialized in ship portraits. Sea captains would often hire these artists to paint pictures of their ships. The term is sometimes used derisively to describe someone who is perceived to be "just a painter," not a real artist.

Pigafetta, Antonio (ca. 1491–1535), Venetian nobleman who sailed with **Ferdinand Magellan** on what was to be the first circumnavigation of the earth (1519–22). After Magellan's death in the Philippines in 1521, Pigafetta returned to Spain aboard the *Victoria*, the only ship to complete the voyage, which was under the command of **Juan Sebastián de Elcano**. Much of what is known of the historic expedition is from Pigafetta's narrative *The First Voyage around the World* (1522), and he is credited with naming the Pacific Ocean, Latin for "peaceful," because he did not encounter any storms on the journey.

Pilar, thirty-eight-foot fishing boat owned by **Ernest Hemingway** and used in the waters off Havana and Bimini. The Wheeler Playmate was built by the Wheeler Shipyard in New York City in 1934. She was painted "pirate's black" and was named for a character in *For Whom the Bell Tolls* (1940).

Pilgrim, eighty-seven-foot **brig** that carried **Richard Henry Dana Jr.** from Boston to California in 1835 and was later immortalized in his seafaring classic *Two Years Before the Mast* (1840).

Pillars of Hercules, name for the two promontories on either side of the **Strait of Gibraltar**—the Rock of Gibraltar and the Jebel Musa at Cueta (Morocco). For centuries, the promontories marked the extreme limits of navigation for Mediterranean seafarers.

Pillsbury, John (1846–1919), U.S. **Navy** oceanographer and **Gulf Stream** explorer. In 1883 aboard USS *Blake*, Pillsbury charted the Straits of Florida and the Gulf Stream and found them remarkably similar to results published by Benjamin Franklin nearly a hundred years earlier.

pilot, person with expert knowledge of tides and obstructions and experience in navigating vessels through local waters. Pilotage is a voluntary or compulsory service provided to a **master** of a ship to assist in maneuvering the vessel when entering or leaving a local port.

The Pilot, 1823 novel by **James Fenimore Cooper**. Subtitled *A Tale of the Sea* and considered the first American novel about the sea, it is the tale of **John Paul Jones** (as the character Long Tom Coffin) and his activities off the coast of England during the American Revolution.

pilot chart, chart of a major ocean area that represents in graphic form information about weather, waves, ice, and other marine data gathered over many years to aid navigators in selecting the quickest and safest routes. First developed in the 1850s by **Matthew Fontaine Maury**, the charts were published by the **Defense Mapping Agency** until it was merged into the **National Imagery and Mapping Agency** in the 1990s.

HMS *Pinafore*, Captain Corcoran's vessel in the 1878 nautical comic opera *HMS Pinafore* by Gilbert and Sullivan.

pinnace, small and fast warship employed in the sixteenth century for scouting and dispatch duties.

Pinta, the smallest of **Christopher Columbus**'s three ships on his first voyage of discovery to the New World in 1492–93. Along with the *Santa Maria* and *Niña*, she reached the Bahamas on October 12. She spent the remainder of the month exploring the islands and then headed south to Cuba before returning to Spain. *Pinta* measured somewhere between fifty-five and seventy-five feet and had a crew of eighteen men.

Piraeus, leading seaport in Greece and the country's third-largest city, behind Athens and Thessaloniki. Piraeus lies along the Saronic Gulf, five miles southwest of Athens. It was an important Greek port in ancient times, and today over half the country's imports and exports pass through its three harbors.

The Pirate, 1821 novel by Scottish romantic writer Sir Walter Scott (1771–1832) that featured pirates and was set among the islands of Shetland and Orkney in the last years of the seventeenth century. The book had a great influence on American authors, most notably **James Fenimore Cooper.**

The Pirate, entertaining 1948 motion picture about a woman on a remote Caribbean island who dreams of her romantic hero, the legendary pirate Black Macocco. To woo her, a traveling actor masquerades as the pirate. The film starred Judy Garland and Gene Kelly and included the Cole Porter songs "Be a Clown," "Mack the Black," and "You Can Do No Wrong."

Pirate Code, written "Articles of Piracy" drawn up and signed by each member of a marauding contingent before the expedition set sail. According to some, **buccaneers** were a well-ordered, democratic group of men sworn to uphold their seagoing social contract, which oftentimes included compensation and disability pay for injuries.

The Pirate Movie, rousing 1982 high-seas adventure musical feature film that, in reality, was an excellent parody of *The **Pirates of Penzance***. The 1982 hit starred Christopher Atkins, Kristy McNichol, and Ted Hamilton.

The Pirates of Penzance, classic 1880 Gilbert and Sullivan comic opera about nineteenth-century pirates and the concepts of good and evil. A traditional rendering of the production

A pilot's license from 1889 for the region between Nantucket, Massachusetts, and Perth Amboy, New Jersey.

was filmed in 1982, featuring Keith Mitchell and Alexander Oliver. However, the following year a much-rearranged version appeared in the mainstream American movie theaters starring Linda Ronstadt, Angela Lansbury, and Kevin Kline.

Pirates of the Caribbean, wildly popular multi-million-dollar attraction first introduced at Disneyland in which guests take a boat ride through the re-created world of eighteenth-century **buccaneers**, plunder, and gold **doubloons**. The 1966 extravaganza drew criticism from the outset for its lighthearted view of pillage, rape, and murder, which is essentially what most of the audio-animatronic experience is celebrating. But nonetheless it is a near impossibility to experience the journey and not come out singing "Yo-ho, yo-ho, a pirate's life for me."

pirogue, small double-ended, flat-bottomed boat with rounded sides, usually hollowed from a single log up to about eighteen feet, used for fishing in sheltered waters of the Gulf Coast and up the East Coast as far as the **Hudson River** in times past.

Pisces, the twelfth sign of the zodiac, which is symbolized by two fish swimming in opposite directions. Pisces, along with Cancer and Scorpio, is a water sign.

Pitcairn Island, isolated two-square-mile island in the South Pacific Ocean lying about five thousand miles east of Australia, famous as the home of the mutineers of HMS *Bounty*. In 1767 English navigator Philip Carteret named the uninhabited island after Robert Pitcairn, the crew member who first sighted the island. In 1790, nine of the mutineers from HMS *Bounty* brought nineteen Polynesians with them—six men, twelve women, and a young girl—to the island. Disputes over women eventually led to fighting among the men. By 1808, when the American ship *Topaz* discovered the mutineers' hideout, all the men except the mutineer John Adams were dead. The mutineers had left twenty-five children, and in 1856 many of Pitcairn's people moved to **Norfolk Island**.

Pitcairn's Island, third installment of the *Mutiny on the Bounty* trilogy written by **Nordhoff and Hall**. The 1934 novel is a much-fictionalized account of the violence in **Fletcher Christian**'s island colony. The other novels are *Mutiny on the Bounty* (1932) and *Men against the Sea* (1934).

pitchpole, term for when a vessel is cast stern over bow in a half somersault by a very large following sea or surf.

Pitt, Dirk, the fictional hero of twenty fast-paced, high-adventure thriller novels by American author **Clive Cussler** that revolve around the sea.

plankowner, member of the commissioning crew of a ship. In the days of wooden vessels, a member of a ship's initial crew had the right to take a plank from her deck when the ship was decommissioned.

Plimsoll marks, **load lines** painted at the midpoints on both sides of a merchant vessel to indicate the maximum depths to which the vessel may be loaded, depending on the season and whether the water is salt or fresh. Samuel Plimsoll (1824–1898) introduced the regulations to Britain's Parliament, and they were ratified under the Merchant Shipping Act of 1876. Until that time, overloading vessels was a major cause of accidents at sea.

pocket battleship, one of three German warships—*Admiral Graf Spee*, *Deutschland*, and *Admiral Scheer*—designed in 1928. Because the German fleet was badly depleted following World War I and was unable to construct traditional battleships because of the restrictions imposed by the 1919 **Treaty of Versailles**, these warships were well engineered to be smaller and faster than a traditional battleship and more powerful than a **cruiser**. The German term for these vessels was *panzerschiff*, meaning "armored ship."

Pocock, Nicholas (1740–1821), British merchant mariner who became a highly successful marine painter. He was largely self-taught and often included small drawings of his vessel in each day's log entry, noting the condition of the weather and the ship. He went on to become one of the most celebrated painters of naval actions and general shipping scenes in both oil and watercolor. His two sons were also painters.

Poe, Edgar Allan (1809–1849), American writer of poetry and short stories who specialized in mystery fiction and the macabre. His story *MS: Found in a Bottle* (1833), about a hurricane and a mystery ship, was his first notable work. His *The Narrative of Arthur Gordon Pym of Nantucket* (1838) is a gloomy tale of a shipwreck in the **South Seas** and the Antarctic region, and his short story "Descent into the Maelstrom" is about a Norwegian fisherman who relates how he got caught in the famous whirlpool and survived.

points of sailing, principal headings of a sailboat in relation to the wind. These include **tacking; close-hauled** or beating; close reach; reach; broad reach; run; and **jibing**.

Polaris, first intercontinental ballistic missile launched by underwater submarine. The first successful launch, on April 14, 1960, from USS *George Washington* off San Clemente Island, California, ushered in the era of Polaris-class submarines.

USS *Polaris*, U.S. **Navy** tug that was loaned to explorer **Charles Francis Hall** in 1871 for a expedition to the North Pole. In August 1871 *Polaris* reached 82°11′ North, a record for the time. Hall died a few months later, and in June 1872 the expedition again pushed on to reach the pole. *Polaris* became caught in the ice and was later crushed. Nineteen crew members who had abandoned ship early drifted 1,500 miles on ice floes and were rescued six months later.

pollywog, sailor—also referred to as a "wog"— who has not crossed the equator or been initiated in the Kingdom of **King Neptune** at some other **crossing the line** ceremony.

Ponce de León, Luis (1474–1521), Spanish explorer who in 1513 set out to find a fountain whose waters would restore the youth of all who drank from it. On Easter Sunday 1513, Ponce de León sighted the east coast of Florida and, claiming it for Spain, named it Pascua Florida for the Easter feast of flowers. He was later appointed governor of the territory and given sole right to conquer and colonize the region. He was wounded and died in an Indian attack in 1521.

Pook, Samuel H. (1827–1901), American naval architect of **clipper ships** and **ironclads**. He designed the clipper ship *Red Jacket*, which was built in 1853, and during the Civil War he designed a series of seven 175-foot ironclads, each propelled by covered sternwheels and carrying thirteen guns. Known as "Pook Turtles," they were used by the Union navy to control the **Mississippi River** and its tributaries. One of those ships, USS *Cairo*, was **salvaged** in 1964 and is presently on display within the Vicksburg National Military Park in Mississippi.

poop deck, deck on a ship that extends from side to side above the after part of the main deck or, if the ship has two decks above the main deck aft, above the **quarterdeck**.

Pope, Dudley (1925–1997), English author and respected naval historian. His novels' main character, **Royal Navy** officer Nicholas Ramage, was the continuum between **Cecil Scott "C. S."** **Forester**'s **Horatio Hornblower** and **Patrick O'Brian**'s **Jack Aubrey**. Pope's first book, *Ramage*, was published in 1965 and was followed by seventeen other Ramage novels, including *Ramage's Diamond* (1976), *Ramage and the Rebels* (1978), and *Ramage and the Renegade* (1981). Pope is also author of *The Black Ship* (1963), *Life in Nelson's Navy* (1981), and *Graf Spee: The Life and Death of a Raider* (1995), among others.

Popeye, live-action feature film directed by Robert Altman retelling the saga of the cockeyed American sailor. The 1981 movie was panned by critics but received praise for its cartoonish set design, namely Sweethaven, a faux village created on the island of **Malta**. The film starred Robin Williams, Shelley Duvall, and Ray Walston.

Popeye the Sailor, cartoon character created by E. C. Segar in 1929. At first, Popeye was a support character for the Thimble Theater comic strip, but the 1933 theatrical cartoon

Popeye the Sailor—part of the Betty Boop series—started the popularity of the cocky little spinach-eating sailorman. The hundreds of theatrical shorts, made until the 1950s, introduced the classic characters J. Wellington Wimpy, Olive Oyl, Bluto, Castor Oyl, the Sea Hag, Alice the Goon, the Jeep, Swee'pea, Poop-deck Pappy, and Popeye's mischievous nephews Pipeye, Peepeye, Pupeye, and Poopeye. Popeye was also the subject of made-for-television cartoons.

Porcellis, Jan (ca. 1584–1632), Dutch marine painter who was married to the daughter of renowned marine artist **Cornelisz Hendrick Vroom** and was one of his students. Porcellis is best known for creating atmospheric effects in his works.

portage bill, statement made out at the end of a voyage by the **master** showing the earnings of each member of the crew, including overtime and shares, if any.

Port Arthur, strategic deepwater harbor that for years was Russia's only ice-free port on the Pacific. Port Arthur was captured by Japan in the **Russo-Japanese War** (1904–5) and subsequently ceded to Japan with the Treaty of Portsmouth (New Hampshire), which ended that war. Today it is located on the tip of the Liaodong Peninsula in what is now China.

Port Chicago Mutiny, incident occurring on July 17, 1944, after two ammunition transport ships, *E. A. Bryan* and *Quinault Victory*, exploded at Port Chicago in Suisun Bay, twenty-five miles from San Francisco, California, killing 320 men and injuring 390. The incident was the largest domestic loss of life in World War II; two thirds of those killed were black U.S. **Navy** seamen assigned to load bombs onto the ships. Following the accident, fifty black seamen refused to return to work because whites were given leave before returning and they weren't. They were court-martialed, convicted, and imprisoned until the end of the war. The mutiny helped lead to an executive order in 1948 ending segregation in the U.S. armed forces. Most of the "mutineers" were cleared in the late 1990s.

Porter, David (1780–1843), U.S. **Navy** commodore and hero of the **War of 1812**. In 1803 Porter's ship, the **frigate *Philadelphia***, was captured in the **Barbary Wars** and he was held prisoner until peace was declared in 1805. In the War of 1812, he commanded USS *Essex*, capturing several British ships. With his informally adopted son **David Glasgow Farragut** on board, Porter sailed *Essex* around **Cape Horn**, becoming the first U.S. Navy ship to enter the Pacific, and nearly destroyed the entire British whaling industry in the Pacific. Porter was court-martialed and briefly suspended in 1824 for disobeying orders while commander of the **West Indies** Squadron, and he resigned his commission in 1826 to become head of the Mexican navy. He returned to the United States in 1829 and later held diplomatic posts.

Porter, David Dixon (1813–1891), U.S. naval officer who distinguished himself in the Civil War and son of **David Porter**. In 1865, he commanded a fleet of sixty naval vessels, the largest ever assembled during the war, and took part in the capture of **Fort Fisher**. Porter served as superintendent of the U.S. **Naval Academy** from 1865 to 1869 and was promoted to vice admiral in 1866. In 1870, he succeeded his adopted half-brother **David Glasgow Farragut** as an admiral, becoming the second person in the history of the U.S. **Navy** to hold that rank.

Porter, Katherine Anne (1890–1980), American writer noted mainly for her short stories. Her *Collected Stories* (1965) won the 1966 Pulitzer Prize for fiction. Her only novel, ***Ship of Fools*** (1962), is a moral allegory that describes an ocean voyage from Mexico to Germany during the early 1930s and reflects the social and political turmoil of that time.

Portland Gale, storm that struck New England on November 26–27, 1898, killing more than two hundred persons and wrecking or sinking at least 140 major vessels (some counts go as high as 400 vessels). The largest loss was the overnight steamer *Portland*, which was en route from Boston to Portland, Maine, crowded with passengers returning home after the Thanksgiving holiday. Upwards of 191 people died when the ship went down off the coast of **Cape Cod**. *Portland*'s remains on the seabed have since been located and explored.

Portobello, formerly Porto Bello, a seaport town in Panama on the Caribbean Sea. Its harbor was visited by **Christopher Columbus**, and it later became a thriving colonial city because it was connected by a stone highway to Panama City and served as a transshipment point for riches from the Spanish Pacific domains. Sir **Francis Drake** died of fever at sea off the city, which was sacked numerous times by English **buccaneers**. The city's fortunes declined with the building of the trans-Panama railroad and the **Panama Canal**.

Port Royal, seventeenth-century capital of Jamaica that served as a center of British colonial activity and a **home port** for piracy in the Caribbean. In June 1692, a series of violent earthquakes struck, and two thirds of the city tumbled into the sea, killing thousands. Located on a sand spit at the entrance to Kingston Harbor, it is today known as the City Beneath the Sea, and the foundations of houses, inns, shops, and their contents are preserved in ten to thirty feet of water.

Portuguese man-o'-war, large cluster of marine organisms called "siphonophores" attached to a large bladderlike float. Long dangling tentacles—sometimes up to twelve feet long—extend from the organisms and contain stinging cells that are lethal to small fish. Its name derives from its viciousness and the fact that it resembles the style of **caravel** used by the Spanish and Portuguese in the fifteenth and sixteenth centuries.

Poseidon, Greek name for Neptune, the Roman god who ruled the sea.

The Poseidon Adventure, best-selling 1969 novel by Paul Gallico (1897–1976) about an aging express **liner** that capsizes in midocean after being broadsided by a **tidal wave**, and the subsequent struggle for survival by those trapped inside the still-buoyant upside-down vessel. An Academy Award–winning film version, adapted by Irwin Allen in 1972, featured an all-star cast headed by Ernest Borgnine, Gene Hackman, Stella Stevens, and Shelly Winters. Some sequences were filmed aboard RMS *Queen Mary* in Long Beach, California, because Gallico had envisioned the disaster happening while he was aboard the famous **Cunard** liner during a rough 1937 westbound passage. Gallico's 1978 sequel, *Beyond the Poseidon Adventure*, was also made into a movie.

posh, meaning "luxurious" or "**first class**," believed by many to be an acronym used by the **P&O** line before the days of air conditioning. A premium fee was paid by passengers wishing to be quartered on the shaded side of the ship to escape the intense heat of the tropical sun, which beat down upon the steel plates of the hull during round-trip passage from England to India. Such requests were marked "port out—**starboard** home," which was eventually abbreviated into a stamp that affixed "P.O.S.H." to the steamer tickets.

Potemkin, Russian **cruiser** whose crew mutinied at Odessa on the **Black Sea** during the revolution of October 1905. The crews of other Russian warships refused to fire on her when she hoisted the red flag. The incident was the subject of *The Battleship Potemkin* (1925), a classic Soviet film. Directed by Sergei Eisenstein, it was commissioned to celebrate the twentieth anniversary of the uprising, which was seen as a direct precursor of the October Revolution of 1917.

USS *Potomac*, 165-foot ex–**Coast Guard cutter** *Electra* converted in 1936 to a presidential yacht for **Franklin D. Roosevelt**. In presidential service until 1946, she was replaced by USS *Williamsburg*. Her career continued as a fishery commission vessel and a ferry, and in 1964 she was purchased by Elvis Presley and donated to a children's hospital in Memphis, Tennessee. Later sold, she was seized by U.S. Customs in a San Francisco drug raid. Purchased by the Port of Oakland (California) in the 1990s, she is undergoing restoration.

Pound, Sir Dudley (Alfred Dudley Pickman Rogers Pound) (1877–1943), British admiral who served as **First Sea Lord** and chief of the British naval staff from 1939–43. At the outbreak of World War II, he effectively handled the German **U-boat** threat. Later though, suffering from a brain tumor, his judgment lapsed and he made a number of grave errors. He resigned in October 1943 and died a few weeks later.

pound net, fixed fishing enclosure of netting supported by stakes and used close to shore in shallow water. Fish swim into the interior pound, where they are trapped.

powder monkey, young boy used aboard sailing warships to transport gunpowder from the powder keg to the cannons. Due to the limited space between decks boys could move more quickly than men.

U.S. Power Squadrons, nonprofit educational organization of amateur boaters incorporated in 1915, whose objectives are to promote safety afloat, boathandling, and piloting.

PQ, British identity symbol for numbered **convoys** run from Great Britain to **Murmansk** and **Archangel**, carrying British and American nationals to the hard-pressed Soviet forces fighting Germany in 1941–45. After atrocious losses in PQ17 in July 1942, when only eleven ships out of a convoy of thirty-five reached the USSR, sailings were restricted to winter months, providing long nights for cover from attacking German **U-boats**.

Praise of the Two Lands, earliest known ship name. It was given to a large cedarwood Egyptian vessel in about 2680 B.C.

"Praise the Lord and pass the ammunition", quote attributed to Howell M. Forgy, chaplain aboard the **cruiser** USS *New Orleans*, when the Japanese attacked **Pearl Harbor** on Sunday morning, December 7, 1941.

"Praise the Lord and Pass the Ammunition", hit song performed by Kay Kyser and His Orchestra that hit number one in 1943 (it previously hit number eight in 1942 for the Merry Macs). One of the verses goes like this: "Shouting Praise the Lord, we're on a mighty mission, All aboard, we ain't a-going fishin', Praise the Lord and pass the ammunition, And we'll all stay free."

pram, small open boat with a square bow and stern and gently curved sides and a flat or V-shaped bottom, often used as a **tender** by yachts.

Preble, Edward (1761–1807), U.S. **Navy** officer who was instrumental in the **Barbary Wars**. In 1803, he took command of a squadron sent to the Mediterranean Sea to protect American ships and sailors from the **Barbary pirates**. After the Barbary forces captured the **frigate** *Philadelphia*, he sent **Stephen Decatur Jr.** on a surprise mission to destroy the frigate. Preble later obtained light gunboats in Italy and bombarded **Tripoli**. Many of the young naval officers who served under him, called "Preble's Boys," led the U.S. Navy in the **War of 1812**.

Premier Cruise Lines, Miami-based multiday cruise operation founded in 1984 that expanded into a major collection of vintage **liners** that are being maintained in cruise operation until their forced retirements due to new **SOLAS** regulations. For ten years the company served as the "Official Cruise Line of Walt Disney World" (until Disney launched its own cruise line) and later called itself the "Big Red Boat." As of 2000, it was operating the *Ocean Breeze* (formerly **Southern Cross**), *Island Breeze* (formerly *Transvaal Castle*), *Rembrandt* (formerly **Rotterdam**), and the *Oceanic*.

USS *President*, one of the U.S. **Navy**'s original **frigates** authorized under the **Navy Act of 1794**. The frigate put to sea in 1800 under the command of **Thomas Truxton**. She was sent to the Mediterranean to fight the **Barbary pirates** and later sailed the Atlantic to prevent the impressment of American sailors. *President* fought in the **War of 1812** and was captured by a British squadron blocking New York City on January 18, 1815. Taken into the **Royal Navy**, she was soon condemned as structurally unsound. Her name was transferred to a succession of Royal Navy ships, and a *President* lies in the Thames at London to this day.

President Coolidge, transpacific **liner** built in 1931 for the **Dollar Line** along with her sister ship, the *President Hoover*. They were both transferred to **American President Lines** in 1938 when the latter assumed the operations of the Dollar Line. Converted for U.S. Army service, she struck a mine while in the New Hebrides Islands in 1941 with more than 5,340 troops aboard. She sank with the loss of only two lives. The wreck site continues to be a popular **scuba** diving destination.

President Roosevelt, substitute for the never-built *President Washington* of **American President Lines**. She was purchased from the U.S. government as the *Leilani*, and her new owners spent over $12 million refitting her in 1962 for luxury transpacific service. Her origins as the troopship **General W. P. Richardson** could never be adequately adapted for

President Roosevelt. (Courtesy Gordon R. Ghareeb)

passenger service while under the American flag, however, and she was not really successful. She was sold for further trading—and extensive rebuilding—to the **Chandris Line** in 1970 and renamed *Atlantis*.

President Washington, ship intended to be the largest **liner** ever built for **American President Lines**. Congress approved $73 million for the construction of the 43,000-gross-ton ship in 1958, but President **Dwight D. Eisenhower** refused to sign the bill into law.

press gang, group of men, commanded by an officer, who forced men into service in a navy or army. They were primarily used to recruit for the **Royal Navy**.

Preussen, 408-foot, five-masted **square-rigger** —the largest **full-rigged ship** ever to sail the oceans—launched in 1902 at Gestemunde, Germany. She was built for the nitrate trade between Europe and Chile, and her forty-three sails, with an area of almost sixty thousand square feet, pushed her along at speeds approaching twelve **knots** on many successful runs. Outbound from Germany in November 1910, *Preussen* was damaged after ramming a cross-channel steamer. Her size proved too formidable for her three tugboat escort, and she grounded on a reef, ending her career. Captain Hans Moethe, **skipper** of her running

Princess Carla. (Courtesy Gordon R. Ghareeb)

mate, the five-masted **bark** *Potosi*, had earlier refused to accept command of the giant ship because of her handling problems.

Pribilof Islands, islands off Alaska that are breeding grounds for seals, acquired by the United States with the purchase of Alaska in 1867. To limit slaughter of seals, in 1911 an international convention allowed quotas to the United States, Canada, Japan, and Russia. Suspended during World War II, this was renewed in 1957 by a convention establishing a North Pacific Fur Seal Commission composed of the same four powers. Seal population, at 125,000 in 1911, is 1.5 million today.

Pride of Baltimore, replica of a nineteenth-century Baltimore **clipper** constructed in downtown Baltimore by Melbourne Smith and launched in 1977. Having sailed more than 150,000 miles at sea, the sail training topsail **schooner** departed Saint Thomas on May 11, 1986, en route to Chesapeake Bay. On May 14 the *Pride* was hit by hurricane-force winds, and she sank, taking with her four of her crew of twelve. A replacement ship, *Pride of Baltimore II*, was commissioned by the State of Maryland in 1988 and continues to sail.

prime meridian, meridian that is designated 0° **longitude**, from which all other longitudes—

180° East or West—are measured. The International Prime Meridian Conference, held in October 1884, fixed the meridian passing through the Royal Observatory at Greenwich, England—the leading science center of the time—as the prime meridian. It is sometimes called the **Greenwich meridian**.

HMS *Prince of Wales*, 745-foot World War II British battleship that had a short life. Fresh from her building yard, she sailed with HMS *Hood* and engaged the *Bismarck* on May 24, 1941. *Hood* exploded and sank, and *Prince of Wales* was damaged. Two months later, she carried Prime Minister **Winston Churchill** to meet President **Franklin D. Roosevelt** aboard USS *Augusta* in Argentia Bay, Newfoundland, where the two leaders signed the famous Atlantic Charter. On December 10, 1941, *Prince of Wales* and the World War I battle **cruiser** HMS *Repulse* were sunk off the coast of Thailand by eighty-five Japanese bombers in three separate attacks.

The Princess and the Pirate, 1944 American film comedy reviving the age-old oceanic tale of the damsel in distress who is rescued from marauding eighteenth-century pirates by her true love. The film starred Bob Hope, Virginia Mayo, and Walter Brennan.

Princess Carla, advertised and unofficial working name of the **Costa Line liner** *Carla 'C'* while under charter to southern California–based **Princess Cruises** from 1968 to 1970. Originally the **French Line**'s *Flandre* of 1952, the ship was extensively rebuilt by Costa just prior to her assignment to Princess. The now-famous Princess Cruises logo of the woman with her hair billowing out behind her was originally designed as a decorative **funnel** device for the *Princess Carla.*

The Princess Comes Across, 1936 American comedy feature film about midocean mayhem and high jinks aboard an ocean **liner** headed to New York. It featured magnificent footage of SS *Normandie* leaving **Le Havre** and starred Fred MacMurray, Carole Lombard, and William Frawley.

Princess Cruises, inauspicious charter cruise line that began in 1965 with West Coast runs to Acapulco undertaken by the ***Princess Patricia***. The success of the initial season led to another charter of the vessel and the adaptation of her name to the company moniker. Continued success brought the year-round charter in 1967 of the new *Italia*, which was marketed as the *Princess Italia* to maintain the company's identity. With the charter of the ***Princess Carla*** in 1968 came the introduction of the famous "whore in the wind" logo (so named by Los Angeles longshoremen of the time), for which the cruise concern has become instantly identifiable. The company was sold to **P&O** in 1974 and became phenomenally popular with the production of *The Love Boat* television series in 1977.

Princess Kathleen, well-patronized three-**funneled** steamer of the **Canadian Pacific Railway** built in 1925 for service from Vancouver to Alaska and to Seattle in the off-season. She served as a British troop transport in the Mediterranean during World War II. While sailing the **Inland Passage** north of Juneau in 1952—not far from where the *Princess Sophia* went down in 1918 —she strayed a mile and a half off course and went aground on the rocky shore. The entire ship's company was removed to safety and, twelve hours after she stranded, the incoming tide flooded the 5,875-gross-ton **liner**, causing her stem to rear high out of the water as she spectacularly plunged stern first to the floor of the waterway.

Princess Louise, **Canadian Pacific Railway** steamer completed in 1921 for passenger excursions through Alaska's **Inland Passage**. When retired from active service in 1965, the 4,032-gross-ton **liner** became a well-known restaurant ship in Los Angeles Harbor. She cap-

Princess Louise at her berth in Los Angeles. (Courtesy Gordon R. Ghareeb)

sized in dry dock during maintenance work in 1989, and her hulk was **scuttled** at sea west of Catalina Island in 1990.

Princess Marguerite, Scottish-built sister ship to the ***Princess Kathleen*** for the **Canadian Pacific Railway**'s northern West Coast service. She sailed with her sister to the Mediterranean in 1941 to become an aircraft carrier support ship. Bound for Cyprus with over fifteen hundred men on board in 1942, she was torpedoed by a German **U-boat** and sank forty minutes after the attack, with the loss of fifty-five lives.

Princess Patricia, unassuming little 5,911-gross-ton coastal **liner** built in 1948 for the British Columbian coastal service of the **Canadian Pacific Railway**. Chartered in 1965–66 for seasonal cruises to the Mexican Riviera, she lent her name to the operation that later came to be known worldwide as **Princess Cruises**.

Princess Sophia, small **Canadian Pacific Railway** coastal steamer operated on the Vancouver to Skagway run. Completed in 1911, the 2,320-gross-ton ship was stranded on Alaska's Vanderbilt Reef in 1918 during a violent storm. Although surrounded by rescue craft, the 333 people aboard the *Princess Sophia*, as well as the fifty horses being carried in the hold, could

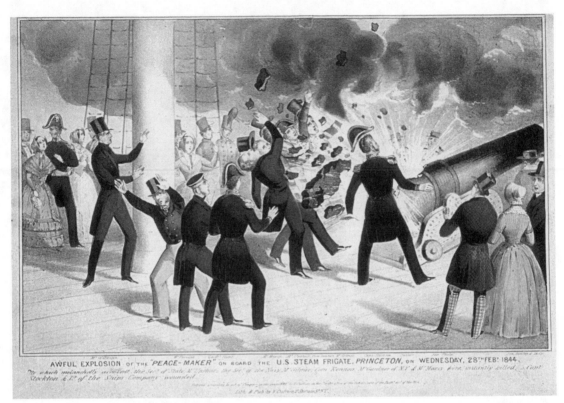

AWFUL EXPLOSION of the *"PEACE-MAKER"* on board the U.S. STEAM FRIGATE, *PRINCETON*, on WEDNESDAY, 28TH FEB: 1844.

Explosion of the Peacemaker aboard USS *Princeton* on February 28, 1844. (Courtesy The Mariners' Museum, Newport News, Virginia)

not be removed to safety because of the sea conditions and snowfall. One of the last messages sent out of her wireless room read, "For God's sake come and save us." Nearly two days after grounding, the weather worsened still, and the **liner** slipped off the reef and sank, taking everyone on board with her.

Princess Victoria, 310-foot British ferry that provided passenger, vehicle, and cargo service between Northern Ireland and Scotland. The **liner** was lost in a gale off the coast of Ireland in January 1953, and 128 of the 172 people on board died.

USS *Princeton*, steam **sloop** and the U.S. **Navy's** first screw-driven warship, designed by **John Ericsson** and launched in 1843. During an ordnance demonstration on the Potomac River in February 1844, one of the ship's "Peacemaker" twelve-inch guns shattered, killing four people, including the secretary of the navy and the secretary of state, and wounding nine others. President John Tyler was on board but below decks at the time. The incident, described as one of the U.S. Navy's worst peacetime tragedies, led the navy to adopt the **Dahlgren gun**, which was later widely used in the Civil War.

USS *Princeton* (CV-23), **Independence**-class aircraft carrier originally laid down as the heavy **cruiser** USS *Tallahassee* in 1941. The hull was converted on the stocks into an aircraft carrier. The thirteen-thousand-ton vessel was commissioned in 1943 and dispatched to action in the South Pacific. While cruising off the Philippines in 1944, the 622-foot ship was hit by a Japanese bomber, resulting in fires that eventually touched off enormous explosions. She sank, taking 208 crew members with her.

Principessa Jolanda, 9,200-gross-ton Lloyd Italiano Line passenger **liner** that capsized upon leaving the launching ways near Genoa, Italy, on September 22, 1907.

Principessa Mafalda, passenger **liner** delivered in 1909 for the South America service of the Lloyd Italiano Line. While the ship was en route to Rio de Janeiro, her port propeller shaft snapped, setting off a sequence of events that led to the deaths of 303 people when the 9,210-gross-ton liner capsized on October 25, 1927.

MS *Prinsendam*, motor **liner** built in 1973 as a prototype for a new cruise ship class for the **Holland America Line**. The 8,566-gross-ton vessel caught fire in October 1980 in the Gulf of Alaska while on a cruise from Vancouver to Singapore with 320 passengers on board. All passengers and crew were evacuated by lifeboats into heavy seas and rough weather and then rescued by the U.S. **Coast Guard**. No one died, but many passengers suffered from hypothermia and exposure. The *Prinsendam* sank four days later while she was being towed to Portland, Oregon.

Prinz Eugen, German heavy **cruiser**, completed in 1940, that accompanied the *Bismarck* at the outset of that battleship's one and only foray into battle. The ten-thousand-ton cruiser was the only major German warship to survive the war in steaming condition and was taken over by U.S. forces. She was sunk during atomic bomb testing in 1946 at the **Bikini Atoll** in the South Pacific.

Priscilla, magnificent **side-wheel** passenger steamer built in 1893 for the **Fall River Line** to provide passenger service between New York and New England. The 441-foot vessel could accommodate fifteen hundred passengers overnight in her opulent interior. She was one of the largest vessels built for service on Long Island Sound, being surpassed only by her running mate *Commonwealth* in 1908, and her career spanned nearly half a century.

prisoner of war model, ship model made by hundreds of French sailors who were prisoners of the British during the **French Revolution** and **Napoleonic Wars**. The sailors would carve the intricate models in order to supplement their wages and rations. Most models were made from animal bones, but often ivory and mahogany were provided for commissioned work.

privateer, privately owned armed vessel authorized by a government by a **letter of marque** to attack enemy shipping. The commander of such a vessel was also called a "privateer." A vessel captured by a privateer was brought to a friendly court, and if the capture was declared legal by a prize court, the vessel and cargo were generally sold and the proceeds were divided among owners, officers, and crew. The practice was abolished by international agreement in 1856.

prize money, profits stemming from the sale of a ship and its cargo that was captured by a warship or a **privateer**. The ship was usually sent back with a prize crew to a port with a prize court, which awarded the prize money. The money would be divided up between the privateers' owner, officers, and crew.

Proceedings, magazine published by the U.S. **Naval Institute** that serves as the main public forum for discussion and debate of subjects affecting the U.S. **Navy**. The U.S. Naval Institute was established in 1873 by a group of concerned naval officers to discuss the serious implications of a smaller, post–Civil War Navy and other matters of professional interest. The "proceedings" of those discussions were eventually published and circulated throughout the fleet.

Propeller Club of the United States, organization founded in 1927 to promote a strong American **merchant marine** on the oceans, **Great Lakes**, and inland waterways. Today there are Propeller Club Ports (chapters) in most major cities in the United States as well as overseas. The "Propeller" in the name, in addition to referring to the propulsion of vessels, is symbolic of the driving force required to maintain a strong private merchant fleet.

protection and indemnity, traditional name for insurance to cover shipowners and charterers against their legal liabilities to third parties. Usually arranged through a **P&I club**, the insurance applies particularly to protection against loss of life and injury, and that portion of collision liability not covered by regular policies.

protest flag, international signal code flag B, which is flown by a yacht during or just after a race if a violation of the rules is claimed by a competitor. The race committee must note the complaint and make a ruling before the winner of the race is declared.

Proteus, in Greek mythology, a prophet who was the son of **Neptune**. He was also called the **Old Man of the Sea**. He was capable of assuming different forms at will in order to escape capture. If captured, Proteus would predict the future truthfully and return to the sea.

Prouts Neck, small coastal town in southern Maine that from 1884 until his death in 1910 was home to artist **Winslow Homer**. Its rocky coast was the subject of a series of seascapes by the artist.

proximity fuse, little-known invention that brought World War II to a quicker end. The fuse, mounted in an artillery shell, used a tiny radio to transmit a signal, which reflected from the target and detonated the shell when close enough to do real damage, converting many potential "near misses" to effective "hits." It was first used as an anti-aircraft fuse in the Pacific by the U.S. **Navy** and helped to bring down many Japanese aircraft.

PT-109, standard torpedo patrol or **PT boat** that was under the command of Lieutenant (j.g.) **John F. Kennedy** in World War II. On the night of August 2, 1943, the craft was cut in two by the Japanese **destroyer** *Amagiri* while off the coast of the Solomon Islands, resulting in the death of two of the boat's twelve crew members. Although Kennedy's seamanship and ability as a **skipper** were questionable, his heroism and cunning were exemplary, resulting in all the survivors being rescued. His actions were cited by the U.S. government, and the event was often recalled during his campaign to become the thirty-fifth president of the United States.

PT 109, well-done Hollywood effort detailing how **John F. Kennedy** managed to get his **PT boat** crew rescued after being run down by a Japanese **destroyer** in 1943 while on night patrol off the Solomon Islands in the Pacific Ocean. Based on the book of the same title, by Robert J. Donovan (1961), the early 1963 film starred Cliff Robertson as the heroic young skipper of PT-109 and also featured Ty Hardin, James Gregory, and Robert Culp. "PT 109" was also a Top 40 song by country singer Billy Dean in 1962.

PT boat, swift, light, easy-to-maneuver U.S. **Navy** patrol craft (PT stood for "patrol torpedo") made famous during World War II. Made of wood, it carried either two or four torpedoes launched from tubes on deck, and one or two 20 mm guns. Between 1939 and 1945, more than eight hundred of the forty-five-ton, seventy- to eighty-foot boats were constructed with 1,500 horsepower engines capable of forty-five **knots**. U.S. Navy PTs were predominantly built by the **Elco** Navy Division of the

Electric Boat Company in Bayonne, New Jersey; Higgins Industries in New Orleans; and **Huckins** Yacht Corporation in Jacksonville, Florida.

Ptolemy, Claudius (100–170), early Greek-Egyptian mathematician, astronomer, and cartographer whose work *Geographia* included a collection of maps that contained nearly eight thousand places identified by **latitude** and **longitude**—words he also was said to have coined. He set a standard for geographic representation, and his maps, continually updated, were known as "ptolemies" in medieval times.

U.S. Public Health Service (PHS), government service established in 1798 to encourage the expansion of the **merchant marine** and to protect ill and injured seamen. Congress established the Marine Hospital Service under the Treasury Department to provide health care to seamen. The first hospital was established in Boston, and others followed in most major ports. The hospitals provided care for sailors during the **War of 1812** and the Civil War. The service turned to public health work in 1870s because of such diseases as smallpox, yellow fever, and cholera, and in 1889 it officially established the commissioned corps along military lines with ranks corresponding to the navy and army. Today the PHS is part of the Department of Health and Human Services and is headed by the U.S. surgeon general.

USS *Pueblo*, one of seven general-purpose supply vessels built in 1944 for the U.S. Army. Originally named the *Duvall*, the 935-ton ship was **laid up** in 1954. Reassigned to the U.S. Navy in 1966, she was rebuilt as a research vessel and renamed *Pueblo*. While on an intelligence mission in 1968, she was attacked and intercepted by North Korean fighter planes and naval craft off the coast of North Korea. The seized vessel was brought to Wonsan, where the eighty-two crew members were held captive in a North Korean prison for eleven months before being returned to U.S. authorities.

Puget, Peter (1762–1822), British naval officer and explorer who sailed with Captain **George Vancouver** on a four-year voyage around the world (1791–95). He played an important part in the exploration of the north Pacific Coast of North America. Puget Sound (Washington), Cape Puget (Alaska), and Puget Island (Columbia River) were named for him.

SS *Pulaski*, American **steamship** that exploded off the coast of North Carolina on June 14, 1838, with a hundred lives lost. The accident was one of several that convinced the U.S. Congress to establish the **Steamboat Inspection Service** that same year.

Punic Wars, three wars fought between Rome and Carthage (264–241 B.C., 218–201 B.C., and 149–146 B.C.) in which Rome was finally victorious. The first war honed Rome's seafaring skills as it was forced to build a fleet to match the skillful Carthagenians. The second war saw Hannibal cross the Alps on elephant. At the end of the third war, the Romans destroyed Carthage. In the end, the wars proved that a strong naval presence was essential for maintaining national trade.

Puritan, ninety-four-foot **cutter**, designed by **Edward Burgess**, that held off the English challenger ***Genesta*** in two races to win the 1885 **America's Cup**. The **New York Yacht Club** defender was owned by a Boston-based syndicate headed by General **Charles J. Paine**.

purse-seine, method of commercial fishing in which fish are encircled using a large stationary net drawn together at the bottom by a purse line. The top of the net is maintained at the surface by a number of floats or buoys.

Pursuit, 1974 book by Ludovic Kennedy about the pursuit and sinking of the German

Kidd on the Deck of the Adventure Galley, circa 1903, by Howard Pyle. (Delaware Art Museum)

battleship *Bismark* by British **Royal Navy** forces in 1941, during World War II.

Pursuit of the Graf Spee, British-made 1957 film, released in England as *The Battle of the River Plate*, about the chase and sinking of the German **pocket battleship** *Admiral Graf Spee*. Peter Finch played Captain Hans Langs-

dorff, and the **cruiser** USS *Salem* starred as the *Graf Spee*.

Pursuit to Algiers, 1945 Sherlock Holmes movie that is set aboard a passenger **liner** tainted with intrigue, assassins, and mystery. It starred Basil Rathbone as the British sleuth and Nigel Bruce as Dr. Watson.

pusser, **Royal Navy** term for the supply officer, a corruption of the term "purser," which originated from the word "disburse" or "disburser" —for the officer's primary function of doling out money and supplies.

Pyle, Howard (1853–1911), one of the foremost American illustrators and author of adventure books. A master of pen-and-ink drawings, he was also prolific in oil paintings and watercolors. His presentation of **buccaneer** life in his *Book of Pirates*, while often fictional (walking the plank was not a pirate predilection), still serves as the basis for modern perceptions of pirate life. Other books of his include *In the Wake of the Buccaneers*, *Memoirs of a Buccaneer*, and *Buccaneers & Marooners of America* (1905).

Pytheas (ca. 320 B.C.), Greek scholar and explorer who sailed from Marseilles, France, to Britain and back, with side excursions. He discovered that the Pole Star does not exactly mark the North Pole and, observing the tides of the **Atlantic**, which are much larger than those in the Mediterranean, correctly theorized that they are caused by the moon. His account of his voyage was widely quoted, but no copy of the entire account has been recovered.

Q

Q3, traditional quadruple-screw transatlantic superliner designed by the **Cunard Line** to replace RMS *Queen Mary* by 1966. The streamlined, twin-**funneled** vessel was expected to be 990 feet long and nearly eighty thousand gross tons. With a passenger capacity of 2,250 in three classes, she would have been no more than a modernized version of the **liner** she was intending to replace. The rise of passenger jet traffic on the **Atlantic** run led the Cunard Line, in 1961, to postpone the contract signing for the unnamed Q3 indefinitely, and construction never began.

QMED, acronym for qualified member of the engine department, an unlicensed member of the engine department with qualifications above the entry level of wiper.

Q ship, ship camouflaged as a noncombatant ship, with its armament and other fighting equipment hidden and with special provisions for unmasking its weapons quickly. Also called a "decoy ship," this type of ship was used by the British **Royal Navy** in the early days of World War I to combat the **U-boat** threat. Limited trial of the concept was made by both Great Britain and the United States during World War II, but it was soon abandoned as ineffective.

quadrant, simple navigational instrument consisting of a quarter circle with a 0-to-90-degree scale, two sights, and a **plumb line**. It was used from the mid-fifteenth century to measure the altitude of heavenly bodies. Later developments included the **Davis quadrant** and **Hadley's quadrant**.

quadrantal spheres, round iron balls mounted on each side of a magnetic compass to correct the induced magnetism of the ship. They are often referred to as the "navigator's balls."

quahog, a hard-shell clam found on the U.S. **Atlantic** coast whose sizes can range up to six inches.

quarterdeck, part of the upper deck, usually extending from the mainmast to the stern, reserved for officers. It is also the ceremonial

RMS *Queen Elizabeth* is eased through an ice-clogged Hudson River to her berth at Pier 90. (Courtesy Gordon R. Ghareeb)

area near the bow on the main deck that is used for receiving visitors.

Quasi-War, unofficial war waged between France and the United States from 1797 to 1801, which was fought entirely at sea in the **Atlantic Ocean** and the **West Indies**. The French, angered at improved U.S. relations with Great Britain—with whom they were at war—sought to capture American ships, while the U.S. **Navy** protected American merchants and hunted down French **privateers**. During this time, the U.S. Navy Department was established in 1798. This war is also referred to as the Undeclared Naval War with France.

Queeg, Captain, mentally questionable commanding officer of the USS *Caine* in **Herman Wouk**'s Pulitzer Prize–winning novel *The **Caine Mutiny*** (1951). Humphrey Bogart portrayed Queeg in the 1954 film based on the book.

The Queen and I, shipboard television fare set aboard the fictitious **liner** *Amsterdam Queen.* Seen in retrospect, this short-lived 1969 series was a transitional piece linking the *The **Gale Storm Show*** and *The **Love Boat***. The *Statendam*, operating a string of cruises from Los Angeles at the time, provided much of the at-sea footage. The show starred Larry Storch and Billy De Wolfe.

Queen Anne's Revenge, three-masted former slave ship that became the **flagship** of notorious pirate **Edward Teach**, also known as **Blackbeard**. The former French merchant ship carried forty guns and was as powerful as any naval vessel of similar size. She was wrecked in Beaufort Inlet in North Carolina in 1718, and what are thought to be her remains were uncovered in 1997.

RMS *Queen Elizabeth*, passenger **liner** built by the **Cunard Line** to provide transatlantic service along with RMS *Queen Mary*. Completed as the world's largest vessel in 1940, she was requisitioned by the **Royal Navy** and served the Allies as a troopship during World War II. She made her peacetime **maiden voyage** in 1946 and was retired in 1968. After being taken to Florida for an ill-fated stint as a tourist attraction, she was purchased in 1970 by Orient Overseas Lines and renamed the *Seawise University*. The 83,673-gross-ton giant was totally destroyed by fire before capsizing in Hong Kong Harbor in January 1972 on the eve of her reemergence into passenger service.

Queen Elizabeth 2 *(QE2)*, conceived as a running mate to the first **Queen Elizabeth**, the 65,863-gross-ton *QE2* was completed in 1968 as a replacement for both of the giant **Cunard Line** "Queen" **liners**. She made her **maiden voyage** in 1969 after scandalous trouble with her Scottish builders led to the refusal by Cunard to accept her until all problems had been set straight. Continually updated and redec-

Queen Elizabeth 2. (Courtesy Gordon R. Ghareeb)

orated, the now-grand liner has lost nearly all semblance of her "swinging sixties" decorative origins. She is scheduled to retire from service in 2005.

RMS *Queen Mary*, crack 1936 passenger steamer of the **Cunard Line**. She was the fastest ship in the world from 1938 to 1952, with top speeds of over thirty-two **knots**, and she made 1,001 crossings of the North Atlantic, 18 pleasure cruises, and 72 government voyages as a troopship during World War II. She holds the all-time record for the most people—16,683—ever embarked for a single voyage, set in 1943, and is for many the most loved and exalted vessel of all time. Her retirement, more than any other luxury **liner**, signaled the end of the transatlantic seagoing era. She was sold amid great hoopla in 1967 to the city of Long Beach, California, where the 81,235-gross-ton liner still

RMS *Queen Mary* entering Long Beach in 1967. (Courtesy Gordon R. Ghareeb)

serves as a hotel and attraction, with modest but effective museum installations representing her unique career as the premier ocean liner.

Queen Mary 2, $780 million dollar transatlantic luxury **liner** to be built in France by **Carnival Cruise Lines** for operation by the **Cunard Line** in late 2003. Intended to be the largest and longest liner ever built, she will measure just over 1,130 feet in length—117 feet shorter than the Empire State Building is tall. The 150,000-ton ship will carry 2,620 passengers and will run between New York and Southampton in the summer, then out of Miami in the winter.

Queen of Spain Cup, name for the 1928 **Transatlantic Race** from New York to Santander, Spain, for yachts from thirty-five to fifty-five feet on the waterline. In conjunction with the **King of Spain Cup**, this smaller class started a week before the larger boats and the two winners arrived the same day. The **Starling Burgess**–designed *Niña*, with an amateur crew, scored a close victory.

Queequeg, fictional tattooed **South Seas** islander, and onetime cannibal who is a har-

pooner aboard the whaleship *Pequod*, in the novel *Moby-Dick* (1851) by **Herman Melville**.

Quiberon Bay, Battle of, important battle of the **Seven Years' War** fought between British and French forces close in to the coast of France on November 20, 1759. The decisive British victory, in which eleven of twenty-one French ships were sunk or captured, destroyed any possibility of a French invasion of England.

A Quiet Voyage Home, best-selling 1970 novel by Richard Jessup that is set contemporaneously aboard the fictitious westbound American **liner** *New York*. It features antiestablishment sentiment, political renegades, and hippie subculture on the **Atlantic** in the Vietnam era of peace demonstrations and revolution rallies.

Quonset hut, semicylindrical steel building used by the U.S. **Navy** during World War II in the Pacific for shelter and storage. The huts were named for Quonset Point, Rhode Island, where they were first manufactured.

R

Ra II, named after the sun god Ra, this copy of an ancient Egyptian papyrus vessel was built by anthropologist **Thor Heyerdahl** to prove that contact between old civilizations and the Americas was possible. The first *Ra* was forty-five feet long and built of papyrus in 1969 in Egypt. It was transported to Morocco, where it set sail for Barbados. Due to problems, *Ra* had to be abandoned a short distance from Barbados. *Ra II*, a reed vessel built ten months later in Bolivia, was shipped to Africa and had a successful transatlantic crossing in 1970, covering the four thousand miles to Barbados in fifty-seven days. *Ra II* is on display at the **Kon-Tiki** Museum in Oslo, Norway, near the **Fram** Museum.

Rackham, John (d. 1720), English pirate, known as "Calico Jack" for his habit of wearing colorful clothing, who became an active raider along the colonial American seaboard and in the Caribbean from 1718 to 1720. Among his crew were the female pirates **Mary Read** and **Anne Bonny**, with whom he was romantically linked. Rackham was captured in 1720 and taken to Jamaica, where he was tried and hanged for offenses to the crown.

racon, also called a **radar** beacon or radar transponder, a receiver-transmitter device used as a navigational aid to identify landmarks, structures, or buoys and designed to produce distinctive images on the screens of radar sets.

radar, a shortening of "radio detection and ranging," the name of a device that works by sending radio waves toward an object and receiving the waves that are reflected from the object. The time it takes for the reflected waves to return indicates the object's range. The direction from which the reflected waves return tells the object's location.

Radford, Arthur William (1896–1973), U.S. **Navy** admiral who served during World Wars I and II and won recognition as an expert on naval aviation and aircraft carrier warfare. He was commander in chief of the U.S. Pacific fleet from 1949 to 1953 and served from 1953 to 1957 as chairman of the Joint Chiefs of Staff.

Radio Bikini, 1987 Academy Award–winning documentary that graphically relives the events and horror of the atomic bomb tests at the **Bikini Atoll** following World War II. Quite scary stuff is all captured here in graphic Technicolor. The glimpse of a battle **cruiser** being upended by the force of the detonation is sobering.

Raeder, Erich (1876–1960), German admiral who served as Germany's naval commander in chief from 1935 to 1943. He resigned after disagreements with Adolf Hitler, who had lost faith in the heavy surface ships Raeder believed in, and was replaced by Admiral **Karl Dönitz**. Raeder was sentenced to life imprisonment at the Nuremberg trials in 1946 but was freed in 1955 because of poor health.

Raffaello, attractive 45,933-gross-ton **Italian Line** passenger vessel built in 1965 for the North Atlantic service. She and her sister ship *Michelangelo* always looked odd in profile because their massive hulls contained only two rows of portholes where other **liners** of these dimensions would have had at least five decks demarcated by ports. This was done as a measure to anticipate changing safety regulations and to make the two ships as seaworthy as possible. She was **laid up** in 1975 because of the loss of government subsidy and was sold to Iran the following year as an accommodations ship. In 1983 she was sunk by Iraqi air attacks.

Raft of Medusa, 1819 painting by French painter Theodore Gericault that depicts survivors of the wreck of the French naval **frigate** *Medusa*, which ran aground and sank while on its way to Senegal in July 1816. Approximately 150 men scrambled onto the raft; after thirteen days of rough seas, murder, and cannibalism, only 10 men survived to be rescued by the ship *Argus*. Survivors' accounts horrified France in 1817. Measuring seven by eight and a half feet, Gericault's painting prompted French historian Jules Michelet to state that "the whole of France had gone to sea in the *Medusa*."

Rainbow, 128-foot American **J-boat** designed by **W. Starling Burgess** and built by the **Herreshoff** Manufacturing Company for **Harold Stirling "Mike" Vanderbilt**. She defeated the British challenger *Endeavour* in the 1934 **America's Cup** competition, four races to two.

Rainbow Warrior, oceangoing protest vessel (former British research vessel *Sir William Hardy*) operated from 1977 to 1985 by the international activist environmental organization **Greenpeace**. The vessel was sunk in 1985 by the French Secret Service in Auckland, New Zealand, while it was protesting French nuclear testing in the Pacific Ocean. Beyond repair, the vessel was stripped and **scuttled** at sea. The name *Rainbow Warrior* was inspired by a North American Indian legend that prophesies that when man has destroyed the world through his greed, the Warriors of the Rainbow will arise to save it again.

Raise the Titanic!, third novel by **Clive Cussler** featuring **Dirk Pitt** as the hero who is in a race to be the first man aboard the hulk of RMS *Titanic* when resurrected from the Atlantic floor. It was made into a rather forgettable 1980 movie featuring Jason Robards.

Rajula, British-India colonial **liner** built in 1926 and sister ship to the **Rohna**. Both ships were notable for holding certificates to carry 5,267 passengers—more than any other peacetime ship—in cabins and on deck. Scrapped in 1974, when she was fifty years old, the 8,704-gross-ton liner was the longest lived of all British-India Steam Navigation Company ships.

Raleigh, Sir Walter (1554–1618), English adventurer, navigator, and historian who engaged in many voyages of discovery and piracy and played an important role in England's victory over the **Spanish Armada** in 1588. He named

Raffaello. (Courtesy Gordon R. Ghareeb)

much of what is now the eastern United States "Virginia," in honor of Queen Elizabeth, known as "the Virgin Queen." He promoted many settlements in the New World and organized the 1584 colony at Roanoke Island, off the North Carolina coast. The colony failed for reasons still mysterious, and it became known as the Lost Colony. Raleigh was imprisoned and later beheaded by King James I.

Ramage, Nicholas, fictional **Royal Navy** officer serving in the **Napoleonic Wars** in eighteen novels by English author **Dudley Pope**.

Rambouillet Decree, order signed by Napoleon in March 1810 ordering the seizure and confiscation of all American shipping in any French port. Two years earlier, he had authorized the French seizure of American shipping.

Ran, Norse goddess of the sea, wife of **Aegir**.

USS *Randolph* (CV-15), **Essex**-class aircraft carrier, completed in 1944, that was attacked by a **kamikaze** on her first tour of duty in the South Pacific, killing 25 men and wounding 106. She participated in assaults on the Japanese main islands. In 1960 she retrieved astronaut Virgil Grissom after splashdown following the second manned flight into space. The 888-foot ship was decommissioned in 1969 and sold for scrap in 1975.

Random, Roderick, reckless young hero of the semiautobiographical novel *The **Adventures of Roderick Random*** by **Tobias Smollett**.

Ranger, newly launched **Continental Navy** vessel dispatched to France under **John Paul Jones** in 1778 to disrupt British shipping and engage the **Royal Navy**. *Ranger* received from the French the first salute to the new American flag by a foreign warship. She later returned home, and Jones took command of a war prize he later named ***Bonhomme Richard***. *Ranger* was later captured and renamed HMS *Halifax*.

Ranger, Harold Stirling "Mike" Vanderbilt's legendary **America's Cup** defender in 1937, which defeated Britain's ***Endeavour II***, four races to none. Designed by **W. Starling Burgess** and **Olin James Stephens II**, at 136 feet she was the largest **J-boat** ever built. She was constructed at **Bath Iron Works** in Bath, Maine, the first defender in forty years not built by the **Herreshoff** yard in Bristol, Rhode Island.

USS *Ranger* (CV-4), completed in 1934, the 14,500-ton ship was the first aircraft carrier specifically designed for the purpose (others had been converted for use as carriers). *Ranger* played a major role in the Casablanca beach-head during the World War II Allied invasion of Morocco in 1942 and was later dispatched for further combat duty in the Pacific. Decommissioned in 1946, the 769-foot vessel was scrapped the following year.

Ransome, Arthur (1884–1976), British journalist, yachtsman, and author of the *Swallows and Amazons* series of books for young readers. An accomplished mariner, Ransome was able to translate his experience with boats, islands, and adventures at sea for a young audience. His *Racundra's First Cruise* (1923) is about sailing on the Baltic Sea.

rates, six classifications into which warships of sailing navies were usually grouped according to the number of guns carried. Developed by the British in the eighteenth century, ratings changed as ships grew bigger. At the Battle of **Trafalgar**, they were as follows: first rate—100 guns or more; second rate—90 to 100 guns; third rate—70 to 90 guns; fourth rate—50 to 70 guns; fifth rate—32 to 50 guns; and sixth rate—any number up to 32 guns. Only a vessel of the first three rates could be considered a **ship of the line**.

rat guard, large conical disc through which a mooring line is run so that rats cannot board a vessel by climbing up the line.

rating rule, in yacht racing, a rule used to classify sailing yachts of different designs to enable them to compete on relatively equal terms. Such rules are based on measurement formulas that take into account a yacht's length, beam, displacement, sail area, and other design factors that affect its potential speed.

Ratsey, Thomas White (1851–1935), British sailmaker and yachtsman who expanded his family's sailmaking business. In 1890 Ratsey of Cowes merged with Lapthorn of Gosport to form Ratsey and Lapthorn. Both family firms

were established in 1790 and made sails for HMS **Victory**, among many other vessels. Opened in 1902, the **City Island**, New York, branch of the Ratsey and Lapthorn was an institution among American yachtsmen for most of the twentieth century until its closing in 1981.

HMS *Rattler*, screw-propelled **sloop** that in 1845 engaged in a tug-of-war with the **side-wheeler** HMS *Alecto* to prove which propulsion system was superior. *Rattler* won the head-to-head battle by pulling the **paddle wheeler** astern at three **knots**.

Rattlin, Jack, fictional naval character in **Tobias George Smollet**'s novel *The Adventures of Roderick Random* (1748).

Rawalpindi, P&O passenger steamer built in 1925. Converted into an armed merchant **cruiser** in 1939, she was attacked by the German battleships *Gneisenau* and *Scharnhorst* between Iceland and the Faroe Islands on November 23, 1939. In the first surface naval action of the war, the British **liner** went down with the loss of 260 lives. The German vessels managed to take on board 26 survivors before approaching British ships, summoned by *Rawalpindi*'s radio, caused them to leave the scene. HMS *Rawalpindi* achieved her mission, because the German ships failed to break out into the **Atlantic** as planned and were forced to return to port.

Reaching for the Moon, classic 1931 musical comedy at sea about a businessman who falls for liquor and a woman on a transatlantic voyage. Music by Irving Berlin served to embellish the spectacular art-deco ocean **liner** movie sets. The film starred Douglas Fairbanks Sr., Bebe Daniels, Edward Everett Horton, and Bing Crosby.

Read, Mary (d. 1721), English pirate who fought in the army and navy disguised as a man before turning to piracy. She sailed with

Anne Bonny under **John Rackham** and was captured along with the rest of Rackham's crew in 1720 and taken to Jamaica. Mary was spared the hangman's gallows because she was pregnant at the time, but she died in jail of a fever shortly after the birth of her child.

reading both pages, see **wing and wing**.

Ready Reserve Force (RRF), a force of combatant sealift ships within the **National Defense Reserve Fleet** that are maintained in a high state of readiness and can be made available without mobilization or congressional declaration of a state of emergency. RRF ships are crewed by civilian mariners employed by a U.S. **Maritime Administration** contractor.

the real McCoy, phrase that has worked its way into American vernacular and come to mean something authentic, not a cheap imitation. The origin of the phrase is credited to Captain Bill McCoy, a **rumrunner** who won renown as an honest man during Prohibition. When spirits of questionable quality were passed off as the good stuff, whatever sailed with—or was smuggled by—Bill McCoy was guaranteed to be the genuine article.

Reap the Wild Wind, epic 1942 Technicolor motion picture, directed by Cecil B. DeMille in his famous panoramic style, about **clipper ships** and pirates off the Florida Keys in the mid-nineteenth century. The salty cinematic blockbuster starred John Wayne and Rita Hayworth, and the giant squid won the movie an Academy Award for best special effects.

Redburn, 1849 novel by **Herman Melville** about Wellingborough Redburn, a boy from New York City, and his rough initiation into a life as a sailor. It was based on Melville's 1839 voyage to Liverpool aboard the merchant ship *St. Lawrence*.

USS Redfish, U.S. submarine that sank a number of Japanese ships, including an aircraft carrier, off the coast of China during World War II. She supported U.N. forces in the Korean conflict, and in the mid-1950s the decorated sub appeared in the motion pictures *Twenty Thousand Leagues under the Sea* (1954) and *Run Silent, Run Deep* (1958).

red lead, anticorrosive primer paint used aboard most vessels. Red in color, it once contained heavy amounts of lead.

Red Oak Victory, 7,612-gross-ton **Victory ship** constructed in 1944. The vessel served in World War II as an ammunition supply ship and was operated by various owners from 1947 to 1968 when she entered the **National Defense Reserve Fleet** lay-up fleet at Suisun Bay. In 1998 she was acquired by the Richmond (California) Museum of History as a museum ship to be permanently moored in the California port, not far from the Kaiser Shipyard, where she was constructed.

red, right, returning, phrase used to remind **pilots** on which hand to leave nun buoys in the **lateral system**. Some people used "back to port, black to port" when can buoys were painted black; they're now green, however.

"Red Sails in the Sunset", hit song performed by Bing Crosby that reached number one in 1935. It was also recorded by Guy Lombardo, Mantovani, Nat King Cole, Louis Armstrong, the Platters, and Fats Domino. The chorus goes, "Red Sails in the sunset, way out on the sea, Oh carry my loved one home safely to me, She sailed at the dawning, all day I've been blue, Red Sails in the Sunset, I'm trusting in you."

red sky at night, weather proverb followed by "sailors' delight." It continues "red sky in the morning, sailors take warning."

Red Star Line, U.S. shipping line established in 1871 to operate vessels under the foreign flags on the Philadelphia to Antwerp route. Formally called the International Navigation Company, it acquired the **American Line** in

1884 and merged with the **Inman Line** in 1886. In 1902 it became part of **John Pierpont "J. P." Morgan**'s **International Mercantile Marine**.

reef, a reduction of sail area, usually by partially lowering the sail and tying part of it off at a reef point, or by rolling some of it up. The task is usually performed to reduce the area of sail during heavy winds.

Reeman, Douglas (b. 1924), English novelist writing nineteenth-century-period naval fiction under the pen name **Alexander Kent**.

regatta, race or series of races organized for sailing, power, or pulling boats.

registered tonnage (also called "net registered tonnage"), gross tonnage minus the volume of noncargo spaces (engine room, machinery spaces, fuel and water tanks, berthing spaces, and so forth). It is used in the documentation and registration of vessels as well as for measuring cargo-carrying capacity.

registry, enlistment of a vessel with a nationality, making it subject to the laws of the country, regardless of the nationality of the ship's ultimate owner.

Reliance, U.S. **America's Cup** defender in 1903. **Cornelius Vanderbilt** and William Rockefeller headed the syndicate that built the largest and most impressive of the Cup contenders. Designed and built by **Nathanael Greene Herreshoff**, the 143-foot bronze-and-steel **sloop** had a 116-foot boom and carried in excess of 16,000 square feet of sail—the most ever in the history of the race. *Reliance* handily defeated Sir **Thomas Lipton**'s *Shamrock III* three races to none.

remember the *Maine*, slogan adopted during the **Spanish-American War** after Spain was blamed for the sinking of the battleship USS *Maine* in the harbor of Havana, Cuba, on February 15, 1898.

Republic, **White Star Line liner** that collided with the Lloyd Italiano steamer *Florida* off Nantucket on January 23, 1909. *Republic* was outbound from New York with relief supplies for earthquake victims in southern Italy, and *Florida* was en route to New York with earthquake survivors. *Republic* transmitted the initial wireless distress call while her passengers were first transferred to the *Florida*. A total of seven vessels responded to the call, and only three *Republic* passengers and three *Florida* crew members were killed in the accident. *Florida* limped on to New York while *Republic* was taken in tow with hopes of beaching her on Martha's Vineyard. The 585-foot liner sank just south of the island in 250 feet of water.

USS *Requin* (SS-481), Tench-class submarine commissioned in 1945 and adapted for Cold War use as **radar picket** submarine. The 311-foot diesel vessel was employed to provide missile guidance as well as early detection of enemy air attacks. Retired from active duty in 1969, she opened as a museum in Tampa, Florida, in 1971. In 1990 she was moved up the **Mississippi River** to the Ohio River, where she opened as an attraction at the Carnegie Science Center in Pittsburgh, Pennsylvania.

ResidenSea, innovative condominium cruise line established in 1997 to promote and market its ship *The World*. The ship was intended to be online in 2000, but the company has had several setbacks, resulting in the postponement of its new "oceangoing luxury resort." Plans call for 110 spacious "residences" and 88 guest suites, with a full-time crew of 343 seafarers and hospitality staff members to help run the ship and serve the residents.

Resolute, 106-foot **Nathanael Greene Herreshoff**–designed **America's Cup** defender of 1920. **Skippered** by **Charles Francis Adams**, she defeated Sir **Thomas Lipton**'s *Shamrock IV*, three races to two. The race had been postponed six years because of World War I, and

Reliance, winner of the 1903 America's Cup. (Hart Nautical Collections at MIT)

the series marked the move of the racing from the waters off New York to Newport, Rhode Island.

HMS *Resolute*, British ship that was one of five vessels dispatched in 1852 in search of the lost **Franklin Expedition**. After becoming stuck in the ice, *Resolute*'s crew was forced to return to England aboard the other four vessels. She was retrieved by an American whaleship in 1855, brought to the United States, and eventually returned to Britain. In 1879 when *Resolute* was broken up, a desk was fashioned from her timbers and presented by Queen Victoria to U.S. President Rutherford B. Hayes. The desk has been used by various presidents in the Oval Office of the White House. In 1965 the British prime minister presented President Lyndon B. Johnson with the bell from *Resolute*.

HMS *Resolution*, ship commanded by Captain **James Cook** on his second (1772–75) and third (1776–79) voyages of discovery. Having learned from his first voyage aboard HMS ***Endeavour***, Cook took two ships on each of these expeditions so that he could continue if one were damaged. *Resolution* was accompanied by HMS *Adventure* on the second voyage and HMS *Discovery* on the third. Cook was killed on the third voyage during an altercation with a group of Hawaiians.

USS *Reuben James* (DD-245), U.S. **destroyer** that was torpedoed by a **U-boat** in October 1941 while escorting a Britain-bound **convoy** from Halifax, becoming the first U.S. warship sunk during World War II before U.S. entry into the war. More than 115 sailors lost their lives, and the sinking prompted U.S. government officials to arm merchant vessels, among other measures.

HMS *Revenge*, Sir **Francis Drake**'s **flagship** in defeating the **Spanish Armada** in 1588. In 1591, under the command of Richard Grenville (1542–1591), *Revenge* alone faced a force of fifty-three Spanish ships in the **Azores**. Her thirty-six-hour fight and subsequent sinking are the subject of **Alfred, Lord Tennyson**'s 1880 poem "The Last Fight of the *Revenge*."

U.S. Revenue Cutter Service, name used for the **Revenue Marine** that was not made official until 1863. In 1915 the Revenue Cutter Service was combined with the U.S. **Life-Saving Service** to form the U.S. **Coast Guard**. The term "**cutter**" continues to be used to describe most Coast Guard vessels.

Revenue Marine, service established in 1790 under the Treasury Department to enforce the customs laws of the new United States. **Alexander Hamilton** had proposed building ten ships—**cutter**-rigged for speed—to safeguard import revenue by combating smuggling; Congress authorized their construction on August 4, 1790. The first officer of the new service was **Hopley Yeaton**, who commanded the *Scammel*, the first revenue cutter. While often referred to as the U.S. **Revenue Cutter Service**, the name was not made official until 1863.

Reversing Falls, waterfalls that flow in alternating directions in a narrow channel in the Saint John River, New Brunswick, Canada, because of the large range of tide and a constriction in the river.

SS *Rex*, magnificent 51,062-gross-ton **flagship** of the **Italian Line** fleet that was completed in 1932 for the company's North Atlantic service and partnered with SS *Conte di Savoia*. She captured the **Blue Riband** in 1933 for the fastest crossing of the Atlantic Ocean and held onto that honor until eclipsed by SS *Normandie* in 1935. **Laid up** for the duration of World War II, the Italian **liner**—bombed and set afire by British planes—capsized in the shallow water of her sanctuary near Trieste on September 8, 1944. Scrapping of the wreck was finally completed in 1958.

Rhodes, Philip L. (1895–1974), prolific American boat designer whose career spanned more than five decades. His designs ranged from large motor yachts to small dinghies, and from **hydrofoils** to the 1962 **America's Cup** defender *Weatherly*.

rhumb line, a straight-line compass course between two points on a **Mercator** chart. Because of the curvature of the earth, it is usually not the shortest distance between two points. The shortest route is calculated by plotting a **great circle** course.

Richardson, James Otto (1878–1974), U.S. **Navy** admiral who was relieved of his position as commander in chief of the U.S. fleet in February 1941. He opposed moving the Pacific fleet to **Pearl Harbor**, insisting that Japanese expansion in the Pacific was of little concern to the United States and that the fleet could be kept in a better state of readiness in mainland ports.

Rickover, Hyman George (1900–1986), Polish-born U.S. naval officer who served in World War II as head of the Bureau of Ships and who later pioneered the development of the nuclear-powered submarine. In 1947, Rickover became head of the Naval Reactors Branch of the U.S. Atomic Energy Commission and also served as head of the Nuclear Power Division of the U.S. **Navy**. He was instrumental in building USS *Nautilus* in 1954. He was promoted to the rank of vice admiral in 1959, and when he reached compulsory retirement age in 1964, his active duty was extended. In 1973, he was promoted to the rank of admiral and continued to serve in the navy's nuclear propulsion program until his retirement in 1982.

The Riddle of the Sands, 1903 novel by **Robert Erskine Childers** that is a masterpiece of suspense and intrigue. It is a story of two British yachtsmen who, while cruising along the sandbank of the North Sea, stumble upon a German plot to mount an amphibious invasion of England. The 1984 movie starred Michael York and Simon MacCorkindale.

Riders to the Sea, 1903 one-act drama by Irish playwright John Millington Synge (1871–1909) about a woman who loses all of the male members of her family to the sea. It was made into a film in 1988 starring Geraldine Page and Amanda Plummer.

Riesenberg, Felix (1879–1939), American engineer, mariner, and author who went to sea from 1896 to 1907 and served in the U.S. **Navy** during World War I. As an accomplished seaman who himself made the transition from sail to steam, he was able to relate firsthand the age of sail. His books include *Under Sail: A Boy's Journey around Cape Horn* (1919), *Standard Seamanship for the Merchant Service* (1922), *Vignettes of the Sea* (1926), and *Mother Sea* (1933). The *New York Times* called his *Cape Horn* (1939) "one of the truly great contributions to the literature of the sea." His son, Felix Jr., was also a mariner and prolific maritime author.

"The Rime of the Ancient Mariner", epic 1798 poem by **Samuel Taylor Coleridge** about an old sailor recounting a story from his youth. In seven parts, the mariner tells of his slaying of an **albatross** and bringing a curse upon his vessel. The bird is hung around his neck, and a passing ghost ship causes the deaths of all his shipmates. After much suffering, he sees the errors in his ways and the albatross drops into the sea. His penance is to travel the world telling the tale. Many believe Coleridge was inspired by the legend of the **Flying Dutchman**.

Riva, Italian maker of luxurious mahogany **runabouts**. The legendary Riva family has manufactured different models of boats since 1842 in Sarnico, a small town on Lake Iseo in northern Italy.

River-Horse, 1995 chronicle by William Least Heat-Moon about his five-thousand-mile, four-month journey from Astoria, New York, to Astoria, Oregon, in a twenty-two-foot boat named *Nikawa* ("river horse" in Osage).

River Plate, English name for Río de la Plata, the estuary lying between Uruguay and Argentina, which is the site of the 1939 Battle of the **River Plate**.

River Plate, Battle of the, naval engagement of December 1939 in which the British **cruisers** HMS *Ajax*, HMS *Exeter*, and HMS *Achilles* forced the German **pocket battleship** *Admiral Graf Spee* to take refuge in Montevideo, Uruguay, after a running fourteen-hour fight. *Admiral Graf Spee* was given seventy-two hours in neutral port in accordance with international law. When the German ship came out on December 17, she **scuttled** herself in the River Plate. Captain **Hans Langsdorff** committed suicide the following day.

Rivers of America, series of sixty-five books published by Farrar and Rinehart and its successors between 1937 and 1974 that described the history, lore, and legend of America's major rivers. The books were written by novelists and poets and were illustrated by professional artists. Editors of the series included Stephen Vincent Benét and Carl Carmer. Other book collections by the same publisher included the American Lakes Series and Seaports of America.

RMS, prefix for Royal Mail Steamship. It preceded the names of British ships that carried the mail and was regarded as a mark of speed and reliability. Companies that owned such ships used the RMS title in their advertising.

RNLI, see **Royal National Lifeboat Institution**.

roaring forties, area of the oceans between 40° and 50° South **latitude**, where strong westerly winds prevail.

Rob Roy, double-paddle canoe developed by Scotsman **John MacGregor** in the 1860s, which had an enormous effect on the sport of canoeing in Britain and America. MacGregor paddled *Rob Roy* thousands of miles in Europe and wrote about his many voyages.

Roberts, Bartholomew (1682–1722), former Welsh slave who became one of the most successful and flamboyant pirates of all time. Known as Black Bart, he captured more than two hundred ships in a thirty-month period from 1719 to 1722. He was renowned as a fine dresser and never drank alcohol. Roberts was killed in a battle with HMS *Swallow* off the coast of West Africa.

Robertson, Morgan (1861–1915), American author who spent his early career at sea. His novels were known for their technical accuracy. He is most famous for his novel *Futility: Or, the Wreck of the Titan* (1918), which eerily prefigured the wreck of RMS *Titanic*. His other works include *Masters of Men* (1901), *Shipmates* (1901), and *Down to the Sea* (1905).

Robinson Crusoe, **Daniel DeFoe**'s classic 1719 novel in which the title character leaves his home in England, goes to sea, and is shipwrecked on an island for twenty-eight years.

The book chronicles Crusoe's adventures on an uninhabited island as he clothes himself, grows crops, and builds and furnishes a house. Eventually he is joined by his servant Friday, a man he has saved from cannibals. Defoe based his tale on the story of **Alexander Selkirk**, a Scottish sailor who was left for four years on Más-a-tierra, one of the Juan Fernández Islands, in 1704 with only his gun, his axe, and a little ammunition.

Robt. E. Lee, 286-foot **Mississippi River paddle wheeler** that was crowned the fastest **steamboat** on the Mississippi after winning the **Great Steamboat Race** against the *Natchez* in 1870. The *Robt. E. Lee* made the passage from New Orleans to Saint Louis in three days, eighteen hours, and fourteen minutes.

Rocks and Shoals, term for those parts of the U.S. **Navy** regulations that concern punishment for offenses, officially the Articles for the Government of the Navy. They were formally read periodically by the executive officer of a ship to the assembled crew. They were superseded by the **Uniform Code of Military Justice**.

Rock the Boat, made for cable television movie about the true story of a band of ten men sailing in the **Transpacific Race** from southern California to Hawai'i. The twist of the story is that all of the crew members are HIV positive. The 1998 film, starring Robert Hudson, John Plander, and Mike Schmidt, was nominated as Best Documentary at the 1998 Academy Awards.

Rodgers, John (1773–1838), U.S. naval officer who played a senior role in the **Barbary Wars** and the **War of 1812**. From 1815 to 1837, he served as president of the Board of **Navy** Commissioners, except for his two years (1825–27) served as commander in chief of the Mediterranean squadron.

Rodney, Sir George Brydges (1718–1792), British naval officer, admiral, and fleet commander who led the British fleet to victory over the French Atlantic fleet, commanded by Admiral **François Joseph Paul de Grasse**, at the Battle of the **Saints** off Dominica on April 12, 1782.

HMS *Rodney*, 38,000-ton British battleship completed in 1927. With a main armament of nine 16-inch guns, she stalked the German battleship *Bismarck* in 1941 along with the *King George V* and helped to send the Nazi predator to the bottom of the Atlantic. She also participated in the shelling of the Normandy beachhead in 1944. Sister ship to HMS *Nelson*, the 710-foot vessel was **laid up** in 1945 and scrapped three years later.

Rogers, Woodes (1679–1732), British **privateer** who in 1709, during a voyage around the world in the ships *Duke* and *Duchess*, rescued **Alexander Selkirk**, who was living on one of the Juan Fernández Islands in the Pacific four hundred miles west of Chile. Rogers returned Selkirk to England, where Selkirk became a celebrity. Rogers was appointed governor of the Bahamas in 1718 and was ordered to rid the area, particularly the port of **New Providence**, of pirates. He wrote about finding Selkirk in his book *A Voyage around the World* (1712).

rogue's yarn, colored yarn worked in rope for identification purposes.

rogue wave, wave produced when two or more wave trains unite to produce a huge single wave. Also called a "freak wave," two 40-foot waves could combine to produce a 60-foot wave.

SS *Rohna*, British-India Steam Navigation Company **liner** built in 1926 and sister of the *Rajula*. While transporting American troops out of Algeria during World War II, she was hit by a German radio-controlled glider bomb on November 26, 1943, and sank, claiming the lives of 1,149 men, most of them U.S. soldiers. It was the third-worst Allied shipping loss of the war, ranking behind the destruction of SS *Lancastria* and SS *Laconia*.

roll on, roll off, see **ro/ro**.

Romance on the High Seas, 1948 musical comedy film about a struggling nightclub singer—Doris Day in her first feature role—who takes a cruise posing as a wealthy socialite. Set aboard a **Grace Line** cruise to South America, it includes excellent footage of the Santa Rosa–class **liners** of 1932. The film received a best song Oscar nomination for "Romance on the High Seas."

USS *Ronald Reagan* (CVN-76), sixth sister ship of the **Theodore Roosevelt**–class aircraft carriers. The ship, expected to cost well over $5 billion, was laid down in 1998. She was christened by former First Lady Nancy Reagan in March 2001 and is due on line in 2002, for assignment to the Pacific fleet out of San Diego.

Rope Yarn Sunday, time allowed at sea for the crew to tend to personal matters such as clothing repairs.

Roosevelt, Franklin D. (1882–1945), thirty-second president of the United States, who served from 1933 to 1945 and whose avocation was ships and naval history. Roosevelt's first position in government was as assistant secretary of the navy under Woodrow Wilson. When Roosevelt was appointed in 1912, the secretary was **Josephus Daniels**. Roosevelt became governor of New York in 1928 and in 1932 was elected U.S. president. After Germany declared war on the United States following the Japanese attack on **Pearl Harbor** on December 7, 1941, Roosevelt declared war on Germany and Italy on December 11.

Roosevelt, Nicholas J. (1767–1854), American inventor and engineer who pioneered the development of **steamboats**. In 1809, Roosevelt and **Robert Fulton** joined in a venture to introduce steamboats on **Western rivers**. In 1812, Roosevelt completed a voyage from Pittsburgh to New Orleans in their boat, the

New Orleans. Roosevelt patented the use of vertical paddle wheels in 1814, which became the chief method of propelling steamboats.

Roosevelt, Theodore (1858–1919), twenty-sixth president of the United States, who served from 1901 to 1909. During his terms, he strengthened the U.S. **Navy**, began the construction of the **Panama Canal** (inspiring the palindrome **"A man, a plan, a canal: Panama!"**), helped end the **Russo-Japanese War**, and became the first American to receive the Nobel Peace Prize. He was appointed assistant secretary of the navy in 1897 but resigned a year later so he could command the famed Rough Riders in the **Spanish-American War**. In 1906 Roosevelt made the first foreign trip by a president by sailing on the battleship USS *Louisiana* to inspect the Panama Canal, and in 1907 he sent the **Great White Fleet** on a goodwill tour of the world. He wrote *The Naval War of 1812* (1882).

Roosevelt, U.S. **steamship** specially designed and constructed in 1905 for Arctic expeditions. The 185-foot ship served as the base for polar explorer **Robert Edwin Peary** for his unsuccessful 1905–6 attempt to reach the North Pole, and again for his successful 1908–10 journey.

ro/ro, a contraction of the term "roll-on roll-off," a vessel equipped with large openings at the bow and stern, and sometimes the side, that with the use of ramps, permit the rapid loading and discharge of wheeled cargo without cranes.

HMS *Rose*, replica eighteenth-century **Royal Navy frigate** constructed in 1970 in **Lunenberg**, Nova Scotia. The 179-foot *Rose* is the world's largest active wooden sailing vessel and conducts adventure education programs open to the general public. The original HMS *Rose* was built in Hull, England, in 1757 and cruised the American coast during the American Revolution.

Rosenfeld, Morris (1885–1968), scion of the preeminent family of American maritime photographers. Morris Rosenfeld began his photography career in the 1890s and was always drawn to yachts and yachting. His passion was shared by his sons David, Stanley, and William, and for nearly a century the father and sons team, Morris Rosenfeld & Sons, chronicled steam and sailing vessels in American waters. Fixtures on the waters in a series of boats named *Foto*, they specialized in harbor scenes, speedboat races, sailing races, and **America's Cup** competitions. Nearly one million Rosenfeld images—the largest single collection of maritime photographs in the world—is now preserved at **Mystic Seaport**.

Ross, James Clark (1800–1862), British polar explorer who led an expedition to the Antarctic aboard the ships *Erebus* and *Terror* from 1839 to 1843 and discovered the Ross Ice Shelf—the world's largest body of floating ice—and Mount Erebus, an active volcano. Ross reached 78°10′ South **latitude**, a record for the time. Ross was the first man to stand on the magnetic North Pole in 1831 while serving under his uncle, explorer Sir John Ross (1777–1856).

Roth, Hal (b. 1927), American journalist and author. He and his wife, Margaret, started sailing in their midthirties and began writing about their adventures. The Roths' books include *Two on a Big Ocean* (1972), *Two against Cape Horn* (1978), and *Always a Distant Anchorage* (1988). Hal wrote *The Longest Race* (1983) about single-handed voyaging and competed in the 1986–87 and 1990–91 **BOC Challenges**. Their book *We Followed Odysseus* was based on a two-year voyage that traced the route of the Greek warrior.

Rotterdam, the second-largest city in the Netherlands (behind Amsterdam) and the world's busiest seaport. The city lies on both banks of

HMS *Rose.*

the Nieuwe Maas River about nineteen miles south of the North Sea. The Nieuwe Maas, a branch of the Rhine River, links Rotterdam with other cities in Europe. Most of the port facilities and buildings in Rotterdam have been constructed since World War II because German bombs destroyed most of the city's central area during the war.

SS *Rotterdam*, 1959 **Holland America Line** consort to the *Nieuw Amsterdam* of 1938. Her revolutionary profile without **funnels**—she had twin mastlike uptakes situated side by side instead—made the 38,644-gross-ton **liner** a favorite among American clientele. She was sold in 1998 to **Premier Cruise Lines** and renamed the *Rembrandt.*

roustabouts, **steamboat** deckhands—often black men—working on the **Mississippi River** and other rivers during the nineteenth and twentieth centuries.

Roux family, important and successful family of French marine artists and ship portraitists based in Marseilles. Their watercolor works were highly prized by sea captains—particularly Americans. The most successful family member was Antoine (1765–1835), who fathered two artist sons, Frederic (1805–1870) and Francois (1811–1882). The grandfather, and founder of the family business, was Joseph Roux (1725–1793).

Royal Caribbean Cruise Line (RCCL), passenger operation established in 1969 by three well-known Norwegian shipping houses—I. M. Skaugen, Anders Wilhelmsen, and Gotaas-Larsen—to offer seven- and fourteen-day cruises out of Miami. RCCL's sleek cruise ships immediately became identifiable because of the Viking Crown Lounge cantilevered from the top of their **funnels**. In 1988 the company introduced the 73,129-ton

Sovereign of the Seas, the largest cruise ship ever built at the time.

Royal Cork Yacht Club, the world's oldest yacht club, founded in 1720 as the Water Club of the Harbour Cork, in Cork, Ireland. In 1831 King William IV granted the club the privilege of using the prefix *Royal*, and despite the club's location in the Republic of Ireland, the prefix has been retained.

Royal Cruising Club, British organization founded in 1880 as the Cruising Club, a club for cruising yachtsmen rather than racers. In 1902 the club obtained permission to use the "Royal" prefix, and its name became the Royal Cruising Club.

HMS *Royal George*, British **ship** of one hundred guns that capsized and sank at **Spithead**, England, on August 29, 1782, while undergoing repairs. More than eight hundred sailors and visitors drowned. The incident is commemorated in the poem "On the Loss of the Royal George," by William Cowper (1731–1800).

Royal Hawaiian Hotel, the "Pink Palace" of Waikiki Beach, which was built in 1927 by the **Matson Line** to match the luxury of its brandnew **liner** SS *Malolo* and to give the line's passengers a destination worthy of their conveyance from California to Hawaii.

Royal National Lifeboat Institution (RNLI), registered British charity founded in 1824 that exists to save lives at sea. The British equivalent of the U.S. **Coast Guard**, it provides, on call, the twenty-four-hour service necessary to cover search-and-rescue requirements to fifty miles out from the coast of the United Kingdom and the Republic of Ireland. With some 224 lifeboat stations, the RNLI depends entirely on contributions and trusts for its income.

Royal Navy, term for the British navy that was first used around 1670 during the **Anglo-**

Dutch War. Britain's naval service dates back over a thousand years to King Alfred's first battle at sea in 882, and the Royal Navy eventually established Britain as the dominant world sea power in the nineteenth century. Today the Royal Navy's primary role is peacekeeping, fighting piracy, and preventing drug trafficking.

HMS *Royal Oak*, **Royal Navy** battleship built in 1916 that was used to transport German sailors to Germany after the **scuttling** of the German fleet at **Scapa Flow** following World War I. In 1939 *Royal Oak*, anchored at Scapa Flow, was torpedoed and sunk by the German submarine U-47, commanded by the **U-boat** ace Gunther Prien, which had slipped into the protected basin. The great irony took the lives of 834 sailors.

Royal Ocean Racing Club, British yacht club founded in 1925 and granted a royal charter in 1931, which has international membership and sponsors the 635-mile **Fastnet Race**, among other functions. The Fastnet Race is run from Cowes, England, around the Fastnet Rock off Ireland, and to Plymouth in odd-numbered years.

Royal Society, organization incorporated by Britain's Charles II (1630–1685) in 1662 for the pursuit and advancement of the physical sciences, including navigation. Sir **Joseph Banks** served as president of the society from 1778 to 1820. The society was influential in the building and outfitting of the ocean exploration vessel HMS *Challenger*.

Royal Viking Line, upscale cruise endeavor begun in 1970 by a Norwegian shipping consortium and absorbed into the **Norwegian Cruise Line** fleet in the early 1990s.

Royal Yacht Squadron, premier British yacht club founded in 1815 at Cowes on the **Isle of Wight**. Five years later it gained royal status, and in 1829 the **Admiralty** allowed members the privilege of wearing the White Ensign of the **Royal Navy**.

Rozinante, twenty-eight-foot double-ended **ketch** designed by **L. Francis Herreshoff**. She was his idea of the perfect cruising vessel and was described in his book *The Compleat Cruiser* (1956). The name of the ketch alludes to the hero's faithful horse, Rosinante, in Miguel de Cervantes's novel, *Don Quijote de la Mancha*.

RRF, see **Ready Reserve Force**.

R Type, a series of forty-one refrigerated cargo ships designated by the U.S. **Maritime Commission** and built in 1945.

Rubicon, small river in North Italy that flows into the Adriatic Sea. In Roman times it marked the boundary between Cisapline Gaul and the Roman Republic. In 49 B.C. Julius Caeser crossed the Rubicon to march against General Pompey, and in doing so committed himself to conquer Rome. The phrase "to cross the Rubicon" had come to mean risking it all.

Rudder, the first successful American boating magazine, which was founded in 1894 by **Thomas Fleming Day** as a journal for aquatic sports. In addition to news and events, it contained the plans and writings of many of the leading boat designers, including **L. Francis Herreshoff**. Other magazines followed, and the *Rudder* ceased publication in 1983.

"Rule Britannia", the official march tune of Britain's **Royal Navy**. Written by James Thomson and first performed in 1740, it was often played on board navy vessels as they sailed in to battle.

rules of the road, regulations for the proper handling of vessels. Comprised of **COLREGS** and **Inland Rules**, they are published by the U.S. **Coast Guard** in *Navigation Rules*.

Rum Row, during Prohibition (1920–33), areas extending along the approaches to New York, Boston, and other metropolitan areas, just outside the three-mile (later twelve-mile) territorial limit. Liquor-smuggling vessels of various types, mostly foreign flagged, drifted or anchored outside of this line, waiting to move into shore or transfer their illegal cargo to smaller, speedier **rumrunners** for delivery to shore.

rumrunner, a boat or individual involved in the highly profitable practice of smuggling illicit cargo during the fourteen years that the Eighteenth Amendment to the U.S. Constitution was in force (1920–33). Rumrunners operated on all coasts as well as the **Great Lakes**. One of the most notable rumrunners was Bill McCoy, for whom the phrase "**real McCoy**" was coined. The U.S. **Coast Guard** was at the forefront of the "rum war," the effort to prevent smuggling of liquor from the sea.

runabout, small powerboat used for fishing, recreation, or water taxi service but not fitted for overnight use.

Run Silent, Run Deep, best-selling 1955 novel by U.S. **Navy** captain **Edward L. Beach** about the officers aboard the fictitious submarine USS *Nerka* in the Pacific during World War II. Arguably the best submarine novel ever written, it was the basis for the successful 1958 movie about a sub commander battling his officers and crew while stalking the Japanese **destroyer** that sank his former command. The production starred Clark Gable, Burt Lancaster, Jack Warden, and Don Rickles.

Russell, William Clark (1844–1911), novelist who is considered among the finest American writers of sea stories. Early in his career, he shipped out in the British **merchant marine** and later turned to writing. His *Wreck of the Grosvenor* (1877) established his reputation as a writer of maritime tales, and he completed twenty-two books during his lifetime.

Herman Melville dedicated one of his books to him, and Russell's *An Ocean Tragedy* (1899) was dedicated to Melville.

Russo-Japanese War, war fought in 1904–5 that included the first conflict at sea in which both participants were equipped with modern, armored warships. On May 29, 1905, the Russian fleet was soundly defeated by the Japanese in the Battle of **Tsushima**, costing Russia the war. The conflict ended with the Treaty of Portsmouth, which was brokered by U.S. president **Theodore Roosevelt** at the Portsmouth, New Hampshire, navy yard. Roosevelt was awarded the Nobel Peace Prize, and Japan was recognized as a major world power.

SS *Ruth Alexander*, passenger **liner** originally constructed in 1931 as the *Sierra Cordoba* for the **North German Lloyd** run to South America. Acquired by the **Dollar Line** after World War I, she became the first American passenger ship to be sunk in World War II, when she was attacked by Japanese bombers off Borneo on December 31, 1941, with the loss of one crew member.

rutter, medieval term for a book of sailing directions describing harbors and routes and containing natural landmarks and navigational information.

de Ruyter, Michiel Adrienszoon (1607–1676), Dutch admiral during all three **Anglo-Dutch Wars** who is considered the greatest fighting seaman of his time. In a daring raid on the British fleet **laid up** in the Medway in 1667, during the second war, he destroyed or captured sixteen ships, including the **flagship** *Royal Charles*, whose stern carvings are preserved in the Marine Museum in Amsterdam today. He distinguished himself in the third **Anglo-Dutch War** by saving his country from invasion and breaking all attempts at blockade. He was killed while fighting the French in the Mediterranean.

Ryder, Albert Pinkham (1847–1917), American painter well known for romantic, moonlit marine scenes. His ***Toilers of the Sea*** series was especially popular and has been widely reproduced. Ryder's *The Flying Dutchman* is in the National Gallery of Art in Washington, D.C.

S

S-4, U.S. **Navy** submarine that collided with the U.S. **Coast Guard cutter** *Paulding* on December 17, 1927, while trying to surface off **Cape Cod**, Massachusetts. The sub sank to the bottom, taking her entire forty-man crew with her. Divers reported they could hear tapping from the inside of the sub and pleas for help for three days but could not free the trapped men.

S-51, U.S. **Navy** submarine that was rammed by the steamer *City of Rome* on the night of September 25, 1925, while running on the surface in Block Island Sound. The submarine sank with all but three of her crew members. This was the submarine service's first peacetime disaster, and it took almost a year to raise the wreck. In July 1926, eighteen bodies were removed from S-51 after it was towed to the Brooklyn Navy Yard.

Sabatini, Rafael (1875–1950), prolific historical romance author of English and Italian extraction. His high-seas tales of pirates in *The Sea Hawk* (1915) and ***Captain Blood*** (1922) forever ensured him the nickname of "the modern Dumas." Two further volumes of Captain Peter Blood stories, *The Chronicles of Captain Blood* (1931) and *The Fortunes of Captain Blood* (1933), reinforced his popularity in literary circles.

Sable Island, narrow, twenty-mile-long sandy island in the Atlantic Ocean, ninety-five miles southeast of Nova Scotia. The uninhabited island was the site of many shipwrecks and is noted for its wild ponies.

Safety of Life at Sea (SOLAS), international convention prompted by the loss of RMS *Titanic* and first held in 1914. It established international standards for safety and lifesaving equipment, required the use of radio, established the **International Ice Patrol**, and recommended the use of established routes on the North Atlantic. It has been updated and expanded in 1929, 1948, 1960, and 1974.

USS *Saginaw*, U.S. **Navy side-wheel** steamer that in 1870 was wrecked on Ocean Island (today Kure Atoll) in the Pacific Ocean, marooning its crew of ninety-three. With little chance of being rescued, five men set out on a voyage of eleven hundred miles in the ship's **gig** to reach the Sandwich Islands (today the Hawai'ian Islands) to get help. One crewman, William Halford, survived the trip, and the king of Hawai'i soon dispatched his steamer *Kilauea* to rescue the other eighty-eight men left on the island. Halford received the **Medal of Honor** for his devotion to his shipmates.

Sagres II, 293-foot sail training **tall ship** representing Portugal. Built in 1937 at the **Blohm & Voss** shipyard in Hamburg, Germany, she first entered the service of the German navy as the *Albert Leo Schlageter*, named for a German Nazi hero. The ship struck a mine during World War II and was put in a shipyard in Bremerhaven, where she was taken by the U.S. **Navy** in 1945. The navy turned the vessel over to Brazil, who turned her over to Portugal in 1962. The sister ship to the *Eagle*, *Mircea*, *Tovaritch*, and *Gorch Foch II*, *Sagres II* is named for a sail training predecessor and the historic port in Portugal. Her **figurehead** is a carving of **Henry the Navigator**.

Sail a Crooked Ship, 1961 comedy film about a bunch of thugs trying to heist a **Liberty ship** out of **lay-up**. Featuring good footage of the freighter as a background to the onboard high jinks, the movie starred Robert Wagner, Ernie Kovacs, Carolyn Jones, and Frankie Avalon.

Sail Away, Broadway musical comedy by Noel Coward set aboard the *Coronia* (read: *Caronia*, because the **Cunard Line** denied the producers permission to use its **liner**'s name and reputation). Elaine Stritch starred in the 1961 film, which is filled with biting Cowardesque views of American tourists aboard British ocean liners, culminating with the singing of "The Passenger's Always Right" by the captain to his very disgruntled crew.

"Sailing", popular song performed by Christopher Cross that hit number one on the pop charts in 1980. It begins, "Well it's not far down to paradise, at least it's not for me, And if the wind is right you can sail away and find tranquillity, Oh, the canvas can do miracles, just you wait and see. Believe me."

Sailing Alone around the World, Joshua Slocum's classic 1899 account of his epic single-handed passage around the world. Slocum departed Boston on April 24, 1895, in his thirty-seven-foot **sloop** *Spray* and returned to Newport, Rhode Island, on June 27, 1898, after traveling a total of forty-six thousand miles. The book, an instant best-seller, has been translated into many languages and remains in print today.

sailing card, see **clipper card**.

Sailing Directions, publication produced by the U.S. government that provides detailed information about the coasts of the world and adjacent waters. First published in 1848 by U.S. **Navy** lieutenant **Matthew Fontaine Maury**, *Sailing Directions* contains much useful information about international port entry, pilotage conditions, channels, anchorages, approach land features and landmarks sketches, tides and currents, winds, hazards, aerial photos, language glossaries, and more.

sailing on her own bottom, phrase used to describe a vessel that has paid for herself.

"Sailing, Sailing", nursery rhyme whose author and date written are unknown. It begins, "Y'heave ho! My lads, the wind blows free, A pleasant gale is on our lee, And soon across the ocean clear our gallant bark shall bravely steer." The well-known refrain is, "Sailing, sailing, Over the bounding main, For many a stormy wind shall blow ere Jack comes home again!"

Sailmaker, Isaac (1633–1721), influential painter who was the earliest recorded marine artist working in England. Sailmaker emigrated from Holland when he was very young and in 1657 fashioned a painting of the English fleet off Mardyke for Oliver Cromwell (1599–1658), who ruled England from 1653 to 1658.

Sailor Beware, 1951 film about fun and mayhem aboard a submarine, with a few songs thrown in for good measure. The movie starred Jerry Lewis and Dean Martin, with appearances by Betty Hutton, Vince Edwards, and even James Dean.

Sailor of the King, 1953 World War II action film about a shipwrecked sailor who unwittingly helps his estranged naval commander father sink a German **cruiser**. Based on **Cecil Scott "C. S." Forester**'s novel *Brown on Resolution* (1929), it starred Jeffrey Hunter, Wendy Hiller, Bernard Lee, and Michael Rennie.

Sailors' Snug Harbor, charitable trust founded in 1801 that is dedicated to the care and support of "aged, decrepit and worn out seamen." A result of a bequest of Captain Robert Richard Randall, it was founded on Staten Island, New York, and is today located in Sea Level, North Carolina, and provides residential retirement services for seamen in need. It also offers other assistance programs that give a retiree supplemental services and income after a career at sea.

Sailors' Union of the Pacific (SUP), maritime labor union formed in San Francisco in 1891 to represent West Coast seamen.

Saint Augustine, city in Florida that was the first permanent European colony on the U.S. mainland. It was founded in September 1565 by the Spanish under Pedro Menendez de Avilés, a naval officer, to help guard sea lanes to the **Spanish Main**.

Saint Brendan (486–577), sixth-century monk who, according to some, discovered America nine hundred years before **Christopher Co-**

lumbus. The story of his voyages is contained in the book *Navigatio Sancti Brendani* (*The Voyage of Saint Brendan the Abbot*).

Saint Elmo's fire, luminous atmospheric discharge of electricity from objects such as masts and rigging. It was looked upon by sailors as a good omen because Saint Elmo was a patron saint of sailors, and Saint Elmo's fire was taken as a sign that the ship had come under his protection.

Saint Helena, small island in the South Atlantic, one thousand miles off the coast of Africa. The British government exiled **Napoleon I** to the remote island following his defeat at Waterloo and abdication in 1815. He remained there until his death in 1821.

Saint Lawrence Seaway, system of canals and locks, the Saint Lawrence River, and several lakes that links the **Great Lakes** and the **Atlantic Ocean**. Opened in 1959 and operated jointly by the United States and Canada, it permitted large oceangoing ships to enter the Great Lakes and to travel the 2,342 miles between the Atlantic Ocean and Duluth, Minnesota. The seaway extends for about 450 miles from the eastern end of Lake Erie to Montréal, Québec, and includes the **Welland Ship Canal**.

St. Louis, passenger steamer of the **American Line** built in 1895 for transatlantic service. She and her sister ship *St. Paul* are considered the first modern ocean **liners**. She was used as an armed **cruiser** and for troop transport during the **Spanish-American War** and as the *Louisville* for yeoman duties during World War I. She was scrapped in 1924 following **lay-up** resulting from a fire on board while refitting her for passenger operation in 1920.

SS St. Louis, the first in a trio of motor ships built in 1929 for the **Hamburg-America Line**. The 16,732-gross-ton **liner** sailed from Hamburg in 1939 with six hundred Jewish refugees seeking asylum in Cuba. However, the Cuban government denied the emigrants permission to land and, in a shocking decision, the United States also refused entrance to the homeless Jews. With no other alternative, the ship was eventually ordered home and the passengers were allowed to land in Belgium, England, France, and the Netherlands—many of them later perished in the Holocaust. In 1940 the ship became a German naval accommodations vessel in Kiel. Damaged by Allied bombers in 1944, the partially burned-out liner was towed to Hamburg for use as an interim hotel. She was scrapped in 1952.

USS *St. Marys*, 150-foot U.S. **Navy sloop of war** that in 1874 was transferred to the New York Nautical School, later to become the State University of New York Maritime College. It served as a school ship until 1908, when she was sold and broken up. After operating from ships for sixty-four years, the school was moved to its present location at historic **Fort Schuyler**, in the Bronx, New York.

Saint Nicholas (d. ca. 348), Christian saint who is considered the patron saint of sailors. On a trip to Palestine, the boat on which Nicholas was traveling encountered a fierce storm. After a number of sailors fell overboard, Nicholas extended his arms and quieted the water so that the drowning sailors could be saved. Over the years, he has also been known as the patron saint of Greece, Russia, and prisoners and is the namesake of Santa Claus.

St. Paul, **liner** built in 1895 along with her sister ship ***St. Louis*** for the **American Line**'s North Atlantic passenger service. The two ships were the largest liners built in the United States in the nineteenth century. *St. Paul* was operated as an **auxiliary cruiser** during the **Spanish-American War**, and in 1908 she collided with the British cruiser HMS *Gladiator*, which sank with some loss of life. *St. Paul* became an armed transport during World War I,

for which she was renamed the *Knoxville*. She later provided passenger service and then was scrapped in 1923. In 1899 *St. Paul* became the first ship in the world to have a wireless telegraph on board.

Saint Paul's shipwreck, incident in which a ship carrying Saint Paul the Apostle was wrecked on the island of Malta. The wreck is described in the Bible in Acts of the Apostles: 27, 28. Saint Paul preached the Gospel during his three-month stay on Malta and converted many Maltese to Christianity during this time. The feast of Saint Paul's shipwreck is celebrated on February 10 on Malta.

St. Roch, Royal Canadian Mounted Police (RCMP) **schooner** that in 1940–42 completed the first west-to-east voyage of the **Northwest Passage** (the second to ever have made the passage in either direction after ***Gjøa***). *St. Roch* arrived in Halifax in October 1942 and in 1944 returned to Vancouver via a more northerly route, covering 7,295 miles in eighty-six days. The voyage demonstrated Canadian sovereignty in the Arctic during World War II but did not lead to effective utilization of this route until after World War II, when large icebreakers came into use. *St. Roch* was built as a supply ship for the RCMP's isolated, far-flung Arctic detachments and to itself serve as a floating detachment when frozen in for the winter. Today *St. Roch* is the centerpiece of the Vancouver Maritime Museum.

Saints, Battle of the, decisive British naval victory over the French on April 12, 1782—the last major sea battle of the American Revolution. The battle occurred off the islands of Les Saintes in the channel separating Dominica from Guadeloupe in the **Windward Islands**. The battle, which pitted the admiral Sir **George Brydges Rodney** against Admiral **François Joseph Paul de Grasse**, reasserted British naval supremacy in the Western Hemisphere and led to the restoration of Britain's possessions in the **West Indies** through the 1783 **Treaty of Paris.** French losses numbered some three thousand casualties and eight thousand prisoners.

Saipan Invasion, monthlong World War II U.S. amphibious assault on an island in the Marianas in the western Pacific that began on June 15, 1944. Rather than being captured, much of the island's Japanese civilian population committed mass suicide, several hundred of whom threw themselves over a cliff. The possession of the island gave U.S. forces the locale needed for a land-based B-29 bomber squadron within striking distance of the Japanese home islands.

Sakura Maru, Japanese exhibition ship built in 1962 for the worldwide display of Japanese products. It was operated by **Mitsui O.S.K. Lines** on transpacific passenger service to California when not on exhibition duty. The 12,470-gross-ton **liner** was sold in 1971 to Mitsubishi and renamed *Sakura* for passenger cruise operation from Tokyo. In 1982 she was sold again to the People's Republic of China and renamed *Ziluolan* for further passenger service.

Salacia, Roman goddess of the sea, wife of **Neptune.**

Salamis, Battle of, naval engagement of 480 B.C. fought ten miles west of Athens in which 370 Greek **galleys** under the command of Athenian Admiral **Themistocles** destroyed half the 1,000-ship Persian fleet of **Xerxes I**, leading ultimately to the abandonment of the Persion invasion of Greece.

USS *Salem* (CA-139), first and namesake vessel of a class of twelve heavy **cruisers** built for the U.S. **Navy.** Commissioned in 1949, the 21,500-ton ship was never assigned to combat duty although she did serve for ten years as the **flagship** of the Atlantic and Mediterranean fleets. She was decommissioned in 1959 and sent to **lay-up.** In 1994 the vessel was brought

to Quincy, Massachusetts—where she had been built forty-five years earlier—to become the focal point of the U.S. Naval and Shipbuilding Museum.

Sallee pirates, a terrifying band of sixteenth-century **corsair** raiders based in Sallee, a seaport on the west coast of Morocco on the north side of the mouth of the Bu-Ragreb River, opposite Rabat.

sallying ship, evolution that includes having the crew run in unison from side to side to create a rolling motion. It is used to float a ship that is aground or to help it make way when beset by ice.

Salmon, Robert (1775–1845), British marine artist who fashioned many finely detailed paintings of ships and waterfront architecture. He moved to Boston in 1829 and recorded the harbor life and activities on the wharves. He had a profound influence on American marine artists, including **Fitz Hugh Lane.** Eventually Salmon's eyesight became impaired; he moved back to England in 1842.

saloon, large social room on a passenger **liner** or yacht. The word comes from the French *salon* for a large hall or room. See illustration next page.

Salt-Water Ballads, first published volume of poems by **John Masefield.** The 1902 compilation includes the moving poem **"Sea Fever,"** which Masefield wrote when he was twenty-two years old.

saltworks, coastal installation where salt is produced commercially. The world's largest salt evaporation facility is located at Laguna San Ignacio on the west coast of Baja California, Mexico.

salvage, action taken to rescue a ship and property from peril—such as fire, shipwreck, or capture—at sea. It is also the compensation

The Grand Saloon of SS *Great Eastern* (see entry previous page). (Courtesy National Maritime Museum, Greenwich, England)

that the owner must pay for having the vessel or cargo saved.

sampan, flat-bottomed boat used as a **lighter** on rivers and harbors of eastern Asia. Equipped with a roof, it can also be used for housing.

Sampson, William Thomas (1840–1902), U.S. **Navy** officer who was involved in a dispute over which American officer was responsible for the victory at the Battle of **Santiago** during the **Spanish-American War** in 1898. Sampson and his **flagship** had left the squadron charged with blockading the harbor to meet with army commanders. When the battle began, he quickly returned to his ships. But because Commodore **Winfield Scott Schley** gave the first orders and

played a key role in the battle, he was credited most with the victory.

sandbagger, wide, shallow-draft centerboard sailboat with a large sail area. Raced extensively in New York City in the late nineteenth century, its ballast included a fifty-pound sandbag for each crew member. The sandbags were shifted to the weather rail after each **tack**. Sandbags and crew members were often jettisoned as conditions required.

Sand Island, immigration station at Honolulu, Hawaii.

The Sand Pebbles, best-selling 1962 semiautobiographical novel by **Richard McKenna** describing the experiences of a group of U.S.

Santa Lucia in 1940. (Bruce Vancil)

sailors on the navy gunboat USS *San Pablos*, which is caught up in the turmoil of the 1926 Bolshevik revolution in China. In 1966 it was made by Robert Wise into an acclaimed Hollywood movie starring Steve McQueen, Richard Crenna, Candace Bergen, and Richard Attenborough. It was McKenna's first and only novel; he died in 1964 at age fifty-one, less than two years after the book was published. The film was nominated for eight Academy Awards.

Sansinena, a 35,633-gross-ton tanker built in 1971. The 790-foot ship blew up in 1976 while at berth 46 in the San Pedro district of the Los Angeles Harbor. The explosion shattered windows throughout the harbor town for several square miles. The tanker, ripped in half and engulfed in flames, lost nine crew members with eighteen more wounded.

Santa Cruz Islands, Battle of the, World War II naval engagement between U.S. and Japanese forces north of the Solomon Islands in the South Pacific on October 26–27, 1942. In the action, USS *Hornet* was sunk and USS *Enterprise* was damaged, leaving the United States without an operational aircraft carrier in the Pacific. Two Japanese carriers were severely damaged in the fighting.

Santa Elena, one of four **Grace Line** passenger ships designed by **William Francis Gibbs** and built in the early 1930s (along with *Santa Rosa*, *Santa Paula*, and **Santa Lucia**) for the service to Latin America. She entered service in 1933 and in 1941 was taken over by the U.S. government for use as a troopship during World War II. The **liner** was torpedoed in the Mediterranean in 1943, and only 4 of the 2,167 people onboard were lost, largely due to the skill and courage of the captain of the U.S. troopship *Monterey*, who despite enemy fire maneuvered his ship quickly into position to recover the survivors.

Santa Lucia, one of four **Grace Line** passenger ships designed by **William Francis Gibbs** and built in the early 1930s (along with *Santa Rosa*, *Santa Paula*, and **Santa Elena**) for the service to Latin America. She entered service in 1933 and was requisitioned by the U.S. **Navy** for troopship duty in 1941. Torpedoed off of Algiers in 1942, she became the first ship sunk in the North African Invasion.

Santa Maria, the **flagship**—and largest vessel—of explorer **Christopher Columbus** on his 1492 voyage to the New World. The decked merchantman of between 100 and 250 tons, with a crew of fifty-two, was wrecked on Christmas Eve 1492 off the coast of Hispaniola.

SS *Santa Maria*, Portuguese **liner** launched in 1953 for service on the South Atlantic. In 1957 her route was changed to include regular ports calls in the Caribbean, including Port Everglades, Florida. Soon after the ship left Curaçao in January 1961, a band of twenty-six Spanish, Portugese, and South American activists posing as tourists hijacked the ship in an effort to draw attention to the dictatorships of Spain's Francisco Franco and Portugal's Antonio de Salazar. Spanish and U.S. warships pursued the liner, and the eleven-day standoff ended when the rebels were granted asylum in Brazil. *Santa Maria* landed her six hundred passengers at Lisbon and resumed service shortly thereafter. The liner was scrapped in 1973.

Santiago, old Cuban fisherman who finally catches a magnificent fish after weeks of not catching anything in **Ernest Hemingway**'s novel *The **Old Man and the Sea*** (1953).

Santiago, Battle of, July 3, 1898, naval engagement that occurred when the Spanish fleet attempted to leave Santiago harbor in Cuba to run the U.S. blockade. The battle lasted four hours, and the Spanish fleet was destroyed. Spanish losses were 474 killed and wounded and 1,750 taken prisoner. U.S. casualties were one killed and one wounded. This **Spanish-American War** battle led to the U.S. acquisition of Puerto Rico and the capitulation of Spain on August 12, 1898.

Sappho, American **schooner** that, in 1871, under existing rules, was allowed to race the final two races against the British schooner *Livonia* to successfully defend the **America's Cup**. The first American vessel, *Columbia*, had lost a jibstay and her steering gear in the third race of the seven-race series.

Sargasso Sea, oval-shaped area of the North Atlantic Ocean east of the Bahamas and west of the Azores where the **Gulf Stream** and equatorial currents cause the sargassum weed to collect in vast quantities and float to the surface. An area roughly two-thirds the size of the United States, it was first reported by **Christopher Columbus** in his accounts of his voyages to the New World.

Sarnoff, David (1891–1971), radio and television pioneer and head of the Radio Corporation of America (RCA). In April 1912 the twenty-year-old Sarnoff was a wireless operator working at the private station atop New York City's Wanamaker's Department Store. Early on the morning of April 15, he caught the first signals of the RMS *Titanic* disaster. He listened and recorded all the messages he could hear, and it was from this source that many newspapers and wire services obtained their first accurate news of the accident. He also helped to coordinate World War II Allied communications for **D-Day**.

USS *Sassacus*, lead ship of a twenty-eight-vessel class of double-ended **side-wheel** gunboats built for the U.S. **Navy** between 1862 and 1864. Designed for river operations during the Civil War, it was the largest class of U.S. Navy vessels built before World War I.

NS *Savannah*, world's first nuclear-powered merchant ship. Conceived in the mid-1950s under the Eisenhower Administration's Atoms for Peace program, *Savannah* was developed to demonstrate peaceful and commercial application of nuclear power and to open ports throughout the world to visits from nuclear-powered vessels. Named after America's first transatlantic **steamship**, the SS *Savannah*, *Savannah* was launched in 1959 in Camden, New Jersey, and debuted in 1962. Deemed a commercial failure, the ship was in service until 1969, refueling only once. *Savannah* was exhibited at the Patriot's Point Naval Museum in Charleston, South Carolina, until the mid-

1990s, when she was again mothballed in the James River in Virginia.

SS *Savannah*, American paddle steamer that was the first **steamship** to cross the Atlantic. Built in New York, she sailed from Savannah, Georgia, on May 22, 1819, and reached Liverpool in twenty-five days. Even though she made little use of her wood-fueled boilers and detachable paddles—instead sailing most of the way—her success made steam viable and ushered in the era of transatlantic steam travel. After her transatlantic voyage, she was converted to a sailing vessel and was wrecked on Fire Island, New York, in 1821.

Savarona III, one of the largest private yachts ever constructed, commissioned by American heiress Mrs. Emily Roebling Cadwalader, whose grandfather had built the Brooklyn Bridge. Designed by Gibbs & Cox of New York and delivered in 1931 by **Blohm & Voss** in Hamburg, Germany, she was built to replace Cadwalader's 294-foot *Savarona II* and to surpass all other yachts of the day. At 408 feet in length, with a beam of 53 feet, she had a crew of 107. To avoid paying taxes, she was never brought to the United States. In commission for just two years as a private yacht, *Savarona* was sold in 1933 and became the presidential yacht of Turkey's Kemal Ataturk and later a training ship for the Turkish navy. Today she continues in service in the Mediterranean as a cruise vessel, carrying thirty-four guests in seventeen palatial suites.

Savo Island, Battle of, August 9, 1942, Japanese World War II naval victory in the South Pacific in which a Japanese task force achieved complete surprise and sank one Australian and three U.S. heavy **cruisers** at **Ironbottom Sound**. The loss of HMAS *Canberra*, USS *Astoria*, USS *Quincy*, and USS *Vincennes*, along with a thousand men, was a bitter blow to the Allied forces and was the severest defeat the U.S. **Navy** had ever suffered in battle. The enemy did not suffer a single loss or any note-

NS *Savannah*. (Courtesy Gordon R. Ghareeb)

worthy damage to any of the ships in their task force.

scandalize, to reduce sail by dropping the peak of a fore-and-aft sail.

Scandinavian Star, Bahamian-flagged combined passenger ship and car ferry that suffered a fire while en route from Oslo, Norway, to Frederikshavn, Denmark, in 1990. Within forty-five minutes, 158 people died.

scantlings, the dimensions of a vessel's structural parts, such as frames, girders, stringers, plating, and so forth.

Scapa Flow, protected sea basin enclosed by the Orkney Islands off Northern Scotland, long used as a British naval base. At the end of World War I, the German fleet was interned at Scapa Flow after its surrender in 1918. On June 21, 1919, in protest of the **Treaty of Versailles**, German Vice-Admiral Ludwig von Reuter (1869–1943) ordered that all seventy-two ships there be **scuttled**.

Sceptre, **twelve-meter** British challenger to the **America's Cup** in 1958—the first contest since 1937. The sixty-nine-foot **sloop** was defeated four races to none by the American defender *Columbia* on a course off Newport, Rhode Island.

Scharnhorst, German World War II battle **cruiser** launched in 1936 with its sister ship *Gneisenau*. Involved in the Norway campaign in 1940, the ship went on to terrorize the North Atlantic, sinking twenty-two merchant ships. It was damaged by gunfire and sunk by **torpedoes** in the Battle of North Cape in December 1943, with the loss of 1,839 sailors. During the World War I Battle of the **Falkland Islands**, Admiral **Maximilian von Spee** drowned when his **flagship**, the earlier **cruiser** *Scharnhorst*, was sunk.

Scheherazade, symphony by Russian composer and former naval officer Nikolai Rimsky-Korsakov (1844–1908) that was inspired by his reading the *Arabian Nights*. At times the work imparts to the listener a vision of the sea. The first movement is titled "The Sea and Sindbad's Ship," and the fourth movement features the "Wreck"—one of the classical depictions in music of the sea's fury.

Scheer, Reinhold (1863–1928), German admiral who was commander in chief of the German High Seas Fleet in World War I. He faced Britain's Admiral **John Rushworth Jellicoe** at the Battle of **Jutland** on May 31, 1916.

Schetky, John Christian (1778–1874), Scottish artist who was a prolific painter of nautical scenes and a teacher of marine art to **Royal Navy** officers. As a marine painter to King George IV, William IV, and Queen Victoria, he was required to sketch and paint diplomatic and state occasions as well as reviews of the fleet at **Spithead**.

Scheveningen, Battle of, August 10, 1653, battle off the coast of the Netherlands in which the English fleet overwhelmed the Dutch fleet. It was the last battle of the first **Anglo-Dutch War**, and Dutch admiral **Martin Tromp** was killed.

Schley, Winfield Scott (1839–1911), U.S. **Navy** officer who commanded the U.S. naval forces at the 1898 Battle of **Santiago** in the **Spanish-American War**. He was involved in a famous dispute with **William Thompson Sampson** over credit for the victory. In 1884 he commanded the expedition that rescued Arctic explorer **Adolphus Washington Greely**, and he later coauthored *The Rescue of Greely* (1885).

schooner, **fore-and-aft rigged** sailing vessel with from two to seven masts. Schooners were first constructed in colonial America and proved effective and popular due to their speed, ability to sail close to the wind, and small crew requirements. They were widely used in fisheries and the coastal trade until the 1920s.

Schuyler, George L. (1811–1890), American **steamship** company owner, yachtsman, and a founding member of the **New York Yacht Club**. He was the last surviving owner of the **schooner** *America* and a part of the syndicate that deeded the **America's Cup** to the New York Yacht Club. He designated the New York Supreme Court as arbiter over any Cup disputes, and he is credited with keeping alive the spirit of the challenge. He died in a stateroom aboard Elbridge Gerry's steam yacht *Electra* at Newport, Rhode Island.

Schuyler Otis Bland, unique prototype merchant ship developed after World War II by the U.S. government. She was a larger, faster, and more efficient type of cargo ship than the **C3 freighter**. An all-welded design, she had elaborate cargo handling gear and folding steel hatch covers. She was delivered in 1950, but the events of the Korean War exposed the need for something better. After years of service, she was scrapped in 1979. The ship was named in honor of Bland (1872–1950), a congressman, chairman of the House Merchant Marine and Fisheries Committee, and architect of the **Merchant Marine Act of 1936**.

scientae cedit mare, motto of the U.S. **Coast Guard Academy**. It is Latin for "the sea yields to knowledge." See also *ex scientia, tridens*.

Scorpion (B-440), 2,550-ton Soviet Foxtrot–class diesel submarine completed in 1970. The vessel, manned by a crew of seventy and capable of sailing at sixteen **knots**, patrolled Pacific regions, including the coast of North America, during the Cold War. Decommissioned in 1994, the 299-foot craft was purchased for display as a museum ship at the Australian National Maritime Museum in Sydney. Brought to California in 1998, the sub opened for tours alongside the former luxury **liner** RMS *Queen Mary* in Long Beach.

USS *Scorpion* (SSN-589), nuclear-powered attack submarine commissioned in 1959. In 1968, while four hundred miles southwest of the **Azores**, the submarine exploded and sank in over ten thousand feet of water, killing all ninety-nine crew members. One initial explanation was that a mechanical malfunction resulted in her electrical batteries exploding. However, there is a substantial amount of evidence to indicate that the 251-foot submarine was sunk by her own accidentally launched Mark-37 torpedo.

Scott, Michael (1789–1835), Scottish merchant and novelist who migrated to Jamaica. He wrote *Cruise of the Midge,* and his ***Tom Cringle's Log*** is considered one of the greatest seagoing novels. Both were first serialized in *Blackwood's Magazine* and published in book form in 1836.

Scott, Robert Falcon (1868–1912), English naval officer and explorer who led an expedition to Antarctica aboard HMS *Discovery* from 1901 to 1904. In 1910 he returned to Antarctica aboard HMS *Terra Nova* and made many important scientific observations. During the expedition, Scott and four others set out on foot and reached the South Pole on January 18, 1912—one month after Norwegian explorer **Roald Amundsen**'s arrival there on December 14, 1911. All of the men died of exposure on the return trek. *Terra Nova* returned to Britain, and Scott's diary was found the following November.

Scrimshaw pie crimpers. (Old Dartmouth Historical Society Whaling Museum, New Bedford, Massachusetts)

Scott, Samuel (1710–1773), one of the most admired English painters of his time. He is best known for his detailed and accurate descriptions of ships and their actions. He was influenced heavily by **Willem van de Velde** the Elder and the Younger.

scow, flat-bottomed boat with square ends used chiefly for transporting bulk materials.

"scratch one flat-top", quote attributed to U.S. **Navy** commander Robert Dixon, spoken during a radio report as the Japanese aircraft carrier *Shoho* blew up and sank while under attack from U.S. aircraft during the Battle of the **Coral Sea.**

scrimshaw, folk art practiced primarily by whalemen who used sperm whale teeth and "whalebone" (baleen) on which to engrave pictures or to make pie crimpers or other articles that they took home to their wives or sweethearts. The craft reached its peak between 1830 and 1850. With the decline of large-scale whaling at the beginning of the twentieth century, the art of scrimshaw faded, and existing pieces rose in value. Today it is illegal to make scrimshaw on whalebone, a measure taken to protect the surviving population of whales.

Scripps, Edward Wyllis (1854–1926), California newspaper publisher who organized the first major chain of newspapers in the United States (Scripps-Howard) and later established the United Press. Scripps privately funded scientific research of marine life in the Pacific Ocean. In 1903 he and his half-sister Ellen Browning Scripps (1836–1932) endowed the San Diego Marine Biological Association, and he provided his private yacht for the association's scientific work. Later the association became the **Scripps Institution of Oceanography**.

Scripps Institution of Oceanography (SIO), public institution for research and graduate instruction in the marine, atmospheric, and space sciences. Located in La Jolla, California, it was founded in 1903 by **Edward Wyllis Scripps** and his half-sister Ellen Browning Scripps (1836–1932) as an independent laboratory. It became part of the University of California in 1912 and received its present name in 1925.

scrod, not a type of fish but a market name used interchangeably for young cod, haddock, and sometimes cusk and pollock.

scuba, acronym for self-contained underwater breathing apparatus. Scuba was coinvented in 1943 as the **aqualung** by two Frenchmen, **Jacques-Yves Cousteau**, a naval officer, and Émile Gagnan, an engineer.

scull, a shell or light narrow racing boat used with up to eight rowers, or the name of one of the oars. To "scull" means to propel a boat by working a single oar at the stern.

scurvy, a disease common aboard ship until the late eighteenth century that was attributable to a deficiency of vitamin C (ascorbic acid). This "plague of the sea" was characterized by lethargy, foul breath, extreme tenderness of the gums, loss of teeth, and pain in the limbs. Scurvy, or scorbutus, was common on long voyages because the diet included few, if any, fresh fruits or vegetables.

scuttle, to sink a vessel intentionally, usually by opening sea valves or cutting holes in the bottom. Also the name for a small hatch on a vessel.

scuttlebutt, nautical slang for gossip or rumors. Its name comes from the cask of drinking water on ships, called a "scuttlebutt," and the fact that sailors exchanged gossip when they gathered for a drink, much like modern-day office workers around the water cooler.

Scylla and Charybdis, threats encountered by **Odysseus** on his journey home in **Homer**'s *Odyssey*. Scylla was a dangerous rock on the Italian side of the Strait of Messina, and Charybdis was a whirlpool on the Sicilian side. In the *Odyssey*, Homer portrays the Sicilian side of the strait as low rock containing an immense fig tree, under which dwelt Charybdis, who thrice every day swallowed down and sucked in the waters of the sea and three times threw them up again. The phrase "between Scylla and Charybdis" consequently means to be beset by danger whichever way one turns.

The Sea and the Jungle, 1912 classic travel novel by **H. M. (Henry Major) Tomlinson** about a man who leaves his humdrum life in London and boards a freighter in Wales bound for the upper reaches of the Amazon River. Three years later, the man becomes famous after publishing a book of his adventures.

The Sea around Us, important 1951 book by **Rachel Louise Carson** about the oceans and the marine environment. This scholarly work topped best-seller lists for months and won numerous awards. A 1952 film of the same name, based on Rachel Carson's studies, won

Sea biscuit from circa 1784. (Courtesy National Maritime Museum, Greenwich, England)

an Academy Award for best feature documentary.

Seabees, nickname for U.S. **Navy** Construction Battalions (CBs). Organized in World War II, the first Seabees were recruited from civilian construction trades for the primary role of constructing airfields and support facilities on captured Pacific islands. Since then, they have participated in all wars and conflicts and have built U.S. naval bases around the world. The Seabee fighting bee logo, adopted in 1944, was designed by Walt Disney studios, and their motto is, "Can Do!"

sea biscuit, hard unsalted biscuit (also referred to as "**hardtack**" or as "ship's biscuit") made with only flour and water that is used as a cheap form of nourishment for seamen aboard ship because of its long shelf life. Seabiscuit, one of the most successful racing thoroughbred horses of the 1930s, was the son of Hard Tack, who in turn was the son of the famous Man o'War and Tea Biscuit.

Sea Cadets, youth education program established in 1958 in cooperation with the U.S. **Navy** and U.S. **Navy League** for young men and women ages eleven to eighteen to learn patriotism and skills aboard navy ships and air stations. Today there are Sea Cadet organizations in most of the maritime nations of the world.

sea change, phrase that today is used to describe a major transformation. Its origin is a change wrought by the sea marked as a transition to something "rich and strange." William Shakespeare first used the phrase in *The Tempest*, in which the sprite Ariel sings of a change from the ugliness of a drowned and decomposing body into the lasting beauty of pearls and coral in the poem **"Full Fathom Five."**

The Sea Chase, 1955 movie about a German freighter captain attempting to return his ship and its crew to their homeland during the opening days of World War II. It starred John Wayne (as a Nazi no less) and Lana Turner as his girlfriend.

Sea Cloud, 316-foot four-masted **auxiliary bark** launched in 1931 as *Hussar*. Designed by Cox & Stevens of New York, and built in Germany, she was the private yacht of cereal heiress Marjorie Merriweather Post, who was then married to E. F. Hutton. *Hussar* was renamed *Sea Cloud* when Post married U.S. diplomat Joseph E. Davies in 1935. *Sea Cloud* served in the U.S. **Coast Guard** during World War II, and Post used the yacht until 1955. After nearly twenty years of different owners and name changes, the grand vessel was purchased by a German company in 1974 and refitted for the cruise trade, where she now sails the Mediterranean by summer and the Caribbean by winter.

sea daddy, an older sailor who takes an interest in and advises young sailors.

sea dog, slang for an experienced seaman.

Sea Education Association (SEA), organization founded in 1971 to provide college undergraduates the opportunity to spend a semester at sea learning about the oceans and the maritime experience. Headquartered on a thirteen-acre campus in Woods Hole, Massachusetts, SEA operates the sailing vessels *Westward* and *Corwith Cramer*. A new vessel, the *Robert C. Seamans*, began operating on the West Coast in 2001.

Sea Empress, Liberian-flagged crude oil tanker that grounded off the coast of Southwest Wales in 1996 and discharged 72,000 tons of oil into the seas. The magnitude of the accident approached that of the *Torrey Canyon*, which spilled 117,000 tons around Cornwall, England, in March 1967. The *Amoco Cadiz* spilled 223,000 tons of oil when she was wrecked off the Brittany coast in March 1978.

Seafarers International Union (SIU), maritime labor organization chartered in 1938 that represents unlicensed U.S. mariners aboard U.S.-flag commercial vessels. Based in Piney Point, Maryland, today it is the largest North American union representing **merchant mariners**.

"Sea Fever", famous 1914 **John Masefield** poem contained in his volume *Salt-Water Ballads*. It begins with the line, "I must go down to the seas again, to the lonely sea and the sky, And all I ask is a tall ship and a star to steer her by."

A Sea Grammar, 1627 book by English explorer Captain **John Smith** that is essentially an indoctrination text for soldiers aboard ship. In addition to detailing seafaring terms and techniques, it also describes how ship-to-ship combat was executed in the early seventeenth century. Smith is best known for his exploration of the East Coast of the North American continent.

Sea Grant, national program administered by the U.S. government since 1966 that encourages the wise stewardship of marine resources through research, education, outreach, and technology transfer. It is a partnership between nearly thirty universities and the **National**

Oceanic and Atmospheric Administration that focuses on marine research and the sustainable development of marine resources.

The Sea Hawk, 1915 **Rafael Sabatini** novel about a pirate who returns home to defend his native England against the **Spanish Armada** and finds romance along the way. The adventure epic was adapted for the silver screen in 1940, starring Errol Flynn, Claude Raines, and Alan Hale.

Sea History, colorful quarterly journal of the **National Maritime Historical Society**. Founded in 1971, the journal features the "art, literature, adventure, lore and learning of the sea," including timely news of historic ships, sail training voyages, marine art shows, and maritime museum exhibitions.

Seahorse, international sailing magazine based in Great Britain. Founded in the 1980s, it is the official publication of the **Royal Ocean Racing Club**.

Sea Hunt, popular U.S. television action-adventure series that ran from 1958 to 1961, starring Lloyd Bridges as **scuba** diver Mike Nelson. Operating from his high-tech boat, *Argonaut*, Nelson hunted down criminals from the undersea underworld and performed rescues and **salvage**—all the while dodging sharks, manta rays, and octopuses.

Sea Islands, chain of more than a hundred islands off the Atlantic coast of South Carolina, Georgia, and Florida. Some uninhabited, they include Isle of Palms, Hilton Head, Edisto, and Cumberland.

SEAL, U.S. **Navy** elite corps formed in 1962 to provide special services and demolition teams for use in warfare. SEALS are trained to conduct unconventional warfare, counterguerrilla warfare, and clandestine operations at sea and in enemy waters. The name is a loose acronym for the "Sea-Air-Land" team.

Sealab, underwater laboratory-living station program initiated by the U.S. **Navy** in 1964. Aboard *Sealab I*, at a site off Bermuda, divers stayed underwater for eleven days at an average depth of 193 feet. In 1965, aboard *Sea Lab II* off La Jolla, California, at an average depth of 205 feet, aquanaut Scott Carpenter communicated with astronaut Gordon Cooper, who was in a Gemini spacecraft orbiting two hundred miles above the earth.

Sea-Land, American shipping company founded in 1960 by **Malcolm McLean** to pioneer his idea of using containers on ships to move cargo. Sea-Land was purchased by the tobacco company R. J. Reynolds in 1969 and spun off as a separate company in 1984. In 1986 it was purchased by the railroad company CSX and in 1998 was acquired by the Danish shipping giant **Mærsk Lines**, creating Mærsk-Sealand.

sea lawyer, sailor who habitually argues against authority and tries to twist the regulations around to favor his or her side of the argument.

sea legs, colloquial term for physical and physiological accommodation to the motion of the sea.

sea letter, ship's passport issued in time of war to a neutral vessel upon leaving a port. It contained information on the **master** and crew, cargo, owners, place of lading, destination, and port of **registry**, and entitled the vessel to sail freely. Use of sea letters was discontinued by Presidential proclamation on April 10, 1815. The last one was issued in New York on December 24, 1806. Sea letters proved ineffective in halting British and French boarding and search of U.S. vessels during the Napoleonic Wars. A sea letter was also, in commercial usage, a report from the captain to a vessel's owners, mailed home when the ship touched port.

Seaman's Act, legislation approved by the U.S. Congress in 1915 to regulate working conditions for seamen. It is widely referred to as the **La Follette Seamen's Act.**

The Seaman's Friend, sailor's handbook written by **Richard Henry Dana Jr.** in 1841 based on his seafaring experiences, which he recounted in *Two Years before the Mast*, as well as on his legal practice. Subtitled *A Treatise on Practical Seamanship*, it served for many years as an authoritative guide to the legal rights and duties of seamen.

seamen's bethel, a church, sometimes affiliated with a particular denomination, that served sailors and their families. Bethels often incorporated schools, savings banks, libraries, and temperance boardinghouses.

Seamen's Church Institute, organization founded in 1834 as the Young Men's Church Missionary Society to focus on the plight of seafarers in the Port of New York. Through the years, it has provided hospitality and legal services and maritime training, and has tended to the spiritual and moral needs of mariners. Formally the Seamen's Church Institute of New York and New Jersey, it is now a worldwide resource for legal research, education, advocacy, and assistance on seafarers' rights issues.

Sea of Tranquility, area on the moon's surface once thought to be water that is the site where Apollo 11 landed on July 20, 1969. Other low-lying areas on the moon once thought to be water include the Sea of Cold, Sea of Rains, Sea of Serenity, Sea of Crises, Sea of Vapors, Sea of Fertility, Sea of Nectar, Sea of Clouds, Sea of Moisture, Ocean of Storms, and Lake of Dreams.

sea power, the total maritime strength of a nation, including naval and **merchant marine assets** and port, harbor, and repair facilities.

sea room, space in which to maneuver without danger of grounding or collision.

Seascape, 1975 Pulitzer Prize–winning drama by Edward Albee (b. 1928) about a couple who, while picnicking by the ocean, meet two giant sea lizards who wish to evolve. The dialogue provides an examination of humans as a species.

Sea Scouts, coed nautical branch of the Boy Scouts, founded in 1912, with an emphasis on boating and seamanship.

Sea Scouts, theatrical cartoon short turned out by Walt Disney in 1939 about the misadventures of an inexperienced seaman out in his sailboat. It starred **Donald Duck** as well as his nephews Huey, Dewey, and Louie.

Sea Shadow, U.S. **Navy** "stealth ship" developed in 1985 and used as a testbed for **radar**, hydrodynamics, and ship controls. The seaborne equivalent of the F-177 stealth fighter, the 160-foot **SWATH** vessel was constructed with no military capabilities. It was placed in storage in 1995 and then reactivated in 1999.

Seaspeak, international language for seafarers developed for use by deck officers and maritime authorities in busy sea lanes. The idea of seaspeak is to reduce to a minimum the possibilities of confusion by establishing set phrases for ideas that are normally expressed in English in a variety of ways.

sea squirt, bottom-dwelling marine animal with no head, no eyes, and no mouth, which resembles a potato. Found in all oceans, sea squirts attach themselves to almost anything.

sea state, the wave condition on the surface of the sea.

"A Sea Symphony", 1910 musical work for choir and orchestra by English composer Ralph Vaughan Williams (1872–1958). The music was directly inspired by the sea, and all lyrics were taken from poems contained in **Walt**

Whitman's *Leaves of Grass*, including "A Song for All Seas, All Ships."

Sea Wife, melodramatic tale of two shipwreck survivors, one a nun, who fall in love while sharing a lifeboat in the Indian Ocean after their vessel was torpedoed by a Japanese submarine in World War II. The 1957 motion picture starred Richard Burton and Joan Collins.

Seawise University, 1970 reincarnation of the former **Cunard liner** RMS *Queen Elizabeth*. The ship was purchased by Chinese Orient Overseas Line shipping magnate C. Y. Tung after the ship failed as a static tourist attraction in Port Everglades, Florida. *Seawise* (read: "C.Y.'s") *University* was taken to Hong Kong for refurbishment into a floating college campus and cruise ship. The ship was torched by arsonists in January 1972, only a few days before her anticipated maiden Pacific cruise. The twisted, capsized wreck in Hong Kong Harbor served as a secret headquarters in the James Bond film *The **Man with the Golden Gun***.

Sea Witch, 192-foot **clipper ship** designed by **John Willis Griffiths** and launched in 1846 for the **China trade** of the New York firm Howland and **Aspinwall**. Beginning with her **maiden voyage**, *Sea Witch* established a series of sailing records on the China run as well as between New York and San Francisco. On the return leg of her ninth voyage, she struck a reef and sank off Havana, with five hundred Cuba-bound Chinese workers on board.

The Sea Wolf, popular 1904 seagoing novel by **Jack London** that follows Wolf Larsen, the satanic captain of the *Ghost* who saves wealthy castaway Humphrey Van Weyden and fugitive Ruth Webster after their steamer capsizes. The two escape in a small boat only to return to the *Ghost*. The classic saga was adapted for the silver screen many times, the most notable of which is the 1941 version that starred Edward G. Robinson. A 1993 remake made for television starred Charles Bronson and Christopher Reeve.

USS Seawolf (SSN-21), 9,137-ton, nuclear-powered submarine commissioned in 1997. The 353-foot vessel is run by a crew of 127 men. The world's most advanced sub, *Seawolf* emits less noise when running at cruising speed than a **Los Angeles**–class sub gives off while tied up dockside. *Seawolf* was also the name of the U.S. **Navy**'s second atomic submarine, which was launched March 30, 1957.

The Sea Wolves, motion picture epic based on true accounts from World War II involving Nazi radio vessels, British undercover intelligence, and decoy fishing ships. Filmed in the Indian Ocean off the great subcontinent, the 1981 action-packed movie starred Gregory Peck, Roger Moore, David Niven, and Trevor Howard.

SeaWorld, America's leading chain of aquatic marine life entertainment parks. Founded in 1964 by four UCLA fraternity brothers who dreamed and developed a few shows and saltwater aquariums, it has become famous for Shamu the killer whale and other maritime theme rides and attractions. SeaWorld is today owned by Anheuser-Busch; there are SeaWorlds in San Diego, California; San Antonio, Texas; Orlando, Florida; and Cleveland, Ohio.

securité, word used in radio communications, repeated three times, to precede a safety message.

Sedov, 386-foot Russian **tall ship** that, with masts rising 184 feet above deck, is the tallest sailing ship in the world. Built in Germany in 1921 as the cargo carrier *Magdalene Vinnen*, she was acquired by the Soviets after World War II and converted to a sail training vessel. Home ported in **Murmansk**, the ship was renamed for the Russian polar explorer and oceanographer Georgij Sedov (1877–1914).

Seeadler, Germany's only sailing warship in World War I. Commanded by the colorful Count **Felix von Luckner**, she was disguised as a Norwegian lumber ship and sank about twenty Allied ships. *Seeadler* ("Sea Eagle") was wrecked when she went aground on a coral reef in the Society Islands.

Seeandbee, the only four-**funneled** passenger steamer built for **Great Lakes** operation. Designed by **Frank Kirby**, the 485-foot **side-wheeler** was completed in 1913 for the Cleveland and Buffalo (C&B) Transit Company. *Seandbee*'s 510 staterooms could accommodate some 1,500 passengers on her Lake Erie route. She was taken over for naval service on the Great Lakes in 1942 and was rebuilt into the training aircraft carrier USS *Wolverine*. She was scrapped in 1947.

Selkirk, Alexander (1676–1721), Scottish seaman who achieved literary immortality when author **Daniel Defoe** based his novel ***Robinson Crusoe*** (1719) on him. In 1704 Selkirk was engaged on a privateering expedition and was set ashore at his own request on Más-a-tierra, one of the Juan Fernández Islands in the Pacific Ocean four hundred miles west of Chile. He was discovered by Captain **Woodes Rogers** and the **privateer** *Duke* in 1709 and returned to England where he became a celebrity.

Semmes, Raphael (1809–1877), U.S. naval officer who commanded USS *Somers* when she capsized and sank in 1846. He joined the Confederacy during the Civil War and in 1862 took command of the **Confederate raider** CSS *Alabama*. He soon became the scourge of Northern commerce, and his two-year cruise in *Alabama* ended when the ship was sunk in an engagement with USS *Kearsarge* off Cherbourg, France, in June 1864. The English yacht *Deerhound* rescued Semmes and several of his crew and took them to England. He returned to the South, where he was promoted to rear admiral. After the Civil War, Semmes practiced law in Mobile, Alabama. He wrote *Service Afloat and Ashore during the Mexican War* (1851), *The Cruise of the Alabama and Sumter* (1864), and *Memoirs of Services Afloat during the War between the States* (1869).

semper paratus, U.S. **Coast Guard** motto, which is Latin for "always ready" or "ever ready." It is also the Coast Guard service song, with words and music written by Coast Guard captain Francis Saltus Van Boskerck in the 1920s.

Sequoia, 104-foot presidential yacht that from 1933 to 1976 served seven presidents, from Herbert Hoover to Gerald Ford. Designed by John Trumpy in 1925, the classic wooden motor yacht entered government service in 1931 and was used as a decoy ship to trap **rumrunners** in the **Mississippi River**. She is a national historic landmark and currently runs charters in Alexandria, Virginia, on the Potomac River, not far from the Washington Navy Yard, her historic home for forty-three years.

HMS *Serapis*, British **frigate** under the command of Captain Richard Pearson that was escorting a **convoy** when she was attacked off Flamborough Head, England, on September 23, 1779, by **John Paul Jones** in *Bonhomme Richard*. In the most famous naval engagement of the American Revolution, *Serapis* was captured, and Jones sailed the vessel to Holland after the shot-riddled *Richard* sank.

Serpens, U.S. **Coast Guard**–manned cargo ship that exploded and sank while loading depth charges at **Guadalcanal** in January 1945. The blast killed 196 Coast Guard personnel and the entire crew of 57 U.S. Army stevedores working on board. It was the largest single loss of life in the history of the U.S. Coast Guard.

Serres, Dominic (1722–1793), French marine artist who moved to England in the 1750s and became one of the most successful painters of naval scenes of the **Seven Years' War** and the American Revolution from the British perspective. His well-crafted paintings are often deemed more accurate than written accounts of the time. He later became marine painter to King George III.

set and drift, refers to the behavior of a ship under the influence of wind and current. "Set" is the direction the ship is deflected from its intended course; and "drift" is the speed in **knots** of the displacement.

Sevastopol, port city in the Ukraine, located on the Crimean peninsula and the Bay of Sevastopol, an inlet of the **Black Sea**. Historically it has served as an important naval base. It was of great strategic importance during the **Crimean War** and World War II.

seven seas, figurative expression relating not to the seas but to the oceans: the Arctic, Indian, North Pacific, South Pacific, North Atlantic, South Atlantic, and Antarctic (which is not a separate ocean but an extension of the Atlantic, Pacific, and Indian Oceans).

Seven Years' War, European conflict (1756–63) that involved many nations but was chiefly a war of Great Britain against France and Spain. In America, it was called the **French and Indian War**. Many of its important battles were fought on the sea to win control of overseas colonies. The **Treaty of Paris** settled disputes between the three countries on February 10, 1763, and Britain emerged as the dominant European power, having made territorial gains in North America, the Caribbean, and India.

Severin, Tim (b. 1940), British adventurer, historian, writer, and lecturer who specializes in recreating legendary and historical expeditions. He re-created the voyage of **Saint Brendan** in 1976–77, and in 1980 he sailed six thousand miles from Oman to China in a replica tenth-century Arab merchant ship to recount the

seven voyages of **Sinbad the Sailor**. In 1984 he retraced the **Black Sea** route taken by Jason and his Argonauts and to follow Ulysseus's homeward-bound voyage from Troy to Ithaca. He has set out to find the great white whale of **Herman Melville**'s *Moby-Dick* and has sailed the Pacific on a bamboo raft. He has written nearly fifteen books on his adventures.

sextant, navigational instrument whose scale is on an arc that is one sixth the circumference of a circle, but through the use of mirrors, can measure angles of up to 120 degrees. Developed from **Hadley's quadrant** by **Royal Navy** Captain John Campbell around 1757, it is used to make observations of the sun, moon, planets, and stars. From these observations it is possible to estimate **latitude**, and with an accurate timekeeping device, the **longitude** of a vessel. The sextant is also used to measure horizontal angles and distances.

Shackleton, Sir Ernest (1874–1922), Irish-English Antarctic explorer. He participated in expeditions with **Robert Falcon Scott** and commanded a 1907–9 expedition that ascended Mt. Erebus and located the magnetic South Pole. Knighted in 1909, he was commander of the ill-fated **Shackleton Expedition** intending to traverse Antarctica in 1914. Following the ordeal, he authored *South* (1919), an account of the whole expedition. Shackleton is considered the last explorer of the heroic age of exploration and one of history's exemplary leaders. In 1921 he sailed on the research ship *Quest* to pursue further Antarctic study but died on board and was buried on South Georgia Island.

Shackleton Expedition, expedition organized and led by Sir **Ernest Shackleton** to make a 1,500-mile crossing of Antarctica. Shackleton and a crew of twenty-seven sailors and scientists set out from Britain in August 1914 aboard the *Endurance* and by January became caught in the ice in the Weddell Sea—one day's sail from their destination. *Endurance* sank eleven months later, and Shackleton led his men 180 miles to **Elephant Island**. Faced with certain death, Shackleton and his strongest men set out on a grueling seventeen-day, eight-hundred-mile voyage aboard the lifeboat *James Caird* to South Georgia Island to get help. Shackleton returned three months later to rescue the other men. The entire ordeal lasted nearly two years and, as Shackleton later wrote, "Not a life lost and we have been through Hell."

shaft alley, long compartment surrounding a ship's propeller shaft aft from the engine room to the **stuffing box**, where the propeller shafts pass through the hull. Mariners have traditionally used this usually empty space as a place for private conversation.

shakedown, to run a new or overhauled vessel through a series of tests. On a shakedown cruise, the crew is trained or retrained.

Shall We Dance?, lighthearted shipboard song-and-dance romance motion picture. While no actual passenger vessel was used for a set, the 1937 film captures a good deal of the aura of luxury shipboard living before World War II. Starring Fred Astaire, Ginger Rogers, and Edward Everett Horton, with songs by George and Ira Gershwin, what better place than a transatlantic **liner** for Fred and Ginger to dance to "The Continental" or to pose the classic musical query "Let's Call the Whole Thing Off."

Shalom, **flagship** of the **Zim** Line, a French-built Israeli **liner** completed in 1964 for transatlantic service. Her popularity never caught on largely because during her first year in service, only kosher food was available on board. Although the menu was later changed, popular opinion had already snubbed the 25,338-gross-ton beauty and she was sold to the **Hamburg-America Line** of Germany in 1967. Renamed the *Hanseatic*, she has since seen operation as the *Doric* and the *Royal Odyssey*.

Shamrock, the first of the succession of five British racing yachts of the same name that Sir **Thomas Lipton** sent over to challenge for the **America's Cup** between 1899 and 1930. A steel **cutter** built in 1899 by Thorneycraft & Company of Millwall on Thames to **William Fife Jr.**'s design, *Shamrock* lost to *Columbia* in three straight races on a course off the New Jersey shore. The 1899 race was the first news event to be transmitted by the **Marconi** wireless telegraphy.

Shamrock II, **America's Cup** challenger in 1901, again against *Columbia* and her **skipper Charles Barr**. Designed by **George L. Watson**, the yacht was constructed with a lightweight alloy called "immadium." The course was again off the coast of New Jersey, and *Shamrock II* lost in three races by close margins. The boat did not return to Britain but was instead left behind in New York and broken up two years later. Lipton desired an all-Irish challenge to the Cup, but naming the vessel *Shamrock*, painting it green, and representing the Royal Ulster Yacht Club of Ireland was the closest he came.

Shamrock III, **Thomas Lipton**'s 1903 **America's Cup** challenger, which was outmatched by the **New York Yacht Club** defender, *Reliance*. The 134-foot **sloop**, designed by **William Fife Jr.**, lost in three straight races on a course south of Long Island.

Shamrock IV, **Thomas Lipton**'s **America's Cup** challenger in 1920 against the U.S. defender, *Resolute*. It was the first contest in which amateurs **skippered** the boats, and Lipton was edged out three races to two. The 110-foot **Charles E. Nicholson**–designed **sloop** was sailing to the United States for a contest in 1914 when World War I broke out. She was **laid up** in New York and recommissioned again six years later.

Shamrock V, 120-foot British **J-boat** designed by **Charles E. Nicholson** that challenged for the **America's Cup** in 1930. It was **Thomas Lipton**'s fifth challenge, and the results were all the same. *Shamrock V* was defeated by the **New York Yacht Club** defender *Enterprise*, four races to two, on a course off Newport, Rhode Island. Lipton had considered a sixth challenge, but he died the following year. *Shamrock V* was later purchased by **Thomas Octave Murdoch "T.O.M." Sopwith** to help with his quest for the Cup and went on to have various owners. She was fully restored in the 1980s, and today sails charters out of Newport.

shanghai, to abduct a sailor by force, usually with the help of drink or drugs, so as to enlist him on another vessel. The use of the term probably derived from the phrase "ship him to Shanghai" (China), which meant to send a seaman on a long voyage to keep him out of trouble. The practice disappeared when sailors became organized in unions.

USS *Shangri-La* (CV-38), **Essex**-class aircraft carrier commissioned in 1944, and named after the code-moniker for Colonel **James Harold Doolittle**'s daring aircraft carrier–launched raid on Tokyo. The 888-foot vessel arrived in time to see action against the Japanese off of **Okinawa**. She participated in the atomic bomb tests at the **Bikini Atoll**, using her crewman as guinea-pig observers in 1946. The 27,100-ton ship was decommissioned in 1971 and sold for scrap in 1988.

HMS *Shannon*, British **frigate** that captured USS *Chesapeake* in June 1, 1813, during the **War of 1812**, despite Captain **James Lawrence**'s dying plea, "**Don't give up the ship!**" Sixty-five *Chesapeake* sailors were killed in the action, and eighty-five were seriously wounded.

Sharpe, Bartholomew (1650–1690), English **buccaneer** who, along with Sir **Henry Morgan**, was involved in the attack on **Portobello** in 1679. During the 1680s, he led an expedition that plundered several Spanish settlements along the western coast of South America.

sharpie, sail workboat distinguished by a long, narrow, flat-bottomed hull, twenty-eight to thirty feet in length; two masts; and a centerboard. Sharpies were first used by oystermen in the mid-nineteenth century in New Haven, Connecticut.

sheer, traditional marine architectural feature that slopes a vessel's deck upward toward the bow and stern from a central point. This design allows the structure to ride up and over an oncoming swell like a duck and also results in the fore/aft stateroom corridors aboard large passenger ships curling up toward the nether ends and disappearing from sight.

sheet anchor, large anchor kept for emergency use, so called because it was usually stowed abaft the fore rigging, where the foresheet was secured. The phrase is also used to describe something that provides security. One example of this usage is in the title of a book on rigging and practical seamanship, *The Young Officer's Sheet Anchor* (1819), by Darcy Lever.

HMS *Sheffield* (D-80), 410-foot guided-missile **destroyer** commissioned in 1975 for the **Royal Navy**. In 1982 she was part of the fifty-one-ship armada—which included the ocean **liner**–troop carriers *Queen Elizabeth 2* and *Canberra*—sent by the British government to recover the Falkland Islands following the Argentine invasion of 1982. *Sheffield* was hit in the opening days of the war by a French-built Exocet missile. The projectile failed to detonate, but resulting fires caused the ship to sink with the loss of twenty crew members.

Shelikhov, Grigory (d. 1795), Russian fur trader who in 1783 sailed with three ships and claimed Alaska for Russia. Called "the Russian Columbus," he built forts and settlements along the southern coast and islands. In 1867 Alaska was sold to the United States for two cents an acre.

shellback, an experienced sailor or veteran hand. The term is also used to describe a sailor, a "**pollywog**," who has crossed the equator and has been initiated into the realm of **King Neptune**.

CSS *Shenandoah*, Confederate Raider of the American Civil War. For several months after the surrender of ground forces, *Shenandoah* had been burning Union shipping, with her captain, James I. Waddell, still thinking the war was in progress. After destroying twenty-four American whaleships in the Bering Sea, *Shenandoah* became the object of a worldwide search. Once Waddell learned that the war had ended, he put guns below decks and sailed twenty-three thousand miles to England to surrender the ship to the British **Admiralty**. On November 6, 1865, the last sovereign Confederate flag was hauled.

Sheppard, Warren (1858–1937), American marine painter, sailor, and writer. In addition to painting scenes of the New England coast, he designed yachts and published a text on navigation.

Shinano, Japanese warship laid down as a sister ship to the battleships ***Musashi*** and ***Yamato*** in 1940. *Shinano* was redesigned in 1942 after the Battle of **Midway** to be completed as a sixty-two-thousand-ton aircraft carrier. Structural steel, which was in short supply in Japanese yards at the time, was taken from her uncompleted fourth sister battleship, which was dismantled for that purpose. Hastily built and commissioned in 1944, *Shinano* was struck ten days later by torpedoes from the submarine USS *Archerfish* off Cape Muroto. She sank several hours later.

ship, in the age of sail, a vessel with three or more masts with square sails on all masts; more precisely, a **full-rigged ship**.

Ship Ahoy, motion picture featuring spies, espionage, and Tommy Dorsey's Orchestra aboard a cruise ship bound for Puerto Rico. In addition to the footwork of Eleanor Pow-

ell and the singing of Frank Sinatra, the 1942 musical starred Red Skelton, Bert Lahr, and Buddy Rich.

shipbreaking, intentional scrapping of a ship that has become obsolete or too old for service.

ship brokerage, the practice of matching cargoes and **carriers** and arranging charter agreements.

A *Ship of Fools*, 1962 best-selling novel by **Katherine Anne Porter** (1890–1980) that is an excellent study of juxtaposed passengers aboard the German luxury **liner** *Vera* headed for pre-Hitler Germany from Veracruz, Mexico. The 1965 classic movie—which starred Vivian Leigh (in her last film role), Jose Ferrer, and Lee Marvin—was nominated for eight Academy Awards.

"The Ship of Fools", German poem ("Das Narrenschiff") written in 1494 by Sebastian Brant (1458–1521) that concerns incidents on a ship carrying people to Narragonia, the fool's paradise. It is a satire of the times and was particularly directed at corruption in the Roman Catholic Church.

Ship of Gold in the Deep Blue Sea, best-selling 1998 narrative by Gary Kinder (b. 1946) about the loss and recovery of SS ***Central America***, a **steamship** returning from the California gold rush filled with $1 billion in gold that sank off Cape Hatteras in 1857.

The Ship of Lost Men, 1929 silent film, starring Marlene Dietrich and Fritz Kortner, about a pilot who is rescued by a ship of escaped convicts after crashing his plane in the **Atlantic**.

ship of state, metaphor for a country and its affairs. In **Henry Wadsworth Longfellow**'s poem "The Building of the Ship" (1850), the newly built ship symbolizes the nation. The final stanza begins with the lines "Thou, too, sail on, O Ship of State! / Sail on, O Union, strong and great!" President **Abraham Lincoln** was deeply moved by these lines and frequently used the phrase, describing himself as a **pilot**.

ship of the line, historical term for a major warship, with at least two full gundecks, that would engage in **line of battle** tactics. Historically, sailing navies had six **rates** of ships, the first three of which would usually be considered ships of the line.

Shipping Act of 1916, act of Congress to address the fact that at the outbreak of World War I in late summer 1914, 90 percent of U.S. foreign trade was carried in foreign-flag ships. The act established the U.S. **Shipping Board** and authorized it to form the **Emergency Fleet Corporation** to build a U.S. fleet. Because the war caused severe shipping shortages, the act also sought to establish a means to regulate **shipping conferences** so that U.S. shippers would be protected from discriminatory or unfair rates.

shipping articles, written agreement between the **master** of a ship and the crew concerning employment. It includes rates of pay and capacity of each crewman, the date of commencement of the voyage, and the voyage's duration.

U.S. Shipping Board, independent agency created by the U.S. Congress under the **Shipping Act of 1916** that was the first government agency to both regulate shipping and promote the **merchant marine**. The board was given authority to purchase, construct, lease, charter, and operate merchant ships. When the United States declared war on Germany on April 15, 1917, the Shipping Board shortly thereafter seized 103 German and neutral merchant ships that had taken refuge in U.S. ports. The **Emergency Fleet Corporation** was also organized under the board to expedite new ship construction. In 1920 the board was empowered to develop and maintain essential foreign trade routes. In 1933 its functions were transferred to a new Shipping Board Bureau within the Department of Commerce.

Shipping Commissioner's Act of 1872, an attempt by the U.S. Congress to improve conditions for U.S. seamen by providing for the appointment of shipping commissioners at the more important ports in the United States to oversee the shipping, discharge, and care of seamen on American merchant vessels. The failure of the act led to the establishment of the **Bureau of Navigation** in 1884.

The Shipping News, 1993 novel by Annie Proulx (b. 1935) that won both the Pulitzer Prize and the National Book Award. The story is about a widower journalist, Quoyle, who flees upstate New York and moves to Newfoundland, Canada. His "Shipping News" column becomes a hit, and he "finds" himself.

Ship Rock, steep hill in northwestern New Mexico that resembles a ship under full sail. The famous landmark rises 1,678 feet above the flat land around it.

ship's husband, legal term for the general agent appointed by the owner of a vessel who is authorized to make repairs, outfit the vessel, hire officers, and enter into contracts. More generally, a ship's husband is the person who sees to a ship's outfitting and marine supplies.

"Ships that pass in the night", phrase immortalized in **Henry Wadsworth Longfellow**'s 1863 poem "Tales of a Wayside Inn." The full stanza reads as follows: "Ships that pass in the night, and speak each other in passing, / Only a signal shown and a distant voice in the darkness; / So on the ocean of life we pass and speak one another, / Only a look and a voice; then darkness again and a silence." It is also the title of an 1895 poem by Black American poet Paul Lawrence Dunbar (1872–1906).

The Ship That Died of Shame, 1955 feature film comedy about a group of World War II shipmates who obtain their old vessel for endearingly illicit purposes. The movie starred Richard Attenborough and George Baker.

shiver me timbers!, a nautical expression of surprise or disbelief. By some accounts, it described a ship running aground so hard that the timbers shivered.

Shokaku, Japanese aircraft carrier that was part of the task force sent to attack **Pearl Harbor** on December 7, 1941. Built in 1941, the 25,675-ton vessel was sunk in 1944 during the Battle of the **Philippine Sea** by torpedoes from the sub USS *Cavalla* off Yap Island. Her name means "happy crane," and she was sister ship to the *Zuikaku*.

Shore Patrol (SP), a ship detail assigned to police duty ashore to maintain discipline and aid local police in handling U.S. **Navy** personnel on liberty and leave.

short-timer's chain, length of chain carried by a **Navy** or **Coast Guard** sailor who has a limited time left in his or her service commitment. The number of links on the chain equals the days remaining before discharge, and each day the short-timer cuts off another link.

shot, a length of anchor chain equal to fifteen **fathoms**, or ninety feet.

Shout at the Devil, 1976 film about two men who seek to blow up a German battleship out for repairs in East Africa in 1913. Based on the 1968 novel of the same name by Wilbur Smith, which in turn was based on an actual incident, the movie starred Lee Marvin and Roger Moore.

Show Boat, popular 1926 novel by Edna Ferber (1887–1968) that chronicles three generations of a theatrical family who live and perform on a **Mississippi River steamboat**. It was made into a successful Broadway musical in 1927 by Jerome Kern and Oscar Hammerstein and was produced several times for film and television. The famous score includes the song "Old Man River," among others.

Shreve, Henry Miller (1785–1851), American trader and pioneer of **steamboat** navigation on the **Mississippi River**. Shreve pioneered the high-pressure engine on a flat-bottomed hull that made upriver navigation against the swift currents of inland rivers possible, making him the person most responsible for the opening of the inland waterways of the United States. He opened the Red River to navigation in the 1830s by clearing it of a logjam that was more than 160 miles long. Shreveport, Louisiana, is named for him.

Sicily Invasion, July 9–10, 1943, amphibious European assault in which 1,400 ships of the U.S. and British navies landed 120,000 Allied troops on the island beachheads in the largest amphibious mission ever undertaken up to that time.

sick bay, the infirmary or medical office on U.S. **Navy** and **Coast Guard** vessels.

side-wheeler, a paddle wheeler with paddles on the sides instead of the stern.

Siebe, Augustus (1788–1872), German inventor who is considered the father of the modern deep-sea diving **dress**. He developed the first deep-sea diving helmet in the 1830s, and in 1839 his hardhat system was used to **salvage** HMS *Royal George* from the harbor at **Spithead**, England. He later won an endorsement by the **Royal Navy**, and his firm, Siebe, Gorman & Company, became a leading manufacturer of diving equipment.

"Sighted sub, sank same", message sent by U.S. **Navy** pilot David F. Mason while on a mission off Argentia, Newfoundland, in January 1942. Mason believed, mistakenly, that he had sunk a German **U-boat**.

Sight Reduction Tables for Marine Navigation, commonly referred to as "Pub. 229," a six-volume U.S. government publication designed to facilitate the practice of celestial navigation at sea.

Sigmund and the Sea Monsters, 1973–75 Saturday morning live-action television series about two brothers who take in a refugee sea monster. The Sid and Marty Krofft production included underwater puppet-related fun.

Sigsbee, Charles Dwight (1845–1923), U.S. **Navy** officer who commanded the ill-fated battleship USS *Maine* when she exploded in Havana Harbor in February 1898, one of the catalysts of the **Spanish-American War**. Sigsbee was in his cabin and survived the incident. Later, in 1905, he commanded a special squadron to carry the remains of **John Paul Jones** from Cherbourg, France, to the U.S. **Naval Academy**. Among his retirement writings was *The Maine, An Account of Her Destruction in Havana Harbor* (1899).

Silent World, 1952 best-selling book by **Jacques-Yves Cousteau**, Frédérick Dumas, and James Dugan about the early days of **scuba** diving. The 1956 documentary film introduced the world to Cousteau's research ship *Calypso*.

Silver, Long John, fictional pirate in **Robert Louis Stevenson**'s novel *Treasure Island* (1883).

Simmons sea skiff, small, seaworthy, outboard-powered fishing boat first built in the 1950s by T. N. Simmons of Myrtle Grove, North Carolina. Designed for the inlets, bars, and open waters of North Carolina, the boats have the bow of a traditional New England dory, a shallow V-bottom, and a high-raking transom with the motor mounted in a well.

Simón Bolívar, 270-foot Venezuelan sail training vessel completed in 1980 and named for Simón Bolívar (1783–1830), the liberator of northern South America. Her sister **tall ships** are *Gloria*, of Colombia; *Guayas*, of Ecuador; and *Cuauhtemoc*, of Mexico.

Sims, William Sowden (1858–1936), U.S. **Navy** officer and commander of all U.S. naval operations in European waters in World War I. The navy, which had a wartime strength of approximately five hundred thousand men, **convoyed** troop transports, chased submarines, and

helped British forces keep German vessels out of the North Sea. During his career, Sims had a profound influence on the administration of the navy and on the development of the officer corps. He coauthored *Victory at Sea* (1920), which won a Pulitzer Prize.

Sinbad the Sailor, hero—along with Ali Baba and Aladdin—in the *Arabian Nights* tales who relates seven incredible and fabulous voyages of Indian Ocean piracy, hidden treasure, and beautiful maidens. The stories were magnificently translated into film in 1947's *Sinbad the Sailor*, starring Douglas Fairbanks Jr., Maureen O'Hara, and Anthony Quinn.

"Sink the Bismarck!", inspired by the motion picture of the same name, a Western ballad composed by American country singer Johnny Horton that accurately—and very simply—recounts the British hunt and destruction of the famous Nazi warship to a toe-tapping tune. Recorded in 1960, the song made it to the number three spot on the popular charts.

Sink the Bismarck!, an excellent 20th Century Fox war room drama released in 1960 that retells the tale of how the German battleship *Bismarck* was intercepted and sunk by the British. The movie featured Kenneth Moore in the lead role.

Sirens, in mythology, sister nymphs who live on an island near Sicily and entice sailors to shore with their beautiful singing. Shipwrecks and death are sure to follow their call. In the *Odyssey*, **Odysseus** had the ears of his crew stuffed with wax and himself lashed to the mast to escape the fatal effects of the Sirens' song.

six-meter, racing **sloop** designed to rate six meters (approximately twenty feet) under the **International Rules** for measurement. Formerly a very important class in international racing, after World War II the six-meters proved too expensive and exotic to continue their dominance of the sport.

six pack, nickname for an uninspected passenger vessel carrying six paying passengers.

USS *Skate* (SSN-578), U.S. **Navy** atomic submarine launched in May 1957, the first designed for assembly-line production. She set underwater endurance records during her initial cruises, and on March 17, 1959, she surfaced at the North Pole—the first ship to be on the surface at the polar icecap. The voyage was chronicled in *Surface at the Pole* (1960), written by her captain, **James F. Calvert**.

Skeleton Coast, southwestern edge of Africa, where the combination of heavy winds, thick fog, and fast currents have made it a maritime graveyard for unwary ships. Survivors who made it ashore had to face the harsh Namib Desert.

skipjack, type of V-bottomed, centerboard, single-mast sailboat about thirty-five to sixty feet in length. Developed in Chesapeake Bay about 1880 for oyster dredging and fishing, the design has since been adapted for recreational use.

skipper, nickname for a captain of a vessel or the person in command of a yacht or small craft. The word comes from the Dutch *schipper*, meaning captain of a small vessel.

skysail, light sail set above the royal on **square-rigged** vessels, which is usually used in light favorable winds.

skyscraper, triangular sail set above a **skysail** to maximize the advantage of light, favorable winds.

Slave Ship, adventure movie about slaving off the African coast in 1860. The 1937 film starred Wallace Beery, Mickey Rooney, George Sanders, Jane Darwell, and Lon Chaney Jr., who opens the film by being crushed during the ship's launching.

Slocum, Joshua (1844–1910), Canadian-born seaman and adventurer who commanded many **tall ships**, including the **clipper** *Northern Light*, in his day. He was wrecked with his family and crew in 1886 in South America and built the **junk**-rigged "canoe" *Liberdade* to return to the United States with his family. He was the first man in recorded history to sail solo around the world. On April 24, 1895, he set sail from Boston in the thirty-seven-foot **sloop** *Spray*, and on June 27, 1898, he returned to Newport, Rhode Island, to complete his circumnavigation. In 1899 he wrote the classic narrative ***Sailing Alone around the World***. He set sail again in 1909 on a voyage to South America and was lost at sea.

sloop, single-masted sailing vessel. Its mast is set farther forward than that of a **cutter**, and it carries fewer **headsails**, usually just one.

"Sloop John B", traditional seafaring song arranged by Brian Wilson in 1966 and recorded by the Beach Boys that recounts a most disconsolate voyage to the Bahamas. The contemporary contrapuntal melody worked into the sea chantey and carried aloft by the amazing harmony of the famous singing group ensured the song's place in American pop culture.

sloop of war, small warship that did not fit into other categories, usually carrying guns on the deck only.

slop chest, supply of tobacco, clothes, knives, and sundries carried on board ship for the crew to purchase, the price being charged against their work and settled up when they were paid at the end of the voyage. The captain usually reaped the profits.

the Slot, the seaway between the Solomon Islands during World War II (New Georgia Sound). Japanese runs down "the Slot" to resupply **Guadalcanal** became known as the "**Tokyo Express**."

"Slow Boat to China", hit 1948 song written by Frank Loessner and performed by Kay Kyser and His Orchestra. It begins, "I'd love to get you, On a slow boat to China, All to myself alone."

smack, small fishing vessel with either a **cutter** or a **sloop** rig. At times in the United States, the term was used for a sloop or **schooner**-rigged fishing vessel with a well for keeping its catch alive.

small craft advisory, alert issued to mariners by the National Weather Service for sustained weather or sea conditions that might be hazardous to small boats. The threshold is usually eighteen **knots** of wind or higher. See also **gale warning**.

Smeeton, Miles (1906–1988), Canadian yachtsman, explorer, and author who, along with his wife Beryl, is credited with pioneering the oceangoing gypsy life. His books include *Once Is Enough* (1959) and *Because the Horn Is There* (1970).

Smith, Archibald Cary (1837–1911), American marine artist and pioneer yacht designer. He gave up his brush and canvas to design many successful sailing yachts, including *Mischief*, the 1881 **America's Cup** winner.

Smith, Edward J. (1850–1912), captain of RMS *Titanic* on her ill-fated 1912 **maiden voyage**. Smith was known as the "Millionaire's Captain" for his experience and skill. The *Titanic* voyage was to have been his last before retirement. The fate of Smith remains a mystery because his body was never found. Most accounts had him on the bridge until he went down with his ship.

Smith, Frank Vining (1879–1967), American marine artist and illustrator who specialized in nineteenth-century sailing ships. His body of work includes more than a thousand paintings. His success was such that he was able to paint in the winter and sail during the summer. He was made a lifetime member of the **Cruising Club of America** in 1956.

A Chesapeake Bay skipjack. (Courtesy The Mariners' Museum, Newport News, Virginia)

Smith, John (ca. 1580–1631), English explorer, soldier, and founder of the **Jamestown** colony in 1607, who also surveyed the coast around **Cape Cod** in a later expedition. The author of *A Sea Grammar* (1627), he is best known for his exploration of the East Coast.

smoking lamp, in the old days, a source of flame for men to smoke. In modern times, the term was used figuratively aboard U.S. **Navy** and U.S. **Coast Guard** ships to denote certain times when smoking was permitted. Today, smoking is permitted only on the weather decks.

smoking room, **saloon** aboard passenger **liners** that was almost always situated aft on the main public room deck. In the era before World War I, the smoking room was usually recognized as a male preserve for drinking, gambling, and—of course—smoking, all away from the delicate eyes of the ladies. Male predominance was certified by the fact that virtually every shipboard smoking room of the period had a men's toilet attached or adjoining, while the women's facilities were located much farther forward. The smoking room's location aft helped to ensure that the draft made by the ship's forward movement would carry the tobacco smoke away from the deckhouses.

Smollet, Tobias George (1721–1771), English novelist who drew from his experience as a surgeon's mate in the **Royal Navy** to write *The Adventures of Roderick Random* (1748), a story of British naval life.

SMS, former prefix for warships of the German Imperial Navy. It is an abbreviation for Seiner Majestät Schiff ("His Majesty's Ship"). Its use ended with the abdication of **Wilhelm II** in 1918.

SNAME, see **Society of Naval Architects and Marine Engineers**.

sneakbox, a light, shoal-draft duckboat developed on Barnegat Bay, New Jersey, for use by duck hunters in marshes and shallow water. Usually wood, of open construction with a deck forward and around the sides, the type was adapted to sail and used primarily for racing.

snipe, seagoing service term for crew members who work in engineering spaces and are seldom seen topside when under way.

Snipe, popular international **one-design** class of racing sailboats. Designed by William F. Crosby and introduced in 1931, Snipes measure fifteen feet, six inches in length and have a beam of five feet.

snug harbor, a well-protected harbor or a safe secure place. The term has also come to mean a place where sailors go after they **swallow the anchor**.

Society of Nautical Research, British maritime organization established in 1910 to encourage research into matters relating to seafaring and shipbuilding in all ages and among all nations. The society supports the survival of HMS *Victory* and has been closely associated with her restoration. It helped found the **National Maritime Museum** at Greenwich, England, and it publishes the *Mariner's Mirror*, a quarterly scholarly journal devoted to ships and the sea.

Society of Naval Architects and Marine Engineers (SNAME), membership organization of professionals involved in ship design and engineering. It was founded in 1893 by individuals concerned about the future of U.S. ship design and construction and its **Navy** and **merchant marine**.

Society of Sponsors, membership organization established in 1908 that is open to any woman who has bestowed a name on a U.S. naval vessel.

SOLAS, see **Safety of Life at Sea**.

Solent, narrow passage between the **Isle of Wight** and the southern mainland of England that provides access to the Port of Southampton, the **Royal Navy** base at Portsmouth, and the yachting center at Cowes.

Soling, popular international **one-design sloop** sailboat. Designed by Jan Herman Linge and introduced in 1965, Solings became an Olympic class in 1972. The keel boat measures twenty-six feet, eleven inches in length.

solstice, the two times of the year when the sun reaches its maximum declination. The summer solstice occurs on or about June 22, and

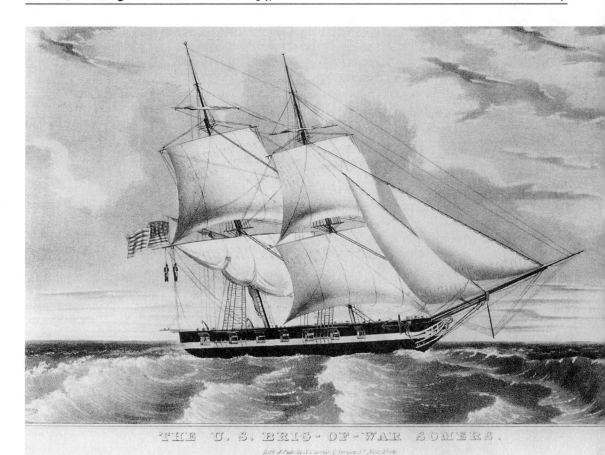

Brig-of-war *Somers*, site of the *Somers* Mutiny.

the winter solstice on or about December 22. The midway points between the solstices are called "equinoxes."

Somers, Sir George (1554–1610), English naval commander and **privateer** who was knighted in 1603. In 1609 he set out with settlers bound for Virginia but was shipwrecked in Bermuda, which he claimed for Great Britain. Versions of the shipwreck written at the time may have inspired William Shakespeare's play *The **Tempest***.

USS *Somers*, U.S. **Navy** training ship that was the site of the 1842 *Somers* **Mutiny**, which resulted in the hanging deaths of three sailors.

Rumors persisted that the vessel was doomed, and the **brig**, under the later command of **Raphael Semmes**, capsized and sank four years later off the coast of **Veracruz**, Mexico, with great loss of life.

***Somers* Mutiny**, 1842 incident aboard the U.S. **Navy** training ship USS *Somers* in which Captain Alexander Slidell Mackenzie discovered what he thought was a planned mutiny. He arrested fourteen trainees and sailors and on December 1, 1842, hanged midshipman Philip Spencer, the eighteen-year-old son of secretary of war John Spencer; boatswain Samuel Cromwell; and seaman Elisha Small. Since there was no declared war at the time, Mackenzie had no authority to carry out the executions, and he was court-martialed. He was found not guilty at two courts-martial—**Matthew Calbraith Perry**, Mackenzie's brother-in-law, was president of the court. The event shocked the country and led the U.S. government to establish the U.S. **Naval Academy** in 1846.

Somerscales, Thomas Jacques (1842–1927), British marine artist who excelled at painting merchant ships under sail. He served in the **Royal Navy** for several years and in 1867 was discharged for health reasons in **Valparaiso**, Chile. He returned to England in 1892 and documented the demise of the sailing ship.

sonar, device used for locating submarines, submerged objects, underwater hazards to navigation, and schools of fish, and for communication. A sound wave is emitted, and the projector listens for an echo. The term is an acronym for "sound navigation and ranging." The early British name for it was **ASDIC**.

son of a gun, a male child born, or conceived, at sea. In the days of sail, seamen were not allowed to go ashore for fear of desertion, so women were let aboard or even carried at sea for a time.

"Son of a Son of a Sailor", hit 1978 song by **James "Jimmy" Buffett** that features rhythms of the sea, images of sailing ships, and the sounds of buoy bells.

Son of Captain Blood, 1962 film sequel in which the son of the famous pirate meets up with his father's enemies on the **high seas**. Sean Flynn, son of Errol Flynn, played the son of the character the elder Flynn played in the classic ***Captain Blood***.

Sons of the Sea, 1941 British film, set in 1837 and starring Michael Redgrave and Valerie Hobson, about two brothers who compete against each other—one in a sailing ship and the other in a **steamship**—by setting up regular shipping service between England and the United States. They also vie for the love of the same woman.

Soo Locks, short stretch of water that is the gateway to navigation between Lake Superior and the other **Great Lakes**. First opened in 1855 at Sault Sainte Marie, Michigan, to bypass the rapids on the Saint Mary's River, it was among the busiest waterways in the world at the end of the nineteenth century as ships carried iron ore from Michigan's upper peninsula to industrial centers of the lower Great Lakes. Enlarged often to accommodate larger ships, it is today the busiest inland waterway in the world. Its centennial was commemorated on a U.S. postage stamp in 1955.

Sopwith, Sir Thomas Octave Murdoch "T.O.M." (1888–1988), British engineer, aviation pioneer, and sailor who mounted two costly challenges to the **America's Cup**. Having built Sopwith "Pups," "Snipes," and "Camels" for World War I, he cofounded the aviation company Hawker after the war. With cash from his successful ventures, Sopwith picked up where Sir **Thomas Lipton** left off and challenged for the America's Cup in 1934 and 1937 with his **J-boats** *Endeavour* and *Endeavour II*. Sopwith's underwriting of a hundred Hurricane fighter planes just before World War II got the production line going for this plane, which was vital both to Great Britain's winning the Battle of Britain in 1940 and to that nation's survival and ultimate victory in World War II.

Soryu, one of the six Japanese aircraft carriers involved in the surprise attack on **Pearl Harbor** on December 7, 1941. Completed in 1937, the 747-foot ship was blown up by planes from the carrier USS *Yorktown* during the Battle of **Midway** in 1942. Her name means "Blue Dragon."

SOS, international signal designating distress that was adopted in 1908. It was selected for its simplicity to read and write in the days of Morse code. Contrary to popular belief, the letters do not stand for "save our ship" or "save our souls."

SOSUS, acronym for Sound Surveillance System, a network of listening and recording arrays employed by the U.S. **Navy** in the 1950s to monitor the movement of Soviet submarines and warships. The system was turned over to the **National Oceanic and Atmospheric Administration** in the 1990s for oceanographic use.

Souls at Sea, 1937 courtroom drama set in 1842 Philadelphia that tells the story of Nuggin' Taylor, who is tried and convicted for mass murder at sea before evidence arrives that the queen of England enlisted him to sabotage the slave trade. Based on the true story of the William Brown murders, the film starred Gary Cooper and George Raft and included vital footage of the American **bark** *Kaiulani* under sail. *Kaiulani* survived "sinking" in the movie to become the last Yankee **packet** to round **Cape Horn** on a commercial voyage, in 1941–42.

South, 1919 account of the **Shackleton Expedition** written by Sir **Ernest Shackleton** himself. It is also the name of the original film shot during the ill-fated Antarctic expedition by the ship's photographer, Frank Hurley. Subtitled *Ernest Shackleton and the Endurance Expedition*, the eighty-eight-minute film was released commercially in 1920 and was restored in 1998.

South China Sea, Battle of the, series of sorties carried out by the U.S. **Navy** starting on January 10, 1945. The ten-day hunt resulted in the sinking of fifteen Japanese navy ships and twenty-nine Imperial merchant vessels.

Southern Cross, southern constellation whose four most prominent members—among the brightest in the sky—form a Latin cross. The long arm of the cross points almost directly at the South Pole. It is not visible above 25° North **latitude**.

Southern Cross, **twelve-meter** Australian contender for the **America's Cup** in 1974. Although she was routed by the American defender, *Courageous*, four races to none, her challenge was the beginning of an Australian tide that would eventually capture the Cup in 1983. The team of **Alan Bond** and Robert Miller (see **Ben Lexcen**) would challenge again in 1977 and 1980 with *Australia*, and in 1983 with *Australia II*.

Southern Ocean, all-encompassing term for the body of water that surrounds the Antarctic Continent. It is actually the southern portions of the **Atlantic**, Indian, and Pacific Oceans. Often used by scientists, the term has also been used to refer to the Antarctic Ocean.

South Pacific, one of the biggest smash-hit Broadway productions of all time, based on the novel *Tales of the South Pacific* by **James Michener**, with music and lyrics by Richard Rodgers and Oscar Hammerstein. The show centers around a band of **Seabees** and **Navy** nurses stationed in the South Pacific during World War II. Mary Martin and Ezio Pinza starred in the 1949 stage production, which included the songs "Some Enchanted Evening" and "I'm Gonna Wash That Man Right Outa My Hair." It was adapted to the screen in 1958, with Mitzi Gaynor and Rossano Brazzi in the lead roles. It was remade for television in 2001, starring Glenn Close and Rade Sherbedgia; Harry Connick Jr. played Lieutenant Joe Cable.

South Sea Bubble, name applied to speculation in Britain's South Sea Company, which failed disastrously in 1720. The company, formed in 1711, was given a monopoly of British trade with the **South Seas** and South America, and holders of government bonds were allowed to exchange them for stock in the new venture. In 1720, the company, knowing it was failing, proposed assuming the entire national debt, offering its stock in exchange for government bonds. The government accepted, and the company's stock rose nearly 800 percent. Soon the bubble burst as banks failed when they could not collect loans made on the inflated stocks.

South Seas, name given by early explorers to the Pacific Ocean. In recent times, it has come to mean the Central and South Pacific. **Schooners** trading in this region in the nineteenth and early twentieth centuries were known as South seamen.

South Street Seaport Museum, maritime museum founded in 1967 in lower Manhattan to trace the history of the Port of New York. The eighteenth- and nineteenth-century buildings and historic vessels are adjacent to the **Fulton Fish Market**—the nation's largest operating wholesale fish market. Ships on exhibit include the original Ambrose lightship of 1907 and the **Cape Horn square-riggers** *Wavertree* (1885) and *Peking*, as well as the fishing **schooner** *Lettie G. Howard* (1893) and the coastal schooner *Pioneer* (1885).

sou'wester, an oilskin hat with a wide brim, elongated in the back, for heavy weather.

Sovereign, **twelve-meter** British challenger for the **America's Cup** in 1964. The sixty-nine-foot **sloop** was soundly defeated, four races to none, by the American defender, *Constellation*, on a course off Newport, Rhode Island. *Sovereign* was **skippered** by Peter Scott, son of the explorer **Robert Falcon Scott**.

Sovereign of the Seas, 232-foot, lavishly ornamented, three-deck warship designed and built by shipbuilder Peter Pett for England's Charles I and launched in 1637. The king ordered that she be the most powerful vessel of her day as an instrument of propaganda against his many

enemies—including the Dutch, French, and Spanish, and the **Barbary pirates**. Her name was changed to *Royal Sovereign* and she was rebuilt several times before being accidentally destroyed by fire in 1696.

Sovereign of the Seas, 258-foot **clipper ship** built in 1852 by **Donald McKay** at East Boston that set many speed records. Her performance so impressed the British **Black Ball Line** owner James Baines that he ordered four more clippers—*Lightning*, *Donald McKay*, *James Baines*, and *Champion of the Seas*. *Sovereign of the Seas* went aground in 1859 and was a total loss.

Spanish-American War, brief conflict between the United States and Spain that took place between April and August 1898. It was precipitated by the explosion of USS *Maine* in Havana Harbor on February 15, with the loss of 260 sailors. The first important battle of the war was the Battle of **Manila Bay**, in which a squadron of six ships under Commodore **George Dewey** sailed to the Philippines and destroyed the entire Spanish fleet of ten vessels. During the course of the war, the United States won Guam, Puerto Rico, and the Philippine Islands, and Cuba was granted its independence. The conflict marked the emergence of the United States as a world power.

Spanish Armada, fleet of 130 heavily armed ships carrying twenty-seven thousand troops that was sent by King Philip II of Spain on July 21–30, 1588, to secure the English Channel as a prelude to an invasion of England to install Catholicism. The smaller but superior warships of Great Britain, under the command of Lord Charles Howard, supported by Sir **Francis Drake**, **John Hawkins**, and Sir **Martin Frobisher**, harassed and ultimately defeated the Spanish fleet, which was under the command of the Duke of Medina Sidonia. The scattered armada, forced to retreat around the north of Scotland and west of Ireland, encountered stormy seas and wrecked an additional twenty-eight ships. In all, the Spanish lost more than seventy ships, and the English only one.

"Spanish Ladies", old **Royal Navy** song written in the 1690s that paints a vivid picture of the British fleet under sail in the English Channel.

Spanish Main, the Spanish possessions in America, particularly the coast of South America from the isthmus of Panama to the mouth of the Orinoco River. The term also referred to the Spanish-controlled section of the Caribbean Sea.

The Spanish Main, standard swashbuckler saga cranked out by Hollywood during the war years. This 1945 RKO color extravaganza starred Paul Henreid, Maureen O'Hara, and Walter Slezack.

spanker, the after mast and its sail on a **schooner**, or a quadrilateral **fore-and-aft** sail set on the mizzenmast or aftermost mast of a **square-rigger**.

SPAR, U.S. **Coast Guard**'s Women's Reserve, authorized in 1942 to serve in administrative and support roles, thereby freeing desperately needed men for sea duty. Captain **Dorothy Constance Stratton** derived the name from the Coast Guard motto *semper paratus* ("always ready"). Approximately twelve thousand SPARs, including one thousand officers, served during World War II, making a significant contribution to the American war effort. The Women's Reserve program was inactive from the end of World War II to 1973, when women became eligible for active duty in both the Coast Guard and the **Coast Guard Reserve**.

USCG *Spar*, 180-foot U.S. **Coast Guard** buoy **tender** that in 1957 was the first vessel to circumnavigate the North American continent on a continuous voyage. She started in Bristol, Rhode Island, traveled south to the **Panama Canal**, then up the Pacific Coast, through the **Northwest Passage**—with two Canadian Coast Guard ships—and back to Bristol.

Sparkman & Stephens (S&S), world-renowned yacht design firm established in New York City in 1929 when twenty-one-year old **Olin James Stephens II** entered into a partnership with yacht broker Drake Sparkman. Since its establishment, S&S has completed more than 2,600 designs in the pleasure, commercial, and military sectors. Best known for its design of sailing vessels, the firm's list of successful designs range from the small-stock day sailors *Blue Jay* and *Lightning* to the famous ocean racers *Dorade* and *Finnesterre* to six **America's Cup** defenders.

Spartina, 1989 award-winning novel by American author John Casey (b. 1939) about a struggling Rhode Island fisherman.

Spee, Maximilian, von (1861–1914), German admiral who was considered a brilliant naval tactician and model officer. During World War I, he commanded a squadron in the Pacific and in November 1914 soundly defeated a British squadron off the coast of Chile—with the British losing two **cruisers** and fifteen hundred men. One month later, von Spee's squadron was defeated in the Battle of the **Falkland Islands**, and he went down with his **flagship**, the heavy cruiser *Scharnhorst*. The incident became famous in German tradition, and the **pocket battleship *Admiral Graf Spee*** was later named for him.

Speed 2: Cruise Control, 1997 action movie using the cruise ship *Seabourne Pride* as a backdrop for a midocean luxury **liner** hijacking. The film starred Sandra Bullock, Jason Patric, and Willem Dafoe.

Sperry, Elmer Ambrose (1860–1930), American engineer and inventor who is best known for his work on the **gyrocompass** and his contributions to navigation. In 1908 he patented the gyrocompass and in 1910 established the Sperry

Gyroscope Company, later **Sperry Marine**. In 1911 the first Sperry gyro was installed aboard the Old Dominion Line's *Princess Anne* for a trial run from New York to **Hampton Roads**, Virginia. The gyro was later installed on USS *Delaware*, and after its success Sperry began to fulfill orders for the U.S. and foreign navies. Sperry later adapted the technology to gunfire control systems; "**metal mike**," the first ship's autopilot; and a gyro stabilizer system.

Sperry Marine, American marine electronics manufacturer that pioneered the **gyrocompass** and related technologies for shipboard and aviation use. The company grew out of the Sperry Gyroscope Company founded in Brooklyn, New York, in 1910 by **Elmer Ambrose Sperry**. Sperry Gyroscope played a key role in World War II and in 1943, at peak employment, had over a hundred thousand people working for it. It later became part of the Sperry Corporation and Sperry Rand. When Sperry Rand merged with Burroughs to form Unisys, the marine division was spun off to Tenneco/Newport News. Renamed Sperry Marine, it was purchased in 1993 by an investment group headed by former secretary of the navy John F. Lehman. In 1996 it was sold to Litton, which was acquired in 2000 by Northrup-Grumman.

spinnaker, large light sail boomed out forward of the mainsail with a pole, and on the opposite side when sailing before the wind or when reaching. It was first used on the British **cutter** *Sphinx* in 1866 and was referred to as "*Sphinx*'s acre."

Spithead, stretch of water lying off the British naval base at Portsmouth that served as the fleet assembly point for the **Royal Navy**.

Spithead Mutiny, famous naval incident of April 16, 1797, in which every ship in Great Britain's Channel Fleet refused to weigh anchor and put to sea during the **French Revolution** until the seamen's demands were met. It coincided with the age of revolution following the American Revolution, the French Revolution, slave revolts, and Britain's own working-class movement. By mid-May, the demands—better pay, better food, and the removal of a few hated officers, along with a royal pardon—were met.

splice the main brace, to be issued an extra ration of **grog**. Use of the phrase was reserved for special occasions, such as the birth of children of the sovereign or after sinking an enemy vessel. Today it means to have or serve alcohol aboard ship, usually in celebration of something.

Spray, thirty-seven-foot, nine-inch oyster **sloop** that Captain **Joshua Slocum** sailed around the world. *Spray*, which had been **laid up** in a field in Fairhaven, Massachusetts, for seven years and was badly in need of repair, was given to Slocum by an old friend in 1892. Slocum spent thirteen months repairing the vessel, and two years later he set off from Boston on the first solo circumnavigation. *Spray*'s lines have been copied by hundreds of boatbuilders worldwide.

Sprout, Harold and Margaret, husband-and-wife research and writing team (born 1901 and 1903, respectively), he a longtime Princeton professor who coauthored the important *The Rise of American Naval Power, 1776–1918* (1939) as well as *Toward a New Order of Sea Power: American Naval Policy and the World Scene, 1918–1922* (1946).

Spruance, Raymond Ames (1886–1969), U.S. admiral in the Pacific theater during World War II. During the Battle of **Midway**, he assumed command of U.S. forces when Admiral **Frank J. Fletcher's flagship** was damaged, and he coordinated the sinking of all four Japanese aircraft carriers in that battle. He served as chief of staff to Admiral **Chester W. Nimitz** and in November 1945 succeeded Nimitz as commander in chief of the Pacific fleet.

USS *Spruance* (DD-963), namesake lead unit of a class of thirty-one destroyers constructed for the U.S. **Navy**. The 563-foot craft is powered by four gas turbines and can run at speeds far above her posted top speed of thirty-two **knots**. The 8,422-ton ship was commissioned in 1975.

Spruce Goose, nickname for the eight-engine wooden flying boat designed and constructed by American billionaire Howard Hughes (1905–1976). In 1947 Hughes piloted the seaplane on its only flight, flying one mile at a height of seventy feet. Spruce Goose had room for seven hundred passengers and is still the biggest aircraft ever built. The Hughes Flying Boat is presently housed at the Evergreen Aviation Museum in McMinnville, Oregon.

spun yarn, a sailor's story, or incidents and adventures that were spun as a yarn. The term also refers to lightly twisted line used for a variety of purposes on board ship.

spyglass, handheld telescope that is often referred to as a long glass. In addition to its physical use, it has historically served as a symbol of authority.

USS *Squalus* (SS-192), diesel-electric submarine that suffered a catastrophic valve failure during an initial test dive off the Isle of Shoals, New Hampshire, on May 23, 1939. Partially flooded, the sub sank to the bottom and came to rest in 240 feet of water, with twenty-six crew members dead. Over the next thirteen hours, the remaining thirty-two crew members and one civilian were rescued by a team headed by **Charles Bowers "Swede" Momsen**. *Squalus* was raised, repaired, and recommissioned as USS *Sailfish* in May 1940, going on to play her part in World War II.

square-knot sailor, a mariner who has crossed the equator, the **international date line**, the **Arctic Circle**, and the **Antarctic Circle**, and has completed a circumnavigation of the globe.

Sailors indicate this distinction with a tattoo of a square knot.

square-rigger, vessel with a sail plan that includes square sails set on yards at right angles to the vessel's hull, which can be trimmed to about thirty degrees from the centerline on either side.

SS, prefix for **steamship**, used to distinguish steamers from sailing ships but applied to diesel-powered vessels as well. Originally it meant a screw steamer as opposed to a paddle steamer.

SSBN, U.S. **Navy** prefix for a fleet ballistic missile submarine, a nuclear-powered submarine armed with long-range strategic missiles.

SSN, U.S. **Navy** prefix for an attack submarine, a nuclear-powered submarine designed to seek and destroy enemy submarines and surface ships.

stadimeter, instrument used to determine ranges to objects of known height. Good for distances from two hundred to ten thousand yards, it is mostly used when naval ships are steaming together in station.

Standards of Training, Certification, and Watchkeeping (STCW), international convention sponsored by the **International Maritime Organization** and signed by the world's maritime nations. Under the agreement, which became effective July 28, 1997, each country has committed to change their national rules on sea service, training, and other qualification requirements to meet or exceed the standards in the convention.

stand-on vessel, according to the *Navigation Rules*, the vessel with the right-of-way. The **give-way vessel** is required by the rules to alter course, speed, or both.

Stanfield, William Clarkson (1793–1867), English artist who is considered one of the leading marine painters of the early Victorian era.

He served in both the British **merchant marine** and the **Royal Navy** and later worked in the theater as a scenery painter. His talent combined with his keen knowledge of the sea and ships to earn him many awards and accolades during his lifetime. He was a friend of Charles Dickens and **Frederick Marryat**.

Star, oldest international **one-design** racing sailboat class. Designed by **William Gardner** in 1906, it was the first truly international class of small racing sailboats and is today the oldest Olympic class, used in competition since 1932. The twenty-two-foot, nine-inch keel boats are sailed on both salt water and freshwater.

starboard, the right-hand side of a vessel. The name derives from the fact that on ancient double-ended vessels, the rudder, or "steerboard" was located on the right side of the vessel. Therefore, the left side, or port, then called "larboard," would be toward the dock or pier.

Starbuck, fictional first **mate** of the whaleship *Pequod* in **Herman Melville**'s *Moby-Dick* (1851).

Stark, Harold Raynsford (1880–1972), U.S. **Navy** admiral deep-selected by President **Franklin D. Roosevelt** in 1939 to be chief of naval operations. He held that position until March 1942 when, in a shakeup following the Japanese attack on **Pearl Harbor**, he was replaced by Admiral Ernest J. King. Stark served the remainder of the war as commander of U.S. forces in Europe with noteworthy success. He was criticized for his alleged failure to forward key intelligence to Admiral **Husband Edward Kimmell** at Pearl Harbor before the December 7, 1941, attack, however, and was censured in 1945.

USS Stark (FFG-31), the twenty-fifth unit of fifty-five **Oliver Hazard Perry**–class guided-missile **frigates** constructed for the U.S. **Navy**. Commissioned in 1982, the 4,100-ton gas turbine–propelled vessel was patrolling the Persian Gulf in 1987 when she was struck by two Exocet missiles fired from an Iraqi jet fighter. The frigate remained afloat thanks to the quick reactions of the crew, but the resulting fires from the twin hits killed thirty-seven crewmen. Repaired and returned to active service, the *Stark* was decommissioned in 1999.

Star of India, 205-foot, iron-hulled, **full-rigged** sailing ship built on the **Isle of Man**, Great Britian, in 1863 as the *Euterpe*. After operation on various routes, including being rerigged as a **bark** and used in the Alaskan fish-packing trade, the ship was purchased by a band of San Diego citizens in 1926 for $9,000. It was largely ignored until 1957, when **Alan John Villiers** lectured the city of San Diego as to the historical importance of the ship. Fully restored as a bark and taken to sea in 1976, and periodically thereafter, she remains a magnificent monument to the age of sail as the centerpiece of the San Diego Maritime Museum.

Stars & Stripes, **Dennis Conner**'s **America's Cup** challenger in 1987, which defeated the Australian yacht *Kookaburra III*, four races to none, to regain the **America's Cup**. Conner was now not only the first man to lose the Cup, he was the first to win it back as well, and the Cup's new home became the San Diego Yacht Club.

Stars & Stripes II, **America's Cup** defender in 1988, which easily defeated the New Zealand challenger *New Zealand*. The sixty-foot **catamaran**, built for **Dennis Conner**, represented the San Diego Yacht Club. *Stars & Stripes II*'s victory is considered by many to be the low point in the history of the America's Cup. The New Zealand team claimed that the catamaran boat was illegal and challenged the action in the American courts. In 1989, an American judge disqualified *Stars & Stripes II* and awarded the cup to New Zealand. Later in 1989, a higher American court reversed the decision and returned the cup to the United States.

SS Statendam, luxurious steamer built in 1914 for the **Holland America Line** but requisitioned by the British government for use in World War I before she could be completed. She was converted into the troopship *Justicia* and assigned to **White Star Line** management. She was torpedoed by a German **U-boat** in July 1918 and sank with the loss of sixteen lives.

staysail, a triangular or quadrilateral **fore-and-aft** sail set up on a stay. It can be a jib and/or be used to fill the void between masts on a **square-rigger**. A fisherman's staysail is set above the main staysail.

STCW, see **Standards of Training, Certification, and Watchkeeping**.

steamboat, a river or coastwise vessel propelled by steam power. The term is often used interchangeably with the term "**steamship**," which specifically describes an oceangoing watercraft propelled by a steam engine or a steam turbine.

Steamboat Bill, Jr., classic 1928 silent film starring Buster Keaton, who returns home from the big city to help run his father's old riverboat against a rival's new boat. Keaton falls in love with the rival's daughter, braves a big cyclone, and becomes a hero. Ernest Torrance played Keaton's father, Steamboat Bill.

Steamboat Inspection Service, service created by the U.S. Congress in 1838 within the Treasury Department to provide for the inspection of ships' hulls and boilers and the installation of firefighting and lifesaving equipment. It was reorganized under the Steamboat Act of 1852 to mandate licensing of engineers and pilots on steam vessels carrying passengers. The service was combined with the **Bureau of Navigation** in 1932 within the Department of Commerce, and in 1936 was renamed the **Bureau of Marine Inspection and Navigation**.

Steamboat Willie, the first animated feature film with sound, released in 1928 by Walt Dis-

Star of India. (San Diego Maritime Museum)

ney. The movie introduced Mickey Mouse to the American public.

Steaming to Bamboola, 1982 novel by Christopher Buckley—son of **William F. Buckley Jr.** —about the aged **tramp** freighter *Columbianna* and her crew.

steamship, a vessel using a steam engine as the principal means of propulsion. As opposed to a motor vessel.

Steamship Historical Society of America (SSHSA), nonprofit organization established in 1935 to preserve artifacts and memories of America's **steamboat** past. The society maintains one of the largest libraries in North America devoted exclusively to the history of engine-powered vessels, located at the University of Baltimore. Since 1940 the SSHSA has published the periodical *Steamboat Bill*, a quarterly journal dedicated to **steamship** history.

steamship row, section of lower Manhattan where, until the late 1960s, most of the **steamship** lines had their main offices. The section starts with the U.S. Customs House and runs northward along Broadway and its adjacent streets.

Stebbins, Nathaniel Livermore (1847–1922), one of the leading American maritime photographers, for whom yachting was a particular interest. In a career that spanned some thirty-eight years, working up until his death, Stebbins took about twenty-five thousand photographs, some fifteen thousand of which were maritime. However, only about three thousand glass plate negatives have survived.

steerage, lowest and most inexpensive of all shipboard passenger categories. Often carried in open bunks stacked three high in the tweendecks, steerage passengers made up the bulk of the **steamship** passenger revenues until the implementation of U.S. immigration laws forced shipowners to raise the comfort and sanitary standards found in these bleak passenger quarters. The classification gradually gave way to **third class** by World War I. Steerage was also referred to by some companies as fourth class.

Steinbeck, John (1902–1968), American novelist and Pulitzer Prize winner and author of *Cannery Row* (1945) and *Log from the Sea of Cortez* (1941). He also wrote the story on which Alfred Hitchcock's film *Lifeboat* was based.

Stella Maris, Latin for "star of the sea," another name for Polaris, or the North Star. Christian sailors have traditionally referred to the Virgin Mary as Stella Maris.

Stephens, Olin James, II (b. 1908), yacht designer and cofounder of the renowned design firm **Sparkman & Stephens**. His name is syn-

onymous with the **America's Cup** because he assisted **W. Starling Burgess** on the J-boats in the late 1930s and drew the lines for six **twelve-meter** defenders, from *Columbia* (1958) to *Freedom* (1980). The only defender he did not design during this span was *Weatherly* in 1962. His brother was **Roderick Stephens Jr.**, and his autobiography, *All This and Sailing, Too*, was published by **Mystic Seaport** in 2000.

Stephens, Roderick, Jr. (1909–1995), American yachtsman and **America's Cup** competitor. As one of the most prominent figures in yacht design, yacht construction, and competitive sailing since 1930, he was an expert in the design of rigging, fittings, and making things work aboard a boat. He owned and raced the yachts *Dorade*, *Stormy Weather*, and others in **Transatlantic** and **Fastnet Races**, and he sailed to victory on the America's Cup winners *Ranger*, *Columbia*, and *Constellation*. He was a partner wtih his brother **Olin Stephens II** in the design firm **Sparkman & Stephens**.

Stephens, William Picard (1854–1946), American yacht designer, historian, and builder of yachts and canoes. He served as an editor for *Forest and Stream* magazine and *Lloyd's Register of American Yachts*. His *Traditions and Memories of American Yachting* (1942), first serialized in *Motor Boating* magazine, is considered the single most complete history of yachting in America.

stevedore, person or firm that employs longshoremen and that contracts to load or unload the ship. The term derives from the Spanish *estivador* for a stower of cargo.

SS *Steven Hopkins*, U.S. **Liberty ship** that in September 1942 engaged two German surface raiders in the South Atlantic. The crew of forty **merchant mariners** and twelve U.S. **Naval Armed Guard** returned fire on the *Stier* and the *Tannenfels*, scoring direct hits. Some thirty minutes later, the *Stephen Hopkins* and the *Stier* were sunk and the *Tannenfels* was badly damaged. Forced to abandon ship, nineteen *Hopkins* survivors piled into the one undamaged life raft and rigged the sail. After thirty-one days at sea, the boat made the coast of Brazil. Four men had died on the passage.

Stevens, Edwin Robert (d. 1868), American engineer and younger brother of **John Cox Stevens** who was active in the design and construction of **ironclad** vessels for the U.S. **Navy**. He was a member of the syndicate that built and raced the yacht *America*, and he served as the third commodore of the **New York Yacht Club**. Upon his death, his will provided for the establishment of the college that bears his family name, **Stevens Institute of Technology**, built on the family estate in Hoboken, New Jersey.

Stevens, John (1749–1838), Revolutionary War colonel and early American engineer. In 1803 he patented a propeller and had a multitube, high-pressure steam-driven boat in operation. In 1808 his **steamship *Phoenix*** was the first American steamship to make an ocean voyage, transiting from New York to Philadelphia. The father of twelve children, including **John Cox Stevens**, **Edwin Robert Stevens**, and Robert L. Stevens, he purchased the fifty-five-acre estate in Hoboken, New Jersey, that would later become the **Stevens Institute of Technology**.

Stevens, John Cox (1785–1857), American shipbuilder and yachtsman, often referred to as the father of American yachting. It was aboard his **schooner *Gimcrack*** in July 1844 that the **New York Yacht Club** was founded. As the club's first commodore, he spearheaded the syndicate that built and raced the schooner *America* around the **Isle of Wight** in 1851 to win Great Britain's **Royal Yacht Squadron**'s **Hundred Guinea Cup**. In 1857 Stevens and his syndicate deeded the renamed **America's Cup** to the New York Yacht Club as a trophy for international competition. He was the son of **John Stevens**.

Stevens Institute of Technology, engineering college founded in 1871 that was provided for in the will of **Edwin Robert Stevens**. Located at the Stevens family home at Castle Point in Hoboken, New Jersey, it awarded the first American degree in mechanical engineering. The school's model-towing tank has had a profound influence on the development of yacht and ship design.

Stevenson, Robert Louis (1850–1894), Scottish novelist and author of the classics *Treasure Island* (1883), *Kidnapped* (1886), and *David Balfour* (1893). He also wrote *An Inland Voyage* (1877) about a journey through Europe in a double-paddle canoe, *Dr. Jekyll and Mr. Hyde* (1886), and *The Wrecker* (1892). Stevenson's family was responsible for designing and building most of the lighthouses in Scotland.

Stewart, Charles (1778–1869), U.S. **Navy** officer who was captain of USS *Constitution* in the closing days of the **War of 1812**. Under Stewart, *Constitution* captured the British vessels HMS *Cyane* and HMS *Levant* off the coast of Africa on February 20, 1815, three days after the U.S. Congress had ratified the **Treaty of Ghent** that ended the war, news that had reached neither Stewart nor his opponents.

stinkpot, slang for a powerboat. Originally it was used to refer to a fire bomb used in naval warfare.

Stobart, John (b. 1929), English painter who is considered one of today's leading marine artists. He specializes in reconstructing ports, harbors, wharves, coastal views, and shipping scenes of the seventeenth, eighteenth, and nineteenth centuries. He also does open-air oils of present-day scenes and has issued a series of videos about other artists and himself engaged in this more spontaneous kind of painting.

MS *Stockholm*, motor **liner** built in 1948 for the transatlantic service of the **Swedish America Line**. On July 25, 1956, the 11,700-gross-ton ship sliced into SS ***Andrea Doria***, sending the Italian liner to the bottom, with the loss of forty-seven lives. *Stockholm* was repaired and returned to service. She was sold to East Germany in 1960 and renamed *Völkerfreundschaft*. When sold in 1989 to Italian interests, her arrival for refitting at Genoa, the **home port** of the *Andrea Doria*, was met with less than an enthusiastic reception. Eventually rebuilt, she entered cruise service in 1994 as the *Italia Prima*.

stone fleet, a fleet of nearly forty surplus whaling vessels that were loaded with New England fieldstone and sunk outside southern harbors in an unsuccessful attempt to obstruct navigation and prevent blockade running during the Civil War.

Stormy Weather, fifty-four-foot **Sparkman & Stephens**–designed yawl that is considered one of the most important racing yachts of the twentieth century. Launched in 1934 from the Henry B. Nevins Yard on **City Island**, she participated in many sailing races and was the winner of a **Transatlantic Race** and the **Fastnet Race**. Today she is still sailing and winning races.

The Story of a Shipwrecked Sailor: Who Drifted on a Life Raft for Ten Days without Food or Water, Was Proclaimed a National Hero, Kissed by Beauty Queens, Made Rich through Publicity, and Then Spurned by the Government and Forgotten for All Time, 1986 translation of *Relato de un náufrago*, a novella by award-winning author Gabriel García Márquez. It recounts the true account of a sailor who was washed overboard in 1955 in the Caribbean and turned up ten days later on a beach in Colombia. García Márquez based the narrative on lengthy interviews he performed with the sailor for Colombian newspapers.

Stowaway, classic 1936 American movie musical about a little girl whose missionary parents are killed in a Chinese revolution and who

stows away on a luxury **liner** bound for San Francisco. It includes good scenes of the SS *President Coolidge*. The film starred Shirley Temple, Robert Young, and Alice Faye.

Strait of Juan de Fuca, one-hundred-mile-long waterway running between Vancouver Island, Canada, and northwest Washington State, linking Puget Sound and the Pacific Ocean. It was named in 1592 by Juan de Fuca, a Greek sailor—whose real name was Apostolos Valerianos—in the service of Spain.

Strait of Magellan, 320-mile-long channel of water that separates **Tierra del Fuego** from the mainland of South America. Located north of **Cape Horn**, it was first discovered in 1520 by navigator **Ferdinand Magellan** as he was transiting from the Atlantic to the Pacific Ocean on his round-the-world voyage. Today Chile controls the winding stretch and maintains a naval base on nearby Navarino Island, just north of Cape Horn.

Strait of Gibraltar, thirty-six-mile passage between Spain and Africa that connects the Mediterranean Sea to the **Atlantic Ocean**. The strait is approximately eight miles wide at its narrowest point.

Stratton, Dorothy Constance (b. 1899), captain in the U.S. **Coast Guard Reserve**, she directed the Women's Reserve, or **SPARs**, during World War II. A full professor and the dean of women at Purdue University, she was the first woman accepted into the Women's Reserve, and she devised the name SPAR from the Coast Guard motto *semper paratus*. Stratton also holds the distinction of surviving the entire tumultous twentieth century.

Struma, World War II refugee ship loaded with 778 Romanian and Russian Jews that was refused entry into Palestine in December 1941 and was later detained in Istanbul for more than two months. In February 1942 Turkish officials towed the ship out into the **Black Sea**

and let it drift. It later struck a mine and sank, taking the lives of all but one of the refugees on board.

stuffing box, watertight device through which the propeller shaft passes through a vessel's hull.

USS *Sturgeon* (SSN-637), namesake lead unit commissioned in 1967 of a class of thirty-six nuclear-powered attack submarines. The vessels are 292 feet long and displace 4,640 tons. Their underwater speed is in excess of twenty-six **knots**, and each is manned by a 106-member crew.

Styx, one of the rivers of the underworld in Greek and Roman mythology. *Styx* is a Greek word meaning "hateful." The boatman **Charon** was often described as ferrying the souls of the departed across the Styx.

submarine race, slang for a secluded romantic interlude on a beach.

suck the monkey, to suck liquor from a cask through a straw. This was done to avoid opening the cask and still be able to get a drink without the captain knowing.

Suez Canal, 101-mile waterway opened in 1869 connecting the Mediterranean Sea and the Red Sea. Planned and created under the direction of French engineer **Ferdinand de Lesseps**, the canal, with no locks, runs from Port Said, Egypt, to the Gulf of Suez. The canal cuts more than four thousand miles off the sea route from Europe to Asia. The canal was claimed by Egypt in 1956 and was blocked by sunken ships in 1967, during the Arab-Israeli War. Egypt reopened the canal in 1975.

Suhaili, thirty-two-foot, double-ended **ketch** built and sailed by Sir **Robin Knox-Johnston** to win the Golden Globe award for the first non-stop, single-handed, round-the-world race, in 1968–69. Knox-Johnston continued to sail *Suhaili*, whose name means "southwest wind" in Arabic, on many other world voyages. Today

she is on exhibition in the **National Maritime Museum** in Greenwich, England.

Sullivans, five brothers—George, Francis, Joseph, Madison, and Albert Sullivan—from Waterloo, Iowa, who served together in the U.S. **Navy** to avenge the death of a friend killed at **Pearl Harbor** aboard USS *Arizona*. All five were killed aboard USS *Juneau* during the Battle of **Guadalcanal** on November 13, 1942. Their images were used to recruit sailors, and the tragedy prompted the navy to pass regulations prohibiting siblings from serving together on the same vessel. The loss was considered the largest single sacrifice by one family in U.S. military history, and the were honored when the USS *The Sullivans* **destroyer** was commissioned.

Sultana, **Mississippi River paddle-wheel** steamer that exploded April 27, 1865, killing 1,700 men. It ranks as the worst ship disaster in U.S. history. While plying the river between Memphis, Tennessee, and Cairo, Illinois, her boilers exploded and she quickly burned and sank. Of the 2,300 people on board, 2,134 were Union soldiers returning from Confederate prison camps after the Civil War.

Summit Venture, Liberian-registered freighter that collided with the Sunshine Skyway Bridge over Tampa Bay, Florida, on May 9, 1980, collapsing one of the bridge's twin spans and killing thirty-five motorists.

Sunbeam, 170-foot, three-masted auxiliary steam **schooner**, owned by Lord Thomas Brassey, that set sail from the **Isle of Wight** in 1876 and returned in 1877, becoming the first yacht to sail around the world. The extraordinary forty-six-week circumnavigation was chronicled by Lady **Anna Brassey** in *The Voyage in the Sunbeam* (1879).

Sunfish, the most common centerboard sailing **dinghy** in the world. Introduced in 1955 by Alex Bryan and Cortlandt Heyniger (of Alcort

Inc.), the **lateen**-rigged boat measures thirteen feet, ten inches in length.

sun over the yardarm, old navy expression measuring the time for a morning drink. Judging from the sun's position relative to the fore-yard as seen from the quarterdeck of a **square-rigger**, the time was approximately 1100 hours.

Sun Princess, 77,000-gross-ton cruise **liner** built in 1997 at Fincantieri shipyard in Italy for **Princess Cruises**. The 1,950-passenger vessel was used as the setting for the short-lived 1990s television series *The Love Boat: The Next Wave*.

Sunward, originally completed in 1966 for ferry service between Great Britain and Spain, the 11,000-gross-ton **liner** was sent later that year to test the short-cruise market from Miami under the aegis of **Norwegian Cruise Lines**. Her astounding success paved the way for one of the major cruise ship operations out of America. Sold for European operation, she reappeared in American waters in 1989 as the *Ocean Quest* and as such carried out the first big-ship nudist cruise from Miami the following year.

supercargo, the representative of the owner on board a merchant ship who oversaw the cargo and handled the commercial transactions of the voyage. The term is short for "cargo superintendent."

supertanker, term applied in the 1950s and 1960s to the largest tankers of the day. The closure of the **Suez Canal** in 1967 led oil transporters to develop larger supertankers, which were known as very large crude carriers, or VLCCs.

surface effect ship (SES), a vessel that does not rely on speed for its lift but moves over land and water by means of a downward thrust of air. An SES combines the best features of a hovercraft and a **catamaran** and is primarily employed in amphibious landing ships.

Surigao Strait, Battle of, October 24–25, 1944, naval confrontation in the Battle of **Leyte Gulf** that cost the Japanese Navy six **capital ships** at the expense of damage to one U.S. **destroyer** out of a task force of eleven vessels. The Japanese had hoped—to no avail—that the encounter would defeat the American invasion of the Philippine Islands.

survey, a thorough examination of a vessel to determine seaworthiness. Usually required by insurance companies, it is carried out by a certified marine surveyor.

Survive the Savage Sea, intense account by Dougal Robertson about his and his family's thirty-seven days at sea in an inflatable rubber raft after their forty-three-foot **schooner** *Lucette* was attacked and sunk by killer whales in the Pacific Ocean in June 1972. The family battled twenty-foot waves, sharks, thirst, and starvation. After the raft sank, the Robertsons crammed into a nine-foot dinghy and were eventually rescued by a Japanese fishing boat.

Susan Constant, fifty-five-foot **ship** that in 1607, along with *Discovery* and *Godspeed*, carried 144 English settlers to the **Jamestown** colony, the first permanent English settlement in the New World. Replicas of the three ships were built in the 1980s by the Jamestown-Yorktown Foundation of Williamsburg, Virginia, and the three vessels are depicted on the Virginia commemorative U.S. quarter minted in 2000.

Susan's tooth, scrimshawed sperm whale tooth fashioned aboard the whale-ship *Susan* of Nantucket by whaler Frederick Myrick around 1829 off the coast of Japan. A Susan's tooth is among today's most collectible pieces of scrimshaw. Approximately twenty-two pieces of scrimshaw by Myrick survive.

Suwannee River, waterway that winds for nearly two hundred miles through southern Georgia and northern Florida and empties into the Gulf of Mexico. Stephen Foster called the river "Swanee" in his song "Old Folks at Home"—"Way down upon the Swanee River, far, far away."

Svaap, small **John Alden**–designed **ketch** sailed by William A. Robinson around the world in the late 1920s and featured in his classic book *10,000 Leagues Over the Sea* (1932).

Swallows and Amazons, the first book, published in 1930, in a series of thirteen children's adventure novels by **Arthur Ransome** that revolve around sailing and adventures at sea (*Swallow* and *Amazon* were the names of sailing dinghies). The other books include *Pigeon Post* (1936), *We Didn't Mean to Go to Sea* (1937), and *Missee Lee* (1941).

swallow the anchor, colloquial phrase that means to give up the sea for good. It implies that one has no further use for the implement (the anchor) one has trusted for so long.

SWATH, acronym meaning Small-Waterplane-Area-Twin-Hull. These vessels typically have two submarine-like lower hulls completely submerged below the water surface. Above the water, a SWATH resembles a **catamaran**. The benefits of the design are the stability and speed in rough seas. The technology dates back to the 1880s, and modern SWATH vessels include the *Sea Shadow* and the cruise ship *Radisson Diamond*.

The Sway of the Grand Saloon, 1971 book by **John Malcolm Brinnin**, subtitled *A Social History of the North Atlantic*. It is perhaps the finest novel of transatlantic **liner** travel ever written. The book conveys a vivid impression of life in the passenger quarters and stokeholds of early **packet** ships.

Swedish America Line, shipping house founded in 1915 to operate a scheduled passenger service from Gothenburg, Sweden, to New York. An innovator in extended cruising, the line finished its passenger-carrying years as a notable cruise operator. It ceased passenger operations in 1975 with the sale of its last passenger ship, SS *Kungsholm*.

Sweetwater Sea, colloquial term for the **Great Lakes**.

swing ship, to put a vessel on various compass headings in order to compare each against a known visual bearing to determine the deviation of the compass.

Swiss Family Robinson, classic novel by Johann Rudolf Wyss (1782–1830), first published in 1813, about a family seeking to escape Napoleon's war in Europe who are shipwrecked on a tropical South Pacific island. The castaways are resourceful at constructing a happy life on the island, only to be confronted by a band of pirates. Finally, when rescue comes, they decline to leave. It was captured on film in 1960 in the exceptional Walt Disney production starring John Mills, Dorothy McGuire, James MacArthur, and Sessue Hayakawa.

HMAS *Sydney*, Royal Australian Navy **cruiser** that engaged the German raider *Kormoran* in the South Pacific in November 1941. Curiously, both ships were sunk during the engagement, and *Sydney* lost her entire complement. Many historians believe the *Kormoran* was rendezvousing with a Japanese submarine and *Sydney* had surprised both vessels. Further, it is surmised that the Japanese sub sank *Sydney*—three weeks before Japan entered the war.

Sydney–Hobart Yacht Race, 630-mile ocean race from Australia to Tasmania that has been held annually since 1944. It begins in Sydney Harbor on Boxing Day (December 26) and finishes several days later in Hobart. In 1998 the fleet was hit by vicious winds, necessitating the largest search-and-rescue operation in Australian history; six yachtsmen lost their lives.

T

T-1 tanker, classification given to a series of small coastal tankers developed by the U.S. **Maritime Commission** and built between 1943 and 1945.

T-2 tanker, the most important and numerous of the World War II tankers that provided vital petroleum supplies to U.S. and Allied military forces in Europe, North Africa, and the Pacific. As part of the U.S. **Maritime Commission** shipbuilding program, 481 of the standard tankers were constructed by four shipyards. Measuring 16,600 **deadweight tons**, the 523-foot vessels had a six-thousand-horsepower turboelectric propulsion capable of 14.5 **knots**. The most famous and numerous tanker type ever built in the world, they became workhorses of world tanker fleets for the next twenty years.

Tabarly, Eric (1931–1998), skilled French yachtsman who sailed numerous ocean races, won one **Fastnet Race** and two **OSTAR**s, and set several offshore speed records. He was a fixture on the world racing circuit aboard his five yachts, which he named *Pen Duick*. He was lost at sea after being knocked overboard in the Irish Sea in 1998. He wrote *Lonely Victory* (1967) about his 1964 OSTAR victory, beating Sir **Francis Charles Chichester**'s 1960 transatlantic crossing record.

tack, to change course on a sailboat by bringing the vessel's bow through the wind so that the wind comes from the opposite side. A boat on the port tack using this maneuver ends up on the **starboard** tack.

Taeping, 184-foot British tea **clipper** built in 1863 that won the celebrated **Great Tea Race** of 1866.

taffrail, the rail farthest aft on a vessel.

taffrail log, a rotator towed through the water and attached to a device that registers distance traveled. It is usually attached to the **taffrail** and is sometimes called a **patent log** or a Walker log.

Taiho, Japanese aircraft carrier launched in 1943 and fitted with an armored flight deck that could withstand one-thousand-pound bombs.

Completed in 1944, the 29,300-ton vessel was hit by torpedoes from USS *Albacore* during the Battle of the **Philippine Sea** after only three months of active duty. Although the ship was not seriously damaged, the ship's bunkers were breeched as were the vessel's aviation fuel storage tanks. In an effort to disperse the commingled vapors and fumes that rapidly filled the ship, all ventilating systems were opened fully while the craft continued to steam at top speed. The highly volatile gaseous mixture eventually found a source of ignition, and the resulting explosion blew apart the carrier's flight deck, sides, and bottom simultaneously. She sank quickly, taking most of her 1,751 crew members with her.

Taiyo Maru, well-known 14,458-gross-ton **Nippon Yusen Kaisha** (NYK) passenger steamer originally constructed as the Hamburg–South American **liner** *Cap Finisterre* in 1911. She was seized during World War I and was eventually allocated to Japan in 1920 for service to California. Reassigned to operation in Asia in 1935, she was used to return Japanese citizens to their homeland from Honolulu just days before the attack on **Pearl Harbor**. She was sunk by the sub USS *Grenadier* in 1942.

"Take her down!", the last command of wounded U.S. **Navy** submarine commander Howard W. Gilmore, who was left on the conning tower of the USS *Growler* when it submerged during a February 7, 1943, engagement with a Japanese gunboat.

Talbot, Silas (1751–1813), U.S. **Navy** officer who served during the American Revolution and was captured in 1780 and made a prisoner of war. He was later selected to be the second commander of USS *Constitution* and fought in the **Quasi-War**.

Tales of the Fish Patrol, 1905 collection of adventurous short stories by **Jack London** about the enforcement of fish laws in San Francisco Bay around the turn of the twentieth century.

Tales of the South Pacific, 1947 Pulitzer Prize–winning novel by **James Michener** relating the emotions, frustrations, tedium, and anxiety of men at war in the Pacific during World War II. Michener's first published novel, it was the basis for the 1949 Rodgers and Hammerstein musical *South Pacific*.

tall ship, term used for a deepwater sailing ship in Shakespeare's time, revived by poets and used today for a large, traditionally rigged sailing vessel engaged in sail training. Tall ships are divided into three classes: class A, all vessels over 160 feet in overall length and all **square-rigged** vessels regardless of length; class B, vessels less than 160 feet but more than 100 feet in overall length; and class C, vessels under 100 feet but at least 30 feet long at the waterline.

Tarawa landings, incident on November 20–23, 1943, in which U.S. naval forces successfully landed troops on the three islands in the Tarawa Atoll in the Gilbert Islands. The assault resulted in the loss of 990 marines and a further 2,391 wounded, while only 17 prisoners were taken out of the more than 4,800 Japanese troops defending the positions.

tarpaulin muster, a collection of cash contributions by a group of sailors, usually for a needy seaman or his family. The term sometimes is also used for any meeting involving the entire crew of a vessel, such as when gathering at the main hatch to set watches.

Tarpon Springs, city on the west coast of Florida known for its sponge industry, which started in 1890 when Greek immigrants began to harvest the plentiful beds. Hardhat sponge diving began about 1903. Today Tarpon Springs is the largest natural sponge market in the world.

Task Force 38, U.S. World War II naval strike fleet that comprised eighty-six ships. While the fleet was refueling in the eastern Philippine Sea on December 18, 1944, a typhoon unexpectedly sprang up, causing the ships to lose formation. At the height of the storm, winds were clocked at over seventy-three **knots**, with visibility at times of only three feet. The carrier USS *Langley* took seventy-degree rolls but managed to stay afloat. Three of the fifty **destroyers** in the task force—USS *Hull*, USS *Monaghan*, and USS *Spence*—capsized in the mountainous seas, with only ninety-two men being plucked from the sea after the storm. In all, 146 planes were lost or damaged aboard the carriers, 790 men lost their lives, and a **cruiser**, five aircraft carriers, and three destroyers suffered serious damage.

Tasman, Abel (1603–1659), Dutch mariner who explored the Pacific. In 1645 he circumnavigated Australia and discovered New Zealand; today the Tasman Sea and Tasmania bear his name.

Tatsuta Maru, 16,975-gross-ton Japanese **liner** built in 1930, sister to the ***Asama Maru***, that was employed on the transpacific passenger service to California. Her name changed in 1938 to *Tatuta Maru*, and in 1941 she removed Japanese citizens from San Francisco and Honolulu, arriving home in Yokohama on the day of the Japanese attack on **Pearl Harbor**. She was commandeered in late 1941 by the Japanese government for operation as a troop transport and was torpedoed and sunk by the U.S. submarine *Tarpon* in 1943.

USS *Tautog*, U.S. World War II submarine that sank twenty-six Japanese vessels, more than any other submarine in the war. *Tautog* was at **Pearl Harbor** during the Japanese attack on December 7, 1941, and the sub's gun crew shot down the first Japanese plane of the war.

Taylor, David Watson (1864–1940), U.S. **Navy** officer who pioneered the experimental testing of ship hull shapes. He is often referred to as the "father of American ship research." He was the driving force to establish the Navy's Experimental Model Basin in 1898, which in 1939 became the David Taylor Model Basin.

The enormous white cement building in Carderock, Maryland, is considered a fine example of the art-deco style of the 1930s and was designated as a building of historical importance by the National Trust for Historic Preservation in 1989. Taylor's *Speed and Power of Ships* (1911) remains an important book on ship research and development.

T-boat, a small passenger vessel under one hundred gross tons, named after sub-chapter T of title 46 of the Code of Federal Regulations (CFR), which contains the rules, regulations, policies, and procedures that govern or affect the operation of these vessels.

Teach, Edward (d. 1718), more commonly known as **Blackbeard**. The famous pirate operated from a North Carolina backwater, successfully carrying out raids on Atlantic and Caribbean shipping. The governor of the Virginia colony sent out two British warships to intercept him, and he was killed in the ensuing battle.

USS *Tecumseh*, Union **monitor** that was sunk by a torpedo at the Battle of **Mobile Bay** in 1864 with the loss of nearly ninety men. The loss of the vessel led to Admiral **David Glasgow Farragut**'s famous battle cry, **"Damn the torpedoes! Full speed ahead!"**

The Tempest, play written around 1611 by William Shakespeare (1564–1616) that is the tale of Prospero, a duke who has been overthrown and banished to an island, where he rules with magical powers. When the men who overthrew him pass near the island, Prospero raises a storm, wrecking their ship and casting them ashore. The source of the play was the then widely publicized wreck of the *Sea Adventure* on Bermuda in May 1609.

tender, small attendant vessel used to supply needed stores. Also, a vessel is said to be "tender" when she lacks stability.

Tennessee-Tombigbee Waterway, 234-mile waterway completed in 1985 that connects the Tom-

USS *Tecumseh*. (Museums of the City of Mobile)

bigbee and Tennessee Rivers in Tennessee and Alabama. Often called the Tenn-Tom Waterway, it ranks among the world's largest navigational projects.

Tennessee Valley Authority (TVA), federal corporation created in 1933 under President **Franklin D. Roosevelt**'s "New Deal" to develop the natural resources of the Tennessee Valley. Through the years, TVA has built dams on the Tennessee River to control floods and create electric power, and has deepened rivers for shipping. The valley includes parts of Tennessee, Kentucky, Virginia, North Carolina, Georgia, Alabama, and Mississippi.

Tennyson, Alfred, Lord (1809–1892), English poet and Britain's poet laureate (1850–92), who was often inspired by the sea. He is well known for his poems "The Lotos-Eaters" (1833) and **"Crossing the Bar"** (1889).

teredo navalis, a shipworm, actually a mollusk, that bores into ship bottoms and pilings of piers, mostly in warm waters, and feeds on the wood. Adults can reach a size of eight inches. Wooden ships were sheathed in copper to combat this menace, whose borings can—and did—sink ships.

Terminal Island, central body of land located in the heart of the Los Angeles–Long Beach Harbor complex. Originally a tidal mudflat outcropping known as Rattlesnake Island, the area was reclaimed during World War I for commercial use. It became home to the U.S.

Navy Pacific fleet during World War II with the construction of a major naval supply, dry-docking, and ship repair facility.

terra australis, Latin name for the great unknown southern continent that was imagined for centuries to occupy the southern hemisphere, which turned out to be mostly open water until one reached the frozen wasteland of Antarctica. The term literally means "southern land."

terra nova, Latin for "new land." It was used to describe, and later name, Newfoundland, Canada.

HMS *Terra Nova*, 187-foot research ship used in **Robert Falcon Scott**'s ill-fated but scientifically valuable Antarctic expedition of 1910–13. Scott died after reaching the South Pole—one month after **Roald Amundsen** had reached it.

territorial sea, areas of the ocean lying beyond the coast or boundary of a nation where that nation has sovereign rights. These rights include control of fishing, navigation, and shipping, as well as the use of the ocean's natural resources. Initially the limit was set at three miles—the distance a cannon shot would carry in the late seventeenth century or the line of sight from the shoreline at sea level. The **Law of the Sea** Convention now provides for a territorial sea of twelve **nautical miles**.

TEU, twenty-foot equivalent unit, a measurement of cargo-carrying capacity on a containership, referring to a container size that is eight feet wide, eight feet high, and twenty feet in length.

Tew, Thomas (d. 1695), colonial American **privateer** who attacked slave-staging sites in Africa and in 1693 captured an Arab **sloop** in the Indian Ocean laden with a cargo of gold. In 1694 he was enlisted by the governor of New York as a privateer when he turned to piracy and collaborated at sea with **Henry Every**. He is often referred to as the "Rhode Island Pirate."

Texaco Oklahoma, U.S.-flag oil tanker that split in two off the coast of Cape Hatteras, North Carolina, on March 27, 1971, taking her crew of thirty-two with her.

USS *Texas* (BB-35), 27,000-ton **New York**–class battleship built in 1914 that saw duty in both world wars. Her long career contains many firsts, including the first ship fitted with anti-aircraft guns; the first vessel to control gunfire with range-finders; the first American battleship to launch an airplane; the first warship to be fitted with commercial **radar**; the first ship in the U.S. **Navy** to use talking motion pictures for crew entertainment; and the first battleship to be utilized as a museum ship in the United States. The 573-foot-long **dreadnought** opened as a museum ship in 1948 under the auspices of the San Jacinto State Historical Park in La Porte, Texas, and has since been designated a national historic landmark. The first USS *Texas* was commissioned in 1895.

Texas City Disaster, incident in which the Texas seaport near Galveston was leveled when the **French Line Liberty ship *Grandcamp*** exploded while loading ammonium nitrate on April 16, 1947. The blast killed 561 persons and destroyed $67 million in property, including the cargo ship *Highflyer*.

Texas Navy, sea service started in 1835 by the Republic of Texas to protect the lines of supply between New Orleans and Texas during hostilities with Mexico. The last of the original four **schooners** was destroyed by 1837, and the Second Texas Navy was launched in 1839. In 1846 the ships of the Second Texas Navy were transferred to the U.S. **Navy**, and the service ceased to exist after 1857. In 1958 Texas governor Marion Price Daniel established a Third Texas Navy in Galveston as a nonprofit organization to preserve Texas naval history.

Texel, Battle of, decisive English naval victory over the Dutch fleet that led to the end of the first **Anglo-Dutch War** in 1654. The fighting, which occurred July 31, 1653, off Texel, the most westerly of the Frisian Islands, cost the Dutch eleven ships and 1,300 prisoners. The English lost twenty ships. A second Battle of Texel, fought August 11, 1683, was the final battle of the third Anglo-Dutch War.

thalassocracy, concept that loosely means "maritime supremacy." It derives from *Thalassa*, which is Greek for "sea" and was introduced in the writings of Herodotus and Thucydides.

Themistocles, Athenian naval strategist who was a proponent of a strong navy and the building of defensible harbors. He played a key role in the Greek fleet's victory over the Persians in the Battle of **Salamis** in 480 B.C.

USS *Theodore Roosevelt* (CVN-7), the lead unit of a refinement of the **Nimitz**-class nuclear-powered carrier, often referred to as the "Improved Nimitz class." The 1,092-foot ship was commissioned in 1986 and stationed as part of the U.S. **Navy**'s Atlantic fleet. Her power is much the same as found in the Nimitz-class carriers, but hull improvements result in speed well over thirty-five **knots**. The other seven ships of this class—each costing over $4.5 billion to construct—are the USS *Abraham Lincoln*, USS *George Washington*, USS *John C. Stennis*, USS *Harry S. Truman*, USS *Ronald Reagan*, and the as-yet-unnamed CVN-77 and CVN-78. Each ship is manned by a crew of 3,200 and carries 2,480 men to fly and maintain the eighty-five aircraft carried on board.

Theodore Tugboat, popular children's television program that began its run in the 1990s and centers on the friendship and adventures of the tugboats of the Great Ocean Tug & Salvage Company—namely Theodore, Emily the Vigorous, George the Valiant, Foduck the Vigilant, and Hank.

Thermopylae, 212-foot tea **clipper** launched in 1868 that was the pride of the British **merchant marine**. On her **maiden voyage**, she was sixty-

three days from London to Melbourne, Australia—a record that has never been broken. The *Thermopylae* loaded 1,000 tons of tea and 250 tons of ballast and is particularly remembered for her rivalry with the **Cutty Sark**.

Theroux, Paul (b. 1941), best-selling American novelist and travel writer who has chronicled many adventures at sea and on rivers, including *Kingdom by the Sea: A Journey around Great Britain* (1983), *Sailing through China* (1984), *Sunrise with Seamonsters: Travels and Discoveries 1964–1984* (1985), and *The Happy Isles of Oceania: Paddling the Pacific* (1992). His novel *Mosquito Coast* (1981) was made into a film of the same name starring Harrison Ford.

USS *The Sullivans* (DD-537), **Fletcher**-class **destroyer** built in 1943 and named for five brothers who were killed when the **cruiser** USS *Juneau* (CL-52) was sunk in 1942. The 376-foot ship saw action in World War II and the Korean War and is now a national historic landmark. She is permanently moored on the Buffalo waterfront as a museum ship for the Buffalo and Erie County Naval and Military Park.

HMS *Thetis*, British submarine completed in June 1939 that was headed for sea trials in Liverpool Bay when one of her **torpedo** tubes flooded. Eventually the torpedo room filled with water, and the sub sank bow first in 160 feet of water, leaving the stern of the 275-foot vessel breaking the surface. Four men managed to get out via the escape hatch before air ran out for the other ninety-nine. *Thetis* was salvaged and refitted, and she saw action in World War II as the *Thunderbolt*. She was sunk by an Italian warship, with the loss of sixty-three lives.

"They that go down to the sea in ships, that do business in great waters", oft-quoted lines from the Bible, Psalm 107, verse 23.

They Were Expendable, 1945 film about two American **PT boat skippers** who pit their vessels against the Japanese fleet in the Pacific during World War II. Based on a true story, the classic film, directed by John Ford, starred John Wayne , Robert Montgomery , Donna Reed, and Jack Holt.

third class, lower grade cabin accommodations on passenger ships beginning in 1905 with the *Carmania* and *Caronia*, which carried half their steerage passengers in two- and four-berth rooms. Continually updated and improved conditions resulted in the third-class quarters of RMS *Queen Mary* and SS *Normandie* being superior to the first-class accommodations found aboard earlier **liners**. The term disappeared almost entirely with World War II.

Thirty Seconds Over Tokyo, Academy Award–winning 1944 feature film telling the story of Colonel **James Harold Doolittle** and his heroic band of airborne raiders setting off to bomb Tokyo from the decks of the aircraft carrier USS *Hornet*. The classic motion picture was directed by Mervyn Leroy and starred Spencer Tracy, Van Johnson, and Robert Walker.

Thistle, 109-foot British **sloop**, designed by **George L. Watson**, that challenged for the **America's Cup** in 1887. She was defeated by the U.S. defender, *Volunteer*, two races to none, in the waters off New York City.

Thomas W. Lawson, 395-foot, seven-masted, steel **schooner**—the largest schooner and the only seven-masted vessel ever built. Constructed at the **Fore River Shipyard** in Quincy, Massachusetts, and launched in 1902, she was employed as a coastal coal carrier. Converted to an oil carrier, she was driven ashore on the Cornish coast in a gale in 1907. The masts, fore to aft, were named fore, main, mizzen, jigger, driver, pusher, and **spanker**.

Thoreau, Henry David (1817–1862), American essayist, philosopher, and author who published only two books during his lifetime: *A Week on the Concord and Merrimack Rivers*

(1849) and *Walden* (1854). Other books published after his death were based on trips he had taken and include *Excursions* (1863), *The Maine Woods* (1864), *Cape Cod* (1865), and *A Yankee in Canada* (1866).

Thousand Islands, group of more than 1,700 islands that lie in a forty-mile stretch of the Saint Lawrence River, between northern New York and southern Ontario, as it leaves Lake Ontario. The recipe for Thousand Island Dressing was created on board George Boldt's steam yacht *Louise* while cruising the region. Boldt was the owner of the Waldorf-Astoria hotel in New York City and of Boldt Castle, a palatial Thousands Islands mansion.

Three Little Pirates, theatrical short in which the Three Stooges—Larry, Moe, and Curly Joe—wind up in a time-warped pirate den on a deserted island. It was filmed in 1946 and starred Moe Howard, Larry Fine, and Curly Howard.

three sheets to the wind, euphemism for an individual who is drunk. It refers to the situation in which a sailing vessel's sheets (the lines that control a vessel's sails) have come adrift and fly in the wind.

USS *Thresher* (SSN-593), lead vessel of the later renamed **Permit**-class nuclear-powered submarines. Completed in 1961, the 278-foot vessel was conducting underwater data tests 240 miles east of Boston in 1963 with 129 crewmen and civilian technicians on board. During an underwater maneuver, her reactor shut down, resulting in the vessel's inexorable 8,400-foot dive to the ocean floor. The submarine was crushed with the loss of all on board. After the tragedy, the class assumed the less ominous name of the second ship of the series.

"Throw Out the Life Line", popular spiritual song written by Edwin Smith Ufford in 1888 and arranged by George Coles Stebbins. Ufford's inspiration came from the Bible, Matthew 14:29–31, and a lifesaving drill he observed at Point Allerton near Boston, Massachusetts. The refrain is "Throw out the life line! Throw out the life line! Someone is drifting away; Throw out the life line! Throw out the life line! Someone is sinking today."

Thunderball, 1965 James Bond film that glamorized and updated the image of **scuba** diving while Agent 007 saved the world. The movie won an Academy Award for special effects.

ticket, colloquial term for a marine officer's license.

Ticonderoga, seventy-two-foot clipper-bowed **ketch** designed by **L. Francis Herreshoff** and launched in 1936 as *Tioga*. She finished first in twenty-four of her initial thirty-seven races. She served in the U.S. **Coast Guard**'s **corsair** fleet during World War II and was renamed in 1946. *Ticonderoga* went on to set more elapsed-time records than any ocean racer in history and continues today as a charter vessel.

USS *Ticonderoga* (CV-14), sixth **Essex**-class aircraft carrier to be built, which was commissioned in 1944. The 27,100-ton ship launched planes for strikes in the Battle of **Leyte Gulf**, and in December 1944 the 888-foot vessel was caught with **Task Force 38** in a typhoon, which resulted in the loss of three **destroyers** and nearly eight hundred men. She was severely damaged by **kamikaze** bombers in the Battle of the **South China Sea**. Despite on-board fires and the loss of more than a hundred men, the ten-degree list of the carrier was corrected and she was eventually repaired before launching further air strikes against Tokyo. She sent more than ten thousand strikes against enemy targets in Vietnam and recovered the Apollo 16 space capsule after its Pacific splashdown in 1972. She was decommissioned the following year and scrapped in 1974.

USS *Ticonderoga* (CG-47), lead ship giving her name to the twenty-seven-unit class of Aegis guided-missile **cruisers**. Commissioned in 1983, the 9,590-ton gas turbine–powered vessel can travel at speeds well over thirty **knots**. The 567-foot ship carries a crew of 367 members.

tidal wave, see **tsunami**.

Tide Tables, publication that lists predicted times of high and low water and their heights for reference posts and secondary stations. The annual editions were originally published by the U.S. government, but beginning in 1996, the printing, distribution, and sale of *Tide Tables* has been assumed by private-sector companies.

Tierra del Fuego, group of islands lying off the extreme southern tip of South America. In 1520, **Ferdinand Magellan** named the region Tierra del Fuego (Land of Fire) when, trying to find a passage to the Pacific, he sighted large fires blazing along the shore. Argentina owns the eastern part of Tierra del Fuego island, while Chile controls the western part. The **Strait of Magellan** separates the islands from the mainland, and **Cape Horn** is at the southern tip of the archipelago.

time ball, visual time signal in the form of a ball that was the primary means for disseminating time to ships in the harbor in the nineteenth century so that they could set their chronometers for navigation. Traditionally a time ball, erected on the highest available structure or mast, was dropped every day at noon. The practice continued until well into the twentieth century.

time charter, charter party in which the owner leases his vessel and crew to the charterer for a stipulated period of time.

tin can, U.S. **Navy** slang for a **destroyer**, especially for destroyers from World War II, whose hulls were virtually unarmored, relying instead on speed and maneuverability to avoid being hit.

Tinkerbelle, 13½-foot **sloop** sailed by **Robert Manry** across the Atlantic Ocean from Falmouth, Massachusetts, to Falmouth, England, from June 1 to August 17, 1965. At the time, it was the smallest boat ever to cross the Atlantic nonstop.

tip of the iceberg, phrase that is a hint of a much larger issue or problem. It derives from the fact that the bulk of an iceberg is under water.

Tirpitz, Alfred von (1849–1930), German statesman and naval officer who played a key role in building up Germany's Imperial Navy before World War II.

Tirpitz, German battleship, launched in 1939 as a sister ship to the **Bismarck**. Ready for action in 1941, the ship was assigned to the Baltic fleet and—due largely to the sensational loss of the *Bismarck*—was kept anchored in Norwegian coastal waters and saw limited action. In 1944 she was intercepted and damaged by British submarines and was later subjected to repeated bombing. A final attack by thirty-two British Lancaster bombers carrying special ten-ton bombs shattered her so badly that she capsized at her moorings in Tromsö Fjord, with the loss of 1,204 crew members.

Titanic, engrossing 1953 20th Century Fox Academy Award–winning feature film revolving around the wistful breakup of a snotty English aristocrat and his brash American wife set aboard the doomed **White Star Line** steamer. The film starred Barbara Stanwyck and Clifton Webb, and its special effects are still effective today.

Titanic, 1997 Broadway extravaganza by Peter Stone and Maury Yeston about the one and only voyage of the **White Star Line** ocean **liner**. It won the Tony for best musical by default because it was a very slow year for Broadway musicals. Its popularity was maintained by riding the coattails of the epic film early the following year.

Titanic, 1998 film that is an unbelievably accurate retelling of the legendary tale worked around a few fictitious passengers thrown in for melodrama in its highest form. It is the most successful film of all time and the only film yet to gross over $1 billion. Director James Cameron demanded and got something close to absolute reality. The film won eleven Academy Awards, including best picture.

RMS *Titanic*, now-legendary 46,329-gross-ton **White Star Line** steamer that sank April 15, 1912. The ship has today assumed mythical proportions in folk history but was in fact nothing more than a large vessel constructed as part of a **liner** trio to maintain a regular transatlantic service. Completely overshadowed by the advent of the *Olympic* the previous year, she would have disappeared into the history books as a rather ordinary craft had she not encountered an iceberg on her **maiden voyage** and sank with the loss of 1,503 lives in pathetic circumstances, because there simply were not enough lifeboats to remove all to safety.

Lake Titicaca, world's highest lake navigable to large vessels, lying at 12,500 feet above sea level in the Andes Mountains of South America. The second-largest lake on that continent (after Maracaibo), it lies on the border of west Bolivia and southeast Peru. The first steamer to ply the thirty-two-thousand-square mile body of water was prefabricated in England in 1862 and carried in pieces on muleback up to the lake. This 240-gross-ton vessel has been restored and still steams in the lake today.

Title XI, a program of U.S. government federal loan guarantees to help finance the construction of ships. Established by a 1938 amendment to the **Merchant Marine Act of 1936**, the vessels must be U.S.-built, must operate under the U.S. flag, and can be used in the foreign or domestic trades.

To Have and Have Not, 1937 novel by **Ernest Hemingway** about a Key West charter boat operator who gets involved in gunrunning. It was adapted for the silver screen in 1944 to

RMS *Titanic, Letting Go the Last Line*, Southampton, England, April 10, 1912. (Peabody Essex Museum, Eugene Smith Collection)

take place in Vichy-controlled Martinique during World War II, where an American fisherman helps a group of French freedom fighters. The film version starred Humphrey Bogart, Lauren Bacall (in her first film role), Walter Brennan, and Hoagy Carmichael.

Toilers of the Sea, 1866 novel by renowned French author Victor Hugo (1802–1885) about the rescue of a shipwrecked engine by a lonely dreamer named Gilliatt. In the process, he must battle storms, an octopus, starvation, and solitude.

Toilers of the Sea, a series of oil paintings by **Albert Pinkham Ryder**. It is also the name of a painting by Rockwell Kent and of a well-known painting by French impressionist painter Edouard Manet (1832–1883).

Tokyo Bay, site of the formal surrender of the Japanese Imperial Government aboard the battleship USS *Missouri* on September 2, 1945. *Missouri* flew the same thirty-one-star flag that had flown over Commodore **Matthew Calbraith Perry**'s **flagship** USS *Mississippi* when he steamed into Tokyo Bay in 1853.

Tokyo Express, term applied collectively to the Japanese after-dark stealth supply runs made southward through the Solomon Islands during World War II to reinforce their bases on and near **Guadalcanal**. The seaway—known as "**the Slot**"—was controlled by U.S. aircraft during the day, but at night the Japanese naval supply trains ran with clockwork regularity and precision.

Tom Cringle's Log, 1835 adventure novel by **Michael Scott**, one of the most popular books about the sea, about a young midshipman who is captured by the French, sent to prison in Germany, and escapes to the **West Indies**.

Tomlinson, H. M. (Henry Major) (1873–1958), English novelist who wrote about the sea in many of his works. His first book, *The Sea and the Jungle* (1912), is considered one of the best travel novels ever written. Other works include *Old Junk* (1918), *London River* (1921), *Under the Red Ensign* (1926), and *Gallions Reach* (1927).

ton, unit for measuring either a ship's **displacement** (weight) or its **tonnage** (volume). For calculations, a long ton weighs 2,240 pounds, and one ton equals one hundred cubic feet.

Tongue of the Ocean, deepest region of the **Atlantic Ocean**, located between Andros and Exumas in the Bahamas, where an abyss plunges down more than five miles.

tonnage, the measure of a ship's volume or capacity, described in cubic feet. See **gross registered tonnage** and **net registered tonnage**.

Topaz, American ship commanded by Matthew Folger that was the first to learn of the fate of the mutineers from HMS *Bounty*. In 1808 *Topaz* called at **Pitcairn Island** while in search of seals. By then, only one of the mutineers was still living; the others, including **Fletcher Christian**, had been killed in the course of quarrels and vicious fighting between themselves. The sole mutineer survivor was Alexander Smith, who had changed his name to John Adams, and there were still a few Tahitian women and a score of the mutineers' children.

topgallant, the sail above the topsail on a **square-rigged** sailing ship.

Tora! Tora! Tora!, 20th Century Fox film that presents the Japanese attack on **Pearl Harbor** from both the American and the Japanese points of view. Technologically and historically superb, the picture was filmed at Pearl Harbor in 1970 with near full-scale mock-ups of USS *Arizona* and **Battleship Row**. Starring Martin Balsam, Joseph Cotton, and E. G. Marshall, the film won the 1970 Academy Award for best visual effects.

torpedo, in early days, the name of a stationary or drifting water mine, usually launched from land, as in **David Glasgow Farragut**'s famous command **"Damn the torpedoes! Full speed ahead!"** The mines became self-propelled with the introduction of the **Whitehead torpedo** in 1866. The term, presumably taken from the fish that can produce a jolting electric shock, was first applied by **Robert Fulton** to an underwater mine he developed.

Torpedo Alley, 1953 motion picture about a U.S. **Navy** pilot who signs aboard a submarine for a treacherous mission in order to overcome his inner turmoil about a failed mission that killed his flight crew. The World War II drama starred Mark Stevens and Dorothy Malone.

Torpedo Junction, name applied to the shipping lanes off Cape Hatteras, North Carolina, during the early months of World War II. In 1942 German **U-boats** torpedoed more than one hundred ships off the coast as civilians ashore witnessed the explosions from the beaches.

Torpedo Run, melodramatic movie detailing the efforts and agony of a U.S. submarine that is hunting down one of the Japanese aircraft carriers that carried out the attack on **Pearl Harbor**. The 1958 movie was nominated for an Academy Award for special effects and starred Glenn Ford, Ernest Borgnine, and Dean Jones.

Torrey Canyon, Liberian-flagged tanker that ran aground off the southwest coast of England in March 1967, spilling its entire cargo—more than 17,340 barrels of oil—into the English Channel and polluting the shores of Cornwall, the Channel Islands, and Brittany. Built at Newport News, Virginia, in 1959, the vessel was en route from the Persian Gulf to Milford Haven, in Wales, when it grounded on Seven Stones Reef, causing the world's first major oil spill. Attempts by the Royal Air Force to bomb the wreck and set the huge oil slick—which at its height reached thirty-five miles long by fifteen miles wide—on fire proved only moderately successful. The tanker broke up and sank nine days later.

tourist class, passenger ship accommodation (also referred to as "second cabin") in the 1930s that was one step behind **first class** in appointments, food, and service. It was geared toward middle-income passengers who were used to solid comfort without the excess frills found in first class. Following World War II, the tourist class quarters were restyled as **cabin class**, although few physical changes were apparent,

The wounding of Admiral Nelson during the Battle of Trafalgar. (Courtesy The Mariners' Museum, Newport News, Virginia)

and the term "tourist class" was then used to describe what had been **tourist third** class before the conflict. The confusion over passenger accommodation grades was deliberate to allow companies to charge cheaper fares for better grades of travel during the lean days of the Great Depression.

tourist third, modification of **tourist class** that signified an inexpensive, no-frills—but still substantial and comfortable—mode of accommodation. With the establishment of new American immigration laws in 1924, the transatlantic lines began to offer "college tours" to Europe. Improvements in **third-class** appointments aboard ship, including the proliferation of two-berth cabins, resulted in the new tourist third class. The term was waning by the time of World War II and was eventually recognized by the mid-1930s simply as tourist class.

Tovarisch, 263-foot Ukrainian **tall ship** that was christened *Gorch Foch* in the 1930s at **Blohm & Voss** shipyard in Hamburg, Germany. Sister ship to the U.S. Coast Guard *Eagle* (for-

merly the *Horst Wessel*), *Gorch Foch* survived World War II but was **scuttled** in the waters of Germany in May 1945. She rested in seventy-five feet of water for more than three years until she was raised and refurbished by the Soviet Union. With her new name, meaning "comrade," she was used as a sail training vessel for the Soviet navy in the **Black Sea**.

towboat, vessel used exclusively for "pushing" barges.

Toya Maru, Japanese ferry that sank in the Tsugaru Strait in September 1954, drowning more than a thousand passengers.

trade winds, predictable winds on each side of the equatorial **doldrums**, blowing from the northeast in the Northern Hemisphere and from the southeast in the Southern Hemisphere. The winds' regularity greatly assisted the sailing ships engaged in world trade.

Trafalgar, Battle of, decisive naval engagement of the **Napoleonic Wars** and one of the major naval battles in history. In this battle fought on

October 21, 1805, off Cape Trafalgar, on the southwest coast of Spain near the western entrance to the Strait of **Gibraltar**, Admiral **Horatio Nelson**'s British fleet defeated a combined French and Spanish fleet. British sea supremacy was established and maintained for the next century in an era known as **Pax Britannica**. Nelson was mortally wounded during the battle.

Trafalgar Square, area in Westminster, London, England, named for **Horatio Nelson**'s victory at the Battle of **Trafalgar** in 1805. Completed in 1845, the square includes the 185-foot Nelson memorial column.

tramp, type of ship that operates as needed and not on any scheduled service, in contrast to a **liner**. It is primarily engaged in the movement of bulky, low-value commodities (such as grain, cotton, coal, lumber, ore, phosphates, sulfur, and scrap metal) that have traditionally tended to move in shipload lots.

Transatlantic, 1931 Hollywood motion picture drama set aboard a speeding ocean **liner**. It contains some good shipboard sets and conveys the feel of life at sea. The film starred Edmund Lowe, Myrna Loy, and Jean Hersholt.

transatlantic cable, 1,686-nautical-mile undersea telegraph cable linking Europe and North America. After many failed attempts, a cable running from Ireland to Newfoundland was laid in August 1858. That cable ceased to work after three weeks, and in 1865 a second cable was laid by the *Great Eastern*. That cable broke after 1,200 miles were payed out. A third attempt was successful, and the first message was transmitted in July 1866. *Great Eastern* later retrieved and spliced the second cable. Both cables ceased working in 1872, but by then other cables were in operation. The transatlantic telephone cable was not operational until 1956.

Transatlantic Merry-Go-Round, American musical comedy feature film about a motley group of passengers involved in a murder aboard a luxury express **liner**. The 1934 movie starred Jack Benny, Nancy Carroll, and Gene Raymond.

Transatlantic Race, yacht race across the **Atlantic Ocean** that has been run occasionally since 1866. Usually run from North America to Europe, notable races have included the **Kaiser's Cup**, the **King of Spain Cup**, and the **Queen of Spain Cup**. Notable yachts to win Transatlantic Races have included *Atlantic*, *Dorade*, *Stormy Weather*, and *Niña*.

Transpacific Race, major ocean race for sailing vessels of all sizes. The 2,225-mile event is run from San Pedro, California, harbors to Diamond Head Buoy off Honolulu. Also called the Honolulu Race, it was first run in 1906 and was made a biennial event in 1939. The mostly downwind course allows for high-speed racing.

Trapp, Georg von (1880–1947), decorated Austrian naval captain known to most as the father in the famous stage play and movie, *The Sound of Music*. Von Trapp commanded one of Austria's first submarines, christened by Agathe Whitehead, granddaughter of Robert Whitehead, inventor of the **Whitehead torpedo**. Captain von Trapp and Agathe met and married; she bore the seven children in the Rodgers and Hammerstein classic. Following the loss of the Austro-Hungarian Empire's seacoast at the end of World War I, von Trapp lost his naval position. He died in Stowe, Vermont.

traverse board, navigational device used to record a ship's speed and direction during a four-hour watch. It consisted of a circular board marked with eight holes radiating along thirty-two points of the compass. Pegs would be placed in position to mark the ship's head every half hour.

trawler, traditional name for a fishing vessel that tows baglike nets. In more recent times, the term has been applied to a type of recreational powerboat popular for cruising, voyaging, and living aboard.

Treasure Island, classic 1883 adventure novel of buried treasure and pirates of the Caribbean. Written by **Robert Louis Stevenson**, the story relates the story of young Jim Hawkins, who discovers a map to treasure on the **Spanish Main**. With the local squire and doctor, he sets out to recover the treasure, only to discover that the crew they hired are the pirates that originally buried it. No less than five film adaptations have been made, including the first in 1934, with Wallace Beery as **Long John Silver**, accompanied by Jackie Cooper and Lionel Barrymore. The motion picture was remade by Walt Disney in 1950, with Robert Newton, Bobby Driscoll, and Basil Sydney in the leads, and again in 1989 with Charlton Heston.

Treaty of Ghent, peace agreement signed by Great Britain and the United States on December 24, 1814, in Belgium, officially ending the **War of 1812**. Neither side gained any military advantage, and Britain gave up rights to the lands of the Northwest Territory. In all, the war cost the United States $200 million and the lives of 2,260 American sailors and soldiers.

Treaty of Paris, 1898 agreement that ended the **Spanish-American War**. Spain agreed to cede the Philippines, Puerto Rico, and Guam to the United States for payment and to surrender all claim and title to Cuba. The treaty name is shared by both the 1783 agreement that ended the American Revolution and the 1763 pact that ended the **Seven Years' War**, which was also called the **French and Indian War**.

Treaty of Versailles , peace treaty signed on June 28, 1919, at Versailles, France, to end World War I. By limiting the size and number of German naval warships, it led to the development of the **pocket battleship**.

Treaty of Washington, 1871 agreement that provided for the peaceful settlement of several disputes between the United States and Great Britain. Foremost, the treaty referred the claims

Charlton Heston as Long John Silver in the 1989 film version of *Treasure Island*. (Maritime Museum of San Diego)

that Britain pay for damages caused during the Civil War by CSS *Alabama* and other British-built **Confederate raiders** to a special court of arbitration in Geneva, Switzerland. (In 1872, that court ruled that Britain should pay the United States $15.5 million.) The treaty granted fishing rights to the United States in territorial waters along Canada's east coast and referred a dispute over ownership of the San Juan Islands to the German Emperor **Wilhelm I**, who upheld the U.S. claim.

Trent Affair, naval incident between the United States and Great Britain that almost brought Britain into the Civil War on the side of the Confederacy. In November 1861, the USS *San Jacinto*, commanded by Captain **Charles Wilkes**, seized Confederate diplomatic agents James Mason and John Slidell from the British ship

Trent near Cuba (their mission was to enlist the aid of neutral France and Britain to the Southern cause). Britain maintained that the act violated the principle of **freedom of the seas**. While Northerners considered Wilkes a hero, his actions were disavowed by the U.S. government. The two agents were released, and war with Great Britain was averted.

Trieste, deep-diving research **bathyscaphe** launched in 1953 in Italy by Swiss scientist Auguste Piccard. After several years of operations in the Mediterranean, it was purchased by the U.S. **Navy**. *Trieste* conducted tests in the Pacific Ocean, including her historic dive to the **Marianas Trench** in January 1960. In 1963 she was engaged in the search for USS *Thresher*. *Trieste* was taken out of service shortly thereafter, and today is on display at the Washington Navy Yard in Washington, D.C. A successor, *Trieste II*, is still in service.

trim, the difference in a ship's draft forward and draft aft, expressed in inches.

Trinity House, association of mariners chartered in 1517 by Henry VIII to oversee lighthouses, buoys, and piloting. It grew to be responsible for all **aids to navigation** in Britain and still serves as the licensing authority.

Tripoli, capital and largest city of Libya. Lying along the Mediterranean Sea, with a fine harbor, Tripoli served as the seat of power for the **Barbary pirates**. The **Barbary Wars** are sometimes referred to as the Tripolitan Wars, and the line from the U.S. Marine Corps Hymn "From the halls of Montezuma to the shores of Tripoli" is a reference to the city.

Triton, in Greek and Roman mythology, a merman who is the son of **Neptune**. He is pictured usually with the head and trunk of a man and the tail of a fish and is accompanied by sea deities and attendants upon the sea gods. He rises from the sea blowing on a trumpet made of a conch shell, with the sound of which he raises or calms the waves as he pleases.

USS *Triton*, nuclear-powered submarine commanded by Captain **Edward L. Beach** that made the first undersea voyage around the world. In May 1960 *Triton* completed an epic forty-one-thousand-mile, eighty-four-day circumnavigation of the world while entirely submerged. *Triton*'s voyage was chronicled by her captain in his book ***Around the World Submerged*** (1962).

Tromp, Martin (1597–1653), Dutch admiral who is considered one of the Netherland's greatest seamen. After one victory during the **Anglo-Dutch War**, he was said to have hoisted a broom to the masthead of his vessel. He was killed at the Battle of **Scheveningen**.

Tropic of Cancer, northern parallel reached by the sun at its maximum northerly declination—approximately 23° 27′ North. It is named for the sign of zodiac in which the sun was when its maximum northerly declination was first measured.

Tropic of Capricorn, southern parallel reached by the sun at its maximum southerly declination—approximately 23° 27′ South. It is named for the sign of zodiac in which the sun was when its maximum southerly declination was first measured.

truck, the top of the highest mast on a ship or the top of a flagstaff. Lower masts have caps.

Truk Lagoon, Battle of, victory for the U.S. **Navy** in its drive to eradicate the Southwest Pacific of Japanese occupation. The February 17–18, 1944, attack task force—including USS *Iowa* and USS *New Jersey*—resulted in the sinking of six enemy **capital ships** as well as the destruction of 265 Japanese aircraft at the Imperial outpost.

Truxton, Thomas (1753–1822), American naval officer and **China trade** merchantman. Having commanded a **privateer** in the American Revolution, he was selected to be one of the first captains of the U.S. **Navy** and supervised the construction of USS *Constellation*. During the **Quasi-War**, he captured the French *Insurgente* in 1799 and in 1800 defeated *La Vengeance*. He went on to write books on navigation and naval tactics.

tsunami, large ocean wave produced by an undersea earthquake, landslide, or volcanic eruption. As a tsunami approaches a coastline, it can form a wall of water that rises more than a hundred feet high. In Japanese, the word "tsunami" means "harbor wave."

Tsushima, Battle of, May 1905 **Russo-Japanese War** naval engagement that resulted in a decisive Japanese victory over Russian forces in the Strait of Tsushima (between Japan and Korea). The contest is considered one of the greatest naval battles ever fought, in view of the total victory of an emerging Asian power over one of the great powers of Europe. The Russian fleet had come from the Baltic and **Black Seas** and was hampered by carrying heavy loads of coal on upper decks.

Tugboat Annie, humorous story by Norman Raine (1895–1971) of the adventures of the tugboat *Narcissus* and her colorful captain, Annie, in and around Puget Sound. Published as a book in 1934, it was initially serialized in the *Saturday Evening Post* and was illustrated by **Anton Otto Fischer**. The 1933 feature film was shot largely on Seattle's Elliot Bay. The tug *Arthur Foss* took the part of Annie's *Narcissus*, and the **Alaska Steamship Company**'s *General Gorgas* became the *Glacier Queen* for the cameras. The film is an excellent salty, waterfront yarn directed by Mervyn Leroy and starring Wallace Beery, Marie Dressler, and Robert Young.

tumblehome, the inward and upward curve of the sides of a ship. It is the opposite of flare.

Turbinia, the first steam turbine–powered vessel, which was built in Britain in 1894 by Charles Parsons, the pioneer of the steam turbine. After trying different propellers and shafts, the ninety-nine-foot ship reached speeds of over thirty-four **knots**—unheard of in 1898. The technology was soon embraced by the **Royal Navy**, and steam turbines were ordered in 1905 for HMS *Dreadnought*.

Turk's head, ornamental knot formed of rope strands that is sometimes used as a stopper knot at the end of a line or as decoration on a stanchion or pole.

Turner, Joseph Mallord William (1775–1851), English painter often referred to as "J. M. W. Turner" or as simply "Turner." He is acknowledged by many as England's greatest landscape and seascape artist. Turner is recognized as a giant influence who stands outside any particular tradition. He was said to have had himself lashed to a mast during a storm for artistic purposes.

Turner, Richmond Kelly (1885–1961), American naval commander of amphibious forces in the Pacific Ocean during World War II. He commanded most of the amphibious naval actions in the central and southern Pacific, including **Guadalcanal**, New Georgia, the Gilbert Islands, the **Marshall Islands**, Marianas, **Iwo Jima**, and **Okinawa**. He was promoted to admiral in 1945.

Turner, Robert Edward "Ted" (b. 1938), American media executive, sail racer, yachtsman, and one of the more colorful personalities in the history of the **America's Cup**. He successfully defended the Cup aboard *Courageous* in 1977. Often referred to as the "Mouth of the South" and "Captain Outrageous," he wrote *The Racing Edge* (1979) with Gary Jobson.

Turner, William (1856–1933), captain of RMS *Lusitania* when she was sunk by a German **U-boat** off Ireland in May 1915. From the time

Lusitania sailed from New York on May 1, 1915, to her sinking six days later, twenty-three ships were sunk off the British Isles. Turner chose to ignore recommendations of the **Admiralty** to help merchant ships but was cleared of all blame.

Turtle, the first submarine actively used in war. Constructed by **David Bushnell** in 1776 in Connecticut, she was transported to New York Harbor and on September 6, 1776, engaged HMS *Eagle*, the **flagship** of the British fleet. Bushnell couldn't attach his torpedo because *Eagle*'s copper sheathing resisted his auger. The torpedo detonated short of its target, but the mysterious explosion led *Eagle* and other British ships to anchor farther down harbor, thus accomplishing at least part of the *Turtle*'s original objective. A second attempt to sink British shipping later in the month also failed.

The Tuttles of Tahiti, 1942 film about rival Tahitian families that become rich from **salvaging** a ship. The comedy, based on the novel *No More Gas* (1940) by **Nordhoff and Hall**, starred Charles Laughton, Jon Hall, and Peggy Drake.

Twain, Mark (1835–1910), pen name of **Samuel Langhorne Clemens**, humorist, lecturer, and a major author of American fiction. Clemens adopted his pseudonym around 1863 after having served as an apprentice **steamboat pilot**—later a licensed pilot—on the **Mississippi River** (the phrase "by the mark twain" meant two **fathoms**, or twelve feet, deep). One of his earliest works, *The Innocents Abroad* (1869), an account of his voyage to Europe and the Holy Land, was a great financial success. His other works include *Life on the Mississippi*, *Tom Sawyer*, and *Huckleberry Finn*.

twelve-meter, **sloop**-rigged racing yacht approximately sixty-five feet in length, carrying a crew of eleven. The "twelve" refers to the number that results when the boat's design rule—a ratio of waterline length, sail area, and displacement—is computed. The first twelve-meter was built in 1906, but the class achieved special prominence after 1955, when a legal change in the deed-of-gift of the **America's Cup** permitted a revival of competition in boats smaller than those originally specified. Twelves competed for the Cup from 1958 to 1987 and included *Columbia*, *Weatherly*, *Intrepid*, and *Courageous*.

Twenty Thousand Leagues under the Sea, 1870 novel by French novelist **Jules Verne** is the adventure of **Captain Nemo** and his crew aboard the submarine *Nautilus*. Nemo, who hates war, uses his submarine to destroy all kinds of war-related ships, but a shipwrecked scientist and sailor do their best to thwart his schemes. The popular 1954 Disney remake film, starring Kirk Douglas, James Mason, and Peter Lorre, won Academy Awards for best art direction and best special effects.

T Wharf, famous wharf on the Boston waterfront whose name derived from its shape. During the early twentieth century, it was the busiest fish pier in North America and later became a freight pier and all-around docking space. The low rent of its lofts and apartments made it a favorite hangout for writers and artists before it was demolished in the 1960s. T Wharf was superseded by the South Boston Fish Pier in 1914, which was the world's busiest by the 1920s.

Twilight for the Gods, 1958 adventure film about a group of misfits on a run-down **barkentine** bound for Mexico from the **South Seas**. Based on the 1956 book of the same title by Ernest Gann, the film starred Cyd Charisse and Rock Hudson.

Twilight Zone: "Passage on the Lady Anne", excellent 1963 television episode from the enigmatic series about an aging transatlantic **liner** embarking on a passage with a decidedly aged crew and passenger manifest—except for one youthful couple on their honeymoon. The juxtaposition of young and old becomes more apparent along the way when finally the young pair are set adrift in a lifeboat before the *Lady Anne* sails off and disappears into thin air. The episode starred Joyce Van Patten, Lee Phillips, David Hyde White, and Gladys Cooper.

***Twilight Zone*: "The Thirty-Fathom Grave"**, thought-provoking 1963 installment from the groundbreaking television series in which a contemporary U.S. **Navy Fletcher**-class **destroyer** encounters unexplainable **sonar** pings from a U.S. sub **scuttled** during World War II. The episode contained great shots of the destroyer under way and starred Bill Bixby, Mike Kellin, and Simon Oakland.

two-blocked, to reach the maximum limit of something. The term describes the situation when in using a block and tackle with two opposing blocks, the blocks are drawn together until they touch and can hoist no further.

***The Two-Ocean War*, Samuel Eliot Morison**'s shortened and concise 1963 version of his encyclopedic work *History of United States Naval Operations in World War II* (1947–62).

Two Years Before the Mast*,** classic 1840 narrative by **Richard Henry Dana Jr.** that chronicles his two-year voyage from Boston to California and back on board the **brig *Pilgrim and the **ship *Alert***. Drawn from his journals, the account provides a vivid, detailed account of a common sailor's treatment at sea and of a way of life virtually unknown to the public at the time. It is one of the best American accounts of rounding **Cape Horn** as well as an important original American source on the geography and history of Spanish California. The 1946 film of the same name starred Alan Ladd and Howard Da Silva.

***Typee*,** the first novel by **Herman Melville**, published in 1846. It is a romanticized version of Melville's own experiences in the **Marquesas Islands** following his desertion from the whaleship *Acushnet* in July 1842. It was followed by the sequel, *Omoo*, in 1847.

***Typhoon*,** 1902 novella by **Joseph Conrad** about an English **steamship** captain named MacWhirr, who is pitted against a furious storm off the coast of China. Like Conrad's other works, it is a study of man versus the sea.

U

U-505, 1,152-ton Nazi submarine built in 1941. One of the 1,110 **U-boats** that were operated by the Imperial German Navy during World War II, U-505 was responsible for sending more than forty-seven thousand tons of Allied shipping to the bottom of the Atlantic. In 1944 the 252-foot vessel was captured by American forces off the Cape Verde Islands and is today on exhibition at the Chicago Museum of Science and Industry.

U-571, suspense-filled motion picture released in 2000 detailing the fictional story of a disguised American submarine trying to intercept a Nazi **U-boat** during World War II. The movie starred Matthew McConaughey and Bill Paxton.

U-1105, one of ten World War II submarines the Germans outfitted with experimental synthetic rubber skin designed to counter Allied **sonar**. The experiment proved successful, and the **U-boat** earned the nickname "Black Panther." At the close of the war, U-1105 surrendered to the British and was turned over to the

United States as a war prize for study of its rubber-tiled coating. After examination, it was used for explosives testing and sunk in the Potomac River near Piney Point, Maryland. Today the wreck is a popular dive site.

U-boat, general name for German submarines (from the German Unterseeboot). U-1, the first to be built for the German navy, was launched in 1906. With many different types, ranging from small coastal to large seagoing boats, the U-boat was a vital weapon in both world wars. More than 800 U-boats were built in the course of World War I, 210 of which were lost. In World War II, more than 1,110 were built, with 635 being sunk.

ULCC, acronym for ultra-large crude carrier, a **supertanker** introduced in the 1970s that was larger than a **VLCC**, usually measuring more than three hundred thousand in **deadweight tonnage**.

Ultramarine, 1933 novel by English writer Malcolm Lowry (1909–1957) about a naive young upperclass Briton who goes to sea as a deckhand in the 1920s and is subjected to rough treatment by the crew.

Uluburon shipwreck, wreck discovered in 1982 off the Turkish coast containing eighteen thousand artifacts dated from about 1300 B.C. It is one of the most important Bronze Age excavations ever.

Ulysses, Roman name of the mythological **Odysseus**. Ulysses is a major character in the *Iliad* and the hero of the *Odyssey*, the two great epics attributed to the Greek bard **Homer**. The *Iliad* deals with events that occurred in the last year of the Trojan War. The *Odyssey* describes Ulysses' seafaring adventures as he returns home after the Trojan War.

Unalaska, second-largest island in the Aleutian chain. It is the site of Dutch Harbor, which served as a U.S. **Navy** air base during World War II.

UNCLOS, acronym for the United Nation's Convention on the **Law of the Sea**.

The Undersea World of Jacques Cousteau, weekly American television series, produced by and starring **Jacques-Yves Cousteau**, that ran from 1968 to 1976. It introduced whales, dolphins, sunken treasure, and coral reefs while dramatizing underwater exploration and the need for conservation of ocean life.

Under Siege, 1992 shoot-'em-up action movie actually filmed aboard USS *Missouri* in which a band of terrorists try to take control of the ship. The movie starred Steven Segal, Tommy Lee Jones, and Gary Busey.

Underwater!, 1955 Howard Hughes film about a team of skin divers who face danger when they begin a search for underwater treasure. The movie starred Jane Russell, Richard Egan, Gilbert Roland, and scantily clad Hollywood newcomer Jayne Mansfield.

Uniform Code of Military Justice (UCMJ), body of laws enacted by the U.S. Congress that con-

tains the substantive and procedural laws governing the military justice system. All persons serving in the Armed Forces of the United States, including the U.S. **Navy** and **Coast Guard**, are subject to the UCMJ at all times.

Uniform State Waterway Marking System (USWMS), buoyage system developed by the U.S. **Coast Guard** and state boating administrators to provide aids to navigation on inland state waters that are compatible with the U.S. **aids to navigation** system.

union jack, flag consisting of just the union or upper inner corner of a national flag. In the United States, it is a blue flag with fifty white stars. It is flown at the jack staff in the bow of a vessel in port or at anchor. Aboard commissioned vessels not under way, the union jack goes up and down ceremoniously with the national ensign.

United American Lines, shipping line started by **W. Averell Harriman** that for a brief time in the early 1920s operated the largest U.S. merchant fleet and one of the biggest in the world. Losing money, Harriman soon grew tired of the shipping business, and in the late 1920s pieces were sold off and a large part of the company was purchased by the Germans to restore the **Hamburg-America Line**. The experience of running a shipping line aided Harriman's **Lend-Lease** program efforts in World War II.

United Fruit Company, large company with many interests in Latin America. Its shipping concern, dubbed the **Great White Fleet** for the color of its refrigerated ships, was started in 1899 to carry tropical products, mostly bananas, to the United States to ensure delivery without interruption or spoilage. A series of takeovers and setbacks in the 1960s and 1970s—including the CEO's jump from the forty-fourth floor of the Pan American building in New York City— prompted the new parent company, Chiquita

Brands, to dissolve the United Fruit Company and call the shipping unit the Great White Fleet.

United Seaman's Service (USS), organization founded in 1942 by the U.S. government to provide community services to members of the U.S. **merchant marine**, similar to those offered by the USO to the armed forces. During World War II, many domestic and overseas centers were established. After the war, federal funding dried up and most of the USS domestic centers were forced to close. Headquartered in New York, the USS continues to operate some overseas centers and has increasingly become self-supporting. Since 1970 it has awarded the Admiral of the Ocean Sea Award, the highest honor in the U.S.-flag shipping industry. In 1973 the **American Merchant Marine Library Association**, a lending library for U.S. merchant vessels established in 1921, became an affiliate of the USS.

SS *United States*, the fastest ocean **liner** ever built. On her 1952 **maiden voyage**, the 53,329-gross-ton flyer smashed the existing Atlantic speed record of RMS *Queen Mary* by traveling at an average speed of 35.6 **knots** eastbound and 33.9 knots westbound with a top spurt of over 42 knots. Designed by **William Francis Gibbs** for operation by the **United States Lines**, the heavily subsidized racer was intended from the outset for auxiliary use as a supertroopship and was given power to keep up with the aircraft carriers and battleships, with which she would be traveling in **convoy** should the need arise. **Laid up** in 1969, she is moored in the Delaware River in Philadelphia today, while discussion of plans to restore her continues.

USS *United States*, one of the six original **frigates** (the others being *President*, *Congress*, *Chesapeake*, *Constitution*, and *Constellation*) called for in the **Navy Act of 1794**. Launched in 1797, she served as the **flagship** of Commodore **John Barry** during the **Quasi-War**. Under the command of **Stephen Decatur Jr.** in the **War of 1812**, she captured HMS *Macedonian*. **Herman Melville** served on *United States* for fourteen months, traveling from Honolulu to Boston, and later recounted the experience in *White Jacket* (1850). Decommissioned in 1849, she was refitted in 1861 for service in the **Confederate States Navy**. **Scuttled** in 1862 to block the Elizabeth River in Virginia from the Union navy, she was broken up in 1865.

USS *United States* (CVA-58), aircraft carrier intended to be the ultimate doomsday vehicle to secure U.S. supremacy during the Cold War. Laid down in 1949, the 1,088-foot carrier was designed without a superstructure to provide an extremely wide flight deck in order to handle long-range bombers, each equipped with an arsenal of nuclear weapons. If completed, she would have been capable of normal steaming at thirty-three **knots** and would have been the largest ship in the world. Controversy shrouded every step of her progress and finally caused the project to be aborted. The stillborn vessel was broken up where she lay on the building berth in Newport News, Virginia, and the order for four sister vessels was canceled.

United States Cruises, corporation founded in Seattle in 1978 to operate the **laid-up** SS *United States* after a proposed $40 million renovation. The concept in 1980 was to run the ship on regular Los Angeles to Hawai'i sailings as well as offer time-share condo arrangements on board. Plans escalated until a radical reconstruction costing over $100 million was envisioned in 1981. The company went bankrupt, and the idle **liner** was sold by court order in 1992 to satisfy creditors.

United States Lines, American **steamship** company established by the U.S. government at the conclusion of the World War I to maintain transatlantic passenger service and to operate the former German **liners**, including SS *Leviathan*. It assumed its more recognized no-

SS *United States*. (Courtesy Gordon R. Ghareeb; photo by Beken & Sons, Cowes)

menclature in 1922 with **steamship row** headquarters at One Broadway in New York City. The line was sold to **International Mercantile Marine** (IMM) in 1931, and the liners *Manhattan* and *Washington* entered service in 1932 and 1933. SS *America* was delivered in 1940, and by 1943 IMM changed its name to the United States Lines. After World War II, the line operated surplus freighters to Europe, Australia, and the Far East, and SS *United States* came on line in 1952. United States Lines was sold to **Malcolm McLean** in 1977, and in 1983–84 it acquired the **Moore-McCormack Line** and Delta Lines. United States Lines entered bankruptcy in 1986 and was liquidated.

United States Lines, cruise line set up in 1999 to operate inter-Hawai'ian sailings of U.S.-flagged passenger vessels. Their first ship, the *Patriot*, was re-registered in the United States while two new **liners** of seventy-one thousand gross tons each were being constructed at Pascagoula, Mississippi, to enter service in 2003 and 2004. Each is designed to carry nineteen hundred passengers on weekly Hawai'ian cruises from Honolulu. The $400 million shipbuilding con-

tract will result in the first oceangoing passenger ships to be built on U.S. soil since 1958.

Universal Rule, yacht rating and measurement rule introduced in 1923 for international racing. It was replaced by the measurement rule of the **International Yacht Racing Union**, also called the **International Rules**.

unlicensed seaman, a member of a ship's deck, engine, or stewards department who is not a licensed officer but is required to hold a merchant mariner's document or **Z-card**.

The Unsinkable Molly Brown, hit 1960 Broadway musical by Meredith Wilson showcasing Tammy Grimes in the title role. It forever earmarked **Margaret Brown** as "Molly" Brown and launched her into American folk history as "unsinkable." Debbie Reynolds starred in the 1964 Metro-Goldwyn-Mayer screen version. In both retellings, the sinking of RMS *Titanic*, along with Molly's subsequent heroic actions to save her fellow shipmates, is the climax of the story.

Up Periscope, submarine film revolving around the interpersonal relationships of the ship's crew as they battle the Japanese in the South Pacific. The 1959 World War II drama standard starred James Garner, Edmond O'Brien, and Frank Gifford.

Ushant, small, ten-square-mile French island located ten miles off the coast of Brittany, in the Atlantic Ocean. Its waters have been the site of numerous naval battles, and its lighthouse marks the southern entrance to the English Channel.

USLSS, see **U.S. Life-Saving Service**.

USNS, prefix indicating a "United States Naval Ship" assigned to a fleet of noncombat **auxiliary** vessels in the custody of the navy, manned by a civilian **merchant marine** crew, and operated by the **Military Sealift Command** or a commercial company under contract to them. The fleet includes supply and hospital ships, oilers, oceangoing tugs, **ro/ro**s, containerships, and such special-mission vessels as surveillance ships, survey vessels, and oceanographic research vessels.

USS, prefix for a commissioned U.S. warship indicating "United States Ship." Although already long in use, this designation was made formal by an executive order issued in 1907 by President **Theodore Roosevelt**.

U.S. Sailing Association, organization established to encourage and promote yacht racing and to unify the racing and rating rules in the United States, Canada, and throughout the world. Founded in 1897 as the **North American Yacht Racing Union**, it changed its name to the U.S. Yacht Racing Union in 1975 (the Canadian Yachting Association was organized in 1931). In 1991 the membership voted to change to the current name, US Sailing.

USS VD: Ship of Shame, graphic 1942 U.S. **Navy** training film shown to every recruit until the 1970s. The intention of the forty-six-minute motion picture was to display the results of sexually transmitted disease in such a hideously unappetizing fashion as to override the hormonal urges of the newly enlisted Yankee sailor.

USYRU, see **U.S. Sailing Association**.

USS Utah (BB-31), Florida-class battleship completed in 1911. The 21,825-ton vessel was sunk in the December 7, 1941, Japanese attack on **Pearl Harbor** with the loss of fifty-eight of her crew. The 521-foot vessel was never raised and, along with the remains of USS *Arizona*, comprises the USS *Arizona* Memorial on Ford Island.

UTC, acronymn for Coordinated Universal Time, also known as universal time, an international time standard that reflects the mean solar time along the **prime meridian**. Adopted worldwide in 1964, the time scale is based on atomic time.

Valcour Island, Battle of, small but significant naval battle during the American Revolution that took place around Valcour Island in Lake Champlain in October 1776. While the British scored a decisive victory, the Americans, under General Benedict Arnold, delayed the British advance so much that the British withdrew forces to winter quarters in Canada. The time allowed a stronger Continental Army to score an important victory the following spring at Saratoga. Eleven of Arnold's sixteen vessels, including the gunboat *Philadelphia*, were lost in the engagement.

Valkyrie II, **America's Cup** challenger of 1893 representing Britain's **Royal Yacht Squadron**. Designed by **George L. Watson** for the **Earl of Dunraven**, it was the first to challenge the Cup under a new set of rules that provided new difficulties for the challenger. *Valkyrie II* was defeated handily in three races by the American defender, *Vigilant*. In 1894, with Lord Dunraven at the helm, *Valkyrie II* sank and a sailor was killed when the boat was struck by the yacht *Satanita* during in a yachting challenge on the Clyde River in Scotland. *Satanita* had maneuvered to avoid a spectator craft. *Valkyrie II* was later refloated. The first *Valkyrie* competed in England but was not a challenger for the America's Cup.

Valkyrie III, **America's Cup** challenger of 1895, backed by the **Earl of Dunraven** and a syndicate from the **Royal Yacht Squadron** and, like *Valkyrie II*, designed by **George L. Watson**. The American yacht *Defender* captured the first race in the best-of-five series. In the second race, the two vessels struck each other and *Valkyrie III* was disqualified. At the start of the third race, *Valkyrie III* hauled down the racing pennant and retired from the course, and *Defender* went on to win the race and the Cup. The events of the disqualification and other protests have become known as the **Dunraven Affair**.

USS *Valley Forge* (CV-45), the final **Essex**-class aircraft carrier, which was commissioned in 1946. She was built in the Philadelphia Navy Yard with funds raised from a special war bond drive by the citizens of Philadelphia. In 1948 she was the first U.S. carrier to pass through the **Suez Canal,** and in 1950 she launched the first carrier-based strikes of the Korean War. The 888-foot vessel was **laid up** in 1970 and sold for scrap the following year.

Valparaiso, principal seaport and one of the largest cities of Chile. Valparaiso lies on a wide inlet of the Pacific Ocean about seventy miles northwest of Santiago. It was a colonial possession of Spain before its won independence in 1818, and it was the site of the 1814 engagement in which the British ships HMS *Phoebe* and HMS *Cherub* captured USS *Essex* during the **War of 1812**.

Vancouver, George (1757–1798), British naval officer and explorer who, from 1792 to 1794, aboard his ship HMS *Discovery*, led an expedition to explore the Pacific coast of North America. Vancouver Island and cities in Washington State and British Columbia, Canada, are named for him. He also sailed a hundred miles up the Columbia River as far as the present site of Portland, Oregon. His surveys of the West Coast of North America from San Diego to southern Alaska were pioneering achievements. His book, *A Voyage of Discovery to the North Pacific Ocean and Round the World in the Years 1790–1795*, was published in 1798.

Vanderbilt, 323-foot **side-wheel** passenger mail steamer built in 1857 for Commodore **Cornelius Vanderbilt** to compete with the **Cunard Line**. During the Civil War, Vanderbilt chartered the ship to the U.S. government as a troop transport. In 1862 he presented the *Vanderbilt* to the U.S. **Navy**. She was converted to a **cruiser** and sent on a yearlong search for CSS *Alabama*. Although unsuccessful in this charge, she did capture several **blockade runners**. *Vanderbilt* was later converted to a sailing ship, then used as a coal barge, and was sold for scrap in 1928.

Vanderbilt, Cornelius (1794–1877), often referred to as "Commodore" because of his ship-

ping interests, the most successful and powerful American businessman of his time. After an early career ferrying freight in New York Harbor, he formed a **steamship** company in 1829 and soon dominated shipping along the Atlantic coast. In 1849 he established a steamship line that carried "gold seekers" from New York City to San Francisco, via Nicaragua, and by the mid-1850s, his ships made regular trips across the Atlantic and he had become the leading American steamship owner. He later diversified into railroads but also had investments in manufacturing and banking. In 1853 Vanderbilt had the 270-foot *North Star* built, the first steam yacht of great size constructed in the United States.

Vanderbilt, Harold Stirling "Mike" (1884–1970), great-grandson of Commodore **Cornelius Vanderbilt** and heir to the vast **steamship** and railroad empire. As a yachtsman, he was the first owner to take the helm of his yacht in the **America's Cup** competition. He defended the America's Cup three times—in 1930 (*Enterprise*), in 1934 (*Rainbow*), and in 1937 (*Ranger*)—and assisted the 1958 defense with his **twelve-meter** yacht *Vim*. He wrote of his Cup defenses in his books *Enterprise* (1930) and *On the Wind's Highway* (1939).

Vanderdecken, Captain, cursed **master** of the ghost ship *Flying Dutchman*, which, according to folklore, sails around the **Cape of Good Hope** but never reaches port, doomed to sail on eternally.

Vane, Charles (d. 1720), British pirate known for raiding ships along the American East Coast from Long Island to the Bahamas from 1718 to 1720. His crew replaced him with **John Rackham** because he proved a coward in an encounter with a French warship. He was captured and hanged in Jamaica.

HMS *Vanguard*, 168-foot, seventy-four-gun **flagship** of Admiral **Horatio Nelson** at the 1798 Battle of the **Nile**. The **Royal Navy** scored a decisive victory in this battle, sinking two French ships and capturing six others, out of eleven total.

Vanuatu, island country, consisting of eighty islands, that lies in the southwest Pacific Ocean. From 1906 to 1980, Great Britain and France jointly governed the islands, which were then called the New Hebrides—named by British explorer **James Cook** after the Hebrides Islands of Scotland. The islands served as a major Allied military base during World War II. In 1980 they became the independent nation of Vanuatu. A lack of taxation fostered Vanuatu's development as a financial and banking center as well as a major port of registry for international shipping.

variation, difference in degrees, east or west, between true north or south, and magnetic north or south, at a given place. It is indicated on most charts and, together with **deviation** (induced by magnetic influences aboard the ship), forms magnetic compass error.

Vasa, Swedish warship that sank on her own in 1628 in Stockholm Harbor and was raised in 1961. The delicate **salvage** operation had the entire hull being lifted to the surface. The wreckage reveals details of daily life in the sixteenth and seventeenth centuries, and today she is the only preserved seventeenth-century ship in the world. In 1990 the wreck was placed in a new Vasa Museum, now the most visited museum in Scandinavia.

Vaterland, three-**funneled** steamer built in 1914 for the **Hamburg-America Line**'s transatlantic service. She was seized by the U.S. **Shipping Board** in 1917 and renamed USS *Leviathan*. The 54,383-gross-ton ship served as a U.S. **Navy** transport during World War I and was nicknamed the "Levi Nathan" by her crew. She was transferred to the **United States Lines** in 1922 for reconstruction into America's premier ocean **liner**, the SS *Leviathan*. *Vaterland* was sister ship to SS *Bismarck*.

V-E Day, Victory in Europe Day, which was officially proclaimed by U.S. President Harry S. Truman on Tuesday, May 8, 1945, to mark the surrender of the German armed forces in World War II. **V-J Day** followed three months later.

SS *Veendam*, 15,406-gross-ton steamer built in 1923 for the North Atlantic service of the **Holland America Line** to New York. Seized by Nazi invading forces at **Rotterdam** in 1941, she became an accommodations ship for German **U-boat** crews. She was restored to Holland America Line operation in 1947 and was scrapped in 1953.

Velde, Willem van de, the Elder (1611–1693) and the Younger (1633–1707), Dutch father and son artists who specialized in marine subjects. They emigrated from the Netherlands to England in 1672, where together they entered into the service of King Charles II (1630–1685), James II (1633–1701), and members of the royal court. They are credited with having a profound influence on the development of marine art.

Vendée Globe, French-organized, solo, nonstop race around the world. Held every four years, competitors must sail twenty-six thousand miles using only satellite telephone and e-mail as their contact with land.

The Venturesome Voyages of Captain Voss, 1913 narrative by John C. Voss that includes an account of his 1901–4 voyage from Victoria, British Columbia, to London aboard a thirty-eight-foot Indian dugout canoe, *Tilikum*, which he fitted with three small masts. Voss, a well-traveled sea captain from the great age of sail, hoped to imitate **Joshua Slocum** but abandoned his hopes for a circumnavigation after sailing forty thousand miles across three oceans.

Veracruz, Mexican seaport city on the Gulf of Mexico, two hundred miles east of Mexico City, that was the first Spanish settlement in

Mexico. In the largest amphibious operation carried out before World War I, more than a hundred ships landed twelve thousand U.S. troops in Veracruz during the Mexican War in 1847 and later captured Mexico City (a victory commemorated in the **Marine Corps** Hymn, "From the Halls of Montezuma"). U.S. marines again bombarded and occupied Veracruz for a few months in 1914, after a dispute with Mexico over the arrest of some U.S. sailors.

Verne, Jules (1828–1905), French novelist and author who helped to shape modern science fiction. His masterpiece, *Twenty Thousand Leagues under the Sea* (1870), is the story of **Captain Nemo**, a mad sea captain who cruises beneath the oceans in the submarine *Nautilus*. Nemo reappears in *The Mysterious Island* (1874). In *Around the World in Eighty Days* (1873), Phileas Fogg travels around the earth, much of the time crossing the oceans, in the then-unheard-of time of eighty days, just to win a bet.

Vernet, Claude-Joseph (1714–1789), one of the most celebrated of all French marine painters, he brought witness to the world of sailors, fishermen, merchants, laundresses, and bathers. He was commissioned by King Louis XV (1710–1774) to produce a series of twenty-six paintings of French ports—two per port—but he was unable to complete the entire series because of the outbreak of war with Great Britain. Many of the paintings hang in the **Musée de la Marine** in Paris.

Vernon, Edward (1684–1757), British admiral who in 1740 issued an order that the **Royal Navy**'s daily rum ration be cut with water. The mixture became known as "**grog**" because Vernon was referred to as "Old Grog" for his habit of wearing overcoats made of a material called grogram. George Washington's brother served under Admiral Vernon in the **Royal Navy** in

the **West Indies** and named the family estate in Virginia after him.

Verrazano, Giovanni da (ca. 1485–1528), Italian navigator in the service of France who sailed to North America in 1524 seeking a **Northwest Passage** to China. While unsuccessful in finding the passage, he explored the eastern coast of North America from the Carolinas to Newfoundland. Verrazano later made two more voyages to the New World. Some historians believe Verrazano named Rhode Island when he wrote that it resembled the Island of Rhodes in the Mediterranean Sea.

Vespucci, Amerigo (1454–1512), Italian navigator in the service of Portugal who in 1501 determined that **Christopher Columbus**'s discovery was not connected to Asia but was a new world. Vespucci's travels became more famous in his day than did those of Christopher Columbus, leading mapmakers to use his name to anoint the New World.

vessel traffic service (VTS), system of regulations, communications, and monitoring facilities implemented to improve the safety and efficiency of vessel traffic and to protect the environment. In the United States, systems are operated by the U.S. **Coast Guard** and **marine exchanges**, employing **radar** and voice communication, to facilitate the movement of ships in congested waters.

SS *Vestris*, New York to South America **liner** of the British-owned Lamport & Holt fleet that was completed in 1912. While en route south to the Caribbean with 326 people on board, the 10,494-gross-ton ship was overcome by heavy seas and—compounded by shifting cargo in her holds—capsized on November 10, 1928, killing 102 people. The incident prompted the 1929 conference leading to the International Convention for the **Safety of Life at Sea**.

VHF, acronym for very-high frequency, the frequency range reserved for bridge-to-bridge radiotelephony to provide clear line-of-sight communications. VHF channels are assigned different uses; for example, channel 16 is designated for calling and distress.

Victoria, first ship to circumnavigate the world. Commanded by **Juan Sebastian de Elcano**, it was the only one of the five vessels in **Ferdinand Magellan**'s voyage of discovery to complete the entire trip around the world, returning to Spain in 1522.

Lake Victoria, the world's second-largest freshwater lake, after Lake Superior, located in east Central Africa. The source of the Nile River, it measures approximately 26,828 square miles.

Victoria and Albert, steam yacht that served as the royal yacht for Britain's Queen Victoria (1819–1901) from 1843 to 1855. Often referred to as "V and A," the 225-foot vessel had a **paddle wheel**, one **funnel**, and two masts. With the advent of steam power, Queen Victoria was able to visit previously remote parts of the empire, thereby enabling thousands of her subjects to catch a glimpse of their sovereign.

Victoria and Albert II, the second royal yacht of Queen Victoria, which measured three hundred feet and was supremely fitted out. On February 1, 1901, it had the duty of escorting the queen's body across the **Solent** for her state funeral. The yacht was broken up and burned three years later.

Victoria and Albert III, British royal yacht built in 1899 and used by King Edward VII, King George V, and King George VI. It played an important part in European diplomacy prior to World War I but was seldom used thereafter. It was replaced by HMY *Britannia* and was broken up in 1955.

HMS *Victory*, Admiral **Horatio Nelson**'s **flagship** at the Battle of **Trafalgar** and the most famous vessel in Great Britain's **Royal Navy.** Launched in 1765 and rebuilt in 1801, she distinguished herself in three wars and several major sea battles. Her greatest exploit was at Trafalgar when Nelson was mortally wounded on the quarterdeck of the ship by a musket shot from a sharpshooter in the rigging of the French ship *Redoubtable. Victory* remained in service until 1811 and returned to Portsmouth, England. In 1922 she was restored to her configuration at the time of the famous battle of October 21, 1805. She was permanently dry-docked in Portsmouth and opened to the public.

Victory at Sea, 1920 Pulitzer Prize–winning book by Admiral **William Sowden Sims**, commander of U.S. naval forces in Europe in World War I.

Victory at Sea, award-winning television documentary showing combat footage of U.S. naval forces in World War II. Produced by the U.S. **Navy** in cooperation with NBC, the series consisted of twenty-six 30-minute episodes. Its editors reviewed more than 60 million feet of film from ten different nations in order to compose the final sequence. Narrated by Leonard Graves, the film was accompanied by a musical score composed by Richard Rodgers. It first aired on American television during the 1952–53 season and is still acclaimed as one of the most powerful war expositories ever produced.

Victory ship, standardized class of ships designed and constructed during World War II to improve upon the **Liberty ship**. Built as cargo ships and transports, the 455-foot-long vessels were propelled by steam turbines capable of speeds of fifteen-plus **knots**. The U.S. **Maritime Commission** switched production to the Victory class, anticipating that more commercially oriented vessels would be needed after the war. Delivery began in 1944, and the final output was 531 ships. Officially called VC2, the ships were named for Allied nations, American cities, and educational institutions. While some Victory ships only saw action in the Pacific in World War II, many went on to serve in Korea and Vietnam.

Viez, Everett (b.1913), well-known American photographer of passenger ships, especially in New York Harbor. His collection totaled more than fifteen thousand images when it was donated to the **Steamship Historical Society of America**.

Vigilant, U.S. **America's Cup** defender in 1893, and the first of six defenders designed by **Nathanael Greene Herreshoff**. Manned by a crew of seventy, the 124-foot **sloop** defeated the British challenger ***Valkyrie II***, three races to none. Referred to as the "Bronze Beauty," she was constructed of bronze below the waterline (steel above) and had a hollow bronze centerboard and a bronze rudder.

Viking Princess, cruise ship converted from the former French colonial **liner** *Lavoisier*. Originally built in 1948, the 515-foot ship was refitted for cruising from American ports in 1961. While en route to Miami at the end of a seven-day cruise in 1966, the *Viking Princess* became engulfed in flames following an explosion in her engine room. Two people lost their lives in the conflagration, and the vulnerability of such secondhand cruise vessels, along with the fires aboard the **Lakonia** and **Yarmouth Castle**, prompted the U.S. Congress to overhaul safety at sea laws for ships sailing from U.S. ports.

The Vikings, 1958 blockbuster motion picture about two half-brothers independently seeking the throne of ancient England as well the hand of the same woman. Featuring lots of great Viking ship footage taken in the Norwegian fjords as well as great scenery of Norway and Brittany, the film starred Kirk Douglas, Ernest Borgnine, Janet Leigh, and Tony Curtis.

SS *Viktoria*, ninety-thousand-ton ocean **liner** planned by the Nazis to signify Germany's

resurgence as the major shipping force on the North Atlantic following its anticipated conquest of Europe after World War II. No construction was ever started, although the vessel had been fully designed.

de Villeneuve, Pierre (1763–1806), French admiral who saw action at the Battle of the **Nile** in 1798 and commanded the French squadron at the Battle of **Trafalgar** on October 21, 1805. He was taken prisoner and later released. He was found stabbed at a hotel in France in 1806, presumably a suicide.

Villiers, Alan John (1903–1982), Australian adventurer, **square-rigger** sailor, and sea writer who brilliantly combined his expertise as a professional mariner with his gift as a narrator. In the 1930s he bought the **full-rigged** Danish training ship *Georg Stage*, which he renamed the ***Joseph Conrad*** and sailed around the world as a private school ship. He commanded a squadron of landing craft during **D-Day,** and his photographs of his life at sea form part of the collection at Britain's **National Maritime Museum**. He wrote nearly thirty books during his lifetime, including *By Way of Cape Horn* (1930), *The **Voyage of the Parma*** (1933), *Cruise of the Conrad* (1937), *Sons of Sindbad* (1940), *Monsoon Seas* (1952), *The **Way of a Ship*** (1953), *The New Mayflower* (1958), *Give Me a Ship to Sail* (1959), *The **War with Cape Horn*** (1971), and *Men, Ships, and the Sea* (1973), and lectured for the National Geographic Society.

Vim, twelve-meter yacht designed by **Olin James Stephens II** for **Harold Stirling "Mike" Vanderbilt** in 1939. Vanderbilt, having just won the 1937 **America's Cup** with his **J-boat** *Ranger*, saw that the era of these big boats was coming to an end. With America's Cup competition having been suspended for more than twenty years due to World War II, *Vim* was narrowly edged out by ***Columbia*** to defend the Cup in 1958. "Vim" combined the first letters of the last names of the syndicate's leaders Harold

This photograph of a group of whalers, possibly in Hobart, Tasmania, during the Ross Sea Expedition (1923–24), is one of a large collection taken by Alan Villiers. (Courtesy National Maritime Museum/Villiers Collection, Greenwich, England; photo by Alan Villiers)

Vanderbilt, **Charles Oliver Iselin**, and Charles Morgan.

USS *Vincennes* (CG-49), 567-foot Aegis guided-missile **cruiser** that in 1988, while on patrol in the Arabian Gulf, mistook an Iranian airliner for a hostile aircraft. After issuing ten warnings to the aircraft—all unheeded and unanswered by the Iran Air intruder—*Vincennes* fired two surface-to-air missiles at the plane. Both found their mark, and the Airbus crashed into the gulf, taking the lives of all 290 people on board.

Vinland, name, meaning "vineland" or "wineland," given by early Scandinavian explorers to a region with abundant grapes somewhere on the East Coast of North America. Many historians believe that Norse explorers visited this coastal area almost five hundred years before **Christopher Columbus** sailed to America in 1492. Sites from Newfoundland to Virginia are thought to be the real Vinland, with Nova Scotia and **Cape Cod** the most frequently named.

Vinland map, purported fifteenth-century map depicting Viking exploration of North America centuries before the arrival of **Christopher Columbus**. Its existence was announced in 1965, and its authenticity has been challenged ever since. If genuine, the Vinland map is one of the great documents of Western civilization; if fake, it is an astoundingly clever forgery.

Vinson-Trammell Act, legislation passed by the U.S. Congress in 1934 committing the U.S. government to an expansion of the U.S. **Navy**

despite the Great Depression. Sponsored by Congressman Carl Vinson, of Georgia, and Senator Park Trammel, of Florida, it was prompted by Japan's seizure of Manchuria and by the fact that Japan had built her navy up to 95 percent of the treaty strength set forth in the **Washington Naval Treaty**. U.S. seagoing strength stood at 65 percent.

CSS *Virginia*, Confederate **ironclad** built on the hulk of USS *Merrimack*—and often called by that original name. On March 8, 1862, she destroyed USS *Cumberland* and USS *Congress* in **Hampton Roads**, Virginia, only nine days after being commissioned. The Union ironclad USS *Monitor* arrived from New York the next morning and engaged *Virginia* in the first battle ever to be fought by two ironclad ships. No winner emerged, but the match forever changed the terms of warfare at sea. During the Confederate evacuation of Norfolk less than two months later, *Virginia* was beached on the shore of the James River to avoid capture and was set on fire by her crew.

Virginia of Sagadahock, first oceangoing ship built in America. The fifty-foot **pinnace** was built in 1607 near the mouth of the Sagadahock (now Kennebec) River in Maine by the members of the Popham Colony—the first English settlement in New England. Originally intended for coastal trading, she was used to transport the surviving members of the colony back to England following a severe winter. In 1957 the ship was featured on a U.S. postage stamp commemorating 350 years of shipbuilding in America.

***Virginius* Affair**, 1873 incident that came close to starting a war between the United States and Spain. During a Cuban revolt against Spanish rule, the Spanish gunboat *Tornado* intercepted the ship *Virginius* off Jamaica and claimed the ship was aiding the Cuban rebels. *Virginius* was registered in New York and flew the American flag, and her captain was an American.

Spanish authorities in Cuba executed the captain, thirty-six crew members, and sixteen passengers. U.S. President Ulysses S. Grant threatened military action, and Spain surrendered the ship and the survivors. An investigation later revealed that the *Virginius* was illegally registered and indeed was owned by Cubans. The event spurred the building of the new U.S. **Navy** and the **ABCD Ships**.

MS *Vistafjord*, last ship built for the **Norwegian America Line**. The 24,292-gross-ton motor ship was completed in 1973 for extensive cruise service. Sold to the **Cunard Line** in 1983, she continued operation without a change of name until 2000. Coming under the corporate aegis of **Carnival Cruise Lines**, she was renamed *Caronia* with an eye to cashing in on the transatlantic company's enviable reputation and the legacy of their fabled Green Goddess of 1949.

V-J Day, Victory over Japan Day, which marked the end of World War II. At 7 P.M. on August 14, 1945, President Harry S. Truman announced that Japan had agreed to surrender. **V-E Day** preceded V-J Day by three months. September 2, 1945, has since been declared the official V-J Day because on that day representatives of Japan signed the terms of surrender aboard the battleship USS *Missouri* in Tokyo Bay.

Vladivostok, vital Russian seaport on the Pacific Ocean lying in southeastern Siberia, near the Korean border. A base for naval and fishing fleets, the port was founded in 1860 and became a naval base after Russia lost Port Arthur to Japan in 1905 following the **Russo-Japanese War**.

VLCC, acronym for very large crude carrier, a **supertanker** developed in the 1960s that measured more than two hundred thousand **deadweight tons**. These supertankers were surpassed by the ultra-large crude carrier, or **ULCC**.

Carl Evers's rendering of the Battle of the *Virginia* (nee *Merrimack*) and the *Monitor*, off Newport News, Virginia. (The Greenwich Workshop)

VOC, see **Dutch East India Company**.

Volga River, the longest river in Europe, which flows 2,194 miles through western Russia, from about 200 miles southeast of Saint Petersburg southward to the Caspian Sea. The Volga is frozen for most of its length three months of the year. Ship canals link it with the Baltic Sea, the White Sea, and the **Black Sea** via the Sea of Azov.

Volstead line, the extent of the twelve-mile limit at sea for the enforcement of the Volstead Act, or the Eighteenth Amendment to the Constitution, passed by the U.S. Congress on October 28, 1919, establishing Prohibition (over President Wilson's veto). The line also became known as the "rum line" and "**Rum Row**."

SS *Volturno*, immigrant-cargo ship bound from Rotterdam to New York that caught fire and burned in the mid-**Atlantic** in October 1913. Nine ships responded to the **SOS** calls, but the seas proved too rough to provide assistance. The nearby oil tank steamer *Narragansett* responded to distress calls and, once on scene, released its cargo to reduce the seas so rescue efforts could take place. Of the 657 passengers on board, 136 lost their lives. The loss prompted British officials to prohibit passenger ships from carrying dangerous cargoes.

Volunteer, 1887, painted by Antonio Jacobsen. (Courtesy The Mariners' Museum, Newport News, Virginia)

Volunteer, successful **America's Cup** defender in 1887. Designed by **Edward Burgess** and owned by General Charles J. Paine, the 106-foot **sloop** defeated the British challenger *Thistle*, two races to none.

votive models, ship models that, from as early as the fourteenth century, traditionally hung in the churches of seaports and fishing communities. Suspended from the roofs of the churches, these models were made by sailors as an offering of thanks to a patron saint for having preserved the boat and its crew from the perils of the sea.

voyage charter, charter agreed upon to deliver a particular cargo to a specified port.

The Voyage in the Sunbeam, classic 1879 account of a Victorian voyage around the world in the 1870s in the auxiliary **schooner *Sun-*** *beam*, by Lady **Anna Brassey**, wife of Thomas Brassey, a millionaire member of the British Parliament.

Voyage of Terror: The Achille Lauro Affair, 1990 made-for-television movie retelling the story of the MS *Achille Lauro* hijacking. The tabloid drama was filmed on board the ship at the ports where it all occurred only five years before. The movie starred Burt Lancaster, Eva Marie Saint, and Joseph Nasser.

Voyage of the Damned, novel by Gordon Thomas and Max Morgan-Witts about the story of 937 German-Jewish refugees fleeing Germany aboard the **Hamburg-America liner** SS *St. Louis*. It is also the name of a 1977 film with a star-heavy cast, including Faye Dunaway, Max von Sydow, Malcolm McDowell, and Orson Welles.

The Voyage of the Parma, 1933 narrative by **Alan John Villiers** about the 1932 grain race and his experiences sailing aboard the **bark** *Parma* from Australia to England in 103 days, around **Cape Horn**. Villiers also documented the trip with photographs.

Voyager of the Seas, first of three 142,000-gross-ton passenger ships built for the **Royal Caribbean Cruise Line**. The largest passenger ship ever constructed at the time of her completion, the motor ship made her first cruise from Miami in 1999.

Voyage to the Bottom of the Sea, 1961 science fiction film about the crew of the atomic submarine *Seaview*, who save the earth from a belt of deadly radiation that has set the polar ice caps ablaze. It starred Walter Pidgeon, Joan Fontaine, Barbara Eden, and Peter Lorre, and spurred a popular television series of the same name.

voyageurs, trappers and traders, many of French ancestry, who traveled extensively by canoe along the waterways of the American Upper Midwest in the late eighteenth and early nineteenth centuries.

Vroom, Cornelisz Hendrick (1566–1640), Dutch artist widely regarded as the father of marine painting. His seascapes show a love and understanding of the sea, and his treatment of naval scenes and battles reveals a strong knowledge of ships. His instruction and body of work inspired many followers.

VTS, see **vessel traffic service**.

MS *Vulcania*, beautiful motor vessel built in 1928 for service from Trieste, Italy, to New York, that was absorbed into the creation of the **Italian Line** in 1932. She engaged in various troop services for the Allied forces during World War II and served as a hospital ship. She returned—along with her sister the *Saturnia*—to the transatlantic run in 1947. The 23,970-gross-ton **liner** was sold in 1965 for further trading as the cruise ship *Caribia*, was grounded in 1966 off Nice, France, and was subsequently **laid up**. She was sold for scrap in 1974.

W

The Wackiest Ship in the Army, 1961 motion picture comedy spinning a far-fetched yarn about an old sailing vessel employed during World War II as a decoy to fool Japanese warships. The film starred Jack Lemon and Ricky Nelson.

Waesche, Russell R. (1886–1946), admiral who served as commandant of the U.S. **Coast Guard** from 1936 through 1945. He oversaw the expansion of the service during World War II and is credited with keeping the service's identity intact during its four years under the control of the Navy Department. A total of 231,000 men and 10,000 women served in the Coast Guard during the war.

Wahine, passenger and car ferry completed in 1966 for the interisland service of the Union Steamship Company of New Zealand. She grounded and capsized on April 11, 1968, while approaching Wellington in 123-mile-per-hour gale winds with 750 people on board, 51 of whom lost their lives. The accident prompted serious thought as to the wisdom of having completely glass-enclosed navigating bridge wings, which insulated the ship's officers from the screaming wind, so that the severity of the storm was not at first fully realized by those on duty in the wheelhouse.

USS Wahoo (SS-238), one of the most successful U.S. **Navy** submarines of World War II. During fourteen months of combat duty in the Pacific, *Wahoo* sank nineteen Japanese vessels.

Wake Island, small three-square-mile atoll in the Pacific Ocean two thousand miles west of Hawai'i. The United States claimed Wake in 1898 because it lay on the cable route from San Francisco to Manila, and in 1935, it became a base for air traffic. Two weeks after bombing **Pearl Harbor**, the Japanese captured the island, which at the time had a radio station, a small airstrip with twelve fighters, and a garrison of 525 marines. In taking the island, the Japanese lost two ships, twenty-one aircraft, and 820 men.

The Wake of the Red Witch, 1966 **South Seas** adventure flick that pits a rogue sea captain, played by John Wayne, against a shipping tycoon. The action revolves around a treasure and a beautiful woman.

walking-beam engine, steam engine used aboard **side-wheel** steamers in which an oscillating beam converted the reciprocal motion from the engine to rotary motion for the wheels. It was first used in mills and factories and adapted for use aboard ship.

Walk-in-the-Water, 135-foot **steamboat** designed by **Robert Fulton** that in 1818 introduced steam power to the upper **Great Lakes**. She was built to provide passenger service from Black Rock, New York, above Niagara Falls, to Detroit, Michigan. Her name was derived from the description given by an American Indian after seeing Fulton's *Clermont* ply its way upstream without sails. *Walk-in-the-Water* was wrecked in 1821, but her engine went on to be used in two other steamers.

Walters, Samuel (1811–1882), English marine artist born at sea, the son of marine artist Miles Walters (1774–1849). Often collaborating with his father, he is best known for chronicling the Port of Liverpool during its greatest shipping boom.

Walton, Izaak (1593–1683), English author best known for his book on fishing, ***The Compleat Angler*** (1653). The book, which combines practical information about fish and fishing with songs, poems, and descriptions of country life and the English countryside, went through four revisions during the author's lifetime.

Wanderer, **Sterling Hayden**'s 1963 autobiography. It recounts the story of his 1959 voyage to Tahiti with his children aboard his **schooner** *Wanderer* after a California court threatened to take the children away.

War and Remembrance, novelist **Herman Wouk**'s 1978 follow-up to his epic *The **Winds** of War* (1971). The sequel follows naval events from **Pearl Harbor** through World War II and the effects of war on Victor "Pug" Henry, a U.S. **Navy** officer, and his family. It was made into a lengthy miniseries in 1989, starring Robert Mitchum, Jane Seymour, Polly Bergen, Sharon Stone, Robert Morley, Barry Bostwick, and William Schallert.

SS *Waratah*, 9,339-gross-ton **liner** built for the Australian service of the Blue Anchor Line of London. On her second homeward voyage, the ship disappeared July 28, 1909, during a wild storm off of the **Cape of Good Hope**, taking with her the lives of her crew and all ninety-two passengers. No wreckage was ever found.

USS *Ward* (DD-139), U.S. **Navy destroyer** that on the morning of December 7, 1941, was conducting a precautionary patrol off the entrance to **Pearl Harbor**. She encountered a Japanese midget submarine and sank it, thus firing the first shots of World War II in the Pacific a few hours before the Japanese attack on the U.S. fleet inside the harbor.

wardroom, commissioned officers' mess and lounge area on U.S. **Navy** and **Coast Guard** vessels.

War of 1812, war declared on Great Britain by the United States to defend American interests in North America, including plans to "liberate" Canada; to protect the rights of American ships at sea in the face of British naval impressment of American seamen; and to effect retribution for the capture of American ships carrying neutral goods during the Napoleonic Wars. The firing by HMS *Leopard* on USS *Chesapeake* on June 22, 1807, was one of several provocations building up war tensions. The war ended with the **Treaty of Ghent** in 1814, with no significant gains for either side but with strengthened respect for the American flag at sea.

HMS *Warrior*, 418-foot **Royal Navy frigate** launched in 1860 as the first fully **ironclad** ship and the most technically advanced of her day. Napoleon III of France, calling *Warrior* "a black snake among the rabbits," called off the naval armament race with the British when he learned of her qualities. She was restored in the 1980s and placed on public display at the Portsmouth Naval Base, England.

War Shipping Administration (WSA), **merchant marine** governing body established by the U.S. Congress in early 1942 to control the operation, purchase, charter, requisition, and use of all oceangoing merchant vessels under the flag or control of the United States during World War II. The WSA was terminated in September 1946, and its remaining functions were returned to the U.S. **Maritime Commission**. In all, the United States constructed 5,500 merchant ships during the war, of which 700 were lost and 640 were so badly damaged that they had to be scrapped.

The War with Cape Horn, an account by **Cape Horn** veteran **Alan John Villiers** of various experiences rounding Cape Horn in **square-riggers** in stormy 1905. The work quotes liberally from ships' logs and officers' journals and memoirs as well as personal interviews by Villiers, who was well respected by everyone he interviewed.

SS *Washington*, **United States Lines** steamer built in 1933 for service with her sister ship SS *Manhattan*. She operated as the troop transport USS *Mount Vernon* during World War II, then reverted to *Washington* in 1946 and resumed passenger operations. The 24,289-gross-ton **liner** was **laid up** in 1951 and finally scrapped in 1965.

USS *Washington* (BB-47), final unit of the four Colorado-class battleships, which was laid down in 1919. Construction on the 624-foot battleship was halted in 1922 to comply with the terms of the newly signed **Washington Naval Treaty**. The 75 percent completed ship was towed out to sea to be used in underwater demolition tests and as a target for gunnery practice, during which she was sunk in 1924.

USS *Washington* (BB-56), 729-foot U.S. battleship completed in 1941 as the second of two **North Carolina**–class battleships that were the first designed with high enough speed—over twenty-seven **knots**—to allow them to steam with aircraft carrier task forces. In March 1942 *Washington* sailed for Great Britain as the **flagship** of Rear Admiral John W. Wilcox. During the crossing, Wilcox was lost overboard, presumably after suffering a heart attack. After **convoy** duty in the Atlantic, the 36,600-ton vessel was ordered into the war in the Pacific. Her main armament of nine 16-inch guns pelted the enemy strongholds at **Guadalcanal** and sank the Japanese battleship *Kirishima* off the Solomon Islands. The $77 million vessel participated in further action against the enemy at the Gilbert Islands, the Philippine Sea, **Leyte Gulf**, **Iwo Jima**, and **Okinawa**. Decorated with thirteen battle stars for her performance during World War II, she was decommissioned in 1947 and finally scrapped in 1961.

Washington Naval Treaty, international agreement signed by principal naval powers (the United States, Great Britain, France, Italy, and Japan) in 1922 to limit their naval strength. A product of World War I, the treaty, signed in Washington, D.C., and extended in 1930 in London (often called the London Treaty), set the number of ships permitted to each nation, including **tonnage** and armament limitations. It allowed six months to demilitarize excess vessels and eighteen months to demolish the same. The ship types affected were **capital ships**—battleships and battle **cruisers**. The treaties became widely disregarded as World War II approached.

Washington's Navy, group of vessels chartered by General George Washington and the Continental Army to confiscate military equipment from British ships in order to sustain the siege on Boston. Between April 1775 and March 1776, the seagoing raiders captured a total of fifty-five prizes. The success of Washington's Navy led the Continental Congress to establish the **Continental Navy**.

USS *Wasp*, sloop of war commissioned in 1806. In October 1812, during the **War of 1812**, she engaged in a heated battle with HMS *Frolic* off the entrance to Delaware Bay. *Wasp* was captured when a British **ship of the line** showed up, and she was taken into the **Royal Navy**.

USS *Wasp* (CV-7), aircraft carrier built in 1940 and deployed on the Atlantic and Mediterranean until transfer to the Pacific theater of war in 1942. The 14,700-ton, 809-foot ship participated in the assault on **Guadalcanal.** While off San Cristobal Island in 1942, she was hit by two Japanese torpedoes, which touched off a series of devastating fires on board. After she was evacuated, *Wasp* was sent to the bottom by three coup-de-grace torpedoes from USS *Lansdowne.*

USS *Wasp* (CV-18), 27,100-ton **Essex-class** aircraft carrier commissioned in 1943. The 872-foot vessel sent strikes against the **Marshall Islands, Wake Island**, Saipan, **Iwo Jima**, Mindanao, and the Battle of **Leyte Gulf**. In one week during March 1945, *Wasp*'s planes destroyed twenty enemy aircraft, hit two Japanese carriers with five-hundred-pound bombs, severely damaged two Japanese battleships with one-thousand-pound bomb hits, struck a Japanese **destroyer** with three five-hundred-pound bombs, hit a freighter with a one-thousand-pound bomb, and sank a Japanese submarine. She recovered astronauts James A. Lovell and Edwin "Buzz" Aldrin from their *Gemini XII* space capsule after its splashdown in the Pacific in 1966. The veteran carrier was decommissioned in 1972 and scrapped the following year.

Watch, Quarter and Station Bill, list posted aboard U.S. **Navy** and **Coast Guard** vessels of the crew's assignments, such as watches at sea and in port as well as during emergencies and battle conditions.

Water Music, airy orchestra piece by composer George Frederic Handel (1685–1759) that debuted for King George I during a festival that took place on boats on the Thames River in England.

Waterman, Cameron (1878–1934), American inventor who was responsible for the first water-cooled production portable engine, which he named the "outboard" in 1907.

Waterman Steamship Company, U.S.-flag shipping line organized in 1919 by John B. Waterman to provide ocean transportation services from the Gulf of Mexico to Europe. In 1955 it was purchased by **Malcolm McLean** to provide a platform for his experiment of carrying truck containers aboard ship. Sold again in 1965, the company filed for bankruptcy protection in 1983. The reorganized concern was acquired by the International Shipholding Corporation in 1988 and today operates **LASH** vessels and **liner** service between the U.S. Atlantic and Gulf coasts and the Mediterranean, Middle East, India, and Southeast Asia.

"Water, water everywhere, nor any drop to drink", lines from "The **Rime of the Ancient Mariner**" (1798) by **Samuel Taylor Coleridge**.

Waterworld, wildly expensive 1995 science fiction movie about post–global warming life and survival at sea after the polar icecaps have melted. Often thought-provoking and always innovative, the film has an unexpected twist of historical fate for the ***Exxon Valdez***. The film stars Kevin Costner as the mutant Mariner,

Jeanne Tripplehorne as Helen, and Dennis Hopper as the Deacon.

Watson, George L. (1851–1904), prolific British yacht designer best known for designing the **cutter** *Britannia* for the Prince of Wales (later Edward VII), as well as the **America's Cup** challengers *Thistle*, *Valkyrie II*, and *Valkyrie III*. He used tank testing of scale models for the first time in sailing history for his design of Sir **Thomas Lipton**'s *Shamrock II*. He also designed *Meteor* and *Meteor II* for Kaiser **Wilhelm II**.

Watson and the Shark, powerful 1778 painting by painter **John Singleton Copley** that is considered the first marine painting by an American artist. Copley based the painting on the real-life trauma of Brook Watson, a fourteen-year-old English boy who lost a leg to a shark while swimming in Havana Harbor in 1749. Watson later went on to become the lord mayor of London. The painting, which excited and shocked the public when introduced, hangs in the National Gallery of Art in Washington, D.C.

Waugh, Frederick Judd (1861–1940), celebrated American marine artist who is best known for painting bright, colorful seascapes, filled with sparkling sunlight and great smashing breakers. In 1927 he settled on **Cape Cod** and built a studio out of old ship's timbers. His works hang in many museums in the United States, including the Metropolitan Museum of Art in New York and the Corcoran Gallery of Art and the National Gallery in Washington, D.C.

Wavertree, 270-foot, English-built **square-rigger** launched in 1885 for the cargo trade between Scotland and India. The 2,170-gross-ton vessel was one of the very last to be constructed of iron. It became an Argentine sand barge in 1947 and, through the efforts of **Karl Kortum**, was eventually acquired by the **South Street Seaport Museum** in 1968 for restoration as a museum ship.

WAVES, acronym for Women Accepted for Voluntary Emergency Service, the World War II designation of women serving in the U.S. **Navy**. This was prior to the authorization by Congress in 1948 of the enlistment of women in the regular Navy and **Naval Reserve**.

The Way of a Ship, comprehensive 1953 account by **Alan John Villiers** of how things worked aboard an oceangoing **square-rigged** vessel.

Weatherly, **Philip Rhodes**–designed **twelve-meter** yacht, **skippered** by Emil Mosbacher, that successfully defended the **America's Cup** against the Australian challenger *Gretel* in 1962. President **John F. Kennedy** witnessed the four-to-one race series victory off Newport, Rhode Island, from the decks of the **destroyer** USS *Joseph P. Kennedy* (named for his brother).

weather routing, procedure to use weather and sea forecasts to plot the optimum route for a vessel, given the voyage and the ship's characteristics. Weather routing seeks to maximize safety and crew comfort and to minimize fuel consumption and transit time.

Webb, William Henry (1816–1899), pioneer American naval architect and shipbuilder who is considered the doyen of American shipbuilding. Webb was active at his East River, New York, yard from 1840 until 1869, and during this period he contracted for, designed, and supervised the construction of all types of vessels, including fishing **schooners**, ferryboats, fast sailing **packets**, **clipper ships**, and large ocean and coastwise **steamships**, as well as **ironclad** warships for European navies. Webb spent a long retirement in other pursuits, the most lasting of which were the **Webb Institute** and the **Society of Naval Architects and Marine Engineers**.

Webber, John (1752–1793), British draftsman and artist who accompanied Captain **James Cook** on his third voyage (1776–79) aboard HMS *Resolution*.

Webb Institute, fully accredited college and research institute that offers full-tuition scholarships and undergraduate and graduate degrees in naval architecture and marine engineering and in ocean technology and commerce. Founded and endowed by **William Henry Webb** in 1889, the school was established to provide a more formal and detailed education for the shipbuilding trade. Originally Webb's Academy and Home for Retired Shipbuilders, the name was changed in 1920 to the Webb Institute of Naval Architecture. In 1947 it moved from Fordham Heights in the Bronx, New York, to Glen Cove, Long Island, New York. The name was again shortened in 1994.

Weddell, James (1787–1834), British explorer who discovered the Weddell Sea in the South Atlantic in 1824 and set a long-standing record for the highest southern **latitude** reached (74°15′ South).

We Dive at Dawn, World War II submarine drama filmed in Britain during the war itself. Counted on to lure new recruits into the **Royal Navy**, the film details the fictitious tale of HMS *Sea Tiger* and her underwater hunt for the new Nazi battleship *Brandenburg*. The 1943 motion picture featured John Mills and Louis Bradfield.

A Week on the Concord and Merrimack Rivers, 1849 narrative by **Henry David Thoreau** that chronicles a boat trip he and his brother took to the White Mountains in New Hampshire. The book includes romantic descriptions of nature and thoughtful discussions of literature, philosophy, and history.

Weems & Plath, manufacturer of navigation instruments founded in 1928 as the Weems System of Navigation, Co., by Captain Philip Van Horn Weems, an instructor of navigation at the U.S. **Naval Academy**. The present trade name was first used after World War II, when the company became the exclusive distributor of **sextants** and magnetic compasses pro-

duced in Germany by C. Plath. C. Plath was founded in 1837 by Carl Plath.

Wegener, Alfred (1880–1930), German meteorologist and geologist who in 1912 was the first person to set forth continental drift as a scientific theory. His theory was confirmed in the 1960s by the Deep Sea Drilling Project and the ship *Glomar Challenger*.

"We have met the enemy and they are ours", message sent by Commodore **Oliver Hazard Perry** to Major General William Henry Harrison following the American victory at the September 10, 1813, Battle of **Lake Erie** during the **War of 1812**.

Welland Ship Canal, Canadian canal opened in 1829 that provides a twenty-seven-mile navigable waterway around Niagara Falls between Lake Ontario and Lake Erie. Greatly improved over the years, it today forms an important part of the **Saint Lawrence Seaway**. Lake Erie is about 325 feet higher than Lake Ontario, so ships must be raised and lowered by a series of eight locks.

Welles, Gideon (1802–1878), U.S. secretary of the **Navy** under Presidents **Abraham Lincoln** and Andrew Johnson. Lincoln appointed Welles at the start of the Civil War, in 1861, and under his supervision, the Union navy added about six hundred ships and grew from 7,500 sailors to more than 50,000. It also set up a blockade along the Confederate coast and formed a fleet of gunboats and **ironclad** vessels on the **Mississippi River**.

We're Here, fictional **Gloucester schooner** in **Joseph Rudyard Kipling**'s *Captains Courageous* (1897).

Westerdam, the original 42,095-gross-ton Home Lines *Homeric* built in 1986 for cruise service out of New York. Sold to the **Holland America Line** in 1988 and renamed *Westerdam*, she was cut in half in 1989, and a 128-foot midbody section was inserted to increase her earning capacity, thereby raising her **gross registered tonnage** to 58,872 tons.

Western Ocean, the **Atlantic Ocean**—so named because it stood to the west as seen by the Europeans who first crossed it.

Western rivers, generally used to refer to the 6,500 miles of navigable waterways of the **Mississippi River** system, also encompassing the Ohio, Missouri, Illinois, Tennessee, Cumberland, Arkansas, and White Rivers. This system includes four Louisiana ports that are among the ten top-tonnage ports in the United States: South Louisiana, New Orleans, Baton Rouge, and Plaquemine.

West Indies, chain of islands stretching from the coast of Florida to the coast of South America, separating the Caribbean Sea from the Atlantic Ocean. They are divided into the **Windward Islands** to the south and the **Leeward Islands** to the north. The West Indies were named by **Christopher Columbus** in 1492 because he believed that he had reached the East Indies, then known simply as "the Indies." When the error was discovered, the two Indies became "East" and "West."

USS *West Virginia* (BB-48), last unit of the Colorado-class battleships to be completed. Commissioned in 1923, the vessel was hit by six torpedoes during the attack on **Pearl Harbor** and settled to the bottom of the harbor on an even keel. The "Weevee" was raised and after extensive repairs was ready for action in 1944. She took part in the assaults on **Leyte Gulf**, the Surigao Straits, Mindoro, **Iwo Jima**, and **Okinawa**, and she sailed into Tokyo Bay in 1945 as part of the American occupation forces. **Laid up** two years later, she was sold for scrap in 1959.

Westward, 135-foot **schooner** built in 1910 by the **Herreshoff** Manufacturing Company for New York industrialist Alexander S. Cochran. Known as the "Herreshoff Flyer," she was **skip**-

pered by **Charles Barr**. *Westward* was victorious at the 1910 Kiel Regatta against *Meteor IV* and *Meteor III* (renamed *Nordstern*) and went on to win many other races. When Barr died, *Westward* was purchased by a German and renamed *Hamburg II*. After World War I, she had various British owners, and in the summer of 1947 she was **scuttled** off the coast of Dartmouth, England.

whaleback, steamer or barge with a convex upper deck, cigar-shaped hull, and blunt bow with no masts, spars, or bulwarks. The unorthodox design was pioneered in the United States by **Alexander McDougall** to maximize carrying capacity while minimizing resistance from wind and waves. More than forty of the ships were constructed, mostly for the **Great Lakes**. Often referred to as a turtleback, turtle deck, or pig steamer.

whaleboat, double-ended seaworthy motor boat used aboard ships as a lifeboat and general utility boat. Originally, the design was a pulling boat used for whaling.

whale oil, clear brownish oil extracted from the blubber of whales, which from the sixteenth century to the nineteenth century was used for making soap and as fuel for lighting.

wharfage, charge made to a cargo vessel for the use of a wharf, pier, or dock.

wharf rats, name applied to vagrant petty thieves who loitered near the waterfront. It is also used for several clubs of retired mariners and waterfront workers.

wherry, a light pulling boat with a transom stern.

Whiskey Galore, 1948 British comedy about the residents of a small Scottish isle during World War II who find their liquor supplies suddenly replenished when a ship carrying fifty thousand cases of Scotch flounders off their coast. The film, released as *Tight Little Island* in the United

Whaleback vessel *John Ericsson* in Duluth.

States, was based on the novel by Compton Mackenzie about the real-life freighter *Politician*, which ran aground in the Outer Hebrides in February 1941 while en route to the United States with a cargo of Scotch. The film starred Basil Radford, Joan Greenwood, and James Robertson Justice.

Whistler, James Abbott McNeill (1834–1903), American artist who painted many seascapes and river scenes in addition to his better known *Arrangement in Gray and Black No. 1: Portrait of the Artist's Mother* (1872), commonly called *Whistler's Mother*. From November 1854 to February 1855, Whistler worked as a chartmaker for the **U.S. Coast and Geodetic Survey**, where he received training in the technique of etching.

Whitbread Race, 31,600-nautical-mile, round-the-world, crewed sailing race that is run every four years. Initiated in 1973, the race sets out from Southampton, England, and heads east for six legs. It is officially called the Whitbread Round the World Race and is sponsored by the British brewer Whitbread PLC.

whitecaps, broken water at the top of a wave that is breaking at sea due to wind. They generally begin to form with winds of twelve **knots**. In the old days, they were referred to as "**Neptune**'s sheep."

Whitehall, site of the chief British government buildings, including the **Admiralty**, in the district of Westminster, London.

Whitehall boat, multipurpose rowing boat, named for Whitehall Street at the southern tip of Manhattan, New York, where they were first employed to transport **pilots**, chandlers, and agents.

whitehat, U.S. **Navy** and **Coast Guard** term for an enlisted person.

Whitehead torpedo, the first self-propelled torpedo, which was invented in 1866 by British engineer Robert Whitehead. The Austrian navy acquired rights to the weapon in 1869, and the **Royal Navy** followed in 1871.

White-Jacket, 1850 allegorical novel by **Herman Melville** that depicts the harsh life of a seaman onboard the nineteenth-century U.S. **Navy frigate** USS *Neversink*. His descriptions of the use of flogging as corporal punishment aboard naval vessels helped lead to the U.S. Congress abolishing the practice. The work was based on Melville's stint as a navy seaman aboard the frigate USS *United States*.

white squall, strong, sudden gust of wind coming up without clouds and without warning. It is usually noted by **whitecaps**.

White Squall, epic 1995 action-packed motion picture about the ill-fated cruise of the sail training ship *Albatros* in 1961 with a crew of teenage boys. Based on a true story, the film starred Jeff Bridges and Caroline Goodall.

White Star Line, preeminent British shipping firm founded in 1869 as the Oceanic Steam Navigation Company Limited. Its ships were primarily engaged in passenger transportation and were named with the familiar "ic" ending—*Olympic*, *Titanic*, and *Majestic*, among others. It merged with the **Cunard Line** in 1934 to eliminate British competition on the North Atlantic at the behest of Parliament in return for funds to complete the then-abandoned hull that eventually came to be launched as RMS *Queen Mary*. "White Star" dropped from the Cunard White Star name in 1950, and the *Britannic*, the last ship to built for the White Star Line, went to the scrapyard in 1960.

Whitman, Walt (1819–1892), American poet best known for his work *Leaves of Grass*—a collection of poems that is considered one of the world's major literary works. The seas provided him with endless inspiration, and **"O Captain! My Captain!"**—a poem written about Abra-

ham Lincoln's death—remains popular. Other nautical poems of his include "Song for All Seas," "All Ships," "The Dismantled Ship," "Passage to India," and "Crossing Brooklyn Ferry."

Whitney, William C. (1841–1904), secretary of the navy credited with ushering in the modern U.S. **Navy**. In the years after the Civil War, the navy's wooden ships had fallen into disrepair, and by 1880 the United States stood twelfth among world naval powers. In 1883 Whitney coordinated the construction of four steel **cruisers** known as the **ABCD Ships**—*Atlanta, Boston, Chicago,* and *Dolphin*. By the time Whitney left office in 1889, twenty-two vessels had been built or authorized. Whitney's actions encouraged the development of domestic steelworks, and he is also credited with launching what came to be known as the military-industrial complex.

WHOI, see **Woods Hole Oceanographic Institute**.

Whydah, one-hundred-foot slave ship that was captured by the pirate **Samuel Bellamy** off the Bahamas in 1717. Bellamy made *Whydah* his **flagship** and later attempted to sail her to Provincetown on **Cape Cod**. In April 1717 the ship was wrecked off Wellfleet, and Bellamy and most of his crew were drowned. The wreck of the *Whydah* was discovered in the 1980s, and **salvage** work has been ongoing. *Whydah* was named for the seaport in modern-day Benin, Africa, that was founded as a French trading port in the seventeenth century and was a major center of the African slave trade.

Wianno Junior, **one-design**-class centerboard **sloop** design by H. Manley Crosby. It has a length of sixteen feet, six inches; a beam of six feet; and a fixed draft of one foot, six inches.

Wianno Senior, **one-design**-class keel and centerboard **sloop** design by H. Manley Crosby. It has a length of twenty-five feet, a beam of eight feet, and a fixed draft of two feet, six inches.

widow's walk, railed rooftop platform typically on a coastal house. It was originally designed to observe vessels at sea.

Wilcox, Crittendon and Company, well-known manufacturer of marine hardware, which was founded in 1847 in Middletown, Connecticut.

Wilhelm II (1859–1941), German emperor and king of Prussia from 1888 to 1918. He was a grandson of Great Britain's Queen Victoria and was always impressed with England's mighty fleet and naval history. He was a yachting enthusiast and a proponent of a strong German navy. His personal sailing yachts included five boats named *Meteor*, and he was the sponsor of the 1905 **Kaiser's Cup**. He was aboard his 382-foot, opulent steam yacht *Hohenzollern* upon news of the outbreak of World War I. He abdicated on November 9, 1918, and went into exile in Holland. The Allies declared him a war criminal and demanded his extradition in 1920, but the Dutch refused to comply and he remained in Holland until his death.

SS *Wilhelm Güstloff*, 25,484-gross-ton **liner** completed in 1938 for the Nazi government and operated on state-organized "Strength Through Joy" cruises by the Hamburg–South America Line. Named for a Swiss Nazi leader, she was torpedoed on January 30, 1945, by a Soviet submarine while attempting to evacuate over 6,100 (some accounts go as high as 8,000) refugees from the city of Danzig, in the face of advancing Soviet troops. The liner capsized and sank leaving only 904 survivors.

Wilkes, Charles (1798–1877), American naval officer and explorer who, from 1838 to 1842, led the **Wilkes Expedition**. In 1842, the navy court-martialed Wilkes on numerous charges of poor conduct but found him guilty only of illegally whipping members of his crew. He served on special duty from 1843 to 1861, mainly writing a five-volume narrative of his expedition's findings. Wilkes was a key figure in the **Trent Affair** of 1861, a naval incident that nearly made Britain an ally of the Confederacy in the Civil War.

Wilkes Expedition, U.S. **Navy** expedition of 1838–42, commanded by Lieutenant **Charles Wilkes** aboard the USS *Vincennes*, to collect scientific data, prove Antarctica was a continent rather than a huge ice pack, and seek commercial opportunities in the Pacific. It was also known as the Great United States Exploring Expedition. The three surviving ships of the initial six sailed more than 85,000 miles, charted 280 islands, and sailed along 1,500 miles of the Antarctic coast, proving that it was a continent. The collection of samples brought back by the expedition formed the core of the Smithsonian Institution.

Wilkinson, Norman (1878–1971), British-born marine artist and illustrator who painted many yachting scenes and covered Sir **Thomas Lipton**'s second attempt to win the **America's Cup** in 1901. During World War I, Wilkinson conceived the idea of **dazzle-painting** camouflage to protect ships from the omnipresent **U-boat** threat. The bold abstract patterns were intended to break up the constructional lines so that when viewed through an enemy periscope, a ship's range, course, and speed were difficult to estimate. Wilkinson moved to America to supervise the painting of hundreds of ships.

SS *William G. Mather*, **flagship** of the Cleveland-Cliffs Iron Company when completed in 1925. The 618-foot-long straight-deck bulk carrier remained in service on the **Great Lakes** until **laid up** at Toledo, Ohio, in 1980. In 1987 she was donated by the owners to the Great Lakes Historical Society and, after a $1.8 million restoration, has become a well-patronized museum ship on the Cleveland waterfront.

USS *Williamsburg*, the last grand presidential yacht. The 243-foot ship was built in 1930 at **Bath Iron Works** as the personal motor yacht of paper magnate Hugh Chisholm and was named *Aras* after his wife, Sara. The ship received her new name as a U.S. **Navy** patrol boat in World War II before becoming the presidential yacht of Harry S. Truman. Mothballed by **Dwight D. Eisenhower**, she served as the National Science Foundation vessel *Anton Bruun* and later was employed as a floating restaurant before being towed to Europe in 1994 for an extensive refit.

SS *Willis B. Boyer*, **Great Lakes** iron ore carrier built in 1911 as the *Col. James M. Schoonmaker*. She was sold in 1969 for further inland waterway trading and renamed. The 8,603-gross-ton vessel was **laid up** in 1980 and purchased by the city of Toledo, Ohio, in 1986. She was opened at International Park on the east bank of the Maumee River in 1987 as a museum ship dedicated to the history and lore of the Great Lakes.

Wind, panoramic 1992 adventure movie detailing the efforts of an American sailor determined to win back the **America's Cup** from its Australian defenders. The film starred Matthew Modine, Jennifer Grey, and Cliff Robertson.

The Wind in the Willows, series of animal tales written by Kenneth Grahame (1859–1932) and published in 1908. Considered a classic of children's literature, the book chronicles the adventures of four animal friends: Mole, Rat, Toad, and Badger. The book is well known for the line spoken by Ratty to Mole, "Believe me, my young friend, there is nothing—absolutely nothing—half so much worth doing as simply messing about in boats."

windjammer, a **square-rigged** sailing ship. The term was first used derisively when the advent of **steamships** made nineteenth-century seamen look scornfully upon vessels that still relied on wind power.

The Winds of War, best-selling 1971 **Herman Wouk** novel about Victor "Pug" Henry, a U.S. naval envoy who witnesses firsthand the beginnings of World War II. It was made into a

lengthy award-winning television miniseries in 1983, starring Robert Mitchum, Ali MacGraw, Polly Bergen, and Peter Graves. The story continued into Wouk's sequel, ***War and Remembrance***.

Windward Islands, group of islands in the southeastern **West Indies** that stretch around the eastern end of the Caribbean Sea to South America. So named because they are exposed to northeast trade winds, the Windward group consists of Dominica, Martinique, Saint Lucia, Grenada, Saint Vincent, and the Grenadine chain.

wine-dark sea, a description of the Mediterranean Sea in **Homer's** *Iliad*.

A Wing and a Prayer, somewhat melodramatic and less-than-factual Hollywood rendition of the Battle of **Midway** saga. The 1944 film is loaded with good naval action footage, however. It starred Dana Andrews, Don Ameche, and Sir Cedric Hardwicke.

wing and wing, describes a sailboat under way, running downwind with one sail to one side and another to the other. This arrangement of sails exposes the maximum sail area to a following breeze. It is also known as "reading both pages."

Winslow, Don, fictional naval intelligence officer who originally appeared in the 1930s comic strip "Don Winslow of the Navy" and later was the subject of books and short films. Winslow, assisted by Lieutenant Red Pennington, was assigned to handle the major individual threats to world peace, and he battled the likes of the Scorpion, Dr. Centaur, and the Crocodile. A book series and thirteen episodes of *Don Winslow of the Navy* (1942) and another thirteen of *Don Winslow of the Coast Guard* (1943) made him the hero of many American teenagers in World War II.

Winslow, John Ancrum (1811–1873), U.S. naval officer who commanded USS *Kearsarge* when it sank the **Confederate raider** CSS *Alabama* off Cherbourg, France, in 1864.

USS *Wisconsin* (BB-64), final **Iowa**-class battleship to be completed. The "Whisky" was commissioned in 1944 and saw action while being assigned to carrier task forces in the South Pacific. She was used to shell enemy targets in North Korea in the early 1950s. When she damaged her stem in a 1956 collision, the bow of her unfinished sister ship *Kentucky* was used for a replacement. Decommissioned in 1958, the withdrawal of the *Wisconsin* left the U.S. **Navy** without a battleship for the first time since 1896. She was brought back to service in 1986 for patrols in the Mediterranean and Middle East. As of 2000, the *Wisconsin* was **laid up** at the Norfolk Naval Yard.

wolf pack, group of up to forty **U-boats** that roamed the shipping lanes and sank thousands of Allied merchant ships during World War II. The U.S. **Navy** later modified this tactic to use in operations against the Japanese in the Pacific.

women and children first, phrase known as the **Birkenhead drill**, from the wreck of HMS *Birkenhead* in February 1852.

Women's Royal Naval Service (WRNS), the support units of Britain's **Royal Navy**, which placed women in charge of administrative duties as well as **radar**, radio and specialized communications, and meteorology. Established during World War I, it reached its numerical peak in September 1944, with 74,620 women in uniform. The U.S. equivalents were the **WAVES** (for the U.S. **Navy**) and **SPARS** (for the U.S. **Coast Guard**). The service was fully absorbed into the Royal Navy in 1994.

Wood, Garfield A. "Gar" (1880–1971), American inventor and boatbuilder who was an early pioneer of speedboat racing. In 1905 Wood, nicknamed the "Silver Fox," reached speeds on the water of five miles an hour, and in 1930 he set a

world record of 102.256 miles an hour in *Miss America X*. He won the British **Harmsworth Trophy** every year from 1929 to 1933 and also captured the **Gold Cup** four times between 1917 and 1921. Wood founded the **Gar Wood** Boat Company, which manufactured a line of production **runabouts** from 1921 to 1948. Wood's fortune stemmed from his invention of a hydraulic hoist for dump trucks.

Woodman, Richard (b. 1944), English mariner and author of nautical fiction ranging from the **Royal Navy** of **Horatio Nelson**'s time to the modern day. His highly acclaimed Nathaniel Drinkwater Adventure Series includes some fourteen novels, starting with *An Eye of the Fleet* (1981).

Woods Hole Oceanographic Institution (WHOI), a private, nonprofit research center for marine science located on **Cape Cod**, at Woods Hole, Massachusetts. Founded in 1930, it has a variety of laboratories on shore and several research vessels for exploring the oceans, including a small deep-diving submarine. Scientists at the institution pursue research in such fields as marine biology, chemistry, geology and geophysics, physics, and engineering. The institution awards doctoral degrees and offers programs for advanced undergraduates and postdoctoral students. The town of Woods Hole was the first site of the U.S. Commission of Fish and Fisheries, today the **National Marine Fisheries Service**.

Worden, John Lorimar (1818–1897), U.S. naval officer who commanded USS *Monitor* in battle against CSS *Virginia* at the Battle of **Hampton Roads** in 1862. During the fight, Worden was temporarily blinded. He served as superintendent of the U.S. **Naval Academy** (1869–74), was promoted to admiral in 1872, and commanded the European squadron (1875–77).

The World in His Arms, 1952 action film, set in and around 1850s San Francisco, about a Russian countess fleeing an arranged marriage to a Russian prince who takes passage on the ship *Pilgrim* on a voyage to Alaska—then part of Russia. After she is kidnapped by the prince, Captain Jonathan Clark, played by Gregory Peck, employs the help of rival sealer Anthony Quinn and other **Barbary Coast** vagrants to help rescue her. The film contains some of the best sailing footage ever of fishing **schooners** under way.

World Maritime Day, annual day set aside to focus attention on the importance of shipping safety and the marine environment and to emphasize a particular aspect of the **International Maritime Organization**. The exact date is left to individual governments but is usually celebrated during the last week of September. The United States celebrates National Maritime Day on May 22 to commemorate the sailing of the *Savannah*—the first **steamship** to cross the Atlantic—on that day in 1819.

World Maritime University, higher education institute established by the **International Maritime Organization** in 1983 in Malmo, Sweden, to provide advanced training for men and women involved in maritime administration, education, and management around the world.

A World of My Own, 1970 book by **Robin Knox-Johnston** about his winning the 1969 Golden Globe Race for the first solo, nonstop circumnavigation of the world. He overcame countless setbacks and was the only entrant to finish, also receiving the £5,000 prize for the fastest finish.

World Port Index, biannual U.S. government publication that contains the location, characteristics, known facilities, and available services of major ports, shipping facilities, and oil terminals throughout the world (approximately sixty-four thousand entries).

Worth, Claud (1864–1936), British surgeon, yachtsman, and author. His book *Yacht Cruis-*

ing (1910) is considered a classic among cruising aficionados. He also wrote *Yacht Navigation and Voyaging* (1927).

Wouk, Herman (b. 1915), popular American novelist and playwright who has based many of his most successful books on his experiences serving in the U.S. **Navy** during World War II. Wouk won the 1952 Pulitzer Prize for fiction for *The Caine Mutiny* (1951), and he adapted part of the novel for the play *The Caine Mutiny Court-Martial* (1954). His historical novels *The Winds of War* (1971) and *War and Remembrance* (1978) were made into a popular television miniseries. His *Don't Stop the Carnival* (1995) is about Americans abroad in the Caribbean.

Wrangel, Ferdinand von (1794–1870), Russian naval officer who led an expedition into the Siberian Arctic from 1820 to 1824 that greatly increased knowledge about the region. In 1830 he became governor of Alaska, and later, while serving as the Russian minister of the navy, he opposed the sale of Alaska and was forced to retire. Wrangel Island is named for him.

"Wreck of the Deutschland", poem written by Gerard Manley Hopkins, published posthumously in 1918, that commemorates the death of five Franciscan nuns, exiled from Germany, who drowned when their ship, the *Deutschland*, grounded off England in December 1875.

"The Wreck of the *Edmund Fitzgerald*", hit 1976 folksong by Canadian troubadour Gordon Lightfoot that retells the grim demise of the giant **Great Lakes** ore carrier *Edmund Fitzgerald*. The seven stanzas of unrhyming lyrics capture the unpredictability of the harsh weather that sent the ship to the bottom of Lake Superior, with all twenty-nine crew members, in 1975.

"The Wreck of the Hesperus", one of the most recognizable ballads by **Henry Wadsworth Longfellow**. First published in 1840, it was based upon the events of an 1839 gale in which a young girl washed ashore near Gloucester, Massachusetts. The poem begins: "It was the schooner *Hesperus*, That sailed the wintry sea; And the **skipper** had taken his little daughter, To bear him company."

The Wreck of the Mary Deare, 1956 best-selling novel by **Hammond Innes** about a **salvage** vessel that comes across a **Liberty ship** that has been set afire and abandoned by its crew, with only the crazy captain aboard. Alfred Hitchcock developed ideas to make the novel into a film but eventually gave up on the project, believing that the story was too strong to begin with. In 1959 MGM used the script Hitchcock had worked on to make a movie, starring Charlton Heston and Gary Cooper, that turned out to be an enormous failure.

WRNS, see **Women's Royal Naval Service**.

WSA, see **War Shipping Administration**.

Wyllie, William Lionel (1851–1931), British artist who was one of the most widely admired of all marine painters. Known for his prodigious output, he painted scenes for the **Royal Navy** and chronicled the day-to-day life and views of the Thames. Later in his life, he played an important role in supervising the restoration of HMS *Victory*. His son, Lieutenant-Colonel Harold Wyllie (1880–1973), was also a marine artist of note.

"Wynken, Blynken and Nod", sleepytime poem by American children's poet Eugene Field (1850–1895), about three fishermen who set out in a wooden shoe to fish for herring. One of the last lines reads, "Wynken and Blynken are two little eyes, And Nod is a little head, And the Wooden shoe that sailed the skies is a wee one's trundle-bed." Field is also well known for his poems "Lit-

The Siege of the Round-House, circa 1913, by N. C. Wyeth. (Brandywine River Museum)

tle Boy Blue" and "The Duel" (also known as "The Gingham Dog and the Calico Cat").

Wyeth, Newell Convers "N. C." (1882–1945), American artist and illustrator who was well known for his many murals and altar panels. A student of **Howard Pyle**, Wyeth in turn taught his son Andrew Newell Wyeth. He is best remembered for his illustrations of children's classics and adventure stories, including *Robinson Crusoe* and *Treasure Island*, published in 1924 and still in print seventy-five years later. He also edited *Great Stories of the Sea and Ships* (1940).

X-craft, British midget submarines employed with some success during World War II. Introduced in 1943, they were intended to enter restricted harbors and lay time-fused explosive charges beneath enemy ships.

xebec, three-masted, shallow-draft sailing **ship** rigged with a square rig on the foremast and **lateen** sails on the main and mizzen. It was frequently used by **corsairs** in the Mediterranean in the eighteenth and early nineteenth centuries.

Xerxes I (ca. 519–465 B.C.), ruler of the Persian Empire from 486 B.C. until his death. He spent several years trying to conquer Greece. His army defeated the Greeks at Thermopylae, but his fleet suffered a crushing defeat at the Battle of **Salamis**. Persian forces were again defeated by Greek soldiers and seamen at the mouth of the Eurymedon River in what today is Turkey. As a result, Xerxes was murdered by a group of nobleman.

XYZ Affair, name given to the 1797 incident in which three French agents—X, Y, and Z—demanded bribes from U.S. officials in order to settle a dispute over the French raiding of U.S. ships and cargoes. France was at war with Great Britain at the time and was angered by the **Jay Treaty**. The XYZ Affair ultimately led to the **Quasi-War** with France and gave the U.S. Congress the resolve to finish constructing the last three—*President*, *Congress*, and *Chesapeake*—of the six **frigates** (the others were the *United States*, *Constitution*, and *Constellation*) called for in the **Navy Act of 1794**.

γ

Yacht Cruising, classic 1910 text by **Claud Worth** about the ins and outs of yacht ownership, on-board equipment, and cruising under sail.

U.S. yacht ensign, flag that is a variant of the national ensign in which the union consists of thirteen stars in a ring surrounding a fouled anchor set diagonally. Originally created in 1848, it is today flown by pleasure craft sailing in U.S. territorial waters as an alternative to the national ensign.

Yachting, U.S. boating magazine founded in 1907 that has been the primary publication targeting sail and power yacht owners.

SS Yale, 1906 coastal **liner** built for the Metropolitan Steamship Company's New York to Boston run. She was transferred, along with sister vessel **Harvard**, to California coastal service in 1910 under various owners. Acquired by the **Los Angeles Steamship Company** after service in World War I for continued West Coast operation, the 2,051-gross-ton flyer was noted for her speed, which was in excess of twenty-five **knots**. She ceased active service in 1936, and after serving in Alaskan waters in and after World War II, she was scrapped in Stockton, California, in 1949.

Yamamoto, Isoroku (1884–1943), Japanese admiral who commanded the Imperial fleet at

SS *Yale* at her Los Angeles terminal in 1930. (Courtesy Gordon R. Ghareeb)

the time of the surprise attack on **Pearl Harbor** on December 7, 1941. His plans to trap and destroy the U.S. aircraft carrier force at **Midway** in June 1942 backfired. Yamamoto was later killed in action when U.S. forces intercepted radio signals giving his itinerary and sent out fighters that shot down his aircraft.

Yamato, sixty-four-thousand-ton, 863-foot Japanese battleship completed in 1941 that was constructed with two sister ships, the *Musashi* and *Shinano*, while a fourth sister was broken up on the building ways when nearly 30 percent complete. Mounting nine 18-inch guns—the largest caliber cannons ever fitted to a ship—the vessels were designed to outgun the **Iowa**-class battleships of the U.S. **Navy**. *Yamato* was sunk by the attack of planes from eight U.S. carriers—including USS *Essex*, USS *Hornet*, and USS *Wasp*—after direct hits by eleven torpedoes and seven bombs during the Battle of **Leyte Gulf** in 1945.

Yangtze River, China's longest and most important river and the world's third-longest river. The 3,915-mile waterway flows eastward through central China and enters the East China Sea. About half of China's ocean trade is carried over the Yangtze and its branches, and oceangoing ships can travel 680 miles upstream from the coast.

Yankee, series of three vessels sailed by Captain **Irving M. Johnson** and his wife, Electa, between 1938 and 1968. The first *Yankee* was a **schooner**, the second a ninety-six-foot **hermaphrodite brigantine**, and the third a **ketch**. The couple took young Americans on voyages of discovery at sea, and their voyages were chronicled in their books as well as in articles in *National Geographic*.

Yankee Pasha, 1947 novel by Edison Marshall about a late-eighteenth-century frontiersman who loses his family but later finds love while working the coastal fisheries of New England. He pursues his love when she is captured at sea by pirates and sold into Moroccan slavery. The 1954 swashbuckler feature film starred Jeff Chandler, Rhonda Fleming, Lee J. Cobb, and Mamie Van Doren.

Yankee Station, U.S. **Navy** designation for the operating area one hundred miles off the Indo-Chinese coast at 16° North **latitude**, 110° East **longitude**, during the Vietnam War.

SS Yarmouth Castle, American coastal **liner** constructed for the Eastern Steamship Company as the *Evangeline* in 1927. She became the *Yarmouth Castle* in 1963 and was dispatched on short cruises from Miami to the Bahamas. The 5,002-gross-ton vessel was consumed in flames on November 13, 1965, killing 87 of the 545 people on board. The tragedy was instrumental in prompting the U.S. congressional overhaul of laws regarding passenger ship safety.

yaw, the movement of a vessel when it departs from her set course. Often a following sea will cause this by lifting the vessel's stern and digging in her bow, causing her to swivel around.

Yawata Maru, Japanese **liner** completed in 1940 that entered passenger service between Yokohama, San Francisco, and Los Angeles for four months before being taken over by the Imperial Japanese Navy, which rebuilt her as the escort aircraft carrier *Unyo* in 1942. The 17,128-gross-ton sister ship to the **Nitta Maru** was torpedoed and sunk by the submarine USS *Barb* in 1944.

yawl, **fore-and-aft-rigged** sailboat with two masts, the taller mainmast forward and the shorter mizzenmast, or jigger, stepped aft of the rudder post.

Yeaton, Hopley (c. 1740–1812), the first commissioned officer in what would become the

Revenue Marine and later the U.S. **Coast Guard**. He commanded the revenue **cutter** *Scamme*l, one of the original ten cutters authorized by **Alexander Hamilton** and the U.S. Congress in 1790.

Yellowbeard, 1983 comic film about a pirate who has been released from prison after fifteen years and his efforts to locate a buried treasure. It starred Graham Chapman, John Cleese, Eric Idle, Madeline Kahn, Cheech Marin, Tommy Chong, Peter Boyle, and Marty Feldman, who died during production.

"Yellow Submarine", hit 1968 Beatles song by John Lennon and Paul McCartney about a strange voyage through the Sea of Green. An entire animated, fantasy, full-length film was built around the imaginary voyage of the Yellow Submarine from Pepperland to Liverpool and its return. The pinnacle of op art, the movie featured hit songs by the band.

Yeomanettes, name by which the first U.S. **Navy** female recruits were known. When allowed to join the service beginning in 1917, women were only permitted to hold clerical posts. They were succeeded by the **WAVES** during World War II.

Y-gun, two-barreled antisubmarine gun mounted in the stern of World War II vessels to launch depth charges over the side. The body of the gun and its two barrels form a Y shape, with one barrel extending to either side of the stern.

Yokohama fender, large fender placed between a ship and the pier, named for the manufacturer, Yokohama Rubber Company, Ltd.

Yorkovitch, Vladimir (1886–1964), Russian naval designer and creator of a new hull contour first used in 1912 for the construction of four Russian Borodino-class battleships incorporating a bulbous underwater bow form. He emigrated to France in 1922 and produced the hull design

for the revolutionary ocean **liner SS** *Normandie*.

USS *Yorktown* (CV-5), 809-foot aircraft carrier christened by Eleanor Roosevelt and completed in 1937. The 19,800-ton sister ship to USS **Enterprise** was dispatched to the Pacific immediately following the attack on **Pearl Harbor**. It participated in the raids on the Gilbert Islands and **Marshall Islands** as well as being a major player in the Battle of the **Coral Sea**. Struck by three Japanese bombs and two torpedoes during the Battle of **Midway** in 1942, the ship lay heeled to port with her flight deck touching the waves, but she refused to sink. The following day, a boarding party attempted to set her back to a more even keel. Two days later, the lone Japanese submarine I-168 found the disabled carrier and launched three more torpedoes into her hull, sending her to the bottom.

USS *Yorktown* (CV-10), **Essex**-class aircraft carrier launched in 1943 and named for the carrier lost at the Battle of **Midway**. The 872-foot-long ship received eleven battle stars for her varied roles in the Pacific theater of World War II and another four battle stars for service during the Vietnam War. In 1967 she recovered the crew of *Apollo 8*—the first manned mission to orbit the moon—after splashdown, and in 1968 she was cast in the film *Tora! Tora! Tora!* Retired in 1970, USS *Yorktown* opened five years later as the National Memorial to Carrier Aviation at Patriots Point Naval & Maritime Museum near Charleston, South Carolina.

"You may fire when you are ready, Captain Gridley!", command of Commodore **George Dewey** at the May 1, 1898, Battle of **Manila Bay** during the **Spanish-American War**. He was addressing Captain **Charles Gridley**, captain of Dewey's **flagship** *Olympia*.

Young America, 243-foot extreme **clipper ship** constructed in 1853 by **William Henry Webb**. Operating in the wake of the gold rush of 1849, she set the record on passage around **Cape Horn**, and she voyaged successfully for thirty years—an old age for a clipper—succumbing to an Atlantic gale in 1883.

Young America, Team **Dennis Conner**'s defender yacht that lost the **America's Cup** to New Zealand's ***Black Magic*** in 1995, five races to none. Conner became the first **skipper** to lose the Cup twice.

"Youth", classic 1902 short story by **Joseph Conrad** that is a narrative of a young man named Marlow and his voyage on the **bark** *Judea* from Scotland to Bangkok. Marlow also narrates Conrad's ***Heart of Darkness*** (1902) and parts of ***Lord Jim*** (1900). "Youth" is based on Conrad's personal experiences as second mate of the *Palestine*, which sank off Java Head.

Z

Zanzibar, historic seaport city on the west coast of Zanzibar Island, which is part of Tanzania. It served as a major trading center between Africa and the Arab world.

Z-card, a U.S. Coast Guard–issued merchant mariner's document. Also known as seaman's papers, the name derives from a system that dates back to the Bureau of Marine Inspection and Navigation in which the assigned mariner's numbers would be preceded by the letter "Z." The Z-numbers have been replaced by the social security number.

zebra mussel, striped freshwater bivalve native to the area around the Caspian and Black Seas and introduced into the Great Lakes around 1987 through ballast water pumped out by a visiting ship. Considered a pest, it clogs pipes, covers boat bottoms, and threatens the food

Top portion of a Z-card, circa 1944.

supply of many native species of fish and shellfish.

Zeebrugge, Belgian coastal town that has historically served as a strategic seaport. During World War I, the channel to the German-occupied port was sealed off by the British by sinking three obsolete **cruisers** filled with concrete in the channel.

Zim Israel Navigation Company, Israel's national **carrier** and one of the largest container shipping companies in the world. It was established in 1945 as a passenger service to carry hundreds of thousands of refugees and immigrants to Israel. In the 1950s and 1960s, Zim offered service throughout the Mediterranean, to and from the United States, and to the Caribbean. By the late 1960s, Zim had moved out of passenger shipping and expanded its cargo lines.

Zimmerman Note, secret telegram sent on January 16, 1917, by German foreign secretary Arthur Zimmerman to the German ambassador to the United States that was intercepted by British naval intelligence. In the note, Zimmerman stated that in the event of U.S.–German hostilities, Mexico should be asked to enter the war as a German ally. In return, Germany would restore to Mexico the territories of Texas, New Mexico, and Arizona. He also made remarks concerning unrestricted submarine warfare against the United States. President Wilson released the text of the message to the press, where it, along with the sinking of RMS *Lusitania*, galvanized public support for America's entry into World War I.

zinc, plate of the metallic element zinc that will draw the corrosive effects of yellow metal used in propellers from galvanizing action that eats away steel plates. When a zinc does its job, it gradually wastes away and must be replaced. It is also known as a sacrificial anode.

Zuider Zee, former arm of the North Sea that extended into the Netherlands. The southern section was diked off in 1932 to form Ijsselmeer, a shallow freshwater lake. Since then, more than 850 square miles of fertile farmland have been reclaimed from the sea.

Zuikaku, 845-foot Japanese aircraft carrier that, with her sister ship ***Shokaku***, was part of the attack force that bombed **Pearl Harbor** in 1941. *Zuikaku* saw more action than any other Japanese carrier in World War II but was sunk in 1944 by aircraft from USS *Essex* and USS *Lexington* during the Battle of **Cape Engaño**.

zulu time, letter designation for **Greenwich Mean Time** or Coordinated Universal Time (**UTC**). The Z designation is used in radio traffic to denote the time of a dispatch.

Zumwalt, Elmo Russell, Jr. (1920–2000), U.S. **Navy** admiral who graduated from the U.S. **Naval Academy** in 1942 and saw combat in World War II and Korea. In 1968 he became commander of naval forces in Vietnam and served as **chief of naval operations** from 1970 to 1974. As chief of naval operations, he faced difficult problems of racial integration throughout the navy, and he became famous for his "Z-grams," which summoned all hands to pull together on this and other matters.

Praise for
THE DICTIONARY OF NAUTICAL LITERACY

"A terrific book—full of information in turns basic, arcane, and playful,
all presented with an authority and humor that I'm sure will appeal to many sailors
as well as to lovers of the sea and maritime art and writing.
Any nautical book that includes Nelson, Travis McGee, 'close-hauled,'
Belloc, *USS VD*, Helen of Troy, the Slot, and skipjacks
wins a medal for sweep and imagination."
—John Rousmaniere, author of *After the Storm*;
Fastnet, Force 10; and *The Annapolis Book of Seamanship*

"A vital resource for anyone interested in the ships and people
that stream across the pages of history. How did we ever get along without this book?"
—Peter Stanford, President Emeritus,
National Maritime Historical Society

"The accuracy and variety of entries will delight nautical trivia buffs,
and the book is a solid reference for the rest of us."
—*Offshore*

"One of the most useful books to come across my desk. . . . [It's] also a fascinating read."
—*SAIL*

"I never thought about reading Daniel Webster's dictionary from cover to cover,
the way I did McKenna's *Dictionary of Nautical Literacy*. . . .
Full of knowledge, wisdom, and entertaining factoids."
—*The Log*